MADNESS AND MODERNISM

MADNESS
AND
MODERNISM

Insanity in the Light
of Modern Art,
Literature, and Thought

LOUIS A. SASS

Harvard University Press
Cambridge, Massachusetts
London, England

Excerpt from "Seventh Duino Elegy" from *The Selected Poetry of Rainer Maria Rilke* by Rainer Maria Rilke, trans. by Stephen Mitchell. Copyright © 1982 by Stephen Mitchell. Reprinted by permission of Random House, Inc.

Excerpts from Apollinaire and Blaise Cendrars and other quoted material from Roger Shattuck, *The Banquet Years* (New York: Random House, 1968). Copyright © 1968 by Roger Shattuck. Reprinted by permission of Joan Daves Agency.

This Harvard University Press paperback is published by arrangement with BasicBooks, a division of HarperCollins Publishers, Inc.

First Harvard University Press paperback edition, 1994

Library of Congress Cataloging-in-Publication Data

Sass, Louis Arnorsson.
    Madness and modernism: insanity in the light of modern art,
    literature, and thought/ Louis A. Sass.
        p.   cm.
    Includes bibliographical references and index.
    ISBN 0-674-54137-5 (pbk.)
    1. Schizophrenia 2. Modernism (Art) 3. Modernism
    (Literature) 4. Modernism (Aesthetics)   I. Title
RC514.S316 1992   91–59013
616.89'83—dc20   CIP

Designed by Ellen Levine

For my father, Louis DeWald Sass

*and in loving memory of my mother,
Hrafnhildur Einarsdóttir Arnórsson Sass
(September 11, 1915–January 1, 1964)*

CONTENTS

PART THREE
SELF AND WORLD IN THE
FULL-BLOWN PSYCHOSIS

ACKNOWLEDGMENTS

V arious friends, colleagues, and institutions have offered help and encouragement over the years (too many years, I fear) that I have spent writing this book.

Fellowships from the National Endowment for the Humanities and from the Institute for Advanced Study (School of Social Science) released me from teaching responsibilities at the important beginning stage of the project; the year at the Institute helped set me on a track from which I might otherwise have wavered. I am especially grateful for Clifford Geertz's support at that crucial early point in my work, as well as for the enduring inspiration I have drawn from his writings.

More recently, a Henry Rutgers Research Fellowship granted me valuable stretches of writing time, and a year as a fellow of Rutgers University's Center for Critical Analysis of Contemporary Culture afforded time as well as stimulating interdisciplinary contacts. The Graduate School of Applied and Professional Psychology at Rutgers, where I teach, is an uncommonly congenial and broad-minded environment. I owe a special debt to my colleagues in the Department of Clinical Psychology; for their unwavering interest and support, I would like especially to thank Sandra Harris, Stanley Messer, and Donald Peterson (Dean of GSAPP during most of my time at Rutgers), and also Robert Woolfolk of the Psychology Department. I have also appreciated the collegiality of my fellow fellows at the New York Institute for the Humanities (at New York University), the source of many memorable lunches for some years now.

Margaret Thaler Singer and John Gunderson introduced me to the study of schizophrenia and supported my early research efforts (along quite different lines from the present book). I am extremely grateful to them for their kindness, and for openheartedly encouraging me to follow my own path. My years of clinical training, research, and practice have been fertile and rewarding, and I extend thanks to the supervisors, colleagues, and patients with whom I have worked at several institutions: New York Hospital–Westchester Division (Cornell Medical Center); McLean Hospital–Harvard Medical School; the Psychology Department at the University of California, Berkeley; the Charles Drew Family Life Center; and Boston State Hospital. I am also grateful to several friends and acquaintances who spoke to me of their own experiences with schizophrenia.

Many people were kind enough to read and comment on versions of these chapters over the years. Although I can't thank all of them here, I would like to mention Sidney Blatt, John Boyd, John Broughton, Bertram Cohen, Philip Cushman, Hubert Dreyfus, Allan Eisenberg, Melvin Feffer, Angus Fletcher, John Gittins, Jim Gold, Howard Gruber, Erich Heller, Wolf Lepenies, Michael Leyton, James Phillips, and Michael Schwartz. Philip Fisher, my tutor in English literature when I was an undergraduate, helped inspire my interest in modernism; and my sister, Ann Sass, was an important early influence on my developing interest in the visual arts. My father's influence, particularly in matters of intellectual style, has been especially profound.

Steve Fraser, my editor at Basic Books, has offered astute and invaluable editorial advice at several stages of what turned out to be a very lengthy process. I would like to thank him for his early encouragement, for his patience throughout the writing process, and for a much-needed push toward completion. I would also like to extend my thanks to Linda Carbone for her meticulous and acutely intelligent attention in the final editing and preparation of the manuscript.

Over the years, Jamie Walkup, a generous-spirited friend and incisive critic, cheerfully read drafts of all the chapters. He offered many thoughtful and useful suggestions as well as endless access to his vast store of knowledge in several fields. I thank him for many hours of enjoyable discussion, and also for saving me from more than a few errors of fact and interpretation.

Finally, I am deeply grateful to Shira Nayman, who has aided me immeasurably since an early stage in the project. She has read and reread all my chapters, has joined in worrying through the arguments, and, most important, has helped to quiet my own critical voices. This would have been a less interesting book, and the task of writing it far more onerous, without the benefits of her keen editorial eye and literary judgment, her invigorating curiosity, and the great pleasure of her companionship.

Note: Quoted material from patients that is not otherwise attributed comes from patients I have treated or interviewed, or to whom I administered psychological tests. All patients' names not from the literature are, of course, pseudonyms.

A great deal of supplementary material—supportive references, additional examples, qualifications, elaborations—can be found in the extensive notes section.

The growing consciousness is a danger and a disease.
—Friedrich Nietzsche

PROLOGUE

The Sleep of Reason

T he madman is a protean figure in the Western imagination, yet there is a sameness to his many masks. He has been thought of as a wildman and a beast, as a child and a simpleton, as a waking dreamer, and as a prophet in the grip of demonic forces. He is associated with insight and vitality but also with blindness, disease, and death; and so he evokes awe as well as contempt, fear as well as condescension and benevolent concern. But the variousness of these faces should not be allowed to obscure their underlying consistencies, for there are certain assumptions about insanity that have persisted through nearly the entire history of Western thought.

Madness is irrationality, a condition involving decline or even disappearance of the role of rational factors in the organization of human conduct and experience: this is the core idea that, in various forms but with few true exceptions, has echoed down through the ages. Nearly always insanity has been seen as what one early-nineteenth-century alienist called "the opposite to reason and good sense, as light is to darkness, straight to crooked."[1] And, since reason has generally been seen as the distinctive feature of human nature itself, it would seem to follow that madmen must be not merely different but somehow deficient in essential qualities of humanity or personhood.[2] Indeed, the very word *reason* means both the highest intellectual faculty and the sane mind.

The origin of these concepts has sometimes been located in the seventeenth- and eighteenth-century Enlightenment, time of the Great Confinement when madness, conceived as "a total suspension of every rational faculty,"[3] came to be sequestered behind the thick walls of the asylum. But it can also be traced to the writings of Plato, who imagined insanity as the condition in which the rational soul abdicates its role as charioteer or pilot of the self, failing to exercise harmonizing dominion over the "appetitive soul" and the rest of the human personality. This conception of insanity is actually older still, coinciding with the very earliest speculations on human consciousness. Heraclitus, the pre-Socratic philosopher who lived in the fifth century B.C., was the first Western thinker to treat the psyche as a source or center of human personality and experience, and he conceived of this center as a cognitive or rational entity, which he identified with the element of Fire. In his view, all forms of frenzy, intoxication, or madness were associated with Dionysus, the god of wine; for they all had the deplorable effect of moistening the soul, thus dimming the psyche's pure flame and robbing human awareness of its essential lucidity. ("A gleam of light is the dry soul, wisest and best," wrote Heraclitus; "It is death for souls to become water.")[4]

In one sense, of course, an equation of madness and irrationality can hardly be questioned. If we *define* rationality in pragmatic or social terms— as a matter of practical efficiency in the attainment of goals generally accepted as being reasonable, as a tendency for one's perceptions and judgments to agree with general opinion, or as openness to dialogue—then it is practically a tautology to equate insanity with the irrational; isn't this just what we *mean* when we refer to some person or act as mad, crazy, lunatic, or insane? But prevailing conceptions have gone considerably beyond this simple judgment of mere impracticality, eccentricity, or unreasonableness. It has been assumed that the madman's point of view is not simply idiosyncratic but actually incorrect, or otherwise inferior, according to some universal standard; and that this inferiority reflects some lack or defect of the defining human ability.[5]

Depending on how reason is understood, this lack has been viewed in somewhat different ways: as a diminished capacity for logical inference or correct sequencing of ideas; as incapacity for reflexive or introspective self-awareness; as inability to exercise freedom through independent volition; as loss of contemplative detachment from immediate sensory input and instinctual demands; or as failure of language and symbolic thought—to mention the most common. Its causes have also been imagined variously as due to intercession by deities, biological defects, or factors intrinsic to the psyche itself. In nearly all cases, however, the essential nature of madness itself has been conceptualized as a diminishment or an overwhelming of one's very personhood, as a decline in "freedom of action, conscious reflection and qualities of intellect and spirit [that] have been considered the fundamentals of our humanity since time immemorial."[6] The ubiquitous image of madness as irrationality is one of those pictures that holds us captive. To paraphrase the philosopher Ludwig Wittgenstein, it lies in our language, and language repeats it to us inexorably.[7]

Many writers and theorists have understood this condition of unreason in almost entirely negative terms: as an intrinsic decline or collapse of the rational faculties, a deprivation of thought that, at the limit, amounts to an emptying out or a dying of the human essence—the mind reduced to its zero degree. Thus Nicolas Joubert, a man who vied for the title of Prince of Fools in early-seventeenth-century France, was described by his lawyer as "an empty head, a gutted gourd, lacking in common sense; a cane, a broken brain, that has neither spring nor whole wheel in his head."[8] And Philo Judaeus of Alexandria, an eclectic philosopher of the first century A.D., asked why we should "not call madness death, seeing that by it mind dies, the noblest part of us?"[9]

Sometimes, however, not the weakness of reason *per se* but the power of its opposing forces receives the primary emphasis. For the philosopher Thomas Hobbes, for example, madness was a matter of "too much appearing passion," while François Boissier de Sauvages, a French alienist of the eighteenth century, described this "worst of all maladies" as a "distraction of our mind" resulting from "our blind surrender to our desires, our incapacity to control or to moderate our passions."[10] This view has ancient roots: madness in Greek tragedy is largely of this kind, as in the character of Ajax in Sophocles's play of the same name—a man whose insanity takes the form of an overwhelming envy and rage, a wave of fury that lends him nearly superhuman strength while bearing him forward toward his tragic fate; and in *The Republic*, Plato speaks of madness as a "drunken, lustful, passionate" frenzy, a giving in to one's "lawless wild-beast nature."[11]

We find insanity being conceived of in much the same terms in the nineteenth and twentieth centuries: either as a kind of "dementia" or "mindlessness,"[12] or as "primitive and archaic drives returning from the depths of the unconscious in a dramatic manner."[13] The traditional models and metaphors persist after 1800, but filtered through the more sophisticated evolutionist/developmental and mechanistic perspectives that have continued to dominate psychology and psychiatry up to the present day (most obviously in psychoanalysis and some forms of biological psychiatry).

Here, then, are the poles around which images of madness have revolved for so many centuries: on the one hand, notions of emptiness, of defect and decrepitude, of blindness, even of death itself; on the other, ideas of plenitude, energy, and irrepressible vitality—a surfeit of passion or fury bursting through all boundaries of reason or constraint. These visions are not mutually exclusive; on the contrary, they are frequently combined, as in one of the most common of all images for madness, the waking dreamer or sleepwalker.[14] For madness, like sleep, is assumed to be a twin of death, a darkening or dampening of the (rational) soul that deprives the soul of its most essential feature, its lucidity; yet, also like sleep, it is assumed to be a wakening, a rising into the fresh yet ancient reality of the dream.[15]

The faith in reason that underlies this conception of insanity is central to Western thought, as basic to Plato and Aristotle as to Descartes and Kant, but it has not gone entirely uncriticized, especially in the nineteenth and twentieth centuries. Various writers in the romantic, Nietzschean, surrealist, and poststructuralist traditions have pointed out dangers in this enshrining of reason, such as how it can splinter the unity and authenticity of the human being, stifling imagination and physical vitality while bringing on the paralysis of overdeliberation and self-consciousness.[16] In most cases, however, this antirationalist sentiment has not affected fundamental notions of madness, only the value judgment placed upon it. Such critics may well speak of "the lunatic state called normalcy or common sense";[17] yet, like Nietzsche in his profoundly influential *Birth of Tragedy*, they continue to identify real insanity with the Dionysian side of life—now, however, glorifying the clinical forms of madness for their presumed spontaneity and sensual abandon instead of condemning them for irrationality and evident loss of control.

The madman, in this view, is a personification of the life force, a kind of Blakean tiger of the night, feeling no scruples and nursing no unacted desires. ("*Dementia praecox*—it reminds me of a night-blooming tropical flower," as a character in Tennessee Williams's *Suddenly Last Summer* remarks.)[18] Most of these writers have had little or no experience with the realities of chronic insanity, however; and one suspects their glorification of madness may be fueled by motivations other than the purest desire for truth. For many such people—intellectuals, for the most part—it may serve as a way of announcing, a bit too loudly, that *they* at least cannot be placed among those self-satisfied yet anemic souls whom Nietzsche mocked so pitilessly for staying on the sidelines of life, having no idea "how cadaverous and ghostly their 'sanity' appears as the intense throng of Dionysiac revelers sweeps past them."[19]

The notion that too much consciousness might be a thoroughgoing illness (as Dostoevsky's narrator puts it in *Notes from the Underground*)[20] has been, then, a common enough idea in the last two centuries, yet it has had little impact on the understanding of the psychoses: the truly insane, it is nearly always assumed, are those who have failed to attain, or else have lapsed or retreated from, the higher levels of mental life. Nearly always insanity involves a shift from human to animal, from culture to nature, from thought to emotion, from maturity to the infantile and the archaic. If we harbor insanity, it is always in the *depths* of our souls, in those primitive strata where the human being becomes beast and the human essence dissolves in the universal well of desire.[21]

Another possibility does suggest itself, however: What if madness were to involve not an escape from but an exacerbation of that thoroughgoing illness Dostoevsky imagined? What if madness, in at least some of its forms, were to derive from a heightening rather than a dimming of conscious awareness, and an alienation not from reason but from the emotions, instincts, and the body? This, in essence, is the basic thesis of this book.

Though such a view is not entirely unknown (one finds hints of it in German romanticism, in some of the Victorians,[22] and in the writings of a few twentieth-century psychiatrists),[23] it has seldom been developed in much clinical detail, and has certainly not been taken seriously in clinical psychology and psychiatry; in recent years, in fact, such conceptions have been almost entirely submerged by the more traditional notions of medical-model psychiatry, psychoanalysis, and the literary or antipsychiatric avant-garde.[24]

I must stress, however, that I will not be concerned in this book with *all* forms of insanity or psychosis, but only with certain types. To *some* kinds of madness, such as manic psychosis and certain of the classic organic brain diseases, traditional emphases on passion or irrationality may well be applicable, at least in a general sense.[25] As we shall see, however, the traditional models are woefully inadequate when it comes to accounting for either the experience or the behavior of a great many patients with schizophrenia and related illnesses. The illness of these patients can hardly be encompassed under the twin signs of Dionysus and dementia; and it will be necessary to develop an alternative to the triumvirate of death, sleep, and the passions, with its recurring imagery of darkness, wilderness, and subterranean places.

The traditional vision is evoked in various works by Francisco Goya, such as the etching "The Sleep of Reason Breeds Monsters" and the painting known as "The Madhouse at Saragossa" (see illustration)—the latter work offering not merely an external portrait of lunatics but also a hint of their inner worlds. "The Madhouse at Saragossa," a painting of inmates in an asylum, is done in an extreme chiaroscuro, so dark that we can hardly make out all the figures in its dungeonlike space. One man stands defiant in the foreground, while behind him two others grapple with each other. In the background a man raises his arms in what appears to be supplication; another crawls across the floor. In the murky depths of the scene, other shadowy forms hint of unknown excesses and depravity. This, in effect, is a portrait of the id—a darkly mysterious place, impossible to fathom yet sure to be filled with blind and passionate intensities. The darkness of this setting, we cannot help but feel, suggests the darkness of the minds contained within it; and we can almost hear the beastlike sounds, the grunts, bellows, and moans issuing from somewhere deep within these brutish creatures.

This is a familiar enough vision, and certainly a compelling one; but its accuracy as a portrayal of the inner world of schizophrenic forms of madness is highly questionable. Close attention to what many schizophrenics actually say or write may well lead, in fact, to quite a different, rather stranger impression: of a noonday rather than a midnight world, a world marked less by the mysteries of hidden depths than by the uncanniness of immense spaces and the enigmas of gleaming surfaces and brilliant light, where the purity of the silence and solitude is not broken by bestial cries so much as by

Francisco Goya, *Corral de Locos*, also known as *The Madhouse at Saragossa* (c. 1794). *Algur H. Meadows Collection, Meadows Museum, Southern Methodist University, Dallas, Texas, accession no. 67.01*

the incessant murmur of inner witnesses. Often enough schizophrenics feel not farther from but closer to truth and illumination. One individual (the subject of chapter 2), for example, describes her madness as a land suffused with a bright and preternatural light; another (the subject of chapter 8) recounts how his head was "illuminated by rays"; and a third, the poet Gérard de Nerval, describes a crystal-clear sight in his psychotic episodes: "It struck me I knew everything; everything was revealed to me, all the secrets of the world were mine during those spacious hours."[26] One can dismiss such claims as showing how truly deluded such persons are, as proving they live in a night so dark that they confuse it even with daylight (the reversal of night and day, darkness and light, was a favorite trope of the seventeenth and eighteenth centuries);[27] but such interpretations hardly account for the *feeling of* revelation, or for the quality of electrical illumination that tends to pervade the schizophrenic world.

Schizophrenics can, in fact, be persons of considerable intelligence and mental complexity, and, as the psychiatrist Karl Jaspers has pointed out, their illnesses often bring on processes of religious or metaphysical revelation and the "exhibition of fine and subtle understanding." As they lose contact with normal life and the natural world, schizophrenics often come to believe that "they have grasped the profoundest of meanings; concepts such as timelessness, world, god and death become enormous revelations which when the state has subsided cannot be reproduced or described in any way."[28] One patient spoke, for example, of his experiences as having a "cosmic character" and "a character of the infinite"; another explained that he "became interested in the beauty of the explanation of chaos."[29] Schizophrenics and schizoid individuals can also adopt a critical stance toward social facts that are too encompassing, or too much a part of the taken-for-granted fabric of normal social existence, for the average person even to notice (they may be acutely aware of the subtle patterns of deference among members of a hospital staff, for instance, or of the arbitrary absurdity of social rituals such as shaking hands). In light of these propensities, it seems unfortunate—and ironic—that the patient's own perspective should be accorded so little attention, that it should often be dismissed either as devoid of significance altogether or as the product of the most primitive and rudimentary forms of mental life.[30]

Problems with traditional models might tempt one, however, to give up the quest for psychological explanation or understanding. No less a mind than Karl Jaspers believed, in fact, that any attempt at unriddling the enigmas of schizophrenic consciousness was doomed to failure, and that we ought simply to acknowledge a fundamental unknowability, perhaps restricting ourselves to the investigation of underlying neurophysiological causes. But there would be certain dangers in adopting this attitude of interpretive nihilism, for it risks doing a double disservice: first, to the patient, who would thereby be banished from the community of human understanding; and second, to the rest of us, who would be deprived of all access to what may be an important limit-case of the human condition. An alternative is to take the uncanny and alien qualities of this condition as challenge rather than prohibition, as signs not of the impossibility but of the difficulty of understanding schizophrenic experience—and perhaps also as offering some hint of what kind of interpretation might suffice.

I would argue that schizophrenia does in fact involve a sort of death-in-life, though not of the kind so often imagined: for what dies in these cases is not the rational so much as the appetitive soul, not the mental so much as the physical and emotional aspects of one's being; this results in detachment from the natural rhythms of the body and entrapment in a sort of morbid wakefulness or hyperawareness. Schizophrenic individuals often describe themselves as feeling dead yet hyperalert—a sort of corpse with insomnia; thus one such patient spoke of having been "translated" into what he called a "death-mood," yet he also experienced his thoughts as somehow electric— heated up and intensified.[31]

It would be foolish to deny that the schizophrenic condition can lack orderliness and intelligibility, that it can display forms of violent contradiction and nearly impenetrable obscurity. These qualities have usually been ascribed to the suspension of "higher intellectual faculties," and perhaps to the liberation of an archaic or infantile mentality that ignores the fundamental Law of Contradiction (that something cannot at the same time be both x and not-x) and that allows the most disparate urges and impulses to share the stage of conscious awareness.[32] But perhaps we should not be so quick to evoke these images of a primal and Dionysian chaos. Could the disorganization in question be something more intricate, not a process of being overwhelmed by antagonistic forces but more of a self-undermining—like something turning in upon itself until, finally, it collapses of its own accord? If so, we might find the peculiarities of schizophrenic experience less a matter of brute contradiction than of paradox: the paradoxes of the reflexive.

The interpretive strategy of this book is to view the poorly understood schizophrenic-type illnesses in the light of the sensibility and structures of consciousness found in the most advanced art and literature of the twentieth century, the epoch of modernism (a term used in a broad sense in this book, one that subsumes the so-called postmodernist style and sensibility as a subtype). Modernist art has been said to manifest certain off-putting characteristics that are reminiscent of schizophrenia: a quality of being hard to understand or feel one's way into—what one critic calls *Uneinfühlbahrkeit*.[33] The relevant aspects of such art are, however, antithetical to notions of primitivity and of deficit or defect, for these art forms are characterized not so much by unreflectiveness and spontaneity as by acute self-consciousness and self-reference, and by alienation from action and experience— qualities we might refer to as "hyperreflexivity."[34]

Human action in our time, it has been said, lacks "shape and measure" and is "veined with currents of inertia."[35] If so, this is surely related to a burgeoning of a certain introversion and alienation, the acceleration of an inner process that Kafka, a figure representative of the age, described in his diary as the "wild tempo" of an "introspection [that] will suffer no idea to sink tranquilly to rest but must pursue each one into consciousness, only itself to become an idea, in turn to be pursued by renewed introspection."[36] It is in the modernist art and thought of the twentieth century that this self-generating, often compulsive process has reached its highest pitch, transforming the forms, purposes, and preoccupations of all the arts and inspiring works that, to the uninitiated, can seem as difficult to grasp, as off-putting and alien, as schizophrenia itself. It is this convoluted and paradoxical condition—so self-undermining and seemingly fragile, and yet so persistent and adaptable as to have endured for nearly a century without sign of exhaustion—that provides the most illuminating analogies for the mysterious symptoms of schizophrenia.

✿   ✿   ✿   ✿   ✿

Let me emphasize at the outset that my purpose in this book will be to clarify rather than to evaluate or explain. I do not seek causal explanation but what Wittgenstein calls "the understanding which consists in seeing connections,"[37] the kind of explanation that uses analogy to change the aspect under which given phenomena are seen, so that they will make sense, or make sense in a new way. I am not suggesting that madness and modernism are alike in all important respects; nor is there any intent to denigrate modernism or to imply that such art or such a culture *is* schizophrenic. I certainly do not wish to glorify schizophrenic forms of madness—to argue, for example, that they are especially conducive to artistic creativity, or to deny that they are profoundly dysfunctional and in some sense constitute a disease. Nor am I claiming there is an etiological connection between madness and modernism—for example, that modern culture or the modern social order actually *causes* schizophrenic forms of psychosis. This is not to imply that schizophrenia and modernism should be assumed to be entirely distinct phenomena—moving on parallel paths that never cross or converge. Like all human beings, schizophrenic and schizoid individuals are molded by the cultural contexts in which they live; at the same time, their contributions can also have some effect on these contexts. This book, however, is concerned with the issue of affinities rather than influences. In the epilogue I do take up the fascinating but difficult question of possible causal relationships among modernism, modernity, and madness; but this issue—about which I remain essentially agnostic—is separate from the phenomenological and interpretative issues that are my focus in the following chapters.[38]

My main goal is simply to reinterpret schizophrenia and certain closely related forms of pathology (the so-called schizophrenia spectrum of illnesses, which also includes schizoid and schizotypal, and some forms of schizophreniform and schizoaffective, disorders); to show, using the affinities with modernism, that much of what has been passed off as primitive or deteriorated is far more complex and interesting—and self-aware—than is usually acknowledged.[39] I would like to think that this investigation is in the spirit of Wittgenstein, a spirit captured in the words of a former student who, some forty years later, described Wittgenstein's message in the following way: "first, to keep in mind that things are as they are; and secondly, to seek illuminating comparisons to get an understanding of how they are."[40]

Ordinarily, we understand people in our own culture with little effort; their purposes and meanings seem virtually transparent, since they allude to a world that is shared and taken for granted. Only with those we do not readily understand are we in need of theory; and theory works mainly by analogy, a "seeing-as" that uses something we think we do understand as a model for comprehending less intelligible things. The comparison with the modernist sensibility, no less than the traditional image of the madman as a sort of savage or child, exemplifies what John Locke called this "wary reasoning from analogy." Such reasoning can lead us astray, to be sure, but without it we would hardly be capable of any understanding at all—and, with luck, this wary reasoning "leads us often into the discovery of truths and useful productions, which would otherwise lie concealed."[41]

A careful comparison with modernism suggests that schizophrenic experience may have less in common with the spirit of Dionysus than with what Nietzsche, in *The Birth of Tragedy*, associates with the god Apollo and the philosopher Socrates: it may be characterized less by fusion, spontaneity, and the liberation of desire than by separation, restraint, and an exaggerated cerebralism and propensity for introspection.[42] In the course of this analysis, one of the great ironies of modern thought gradually emerges: the madness of schizophrenia—so often imagined as being antithetical to the modern malaise, even as offering a potential escape from its dilemmas of hyperconsciousness and self-control—may, in fact, be an extreme manifestation of what is in essence a very similar condition.

In this book I will be concerned almost exclusively with phenomenological issues, the forms of consciousness and the texture of the lived world characteristic of many schizophrenics. I seek an integrating vision, an understanding not of patterns of causal interaction but, as the anthropologist Clifford Geertz puts it, "of style, of logical implication, of meaning and value."[43] As such, my argument is not in any necessary conflict with certain other approaches to this illness, such as those that investigate underlying neurobiological abnormalities or the role of genetic or environmental factors in the genesis of schizophrenia. These are just different, not conflicting, perspectives.[44] As the literary scholar Erich Heller has pointed out, however, the "vulgar mental habit" of confusing questions about causes and about the nature of phenomena is widespread in the contemporary world: modern mechanistic science has "overpopulated our minds with most successful answers to questions of *How*, and left little breathing space for questions of *What* even to be asked without a sense of embarrassment."[45] In the medical and psychological professions, this has resulted in a situation where profound issues concerning the nature of these bizarre schizophrenic phenomena—the subject of this book—are often ignored, and nearly all attention focuses on issues of their etiology and pathogenesis.

My interpretation can and does conflict with certain other approaches insofar as these offer a model of the structure and feel of schizophrenic consciousness. This is the case with many influential theories, including psychiatric conceptions of schizophrenia as essentially a kind of dementia, as well as psychoanalytic notions about the dominance of primitive instinctual forces, of "primary-process" modes of thinking, and of self-world fusion akin to infancy.[46]

I am not claiming that characteristics like hyperreflexivity are found *only* in such patients. Like virtually any aspect of mental processes, the forms of reflexivity and alienation that I stress are not unique to any diagnostic group or personality type, but only more prominent or less prominent in them. I certainly do not wish to offer, for schizophrenia, for modernism, or for hyperreflexivity itself, an essentialistic definition—one that would suggest these phenomena have sharp boundaries and a readily definable single essence.[47] No actual schizophrenic person is likely to manifest all of the many modes of experience and expression treated in the chapters to follow; furthermore, these modes will sometimes be present in an attenuated or impure form (especially in patients who are, for example, only schizoid or who have schizoaffective illness—combining traits of schizophrenia with those of mania or depression). For the sake of convenience and clarity, I will be adopting something like an ideal-type approach, allowing me to generalize readily about the schizophrenic individual without dwelling too much on exceptions and qualifications. As Max Weber, who first described the notion of the ideal type, noted, such an approach is unabashedly perspectival and partial in nature: accentuating features that are "typical" of the phenomena at issue but not applying equally well—or in the same way—to all instances of the type.[48]

At the same time, it should be clear that the thesis I am proposing is by no means a modest one. I think it applies to a great many schizophrenic patients, perhaps even the majority of "true" schizophrenics, and to many of those classic symptoms of the disease that have traditionally been seen as defining characteristics or core features. I would argue, in fact, that hyperreflexivity is a kind of master theme, able to subsume many specific aspects of schizophrenic consciousness and to organize our overall picture of the syndrome.[49] But this is not to say that it is the *only* issue of significance for such individuals, or to deny that there are other important aspects that can best be approached from other standpoints.

One final point: given my comparative strategy of argument, it would be ideal if the nature of the supposedly more understood phenomenon—modernism—were absolutely clear and noncontroversial. Otherwise the whole analysis may have a quicksilver quality, both objects of comparison seeming to shift subtly before one's eyes. Unfortunately, in treating issues regarding sensibility and phenomenological structure, the work of interpretation is inevitably hazardous and allows no escape from such ambiguity. In my treatment of modernism, however, I have stuck to widely accepted interpretations so that my view of at least one of the objects of comparison will not be intolerably idiosyncratic. But this is not to say that the comparison has no implications concerning the nature of modernism. When one looks back from schizophrenia and again at modernism, one may well wonder whether one is seeing quite the same modernism as before. Indeed, I think this comparison can help to illuminate, if not the modern condition in general, at least certain of its more disturbing potentialities—as these are refracted through the most exaggerated or pathological of examples. But while I will consider this question in the final chapter, especially in relation to the nature of "postmodernism," my primary concern is to elucidate schizophrenic phenomena; the arrow of interpretation goes from modernism to madness.[50]

Introduction

The fact of the psychoses is a puzzle to us. They are the unsolved problem of human life as such. The fact that they exist is the concern of everyone. That they are there and that the world and human life is such as to make them possible and inevitable not only gives us pause but makes us shudder.
—Karl Jaspers
General Psychopathology

Schizophrenia is, at the same time, the most severe and the most enigmatic of mental disorders. Though not conceptualized as a diagnostic category until the 1890s, surprisingly late in the long history of theorizing about the abnormal mind, this illness or set of illnesses quickly became psychiatry's central preoccupation, the object of countless empirical studies and conceptual treatises. The history of modern psychiatry is, in fact, practically synonymous with the history of schizophrenia, the quintessential form of madness in our time.[1] The attention lavished on this condition seems not, however, to have fathomed its many mysteries; and to this day we remain largely ignorant of the causes, the underlying psychological structure, and even the precise diagnostic boundaries of this most strange and important of mental illnesses—an illness that has been likened to a "cancer of the mind" and that comes to afflict around 1 percent of the population of most modern, industrialized societies.[2]

Even defining the category is no easy task. Emil Kraepelin, who created the diagnostic concept in 1896 and, almost in the same breath, laid the foundation of modern psychiatric classification, described *dementia praecox* (his term for what we now call schizophrenia) as involving "a peculiar destruction of the inner cohesiveness of the psychic personality with predominant damage to the emotional life and the will"; Eugen Bleuler, who coined the term *schizophrenia* in 1908, described a "specific type of alteration of thinking, feeling, and relation to the external world which appears nowhere else in this particular fashion."[3] People with this illness experience various kinds of delusions and hallucinations, and they manifest peculiarities of thought and language; but since this is also true of other severe mental or emotional disorders (manic-depression, paranoia, and the various organic brain syndromes, for instance), it is difficult to specify a distinctive feature or underlying essence that is unique to schizophrenia in particular.

Schizophrenia's elusiveness makes itself felt not only at the theoretical or scientific level but also in the more immediate sphere of the human encounter, in the intense yet indescribable feelings of alienness such individuals can evoke. In the presence of normal people, as well as with patients of nearly every other psychiatric diagnosis, one feels an immediate sense of a shared humanity, whereas the schizophrenic seems to inhabit an entirely different universe; he is someone from whom one feels separated by "a gulf which defies description."[4] European psychiatrists have labeled this reaction the "praecox feeling"—the sense of encountering someone who seems "totally strange, puzzling, inconceivable, uncanny, and incapable of empathy, even to the point of being sinister and frightening."[5]

The changes schizophrenics undergo are especially disconcerting, and agonizing, to those closest to them: a son, daughter, brother, or wife will still be there in the flesh, breathing and speaking, but he or she may no longer seem to have a soul and may seem to treat you like an utter stranger. And, to judge from what schizophrenics report, they themselves are not spared this unnerving sense of aberrancy and alienation. They may experience the most profound alterations in the very structures of human consciousness, in the forms of time, space, causality, and human identity that normally provide a kind of bedrock foundation for a stable human existence. The sense of time or of space may be destabilized or radically transformed; the objective world may loom forth as a solid but strangely alien presence, or else may fade into unreality, or even seem to collapse or disappear. One patient, for example, called himself "a timeless being," describing the past as "restricted, shriveled, dislocated;"[6] another spoke of the external world as "an immense space without boundary, limitless, flat, a mineral, lunar country . . . [a] stretching emptiness [where] all is unchangeable, immobile, congealed, crystallized." Another patient said he was "always being swallowed at long-distance and beheaded at long-distance"; and still another described how, during a catatonic episode, he had had the experience of removing his own head and climbing down through his trachea, there to stroll about gazing at his own inner organs.[7] Perhaps most unnerving of all, however, are certain mutations of selfhood—of the ego's unity, discreteness, or continuity over time, and of the sense of volitional control over thought and action:

When I am melting I have no hands. I go into a doorway in order not to be trampled on. Everything is flying away from me. In the doorway I can gather together the pieces of my body. It is as if something is thrown in me, bursts me asunder. Why do I divide myself in different pieces? I feel that I am without poise, that my personality is melting and that my ego disappears and that I do not exist anymore. Everything pulls me apart. . . . The skin is the only possible means of keeping the different pieces together. There is no connection between the different parts of my body.[8]

Rather than feeling that they control, or even inhabit, their own conscious lives, such persons may seem "to suffer under the yoke of an elusive strange power."[9]

Just as the Church was rent apart by schisms [wrote another such patient], the most sacred monument that is erected by the human spirit, i.e., its ability to think and decide and will to do, is torn apart by itself. Finally, it is thrown out where it mingles with every other part of the day and judges what it has left behind. Instead of wishing to do things, they are done by something that seems mechanical and frightening because it is able to do things and yet unable to want to or not to want to. . . . The feeling that should dwell within a person is outside longing to come back and yet having taken with it the power to return.[10]

It is hardly surprising that these forms of madness should tend to evoke contradictory reactions—composed equally of fascination and repulsion. Like death and ecstasy (states with which, as we have seen, it has sometimes been compared), schizophrenia has often seemed a limit-case or farthest borderland of human existence, something suggesting an almost unimaginable aberration: the annihilation of consciousness itself.

Such deviations from the normal forms of human existence are indeed extreme, and some psychiatrists and psychologists have argued that the condition is totally incomprehensible, closed to the very possibility of human empathy. But others disagree, and, as we shall see, they have most commonly likened schizophrenia's characteristic modes of consciousness to those of people who have lost, or never attained, the higher and more socialized faculties of the mind—including patients with diffuse brain damage (for example, senile dementia), infants or very young children, or else some imagined instance of an utterly unsocialized being, such as the mythical (and sometimes glorified) figure of the Wildman.

Given the prevalence of these traditional models—Wildman, child, or broken brain—it may be surprising to discover that, in many crucial respects, schizophrenia bears a remarkable resemblance to much of the most sophisticated art, literature, and thought of the twentieth century, the epoch of "modernism." In *The Man Without Qualities*, one of the great novels of modernism, for example, the Austrian writer Robert Musil describes transformations of selfhood that strikingly recall certain experiences in schizophrenia:

What has arisen is a world of qualities without a man, of experiences without someone to experience them. . . . Probably the dissolution of the anthropocentric way of relating, which has held the human being for so long at the center of the universe . . . has finally made its way to the self; for the belief that the most important thing about experience is the experiencing of it, and about deeds the doing of them, is beginning to strike most people as naive.[11]

The dissolution Musil describes is but one of many points of resemblance between madness and modernism—one of many parallels or affinities that can help to elucidate the baffling inner lives of schizophrenic individuals, and to account for the singular aura of alienness that hovers about them.

TRADITIONAL TWENTIETH-CENTURY VIEWS
OF SCHIZOPHRENIA

The Doctrine of the Abyss
and the Broken Brain

Oddly enough, schizophrenia's ineffable yet distinctive aura of strangeness has sometimes been made the basis of a crucial diagnostic criterion—thus raising our very bafflement to the status of an essential ordering principle. In *General Psychopathology*, first published in 1913 and still the most important theoretical treatise of modern psychiatry, Karl Jaspers (a psychiatrist before he became a philosopher) describes the "most profound distinction in psychic life [as] that between what is meaningful and *allows empathy* and what in its particular way is *ununderstandable*, 'mad' in the literal sense, schizophrenic psychic life (even though there may be no delusions)."[12]

Jaspers argued that the symptoms of all other types of mental illness were comprehensible as exaggerations of normal states of anxiety, euphoria, depression, fear, grandiosity, and the like. A manic patient, for example, might have an enormously inflated sense of his own power, attractiveness, or virtue—believing, for example, that thousands of women were in love with him or that he was about to make a killing on Wall Street or win a Nobel Prize. A person with paranoid psychosis might claim she was being followed by the CIA and might be impervious to rational arguments showing the purely coincidental nature of the "evidence" she perceived. Such fantasies are not truly bizarre, however: though clearly delusional, they nevertheless presuppose the normal world of space, time, and human identity; and one has little trouble understanding them as extreme exaggerations of relatively normal fears, fantasies, and mood-states. Contrast these with the sheer strangeness of the schizophrenic experiences described earlier, with their uncanny mutation of all normal relationships between self and world—or else with the seeming nonsensicality, the *logical* impossibility, of the following passage from the diary of the dancer Vaslav Nijinsky, who suffered a schizophrenic breakdown in his late twenties: "Once I went for a walk and it seemed to me that I saw some blood on the snow. I followed the traces of the blood and sensed that somebody *who was still alive* had been killed."[13] The defining feature of these experiences, in Jaspers's view, was an irreducible strangeness, and it was futile even to speculate about some central factor or deficit underlying the puzzling variety of schizophrenic symptoms.

It is odd that Jaspers, of all people, should have insisted so adamantly on the utter incomprehensibility of this condition; he, after all, was the most important champion of a *verstehende* psychiatry—one of interpretation or understanding—and he believed that psychiatry's need to study meanings and modes of experience made it as much one of the humanities as a biological science. Indeed, Jaspers was quick to attack certain physicalistic and rationalistic assumptions that are deeply rooted in Western thought—assumptions that, in the psychiatric theory of the last decade or more, have once again come to the fore, in the form of a neo-Kraepelinian revival that has tended to stifle most alternative views.

Kraepelin implied, and sometimes explicitly argued, that the psychological manifestations of schizophrenia were "nothing but 'functions' of the brain," and he maintained that these neurophysiological deficits caused a profound weakening of emotion and volition that caused a virtual destruction of the personality's inner unity and of its very capacity for coherent or meaningful experience.[14] Kraepelin's use of the term *dementia praecox* for what we now call schizophrenia revealed his conception of the illness as a premature form of senile dementia—an "inevitable and progressive mental deterioration" or "enfeeblement" of mental life in which the ego dissolves and the patient becomes "completely incapable of comprehending and developing new ideas." In his view, some kind of neurophysiological deterioration or damage brought about a "destruction of inner concatenation and causation," causing "the whole of active life" to be deprived of its normal coherence, goal-directedness, and rationality, and to receive instead "the stamp of the incalculable, the incomprehensible, and the distorted." And so, instead of being guided by a view of life and a temperament, by "the elaboration of perceptions, by deliberation and moods," the thought and action of such individuals were but the product of "chance external influences, and of impulses, cross impulses, and contrary impulses, arising similarly by chance internally."[15]

Many psychiatrists and psychologists in this century have followed along these lines, viewing schizophrenic disorder as a "lowering of the mental level,"[16] a "primary insufficiency of mental activity,"[17] or a reduction of psychic operations to the simplicity of the reflex arc or the mental automatism (defined as "human activity in its simplest and most rudimentary forms"),[18] or else as little more than the outcome of certain malfunctions of the cognitive apparatus. Such accounts have usually had a mechanistic cast, with schizophrenic consciousness being conceived on the analogy of a malfunctioning computer or machine and its peculiarities ascribed to various kinds of "defect," "deficit," or "failure" (such as impairment of the ability to direct one's attention, defective capacity for abstract thinking, or diminished ability to categorize objects or perceptions). The possibility of a superabundance of cognitive functioning, or of a radical qualitative difference in the nature of the patient's experience, is seldom explored. Nor is there much emphasis on the active role the patient might play in creating his abnormal world and actions.

Such approaches can have the unfortunate effect of legitimating a contemptuous and dismissive attitude: when human beings are viewed as malfunctioning cerebral mechanisms, incapable of higher levels of purposefulness and awareness, it will naturally be assumed that they are not only *difficult* to interpret but in some sense *beneath* interpretation, since their behavior and expression must lack the intentionality and meaningfulness of normal human activity.[19] In criticizing these views, Karl Jaspers was attacking the forms of disenchantment that madness has suffered in the modern world, under the cold gaze of reductionistic science. For him schizophrenic experience remained unintelligible not because it was beneath understanding but because it was beyond it, existing in some unimaginable realm outside the possibility of human comprehension.[20] But those who adopt *either* Kraepelin's notion of dementia or Jaspers's "doctrine of the abyss" have assumed that the essential features of the schizophrenic disorder are the result of some unknown organic cause—a biological factor that intrudes itself into the psychological sphere and thus cannot be understood psychologically. (Obviously, such attitudes are unlikely to encourage therapeutic efforts, and one wonders whether they may actually increase the patient's sense of alienation from the social world.) According to this view, schizophrenia might eventually be *explained* in a causal fashion—as the effect of some "tangible morbid process occurring in the brain"—but is a dubious candidate for empathic understanding or psychological interpretation.[21] The schizophrenic process will always remain beyond the reach of our empathy, Jaspers believed, for its distinctive element is "something inaccessible and foreign which, for this very reason, the language defines as *deranged.*"[22]

The schizophrenic, it would seem, is psychiatry's quintessential other— the patient whose essence is incomprehensibility itself.

The Original Infantile Story

We are victims of a subjective illusion. . . . In the normal course of things, customs varying greatly from our own always seem puerile.
    —Claude Lévi-Strauss
      "The Archaic Illusion," *The Elementary Structures of Kinship*

But these conceptions of dementia and of an unbridgeable alienness are not the only notions to have affected modern attitudes toward madness; and in the more eclectic work of Eugen Bleuler, one of the three great sources of modern psychiatric thinking (the others being Kraepelin and Jaspers), we encounter the most influential alternative to these "medical-model" assumptions. Bleuler, a man who coined the term *schizophrenia* and spent most of his life living with and treating schizophrenics, once remarked that when all was said and done, they remained as strange to him as the birds in his garden.[23] Yet he also wrote the following, in what must have been a very different mood: "There are essentially only quantitative differences between the dream of the youngster who plays general on his hobby-horse . . . the twilight state of the hysteric, and the hallucinations of the schizophrenic in which his most impossible wishes appear fulfilled. All these are but points along the same scale."[24]

In his great monograph of 1911, Bleuler declared a dual allegiance, to both Kraepelin and Freud. And in his work we can see how twentieth-century conceptions of madness have oscillated between two extremes: a declaration of its inherent remoteness or mental debility and the idea that we can understand it if we view it as a return to some kind of childlike, infantile, or even prenatal state.[25]

In 1911 Sigmund Freud described schizophrenia as a profound regression to the most primitive stage of "infantile auto-eroticism,"[26] and since then nearly all psychoanalytic writers have interpreted this type of psychosis as involving some kind of deep regression to the "original infantile story."[27] They see the structures of schizophrenic consciousness as a return to an archaic mode of experience dominated by illogical primary-process thinking, by hallucinatory wish-fulfillment fantasy and raw, untamed instinct, by a state of primal fusion with the world, and by an absence or severe attenuation of "observing ego" (the capacity for self-conscious reflection and ironic distance from experience). There are many variations of this view, all offering the possibility of both a theoretical grasp and an empathic understanding of this seemingly alien mode of being.[28] The effect of such theorizing is to welcome the schizophrenic back into the human fold, but only in the subordinate position of the child.

The regression or fixation in question has sometimes been understood largely as a deficiency, the result of defects of the ego, at other times more as a defense, a way of escaping anxieties that a more mature consciousness would have to recognize. Further, the stage to which one returns (or at which one is fixated) is sometimes conceptualized as being akin to the normal infantile condition, at other times as involving deviations from the developmental norm.[29] But in all these cases, the most distinctive features of schizophrenic consciousness are considered to involve lower stages of psychological existence that are characterized by "deterioration in conceptual powers," "derangement of purposeful and selective attention," and "little capacity to reflect on the self and on immediate experience"; by an inability to distinguish self from environment; and by a dominance of the "most primitive processes of merging with the object."[30] If in the neuroses we discover the lost content of childhood, its yearnings and conflicts, in such psychoses we supposedly encounter something closer to the form of infantile consciousness itself: subjectivity at the very moment of its birth.

Whatever one may think of the validity of these psychoanalytic perspectives on schizophrenia, one can hardly deny their importance, both in the mental health professions and in the culture at large. It is not that these Freudian and post-Freudian notions are radically new—as we have seen, many of their tenets have been with us since Heraclitus and Plato.[31] But psychoanalysis is by far the most influential contemporary vision of human nature, and as such it offers the decisive modern formulation of these views.

While something akin to the Kraepelinian or Jasperian approach remains the dominant view in the biologically oriented psychiatry of the present day, the "primitivity" view is embraced by the vast majority of those who seek a psychological understanding or who advocate psychotherapeutic treatment of such patients.[32] Not only in psychoanalysis but also in other schools of psychological thought—cognitive-developmental, gestaltist, Jungian, interpersonal, and self-psychological—the strategy of explanation often assumes something like a modern and developmental version of the Great Chain of Being: the idea, prominent in Western thought through the Renaissance, of a single hierarchy of being with ascending degrees of perfection, rising "from the dark, heavy and imperfect earth to the higher and higher perfection of the stars and heavenly spheres," from the domain of ignorance and the body to the bracing heights of rational self-awareness.[33] All these schools accept some version of the grand and optimistic Western narrative of progress toward higher levels of consciousness and self-consciousness, and all presuppose a single, unilinear dimension along which all psychological phenomena can be located. At the very top are the reality-adapted, pragmatic, quasi-scientific modes of consciousness presumably obtained by normal socialized adults in modern culture. And, by what seems an inexorable logic, any deviation from this condition is assumed to correspond to an earlier and lower developmental stage.

In this narrative, schizophrenia holds a special place—as an exemplar of the lowest stages and a supposed proof of the correlation between the severity of an illness and its degree of primitivity. Such interpretations can have a powerful appeal—what Wittgenstein, in his lectures on Freud, described as "the attraction which mythological explanations have, explanations which say that this is all a repetition of something that has happened before." And, as Wittgenstein pointed out, "When people do accept or adopt this, then certain things seem much clearer and easier for them."[34] This view has often led to the rather condescending assumption that schizophrenics need to be brought up or socialized, and that a therapist should play the role of a benign and wise parent who gives the patient a second chance to be nurtured toward maturity. (Anna Freud wrote that the appropriate therapeutic techniques in treating schizophrenics "are in many respects identical with the methods used in the upbringing of infants.")[35]

The Wildman: Hero of Desire

Though mainstream psychiatry and psychoanalysis have been the major influences on the understanding and treatment of schizophrenia in this century, they are not the only traditions to have concerned themselves with this condition. As the most severe and prototypical type of madman, the schizophrenic has also been a central figure in the twentieth-century literary, intellectual, and artistic avant-garde (including the tradition of antipsychiatry), where he has been taken to exemplify yearned-for ideals of authenticity or unfettered passion. In *The Politics of Experience*, R. D. Laing describes madness as a release from constraint and a return to "primal man" that may even have the power to heal "our own appalling state of alienation called normality."[36] In works like André Breton's "Surrealist Manifesto" of 1924 as well as in more recent books such as Norman O. Brown's *Love's Body* and Gilles Deleuze and Félix Guattari's *Anti-Oedipus: Capitalism and Schizophrenia,* the schizophrenic is celebrated as a "true hero of desire," a Wildman figure who "is closest to the beating heart of reality" and "the vital biology of the body"; and he is sometimes seen as an "emblem of creative insurrection against rationalist repression linked to social power."[37] Here the prevailing image has been the "Dionysian madness" described in Nietzsche's *Birth of Tragedy*, where ecstatic surrender of self-control obliterates all doubt and hesitation, making way for the raptures of unrestrained instinct and "primordial unity." Since such a condition is generally assumed to be more characteristic of early stages of development or evolution, there is a certain affinity between the Dionysian and primitivity models. The avant-gardists and antipsychiatrists have emphasized the positive side—excesses of passion, vitality, and imagination—yet they, no less than the traditional analysts, assume that the schizophrenic lacks the self-control, awareness of social convention, and reflexivity of "civilized" consciousness. For traditionalists as well as radicals, rationalists as well as romantics, the schizophrenic exists in something akin to the stage of mythical thought—the moment when (in Ernst Cassirer's words) consciousness has not yet raised itself from its stupor.[38]

Such notions of schizophrenia are, in fact, remarkably reminiscent of the evolutionism that once prevailed in cultural anthropology, in which tribal man was assumed to be ruled by rampant instinct and to lack the capacity for abstraction and self-awareness attained in later stages of development or evolution. Lévi-Strauss describes the "traditional picture of this primitiveness," which he finds in Lucien Lévy-Bruhl and other earlier anthropologists, as of a "creature barely emerged from an animal condition and still a prey to his needs and instincts who has so often been imagined . . . [a] consciousness governed by emotions and lost in a maze of confusion and [magical] participation."[39] Compare this to psychoanalyst Marguerite Sechehaye's vision of madness as the triumph of the id:

Freed of social control, stripped of logical and moral imperatives, deprived of conscious directives, [schizophrenic thinking] sends its roots to the very heart of the desires, the dreads and the fundamental drives of which it is the cherished instrument of expression. Invested with an affective potential drawn from reality, it charges the inanimate world of objects with life, energy and the strength of the drives from which it emanates.[40]

Though such assumptions about madness and mind can be traced back to the ancient world, it was the rationalism of the seventeenth- and eighteenth-century Enlightenment that gave them their modern stamp. Once human consciousness came to be defined by the self-awareness of its mental essence, as in Descartes's famous arguments about the certainty of the *Cogito* (*"Cogito ergo sum"*), it seemed especially evident that madness must be understood as a deviation from this condition of self-transparent mentation, that thought and madness must somehow be profoundly antithetical.[41] At the deepest level, then, all three of these models—psychiatric, psychoanalytic, and avant-gardist—share the assumption that schizophrenic pathology must involve a loss of what, in the West, has long been assumed to be the most essential characteristics of mind or subjectivity: the capacities for logic and abstract thinking, for self-reflection, and for the exercise of free will.[42]

Each of these models claims to explain a great deal of schizophrenic symptomatology, and to do so by assimilating bizarre symptoms to conditions more readily understood. Such models can be powerful—too powerful perhaps; in their explanatory zeal, they may distort or oversimplify the phenomena they purport to explain. Through taking a closer and, I hope, less biased look at the lived world of schizophrenic patients, I will present a very different interpretation of their modes of being. For the moment, however, we need to hold all explanations in abeyance and examine the phenomena at issue. As we shall see, there are a number of central features of schizophrenia that do not, even on their face, seem very consistent with the concept of deficient, Dionysian, or primitive states of mind; here I shall mention just three.

ANOMALOUS FEATURES OF SCHIZOPHRENIA

The first feature conflicts most blatantly with the Dionysian image of schizophrenia. This is that schizophrenic persons can often seem nearly devoid of emotion and desire (they display "flatness of affect") and that a sense of alienation may be felt as much by the patient as by the observer. Also, such persons often display a more deliberative and ideational rather than intuitive or emotional style of acting and problem solving.[43] A schizophrenic mentioned earlier (the one who took the imaginary journey down his own trachea) could hardly have been more different from the id incarnate postulated by the primitivity and Dionysian models; this patient was, in fact, so devoid of any real sense of physical grounding or spontaneity that he once described his body as a photocopy machine, and contemplated cutting himself to see whether there might be motor oil in his veins. Many such patients report feeling profoundly distant and lonely—"like a zombie living behind a glass wall," as one put it.[44] Kraepelin, in his *Lectures on Clinical Psychiatry*, spoke of the "peculiar and fundamental want of any *strong feeling of the impressions of life*" as being perhaps the distinguishing quality of *dementia praecox*.[45] As both he and Bleuler have noted, a characteristic feature of the disease is a frequent outburst of laughter; yet there tends to be something stiff, tinny, or affectless about this hilarity: "the fresh joyousness of the manic [patient] is lacking."[46]

The second anomalous feature is the peculiar variability or instability of schizophrenic cognitive disturbances, a fact that conflicts with the concept of schizophrenia as a kind of dementia. Curiously, many patients who have long given the impression of being severely incapacitated may, under the right circumstances, show themselves to be quite capable of intact speech and intellectual functions, of appropriate emotional reactions, and even of making practical decisions and cooperating with others. When a major flood hit Topeka, Kansas, in 1951, one psychologist from the Menninger clinic was "astonished . . . to see chronic schizophrenic patients—some of whom had been hospitalized for over twenty years—not only loading and placing sandbags with the rest of us, but effectively supervising us in the loading and placement of the bags." The patients kept this up for several days; then, once the emergency had passed, they resumed their back-ward existence.[47]

As a general rule, schizophrenics tend to perform somewhat more poorly, often more slowly, than do normal individuals on a wide variety of tests of cognitive functioning (but not always; on some tests their performance can be superior). As Eugen Bleuler, among others, has noted, however, it is all too easy to make the mistake of assuming ignorance or incapacity when one is really encountering indifference, negativism, or reluctance to think, which may make the patient profess ignorance or give random answers. The mistakes made by schizophrenics (unlike those of patients with organic dementia) do not in fact closely correlate with the difficulty of the task: a patient who seems to have trouble with a simple problem of subtraction will, a moment later, solve a much more complex arithmetic problem with ease;[48] a patient who claims not to know what the date is or where she is will, minutes later, write a letter that shows her to be fully oriented. "Whenever the patient has an earnest aspiration," Bleuler observed, "he shows himself capable of making exceptionally sharp-witted and complex deductions to achieve his desired ends."[49]

The poet Friedrich Hölderlin was schizophrenic for the last forty years of his life, and he often spoke to visitors (especially those he didn't like) in a garbled and virtually incomprehensible way, using language that suggested extreme confusion and lack of self-control. But even after "no sensible word had been spoken by him for days or weeks on end," he would compose poems containing not a single meaningless line nor any distortions of syntax or semantics—and this "without rereading them afterwards or correcting anything at all." One of his friends wondered: Could it be that Hölderlin only "wore the *mask* of folly, from time to time, like Hamlet"?[50]

The third feature of schizophrenia that seems inconsistent with the traditional models is of a somewhat different order, for it concerns not any single symptom but the daunting heterogeneity of the entire syndrome.

Actually, many psychiatric categories subsume a certain diversity, and many are probably "family concepts," lacking a single and clear-cut criterion or essential defining feature. But the character traits and symptoms of most diagnostic groups can nevertheless be "comprehended" in two distinct but related senses of the word: "understood" empathically as well as grouped together as a unity of related features. The orderliness, frugality, and stubbornness of the obsessive-compulsive person, for example, do not seem a random congeries but a grouping that has a certain unity (all three traits suggest an excessive need for autonomy and self-control); and even the manifest inconsistency of manic-depressive mood-states can be grasped as a dialectical shifting rooted in a disturbance of emotional control.

It is in the realm of schizophrenia that all the vulnerabilities of taxonomic classification seem to be multiplied and underscored. Here the characteristic symptoms cannot easily be ascribed to disturbance of a single psychological function, whether of thought, emotion, will, or interpersonal judgment; all these faculties seem to be affected, and it would be difficult to say that one is more central than the others. Nor can schizophrenia be described in terms of a single theme, like exaggerated control, labile emotion, or heightened self-love; on almost any dimension one might choose, this kind of person manifests a heterogeneity that is hard to explain on the basis of any common-sensical interpretation or standard model of the illness. Indeed, almost any generalization one applies to such patients will seem, on further consideration, almost counter to the truth. The traditional models of malfunctioning brain or childlike experience suggest that such patients ought to be prone to concrete modes of thinking and animistic ways of perceiving the world. Yet we typically find that, while schizophrenics sometimes manifest seemingly literal or concretistic thinking, they are also given to unusually abstract modes of cognition; while they may sometimes experience the world in an animized fashion (as if even the walls were listening and the clocks staring), they may equally well experience it as deadened and mechanistic (one patient believed that everyone else was an automaton, and that, with his parents, "I had to do all their thinking for them").[51]

Schizophrenics can be hypersensitive to human contact but also indifferent.[52] They can be pedantic or capricious, idle or diligent, irritable or filled with an all-encompassing yet somehow empty hilarity.[53] They can experience a rushing flow of ideas or a total blocking;[54] and their actions, thoughts, and perceptions can seem rigidly ordered or controlled (exhibiting a "morbid geometrism"),[55] but at other times chaotic and formless. They will sometimes feel they can influence the whole universe, at other times as if they can't control even their own thoughts or their own limbs—or, in what is one of the supreme paradoxes of this condition, they may have both these experiences at the same moment.[56] They may be extremely negativistic, responding to requests either by doing the exact opposite or by refusing even to acknowledge the requester's existence; yet it is inaccurate to characterize them, as is often done, simply as oppositional or even as out of contact with their social environment. For, at other times, the same schizophrenic may be afflicted with "suggestion slavery"—veritable "fits of servility" in which he complies instantly with every request (although sometimes exaggerating his performance to a ridiculous degree).[57]

This illness therefore defies all attempts to bring its features within the grasp of any overarching theory or model, or to discover an underlying essence, the " 'something' that underlies the symptoms," as Jaspers calls it.[58] It is easy to feel that we would be wiser simply to admit our incomprehension and leave it at that. Again, Jaspers best sums up this frustrating impasse:

> Among all this ununderstandable material search has been made for *a central factor*. All the unexpected impulses, incomprehensible affects and lack of affect, the sudden pauses in conversation, the unmotivated ideas, the behaviour so reminiscent of distraction and all the other phenomena which we can only describe negatively and indirectly ought to have some common base. Theoretically we talk of incoherence, dissociation, fragmenting of consciousness, intrapsychic ataxia [splitting of thought and emotion], weakness of apperception, insufficiency of psychic activity and disturbance of association, etc. We call the behavior crazy or silly but all these words simply imply in the end that there is a common element of "the ununderstandable."[59]

And so we arrive once again at this strange criterion of strangeness— sheer bizarreness and the "ununderstandable." Yet this criterion is itself problematic. What, after all, is "bizarreness"? Does it designate some positive quality or only an absence, the lack of some difficult-to-define norm? And if the latter, must we accept schizophrenia as but an ad hoc category—a potpourri of phenomena whose only common feature is their deviance from the standard human form of life?

The criterion can also be criticized for its overly subjective nature. How can we know that understanding (the finding of "intelligible relations") is a function of the patient rather than of something in the explainer—his zeal, the elasticity of his interpretive concepts, his empathic skills, or perhaps his ability to find schizoid elements within himself?[60] One may well be tempted to throw one's hands up in despair, declaring schizophrenia an "impossible concept" that should be eliminated from our nosology.[61] But here again Jaspers's position seems the wisest one, and as valid today as ever. Though well aware of the many problems plaguing the schizophrenia concept (how, for example, its borders have vacillated throughout the history of psychiatry, sometimes narrowing but at other times becoming "so impossibly extended [as to] perish with [its] own magnitude"), he maintained that it is nevertheless an indispensable concept for the science of psychopathology.[62] We must recall, however, that in Jaspers's view any discoveries about the nature of schizophrenia would have to come from fields such as psychophysiology and genetics, since the "psychology of meaningful connections" could not be applied to this most alien of mental illnesses.

Although I disagree with Jaspers on this last point, I believe he was quite right to stress the two aspects of schizophrenia that pose the greatest challenge to all interpretive understanding: its extreme diversity and the alienness of its characteristic signs and symptoms. Whatever schizophrenia is, a certain heterogeneity and qualities of strangeness are certainly among its most salient features; models or similes that ignore these aspects of the disease thereby convict themselves of inadequacy. What is needed, then, is an interpretation that can help us to elucidate common features without glossing over the diversity, and to understand schizophrenic patients without downplaying their alienness or the radical contradictions of their inner worlds.

Having introduced the main object of this comparative study, schizophrenic symptoms, suggested their problematic nature, and questioned traditional interpretations, I now turn to the other side of the comparison: the domain of modernist art and thought. At this point a juxtaposition of madness and modernism may seem rather arbitrary, perhaps even outlandish, to some readers. Only the following chapters can really demonstrate the aptness and fruitfulness of the comparison, but one remark here can perhaps help bring the two domains into suggestive alignment: if schizophrenia is to be comprehended psychologically, I would suggest that its interpretation must be intimately tied to its very diversity and incomprehensibility; what better place, then, to seek analogies than in the culture of modernism/postmodernism—that "tradition of the new" where bafflement and pluralism are the rule?[63]

A BIZARRE TRADITION AND A TRADITION
OF THE BIZARRE

"It is high time for us to compare these phenomena with something different"—one may say. I am thinking, e.g., of mental illnesses.
—Ludwig Wittgenstein
Culture and Value

The advent of modernism is, at the same time, the most distinctive and the most elusive of aesthetic revolutions. Virginia Woolf's famous statement, "In or about December 1910 human nature changed," is not, of course, to be taken literally; but it does capture a widespread sense that some profoundly new developments were occurring shortly after the turn of the century—developments concentrated in the realms of avant-garde art, literature, and thought, but echoing simultaneously in many other areas of human life. C. S. Lewis, a man of traditional tastes and tendencies, spoke for many when he wrote that no "previous age produced work which was, in its own time, as shatteringly and bewilderingly new as that of the Cubists, the Dadaists, the Surrealists, and Picasso has been in ours." Along with such critics as George Steiner and Roland Barthes, he saw the decades preceding World War I as marking the greatest rupture in the entire history of Western art and culture; indeed, he considered modern poetry "not only a greater novelty than any other 'new poetry' but new in a new way, almost in a new dimension."[64] The sheer fact of the newness may be indisputable, but defining its nature is a somewhat more difficult proposition.

All period concepts subsume a certain diversity, of course, but the variousness of modernist innovations is somehow more daunting. What, after all, could dadaist art—celebrating chaos and mocking all aesthetic values—have in common with the ordered neoclassical formalism of the later T. S. Eliot? What could the austere rationalism of Mondrian or the Bauhaus share with the neoromantic dream-logic of surrealism? Herbert Read saw the modernist revolution as unique in kind precisely because it did *not* establish a new order; rather, he said, it is "a break-up, a devolution, some would say a dissolution. Its character is catastrophic." And another critic has written that if modernism *were* to establish a prevalent style of its own, it would thus deny itself, "thereby ceasing to be modern."[65]

It would be understandable, then, if one were tempted to abandon entirely the quest for an encompassing definition. Perhaps "modernism" just *has* no unifying characteristics: Might the term designate an utterly diverse set of attitudes and practices, a mere miscellany sharing nothing more than a certain contemporaneity and, perhaps, a general aversion to the nineteenth-century traditions of romanticism and realism? In my view such a conclusion is not warranted, for, though difficult, it is not impossible to discern certain family resemblances running through most central examples not only of the advanced art of the first half of the twentieth century but also of the so-called postmodernist art popular during the last few decades.

I have divided the salient characteristics of modernism (defined broadly to include postmodernism) into seven interdependent aspects or features. Though many of these characteristics will be present in the most representative works, few such works will exhibit them all. Also, the features must be understood not as absolute qualities but as propensities or tendencies that are particularly pronounced in such art. And, as we shall see, several of the qualities have a dialectical, almost contradictory nature, and are quite capable of undermining themselves or even, at times, of turning into their opposites. But this is part of what makes modernism so useful for our purposes—for elucidating forms of psychopathology that are no less startlingly diverse, complex, or paradoxical in nature.

(The term *modernism* is used in this book in a fairly broad sense, one that includes what is called postmodernism as a somewhat-difficult-to-define subgenre. I view postmodernism, rather than as a deviation in some radically new direction, either as being an *exaggeration* of central modernist tendencies [of modernism's reflexivity and detachment], or as involving certain *dialectical reversals* occurring within a shared framework, a framework defined by these same tendencies. In either case, postmodernism looks less like an adversary than like an offspring—or, perhaps, a sibling—of the artworks of the high modernist period and sensibility.)[66]

Avant-Gardism, the Adversarial Stance

The first characteristic of modernism is the one most obviously associated with the heterogeneity just described, and this is its negativism and antitraditionalism: its defiance of authority and convention, its antagonism or indifference to the expectations of its audience, and, on occasion, its rage for chaos. Though precursors can certainly be found, notably in romanticism, it is in the twentieth century that these tendencies seem to have moved from an epidemic to an endemic state, thereby establishing avant-gardism as the "chronic condition" or "second nature" of modern art.[67]

The desire to escape conventional languages and seek as yet undiscovered subjects for expression is present in many classic examples of proto-, early, and high modernism. "To inspect the invisible and hear the unheard-of"—this was the goal espoused by the poet Arthur Rimbaud in 1871;[68] and a great many writers and artists who followed him have adopted similar ambitions, as if only the ineffable and the incomprehensible could be worthy subjects for poetic attention. The twin motives this entails—escape from convention and exploration of the new—have often resulted in an extreme and off-putting degree of obscurity (the famous "difficulty" of modern poetry) or even in a flirtation with silence, with total refusal of communication as well as expression on the grounds that any possible medium is inevitably contaminated by convention and the generic.[69] The negativism and rebellion are at their most intense in a dada polemicist like Tristan Tzara, who spoke of art as "a private affair, [something] the artist . . . produces for himself," and who compared his fellow rebels to "a furious wind, tearing the dirty linen of clouds and prayers, preparing the great spectacle of disaster, fire, decomposition."[70]

A different attitude toward tradition and the possibility of originality has long been present in modernism, and has recently come to the fore under the banner of "postmodernism." Here, instead of being rejected, conventions are actually embraced and exaggerated in various forms of parody and pastiche;[71] hence the avant-gardist element, the alienation from tradition, emerges in a different way, not as an iconoclastic striving for radical innovation and originality but in the bemused and knowing irony, or deadpan detachment, with which conventional forms are mockingly displayed.[72]

The paradoxicality of entrenched avant-gardism is captured in the notion of an "adversary culture" or "tradition of the new," whose only constant is change itself, whose only rule is the injunction to "make it new."[73] By their very nature, such ambitions will incite the most varied forms of expression in an ever-accelerating whirl of real or pseudo-innovation (or in the constant and ironic recycling of familiar forms). For the modern, as Octavio Paz has remarked, is "condemned to pluralism"; characterized by novelty as well as otherness, it is truly "a bizarre tradition and a tradition of the bizarre."[74] We should not be suprised, therefore, that the common thread cannot be found in the forms themselves, but only in the psychological condition, the attitude of defiance or alienation, that underlies them.

Perspectivism and Relativism

A related characteristic of many modernist and postmodernist works is the uncertainty or multiplicity of their point of view. We find works that draw attention to the presence of a particular perspective, thereby displaying a recognition of the inevitable limitedness of that perspective, as well as works that attempt to transcend such limits by inhabiting a variety of perspectives, simultaneously or in quick succession. (Impressionist paintings and novels such as Virginia Woolf's *Mrs. Dalloway* might exemplify the first sort; analytic cubist paintings and novels such as William Faulkner's *The Sound and the Fury* and Woolf's *The Waves* illustrate the second.)

Both tendencies are inspired by the modern realization of the observer's role in both creating and curtailing the world of perception, a realization usually traced to Immanuel Kant's demonstration, at the turn of the nineteenth century, of the central role of the human subject, in particular of the human "categories of understanding," in the constitution of all knowledge. (The critic Clement Greenberg identifies modernism with "the intensification, almost the exacerbation, of this self-critical tendency that began with the philosopher Kant.")[75] This can lead to what Nietzsche called "the most extreme form of nihilism": the view that there is no true world, since everything is but "a *perspectival appearance* whose origin lies in us."[76] And this recognition of one's own centrality can, in turn, be experienced in a couple of different ways: as a vertiginous sense of power inherent in seeing reality as but a figment of one's own, all-powerful self; or as a despairing recognition of the ultimate meaninglessness and absurdity of the human world, a succumbing to what Nietzsche called "the great blood-sucker, the spider skepticism."[77]

Dehumanization, or the Disappearance of the Active Self

The development in the twentieth century of what has seemed a higher sophistication about human consciousness has been accompanied, oddly enough, by a certain fragmentation and passivization, by a loss of the self's sense of unity and of its capacity for effective or voluntary action; this has gone along with an ethic of impersonality that contrasts sharply with the romantic cult of the self.

One variant of this tendency might be termed an impersonal subjectivism or a subjectivity without a subject. In this form of dehumanization (common in novels by Ford Madox Ford, Virginia Woolf, and Nathalie Sarraute, among others), there is a fragmentation from within that effaces reality and renders the self a mere occasion for the swarming of independent subjective events—sensations, perceptions, memories, and the like. The overwhelming vividness, diversity, and independence of this experiential swarm fragment the self, obliterating its distinctive features—the sense of unity and control.[78]

A second variant of modernist dehumanization seems, by contrast, to indulge the most extreme kind of objectivism. Here human activity is observed with the coldest and most external of gazes, a gaze that refuses all empathy and strips the material world of all the valences of human meaning. Though less common than the fragmented subjectivism I have just mentioned, this kind of dehumanization has nevertheless held an important place throughout the twentieth century. It was central to the work of Wyndham Lewis, the radically antiromantic and antihumanist painter and novelist who depicted human bodies in the manner of machines and whose novels portray human activity as the mechanical playing out of clichéd scenarios: "Deadness is the first condition of art," Lewis wrote, "the second is absence of soul . . . good art must have no inside."[79] More recently, this objectivist dehumanization occurs in the fiction of Alain Robbe-Grillet as well as in various other writers of a postmodernist or poststructuralist persuasion.

Derealization and the "Unworlding of the World"

This feature, closely bound up with the dehumanization I just mentioned, could be termed the "loss of significant external reality."[80] It too can occur in at least two different forms—with the emphasis either on the loss of the feeling that reality is external or on the loss of reality's aura of significance.

In many modernist works, the world seems to be *derealized*, robbed of its substantiality or objectivity, its ontological status as an entity or horizon independent of the perceiving subject. Writing of the techniques of twentieth-century abstract painting, the art historian Meyer Shapiro describes "the thousand and one ingenious formal devices of dissolution, penetration, immateriality and incompleteness, which affirm the abstract artist's active sovereignty over objects." In search of a freedom beyond society and nature, such artists negate the "formal aspects of perception—like the connectedness of shape and color or the discontinuity of object and surroundings—that enter into the practical relations of man in nature," thereby denying or overcoming the obdurate independence of the world.[81] In the poet Stéphane Mallarmé's influential ideal of a literature of absence, we find the literary equivalent: a poetry preoccupied with its own sounds and syntax, seeking to negate rather than to evoke a realm of external objects and events.

Often this sovereignty over objects amounts to a kind of solipsism, with experiential objects seeming dependent on the perceiving self or the self expanding to fill the world. Heidegger described the modern age as the "age of the world view," a period when the world is "conceived and grasped" *as* a view, as a kind of subordinated picture. ("Man becomes that being upon which all that is, is grounded as regards the manner of its Being and its truth," he writes. "Wherever this happens, man 'gets into the picture' in precedence over whatever is.")[82] In Alfred Jarry, the turn-of-the-century playwright who inspired the theater of the absurd, we find a more annihilating solipsism, the celebration of an utter self-involvement of the mind: Being, said Jarry, "consists . . . not in perceiving or being perceived, but in that the iridescent mental kaleidoscope *think itself and of itself* [*SE pense*]."[83]

This subjectivist variant is not the only version of modernist worldhood, however; in another mode, external reality loses not its substantiality and otherness but its human resonance or significance, thus bringing about what Heidegger called the "unworlding of the (human) world." One extreme manifestation of this is what has been called the "white style" or "zero degree of literature"[84]—exemplified by the novelist Alain Robbe-Grillet's *chosisme* ("thingism"), his aspiration to depict a world "neither meaningful nor absurd, [that] quite simply *is*," a world where "all around us defying our pack of animistic or domesticating adjectives things *are there* . . . without false glamour, without transparency."[85]

Obviously, there are radical differences between "derealization" and "unworlding," the subjectivist and objectivist variants of modernist worldhood; but there are also important affinities. In both cases, the ego or self is passivized: either it becomes an impotent observer of thinglike yet inner experiences—of sensations, images, and the like (derealization)—or else it is transformed into a machinelike entity placed in a world of static and neutral objects (unworlding). And, in both cases, the objects of human experience are reified, transformed into opaque or intransitive entities that can do no more than manifest their own mere presence (when the objects in question are *subjective* phenomena, they seem incapable of referring to a transcendent external world—one experiences experience, as it were; when they are objective "things," they seem unable to evoke or convey human significance or value—one perceives meaningless bits of matter).[86] Indeed, as we shall see in chapters 5 and 11, the subjectivism and objectivism associated with both dehumanization and derealization are so closely linked that they can actually coexist at the same moment, as complementary facets of a single though highly paradoxical mode of existence. (Heidegger speaks of a "necessary interplay" between subjectivism and objectivism in the modern age, a "reciprocal conditioning" that points back "to events more profound": namely, to the momentous development of a form of self-consciousness whereby the human being loses touch with the reality of practical activity and comes to experience himself as a subjectivity, or *subiectum*—the essential being for whom and by whom the world is represented.)[87]

"Spatial Form"

Given the forms of passivization and reification I have just described, certain traditional ways of organizing literary works become less viable. In a universe where human intentions are nonexistent or inconsequential, and where objects no longer show up as goals, obstacles, or tools but as mere phenomena for contemplation, it is no longer possible for narrative structure, with its presumption of meaningful historical change, to serve as a central unifying principle. Many works of modernist literature therefore seek alternatives to storytelling and to all the standard devices of temporal or narrative form.

In the classic article "Spatial Form in Modern Literature," the literary scholar Joseph Frank describes some of the ways modernist fiction attempts to deny its own temporality and approach the condition of the poetic image, defined by Ezra Pound as "that which presents an intellectual and emotional complex in an instant of time."[88] To achieve this sense of encompassing experiential stasis, writers use a number of devices to draw attention away from both the inherent temporality of language (which by its very nature can only present one word after another, in a temporal sequence) and the implicit temporality of human action itself, with its purposes and causes. These include: the overwhelming of plot by mythic structures used as organizing devices (as in Joyce's *Ulysses*), the movement from perspective to perspective instead of from event to event (for example, Faulkner's *The Sound and the Fury*), and the use of metaphoric images as recurring leitmotifs to stitch together separate moments and thereby efface the time elapsed between them (for example, Djuna Barnes's *Nightwood*).

In the objectivist variants of literary modernism, which are somewhat less common, stasis is sought in events or objects themselves rather than in their human meaning or aesthetic significance. Often, such works will have an almost antiliterary tone—a stylized stylelessness that carefully avoids aesthetic devices such as metaphor, simile, and all the techniques for building suspense. Here, "spatial form" typically means an emphasis on neutral description, preferably of static objects, and a downplaying of any lyrical, narrational, or mythic aspects of literature (as in certain novels by Camus, Beckett, and Gertrude Stein).

Aesthetic Self-Referentiality

Many of the motives and purposes that animated earlier forms of art have lost their force in the twentieth century. Mimesis of external reality, evocation of a spiritual beyond, the conveying of an ethical or intellectual message, even the expression of intense inner feelings—all seem to have been deprived of their ability to compel commitment or belief. As if in compensation, many works of art have turned inward, concentrating instead on the revelation of their own being, whether by focusing attention on their own material existence and internal structure or by displaying the processes of artistic creation and appreciation.[89]

One might distinguish a couple of ways in which these effects have been achieved. The first, more aestheticist mode takes its cue from Flaubert's famous ambition to write a book about nothing, a work without external attachments, held together purely through the internal force of its style. In such cases, representational content is attenuated or excluded in favor of formal elements displayed in relative isolation, as in abstract painting or the symbolist cult of the word (where the word is treated as a kind of word-*object*, an opaque sound-complex blotting out all referential meaning).[90] Art thus "encloses itself within a radical intransitivity . . . curv[ing] back in a perpetual return upon itself, as if its discourse could have no other content than the expression of its own form."[91]

In much recent postmodernist art, another mode of reflexivity is dominant: what the Russian formalist critics called the "baring of the device."[92] Here there is no attempt to escape the referential or representational potential of a given aesthetic medium. Indeed, such works take as their explicit subject matter precisely those representational or narrative conventions that had been banished in so many works of early modernism. Italo Calvino's quasi-novel, *If on a Winter's Night a Traveler,* consists, for example, of a series of evocative and suspense-filled but abortive narrative beginnings. Each beginning follows the conventions of nineteenth-century realism, but, instead of leading on to a climax and a further building of suspense, it just circles back to another beginning; as a result, readers cannot lose themselves in the story and are forced instead to focus on the conventions of storytelling itself.[93]

Whereas the first, or aestheticist, mode of artistic self-referentiality involves withdrawal to a position of security, to the self-validating domain of formal perfection (thus "to entrench [the work of art] more firmly in its area of competence," as Clement Greenberg puts it),[94] the second kind of reflexivism is more likely to have a disruptive, undermining, or deconstructive effect—as a subverting of conventional certitudes. But in both cases we can speak of the work of art as what Paul Valéry called "a form of drama in which consciousness watches itself in action"; and of artists as being, in e. e. cummings's words, "good for nothing but walking upright in the cordial revelation of the fatal reflexive."[95]

Irony and Detachment

In a famous essay, "The Dehumanization of Art," the philosopher Ortega y Gasset treats many of the features of modernism mentioned here, and in closing he turns to a feature of special importance—a particularly profound and pervasive form of irony. As Ortega sees it, one consequence of modern art's retreat upon itself is "a ban on all pathos": given that depicting a realistic world of living beings is no longer a primary goal of modern art, such works can no longer engage compassionately with the sorrows and joys of normal human existence, but must operate instead in an "abstruse universe" of "purely aesthetic sentiments."[96] Instead of being imbued with a sense of sincere or passionate engagement, such art is therefore "doomed to irony," to a spirit of "waggery" that may "run the gamut from open clownery to a slight ironical twinkle, but . . . is always there."[97]

This final aspect of modern art, which is even more prominent in postmodernism than in modernism, is implicit in most of the features already discussed, for they all involve disengagement—whether from the aesthetic tradition and the audience, from the perspective of the artwork or artist, or from experiential objects (be they external entities or reified subjective phenomena).[98]

Irony and detachment were certainly far from unknown in earlier periods of art, but prior to modernism these qualities seem not to have been all-encompassing, but qualified by an underlying seriousness of purpose and positive thrust. The "romantic irony" of Friedrich and August Schlegel, for instance, did require artist and audience to be conscious of the fictional or merely imaginary nature of the work of art; but it was not intended to undermine all faith in the ideals of sincere expression and authentic feeling, or in the possibility of redemption through art and the imagination.[99] Modernism, by contrast, is far more caustic and uncompromising—and, as Lionel Trilling has pointed out, it is only in the modernist era that we find artworks whose most central attitude is not to communicate or to celebrate, but to pour scornful laughter on the whole of existence.[100] Further, this spirit of ironic negation—of detachment, subversion, and unremitting criticism—has been turned not just on "life" but on "art" itself. In no previous era of Western art is it possible to imagine a figure like the proto-postmodernist Marcel Duchamp, most of whose career was devoted to a series of mockeries, of ironic comments on art and its purported relationship to life; or one like Samuel Beckett, the bard of a condition of nearly terminal detachment, who dreams of "an art unresentful of its insuperable indigence and too proud for the farce of giving and receiving."[101]

Modernism: Hyperreflexivity and Alienation

As we have seen, each of these seven aspects of innovative art in the twentieth century can manifest itself in a variety of ways. Taken together, they encompass an enormous range. One could ask the same question I posed earlier about schizophrenia: Might "modernism" be only a negative category, an utterly diverse collection of styles and attitudes, linked by nothing more than that most elusive of attributes—the sheer fact of deviating from a norm (in this case, from the aesthetic conventions of preceding generations)? Actually, there is no need to be so nihilistic; for one can in fact discover a loose sort of unity here—not a single underlying essence, perhaps, but at least a common thread or two. These have to do with the presence of intensified forms of self-consciousness and various kinds of alienation. Instead of a spontaneous and naive involvement—an unquestioning acceptance of the external world, the aesthetic tradition, other human beings, and one's own feelings—both modernism and postmodernism are imbued with hesitation and detachment, a division or doubling in which the ego disengages from normal forms of involvement with nature and society, often taking itself, or its own experiences, as its own object.[102]

Unlike their distinguished predecessors, the German and English romantics of the early nineteenth century, the modernists have not sustained hope in the possibility of unifying subject with object or human being with nature. The central goal of romantic aesthetics, integration of opposites through a higher self-forgetfulness, seems to have been largely abandoned or even reversed.[103] Instead, the modernists have opted either for an extreme inwardness, an egoism or solipsism that would deny all reality and value to the external world, or else for a radical materialism or positivism in which not only nature but man himself is stripped of all human, and even of all organic, qualities.[104] And all these tendencies have only been intensified in that further turn of the screw of self-consciousness called postmodernism—for it is there that one finds the most dogmatic expressions of skeptical disengagement, self-referentiality, and denial of the active ego, along with proud, even brazen expressions of both intense subjectivism and hyperobjectivism.[105]

In my portrait of modernism, I am clearly emphasizing what Nietzsche called the Apollonian and Socratic aspects of art: namely, the (sometimes mutually undermining) tendencies toward a form-seeking and contemplative self-control, toward separation of self from world and from other selves, and toward fragmenting hyperawareness and a kind of cerebral self-interrogation. But before I proceed, a possible objection to this portrait of modern art ought to be considered. After all, it has sometimes been alleged that modern art, perhaps especially in its postmodernist forms, is really a Dionysian phenomenon, its central characteristics being surrender to impulse and pleasure, an eclipse of all forms of distance (psychic, social, and aesthetic), and a regression to early, inchoate forms of psychic organization.[106] If so, the analogies between schizophrenia and modernism, no matter how apt, would hardly contradict traditional interpretations of schizophrenia.[107]

In later chapters I will argue that certain aspects of modern art and consciousness (and also of schizophrenia) that have often been assumed to indicate primitivist or Dionysian trends (such as the dissolution of active, unitary selfhood) may actually result from more Apollonian, Socratic, or hyperconscious forms of experience.[108] Still, it would be foolish to deny the existence of certain truly primitivist or Dionysian inclinations in twentieth-century art—for example, in the work of such figures as Rimbaud, Lautréamont, Antonin Artaud, D. H. Lawrence, and Jean Dubuffet. But I would maintain that the boundary-dissolving, spontaneity-inducing instinctualism they sometimes advocate constitutes only a peripheral trend in modernism. It is not merely that such neoprimitivism is less common than other trends in this age and less characteristic of its most influential figures (a point with which the majority of literary scholars would agree);[109] even more telling is the fact that the primitivist expressions that do occur frequently have a strongly reactionary quality, as if their real motivation were a desire to *escape* a more fundamental hyperreflexivity—that condition Ortega described as the "increasing insomnia of civilized man, the almost permanent wakefulness, at times terrible and uncontrollable, which affects men of an intense inner life."[110] One might question the authenticity of these often rather self-conscious expressions—which, in many cases, are more indicative of primitiv*ism* than of a truly primitive mode of being. Friedrich von Schiller believed that the feeling for nature and the spontaneous did not come naturally to his age but, rather, was akin to "the feeling of an invalid for health."[111] The same goes for the twentieth century, where neoprimitivism has only a secondary status—as one of the masks but not the faces of modern art.[112]

The twentieth century seems, then, to be characterized by the pursuit of extremes, by exaggerated objectivist and subjectivist tendencies or by unrestrained cerebralism and irrationalism. These can be understood either as expressions of an extreme self-consciousness or as rather desperate (and often unavailing) attempts to escape from alienation and hyperawareness. Instead of the synthesis advocated by Nietzsche in *The Birth of Tragedy*, we find, on the one hand, the expressions of a fundamentally Apollonian or perhaps Socratic sensibility and, on the other, occasional reactionary lunges toward the most unrestrained Dionysianism. Such trends have resulted in artworks that, at least to the uninitiated, can seem as difficult to grasp, as off-putting and alien, as schizophrenia itself.

This, in any event, is my modernism, the modernism I shall use as a beacon for exploring the forms of madness at issue in this book.

Each of the following chapters is organized around a single domain of schizophrenic symptomatology. With one deviation, I follow the sequence of an ideal-typical schizophrenic process, beginning with the first disturbing encroachments of an alien world and ending in the more bizarre reaches of insanity: the world-catastrophe experience, where most vestiges of stable or familiar reality are dissolved. (The exception is chapter 3, which backtracks to a discussion of the schizoid personality, the character type most common in those who eventually develop schizophrenia.)[113]

Let us turn, then, to our first topic: the uncanny dawn that heralds the onset of a schizophrenic break.

Giorgio de Chirico, *The Enigma of a Day* (1914). *Oil on canvas, 6′1¼″ × 55″. Collection, The Museum of Modern Art, New York. James Thrall Soby Bequest*

PART ONE

EARLY SIGNS AND PRECURSORS: PERCEPTION AND PERSONALITY

The Truth-Taking Stare

Day is breaking. This is the hour of the enigma. . . . One of the strangest and deepest sensations that prehistory has left with us is the sensation of foretelling. It will always exist. It is like an eternal proof of the senselessness of the universe. . . .

One bright winter afternoon I found myself in the courtyard of the palace at Versailles. Everything looked at me with a strange and questioning glance. I saw then that every angle of the palace, every column, every window had a soul that was an enigma. . . . I had a presentiment that this was the way it must be, that it could not be different. An invisible link ties things together, and at that moment it seemed to me that I had already seen this palace, or that this palace had once, somewhere, already existed. Why are these round windows an enigma? . . . And then more than ever I felt that everything was inevitably there, but for no reason and without any meaning. . . .

Then I had the strange impression that I was looking at all these things for the first time, and the composition of my picture came to my mind's eye.

Above all a great sensitivity it needed. One must picture everything in the world as an enigma, not only the great questions one has always asked oneself. . . . But rather to understand the enigma of things generally considered insignificant. . . . To live in the world as if in an immense museum of strangeness.

—Giorgio de Chirico

A s is the case with epileptic seizures, schizophrenic breaks are often preceded by an aura. Klaus Conrad, a German-speaking psychiatrist, named this preliminary stage the *Trema*, a term of theatrical slang referring to the stage fright an actor feels before the performance begins.[1] At these moments the patient will be suspicious and restless, often filled with anticipation or dread. Normal emotions like joy and sadness will be absent, the mood veering instead between anxiety and a kind of electric exaltation.[2] Generally the person has a sense of having lost contact with things, or of everything having undergone some subtle, all-encompassing change. Reality seems to be unveiled as never before, and the visual world looks peculiar and eerie—weirdly beautiful, tantalizingly significant, or perhaps horrifying in some insidious but ineffable way.[3]

Fascinated by this vision, the patient often stares intently at the world, demonstrating that early sign of illness German psychiatry has named the "truth-taking stare" (die Wahrnehmungstarre).[4] (He may also stare at himself in a glass, as if transfixed by the strangeness of his own reflection—the so-called signe du miroir.)[5] Usually the person becomes quiet and withdrawn, though an abrupt and seemingly senseless breach of decorum or discipline may also occur.[6] This mood is sometimes followed by the development of delusions, especially the symptom called "delusional percept"— where a relatively normal perception is experienced as having a special kind of meaning, a meaning not obviously contained in the percept itself and with a special relevance for the perceiver.[7] A good example is a schizophrenic who noticed that people in a train car were crossing their legs from time to time, and then suddenly concluded that they were all performing some kind of play for his benefit.[8]

This is a strange and enigmatic atmosphere, a mood that infuses everything yet eludes description almost completely. To judge from what patients say, the world appears to be, in some sense, quite normal. At least at first, they experience neither hallucinations nor delusions, nor does their thinking or behavior seem disorganized to any significant extent. Still, everything is totally and uncannily transformed: the fabric of space seems subtly changed; the feeling of reality is either heightened, pulsing with a mysterious, unnameable force, or else oddly diminished or undermined—or, paradoxically, things may seem (as one patient put it) both "unreal and extra-real at the same time."[9]

Patients in these moments may have a feeling "of crystal-clear sight, of profound penetration into the essence of things," yet, typically, "there is no real, clear content to communicate."[10] The experience can involve a kind of conjoint and rather contradictory sense of meaning*ful*ness and meaning*less*ness, of significance and insignificance, which could be described as an "anti-epiphany"—an experience in which the familiar has turned strange and the unfamiliar familiar, often giving the person the sense of déjà vu and jamais vu, either in quick succession or even simultaneously.[11] Aspects of this atmosphere are vividly captured in the quotation that opened the chapter, from the journals of the painter Giorgio de Chirico, a severely schizoid man whose famous early canvases exerted a powerful influence on surrealism and other artistic movements of the twentieth century.[12]

The surrealists were, in fact, profoundly inspired by de Chirico's evocations of this vision, and they actually made a practice of cultivating such a mood or state of mind; meditating on de Chirico's paintings was one method they used to bring on a prototypical surrealist mood (see figure 2.1)—the feeling of living in a vast museum of strangeness that they considered to be the essence of aesthetic inspiration and a route to a kind of secular transcendence.[13] ("There are more enigmas in the shadow of a man who walks in the sun than in all the religions of the past, present, and future," wrote de Chirico in his journals.)[14] Though virtually unknown or undescribed before the twentieth century, something like de Chirico's anti-epiphany is in fact characteristic of a wide spectrum of modernist art and thought.[15] The poet Louis Aragon spoke of it as the "dream contagion" of modern art,[16] and it has played a crucial role in the personal development and literary work of many artists of the early twentieth century—including, among others, Hugo von Hofmannsthal, Rilke, Robert Musil, Kafka, Nietzsche, André Breton, and Jean-Paul Sartre.[17]

De Chirico borrowed from Nietzsche the untranslatable German term *Stimmung* to refer to this mood or state of mind that accompanies the truth-taking stare.[18] (I will use *Stimmung* to refer to the perceptual and emotional experience in question, and "truth-taking stare" to refer to the mode of action—that is, a particular way of looking—that goes along with it.) Though the experiences of the *Stimmung* are particularly common in early or premonitory stages of schizophrenia, they can also persist or recur throughout the course of the illness (and also in milder, schizoid disorders, and in some schizoaffective and schizophreniform psychoses). As we shall see, the *Stimmung* is a key symptom of schizophrenia: it contains, *in nuce*, many of the qualities that persist throughout the entire course of the illness and, in addition, seems to play a pivotal role as the foundation or source for other, better-known symptoms, such as delusions or ideas of reference (the latter involves the belief or sense that one is somehow the center of attention, the object of all gazes and messages).[19]

Most clinicians who work with schizophrenic patients will have encountered these important but subtle symptoms, which often dominate the incipient phases of a psychotic break and can give rise to the famous "praecox feeling"—the sense of radical alienness that some European psychiatrists have considered the best diagnostic indicator of schizophrenia. Experienced therapists will have sensed the importance, but also the difficulty, of trying to grasp what patients are going through at this crucial moment when they begin to move away from a social, consensual world. To patients in this state of mind, the world is stripped of its usual meanings and sense of coherence and it therefore defies any standard description. Everything bristles with a

FIGURE 2.1

Giorgio de Chirico, *Gare Montparnasse (Melancholy of Departure)* (1914). A painting evocative of the *Stimmung*, a prototypical surrealist mood. *Oil on canvas, 55⅛" × 6'5⅝". Collection, The Museum of Modern Art, New York. Gift of James Thrall Soby*

new and overwhelming quality of definiteness and significance, yet patients cannot say what the special meanings they sense are, nor just *what* is important about the details that, in their ineffable specificity, so compel their attention. Even the most articulate schizophrenics are usually reduced to helplessly repeating the same, horribly inadequate phrase: everything is strange, or everything is somehow different.

THE *STIMMUNG* IN SCHIZOPHRENIA

Perhaps the best descriptions of the schizoid and schizophrenic *Stimmung* can be found in *The Autobiography of a Schizophrenic Girl*, a personal memoir written by "Renee," a patient who had such experiences not only at the outset but recurrently throughout her illness. While any such categorization is necessarily somewhat arbitrary, it is possible to distinguish at least four aspects of her *Stimmung* experience: what I shall call the visions of Unreality, Mere Being, Fragmentation, and Apophany. The first three seem to be particularly closely interconnected and, taken together, constitute the *Trema* (anticipatory stage fright), while the fourth tends to occur at a somewhat later moment in the psychotic break.

Unreality

Renee describes "a disturbing sense of unreality" as the first inkling of her schizophrenic psychosis, an illness that first appeared at age seventeen and that manifested features of the paranoid and hebephrenic as well as catatonic subtypes of schizophrenia.[20] For her, the encroaching madness would seem to be out there in the world, embedded somehow in the look of material objects and in the forms of space and time. Typically, this Unreality vision revealed an alien and forbidding world pervaded by a sense of illimitable vastness, brilliant light, and the "gloss and smoothness of material things"—a universe of uniform precision and clarity but devoid of the dynamism, emotional resonance, and sense of human purpose that are characteristic of everyday life.[21] Like many of de Chirico's paintings, Renee's world of Unreality lacked the chiaroscuro of normal forms of perception—the quality in which some objects, those deemed subjectively more important, are as if lit up in the focus of awareness while others recede into obscurity:

> For me, madness was definitely not a condition of illness; I did not believe that I was ill. It was rather a country, opposed to Reality, where reigned an implacable light, blinding, leaving no place for shadow; an immense space without boundary, limitless, flat; a mineral, lunar country, cold as the wastes of the North Pole. In this stretching emptiness, all is unchangeable, immobile, congealed, crystallized. Objects are stage trappings, placed here and there, geometric cubes without meaning.
>
> People turn weirdly about, they make gestures, movements without sense; they are phantoms whirling on an infinite plain, crushed by the pitiless electric light. And I—I am lost in it, isolated, cold, stripped, purposeless under the light. A wall of brass separates me from everybody and everything. . . . This was it; this was madness, the Enlightenment was the perception of Unreality. Madness was finding oneself permanently in an all-embracing Unreality. I called it the "Land of Light" because of the brilliant illumination, dazzling, astral, cold, and the state of extreme tension in which everything was, including myself.[22]

As we can see from the following description of being visited in the hospital by a friend, the experiential mutation Renee experienced did not involve gross perceptual errors or confusion about the real identity of people or objects, but something more subtle and pervasive:

> During the visit I tried to establish contact with [my friend], to feel that she was actually there, alive and sensitive. But it was futile. Though I certainly recognized her, she became part of the unreal world. I knew her name and everything about her, yet she appeared strange, unreal, like a statue. I saw her eyes, her nose, her lips moving, heard her voice and understood what she said perfectly, yet I was in the presence of a stranger.[23]

In other descriptions of so-called Unreality, Renee places less emphasis on the feeling of illuminated emptiness, strangeness, or devitalization and more on some flimsy, false, or doubled quality inherent in things. At these moments, objects could take on the look of "stage accessories" or "pasteboard scenery," and people seemed mere "puppets," "mannikins," or "automatons," or else somehow "in disguise."[24] Patients will sometimes express Unreality by stating that everything seems distant, or as if behind plate glass. Things may seem unreal to them, and they may conclude that the world before them is really some kind of second world, perhaps only a simulacrum of the true one existing elsewhere.[25] One schizophrenic saw everything "as through a telescope, smaller and at a very great distance"; this was not so much a matter of actual perceptual illusion as of some subtle change of atmosphere: things seemed "not smaller in reality," the patient said, "but more in the mind . . . less related to each other and to myself as it were . . . [it was] more a mental remoteness."[26] (It is noteworthy that these alterations of spatial experience in schizophrenia do not have a commensurate effect on behavior: the patient does not walk into things, for example, as persons with distorted spatial experience due to organic lesion are wont to do.)[27]

Mere Being

At other times what astonished Renee and riveted her attention was not so much the absence of a normal sense of authenticity, emotional resonance, or functional meanings, but the very fact that objects existed at all—their Mere Being. Here we encounter an experience so very general in nature, yet at the same time so inherently concrete, so rooted in the mute thereness of the world, as nearly to defy description. Depending on the prevailing emotional tone, such experiences can be akin either to the exalting feeling of wonder, mystery, and terror inherent in what Heidegger considers to be the basic question of metaphysics—Why is there something rather than nothing?—or else to the vertigo, nausea, or sense of utter arbitrariness that made Roquentin, hero of Sartre's philosophical novel *Nausea*, reel before the brute fact of existence itself. To Renee, things looked

> smooth as metal, so cut off, so detached from each other, so illuminated and tense that they filled me with terror. When, for example, I looked at a chair or a jug, I thought not of their use or function—a jug not as something to hold water and milk, a chair not as something to sit in—but as having lost their names, their functions and meanings; they became "things" and began to take on life, to exist.
>
> This existence accounted for my great fear. In the unreal scene, in the murky quiet of my perception, suddenly "the thing" sprang up. The stone jar, decorated with blue flowers, was there facing me, defying me with its presence, with its existence. To conquer my fear I looked away. My eyes met a chair, then a table; they were alive, too, asserting their presence. I attempted to escape their hold by calling out their names. I said, "chair, jug, table, it is a chair." But the word echoed hollowly, deprived of all meaning; it had left the object, was divorced from it, so much so that on one hand it was a living, mocking thing, on the other, a name, robbed of sense, an envelope emptied of content. Nor was I able to bring the two together, but stood rooted there before them, filled with fear and impotence.[28]

Renee makes it clear that she is using the word *alive* in a metaphoric sense; that, despite the impression her doctors sometimes had, the world looming before her was not an animistic one:

> When I protested, "Things are tricking me; I am afraid," and people asked specifically, "Do you see the jug and the chair as alive?" I answered, "Yes, they are alive." And they, the doctors, too, thought I saw these things as humans whom I heard speak. But it was not that. Their life consisted uniquely in the fact that they were there, in their existence itself.[29]

Fragmentation

In the visions of Unreality and Mere Being, one experiences a loss of the normal dynamism and texture of human life; but at other moments of the *Trema*, what is most striking about the perceptual world is a quality of fragmentation. Objects normally perceived as parts of larger complexes may seem strangely isolated, disconnected from each other and devoid of encompassing context; or a single object may lose its perceptual integrity and disintegrate into a disunity of parts:

> I looked at "Mama" [writes Renee, referring to her therapist, Dr. Sechehaye]. But I perceived a statue, a figure of ice which smiled at me. And this smile, showing her white teeth, frightened me. For I saw the individual features of her face, separated from each other: the teeth, then the nose, then the cheeks, then one eye and the other. Perhaps it was this independence of each part that inspired such fear and prevented my recognizing her even though I knew who she was.[30]

Another schizophrenic likened his vision of Fragmentation to being "surrounded by a multitude of meaningless details." "I did not see things as a whole," he said, "I only saw fragments: a few people, a dairy, a dreary house. To be quite correct, I cannot say that I did see all that, because these objects seemed altered from the usual. They did not stand together in an overall context, and I saw them as meaningless details."[31] Another patient said that everything seemed split up, "like a photograph that's torn in bits and put together again," while still another spoke of having "to put things together in my head": "If I look at my watch I see the watch, watchstrap, face, hands and so on, then I have got to put them together to get it into one piece."[32] (For an illustration of the Fragmentation experience, see figure 2.2.)

Unreality, where the world is devoid of feeling or authenticity; Mere Being, where the sheer fact of existence defies speech and understanding; Fragmentation, where details or parts overwhelm the synthetic whole: each of these phases or aspects of the *Trema* challenges the capacity of words and concepts to capture lived experience. With the thrusting into prominence of the brute existence of both objects and words, language and the world shed their normal symbol-referent relationship; objects seem to be stripped of the usual meanings by which they are unified and placed in the human world (in Sartre's vocabulary, *essences* recede while *existence* obtrudes). To speak of things as "alive" was Renee's way of capturing the fact that objects no longer seemed to have the subservience of tools, as if they were rebelling against their normal role as dutiful exemplars of the various categories of human thought and language. And, at the same time, words and syllables themselves will come to seem objectlike: no longer the transparent signifiers of meanings lying beyond themselves, they may turn opaque or come alive—flaunting their immanence and independence, demanding to be paid attention to for their own sake. It is, in fact, quite common for schizophrenics and schizoids to complain of the inadequacy of language. One patient I treated was preoccupied with the insufficiency of words, an effect that seemed to

FIGURE 2.2

Fruit bowl drawn by a schizophrenic patient. Evocative of the Fragmentation vision: objects seen in isolation, separated from one another and from their overall context. *From S. Arieti,* Interpretation of Schizophrenia, *2nd ed. (New York: Basic Books, 1974)*

result from his experiencing the Mere Being of both language and world. "Words have textures, and so do objects," he said, "but sometimes the words don't have the same texture as what they refer to." "But what is a train?" asked a patient treated by the psychiatrist Rachel Rosser. "It's a word. The word has nothing to do with a solid thing like a train."[33]

Though any one of these aspects of the *Trema* may be especially prominent at a given moment, all seem to be tightly intertwined, with no single element more fundamental than the others; indeed, they seem able to transform into one another readily, or even to coexist at a single moment. This interdependence is not hard to understand phenomenologically: after all, in normal modes of experience, focusing on standard functional meanings of objects tends to suppress awareness of the sheer fact of their existence as substances, and also to ensure their discreteness and integrity as perceptual forms; it makes sense, therefore, that a fading away of pragmatic and conventional meanings (Unreality) might lead to the experience of Fragmentation or Mere Being (or the reverse: that a focus on Mere Being might erode awareness of conventional meanings).

Apophany

The other aspect of the schizophrenic *Stimmung*, the fourth vision or mode of experience that is common in early phases of a psychotic break (though it generally occurs slightly after the *Trema*), is a certain abnormal awareness of meaningfulness or of significance that has been termed the apophanous mood (from the Greek word *apophany*, meaning "to become manifest").[34] (The *Stimmung*, then—a mood, which is accompanied by the truth-taking stare—can be thought of as consisting of the *Trema*, whose three aspects are Unreality, Mere Being, and Fragmentation, and the *Apophany*, often occurring slightly later.)

Once conventional meanings have faded away (Unreality) and new details or aspects of the world have been thrust into awareness (Fragmentation, Mere Being), there often emerges an inchoate sense of the as yet unarticulated significances of these newly emergent phenomena. In this "mood," so eerily captured in both the writings and the paintings of de Chirico, the world resonates with a fugitive significance. Every detail and event takes on an excruciating distinctness, specialness, and peculiarity—some definite meaning that always lies just out of reach, however, where it eludes all attempts to grasp or specify it. The reality of everything the patient notices can seem heightened, as if each object were, somehow, being hyperbolically itself; and this in turn can create an air of unavoidable specificity, or a feeling of inevitability that hovers about everything. Alternatively, things may take on an exemplary quality, as if they represented other objects or essences, existing not as themselves but as tokens of types lying elsewhere (in such instances visible objects can appear very precise and very unreal at the same time).[35]

The mood, in either case, is such that no object or occurrence can seem accidental; everything is "just so." That something happened the way it did—the fact that a person in one's vicinity coughed three times, for instance—will seem not a random event but somehow necessary, and perhaps deeply significant, even though one would have had this same experience if the event had happened in some other way (if, for example, there had been one or two or four coughs).[36] Karl Jaspers describes this well:

A patient noticed the waiter in the coffee-house; he skipped past him so quickly and uncannily. He noticed odd behaviour in an acquaintance which made him feel strange; everything in the street was so different, something was bound to be happening. A passer-by gave such a penetrating glance, he could be a detective. Then there was a dog who seemed hypnotised, a kind of mechanical dog made of rubber. . . . Something must be going on; the world is changing, a new era is starting. Lights are bewitched and will not burn; something is behind it. A child is like a monkey; people are mixed up, they are imposters all, they all look unnatural. The house-signs are crooked, the streets look suspicious; everything happens so quickly. The dog scratches oddly at the door. "I noticed particularly" is the constant remark these patients make, though they cannot say why they take such particular note of things nor what it is they suspect. First they want to get it clear to themselves.[37]

"Every single thing 'means' something," said one patient of this mood of "delusional tension." "This kind of symbolic thinking is exhausting. . . . I have a sense that everything is more vivid and important. . . . There is a connection to everything that happens—no coincidences."[38] So freighted with the presence of meaning, yet simultaneously so devoid of any particular, specifiable meaning, the symbols experienced during the Apophany might be called "symbol symbols," for the sole referent of these ubiquitous semiotic pointers seems to be the sheer presence of meaningfulness itself.[39]

Traditional Interpretations

Perhaps because of their subtlety and evanescence, the experiences of *Trema* and *Apophany* have not been major topics for discussion and exploration either in psychiatry or in psychoanalysis (they have received far less attention than have more florid and distinct phenomena such as delusions, hallucinations, and abnormalities of language);[40] and it cannot be said that traditional approaches in these fields, at least the better-known approaches, have done much to illuminate or to explain the actual nature of these peculiar early symptoms. Karl Jaspers (along with his follower Kurt Schneider) considered this mood or vision one of the most important and distinctive features of schizophrenia; but, though Jaspers did offer some interesting descriptions of these experiences, he did not try to explain or to interpret them, since he considered such phenomena to be examples of a fundamental alienness or psychological inaccessibility.

There are, however, a couple of cognitively oriented theories that *have* attempted to explain these phenomena. The first of these theories, which was especially popular in the 1960s and 1970s, postulated some basic defect or deficiency of "selective attention," of the ability to exclude irrelevant sensory input from conscious awareness during the act of perception. In 1961 two investigators, Andrew McGhie and James Chapman, wrote of "a general factor of distractibility": a loss of "the ability and freedom to direct . . . attention *focally*," with the direction of attention coming to be determined "not by the individual's volition but by the diffuse pattern of stimuli existing in the total environmental situation."[41] The forms of experience that are posited by this well-known hypothesis of a defective attentional "filter" are, essentially, states of confusion and sensory overload: McGhie and Chapman speak of consciousness being "flooded with an undifferentiated mass of incoming sensory data," of an "involuntary tide of impressions" that sweeps over "an undifferentiated protoplasmic consciousness"—a consciousness in which, supposedly, there is "no differentiation between the self and the outside world; no self awareness; no consciousness of external objects."[42] This model does not, however, seem particularly apt for explaining the uncanny, highly distanciated, transfixingly significant, and often static world of the *Stimmung*. (Nor does it capture certain associated feelings of hyperintentionality, of a kind of anxious *directedness* of attention, which will be discussed later.)

A much more adequate portrait, at least of the perceptual qualities of the *Stimmung* world, is conveyed by the work of Klaus Conrad and another German psychiatrist, Paul Matussek, each of whom has interpreted these characteristic early-stage experiences as resulting from a breakdown in the capacity for Gestalt perception.[43] Both of these theorists—whose interesting work is too little known in Anglophone psychiatry and psychology—would see Fragmentation as a direct result of this perceptual defect, and would regard the sense of Apophany as a consequence of noticing fragments or facets of the perceptual world that have been released from their usual context. (Mere Being and Unreality may not be quite so easily explained, however.) Like the hypothesis of a defective attentional filter, however, these failure-of-Gestalt-perception theories have a rather mechanistic cast; in both cases, the early perceptual anomalies are interpreted as rather straightforward results of *failures* or defects of cognitive functioning, with the patient seen as playing (and as experiencing) a role that is almost completely passive in nature.

Those few psychoanalysts who have explicitly addressed the issue of the *Stimmung* have tended to view these perceptual changes as manifestations of profound regression to, or fixation at, very early stages of psychological life—as betokening a developmental shift downward, backward, or inward toward highly primitive modes of being.[44]

Marguerite Sechehaye, who was Renee's therapist and the editor of her patient's autobiographical account, sees Renee's *Stimmung* experiences as the first intimations of a "deep regression" of her ego to the earliest evolutionary phases of infancy or even to the "fetal level," to those forms of consciousness that precede internalization of linguistic and cultural categories.[45] Paul Federn, one of the seminal psychoanalytic writers on schizoid and schizophrenic conditions, adopts a similar tack, viewing the estrangement and depersonalization that so often herald psychotic breakdown as involving a weakening of "ego boundaries" akin to what occurs in dreams and in infancy, where, presumably, there is a near-fusion of self and world.[46] More recently, the psychoanalytic psychiatrist Silvano Arieti has argued that the anxiety preceding psychotic breakdown is a response to the resurfacing of repressed traumatic memories of very early threats to the sense of self-worth and organismic integrity, as well as to the reemergence of primitive forms of logic by which the traumatic memories are elaborated and amplified.[47]

Arieti's interpretation is very close to Freud's (1919) own explanation of what he called the Uncanny, a form of experience that would include the Apophany (though Freud in the relevant essay does not directly refer to schizophrenic types of experience).[48] As Freud points out, the Uncanny is felt to be neither simply familiar nor simply novel: as in the well-known *déjà vu* experience, the sense of strangeness is actually bound up with a sense of recognition.[49] Freud argues that this peculiar combination of qualities results from a remembering (a remembering not recognized *as* a remembering by the person) of something that has been repressed—which could involve particular fears or desires, or else overall formal qualities of early experience, such as primary-process thinking or self-world fusion. In either case, Freud tells us, we can define the Uncanny as "that class of the terrifying which leads back to something long known to us, once very familiar."[50]

Given the supposed incomprehensibility and radical alienness, the cognitive defectiveness, and the primitivity ascribed to the *Stimmung*, it may be surprising to discover that closely analogous forms of experience have been extremely common in the art and literature of the twentieth century—in the context of a highly sophisticated and, in certain respects, hyperintentional sensibility that would seem antithetical to all that is connoted by notions of the infantile or of defect.

THE ANTI-EPIPHANY IN MODERNISM

Since the turn of the century, the revelation of the inadequacy of standard meanings and habitual constructions of reality, including conventional language, and the looming up of previously suppressed aspects of the world have become prominent themes. In relatively recent works, such as the novels of Samuel Beckett and the plays of Eugène Ionesco, the vision of meaninglessness is, in fact, so taken for granted, any alternative view so out of the question from the outset, that it is even a bit misleading to speak of a revelation. But elsewhere, especially in early modernism, the realization is felt as something devastating, a sudden and shocking transmogrification of the familiar world. Excellent examples can be found in two works by the Austrian writer Hugo von Hofmannsthal, "Colours" and "The Letter of Lord Chandos," both written in 1901 and both filled with protestations of the near-ineffability of their own subject matter. Most literary scholars consider these to be highly autobiographical works, the chronicles of an aesthetic and spiritual crisis suffered by Hofmannsthal himself.

In a passage from "Colours," Hofmannsthal describes "the crisis of an inner indisposition," attacks of an almost indescribable "Next-to-Nothing" that closely recall both Renee's and de Chirico's experience of Unreality. As for Renee, so for the protagonist-narrator of this fictional work, the world loses all emotion and dynamism, and begins to feel as false and insubstantial as a stage set; eventually he also experiences hints of something akin to the anxiety-laden feeling of the Apophany (at the end of the following quote):

> But how enumerate these occasional attacks of a Next-to-Nothing? . . . Now and again in the morning it happened, in these German hotel rooms, that the jug and wash-basin—or a corner of the room with the table and clothes-rack—appeared to me so nonreal, despite their indescribable banality so utterly not real, ghostly as it were, and at the same time ephemeral, waiting, so to speak temporarily, to take the place of the real jug, the real wash-basin filled with water. . . . it was like a momentary floating above the abyss, the eternal void. . . . such an indescribable wafting of the eternal Nothing, the eternal Nowhere, a breath not of death but of Not-Life, indescribable. . . . all in all [things] took on an aspect, a peculiar ambiguous air so filled with inner uncertainty, malicious unreality: so transitory it lay there—with such ghostlike transitoriness.[51]

While still in this mood-state, the narrator wanders accidentally into a gallery where he encounters a series of paintings by Vincent van Gogh. Gazing about him, the narrator's earlier sense of the flimsiness of reality transfigures into a vision of Mere Being akin to what Renee also experienced. Objects seem to come alive with the sheer fact of their own existence:

> And this innermost life was there, tree and stone and wall and gorge gave of themselves their innermost, almost casting it at me—not, however, the voluptuousness and harmony of their lovely inanimate lives, as sometimes, in days gone by, like a magic atmosphere it had flowed towards me from old paintings: no, only the impact of its existence, the ferocious wonder of its existence surrounded by incredibility, made a dead set at my soul.[52]

In "The Letter of Lord Chandos," Hofmannsthal's focus shifts from the decomposition and transfiguration of perceptual appearances that are so prominent in "Colours" to the actual failure of language and thought. For Lord Chandos, a young writer who feels he is living a life of "barely believable vacuity," words have turned opaque, thereby depriving him of the necessary tools of his vocation: as the substantiality of the words themselves intrudes, they can no longer serve as the vehicle of meanings that transcend them. "I have lost the ability to think or to speak of anything coherently," writes Hofmannsthal's narrator, "because the abstract terms of which the tongue must avail itself as a matter of course in order to voice a judgment—these terms crumbled in my mouth like moldy fungi. Thus, one day . . . the ideas streaming into my mind suddenly took on such iridiscent colouring. . . ."[53]

First words and then ideas seem to take on a life of their own, upsetting the usual functional harmony between the realms of thought and of words. As the story progresses, the narrator's experiential universe further implodes, resulting in a pervasive vision of Fragmentation that affects both language and world:

> My mind compelled me to view all things occurring in such conversations from an uncanny closeness. As once, through a magnifying glass, I had seen a piece of skin on my little finger look like a field full of holes and furrows, so I now perceived human beings and their actions. I no longer succeeded in comprehending them with the simplifying eye of habit. For me everything disintegrated into parts, those parts again into parts; no longer would anything let itself be encompassed by one idea. Single words floated round me; they congealed into eyes which stared at me and into which I was forced to stare back—whirlpools which gave me vertigo and, reeling incessantly, led into the void.[54]

Sections of "The Letter of Lord Chandos" also recall the Apophany, though in a tone more exalted and quasi-mystical, and less overtly paranoid, than in the schizophrenic examples quoted above: "Everything that exists, everything I can remember, everything touched upon by my confused thoughts has a meaning. Even my own heaviness, the general torpor of my brain, seems to acquire a meaning."[55]

Such revelations and anti-epiphanies seem to be symptomatic of a culture in crisis, one no longer comfortable within the armature of its own categories; though virtually unknown before 1900, they are found in numerous works of both early and later modernism. Robert Musil is but one of the many twentieth-century writers who have described the peculiar look of objects suddenly deprived of their usual functional meanings. "Clothes," he writes in *The Man Without Qualities*, "if they are lifted out of the fluidity of the present and regarded, in their monstrous existence on a human figure, as forms *per se*, are strange tubes and excrescences."[56] And Watt, one of Beckett's schizoid protagonists, also experiences the waning of a prior reality:

> Watt now found himself in the midst of things which, if they consented to be named, did so as it were with reluctance. And the state in which Watt found himself resisted formulation in a way no state had ever done. . . . Looking at a pot, for example, or thinking of a pot . . . it was in vain that Watt said, Pot, pot. . . . for it was not a pot, the more he looked, the more he reflected, the more he felt sure of that, that it was not a pot at all. It resembled a pot, it was almost a pot, but it was not a pot of which one could say, Pot, pot, and be comforted. It was in vain that it answered, with unexceptionable adequacy, all the purposes, and performed all the offices, of a pot, it was not a pot. And it was just this hairbreadth departure from the nature of a true pot that so excruciated Watt.[57]

An unsettling mood of Apophany pervades Musil's autobiographical novel of 1906, *Young Torless*, in which the hero is preoccupied with the "double-face" of the world: he is constantly aware of the illusoriness of everyday appearances, and everything around him resonates with mystery, as if harboring some specific, horrible, yet unspecifiable essence. Torless even feels assailed "by inanimate objects, by mere things, as by hundreds of mutely questioning eyes."[58] We find a similar combination of meaninglessness and meaningfulness in the work of Rilke, who is often seen as the bard of a dissociated world where all things are separate and alien and without familiar meaning, yet whose poems also reveal another trend—what the scholar Erich Heller calls an "inflationary" *increase* of "significances."[59] Like the schizophrenic in the *Stimmung*, all of these central modernist writers describe objects that seem alien and incomprehensible—stripped of familiarity and reality, and of any sense of coherence or connectedness, yet bursting with some profound inner significance that always lies just beyond the reach of one's comprehension.

Most developmental theories hold that the world of the infant and young child is imbued with a dynamic sense of visceral and emotional involvement. To the child, everything is utterly real and utterly alive. Knowing and feeling are not yet differentiated; and objects tend to be experienced through their emotional resonance for a perceiver who is not yet capable of more neutral and objective forms of perception. Infantile perception is directed toward human intentions and physiognomies; it attaches itself first to gestures and faces, especially those of the mother and father. Even nonliving objects are perceived animistically, as if they were alive and conscious, and able to echo the yearnings and tremblings of the subject's inner life. Also, space for the infant or young child is not an abstract and homogeneous continuum (this only develops after the advent of the stage of concrete operations, which begins around age seven or eight)[60] but an affect-laden space-of-action, a space dominated by the proximity senses of smell and touch, and where locations are defined by such qualities as whether they are in or out of reach and whether they feel invitingly safe or threatening. It is widely acknowledged that young infants have a less distinct sense of their own separateness, and that their relationship to the surrounding world may even verge at times on a sense of union, a quasi-mystical feeling that what exists is a single unified flux. And, at least in the earliest stages, objects seem to be perceived in an exceptionally global and evaluative fashion, not as overly differentiated, fragmentary, or neutral.[61]

It is an altogether different universe that takes shape in the modernist examples we have been considering; and one that seems to have much in common with the schizophrenic *Stimmung*. The literary scholar Erich Kahler, who has offered what is perhaps the most detailed examination of the modernist anti-epiphany, speaks of "schizaesthesia" and "lucid indifference": far from resonating in affective concert with an animate or magical external world, the modernist observer seems profoundly disengaged;[62] and, accompanying his emotional detachment there is a fractionating focus on details, an unremitting "mental microscopy" that fragments and negates the larger coherencies of human meaning by concentrating too sharply on isolatable elements.[63] This detached hyperconsciousness decomposes all unities— not only abstractions, rational explanations, and pragmatic meanings, but also perceptual objects, time and history, and, finally, the ego-sensation itself.

Obviously, this is a far cry from the oceanic feelings, the dynamic primal oneness of infancy. Though this modernist anti-epiphany has been described as a "mysticism of a new kind,"[64] it might better be labeled an *anti*mysticism. In both their lives and their work, central modernist figures like Rilke and Hofmannsthal reveal what Kahler calls a "transcendence downward," "a piercing analysis of the texture of sensory appearance" or a "cruel, indeed vicious overstress of facts, [a] showing of objects in their inexorable suchness, in a glazed nakedness."[65] Instead of a gathering in of all things or a transcendence to some incorporeal plane, we find the several varieties of alienation so familiar to the modern sensibility: deadness, increased sense of distance between self and world, and a decomposition of all the organic unities of human action and perception.

The schizophrenic-type *Stimmung* clearly has more in common with this kind of alienation than with the dynamism and fusion of infancy. The most prominent qualities of Renee's "Land of Unreality," for example, are stillness, light, deanimation, and a sense of great distances: she describes "an immense space without boundary, limitless," where "all is unchangeable, immobile, congealed, crystallized," "where reigned an implacable light, blinding, leaving no place for shadow." Like the universe of de Chirico, Renee's *Stimmung* world has a certain immobility and neutrality, a benumbed and hardened precision where things seem "artificial, mechanical, electric," and voices have a "metallic [sound], without warmth or color."[66]

Further, what Renee refers to as the "aliveness" of objects is not at all the animism of the young child (as Sechehaye and other psychoanalytic commentators on the case have claimed).[67] It is not the felt presence of living beings but the looming up of Mere Being that she aims to describe. And this is a highly abstract quality, likely to emerge when things no longer appear as tools or threats in a world-of-action, but only as objects for detached contemplation. In fact, those parts of the world that would normally seem alive—human beings—are deanimated: "Only their bodies were left them, moving like automatons."[68] Dr. Sechehaye viewed such schizophrenic symptoms as manifestations of primitive "adualism," breakdown of boundaries between self and world;[69] but by now it should be clear that the world of the *Stimmung* is a profoundly alienated one, where self and world are separated by a vast and unbridgeable gulf.[70]

"TACIT INTIMATIONS": ON THE
FORMATION OF DELUSIONS

A proper understanding of the *Stimmung*, particularly of the Apophany phase, is important not only for its own sake but also because it may help account for the origins of the ideas of reference and of some of the delusional notions that occur so often in schizophrenia.

The experience of the Apophany is shot through with a profound and almost unbearable tension (in some cases combined with exaltation). In this state of pulsing significance, the very ineffability, uncanniness, and precision of everything seem nearly intolerable, as if the human need for meaning and coherence were being titillated only to be frustrated on the brink of its fulfillment. Many patients feel gripped with a profound urge to find some way to account, however inadequately, for the alterations in their world and so to dissipate this disconcerting tension, an impulse Jaspers captures in the following passage:

Gestures, ambiguous words provide "tacit intimations." All sorts of things are being conveyed to the patient. People imply quite different things in such harmless remarks as "the carnations are lovely" or "the blouse fits all right" and understand these meanings very well among themselves. People look at the patient as if they had something special to say to him—"It was as if everything was being done to spite me; everything that happened in Mannheim happened in order to take it out of me." . . . Patients resist any attempt to explain these things as coincidence. These "devilish incidents" are most certainly not coincidences. Collisions in the street are obviously intentional. The fact that the soap is now on the table and was not there before is obviously an insult.[71]

It is easy to see how the apophanous mood might be followed by the development of delusions of reference (for example, the above-mentioned belief that, by crossing their legs, people on a train were performing a play for the patient's special benefit). This sort of delusion postulates the existence of a special situation, but in the midst of a relatively normal lived world; and often it takes on a paranoid cast, positing a pervasive evil intent that is directed toward a passive subject, but in a world where space, time, causality, and the quality of material objects are reasonably normal. Such delusions may help to make a kind of rational sense out of what would otherwise be experienced as a most disturbing change in the very foundations of the normal perceptual world. Indeed, paranoid thinking can be viewed as, in some sense, an almost obvious, logical development—in a world where everything seems cryptic but never vague, where things seem illusory but never insignificant; a world where all events feel interpretable, so that nothing can seem accidental and everything therefore appears to be somehow consciously intended.[72] (Believing in a conspiracy might help to explain why, for example, everyone seems false, as if play-acting for the patient's benefit.)[73]

An urge toward forming delusions, then, may well inhere in the very *form* of the Apophany (a mode of experience that itself derives from the loss of conventional contexts and meanings characteristic of the *Trema*). (As one schizophrenic patient said, "out of these perceptions came the absolute awareness that my ability to see connections has been multiplied many times over.")[74] The most important feature of a given delusion may not be its specific content but its ability simply to offer *some* meaning, thereby to resolve the abstract tension of the Apophany. The early and often neglected "prodromal" experiences of the *Stimmung* and the truth-taking stare (Unreality, Mere Being, Fragmentation, and Apophany) may therefore play a much larger, perhaps even foundational role in the development of the more striking and overtly psychotic symptoms of delusions and paranoid thinking.

FUTURISM, SURREALISM, AND THE
MODERNIST STARE

So far, I have been focusing almost exclusively on the look and feel of unusual perceptual worlds, paying little attention to the person undergoing the experiences in question. I have been describing changes that occur in the external universe of space and time, changes that the schizophrenic individual may appear to be witnessing, like a passive observer. Renee, for example, spoke of feeling "rejected by the world, on the outside of life, a spectator of a chaotic film unrolling ceaselessly before my eyes, in which I would never have a part"; and she wrote of the Land of Unreality as a vision "to which I could only submit."[75]

It would be understandable if the perceptual changes of the *Stimmung* seemed always to be the prior and fundamental event, and the transfixed gaze of the truth-taking stare merely a reaction to a mutation that is passively endured. This, however, would be only part of the truth; and in the rest of this chapter we need to trace the other half of the story: how the perceiver can exacerbate or attenuate these dramatic perceptual alterations, or even bring them on, through adopting various attitudes, modes of action, and forms of attention. A number of questions will need to be considered: What is the existential stance or orientation that accompanies these transformations of the perceptual world? How precisely does the subject's attitude or stance affect the perceptual changes? And to what extent is the subject an active or controlling agent as opposed to a mere victim of these disconcerting perceptual mutations?

In addressing this complex set of issues, I find it useful to consider certain modernists of a somewhat later generation than Hofmannsthal and Rilke, namely, the French surrealists and Russian formalists. Pursuit of a state very like the *Stimmung* was, for them, a conscious goal; and for this reason their aesthetic philosophies and techniques offer special insight into this mode of experience, particularly into the existential attitude or stance that seems to underlie it. Both these artistic schools exemplify what has been called the paradox of the modern conception of volition, with its peculiar "fusion of determinism and free will, [of] automatism and caprice."[76] Both can help elucidate the complicated interpenetrations of activity and passivity, of the intentional and causal factors that are to be found both in modernism and in madness.

For Hofmannsthal (1874–1929) and, to a large extent, for Rilke (1875–1926) and other early or proto-modernists, the dissipation of normal forms of meaning occasioned anxiety and despair. They describe this event as overcoming the perceiver almost against his will, certainly not as something to be wished for or actively pursued. But as the twentieth century wore on, the same vision that destroyed Lord Chandos's capacity for communication and artistic expression came to be seen as desirable, even as providing the new muse and principle of style.[77] In movements as otherwise diverse as Russian futurism, surrealism, (French) existentialism, and the *nouveau roman,* artists actively sought to adopt such forms of consciousness. They suspended the normal trust in words and concepts in order to provide release from contamination by abstract categories, by pragmatic, goal-oriented concerns, and by all conventional patterns of meaning—thus to bring about a fuller appreciation of things in all their concreteness and wondrous particularity.

One of the clearest examples of this aesthetic attitude is to be found in the writings of the Russian formalists, the avant-garde critics who were inspired by the linguistics of Saussure and the poetic experimentations of the Russian futurists (the aesthetic movement that had dominated Soviet cultural life for a brief period after the revolution).[78] Viktor Shklovsky, the leader of the Russian formalists, defined art as defamiliarization ("making it strange"), while the Czech critic Jan Mukařovsky spoke of deautomatization. According to this futurist/formalist view, art's essential role was to overcome the numbing of perception that accompanies the automatizing of actions frequently performed. (In order to do this, it seems necessary to destroy, not memory itself, but all the ways in which memory usually provides an implicit framework, an omnipresent, constantly updated set of expectations or schemas that guides normal forms of awareness.)[79]

Achieving this kind of illuminating awareness naturally requires that one displace oneself from all standard action patterns and familiar modes of perception. Shklovsky describes several techniques for doing this—such as taking a very distant or else fragmentingly microscopic perspective on an object, avoiding standard causal/narrative schemas of meaning, and describing an object in terms of its mere existence or geometrical form (that is, by avoiding use of its name and suppressing all references to its usual functional role in human life).[80] Such techniques are very reminiscent of the truth-taking stare; and the experiences they were designed to bring about involve the same qualities of fragmentation and uncanny hyperclarity that are characteristic of the *Stimmung.*

Like the futurists, the surrealists also strove to jolt their audience out of complacency and unconsciousness. Their works of art were intended to lay bare what the surrealists saw as the essentially discontinuous nature of existence and the inadequacy and absurdity of the rational systems human beings use to give themselves the illusion of coherent understanding. ("Reality," said the surrealist poet Louis Aragon, meaning conventional reality, "is the apparent absence of contradiction. The marvelous [meaning "true" reality] is the eruption of contradiction within the real.")[81] It is within the surrealist tradition, in fact, that we find images and objects most reminiscent of the schizophrenic *Stimmung.* Claes Oldenburg's soft-sculpture renditions of everyday objects—the work called "Ghost Toilet," for instance—suggest Unreality, while the paintings of Yves Tanguy, with their distinct yet unrecognizable, and therefore mysterious, shapes scattered about a lunar landscape, suggest a vision that combines Mere Being with Apophany (see figure 2.3). The uncanny clarity and timelessness of Giorgio de Chirico's cityscapes capture a mood that merges Apophany with Unreality.

The essential element of the surrealist stance is a certain willed passivity. Indeed, surrealist doctrine declared that the individual consciousness was but "a modest recording device" that could best serve the purposes of art by

FIGURE 2.3

Yves Tanguy, *The Furniture of Time* (1939). A painting evoking two aspects of the *Stimmung:* Mere Being and Apophany. *Oil on canvas, 46″ × 35¼″. Collection, The Museum of Modern Art, New York. James Thrall Soby Bequest*

yielding itself up to external influences. André Breton (1896–1966), the impresario and high priest of the movement, announced the "crucial inadequacy . . . of any action which requires a continuous application and which can be premeditated" and celebrated the "great victory of the involuntary over the ravaged domain of conscious possibilities," over the "tremulous ennui" of normal pragmatic perception and action.[82] Breton sometimes advocated a meticulous, unblinking, almost cruel empiricism, an automatism of inner and outer perception that excluded all directed attention and all conventional meanings and judgments of value. In a 1936 essay, "The Crisis of the Object," he speaks of creating "fields of tension" that would allow objects to release "an infinite series of latent possibilities."[83]

Good examples of the actual practice of this surrealist passivity can be found in works like Breton's *Nadja* (1928) and Louis Aragon's *Paysan de Paris* (1926), *Benjamin* two picaresque quasi- or anti-novels that recount not a coherent plot but the authors' aimless and solitary wanderings about Paris in search of surreality— that vision of "an almost forbidden world of sudden parallels and petrifying coincidences" (Breton). According to Breton, this world of "pure observation" is likely to paralyze action—or perhaps, we should say, to depend on such a paralysis. *Nadja* can, in fact, be read almost as a manual for achieving the surrealist vision of inspired alienation. Its author-protagonist is an isolated, receptive being, a perambulating passivity who loses himself in a sort of hyperconscious aimlessness, allowing experience to impinge on him in all its meaningless/meaningful specificity. And the world that looms before this passive, "agonized witness" is very like that of the schizophrenic-type Apophany—of those patients whom Jaspers describes as always saying, "I noticed particularly." As Breton puts it in *Nadja*, the facts "present all the appearances of a signal, without our being able to say precisely what signal"; they are "accompanied by the distinct sensation that something momentous, something essential depends on them."[84]

Whereas the surrealists emphasized the passivity necessary for creative vision, a desisting from normal pragmatic modes of action, the formalists emphasized forms of awareness that would actively penetrate conventional appearances. At first these aesthetic techniques may seem antithetical, but a closer inspection suggests that surrealist automatism and formalist deautomatization are actually complementary, differing mainly over a matter of emphasis. Desisting from normal modes of action allows unconventional perspectives to emerge, just as concentration *within* such unusual perspectives is likely to undermine both the coherence of normal perceptual patterns and the fluidity of standard action-schemas. In both cases, the kind of experience sought involves a certain passivity and disengagement from habitual modes of acting, *along with* exacerbation of a kind of conscious awareness. And in both cases these developments are accompanied by a profound and utter detachment: as the scrutinizing consciousness slips its moorings in normal emotional, practical, and social concerns, it becomes a pure observer in a largely alien world.

In an essay on modernist aesthetics, Susan Sontag contrasts this kind of staring with the mode of attention appropriate to more traditional art, as well as to normal pragmatic perception: "Consider the difference between *looking* and *staring*. A look is voluntary; it is also mobile, rising and falling in intensity as its foci of interest are taken up and then exhausted. A stare has, essentially, the character of a compulsion; it is steady, unmodulated, 'fixed.' Traditional art invites a look. [Modernist avant-garde art] engenders a stare."[85]

The "look" is closer to what might be called the "natural attitude" of everyday life. Emanating from a secure base (and rooted in the lived body), it moves always within stable horizons; it is naturalistic as well as natural, capturing reality as conventionally and pragmatically conceived. And, although the subject of the "look" moves his eyes across the object at will, the look remains faithful, even subservient to the object's integrity, seeming to caress it, following its "natural" contours and respecting standard hierarchies of significance. The "stare," on the other hand, is rigid and fixed—passive, in this sense; yet it bores through, breaks up, or withers its object, dissolving the physiognomy of the everyday world and bringing on the various aspects of the *Trema*. Whereas the "look" is naturalistic, guided by implicit expectancies and reflecting a taken-for-granted reality of shared meanings, the "stare" is analytic; which perceptual element is focused on may be arbitrary, yet once noticed, the element stands forth as if framed for its special significance—and this gives rise to the mood of the Apophany. We might say that the look examines things that have a prior claim to our interest; with the stare, things become interesting (and mysterious) only because they are being looked at.[86] (The latter phenomenon is exemplified by Duchamp's aesthetic—or anti-aesthetic—of the *objet trouvé*, for example, a bottle rack or bicycle wheel chosen not for some special, unappreciated beauty but precisely for its sheer ordinariness: it is the act of looking at it in a special way, thereby declaring it to be an object of perceptual interest, that actually *makes* the ordinary entity into a kind of artwork.)

Particularly revealing examples of this compulsory stare, and of the perceptual changes it can engender (which in turn can motivate the stare), can be found in Jean-Paul Sartre's philosophical novel *Nausea* (1938). The narrator, Roquentin—clearly Sartre's alter ego—becomes aware of certain disquieting alterations in the perceptual world; and, to clarify these for himself, he resolves to observe and record, from a position of the utmost detachment, every detail of his experience: "Not the slightest nuances must escape my attention, none of those tiny little facts, even if they look like nothing at all," he writes.[87] Though Roquentin's scrutinizing gaze is inspired by his desire to get to the bottom of these subtle perceptual changes, it actually has the effect of exacerbating these changes—which he nevertheless watches as if they were happening independently of him, compelling his stare. And with the progressive disintegration of normal perceptual reality, Roquentin goes through virtually all of the modernist experiences I have described: objects lose their normal functional meanings; they begin to seem absurdly substantial; they fragment into parts; they take on curious meanings. Everything that usually links us with our embodied selves, all the emotions of desire, love, hate, and fear, and all the memories and channeled expectations that normally connect us to the social and practical world—all this seems to have disappeared, reducing the protagonist to a state of ontological anxiety, a sort of abstract nausea in the face of the sheer existence of things.[88]

Erich Kahler (writing in the 1940s and 1950s) considers *Nausea* to be the ultimate, culminating example of the drama of the crumbling of normal sensory and emotional reality; he views this drama of "schizaesthesia" and "mental microscopy" as quintessentially modernist—hardly known before 1900, though a virtual commonplace in the twentieth-century avant-garde. And he sees the emergence of these experiences of perceptual uncanniness as demonstrating not regression but a certain *progression*—cruel consequences of a "steady growth of man's self-reflection and psychological introspection," which leads to "utmost detachment" and to "that second, coldest consciousness . . . objectification of life."[89]

In one passage, Kahler beautifully captures the paradoxical nature of these perceptual transformations—where one is both witness and creator, transfixed by the consequences of one's own stare. He describes "how the indiscreet, all too imaginative look disintegrates the organic figuration and texture of surface reality, and how, under its animistic vivification, parts and segments assume an independent, swarming life. This happens as if under a compulsion, and the man who looks seems himself to be just an instrument, or victim, of this irresistible seeing."[90] A passage from Renee's memoir evokes exactly this sort of experience, a mode of scrutinizing bringing on a perceptual transformation that nevertheless seems to be occurring all by itself:

I remained quiet, unmoving, my gaze fixed on a spot or a gleam of light.

But behind this wall of indifference, suddenly a wave of anxiety would come over me, the anxiety of unreality. *My perception of the world seemed to sharpen the sense of the strangeness of things.* In the silence and immensity, each object was cut off by a knife, detached in the emptiness, in the boundlessness, spaced off from other things. Without any relationship with the environment, just by being itself, *it began to come to life.* It was there, facing me, terrifying me.[91]

ACT OR AFFLICTION?

But there is not one common difference between so-called voluntary acts and involuntary ones, viz., the presence or absence of one element, the "act of volition."
—Ludwig Wittgenstein
The Brown Book

The *Stimmung* feels, in one sense, more like an affliction than an act, like something that happens *to* the person: "I feel nameless, impersonal," said one schizophrenic. *"My gaze is fixed like a corpse;* my mind has become vague and general; like a nothing or the absolute; I am floating; I am as if I were not."[92] "I have to stop and look at something," said another such individual, otherwise [the compulsion to look] won't go away. It looks back at you. It fixes on you. It just gets stuck."[93] One extremely intellectual patient, Lawrence, who was seen by a colleague, described going up to a mirror to look at himself, then staring too intensely into his own eyes: "I was admiring myself and then looked into each eye individually and then I got trapped," he explained. "It took an outside stimulus to break the trap. I didn't form a gestalt of my face." (And this, he said, suggested that "the myth of Narcissus has a basis in fact.")

The state *in* which such schizophrenics feel caught is imbued, however, with a kind of "hyperintentionality"—a compulsive rigidity and anxious directness of behavior that could be described as involving "marked intensification of such normal voluntary faculties as attention, muscular control, and, on a different level, purposiveness."[94] The patient, it seems, is plagued not so much by diminished awareness or ability to concentrate as by hyperawareness, a constant, compulsive need to exercise his own consciousness. Thus the illness of the famous schizophrenic Dr. Schreber began with a torturing sleeplessness, and Schreber maintained that there was a "more or less definite intention," emanating from somewhere, to bring about his mental collapse by forcing him always to be awake and aware. Another schizophrenic said, "It's as if I am too wide awake—very, very alert. I can't relax at all."[95]

That such intense concentration should interrupt the natural flow of physical or mental activity is not surprising, for it introduces a potentially disturbing self-consciousness and awareness of choice, a conscious, controlled mode of functioning that disrupts more automatic or spontaneous processes. "If I do something like going for a drink of water," reported one schizophrenic patient, "I've got to go over each detail—find cup, walk over, turn tap, fill cup, turn tap off, drink it. I keep building up a picture." A second schizophrenic spoke of having become "the opposite of spontaneous, as a result of which I became very diffident, very laboured."[96]

What burgeons out of control here is the process of awareness itself and the need to exercise choice, not some lower, instinctual element or the more automatic behavioral or mental processes. Patients like this might be said to be condemned, if not to freedom then at least to a kind of hyperconsciousness and compulsive deliberation; it is as if they cannot choose not to choose or to be aware—no matter how disturbing this state of mind may be. In his novel *Watt*, Beckett captures very well this curious condition in which one is, as it were, afflicted with the need to act (the acting in question being largely mental, a matter of concentrating one's attention and of noticing many things):

> Watt's attention was extreme, in the beginning, to all that went on about him. Not a sound was made within earshot that he did not capture and, when necessary, interrogate, and he opened wide his eyes to all that passed, near and at a distance, to all that came and went and paused and stirred, . . . and he grasped, in many cases, the nature of the object affected, and even the immediate cause of its being so. . . . This constant tension of some of his most noble faculties tired Watt greatly. And the results, on the whole, were meagre. But he had no choice, at first.[97]

This kind of exaggerated consciousness or intentionality is not the sort of condition that, traditionally, has been imagined as being a manifestation of underlying lesions or other abnormalities of the brain. This, however, is mostly a result of the pervasiveness of traditional biases—such as the assumption that the higher and more volitional mental processes must necessarily suffer first in an organically based disorder. Recent work in neurobiology and cognitive psychology clearly shows, however, that the forms of experience we have been considering could in fact have significant neurophysiological underpinnings—for example, in a disruption or underactivation of certain more automatic and less volitional neurophysiological processes, or in an (perhaps related) overactivation of brain processes that might be thought of as "higher" or more intentionally directed.

(Experimentally based neurobiological and cognitive models of schizophrenia that are consistent with the hyperintentionality portrayed here include the following: theories that postulate "a weakening of the influence of regularities of previous input on current perception," an abnormality [perhaps rooted in abnormal functioning of the hippocampus and related brain structures] that would make the perceiver react to all stimuli with the kind of directed, focused attention that is normally turned only toward what is novel, thereby disrupting automatic processing and forcing cognitive activity to "proceed at the level of consciously controlled sequential processing";[98] theories postulating either an overactivation of the more analytic, volitional, self-conscious, executive, or rational parts of the brain [for example, the left cerebral hemisphere, which has been described as "almost obsessed with parts"]—or else an underactivation of the parts that supposedly mediate the more intuitive, emotional, and spontaneous modes of functioning [for example, the right hemisphere];[99] theories emphasizing the role of neurophysiological hyperarousal, possibly combined with anxiety, in bringing on an overfocused, and in some sense passivized, mode of attention;[100] and, perhaps, theories stressing disturbed *maintenance* of attention, which is manifest in the disruption of automatic eye-tracking patterns by more voluntary, saccadic eye movements.[101] For further discussion of traditional assumptions, and of alternative neurobiological models, see the appendix.[102])

We see, then, that, like the modernist anti-epiphany, the schizophrenic *Stimmung* involves not a lowering but a heightening of conscious awareness and, in many instances, not release from a sense of responsibility and control but the heightening of a kind of anxious compulsiveness. This, however, raises another, nonphenomenological question: namely, whether this general *form* of consciousness, this heightened and hyperintentional *mode* of perception, can really be captured by the notion of psychological defect or deficiency. Does it constitute a true *in*capacity, something that leads always to a decline in psychological performance? And is the mode of hyperintentionality and hyperawareness something over which the patient can have, in actuality, any significant degree of volitional control? To pose these questions is to bring attention to the possibility that, in discussing the affinities of madness and modernism, I may have been ignoring a crucial difference between these two realms of phenomena. After all, whatever the *perceptual* analogies between the schizophrenic *Stimmung* and the aesthetic anti-epiphany, and whatever the parallels concerning *feelings* of volition or determinism, isn't there one all-important difference: namely, that whereas the artist chooses, controls, and uses certain states or forms of consciousness, the madman simply suffers them? This latter idea is one that has been with us since ancient times, and, with little doubt, it remains the most widely held assumption about the difference between insanity and "true" creativity.

One famous statement of the view in question is Charles Lamb's essay of 1826, "Sanity of True Genius"; another is Ernst Kris's influential description of artistic creation as involving regression that occurs always *"in the service of the ego."* And Carl Jung once invoked the distinction with James Joyce, who had consulted Jung about his psychotic daughter Lucia. After a lengthy examination, Jung concluded that Lucia suffered from *dementia praecox;* and, defending his diagnosis, he pointed out various linguistic deviances and distortions in her poems. Remembering what Jung had once said about *Ulysses* (in an essay, Jung had compared Joyce's novel to the productions of psychosis, suggesting that both demonstrated *"abaissement du niveau mentale"*—a lowering of the mental level),[103] Joyce now claimed that his daughter's deviances were anticipations of new literary forms; his daughter, he contended, was an innovator, not yet understood. Jung in turn did acknowledge the remarkable quality of some of her neologisms and portmanteau words, but he insisted that they were random productions; he added that while she and her father were both going to the bottom of a river, there was this crucial difference: one of them was diving, the other only falling. "The ordinary patient cannot help himself talking and thinking in such a way," Jung would write some time later, "while Joyce willed it and moreover developed it with all his creative forces."[104]

Despite numerous demonstrations of the role of volition and intentionality in the genesis and shaping of schizophrenic-type experiences[105] (and despite recent deflations, in literary studies, of Promethean myths about the freedom and power of the individual artist or writer), the traditional view remains remarkably persistent. As the authors of one of the best and most influential contemporary studies of schizophrenic thinking put it, "The schizophrenic patient appears to be driven by his thoughts; the artist orders them. The patient's thoughts are peremptory and insistent, the artist's are formed and modulated." In their view it is the presence of "control voluntarism and purposefulness" that distinguishes creative productions from "psychotic ravings."[106]

It cannot be denied that schizophrenia does, in certain respects, involve a loss of freedom, and that, in many circumstances, such individuals do perform less effectively than other people, be they artists or not. Both madness and creativity tend, however, to be seriously oversimplified by this all too tidy distinction; for, on careful consideration, phenomena like the schizophreniclike *Stimmung* and the modernist anti-epiphany appear to be rather complex mixtures of volition and determinism, of capacity and incapacity.

Perhaps the clearest example of a pure deficit or affliction interpretation of the schizophrenic *Stimmung* is the previously mentioned notion that such individuals have an incapacity for selective attention, for focusing awareness on specific objects while ignoring peripheral or irrelevant stimuli because of what is termed their defective perceptual filter. As we have seen, however, many such patients are manifestly able to engage in a very concentrated stare, an act that clearly involves adopting a narrow and exclusionary focusing of awareness; also, research demonstrates that schizophrenic "distractibility" itself is, in some respects, far more selective than this rather mechanistic theory would imply (schizophrenics, compared to normal individuals, were found to be more easily distracted by tape-recorded voices *only* when these voices were speaking of topics related to the patients' delusions; also, schizophrenics seem *less* likely to be distracted by outer than by inner stimuli—that is, by the normally unnoticed workings of their own minds).[107] The gestaltist theories of Conrad and Matussek also portray the schizophrenic largely in defect-oriented and passive terms, as if merely the victim of cognitive incapacities—in this case, an incapacity to form perceptual Gestalts; yet the disturbances or anomalies of attention actually found in most schizophrenics are far less widespread, persistent, and debilitating than this theory would predict.[108]

Current evidence suggests that the distinctive anomaly of schizophrenic attention and perception might, in fact, better be conceived as a matter of perceptual *strategy*. Specifically, one might think of this as an overly analytic, detail-oriented, and intellectual orientation to the perceptual world tending to replace one that is intuitive or holistic; or, perhaps, as a stance that is overly idiosyncratic, goalless, and meandering replacing one that is guided by an ongoing practical sense of what is likely or probable.[109] Such a propensity need not be thought of only as a deficit or defect, for it could equally well be described as involving either a heightening or a diminishment of capacity: thus, schizophrenics do seem to be capable of a kind of concentration, focus, and awareness of anomaly that is very difficult for other people to maintain, and they often take pleasure in this prolonged concentration on objects;[110] but, at the same time, they find it difficult (or they may be disinclined) to shift *out* of this general mode and adopt the more intuitive, spontaneous, or practical mode of everyday life. (Sometimes they also have difficulty with*in* this analytic mode—in shifting attention from one kind of object to another.) The ambiguity about abilities is reflected in their performance in different situations, given that, on certain types of tasks—for example, those requiring an ability to perceive objects in isolation, or to recognize unlikely situations—such patients will actually perform better than do normal individuals,[111] while on many other tasks (such as identifying the conventional, main theme that is expressed in a drawing of human beings interacting with each other) their performance tends to be poorer, probably because an intensive concentration on details prevents a quick intuitive grasp of the overall situation.

Schizophrenics often do find it difficult to move out of this potentially disruptive *mode* of deliberateness and hyperawareness, and this can seriously disturb their ability to cope easily and effectively with many aspects of daily life. Yet it should not be thought that the shifting in or out of such forms of experience is something *entirely* outside the patient's control. As we saw from our examination of Breton's *Nadja* and Sartre's *Nausea*, the surrealist vision does not loom up before a subject engaged in practical action, but occurs instead when he is in some sense inactive or detached. A similar pattern was described by one schizophrenic I treated, who said that he knew he would not have become ill if he had not made the mistake, at the outset of his psychotic break, of sitting back and watching his friends at a party instead of joining in their activities; only then, he explained, had things begun to look "weird." This kind of correlation between particular modes of activity (or *in*activity) and certain forms of experience suggests that the experiences in question could perhaps be controlled, at least in part, through the adoption of one or another stance or mode of activity.

The perceiver might, for instance, make the *Stimmung* diminish or disappear by stepping *out* of his contemplative stance and taking up some familiar activity. Roquentin does this when he stops staring at the chestnut tree, gets up, and walks out of the park. Similarly, to rid herself of the Unreality vision, Renee would sometimes throw herself into familiar activities, such as making a meal, therefore managing, at least partially, to restore a less strange universe—to "make things as they usually were": "What saved me that day was activity. It was the hour to go to chapel for prayer, and like the other children I had to get in line. To move, to change the scene, to do something definite and customary, helped me a great deal. Nevertheless, I took the unreal state to chapel with me, though to a lesser degree."[112] Many schizophrenic patients do in fact report that they will throw themselves into some kind of familiar activity as a way of diminishing their symptoms—whereas manics, to take one counterexample, may be more likely to use withdrawal for the same purpose.[113] (It should also be said, however, that in more extreme cases schizophrenic hyperawareness can be so intense as to *prevent* engagement in such everyday actions.)

Schizophrenics may also bring on some aspect of the *Stimmung* by intentionally adopting a fixed gaze (or by willfully giving in to it). During a period of remission from her psychosis, one schizophrenic girl protected herself against intimacy with others by concentrating on a spot on the wall or a thread in her bedsheets. Though nothing in her outer manner would have made this obvious, the activity clearly had a strongly intentional and defensive quality. "It is silly, how the power of a thread or a spot of rust can absorb me altogether," she said. "In themselves they make a satisfying world for me. Thanks to them I manage not to respond to the doctor's orders. And when they insist . . . I hold fast to my spot and drown myself in it down to its very atoms."[114] It is possible for something analogous to occur on a more general level, as the quasi-choice of an entire existential stance, a mode of experience dominated by contemplative detachment. For, even if one were, in some sense, temperamentally doomed to this stance—perhaps because of innate neurophysiological factors—one might still take it up actively and make it one's own, thereby animating this style with a certain intentionality.

To claim that schizophrenic states are *entirely* under the patient's control, or that they result purely from an attitude of detachment and disengaged concentration, would obviously be absurd. But such reports suggest that the standard understanding of the schizophrenic *Stimmung* as resulting from a simple loss or diminishment of self-control is also too simplistic: like so much about schizophrenia (as well as modernism), the *Stimmung* is difficult to characterize in our standard vocabulary of volition and determinism; it seems to occupy a kind of anxious twilight zone somewhere between act and affliction.

It is significant that Renee should describe her insanity not only as the Land of Unreality and the state of Madness but also as the Land of Enlightenment and Light.[115] Light, after all—along with the associated perceptual mode of vision—has long been the privileged metaphor, at least in Western culture, for conscious awareness, and especially for those modes of awareness in which the distance between subject and object is crucial. We might interpret the "implacable light" that irradiates the bright surfaces and sharp edges of Renee's Land of Madness as a quasi-symbolic manifestation of the central element of her illness: her own unrelenting and disengaged consciousness.

Madness, however, has nearly always been associated with images of primitivity and wildness, with peremptory urges emerging from some dark and subterranean place. The "remorseless light"[116] of the *Stimmung* suggests the existence of other types of madness, Apollonian or even Socratic illnesses whose central features are hypertrophy of consciousness and a concomitant detachment from instinctual sources of vitality. It is in modernist and postmodernist culture that this detachment and heightened awareness have been most extensively explored, so let us end with the words of the poet Octavio Paz, describing, in *The Labyrinth of Solitude*, a "truly modern consciousness"—words that apply equally well to the "electric immobility" and infinite horizons of Renee's *Stimmung* world. Paz speaks of a consciousness "turned in upon itself, imprisoned in its own blinding clarity," and of the poet who, "in a sort of lucid fury, wants to rip the mask off existence in order to see it as it is. . . . Everything is immersed in its own clarity and brilliance, everything is directed toward this transparent death."[117]

CHAPTER 3
· ·

The Separated Self

*Incapable of ruling and of serving, incapable of giving love or receiving it
. . . he wanders like a ghost among the living.*
                                        —Hugo von Hofmannsthal
                                        The Death of Titian

I am hard as ice, and yet so full of feeling that I am almost sentimental.
                                        —August Strindberg

There is a potential for estrangement in every act of consciousness. To
become aware of something, to know it as an object, is necessarily to
become aware of its separateness, its nonidentity with the knowing
self that one feels oneself to be at that very instant. To perceive something
is, *ipso facto*, to cast it outward, into the domain of the not-me that lies at
the farthest reaches of the experiential universe. And since this is an *essential* fact about consciousness, it must surely apply to self-awareness as well:
to know my own self is, inevitably, to multiply or fractionate myself; it is to
create a division between my knowing consciousness and my existence as a
perceivable individual who interacts with others or subsists as a body of flesh
and blood.

This, at least, is one vision of the human condition, a vision rooted in the
philosophy of Descartes but whose more extreme implications were not
elaborated (or lived out) until the era of modernism, or perhaps just
before[1]—a time when engagement in the world can no longer be taken for
granted and the mind withdraws, or turns in upon itself. No one states this
view more clearly than that scrupulous Cartesian of French modernism,

Paul Valéry. In "the final analysis," Valéry writes, "it is the doubling which is the essential psychological fact." He speaks of a brain "too much occupied internally, [and that] deals brutally with external things—rejects them violently, etc.," but also of a brain whose "prime function" is "to take its [own] acts, its modifications as strange and independent things."[2] Such views are of particular relevance for understanding the so-called schizoid personality, the character type most commonly found in persons who will eventually develop schizophrenic forms of insanity. In *The Divided Self*, R. D. Laing describes the schizoid person as an individual whose being is split in two main ways: in the relationship to external reality and in the relationship to the self. Instead of feeling at home in the world or together with others, such a person tends to "experience himself in despairing aloneness and isolation; instead of feeling like a complete and integral whole, he feels 'split' in various ways, perhaps as a mind more or less tenuously linked to a body, as two or more selves, and so on."[3]

In the previous chapter I considered phenomena that were relatively abrupt and violent; now I shall turn toward something more subtle and enduring: pervasive psychological orientations or traits. Thinking in terms of the course of illness, this means a shift from the acute to the chronic dimension and a moving backward in time, to an investigation of the so-called premorbid personality that often precedes the psychotic break (and that, it should be noted, often reemerges into prominence after the psychosis subsides, as a kind of postpsychotic personality). At the same time I shall be moving in another plane: downward or inward to an examination of core personality traits, characteristics that frequently seem to underlie the more florid symptoms of the overt psychosis.

SCHIZOID PERSONALITY

The term *schizoid* was first used around 1910 by Eugen Bleuler and his colleagues at the Burghölzli Hospital in Switzerland. It served as a way of labeling abnormalities seen in the relatives of schizophrenic patients as well as in the patients themselves prior to their psychotic break. The concept encompasses a congeries of qualities that may not seem, at least at first, to have a great deal in common—including both coldness and hypersensitivity, both obstinacy and vacillation, both rebelliousness and timidity. Not all schizophrenics show these characteristics premorbidly; nor, for that matter, do all schizoid individuals eventually develop a schizophrenic psychosis (most, in fact, do not). But the schizoid type is by far the most common prepsychotic personality for this kind of psychotic illness, with up to one-half or even three-fifths of all schizophrenic patients having manifested such features in their earlier lives, according to some estimates;[4] it seems especially common in patients whose schizophrenic illness is more enduring and difficult to cure.[5]

Though no brief example could possibly illustrate the entire syndrome, the following vignette does capture a number of its main features:

> At follow-up, aged 18, he was a mathematics student . . . hooked on computers since 13 . . . reads physics and computer manuals for pleasure as well as poetry and modern, "absurd," plays. . . . never had a close friend of his own age. He . . . saw sex "as a way of disposing of energy." He said his great problem was communication. "A sense of isolation; I bury myself in work; my chief interest is in knowledge." He enjoys acting, but otherwise prefers to keep to himself. "When I myself start coming out, people don't like it. Something puts people off. Maybe I'm a pure intellectual . . . narrow . . . music, poetry, opera, and then computers, nothing in between." He knows he's regarded as an "odd-bod" at the polytechnic and as a "pain in the neck . . . but I can't do anything about it." He gets hurt easily by what people say but "I have taught myself to dissociate from emotion . . . I look at the emotion, and then colour my actions according to the emotions which seem appropriate." He daydreams how to prove his work to the world. He has "guidance" from "voices" he senses within himself. At times incidents have a special significance for him and his mind "fills with images . . . runs ahead of me, things not connecting."
> He is often very unhappy.[6]

The most prominent characteristics of schizoid persons are an apparent asociality and indifference, often combined with introversion. Seldom do such people feel in harmony with their bodies or with the environment, and typically, their emotions do not flow in a natural and spontaneous way; instead they seem forced or stiff, and others may find them cold and unfeeling, perhaps overly cerebral or calculating. Often they will seem detached, "as if something unnatural and strange divided them from the world,"[7] and others are liable to sense something not entirely genuine in their behavior and emotional expression. In fact, many schizoids convey an "as-if" quality, giving the impression that they are only role-playing—perhaps to caricature themselves, to mock those around them, or simply to give an appearance of seamless normality. But beneath an apparent coldness, these people can be excessively sensitive, thin-skinned, and self-deprecatory, highly vulnerable to slights and criticism. Sometimes they will seem docile, submissive, and awkward, at other times arrogant, superior, or rebellious. They have, in any case, an aloof, vaguely mysterious air, suggestive of a realm of experience hidden away from others. Though they may seem circumspect and inordinately controlled, perhaps overly formal or mannered, this can be interrupted by occasional bouts of impulsive or pseudo-impulsive extroversion that smacks of overcompensation—as, for example, when a shy and introverted adolescent boy suddenly turns bold, propositioning girls he would not have dared approach just a few days earlier.

A similar duality characterizes the schizoid cognitive style, which encompasses both excessive doubting and extreme rigidity and obstinacy, and which can sometimes involve subtle peculiarities of thought or language. Here, as in the emotional sphere, schizoid persons seem out of touch with their fellow human beings, and what is practical and obvious to others may be missed entirely by them. Commonly, such individuals are obsessed with abstract, metaphysical, or technical concerns; and, bent on independence and originality, they may pursue these in complete indifference to the opinions of others. One such patient was preoccupied with philosophical topics but made a point of not reading any philosophical books for fear this might "deform" his own thoughts.[8]

Most schizoid persons are well aware of their own detachment. "There is a pane of glass between me and mankind" is a typical remark. The writer August Strindberg, who eventually suffered from schizophrenia, described himself and others like him as seeking loneliness in order to "spin themselves into the silk of their own souls."[9] And one schizophrenic (Lawrence), recalling his earlier life, described himself as having long had the feeling of living "suspended in the plasma" of his own thoughts.[10] Schizoids may also have a sense of detachment from themselves, giving them the feeling that they don't fully exist;[11] or that their feelings or actions are somehow unjustified, disruptive, or vaguely incorrect. One schizoid man was uncomfortable with spontaneous talk. "If I speak a word as soon as it comes into my head," he explained, "I have the feeling as if I were shouting insolently into the blue, just like when you spring over stocks and stones." In going to greet another person, he might draw back suddenly, fearing it would be insulting to grip the other's hand too quickly.[12]

Like so much about the schizophrenia spectrum of illnesses, the significance of these abnormalities of personality, including their precise relationship to full-blown schizophrenia, remains controversial. According to some experts (including Karl Jaspers and Kurt Schneider),[13] the central characteristics of schizophrenia are simply too bizarre to be understood as exaggerations of, or outgrowths from, such traits of character or personality. Jaspers assumed that schizophrenia is a morbid "process," a biologically caused event that supervenes at a certain point and has no particular affinity for any specific personality type; it does not, he thought, grow out of, nor can it be seen as an expression of, individual character or personality (though it can progress to the point of obliterating the patient's original personality traits). Some theorists, Kraepelin, for example, view apparent "premorbid" characteristics as nothing more than early signs of the disease process itself, not "the expression of a disposition to the disease [but] the surreptitious beginnings of the disease itself."[14] But it has been just as common to grant premorbid personality a more central role, and to view schizophrenia not as a process but as what Jaspers would call a "development." According to this view the schizophrenic psychosis is not something one simply *gets* or *has*—like malaria or tuberculosis or cancer; rather, it is something that one *is*, something that, in a profound sense, develops out of or expresses one's basic character or personal mode of being.[15]

THEORIES AND SUBTYPES OF SCHIZOID PERSONALITY

Characteristics such as those I have been describing are central to virtually all conceptions of schizoid personality, but two rather different ways of explaining these traits have been proposed, corresponding to the extremes of the act-affliction polarity I have mentioned previously. In the first approach, which is popular in medical-model psychiatry, the schizoid's apparent asociality and emotional flatness are taken more or less at face value, being attributed to some biological predisposition such as a physiologically based insensitivity, emotional blandness, or imbalance of cognitive and affective functions.[16] Just the opposite tack is taken by the psychoanalysts most interested in schizoid conditions, the British object-relations theorists, for they interpret the apparent insensitivity and asociality as a defense, a way of protecting and masking a deep-lying hypersensitivity and neediness.[17]

The Views of Ernst Kretschmer

The subtlest and most reasonable account is, however, the one offered in *Physique and Character*, a book published in 1921 that avoids this kind of polarization of explanatory principles. The author, Ernst Kretschmer, was a German psychiatrist who was gifted with the descriptive powers of a first-rate novelist (unfortunately, he is seldom read by contemporary psychopathologists). He conceived of the schizoid as being endowed, to a particularly strong degree, with one of two universal and fundamental human tendencies, tendencies that, when particularly pronounced, would eventuate in either the schizophrenic or the manic-depressive forms of psychosis. The first of these he termed *schizothymia*—the propensity to shift between hypersensitivity and insensitivity or coldness in one's reactions to the world.[18]

Like Eugen Bleuler—who had similar, though less elaborated views—Kretschmer distinguished the schizoid or schizothymic person (the latter being a less severe variant) from what could be called the *cycloid* (or, as Bleuler named it, *syntonic*) individual.[19] In contrast with schizoids, cycloid or syntonic people are characterized by relaxation and spontaneity and by a harmonious sense of union both with the world and within themselves.[20] They tend, in Kretschmer's words, "to throw themselves into the world about them"; they may be sensual enjoyers of life or practical go-getters, expansive realists or good-natured humorists,[21] and their dispositions can be predominantly happy or sad or, more likely, prone to shifts between the two (hence a propensity for affective illnesses and, at the extreme, manic-depressive psychoses). In all cases, they are sociable, immediate, and relatively undivided in their being, tending "to be engrossed in their surroundings and to live in the present."[22] All this is in sharp contrast with the schizoid condition, in which "internal multiplicity" and "disharmony" tend to "inhibit a complete, fulfilling, and harmonious devotion to the opportunity of the moment, to a frame of mind, to others, and to the entire world of reality."[23]

In Kretschmer's view, the key to understanding the schizoid temperament is to recognize that most schizoids are, in fact, neither oversensitive nor cold, but "oversensitive and cold at the same time, and, indeed, in quite different relational mixtures"; they are people "full of antitheses, always containing extremes, and only missing out on the means" (the middle positions).[24] And for this reason, he argues, one should not set up too strong an opposition between those schizoid persons whose surface indifference is more active, "cold," as he terms it (that is, a defensive kind of self-anesthetizing, numbing, or cramping) versus those with a more passive or innate "insensitivity," an emotional blindness or deadness based on some intrinsic defect (what he calls "affective imbecility"); indeed, one often observes "within the same schizoid life, how insensitivity turns into coldness, or coldness into insensitivity."[25]

But, though schizoids and schizothymes are best characterized by their propensity to be not at any single point but at the extremes of a dimension indicating degree of sensitivity to the environment,[26] the temperament's center of gravity may still differ from patient to patient (as it can also from moment to moment within a given patient); and for this reason Kretschmer was willing to distinguish two schizoid variants: the (predominantly) "hyperaesthetic" and the (predominantly) "anaesthetic" subtypes.[27] Here is a summary of Kretschmer's distinctions among personality types:

A. Cycloid or Syntonic
   Endowed with a predominantly cyclothymic type of disposition.
B. Schizoid

Endowed with a predominantly schizothymic type of disposition; with two subtypes:
1. Hyperaesthetic
2. Anaesthetic

(*Note:* The terms *schizothyme, schizoid,* and *schizophrenic* can be used to designate persons with progressively stronger degrees of the schizothymic type of disposition.)

Whereas the hyperaesthetic subtype may seem "timid, shy, with fine feelings, sensitive, nervous, excitable . . . abnormally tender, constantly wounded . . . 'all nerves,' " the anaesthetic schizoid may seem "flavorless, boring," as if there were nothing behind the masks but "a dark, hollow-eyed nothing—affective anaemia . . . nothing but . . . yawning emotional emptiness, or the cold breath of an arctic soullessness."[28]

Yet even with the extreme cases, insists Kretschmer, a closer look will nearly always reveal evidence of the other end of the scale. Even with the gentlest manifestations of hyperaesthetic traits, he says, we are likely to feel "a light, intangible breath of aristocratic boldness and distance, an autistic narrowing down of affective responses to a strictly limited circle of men and things, and occasionally we hear a harsh, loveless remark passed on men who lie outside this circle." As for those individuals of the anaesthetic subtype who seem predominantly cold or poor in affective response: "as soon as we come into close personal contact with such schizoids, we find, very frequently, behind the affectless, numbed exterior, in the innermost sanctuary, a tender personality-nucleus with the most vulnerable nervous sensitivity which has withdrawn into itself, and lies there contorted."[29]

Kretschmer, who was particularly interested in the connection between temperament and creativity, believed that neither of his two major personality types could be said to be superior in overall creative disposition or ability, yet he claimed that each was predisposed toward certain *kinds* of creative activity. The cycloid or syntonic individual's acceptance of society and interest in the external world, for example, would incline him or her toward realism and good-natured humor in literary production or, in the sciences, toward careful empirical observation (as examples Kretschmer mentions Émile Zola and Alexander von Humboldt); whereas the introversion and cerebralism of the schizotype (whether hyperaesthetic or anaesthetic) would generally dispose toward aestheticism and mysticism, or toward more abstract or systematizing efforts. It is understandable, therefore, that there should be a predominance of people with one or the other of the fundamental temperaments in certain fields, schools of thought, and aesthetic movements, and among those drawn to a particular artistic style. Kretschmer notes, for instance, the high number of schizothymic individuals to be found in the movements of German idealism and romanticism—among them Immanuel Kant, Friedrich Hölderlin, Johann Gottlieb Fichte, and Friedrich von Schiller.[30]

But if the schizothymic disposition has some affinities with romanticism, it would seem to be even more strongly linked with the modernist movements—where romantic individualism and expressivism have been transfigured into a far more radical aesthetic of isolation and detachment. We can see this in the image of the creative personality that has come to dominate our age. In James Joyce's *Portrait of the Artist as a Young Man,* said to be "the bible of modernism in English,"[31] for example, the central character, Stephen Daedalus, describes the artist as remaining "invisible, refined out of existence, indifferent, paring his fingernails"; and he embraces the artist's destiny as "silence, exile, and cunning"—"not only to be separate from others but to have not even one friend."[32] Such a vision would have seemed very peculiar indeed in the early nineteenth century (a time when Wordsworth could define the poet as "a man speaking to men"),[33] but by the beginning of the twentieth it had come to be a guiding cultural assumption in the West.[34] It seems likely that this reflected widespread cultural changes, changes extending well beyond the domain of aesthetic attitudes. In this respect we might regard the artist as an emblematic as well as ambivalent figure—his inward turn providing an image of nonconformist escape or of rebellion *against* modern society while at the same time illustrating, in exaggerated form, tendencies that pervade this same society.

Later in this chapter I shall consider these cultural tendencies in more detail, but here I would like to dwell on two modern writers who represent Kretschmer's hyperaesthetic and anaesthetic subtypes of the schizoid personality, Franz Kafka and Charles Baudelaire. Each of these writers is an influential as well as an exemplary figure, illustrating, both personally and in his art, certain major trends in modern culture. For the moment we shall focus on these schizoid individuals in relative isolation, in the hope of gaining a more vivid sense of this rather paradoxical mode of being.

Franz Kafka: A Hypersensitive Sensibility

In the works of Franz Kafka (1883–1924) the isolation of the human being seems a condition as fundamental and as ineluctable as gravity, time, or human mortality itself. That his fictions (whatever else they may be) are allegorizations of personal experience is, for anyone acquainted with his letters and diaries, almost too obvious to require defense; Kafka himself was understandably ambivalent about publishing much of what he wrote, fearing it would constitute "personal proofs of my human weakness" and "evidence of solitude."[35]

Solitude, the "power over me which never fails,"[36] was in fact Kafka's most constant theme, something he experienced as both haven and curse. Surely one of the great solitaries of the twentieth century, Kafka, at age ten, already seemed withdrawn and unapproachable. As a classmate would recall many years later, "Something like a glass wall constantly surrounded him. With his quiet kindly smile he opened the world up for himself, but he locked himself up in front of it."[37] Throughout his life Kafka would describe himself in similar terms. In 1911, at age twenty-eight, he wrote in his diary of his "lack of feeling," referring to a hollow space "between me and everything else . . . which I make no attempt at all to pierce;"[38] and in a draft for an early short story, he compares the experience of joining with others in song to "being drawn on by a fish hook" (381).* For his writing, Kafka said, he needed an absolute solitude, not merely the solitude of "a hermit— that wouldn't be enough—but like a dead man."[39]

Kafka seems to have been a predominantly hypersensitive—what Kretschmer would call a hyperaesthetic—person, and his withdrawal was accompanied by conscious feelings of vulnerability and inferiority, by extreme self-consciousness, and by a persistent desire for contact with others. Incessant self-scrutiny could be a source of reassurance, but it would also alienate him from his physical self and actions, rendering him awkward in his movements and hesitant in speech. Kafka's hypersensitivity and sense of being somehow awry in the social world, as well as the intense yearning for contact that existed beneath his aloofness, are apparent in "Investigations of a Dog," a story in which one of Kafka's fictional alter egos, the dog-narrator, describes his persistent experience of

> some discrepancy, some little maladjustment, causing a slight feeling of discomfort which not even the most decorous public functions could eliminate; more, that sometimes, no, not sometimes, but very often, the mere look of some fellow dog of my own circle that I was fond of, the mere look of him, as if I had just caught it for the first time, would fill me with helpless embarrassment and fear, even with despair. . . . I was nevertheless able to carry on as a somewhat cold, reserved, shy, and calculating, but all things considered normal enough dog. . . . Solitary and withdrawn, with nothing to occupy me save my hopeless but, as far as I am concerned, indispensable little investigations, that is how I live; yet in my distant isolation I have not lost sight of my people. [278][40]

Kafka's sense of inferiority is more directly discussed in his posthumously published *Letter to His Father*, a long missive (never delivered) that answers his father's accusation of coldness, estrangement, and ingratitude

*Numbers in parentheses in this chapter refer to page citations in Kafka, *The Complete Stories*.

unbecoming to a son. Without denying these qualities, Kafka tries to explain how the father has played a major role in bringing them about. Whereas he describes himself as "weakly, timid, hesitant, restless," "shy and nervous," "wavering," and "doubtful," to his father he ascribes all the virtues of the syntonic or cycloid person: "will to life, business, and conquest," and "strength, health, appetite, loudness of voice, eloquence, self-satisfaction, worldly dominance, endurance, presence of mind . . . hot temper"[41]—virtues that had an overpowering effect on the sensitive, sometimes envious son who would self-protectively shrink away.

Kafka's introversion does seem largely a response to hypersensitivity, a defensive drawing back from what Kretschmer called "the harsh, strong colours and tones of everyday life." What both normal and cycloid or syntonic people find "welcome and indispensably stimulating elements of existence" are felt, by such a person, as "shrill, ugly, and unloveable, even to the extent of being psychically painful." Kretschmer describes "a cramping of the self into itself," an attempt "as far as possible to deaden all stimulation from the outside"; such people "close the shutters of their houses, in order to lead a dream-life, fantastic, 'poor in deeds and rich in thought' [the quotation is from Hölderlin] in the soft muffled gloom of the interior."[42] There is evidence of this orientation in many of Kafka's fictions, as in his short story "Unhappiness," which begins with the following line: "When it was becoming unbearable—once toward evening in November—and I ran along the narrow strip of carpet in my room as on a racetrack, shrank from the sight of the lit-up street, then turning to the room found a new goal in the depths of the looking glass" (390).

In another, particularly long story called "The Burrow," we find an extended parable of the consequences of this kind of withdrawal. The narrator here is a small animal, perhaps a mole or a groundhog, who calls himself "a connoisseur and prizer of burrows, a hermit, a lover of peace" (337), and who tells, in obsessive detail, of his preoccupation with building a perfect haven from the outside world. As the story progresses, it becomes clear that the burrow should not be understood too literally, that it is not so much a matter of a physical construction as of a psychological condition the narrator takes with him everywhere: "I and the burrow belong so indissolubly together . . . nothing can part us for long"; "You [the burrow] belong to me, I to you, we are united; what can harm us?" (340, 342).

The story also illustrates a point Kretschmer neglects: this kind of inward withdrawal is not all that successful. For the narrator of "The Burrow" does not really lose himself in escapist fantasies of bliss or adventure; what he dwells on are not fantasies of tropical pleasures and exotic escapades but thoughts of a highly obsessional and anxiety-laden nature, involving a perpetual invocation and warding off of all kinds of imagined dangers (a point that could also be made about Kafka's own literary productions). Thus he worries about "hideous protruberances, disturbing cracks" (350), which appear in the walls of his burrow, and he never forgets that its beautiful stillness can be deceptive: "for, despite all my vigilance, may I not be attacked from some unexpected quarter?" (326)

Weakness and vulnerability are, in fact, among Kafka's most prominent experiences, and his fictions present us with parables of such feelings and of the (often futile) measures for self-protection that they inspire. We know from Kretschmer, however, that we should always look for the other side, for the "thin icy sheath" or deep sense of aristocratic superiority that may accompany the feelings of vulnerability and inferiority of the hyperaesthetic schizoid. Kafka himself once said that his deepest feelings toward other people were fear and indifference (which, according to one commentator, makes him a representative modern man);[43] and it would, I think, be simplistic to dismiss the sense of indifference as nothing but a defense against the fear. It is true that Kafka's own self-analysis may sometimes encourage such an interpretation, as when he writes of his own "cold, scarcely disguised, indestructible, childishly helpless, almost ridiculous, brutally self-satisfied indifference—that of a self-sufficient but coldly whimsical child," stating that this was "the only protection against the nervous disturbance that came from anxiety and guilt feelings."[44] But at other times Kafka characterizes his indifference as the more essential trait. Thus in a letter to his on-again, off-again fiancée, Felice, he describes himself as "basically a cold, selfish, callous creature, despite my weakness which conceals rather than mitigates these qualities."[45] And in a diary entry from 1913 he describes hating "everything which doesn't relate to literature. Conversations bore me (even when they are about literary subjects), visiting people bores me, and the joys and sorrows of my relatives bore me to death." "I don't have 'literary interests,' " he wrote in a letter to Felice, "literature is what I'm made of."[46]

The tendency toward withdrawal and a cutting off of sympathy and emotion came to be a deep and enduring aspect of his personality—something that, whatever its defensive origins, eventually created problems of its own. Kafka himself stated the dilemma very well: "You can hold yourself back from the sufferings of the world, this is something you are free to do and is in accord with your nature, but perhaps precisely this holding back is the only suffering that you might be able to avoid."[47] Kafka seems to have sensed the problem early on, for when only twenty or twenty-one, he wrote to a friend of wanting to read only "the kinds of books that bite and sting . . . a book should be an ice-pick to break up the frozen sea within us."[48]

Charles Baudelaire: A New Aesthetics of Disdain

Charles Baudelaire had a vision of solitude that was different but no less emphatic than Kafka's, and in him we find an example of the anaesthetic variant of Kretschmer's schizoid sensibility. Although he lived before the era of modernism (born 1821, died 1867), this poet and critic—whom T. S. Eliot described as "the first counter-romantic in poetry" and as "far in advance of his time"—was the first great harbinger of the modernist spirit, and an artist of almost unparalleled influence on writing in the late nineteenth and early twentieth centuries, as well as on images of the artist's role and personality. Baudelaire was the first to crystallize a form of solitude that was virtually unthinkable before the nineteenth century: a profound, self-generated isolation so unaffected by the presence of others that it is likely to be felt most strongly amid a crowd. And he was the first major poet to revel in the self-imposed, self-glorifying alienation that was to become virtually *de rigueur* in the artistic avant-garde.

As with Kafka, the themes of solitude and detachment permeate Baudelaire's life as well as his literary works. In a collection of autobiographical fragments called *My Heart Laid Bare,* he writes of a persistent "feeling of solitude, since my childhood. Despite family—and in the midst of my friends, certainly—a feeling of being destined to be eternally alone."[49] And, also like Kafka, Baudelaire embraces this solitude, calling it the "privilege of silence, if not of rest," and the sanctuary where "the tyranny of the human face has vanished, and I shall suffer only by myself."[50] Where Baudelaire's solitude differs from that of Kafka is in its mood or tone. In the French poet's case, it is less a matter of fear or envy than of disdain, less of *Angst* than of *spleen*—the latter being Baudelaire's term for a new kind of emotion, a peculiar mix of disillusionment, irony, bitterness, and ennui that he invented as much as described, and that (along with the more Kafkaesque emotion of *Angst*) came to be a frequent constituent of the modernist sensibility.[51] Kafka is preoccupied with a sense of vulnerability and inferiority; Baudelaire's attitude, by contrast, is haughty condescension toward a world he finds less threatening than disappointing, a place of ugliness, futility, and cliché that would be unworthy of the poet's attention—were it not for his invention of what might be called a new aesthetics of disdain.

Baudelaire displays a kind of indifference and scorn that, in Kretschmer's view, is especially common in the anaesthetic or insensitive schizoid type: a disinterest that is "ostentatiously manifested [since the] indifferent knows that he takes absolutely no interest in many things which are important to other people," an attitude sometimes mixed with "traces of baroque humor or sarcasm." Kretschmer compares the impression such people make to that of a "cat that walks by itself," seeming "indifferent and indolent, who joins in too little with his comrades, and who is too pleased with himself."[52]

Baudelaire's persistent scorn has two main objects, the first being the natural world and all the organic, spontaneous processes that it sustains. Nature, he says, is hideous and corrupt: a "swamp of blood, an abyss of mud"[53] whose relentless flourishing and self-renewal strike him as shameful and distressing.[54] His own preference is for "la majesté superlative des formes artificielles," and he insists that "everything that is beautiful and noble is the product of reason and calculation" and, further, that everything created by mind is not only more beautiful but even more living than matter.[55]

The other object of Baudelaire's disdain is the ordinariness and predictability of both the masses and the bourgeoisie—of all who fail to live up to what he sees as the aristocratic ideals of uniqueness, self-control, and self-sufficiency.[56] The problem with the average man, as Baudelaire sees it, is his sociability: his desire to be just like the others, to conform to their expectations, and, worst of all, to lose his separateness by melting in with the crowd. The man of genius, by contrast, always "wants to be *one*, and therefore solitary," for he knows that "to be a great man and a saint by *one's own standards* . . . is all that matters"; "the true hero amuses himself all alone."[57]

The mood of Baudelaire's solitude and withdrawal is, then, less a matter of threat than of gnawing dissatisfaction, what he calls "an irritated melancholy, a nervous postulation, [the feelings of] a nature exiled in an imperfect world which would like to take possession at once on this very earth of a revealed paradise."[58] The sanctuary from so disappointing a world will be, however, not a burrow, appealing primarily for the stoutness of its walls, but a magic, interior space, an aesthetic paradise where it is not the threat but the banality of everyday life that can be conjured away. And, given Baudelaire's aversion to all that is physical or spontaneous, it is not surprising that this paradise should not turn out to be a Dionysian one. We find in him no evidence of the envy and even respect that Kafka could feel for people endowed with strong appetites and sensuality and who (like Kafka's father) have some meat on their bones. Baudelaire disdained sexuality as but the debased and debasing "lyricism of the masses"; to him the true man of nature is purely repulsive.[59]

Baudelaire's aversion to the sexual (in any but the most oblique and rarefied of its expressions) is a revulsion for all that is physical and spontaneous, existing beyond the shaping and distancing powers of the mind, but also for the necessity of contact with other human beings. "What is annoying about Love," he tells us, "is that it is a crime which one cannot do without an accomplice." After all, "to fornicate is to aspire to enter into another," and the true artist "never emerges from himself."[60] Indeed, Baudelaire insists that anything natural, like passion or the "intoxication of the heart," could only disrupt that "human aspiration towards a higher beauty" that is the authentic poetic impulse.[61]

The true antithesis of nature and society is that glorious figure, the dandy, whom Baudelaire defined as "the man brought up in luxury . . . who has no other profession but that of elegance, [and who] will always have a distinctive appearance, one that sets him utterly apart." (He is always a male, since

Baudelaire—an infamous misogynist—viewed woman as a rather pathetic creature, largely at the mercy of the cycles and impulsions of her swollen body.) The way of the dandy is not an easy one, however, for he aspires to a cult of coldness and self-absorption that requires him to be "sublime without interruption; [to] live and sleep before a mirror," always cultivating an "air of reserve, which in turn arises from his unshakeable resolve not to feel any emotion." It seems, however, that the possibility of passionate response is not to be entirely excluded; for Baudelaire does compare the dandy's beauty to "a hidden fire whose presence can be guessed at, a fire that could blaze up, but does not wish to do so." Such a person will make his life into a work of art, a peculiarly controlled and self-absorbed work founded on an invisible relationship of the self to itself; but to do this the gaze of the other must still be attracted, if only as a way of affirming the exquisite subtlety of what cannot be seen. Therefore Baudelaire says that the dandy's "very reserve is a provocation," and he speaks of the "cult of oneself" that allows "delight in causing astonishment, and the proud satisfaction of never oneself being astonished."[62]

Behind such cold and arrogant surfaces, however, there will, as Kretschmer pointed out, usually be indications of a tender core: a "most vulnerable nervous sensitivity which has withdrawn into itself, and lies there contorted."[63] Though evidence of such tenderness is scarce in the most extreme variants of the anaesthetic schizoid, it is fairly easy to see in a person like Baudelaire, whose characteristic irony is often laced with a subdued pathos, a hint of passionate feelings that, like the banked fires of the dandy, seem ever capable of flaring up (even if they never quite do). Thus in the prose poem "One A.M.," there is first a recounting of a series of perverse cruelties the poet has been inflicting on others, almost at random and in a mood of disdain and despair; but the work ends on a rather curious note of semi-confession and prayer:

> Displeased with everybody, displeased with myself, I should like to regain a little self-redemption and self-pride, amidst the silence and solitude of night. . . . O Lord my God, give me grace to produce a few lines of good poetry, so that I may prove to myself that I am not the most abject of men, that I am not inferior to those whom I despise.[64]

PARALLELS WITH MODERN CULTURE: DISCONNECTION

Both Kafka and Baudelaire wrote from a position of estrangement from society—a society seen, in the first instance, as callous and threatening and, in the second, as unknowing and banal. Yet it would be wrong, for this reason, to ignore how their attitudes and modes of experience, so typical of the schizoid individual, can also reflect the culture of which they were a part, a culture whose signature can be most apparent precisely in those who criticize or reject it.

The issue of the affinities between culture and the schizoid attitude has received remarkably little attention in mainstream psychiatry and psychoanalysis. Medical-model psychiatry has focused on cognitive and emotional disorders that are assumed to reflect underlying neurobiological abnormalities, and for various reasons (discussed in the appendix to this book) these disorders have been conceived largely as defects or deficit states. There has therefore been a tendency to view schizoid conditions as lacking the kind of internal complexity and the patterns of intentionality that the parallels with modern culture might suggest.

To generalize about psychoanalytic approaches to schizoid characteristics is more difficult, not only because of their variety but because the theoretical models being proposed are often obscure. It is clear, however, that the most influential authors have relied heavily on versions of the fixation/regression model. Helene Deutsch speaks of "a genuine infantilism," with "arrest at a definite stage in the development of the emotional life and character formation," of instincts that are "crudely primitive" and "untamed," "relationships to objects [that have] remained at the stage of identification," and "a failure to synthesize the various infantile identifications into a single integrated personality."[65] W. R. D. Fairbairn states that "the pattern of the schizoid attitude" is largely determined by "fixation in the early oral phase";[66] and his follower Harry Guntrip describes "schizoid withdrawal and regression [as] fundamentally the same phenomenon." The postulated regression, in Guntrip's view, is particularly profound, for it is aimed at the utter dependence and vegetative passivity of the intrauterine state.[67] Another psychoanalytically oriented writer, the social historian Christopher Lasch, writes about possible parallels between modern culture and various pathologies that could be described as schizoid (he speaks of selves "contract[ed] to a defensive core, armed against adversity"). But he, too, sees such persons as seeking to return to the very early stage of primary narcissism in order "to annul awareness of separation"—"either by imagining an ecstatic and painless reunion with the mother or, on the other hand, by imagining a state of complete self-sufficiency and by denying any need for objects at all."[68]

I would not deny that fantasies of symbiotic union and primitive instinctual satisfaction may exist on some deep, and thus largely invisible, level of the unconscious of schizoid people (as, no doubt, is the case for many of us).[69] A familiarity with the experiences actually described by schizoid individuals suggests, however, that these psychoanalytic interpretations are, at the very least, extremely incomplete. To judge by what patients themselves say, they seem dominated much more by a fundamental awareness of distance, difference, and fragmentation, by forms of "internal multiplicity and disharmony,"[70] than by experiences of boundaryless unity or utter self-sufficiency. And these, the most characteristic features of the schizoid lived world, bear a remarkable resemblance to the modern or modernist sensibility;[71] of all personality types, the schizoid most clearly epitomizes the distinctive elements of the modern condition.

The relevant aspects of the modern social and cultural framework have been described by a small army of sociologists, anthropologists, philosophers, and culture critics of various stripes, writing over the course of the last century or more; and, surprisingly enough, there is considerable consensus on certain central points. It seems clear that one of the most distinctive and pervasive features of modernity is the intense focus on the self (both as a subject and as an object of experience) and on the value and power of the individual—emphases not to be found in the more communal, homogeneous, and organically integrated worlds of contemporary tribal and nonliterate societies or in the culture of premodern Europe. The modern cultural constellation obviously has certain strengths—allowing as it does for freedom of movement and thought, and encouraging individual initiative and self-expression. But, of course, it also has a dark side, forms of alienation summed up in the following list: "isolation, loneliness, a sense of disengagement, a loss of natural vitality and of innocent pleasure in the givenness of the world, and a feeling of burden because reality has no meaning other than what a person chooses to impart to it."[72] The resemblance to the *Angst*- and *spleen*-ridden worlds of Kafka and Baudelaire—those "town criers of inwardness," in Kierkegaard's phrase[73]—and to the overall description of schizoid personality offered at the outset of this chapter, may already seem obvious enough, at least on a general level; but further insights can be gained by considering these parallels in detail.

Let us begin by exploring aspects of the rift in one's connection to the world; later we shall examine the rift in the self's relationship to itself. As labels for these two forms of separation, I shall adopt the terminology used by Peter, a schizoid patient who was treated by the psychiatrist R. D. Laing. *Disconnection* was Peter's word for the separation from the social and external world; the separation from the self he referred to as *uncoupling*.[74]

Interiorizing Trends

The social historian Norbert Elias speaks of "the extraordinary conviction carried in European societies since roughly the Renaissance by the self-perception of human beings in terms of their own isolation, the severance of their own 'inside' from everything 'outside.' "[75] This aspect of modern existence is manifest at many levels of cultural reality, not only in the realm of ideas but in characteristic forms of social organization, in cultural practices, and in the experiential modes of everyday life. For its clearest expression, however, we might look to the doctrines of the two most influential philosophers of the modern era, René Descartes and Immanuel Kant.

Descartes (1596–1650), generally acknowledged as the father of modern philosophy, could be said to have invented the modern concept of mind, or at least to have given it its decisive formulation. It was he who fostered certain dualisms and conceptions of human inwardness that have permeated much of the philosophical, scientific, and ethical thought coming after him. Consciousness in the Cartesian scheme is conceived of as radically distinct from the material plane of extended substances, a plane that includes the body in which this conciousness is mysteriously housed, rather like a ghost in a machine (in Gilbert Ryle's famous phrase). Further, consciousness is assumed to have direct access not to the external world but only to inner "ideas" that somehow represent this world (it is certain, says Descartes, "that I can have no knowledge of what is outside me except by means of the ideas I have within me").[76] Both these aspects of Cartesianism are by now so deeply embedded in prevailing modes of understanding as to seem self-evident and inevitable.[77] We may need to be reminded that very different visions are quite possible, and have in fact prevailed in other cultures and other eras, such as ancient Greece.

The essential implications of Cartesianism for the modern self might be summed up in two words: disengagement and reflexivity. On this account a full realization of one's essential being—which is to say, of one's being as a consciousness—requires detachment from the body and from the passions rooted in it; for only in this way can one achieve the self-mastery inherent in recognizing and exercising the capacity for rational self-control. The achievement of certainty in knowledge also requires disengagement—disengagement from naive acceptance of the existence of the external world in favor of an inspection, by the "Inner Eye" of the Mind, of those "clear and distinct" ideas that can be found within (this is Descartes's famous method of doubt).[78] Going along with this is a reflexive turn, involving recognition of the inevitable participation of one's own mind in every act of awareness (this is the certainty of the *cogito*—I think, therefore I am—the essential realization on which all other knowledge will be founded). In this way, thought, previously associated with dialogue, begins, with Descartes, to seem a quintessentially private event; and knowledge, previously conceived as a communal possession, comes to be associated with a "logic of private inquiry."[79]

Kant's philosophy, which was formulated at the end of the eighteenth century and is sometimes viewed as initiating modern*ist* thought,[80] could be seen as a radicalization of Cartesianism, since it places an even more intense emphasis on reflexivity and disengagement. The *cogito*, the ego's awareness of the fact of its own consciousness, had played a critical role in Descartes's search for certainty in experience; but with Kant its role becomes even more crucial. Consciousness for Kant is not just a touchstone of certainty; now its structures—in the form of the (human) categories of time, space, causality, and materiality—are said to constitute, in a sense to create, the world of our experience. Acceptance of this suggestion had the effect (as Hegel put it) of "withdraw[ing] cognition from an interest in its objects and absorption in the study of them, and . . . direct[ing] it back upon itself; and so turn[ing] it into a question of form."[81] The Kantian vision also encourages a more radical sense of separation than did Cartesianism. In Descartes's scheme, the ideas we experience were certainly inner phenomena, yet nevertheless were assumed to be linked (albeit uncertainly) to an external world. Kant, by contrast, draws an absolute distinction between the realm of all possible human experience (the "phenomenal" realm, as he called it) and that of actual existence or being (the "noumenal"), thus implying an unbridgeable gap that sunders us eternally from the real—leaving us "lonely and forsaken amidst the world, surrounded everywhere by spectres."[82]

I said earlier that these philosophical conceptions of mind and self are echoed at other, more concrete levels of existence, involving social, political, and economic aspects of modern life. While these latter aspects are far too numerous, and their interactions with philosophical ideas and personal experience far too complex, to be covered comprehensively here, I can offer at least a couple of suggestive examples.

Particularly telling illustrations of a growing self-consciousness, and of an increasing interiorization and privatization of daily life, are offered by the historical sociologist Norbert Elias's vivid studies of the history of manners. Elias describes, for instance, how eating came, in Western society, to be the object of increasing strictures that had the effect of emphasizing the separation between individual persons, and of disguising or even denying their natural or animalistic side. Food, which medieval people ate by dipping their hands into a communal bowl or by tearing flesh from a common dish, later had to be ladled out carefully to individual plates, and to be picked up only with certain utensils and at a particular moment in a sequence of courses. Spitting on the table became taboo, then spitting on the floor became taboo; soon enough it was frowned upon to spit anywhere in public. The new forms of etiquette that were developing required the restraint of emotion and spontaneous impulse by internal controls and an increasing dominance of the cerebral over the affective or instinctual side of life. They also led to an ever-growing self-scrutiny and insistence on self-control, which necessarily lowered the threshold of what was felt to be shameful and offensive. Elias suggests that this necessity to restrain the spontaneous expression of affect and impulse led to a feeling of being separated from the external world by an invisible wall, a "self-perception in terms of one's own isolation" that is expressed in the modern philosophical leitmotif of *homo clausus*, the image of a "self in a case" that is so important in the thought of Descartes, Kant, and many other lesser spirits.[83]

The spread of literacy may also have contributed to these interiorizing trends. As the scholar Walter Ong has pointed out, both writing and reading (especially silent reading, a practice that only gradually came to be the norm) allow—even force—a person to think or to encounter thought alone, with a sense of isolation from the group; writing especially tends to require and to encourage silent reflection. The written word could also be said to freeze thought, by organizing and preserving it in a visual space; it thereby offers a new image of an independent mental universe—what Ong describes as a "spectacularly ordered environment for thought, free from interference, simply there, unattended and unsupervised by any discernible person." By the eighteenth century in the West, Ong argues, the commitment of sound to space that is inherent in alphabetical writing had had a noticeable effect on our sense of the world, gradually making possible what Ong calls a new kind of "schizoid" withdrawal—a remoteness from sensory actuality and social interaction that allowed for escape into something other than violent action or tribal magic: the interior of one's own mind.[84]

Schizoid individuals seem to have a special affinity for modes of inwardness and withdrawal akin to those of the modern age.[85] Martin, a young artist who experienced his first schizophrenic episode in adolescence, had long had a profound sense of separateness. "I have always found myself thinking and yet my thoughts were an internal reference," he wrote in his diary. Recollecting what it was like to ride in a car as a child, he wrote, "I was at the center of the universe, the 'real world'—the people in the other cars were outside of my inner world." He remembered being very shy when he was young, and often remaining silent, "thus allowing me to listen not only to conversation between people but also to myself." In his relationship to the external world and to his own activity, there was something reminiscent of the Cartesian notion of an Inner Eye that contemplates sensations and actions from a remove: "Hearing a door creak, a calling jay sends a vibration into the receiver of my mind, and I choose from the phenomena an action," he wrote in his diary; and, in a paper for school, he wrote, "The eye is to watch; the mind watches the eye."

Interestingly enough, Martin felt extremely drawn to Kantian philosophy when he happened to encounter it in a college course, and later he would sometimes insert sentences from Kant into his paintings. Kant's ideas about what Martin termed "the separation we have between the patterns of our thoughts and the existence of the world" were very similar, he explained, to "my own realization of my mind in adolescence." Reading this philosopher was a very calming experience for him; for, as he explained to me, Kant "has been where I'm going," and this provided him with what he described as "security in being in my mind," "the feeling that it was OK to feel what I was feeling." While reading Kant on the nature of judgment, Martin was particularly struck with the uncanny sensation that his own ongoing mental processes, those accompanying the reading itself, were examples of the very thing that he was reading *about* (which is a realization very much in keeping with the spirit of the Kantian work he was absorbing).

A similar inwardness is described by Jonathan Lang (a pseudonym), a patient who in his early twenties developed schizophrenia with paranoid and catatonic trends. When in his early thirties, Lang, who had read a great deal of psychology, wrote about his premorbid schizoid traits in an article that appeared in the journal *Psychiatry* in 1939. "Even before the development of my psychosis, I can remember the existence of a tendency for ideas to possess a higher affective potential than immediate external stimuli such as persons or things," he says. Apparently he had long felt uncomfortable with emotions and with any kind of direct contact with the outer world, whether through passive perception or active interaction. And for this reason, "[I] trained myself to favor ideation over emotion . . . to block the affective response from showing any outward sign." He always preferred reading to direct sensory perception, Lang tells us, and he viewed the senses "largely as means of obtaining information with which to build ideas." "While I played games during the required physical education period at school, I either thought of something else while I played or tried to govern my playing by verbal ideation rather than direct sensory-motor reaction." And, he insists, his withdrawn concentration on ideas—"ideocentrism," as he called it—was "the prime factor influencing the direction and trend along which my psychosis developed."[86]

Loss of Reality

Nietzsche described his own age, and the two centuries to come, as the era of "nihilism"—a word he used, in a complex and idiosyncratic way, to refer to various consequences, personal and cultural, of an exaggerated subjectivism. One central element of this nihilism was the disappearance of a sense of external grounding of values (something that occurs with the advent of Cartesianism and the Galilean scientific revolution); another was that devaluation of our experiential world that occurs when (as in Kant) it is contrasted with some hypothesized "thing-in-itself" from which we are eternally separated.[87] In Nietzsche's view an important distinction had to be made between two types of nihilism: a passive kind that could be read as a sign of weakness, and more active forms that suggested vitality and will.

A similar critique, also focused on subjectivism, is offered in various works by Martin Heidegger, notably "The Age of the World Picture."[88] It is with Cartesian metaphysics, Heidegger says, that the human subject becomes "that being upon which all that is is grounded as regards the manner of its Being and its truth." In the Middle Ages the world was understood to have been brought into being by a Creator-God, but now it is "conceived and grasped" as depending in some essential way on the human beings who know it. This, then, is the "essence of the modern age": "the unconditional dominion of subjectivity" whereby the human being sets himself up as the ultimate subject before whom and for whom the world will appear as a kind of "picture."[89] The main problem with this glorification of the knowing subject, according to Heidegger, is that it necessarily brings with it a devaluation of the world, whose ontological status is made to seem secondary, derivative, and somehow vulnerable: "Where anything that is has become the object of representing, it first incurs in a certain manner a loss of Being."[90] For "how can I know," he asks, "that this world is not simply a dream, a shimmering hallucination, a horizon no longer suffused with its own light but with mine?"[91]

Such a loss of the sense of Being seems especially common in persons with schizoid personalities, and for them too it is often accompanied by a heightened awareness of their own role in experience. "Reality recedes from me. Everything I touch, everything I think, everyone I meet, becomes unreal as soon as I approach," said James, a severely schizoid patient (verging on psychotic) treated by R. D. Laing.[92] Another patient, a schizophrenic, recalled his premorbid self as follows:

I was always a shy, retiring child, not disposed to make myself free with strangers, not much given to prattle. . . . I was very early in life an observer of my own mental peculiarities . . . [there was always] an unsatisfactoriness in my consciousness of what surrounded me. I used to ask myself "Why is it that while I see and hear and feel everything perfectly, it nevertheless does not seem real to me?"[93]

To judge from a diary entry from 1921, Kafka must have had experiences of a very similar kind: "All is imaginary—family, office, friends, the street, all imaginary, far away or close at hand."[94]

These examples seem to illustrate what Nietzsche called passive nihilism, for these individuals appear to experience the states and moods they describe as something suffered rather than actively brought about, as conditions suggesting "decline and recession of the power of the spirit," a sense of being unable to sustain the existence of a world dependent on the self. But other instances of schizoid derealization are more suggestive of Nietzsche's active nihilism; here the experience has a far more willful or purposive cast, bolstering a sense of superiority over the world and serving as a "sign of increased power of the spirit."[95]

We see this often—for example, in the tendency, common in schizoids and many schizophrenics, to be acutely sensitive to the repetitive or hackneyed aspect of what they observe around them, and therefore to react at times with a certain disdain and a sense of disappointment with the world. Henry, a schizophrenic patient to whom I administered various psychological tests, responded to a series of pictures (the Thematic Apperception Test) by asking whether they were "all clichés"—which he then defined, in a most contemptuous tone, as "an exploited kind of pattern that people consider an aspect of experience."[96]

The sense of pervasive unreality experienced by one young man, a patient treated by the psychoanalyst Charles Rycroft, also suggests this kind of active declaration of superiority and indifference. During a thirteen-year period prior to developing schizophrenic delusions, this man maintained an attitude of profound schizoid detachment, declaring that everything he experienced was, as he put it, merely hypothetical and therefore not worth getting too worked up about. Rycroft explains:

> he had the idea that he attended a Dr. Rycroft for psychoanalytical treatment. It was, however, possible that I was not Dr. Rycroft, or that there were two or more Dr. Rycrofts; in any case it didn't really matter whether I was or was not Dr. Rycroft, or whether I was singular or plural. The whole matter was "hypothetical," and no one of the many alternatives was preferable to any other.[97]

The same tentative or purely theoretical quality applied to his fantasies, such as his notion that his actual father might really have been a great mathematician or philosopher like Karl Friedrich Gauss or Bertrand Russell. This sense of hypotheticalness (which could be likened to the technique of phenomenological "bracketing," which suspends the "natural standpoint" whereby we assume the objective existence of the world) seems to have served defensive purposes, enabling him to avoid admitting to himself that any aspect of reality could be truly tempting or dangerous, a possible object of painful loss or frightening attack.

Like Martin, the schizophrenic artist I mentioned earlier, Rycroft's patient also had an explicit interest in philosophy, and his nihilism (in Nietzsche's sense of the word) emerged most clearly in certain solipsistic claims, as when he stated that his thoughts were the only reality and that his thinking was the world itself in action. As Rycroft astutely remarks, these experiences, fantastical though they were, cannot be considered manifestations of the Freudian primary process, for they lack all signs of instinctual or emotional charge. What this young man seemed to enjoy above all was the experience of watching his intellectual processes as they "idled in neutral," devoid of affect and severed from all connection to things external to themselves.

PARALLELS WITH MODERN CULTURE: UNCOUPLING

Disconnection—the sense of being cut off from external objects and other people—is not the only form of separation experienced by the schizoid individual. Typically, such a person's existence is also riven in a second major way, along fault lines running through the self rather than between self and world. And this is often associated with a second major form of self-consciousness: where consciousness focuses on the self not as a knowing center (a subject ranged against a world that seems remote or unreal) but as an actor in the world and a potential object of awareness for others. The "uncoupling" this entails can be suffered by the individual or it can be intentionally induced. In either case, it sets up a division between two different selves: a hidden, "inner" self that watches or controls, usually associated with the mind, and a public, outer self that is more closely identified with bodily appearance and social role and that tends to be felt as somehow false or unreal.[98]

Role Distance

David, a young schizoid man treated by R. D. Laing, distinguished between what he called his "own self" and his "personality," the latter being what others thought he was or wanted him to be. Within himself his ideal was utter frankness and honesty, but with others he needed to feel he was playing a part, even if this was only the part of himself. (The part he saw himself as having played during most of his years in school was that of a precocious and witty schoolboy who was rather cold; on realizing, at age fifteen, that this part was becoming unpopular because, as he put it, "*it* had a nasty tongue," he decided to make his personality more likeable, and did so with what he considered to be "good results.")[99]

Something like this uncoupling can be present in schizoid individuals with the most diverse patterns of overt behavior. They may, for example, be extremely eccentric or else conventional, rebellious, or overtly compliant. They may be highly predictable, perhaps behaving with an excessive formality, or else highly inconsistent, putting on and shedding attitudes, even whole personalities, at a rapid pace.[100] Different as these patterns are, they do have one thing in common: a false or "as-if" quality. David, a sort of dandy with a cloak and a cane, always had a theatrical and contrived quality, as if he were somehow only *playing* at being eccentric.[101] And Kretschmer describes a (predominantly anaesthetic) schizoid man named Ernst Katt, with a mixed dandy/bohemian persona, who rejected any recognized profession or conventional style of life and who would play "the mask of the interesting, bewitched spirit of beauty, which hovers over life"; sometimes he would suddenly say, 'I am a sausage.' "[102]

To the observer, such persons will seem unidentified with or detached from their public performances—uncoupled, if you will—and especially from the inner feelings or qualities of personhood that such roles would normally imply. One may sense an aura of ironic detachment, albeit an ambiguous one, and often an air of mystery suggestive of some hidden intention, or perhaps of an entire private world that is far more significant than anything they reveal.

The term *role distance,* introduced by the sociologist Erving Goffman, captures this phenomenon: one scrutinizes and judges one's behavior from within as well as from the standpoint of an imaginary other, whose reactions one attempts to anticipate and control. And, as Goffman points out, role distance is not so much a denial of the role itself as a rejection of the "virtual self" that is normally felt to animate or inform one's public performance.[103] As with other features of schizoid personalities, this phenomenon seems to have particular prominence in the modern world; let us now consider some of its cultural manifestations and sources.

One of the most fundamental presuppositions of contemporary Western society and thought is that each individual has some kind of inner being or personhood existing apart from or prior to his or her actions or social roles. Historical and anthropological research suggests, however, that this notion is far from universal, being absent not only in traditional societies of the non-Westernized world but also in the West prior to the modern age. In heroic societies like those of the ancient Greeks or the Vikings, as well as in most so-called primitive societies, people's identities were inseparable from their social position, with all its implied rights and obligations. You knew who you were by understanding your place in the web of social statuses, privileges, and duties—and the web itself, the fundamental framework guiding all thought and action, virtually never came into question. Further, what was required of a person, what counted as virtue and what as vice, was always defined in terms of actions. Any concept of a private psychological domain was avoided almost entirely, as though a person simply *had* no hidden depths.[104] Among the Dinka of the southern Sudan, for example, there appears to be no concept that is even roughly equivalent to "our popular modern conception of the 'mind,' as mediating and, as it were, storing up experiences of the self."[105]

It seems likely that a similar absence of the concept or experience of an inner self prevailed in European culture until the end of the Middle Ages, for it is only in the sixteenth century that one begins to find literary evidence of a modern awareness of inwardness and role distance; and philosophical conceptions of the individual person as independent of roles do not come to prominence until the eighteenth century. Historians and sociologists have viewed these as "inner deep-seated changes in the psyche" that betoken "the emergence of modern European and American man."[106] To explain the changes, they point to a number of factors, one of these being the pluralization and segmentation of society—the fact that modern society requires human beings to play a variety of different, even mutually incompatible roles in various reference groups.[107] A related factor is increased social mobility, beginning in the Renaissance and on the increase ever since. This may have encouraged a heightened awareness of the possibility of fashioning human identity in an artful, manipulative way (something that, though common among the elite in the classical world, had been largely absent for a millennium or more).[108]

The polarization of inner from outer or public man has strong evaluative implications, for there is an increasing tendency to value the inner self above its "mere" social roles. We can trace this development in the process whereby the sixteenth-century ideal of sincerity came, by the nineteenth century, to be replaced by an emphasis on a rival ethic—authenticity. Sincerity—the congruence between actual feeling and avowal—does not yet imply an overvaluation of the inner; for, despite the preoccupation with a potential discrepancy between public face and private essence, this ethic nevertheless stresses the honesty and integrity of the performance of public roles. But, as Lionel Trilling shows, this concept of virtue has been displaced over the course of the last two hundred years—to the point where the term *sincerity* has come to have a quaint, even faintly absurd ring to it. For some time now we have lived in a postromantic climate that (at least until very recently) stresses instead *authenticity*—where the point is not so much to be true to other human beings as to be true to oneself, to fulfill one's own inherent being and potential. Similar developments are suggested by the gradual eclipse of the Renaissance category of *passion*—which implied some overt, often violent accompanying action—by the far more "inner" or "subjective" concept of *emotion;*[109] it is also apparent in the growing prominence of notions of *dignity* at the expense of the older concept of *honor.*[110]

One consequence of this inward turn has been a draining of value from public action, at least when the action accords with conventional expectations—for the latter tends increasingly to be seen as irredeemably inauthentic, somehow compromised and contaminated by the demands of conformism and theatricality.[111] More and more the true source of human significance, of what Wordsworth and Rousseau termed "the sentiment of being," is felt to be located not in public action but in the idea of a private or unique self. There seem to be two main ways of responding to this set of cultural attitudes and valuations, the first corresponding to the (predominantly) hyperaesthetic and the second to the (predominantly) anaesthetic kind of schizoid organization. The next two sections will be devoted to an exploration of these tendencies.

Abdication of the Public Self

The first way of responding to this devaluation of the public self is to attempt to abdicate the public self entirely—either through hermitlike isolation or through refusal to interact in a more than perfunctory way—and this is accompanied by a tendency to locate the source of being in the tremors and yearnings of the inner life. Such an attitude is widespread in modernist culture (one thinks, for example, of Virginia Woolf and Ford Madox Ford, among others), and among its most forceful advocates is the contemporary French novelist and essayist Nathalie Sarraute.

Sarraute, a member of the school of the *nouveau roman,* is a harsh critic of conformity to the "impurities" of social convention and tradition. She associates such conformism with a focus, in novel writing, on "literary types" and on "tiresome descriptions" of public events, which she dismisses as but "large empty carcasses" when set beside the "wealth and complexity" of the inner life.[112] Her vision of this inner life is highly reminiscent of Kretschmer's characterization of the exquisitely sensitive hyperaesthetic person, for she describes it as a life of interior stirrings "at once impatient and afraid," of "tiny, evanescent movements" that "blossom out preferably in immobility and withdrawal." Like "little gray insects that hide in damp holes, [these stirrings] are abashed and prudent. The slightest look makes them flee. To blossom out they must have anonymity and impunity. They consequently hardly show themselves in the form of actions." Hence her novels are filled with the most minute descriptions of inner experience—a world of passing images and sensations, of thoughts and velleities fleeting through the private consciousness of her central characters.

Diffident and fragile though they may be, these inner "tremblings" and "recoilings" are nevertheless the essential stuff of human existence, an existence that, in Sarraute's words, is tending in the modern world "to become self-sufficient and, in so far as possible, to do without exterior support." Though Sarraute is speaking principally of the art of the modern novel, of its preoccupation with the inner life of author or character, it is clear that an ethic of living is also being implied. For, in her view, it is the "unceasing play" of inner phenomena—what she elsewhere calls the "subconversation" rather than the "conversation"—that constitutes "the invisi-

ble woof of all human relationships and ⟨...⟩
authentic life is one that attends to this i⟨...⟩
itself in the distractions of action and the p⟨...⟩

This kind of inwardness and alienation fro⟨...⟩
mon in certain kinds of schizoid patients.[113] ⟨...⟩
reflections published in 1917, when its author ⟨...⟩
schizophrenic patient named Mary MacLane offer⟨...⟩
description of the introversion that had marked her ⟨...⟩

> The least important thing in my life is its tangibleness.
> The only things that matter lastingly are the things that ha⟨...⟩
> If I do a cruel act and feel no cruelty in my Soul it is nothing. I⟨...⟩ ⟨...⟩elty
> in my Soul though I do no cruel act I'm guilty of a sort of butc⟨...⟩ and my
> spirit-hands are bloody with it.
> The adventures of my spirit are realer than the outer things that befall me.

In phrases that recall Nathalie Sarraute's apostrophe of the inner life, Mary MacLane speaks of "dwell[ing] on the self that is known only to me—the self that is intricate and versatile, tinted, demi-tinted, deep-dyed, luminous"; such an experience gives her "an intimate delectation, a mental inflorescence and sometimes an exaltation," whereas thinking of "the mass of outer events that have made my tangible life darkens my day."[114]

Later in her book, *I, Mary MacLane*, Mary describes a time when she went walking by herself on a night that made "solitude a delectation," a night when "[m]y thoughts as I walked were all of Me: how fascinating is Me." Coming indoors, she sat down before a mirror on a bureau and tipped forward to get closer to herself: "Lovingly, tenderly . . . I looked at Me in the mirror. 'You enchanted one!' said I, 'You're my Companion, my Familiar, my Lover, my wilding Sweetheart—I love you! . . . I love your beauty-sense and your proud scornful secret super-sensitiveness."[115]

At least in her nonpsychotic periods, Mary MacLane is a clear example of the hyperaesthetic schizoid, the kind who turns inward and develops a layer of indifference largely as a means of self-protection. This she makes clear in an earlier book, written at the age of nineteen, where she speaks of having been, until a few years before, "an exceedingly sensitive little fool" who was deeply hurt when her acquaintances found her odd. But, she tells us, "that sensitiveness, I rejoice to say, has gone from me"; for some time now the opinions of others have been "quite unable to affect me."[116] And this invulnerability was largely achieved by cultivating the split between the inner and outer selves: "I never disclose my real desires or the texture of my soul," she explains. "And so every day of my life I am playing a part; I am keeping an immense bundle of things hidden under my cloak." "My inner life is never touched." But this extreme dissociation from the outer persona

form of painful feelings of fraudulence: "When one
—a false part—all one's life, for I was a sly, artful little liar
days of five and six; then one is marked." "[I am] in no small
, I find, a sham—a player to the gallery," she insists; there was always
a spirit of falseness that rose and confronted me and said, 'hypocrite,'
'fool.' "[117]

Such preoccupations were especially intense for another of Laing's schizoid patients, a twenty-eight-year old chemist named James who maintained
a particularly extreme split between what he considered to be his true and
false selves. Generally, James would try to protect his inner being by appearing like everyone else, falling in step with them and copying their behavior.
The result, however, was that nearly everything he did felt inauthentic, only
a mimicry of the way "they" thought, perceived, or acted. "If I open the
door of the train and allow someone to enter before me," he said, "this is not
a way of being considerate, it is simply a means of acting as much as I can
as everyone else." Further, the outer self, instead of feeling under the actor's
control, came to seem increasingly independent and removed, taking on a
mechanical life of its own. If his wife gave him a cup of milk, James would
notice himself responding with an automatic smile and a "Thank you"; and
immediately he would feel revulsion at how he and his wife were behaving,
as if in response to a kind of "social mechanics": "Did *he* want the milk, did
he feel like smiling, did *he* want to say 'Thank you'? No. Yet he did all these
things." Eventually such persons may come to sense they have no self at all,
no weight or substantiality as an independent being: "I am only a response
to other people," James said. "I have no identity of my own . . . no self
. . . I am only a cork floating on the ocean."[118]

Another of R. D. Laing's schizoid patients would begin to feel too caught
up or trapped in whatever group or social circle he joined; he would then go
and live by himself in a single room for months at a time, subsisting on his
small savings and daydreaming in almost total isolation. The problem, however, was that this would eventually make him feel empty or dead, bringing
on what he called "a progressive impoverishment of my life mode."[119]
Another problem for patients who withdraw from their public or performing
selves is that they may come to feel clumsy and awkward, and to worry that
others may see through their shamming and pretense.[120]

Not surprisingly, perhaps, patients like these will often assume that other
people's behavior is just as contrived or mechanical, in any case as devoid of
spontaneous involvement, as their own. David, for example, simply took it
for granted that everybody else was also an actor. James was a more extreme
case. He often perceived the actions of his wife—a vivacious and lively
woman—as those of a kind of robot, an "it" devoid of inner life. If he told
his wife a joke and she ("it") laughed, this showed no real feeling but only
her "conditioned" or mechanical nature.[121] (A similar sense of inauthen-

ticity can occur with frankly psychotic schizophrenic patients—as, for instance, with one patient, diagnosed as having a hebephrenic form of schizophrenia, to whom the farmers in the fields looked as if they "were not really working but merely going through the gestures.")[122]

Unconventionality and Inauthenticity

There are other, more active modes of being that also stem from the modern emphasis on individuality and the separation between inner and public selves. Instead of shrinking back from overt action, as from something inevitably contaminating, one may seek to act in ways that display the sovereignty of the inner person or unique self. Usually, this will involve one of two characteristic ways of acting (or both, for they are easily combined): a radical contrariness, in which one declares one's freedom from social constraint through the unconventionality of one's behavior; or a blatant inauthenticity, in which one flaunts the falseness of one's behavior (which may itself be either conventional or unconventional) as a way of suggesting the existence of a hidden true self (or, at least, of emphasizing the illusory and superficial nature of the self that *is* visible).

We find particularly influential statements of this ethic of antinomianism and inauthenticity in the works of Nietzsche, that champion of self-invention and the mask. Nietzsche's conception of heroic behavior certainly differs sharply from that of more traditional societies: instead of praising loyalty to one's compatriots and bravery in the service of one's culture, he extols "human beings who are new, unique, incomparable, who give themselves laws, who create themselves"[123]—beings who glory in unconventionality and in their own refusal to be honest or sincere. In *The Will to Power* Nietzsche describes the "Great Man" in the following terms:

colder, harder, less hesitating, and without fear of "opinion"; he lacks the virtues that accompany respect and "respectability," and altogether everything that is part of the "virtue of the herd." If he cannot lead, he goes alone; then it can happen that he may snarl at some things he meets on his way. . . . he wants no "sympathetic" heart, but servants, tools; in his intercourse with men he is always intent on *making* something out of them. He knows he is incommunicable: he finds it tasteless to be familiar; and when one thinks he is, he usually is not. When not speaking to himself, he wears a mask. He rather lies than tells the truth: it requires more spirit and *will*. There is a solitude within him that is inaccessible to praise or blame, his own justice that is beyond appeal.[124]

But it is in a passage from Hegel's *Phenomenology of Mind* (1807) that we find the clearest analysis of the inner logic of this modern aspiration toward inauthenticity. In these pages, an early attack on the ideals of sincerity and integrity, which Lionel Trilling has described as a "paradigm of the modern cultural and spiritual situation,"[125] Hegel anatomizes the reasons why sincerity and integrity came to be seen as barriers to self-fulfillment, and why fulfillment would increasingly be sought not only in unconventionality but through strategies of inconsistency, irony, and self-division.

The passage is called "The Spirit in Self-Estrangement," and it discusses a work that had impressed Hegel greatly: Denis Diderot's *Rameau's Nephew*, a theatrical dialogue composed between 1761 and 1774 but not published until 1805. Diderot's play poses a sharp opposition between two attitudes concerning selfhood: that of the *Moi* of the dialogue—an older man who believes in sincerity and personal integrity, the value of striving for a single self consistent across time and unified in being and appearance; and that of the nephew—the *Lui* of the dialogue, who disdains such a possibility, which to him is but an illusion masking an actual subservience to externally imposed and limiting social roles. At one point the nephew demonstrates his view by pantomiming the roles on which he, a brilliant and compulsive mime and a hanger-on at the tables of the rich, has long depended for survival. Though the nephew compares his own behavior with "the flatterer's, the courtier's, the footman's, and the beggar's," he sees it as not differing in essence from that of all people. After all, he asks, is it not the case that even the king himself "takes a position before his mistress and God," that he too "dances his pantomime steps"?

The climax of the dialogue comes a bit later, in an operatic performance where the nephew manages to escape the demeaning potential of the theatricality that is so inescapably a part of life. Here the nephew takes on a series of different voices and roles: priest, king, tyrant, slave, madman, woman in grief, ballerina—roles so astonishing in their variety, and played out so unabashedly and compellingly, as to refute the very idea of a unitary self. Though Diderot's own attitude to this marvelous yet appalling display seems to have been equivocal, Hegel's was not, and it is his response that foretells much about the coming sensibility of the modernist and postmodernist age.

To Hegel, this performance demonstrates the accession of Spirit to a "higher level of conscious life" characterized by Spirit's self-recognition of its own freedom and autonomy and by a concomitant estrangement from society as well as from itself. He points out that in earlier stages of society (in the Middle Ages, for example), people were likely to be in a state of unquestioning harmony with the social order, feeling at one with their roles and rendering "obedient service" to an external power for which they felt "inner reverence." But it is the nature of individual consciousness or Spirit to strive toward self-realization, to seek "existence on its own account"; eventually this leads to resentment of any limitation on one's own identity that is imposed by the social order, whose dictates are now obeyed only "with secret malice and stand[ing] ever ready to burst out in rebellion."

It is through this continual uncoupling from any single identity that the nephew manages to declare his ultimate freedom and autonomy—and this is why Hegel can speak of the existence of the self "on its own account" as being "strictly speaking, the loss of itself" (meaning the loss of any *particular* identity). In this sense, to negate the self is the only way to find it, the only way to affirm its true (if paradoxical) nature. Thus it is by flaunting the most problematic aspects of the social self—its theatrical self-consciousness, its inconsistency, its separation from the inner life— that one achieves a higher integrity, almost, in fact, a new kind of authenticity. For, as Hegel explains at the end of his section on Spirit in self-estrangement, "only by self-consciousness being roused to revolt does it know its own peculiar torn and shattered condition; and in its knowing this it has *ipso facto* risen above that condition."[126] It would be wrong to confuse Hegel's claims with an analysis of the conflict between individual and society of the kind that Freud offers in *Civilization and Its Discontents*. The nephew's rebellion is no lapsing back into polymorphous perversity and the primary process under the sway of the id.[127] His behavior (at least as Hegel reads the dialogue) is ultimately in the service not of bodily pleasure but of a kind of self-creation or preservation; and this involves rising to higher and more complex levels of self-consciousness and self-alienation rather than anything that could be called *regression* or a kind of fusion.

It is also significant that Hegel conceives of Spirit as becoming aware not only of its *self*-estrangement but of estrangement as a nearly universal presence in all of social existence, whether people recognize it or not. This is why Hegel can refer to the Spirit in self-estrangement, epitomized by the nephew, as "this self-apprehending vanity of *all* reality"; for, in knowing himself the nephew knows "the contradiction that lies in the heart of the solid elements of reality," the fact that *"everything* [is] estranged from itself."￼It follows that for Spirit to "be conscious of its own distraught and torn existence," as Hegel puts it, "and to express itself accordingly—this is to pour scornful laughter on existence, on the confusion pervading the whole and on itself as well."[128]

We saw earlier how central this kind of scorn was for Baudelaire, whose notion of the dandy certainly exemplifies this detached and irony-laden stance. As its credo, however, one might choose the famous assertion by Oscar Wilde: that "the first duty in life is to be as artificial as possible" ("What the second duty is no one has yet discovered," he added.)[129] Wilde's flamboyance and cheeky politesse have much in common with the exhibitionistic reticence of Baudelaire's dandy: always polite, reserved, and exquisitely formal in his demeanor, while giving one to feel that his persona is nevertheless an insult, an exquisite white glove protecting his real self from any contamination by lesser beings.

This, however, is but one of many kinds of behavior that can express this ethic of inauthenticity. Some of the other possibilities are represented by the raucous outrageousness of Père Ubu, the mask—half wildman, half robot—that the absurdist playwright Alfred Jarry habitually held up between himself and the world; and by the ever-shifting personae of Jacques Vaché, a young soldier whose bemusement and flaunted indifference had such a great influence on André Breton and the entire surrealist movement. Such an individual may be either completely outrageous or studiously conventional, either mercurial or eerily consistent and predictable. The one shared feature is a certain coldness and, going along with this, a sense of absence—as if the person did not actually inhabit his actions, at least not in a full-blooded way, but instead stood apart, manipulating like a puppeteer, or perhaps only observing from somewhere far above.

The uncanny predictability of Andy Warhol represents what is perhaps the zero degree of this way of being. Certainly Warhol was a member of what Baudelaire called "a caste whose very reserve is a provocation," committed both to causing astonishment and to having "the proud satisfaction of never oneself being astonished."[130] Yet his nearly catatonic demeanor divested him not only of all outer signs of flamboyant rebellion but also of any hint of that controlled inner fire that seems to lurk, at least as a potentiality, behind the dandy's haughty reserve. For Warhol came across as infinitely empty—as if the inner self had been rendered contentless and anodyne, reduced to the mere fact of its sense of detachment from the body, from the world, and from its own bland mask.

This kind of artificiality is common enough among schizoid persons, whose behavior is often characterized by an all-pervasive yet somehow cryptic form of irony. Laing's patient David, for instance, seems to have found a kind of self-protective reassurance in exaggerating his theatricality, in a way that reminded both himself and his audience that he transcended whatever part he played. James would also exaggerate roles—for example, when he mimicked his father's pseudo-politeness by asking guests if they'd had enough to eat, but repeating the question over and over until it was clear that he was really offering a satirical comment on his father's veiled aggression.[131]

A similar irony imbued the actions of Philip, a young man I knew very well; yet in his case the overt behavior was more flagrantly unconventional. Philip was a markedly schizoid person (of the predominantly anaesthetic type) who developed schizophrenia in his early twenties and committed suicide a few years later. Since early adolescence he had dedicated himself to the heroism of rebellion, and his defiance could reach the most flamboyant extremes. In the following passage from a letter, which sarcastically alludes to his father's nagging insistence that he settle on some serious life-goal, the quality of both his irony and his defiance is very evident:

Speaking of shit, I've finally found a goal (my father has offered to pick a goal for me, again). Have you heard of the refined art of copromancy? copro = shit. I've decided to prophesy my future by careful regulation of my diet. Of course the artistic possibilities are limitless—polka-dots and peppermint swirls, not to speak of medium and method (plop in gelatin—from what height?—up against the wall). And just think, one wrong image in my subconscious and I fuck up the works. The most stringent require-ment will be the boredom of eating only slightly varied diets from day to day. (My father said that, for him, the goal was not really satisfactory, but that he would not stop me from being anything I wanted to be. Of course you must realize that he has always been a man of meagre artistic sensibili-ties. . . .) (As young Ben Franklin said, "If it's worth doing at all, it's worth doing well.")

Virtually everything in this lengthy letter is very reminiscent of Nietz-sche's vision of the Great Man, the one who flaunts his coldness and disdain for "sympathy," haughtily arrogating to himself the right to "make some-thing" of others and living by the ethic of the mask. With the coldest pride, Philip tells of seducing various women in his hometown, largely by playing out, in a most calculating manner, roles that either mesmerized them or mollified their fears; and he seems disgusted by the sheer ease of these seductions, which he goes on to compare to "shooting swans in cesspools."

Later in his letter, Philip speaks of thoughts of having sex with both his parents. A psychoanalyst might be tempted to view this oedipal fantasy as essentially expressing the primitive, polymorphous-perverse yearnings of early childhood, now emerging to overwhelm a weakened ego (and a similar point might be made about anal themes implicit in the just-quoted passage about the "art of copromancy"). A careful reading of this young man's actual words suggests, however, that they might better be understood as expres-sions of an extreme contrariness, which steers him unerringly toward the ultimate taboos and makes him feel duty-bound to break them, rather than as the welling-up of unbridled desire; indeed, he lived in accord with a perverse but unyielding sense of duty—a code that required him to disman-tle all conventions, to defy all codes of human conduct, and always to behave as scandalously as he possibly could. He wrote, for example, that he just didn't know how he could justify to himself his living at home during the summer without having slept with either of his parents: "There's no ques-tion in my mind that they both want it—a little less sublimated in my mother, as is natural—and I suspect I do too, though I never get horny seeing or thinking about them. What's possibly even worse is that I haven't killed either of them. (Typical guilt feelings.) A modern version of the Oedipus myth. . . ."

This is a peculiar, and distinctively modern, form of guilt—not over feelings of forbidden lust or anger but over the *lack* of such feelings and, perhaps, over failing to have transgressed enough of the sacred taboos.

THE PATH OF MOST RESISTANCE: SCHIZOID TRAITS IN OVERT SCHIZOPHRENIA

One of the most characteristic features of the disease [dementia praecox] is a frequent, causeless, sudden outburst of laughter. . . . "His thoughts always made him laugh," said the relatives of a patient.
—Emil Kraepelin
Dementia Praecox and Paraphrenia

We have now surveyed the schizoid personality, but we have not yet considered the relationship between this mode of being and the overtly schizophrenic condition. This is a controversial issue, for it brings out one of the fundamental polarities or dilemmas of psychiatric knowledge: the conflict between disease and dimensional ways of viewing psychopathological conditions, or between explaining an illness as a process versus understanding it as a comprehensible development.

Many psychopathologists have adopted a position like that of Kretschmer, who considered schizoid and schizophrenic characteristics to exist on a continuum, with the florid symptoms of overt schizophrenia being exaggerations or exacerbations of milder schizoid traits that tend to be evident prior to the development of the psychosis. Perhaps more popular, however, has been the view of Jaspers, who chided Kretschmer for having "lost his sense of the differences that gape between personality and process psychosis"—"personality" involving exaggerations or decreases of normal traits, and "process psychosis" involving something of a different order (in Jaspers's opinion, quite inaccessible to normal people). Jaspers did recognize that schizoid traits (broadly defined) are especially common in the premorbid histories of schizophrenics as well as among their relatives, but he insisted on a sharp qualitative difference, pointing out that we seldom have difficulty deciding whether actual schizophrenia or only schizoid personality is present. "If there is any relationship between schizoid personality and psychosis, it is certainly not of the nature of a transition but a sort of leap," wrote Jaspers's follower Kurt Schneider. According to this view, schizophrenia is not simply an exaggeration of schizoid traits; it involves some kind of decisive move into another dimension.[132]

Jaspers's and Schneider's arguments cannot be ignored: true schizophrenia *does* seem to involve something more than a merely quantitative shift, and it *can* develop in the absence of a clearly schizoid predisposition. But, having granted these objections to any straightforward Kretschmerian interpretation, one must also acknowledge the remarkable affinities that exist between the two conditions. After all, the most prominent signs of the schizoid personality—an apparent asociality and indifference, and a propensity for introversion—are also characteristic of schizophrenia, where they generally appear in more extreme forms. The psychiatrist H. C. Rümke (the Dutchman who introduced the notion of the praecox feeling) has argued, in fact, that the "fundamental phenomenon" of schizophrenia is the weakening of the "rapprochement-instinct," the source of normal directedness toward people and the environment—which clearly recalls Kretschmer's description of the anaesthetic schizoid.[133] Other writers have emphasized more hyperaesthetic (in Kretschmer's sense) and defensive reasons for the schizophrenic's seeming affectlessness and detachment, such as an exquisite sensitivity and consequent withdrawal, acutely described in just these terms by one such individual (Rosser's patient): "I can't feel or relate. . . . I used to feel emotions like physical pain and I couldn't stand it. So I blocked off. I can't empathize with people."[134] And so, while schizophrenia cannot be viewed simply as a matter of schizoid personality writ large, it does appear to incorporate some schizoid tendencies that deserve to be considered.

We have seen that, on the most general level, schizoid personality is characterized by an essential disharmony, a proneness to fragmentation and conflict, both with the world and within the self. Similar qualities appear to be central to schizophrenia, a condition that has been described as a form of "intrapsychic ataxia" (a separation of cognition and emotion) and as "a peculiar destruction of the inner cohesiveness of the psychic personality."[135] More specific manifestations, involving disconnection from the world, have already been discussed in chapter 2, and part three will examine what could be considered more extreme instances of both uncoupling and disconnection. Here I would like to focus on two other manifestations of schizoidlike disharmony that are common in schizophrenia, aspects having more to do with social attitudes and forms of emotional expression: a propensity for willful unconventionality and flaunted inauthenticity, and a pervasive attitude of ironic detachment.

A Counter-Etiquette

Rejection of societal norms and conventional roles, and of the normal expectations of a social encounter, is certainly common enough in schizophrenia. Cross-cultural research has shown, in fact, that schizophrenics generally seem to gravitate toward "the path of most resistance," tending to transgress whatever customs and rules happen to be held most sacred in a given society. Thus, in deeply religious Nigeria, they are especially likely to violate religious sanctions; in Japan, to assault family members.[136] The Swiss psychiatrist Manfred Bleuler (son of Eugen Bleuler) has interpreted this antinomianism as indicating the patient's "ruthless bent to live his life according to his own nature." The negativism of such patients is, he argues, an attempt to outstrip "the conventional ego in a schizophrenic search after a more 'genuine' ego"; he even goes so far as to imagine a patient having the following thoughts: "If I present myself candidly, as I am, perhaps they'll understand me better than behind a mask of conventionality that alienates me from my own nature. . . . Please—O please!—for God's sake, accept me as I am."[137]

Manfred Bleuler's interpretation may capture one element of schizophrenic negativism, but our study of schizoid phenomena should alert us to the possibility that the bent toward originality or authenticity may often be a bit more compromised than his reading would suggest. As we know, such behavior can be motivated as much by antagonism as by any simple urge to self-expression; and what results can be a form of action by negative reaction, a kind of counter-etiquette riveted on the conventions it is trying to subvert. The focused and oppositional quality of schizophrenic negativism comes across clearly in one of Eugen Bleuler's descriptions of schizophrenics' behavior:

> In short, they oppose everyone and everything and, consequently, become exceedingly difficult to handle. . . . They may eat only secretly or at unusual times. They grumble about the food but when asked what they would like to have, their only answer is: "Something else, not what we have." . . . To "Good day" [such patients] say, "good-bye." They do their work all wrong; sew buttons on the wrong side of their clothes. They eat their soup with a fork and their dessert with a soup spoon. They continually sit down in somebody else's place, enter every bed but their own. . . . A hebephrenic . . . is supposed to go down the staircase but resists; then suddenly takes the whole flight in one great leap. .. . Frequently, a request will be complied with as soon as the proper time for it has gone by.[138]

The unconventionality of such persons seems too studied or reactionary, too suggestive perhaps of a kind of "devious perversity,"[139] to be the natural welling up of something truly spontaneous, authentic, or original. Schizo-phrenic behavior, in fact, is more likely to seem affected or mannered than natural and spontaneous; and, as Eugen Bleuler has noted, such individuals are "entirely conscious of many of their mannerisms."[140] Indeed, one cannot escape the impression, with many such individuals, that they are engaged in a kind of mockery and "chronic 'clowning.' "[141] Jaspers describes a patient, Nieber, who was "well orientated, in his senses, lively, chatty and jovial, always on the alert for smart and apt remarks," and who seems to have devoted his whole life to a kind of facetious play. Not acutely disturbed, Nieber wrote poetry, letters to all sorts of authorities, and applications of various kinds. He once drew an elaborate picture of a check, including all the usual ornamentation, and sent it to his previous hospital in payment for his care there. He also wrote a lengthy "dissertation" called " 'The Toilet Paper'—extempore essay by R. H. Nieber," from which the following is extracted: "Essays have already been printed and printed about the immor-tality of the may-fly, about the risks of the shot-gun, about the disputability of Darwin's theory of descent. Why should an essay on toilet paper not find a recognition and reward?"[142]

With some schizophrenics, one may even feel that they are *pretending* to be mad (which would not, of course, exclude the possibility that they may in fact also *be* mad). Eugen Bleuler describes, for example, patients with a special form of hyperkinetic catatonia, who constantly make disconnected, caricatured grimaces and gestures:

> One has the impression that these patients want to play the buffoon, though they do this in a most awkward and inept fashion. They contrive any number of stupidities and sillinesses, such as beating their own knees, interchanging pillows for blankets when they go to bed, pouring water out on the floor instead of into a cup, lifting doors off their hinges. The patients will do all this while they are seemingly well oriented. As a rule they speak very little or not at all and what they have to say is, in the main, completely illogical cursing or other nonsense. . . . the "faxen-psychosis" [buffooner-ies-psychosis] . . . usually involves individuals who for some unconscious reasons *pretend* to be mentally deranged.[143]

It is not uncommon for patients whose illness is very real nevertheless to feign or exaggerate symptoms, perhaps as a way of avoiding intimate contact with others, or of preventing discharge from the safe environment of a hospital ward (the "flight into disease," as Eugen Bleuler calls it).[144] Of more interest in the present context are those instances where the simulation of schizophrenic symptoms is really in the service of a kind of *dis*simulation of the condition. I am speaking of patients who, by exaggerating a certain bizarreness, or an artificiality or falseness of demeanor, may actually feign the *feigning* of symptoms, as a way of pretending (to themselves as well as to others) that they are really much more sane or in control than is truly the case.[145] It would be foolish, by taking this kind of feigning at face value, to conclude that the madness they display is but an act;[146] it would be equally simplistic, however, to ignore what the very use of this ploy suggests about the person in question: for it does reflect an essential dividedness, qualities of self-detachment and irony that are too seldom recognized as central to the schizophrenic way of being.[147]

The "Famous Empty Smile"

The schizophrenic's facetiousness, antagonism, or mockery can also be expressed in more muted fashion—in, for instance, sardonic comments, often delivered in deadpan style ("I not only delighted in hunting but also in being a burden to my father," said one patient; "You have been just like a mother to me," wrote another patient in a postcard to his mother),[148] or, more subtly, in the queer smile that often plays about the features of a schizophrenic's face. Often dismissed as no more than a kind of idiotic grimace, this "famous empty smile," in the view of H. C. Rümke, is not really empty at all; it expresses a certain irony and shyness stemming from preoccupations with a private inner world.[149] Manfred Bleuler has noted that schizophrenics whom one is concerned about seem to smile in "a soulful, expressive way," their smile telling us something like: " 'Dear friend, it's all just an act. Somehow, in some other world, we'll get along with one another.' "[150] Perhaps more common, however, is the sardonic and off-putting yet somehow perplexed irony of patients who feel profoundly alienated from any normal activity or human encounter—who may, for example, shake hands as if they were engaging in some totally absurd and arbitrary action or may respond to questions as if condescending to petty and useless demands. No one who has interviewed schizophrenics will have failed, at times, to have the sneaking suspicion that the whole interaction is, to the patient, something of a joke. Often this tone is quite subtle, and the interviewer is left wondering whether the patient is really involved in the conversation, or is essentially detached, watching and mocking the whole event as if from somewhere far above.

Given how common this disconcerting and ambiguously ironic posture can be, it is surprising it receives so little attention in the literature on schizophrenia. (Schizophrenic affect is often described as "flat," "shallow," or "inappropriate," but it is too infrequently stressed that the "inappropriate affect" is usually of a particular kind—involving laughter, giggling, grinning, an ironic or perhaps self-absorbed and self-satisfied smiling, a lofty manner, and the like.)[151] Considering the standard models of the illness, however, this may be understandable—irony, after all, is an intensely directed and meaningful mode of consciousness or expression, and one can hardly attribute it to an individual without acknowledging a distinct degree of awareness, and particularly of meta-awareness, on that person's part. "Irony," the literary critics tell us, is "our most general term for indicating [the] recognition of incongruities" in experience; it is "that arrangement of experience . . . which permits to the spectator an insight superior to that of the actor";[152] and often it suggests a kind of inner distance, an ability to separate from the self—none of which is very congruent with standard conceptions of cognitive breakdown, or of primitive fusion, instinct domination, and primary-process thinking. (It is one thing for the schizophrenic to *embody* incongruity and paradox, but quite another for him to recognize these phenomena—and even to play with them, perhaps at our expense.)

Significantly, irony is one of the salient features of modern art and consciousness. In 1800 Friedrich Schlegel spoke, very presciently, of "such a quantity of great and small ironies of different sorts" that seemed to be springing up recently, and he warned of the dangers of these tendencies he saw burgeoning all around him, asking: "What gods will rescue us from all these ironies?"[153] But irony, of course, comes in many forms, and what seems fairly distinctive about the schizophrenic variety, when it is present, is, first, its totalizing character—like the irony of Marcel Duchamp or Alfred Jarry, it is all-encompassing, not a criticism of one thing in favor of another but a universal mockery—and, second, its withholding, confusing, and ultimately off-putting effect.

Often, we will not find the same things incongruous as a schizophrenic does; we may not share the jaundiced or absurdist perspective. This, together with the affectless, uninviting, and ambiguous character of his or her demeanor and delivery, can all too easily prevent us from getting the joke. Certainly the schizophrenic's irony lacks the infectious quality of a manic person's hilarity;[154] and it is hardly the sort of good-natured belly laughter that builds a sense of solidarity. Rümke remarked on the stiff and ceremonious quality of schizophrenic body movements, and on the near-impossibility of engaging such patients in playful or joking relationships, which require a natural attunement with, and an openness to, others.[155] Indeed, the schizophrenic's cues can be so ambiguous that we may not even be sure that it *is* irony, so we can hardly take it as an invitation to join the speaker in his privileged observation post.[156] Then again, it is not obvious that the schizophrenic actually *wants* us to get the point (or even to be sure there *is* a point), the jokes and sardonic remarks perhaps being addressed more to himself than to the social world; and we may end up suspecting we are more the object of the remarks than their intended audience. All of this can clearly serve defensive purposes, allowing the patient to declare his indifference to interactions and activities that, in fact, he may find highly threatening. The irony may be a way of declaring, to oneself as well as to the other, that one is superior to, rather than inept at or frightened by, the social encounter. (If one cannot be part of the flow, at least one can declare one's indifference to it; one's irony need not have anything terribly focused or insightful about it to serve this purpose.) While this kind of irony may provide a bizarre form of satisfaction, not surprisingly its usual effect is further to alienate the patient from the possibility of a satisfying intimacy with others.

During the long psychotic period of Hölderlin's life, the friends who visited him were often treated in just this way. If persistently questioned, Hölderlin was generally unwilling, or afraid, to respond, and he would echo the question back to the questioner, or else would address his visitors with grand and royal titles and a bombastic tone: "Your majesty, I must not, I cannot answer this," he would say; and his visitors, who did not have the impression that Hölderlin was truly confused about their real identities, would have to wonder whether they had been the butt of some indirect and cosmic joke.[157] Harry Stack Sullivan has described the effect of this ambiguous kind of behavior very well: "It looks as if the schizophrenic were laughing at you, and you do not like to be reminded that you might be that humorous; and, anyway, he is too sick to be having such a good time at your expense. Thus it has the effect of separating him from what might otherwise be a slightly reassuring contact that might, in turn, go into more reassuring contact."[158]

When schizophrenic irony, mockery, facetiousness, sarcasm, and the like have been considered in the psychiatric and psychoanalytic literature, they have generally been treated as secondary or peripheral features of the illness. The patient's sense of alienation from his own bizarre behavior, for instance, has sometimes been attributed to the survival of an island of normality, a fragment of mature "observing ego" that somehow survives amid the general collapse and regression to which it simply bears witness.[159] The propensity for playing roles has been seen as little more than a mindless aping of whatever persons happen to be encountered in the immediate vicinity. And the witty impact that schizophrenic speech can sometimes have has often been dismissed as mostly unintentional, a mere by-product of fluid associative processes, or of release from the inhibiting effects of conscience and convention.[160] The assumption seems to be that, if there is real method in speech or action, then it is not truly madness; thus to *play* at madness, or within one's madness, is not to be truly mad—and only in such literary artists as Diderot and Pirandello do we have the suggestion (never taken seriously by the mental health establishment) that an authentic madness might, in some essential way, involve just such a playing.

It would obviously be foolish to view schizophrenics as purely volitional and entirely self-aware, or to attempt to reduce madness to the feigning of madness. Still, one must question whether these qualities of alienation, irony, and masquerade are really so peripheral to the schizophrenic condition as is often assumed. Some of these forms of behavior—facetiousness, equivocation, the flaunting of affectation and absurd decorum—are ways of disowning one's actions, of distancing oneself from everything that one appears to be, from all social roles, and even from biological destiny; in this sense they are expressions, or declarations, of freedom. Yet, paradoxically, these modes of behavior may also reflect what are in fact deeply ingrained elements of the schizoid character, the true stigmata, and the burden, of a particular kind of temperament: a disconcerting awkwardness and rigidity, a lack of free-flowing activity and syntonic social ease. Far from running counter to the general progression of schizophrenic pathology, these schizoid phenomena, and the forms of inauthenticity and self-detachment they presuppose, may, in fact, be closely bound up with the core of the disease itself.

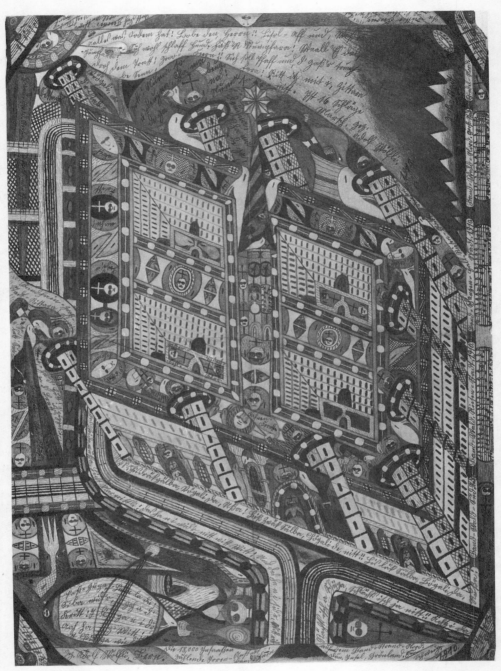

Adolf Wölfli, *Mental Asylum Band-Hain* (1910). *Courtesy of Adolf-Wölfli-Foundation Museum of Fine Arts, Berne*

PART TWO

ASPECTS OF MADNESS: THOUGHT AND LANGUAGE

CHAPTER 4

Cognitive Slippage

Consider any morality with this in mind: what there is in it of "nature" teaches hatred of the laisser aller, of any all-too-great freedom, and implants the need for limited horizons and the nearest tasks—teaching the narrowing of our perspective, and thus in a certain sense stupidity, as a condition of life and growth.

—Friedrich Nietzsche
Beyond Good and Evil

Ma position est l'absence de position.   —Marcel Duchamp

Je sens que je raisonne bien, mais dans l'absolu, parce que j'ai perdu contact avec la vie.

—Schizophrenic patient
In Eugene Minkowski, *La Schizophrénie*

In his preface to *The Order of Things,* the philosopher and historian Michel Foucault offers a quotation from the Argentine writer Jorge Luis Borges that we might view as a kind of hyperbolic portrait of both the schizophrenic and the modernist minds. In these lines, the study of concepts and categories—normally a rather abstract, even academic enterprise (and one that risks sounding the dullest of topics)—emerges as something exotic and exciting, enticing us with the romance of worlds that are not elsewhere but Other. This astonishing passage is, in fact, what inspired Foucault to write *The Order of Things,* a study of the radical, and nearly incommensurable, differences in the forms of understanding that have permeated succeeding epochs of European thought since the Renaissance. It forced him, Foucault explains, to question all the familiar landmarks of his own thinking—to doubt the distinctions between the Same and the Other that he had previously taken for granted and to embark on his own attempt to imagine the unimaginable.

In the passage, Borges pretends to be quoting from "a certain Chinese encyclopedia," where it is written that animals are divided into the following set of categories:

(a) belonging to the Emperor, (b) embalmed, (c) tame, (d) sucking pigs, (e) sirens, (f) fabulous, (g) stray dogs, (h) included in the present classification, (i) frenzied, (j) innumerable, (k) drawn with a very fine camelhair brush, (l) *et cetera*, (m) having just broken the water pitcher, (n) that from a long way off look like flies.[1]

There is something hilarious but also freakish about this "Chinese" system of classification. As Foucault points out, it is stranger—more disruptive to our normal sense of order—than the mere juxtaposition of extremely disparate entities, of which the prototypical example would be the line from the poet Lautréamont so admired by the surrealists: "Beautiful as the chance encounter on a dissecting table of a sewing machine and an umbrella." With Lautréamont's line (from *Les Chants de Maldoror*) we encounter what Foucault terms "the incongruous": an unexpected juxtaposition of objects occurring in a coherent and familiar domain. But this seems tame indeed next to Borges's encyclopedia, which transports us to an entirely different universe. There it is not so much the particular objects that are classified together as the perspective, or perspectives, in which they are classified that is odd—indeed, almost unimaginable.

What, one asks oneself, is the point of view, the thought world, that could conceive such species as "having just broken the water pitcher" and "included in the present classification" (the first with a peculiar focus on immediate and seemingly accidental facts, the second more abstract, alluding to certain paradoxes of reflexivity familiar to modern philosophy)? Even harder to imagine is the perspective that could draw all such categories or perspectives together into one encyclopedia, a single system far stranger than any of its component parts. What, after all, is the dissecting table, the common ground or field of consciousness, on which "sucking pigs," "fabulous" beasts, animals "drawn with a very fine camelhair brush," and "that from a long way off look like flies" could possibly meet? Alone, each contains the principle of an understandable ordering, a possible perspective. But together they seem inconceivable; and one can hardly imagine the consciousness that could contain such a monstrosity. This, as Foucault says, is the anti-utopia of the "heteroclite": a perverse disorder or nonplace in which "fragments of a large number of possible orders glitter separately," where "things are 'laid,' 'placed,' 'arranged' in sites so diverse that it is impossible to find a place of residence for them, to define a *common locus* beneath them all."[2]

In the previous chapters I investigated the perceptual changes that frequently herald the onset of a schizophrenic episode, as well as certain underlying personality traits, especially social attitudes and emotional tendencies that can be apparent both before and after the schizophrenic break. Now I shall turn to certain abnormalities of cognition, thus taking up a set of signs and symptoms that are often assumed to lie closer to the heart of the disease itself, perhaps to constitute its core or defining feature.[3] Paul Meehl coined the phrase "cognitive slippage" to capture the full spectrum of anomalous thinking in schizophrenia, including its milder forms.[4] This term brings out the unanchored and vacillating quality of schizophrenics' thinking that I wish to emphasize in this chapter.

In his famous monograph of 1911, *Dementia Praecox, or the Group of Schizophrenias*, Eugen Bleuler described certain characteristic anomalies of thinking as "fundamental" features of schizophrenia, present in all cases and all phases of the illness. He viewed these as involving loss of the normal hierarchical organization and goal-directedness of thought, and as being caused by an interruption or loosening of the continuity of normal threads of association.[5] Many subsequent theorists have disputed Bleuler's way of explaining these phenomena, but few have disagreed with his emphasis on the crucial importance of disturbances in this particular domain of human functioning. We should describe the disturbances in question as *formal* thought disorders, for they concern not so much the content of thought (the presence of delusions or overvalued ideas) as the patient's entire mode or style of thinking—including aspects of categorization, concept formation, and logical inference, as well as anomalies in the temporal or spatial ordering of experience and in the comprehension and manipulation of symbol-referent relationships.[6]

This and the following chapter are devoted to this broad, rather ill-defined set of disturbances. In the present chapter I will concentrate on a particular aspect of cognition: the schizophrenic's characteristic ways of manipulating concepts and categories; whereas in the next, the focus will broaden considerably, to encompass the structuring of temporal, spatial, and symbolic relationships, and to allow for a more general exploration of the existential conditions and experiential feel of the schizophrenic world.

A great many studies of schizophrenic cognition have investigated the processes foregrounded in Borges's Chinese encyclopedia: namely, modes of classification and identification, the ways in which perceived identities, differences, and similitudes are used to form categories. Here I shall suggest that the most salient tendencies of schizophrenic thinking are much the same as those revealed in Borges's epistemological fantasy. The first of these is the sheer strangeness in the classificatory principles or perspectives such patients tend to adopt, which often seem idiosyncratic or even bizarre (and either abnormally concrete or abnormally abstract, an issue analyzed in depth in the following chapter). The second is a tendency to shift vertiginously among, or to make paradoxical combinations of, incompatible perspectives, thus leading to an oddity of a higher logical type—a sort of meta-strangeness, if you will. A third feature is less prominent in the Chinese encyclopedia (though it is suggested by the category "included in the present classification") and may be somewhat less obvious in many schizophrenics; this is a certain self-consciousness, the effect of which is more often confusing than clarifying, for the thinker as well as for anyone who listens to him. The whole passage by Borges is, in fact, suggestive of a kind of perspectivism, of the realization that there is no "thing-in-itself"; that, in the words of Nietzsche, the greatest modern student of this phenomenon, the so-called essence or essential nature of a thing is really "something perspectival and already presupposes a multiplicity," the possibility of other perspectives, and that "at the bottom of it there always lies 'what is it for *me?*' "[7]

This is hardly a standard vision of schizophrenic thinking in psychology or psychiatry. Before proceeding further, let us consider some of the more influential theories that have been proposed.

SCHIZOPHRENIC THINKING

Traditional Theories

Perhaps the most famous interpretation of schizophrenic thinking was formulated some fifty years ago by Kurt Goldstein, a neurologist who treated many brain-damaged casualties from World War I. Goldstein argued that the core disturbance in schizophrenia was a certain "concreteness," a loss of the "abstract attitude" similar to what he had observed in patients suffering from organic brain syndromes.

Schizophrenic reality, in Goldstein's view, is "more dynamic than static," for he claimed that such patients "have a marked tendency to do something," preferring "situations of activity" and experiencing objects as "things for definite use."[8] He thought, however, that, like many organic patients, schizophrenics tended to be deficient in a wide range of mental abilities, such as the capacity to distance oneself from sensory immediacy in order to develop general concepts; to shift from one aspect of an object or situation to another, or to hold several aspects simultaneously in mind; and to contemplate hypothetical possibilities, exercise choice, or anticipate future events. What such persons lacked was the so-called abstract attitude, which, for Goldstein, encompassed virtually all of the higher functions of mind—not only the capacity for theoretical or abstract awareness but also the closely intertwined capacities for volition and reflection (reflection being necessary if one is to make choices rather than to engage in reflexlike activity).[9]

At its extreme, schizophrenic concreteness would be a state in which credulousness, utter certainty, and immediacy of response have replaced deliberation, doubt, and the capacity for self-criticism.[10] This hypothesis of schizophrenic deficiencies of abstraction is perhaps the classic formulation of the deficiency view of medical-model psychiatry, and it has also been influential in psychoanalysis, where "concreteness" has usually been seen as a manifestation of regressed ego functions.[11] Despite a series of cogent critiques it still enjoys considerable popularity, and in recent years has been enjoying something of a renaissance, though in somewhat disguised form.[12]

Another influential view, put forward by the psychiatrists E. von Domarus and Silvano Arieti, argues that schizophrenics suffer from a fairly specific failure of logic, an error of syllogistic reasoning. According to this view, such patients make the mistake of equating phenomena that may share only a single feature; they assume, for instance, that stags and Indian braves are the same because they are both fast. Von Domarus referred to this kind of reasoning as "paralogical"; but Arieti, a psychoanalyst, preferred to call it "paleological," since he believed this loose form of inference constituted the essence of all immature forms of consciousness, including those of higher animals, children, the brain-damaged, and preliterate humans.[13] A related theory, first propounded by the psychiatrist Norman Cameron, proposes that schizophrenics are "overinclusive": they tend either to *employ* categories in an insufficiently restrictive way or else to *create* categories that are overly general. (Overinclusion can refer to the addition of inappropriate items to a classification—putting "bat" and "claw" in the category of "birds," for example; or to the use of categories that are too broad—for example, calling an orange and a banana similar because "they both contain atoms.")[14] This view of schizophrenic thinking has affinities with psychoanalytic and other organicist-developmental theories that postulate a primitive incapacity to constitute boundaries—whether between self and world, between figure and ground, between objects of different sorts, or between one category and another.[15]

A final approach, popular in the 1960s and 1970s but waning somewhat in influence more recently, emphasizes defects of "selective attention," a breakdown in the mechanisms by which the mind is able to focus on certain stimuli, objects, or trains of thought. It is said that the schizophrenic cannot screen or filter out thoughts or perceptions that are irrelevant to the activity at hand, and instead is pulled every which way by whatever stimuli, internal or external, happen to pop into his head or to occur in his immediate vicinity.[16]

These theories, along with other, less influential ones, have spawned a vast literature of empirical and clinical studies. But, though useful in many ways (particularly in highlighting the sheer variety of characteristic deviances), it seems fair to say that the overall attempt to discover some central deficit or tendency must be deemed a failure.[17] The characteristic anomalies of schizophrenic thinking appear to be too diverse to be ascribed to any single factor, and too bizarre to be accounted for as simple errors or consequences of regression.

Eccentricity of Perspective

Goldstein claimed that schizophrenics lack "generic words which signify categories or classes" and that, when asked to classify objects, they are less likely to do it in a truly abstract way—that is, by means of a conscious and volitional singling out of some common property that (in Goldstein's estimation) is truly essential and conceptual in nature. Instead they tend to classify in a rather stimulus-bound and automatic fashion and on the basis of relatively concrete features, which for Goldstein included the perceptual appearances of these objects, their practical uses, and the situations where they had previously been encountered.[18] On an object-sorting task, for example, a concretistic patient might put a screwdriver, pliers, and toy hammer together because all three can be used to smash things, because all three are found in the toolbox, or perhaps because all three are silver-colored—rather than because they are all tools, a similarity Goldstein considered to be "abstract."[19] This theory of schizophrenic thinking has some serious drawbacks, not least of which is the murky and, at times, rather arbitrary nature of Goldstein's rationale for distinguishing concrete from abstract.[20] But even if one does accept his definition of concreteness and abstractness, evidence gathered by subsequent investigators is not very supportive of his claims for where schizophrenics fall on this dimension.[21]

True, schizophrenics will sometimes categorize objects according to their practical uses, and will sometimes become fascinated by the immediate or literal sensory reality before them. But the former tendency is common enough in normal adults, while the latter (as we shall see in the next chapter) need not indicate the kind of deficient or primitive cognitive capacity that is implicit in Goldstein's notion of concretistic functioning. Studies done in recent decades have shown, in any case, that such seemingly concrete tendencies are by no means the only anomalies of schizophrenic performance, nor even the most common. Indeed, it seems that schizophrenics will often opt for categories and forms of description that are *more* abstract or general than is usual. Typical schizophrenic responses on a similarities test, for example, include the description of "orange and banana" not as fruit (the common and "correct" response) but as "nature's produce"; "coat and dress" not as clothing but as items to "maintain human modesty"; "fly" and "tree" not as living things but as things that "occupy space in our world"; "air and water" not as elements but as "states of molecular density"; and "table" and "chair" not as furniture but as "objects in the universe." On an object-sorting test, objects may be grouped together as "forms of energy."[22] Word choice may suggest a similar heightening of abstraction—as, for instance, when a candle is referred to as a "night illumination object," a watch as a "time vessel," or a dustpan as a "domestic utensil."[23] Impressed with responses like these, a few theorists have taken the opposite tack from Goldstein, proposing that the central tendency of schizophrenic thinking is actually its quality of pathological overabstractness.[24]

Similar problems confront Cameron's "overinclusiveness" hypothesis. While some schizophrenics' responses may suggest overly broad categorizations (things that "occupy space in our world" is a good example), they can also tend—though probably to a lesser extent—to be overexclusive at times, using categories of an exceptionally narrow type; and this has given rise to theories about the supposedly *under*inclusive nature of their thinking.[25] One should not suppose, however, that hypotheses either of overabstractness or of overexclusiveness would be much of an improvement over Goldstein's or Cameron's original characterizations of schizophrenic thought. It may be true that schizophrenics are more often overly abstract than overly concrete,[26] and (perhaps) more often overinclusive than underinclusive;[27] but at least as important as either of these facts is their propensity to give responses at *both* extremes of these dimensions. Any adequate model or theory of schizophrenic thinking will have to account for this curious but characteristic heterogeneity.[28] (Some possible reasons for it will be discussed in the next chapter.)

It must also be recognized that there are many schizophrenic responses whose anomalous qualities cannot be captured in terms of either the abstractness *or* the inclusiveness dimension, *even if* one allows for the possibility of falling at both extremes. In these cases the salient feature seems to be simply the sheer peculiarity of their generalizations and sortings—the use of principles that are highly personal, private, or bizarre, less likely to be shared, or readily understood, by other members of the culture.[29]

Consider, for example, a young schizophrenic man to whom I administered an object-sorting task—a diagnostic test that requires the patient to select objects from an array that includes a cigarette, a cork, a sink stopper, a nail, a pair of pliers, a padlock, a screwdriver, pieces of colored paper, and a variety of other items; and then to explain what the selected items have in common. Instead of choosing groups of objects that share some fairly obvious and commonly noticed characteristic—tools, for example, or red objects, or things made of paper (the normal kind of response)—he selected the sink stopper, the padlock, and a circle of red paper, explaining that they were similar because all three "stopped flows or processes" (the red circle, he explained, could stand for a stoplight halting the flow of traffic). On a different sorting task, which uses words instead of objects, another patient put "trumpet," "umbrella," and "whistle" together because all three refer to "noise-producing objects," and, to explain why he excluded the word "beret" from this group, he singled out the feature of "noiselessness." On a similarities test, another schizophrenic patient, asked what a pencil and a shoe had in common, replied that both items "leave traces."[30]

The qualities of stopping flows, producing noises, and leaving traces do not seem to be particularly abstract or particularly concrete in nature, nor, for that matter, do they constitute categories of an especially wide or narrow breadth. They are not especially illogical, or indicative of primitive, drive-dominated thinking; and they certainly don't suggest a concretistic mentality in Goldstein's sense, with "passive indifferent surrender to the total impression" or inability to distance oneself from habitual and practical schemata.[31] In fact, responses like these would seem to have sprung from an enhanced ability to perceive nonobvious similarities, those unlikely to leap out at a (concretistic) person unable to disembed himself from clichés or standard modes of practical activity.[32] What *is* striking and undeniable about such responses is their sheer unconventionality; like certain categories in the Borgesian encyclopedia ("having just broken the water pitcher"; "that from a long way off look like flies"), they suggest a tendency to order the world in accordance with highly idiosyncratic and impractical perspectives, on the basis of criteria different from those usually singled out as salient and fundamental in our culture.[33] Some researchers on selective attention in schizophrenia have been led to similar views, concluding that what is characteristic of such patients is not so much an incapacity for selective attention as an unusual manner of *allocating* attention—a quality likely to derive from their unusual set of interests and their eccentric and often impractical or goalless orientation to the world.[34] As so often with this strange disease, we find ourselves obliged to describe its characteristic signs in negative terms: as involving the replacement of normative responses by all manner of odd alternatives, by attributes "hardly dreamed of by the normal subjects."[35]

It would certainly be wrong to think of the eccentricity of schizophrenics as involving the simple failure or lowering of an intellectual function. (This, of course, is not the same as denying that these phenomena may have a physiological or neurological basis; see appendix.) Eugen Bleuler pointed out long ago that the errors made by schizophrenics, in contrast with those of mentally deficient and most brain-damaged patients, are not highly correlated with the relative difficulty of the task. Sometimes the errors they make seem willful, the result of defiance or refusal to engage in the task; at other times they seem related to anxiety aroused by the private symbolic significance of the question; and at still other times they appear to be simply random. Some experts have suggested, in fact, that schizophrenics are actually more capable of creating generalizations than are most normal individuals;[36] and it is noteworthy that the test responses taken to indicate schizophrenic "deficit" are frequently indistinguishable from those given by normal but highly creative subjects in studies of creativity.[37] One might describe the central feature of the schizophrenic mind as a disconnectedness, an unmooring from practical concerns and accepted practices that allows consciousness to drift in unexpected and unintended directions, and to come to rest in strange orientations. Significantly, it appears that schizophrenics actually perform better than do normal people on the kinds of cognitive tasks for which such an unmooring might be expected to provide an advantage.

Consider, for instance, a series of experiments done in the laboratories of the Russian researchers U. F. Polyakov and I. M. Feigenberg. Normal individuals and chronic schizophrenics were compared in their ability to identify stimuli presented in an unclear way—the final word of a sentence when this word was masked by white noise, for example, or the content of blurry pictures projected on a screen. When that final word was a highly probable one ("Along the street sped a *car*") or when the blurred picture depicted a standard or expected situation, the normal subjects were quicker and more accurate in making these identifications. But when the sentence was more improbable ("The photographer made a pretty *box*") or when the pictures were unusual (an upside-down eagle, or a man lying on his back and drawing a picture with his feet), the performance of the schizophrenics was superior. Schizophrenics were also better at solving problems that required focusing on attributes of objects that are not salient in everyday life (for example, the fact that a candle loses weight as it burns).[38]

The Polyakov group describes these results in rather technical terms (as a difficulty with "probability prognosis"),[39] but they can be seen more broadly as suggesting a failure to adopt the practical perspective of everyday, commonsense reality, which normally attunes one to the highly probable and canonical properties of objects and situations.[40] In most circumstances this kind of framework facilitates recognition of familiar objects, while at the same time making one less prone to expect the unexpected. By contrast, it appears that schizophrenics tend to enter each situation as if almost anything were possible—thus manifesting what has been called the "pathological freedom" of schizophrenic thinking[41] (a quality evoked in figure 4.1, where a person sprouts a branch with a flower-hand).

FIGURE 4.1

Heinrich Anton Müller, *L'Homme aux Mouches et le Serpent* (*Man with Flies and Serpent*) (1925–27). "Pathological freedom" illustrated in a work by a schizophrenic. *Collection de l'Art Brut, Lausanne*

This may help to explain why practical or commonsense social understanding (as opposed to knowledge of factual information) is so likely to suffer in schizophrenia,[42] and why such patients may readily adopt delusional or quasi-delusional notions that seem radically implausible to the normal person. One patient I interviewed, for example, was preoccupied with doubts about the trustworthiness of history. He justified his skepticism by asking how one could ever be sure that people weren't going into the archives and altering or replacing the pages they found there. It wasn't that these deceptive practices necessarily *did* occur; for him the fact that they were at least theoretically *possible* was quite sufficient, for he would then collapse any difference of degrees of probability, treating probable events and just barely possible ones in exactly the same way. A similar attitude was apparent in his response to a picture-arrangement test that requires one to put a series of cartoon scenes in an order that tells a story (a test on which schizophrenics do especially poorly). This patient had difficulty coming up with what is usually deemed the "correct" response (the sequence most people find to be most plausible) because, as he said, "any order would make sense." This, of course, is perfectly true; for, as he himself demonstrated with the stories he made up to explain his idiosyncratic and technically "incorrect" arrangements, one can always come up with a narrative line—albeit an improbable one—to justify any imaginable sequence of scenes. Obviously, however, this patient's mentality was not restricted to a concretistic level; if anything he seems to have been overly inclined toward the abstract functions of keeping several possibilities in mind simultaneously, of assuming a hypothetical attitude, and of detaching himself from immediate practical realities and stimulus demands.[43]

Vacillation and Inconsistency

Another distinctive characteristic that is often manifest in schizophrenic thinking is a striking inconsistency or a tendency toward vacillating among alternative responses to the world. One researcher describes the extreme variability of a given individual's responses—attributed to the tendency to keep changing his mind—as the main way in which various groups of schizophrenics differed from patients with affective illness across seven different tasks.[44] On the object-sorting task schizophrenics will often show "endless hesitancy and vacillation between various aspects of the material," a tendency attributed to the patient's "inability to abstract one principle of the given material while he neglects the others." The schizophrenic often seems aware of a vast number of possibilities; but instead of focusing on only one, such as color or shape, it is as if he takes "all the possibilities into simultaneous consideration," thus leading to a competition among incongruous and incompatible modes of response.[45] At times this may derive from a kind of "intellectual ambivalence"—what a patient of mine called a "countervailing tendency" of the mind. One of Eugen Bleuler's patients (a man educated in philosophy) described his experience in the following way: "When one expresses a thought, one always sees the counter-thought. This intensifies itself and becomes so rapid that one doesn't really know which was the first."[46]

Analogous phenomena occur fairly often on the Rorschach test (a projective test that requires subjects to describe what they see in a series of symmetrical inkblot patterns). A part of the inkblot that is perceived in one way may come to be seen under another aspect, even appearing to transform into something else or to rotate perspectives before the schizophrenic person's eyes, sometimes leaving a subject uncertain about what he or she sees. One patient couldn't decide whether he saw poodles or ladies; another described "two people . . . one minute this appears like their eyes and the next this appears like their entire body holding on." A third perceived "a bat flying away"; then, on looking at it again, saw "a bat coming toward me."[47] In the so-called contamination percept, a rare type of response that occurs almost exclusively with schizophrenics,[48] two objects or perspectives appear to be present simultaneously, as if overlaid on each other as in a photographic double exposure. One patient perceived a red part of the third Rorschach inkblot as blood but also as an island, and said he saw the pattern as a "bloody island"; another, looking at Card #6, said that it "reminds me of a dog and also of a rug, so it's a *dogrug";* while a third saw the whole of the first inkblot pattern as both a butterfly and the world, hence "a butterfly holding the world together."[49] Schizophrenic artwork often displays a similar quality, with a contaminatory fusion of two or more objects or perspectives (see figures 4.2 and 4.3). If asked to draw a picture of a human being, schizophrenics will often show the figure from external and internal standpoints at the same time, with both clothing and inner organs visible in an incongruous combination of perspectives, or from two different angles (these are called "rotations").[50]

According to the psychologist David Rapaport and his co-authors, the schizophrenic's frequent shifting among conceptual frames of reference that are not regulated with each other leads to a loss of "solidity and coherence."[51] In his view many schizophrenics, like many obsessional patients, seem to lack a quality of "automatic steering" and to be afflicted with an often debilitating self-awareness and need to exercise volition: "Their attempts to decide from occasion to occasion the level of discourse in which to move result either in shifts of the sort we have seen [that is, shifts not simply between one object of attention and another but between perspectives or orientations] or in an inability to make a shift when it is appropriate, or in a state of hopeless confusion."[52] (This kind of perspectival shifting and deliberation may account, in part, for the slowing of reaction time and response selection that is so common in schizophrenia.)[53] Schizophrenics can demonstrate "astonishing shifts in level of psychic functioning" of a kind not found in other patients, and where it can seem as if such a patient's "relation to internal and external reality [is] altered from one response to the next . . . [and] there is a new definition of the test situation and of his role in life with each response."[54] Such vacillation among widely divergent perspectives or orientations (sometimes involving movement between what appear to be highly abstract and highly concrete or literalist modes of response) seems suggestive not so much of incongruity as of the heteroclite (as Foucault defines these terms), since each Rorschach response (like each animal in the Chinese encyclopedia) appears to exist within an entirely different thought world.

Schizophrenics' vacillation distinguishes their performance from those organic patients (this is by no means all) who are truly concretistic, for such persons do not as readily set up or move among alternative hypotheses,[55] nor do they show the same sense of ambivalence, conflict, hesitation, or self-awareness. Such organic cases have been described as solving problems "in a cheerful, direct, and frequently incorrect manner without really comprehending the task involved," whereas the schizophrenic seems more aware of the problems of perspectival choice that present themselves.[56] This was particularly evident in the "chief complaint" offered by one schizophrenic patient (Carl) on his admission to the hospital: "I have conflicting feelings and processes in decision making. The way manifests itself functionally at present in choices of alternatives for action. I hold out for seemingly better representations of the problem."

We must also distinguish schizophrenic vacillation and inconsistency from the distractibility of mania, in which attention moves rapidly but usually in a less radical, confusing, and self-paralyzing way. There is generally something fluid, spontaneous, and exuberant about the manic person's rapidly shifting attention; and, typically, it appears to move among ideas or stimuli that exist within a single context or domain—as in Foucault's "the incongruous." (The Rorschach test manifestation of this way of thinking would not be the above-mentioned "contamination"-type response, with its fusing of *perspectives*, but the "incongruous" or "fabulized combination" response, which brings objects together in unlikely or impossible combinations—as when a person sees, for example, "a mastadon wearing shoes" or "two crows with afros . . . pushing two hearts together.")[57] Also, though the manic person's attention may not rest for long on any particular topic, he does not seem as likely to experience the object of awareness as dependent on the standpoint he adopts toward it; and in this sense he is less reflective and wavering, less inclined toward the consciousness of a perspectivist, and less likely to feel a sense of turmoil and confusion. The schizophrenic, by contrast, seems more often to have a simultaneous awareness of several possibilities, frequently moving, or hesitating, among what are experienced, at least implicitly, as alternative worlds or orientations toward experience, thereby demonstrating what one theorist has described as a characteristically schizophrenic tendency to shift not merely among a variety of objects or topics but among alternative frames of reference, universes of discourse, or semantic strata (Foucault's "heteroclite").[58] If consciousness can be compared to a searchlight beam, we might say that manic consciousness tends to pivot rapidly as it shifts focus from one object of attention to another, whereas schizophrenic consciousness actually slips out of any anchor point, floating about unstably among varying points of view.[59] (This is evoked in the

FIGURE 4.2

Carl Lange, *Das heilige Schweisswunder in der Einlegesohle (Holy Sweat Miracle on the Insole)*. Simultaneity of several perspectives ("contamination") in a drawing by a schizophrenic. *Courtesy of Prinzhorn-Collection of the Psychiatric Clinic, University of Heidelberg; Foto Klinger Kunsthist., Inst. Inv. Nr. 98*

schizophrenic Adolf Wölfli's portrayal of a mental asylum, reproduced on page 116.)

Schizophrenic consciousness, then, appears to resemble the unlikely and curiously fluctuating thought world of Borges's Chinese encyclopedia in at least a couple of ways: in both we find perspectives that strike the normal person as peculiar or unworldly, and in both there is a tendency to shift among, or to combine and confuse, diverse or even incompatible vantage points. And so we arrive once again at the two qualities that so often emerge

FIGURE 4.3

Scottie Wilson, *Greedies* (1940–45). Simultaneity of several perspectives ("contamination") in a drawing by a schizophrenic. *Collection de l'Art Brut, Lausanne*

from a critical consideration of schizophrenic illness: a certain alienness and a radical kind of heterogeneity—qualities that may seem to defy attempts at further understanding or explanation. In fact, many psychological studies of schizophrenic thinking have concluded that, while one can assert that "schizophrenics are idiosyncratic, unique, inappropriate or bizarre in their responses, . . . any further elaboration is impossible."[60] But is this really the case: Must we be content to rest with the praecox feeling, with a simple acknowledgment of the sheer fact of the bizarre?

Any explanation that would reduce schizophrenic thought disorder to the working of some simple factor, whether mechanistic or regressive, seems unlikely to capture its variety or subtlety. But, as with other aspects of schizophrenia, it does not follow that all possibility of understanding is foreclosed. There are, once again, features of the modernist sensibility that appear to be closer to schizophrenic thinking than is the thought of the child or the (mythical) Wildman, or the patient with one of the classic organic brain syndromes. And, while these parallels may not provide an *explanation* of schizophrenic consciousness, they can at least serve to illuminate its structure and mood—helping in particular to clarify the reflexive and volitional aspects that are so often neglected by traditional theories.

PARALLELS WITH MODERNISM

Lucidity came to me when I at last succumbed to the vertigo of the modern.
                                                                    —Louis Aragon

Oddity and fluidity of perspective are widespread features of the culture of modernism and postmodernism. They have, in fact, often been seen as necessary features of authentic or creative modes of experience and expression. A particularly emblematic as well as influential figure in this regard is Alfred Jarry, the author of *Ubu Roi* and other plays that inspired the theater of the absurd.

Jarry was a most unusual personality, with schizoid tendencies of nearly psychotic proportions. He took on—and eventually seems to have been taken over by—a robotlike persona, a sort of mechanical, proto-Warholian antipersonality who spoke in mock-heroic and periphrastic prose. In a peculiar, machinelike monotone he would emit his zany witticisms, generally expressing sudden ironic reversals that emanated from a position of utter emotional indifference and absolute disengagement from logic or practical realities. After a friend had published an analysis of thirty-six dramatic situations, Jarry created a thirty-seventh: "To perceive that one's mother is a virgin"; and when he wrote an article on the Crucifixion, he adopted an odd and typically deflationary standpoint: "The Passion Considered as an Uphill Bicycle Race." One typically Jarryesque passage manages to overturn several assumptions at once, and to transcend the sometimes schoolboy level of his wit: "Antialcoholics," he wrote, "are unfortunates in the grip of water, that terrible poison, so solvent and corrosive that out of all substances it has been chosen for washings and scourings, and a drop of water, added to clear liquid like absinthe, muddies it."[61]

A similar antinomianism is pervasive in the early-twentieth-century avant-garde. The dadaist Marcel Duchamp, for instance, expressed tempt for standard orientations and declared his devotion to his new c gory of the *"infra-mince,"* which included such unfairly neglected phenon ena as the difference in space taken up by shirts before and after they have been laundered.[62] The surrealist Louis Aragon defined poetic imagery as an instrument of radical reversals and caustic irony that would annihilate the world of convention: "The image is a vehicle of humor," he wrote, referring to something like the black humor of surrealism; "every image ought to produce a cataclysm . . . for every man there must be found an image which annuls the whole universe."[63]

Desire to escape the blinders of conventional perception is, of course, far older than the traditions of dadaist and surrealist mockery and absurdism; and, in romanticism's rejection of the universal standards of neoclassical aesthetics, we already find the association of aesthetic value with originality or eccentricity of point of view. This valuing of originality remained a dominant attitude throughout the 1800s and beyond—so that even Émile Zola, the great naturalist of the nineteenth century, conceived of the work of art as "a corner of nature seen through a temperament," while Rémy de Gourmont could say that the sole excuse for writing is "to unveil for others the sort of world which mirrors itself in [one's] individual glass."[64] The impersonal aesthetic of early modernism, exemplified by figures as diverse as Jarry, Duchamp, and T. S. Eliot ("Poetry is not the expression of personality, but an escape from personality"),[65] was soon to eclipse this romantic and postromantic concern with an inner or unique self. But in its place was instituted the self-undermining impulse of radical avant-gardism, a make-it-new aesthetic that placed, if anything, even more emphasis on novelty of perspective.

Many instances of schizophrenic eccentricity and cognitive slippage closely resemble these modernist examples, with their reversals and their concentration on what is usually ignored by the person engaged in normal activity. One patient I knew said she found it curious that we always walk on the treads rather than the risers of a staircase. Another contemplated how one could tell the back from the front of a blouse—surely a candidate for inclusion in Duchamp's category of the *infra-mince*.[66] The psychiatrist Harry Stack Sullivan has pointed to these "particular slants of the cognitive or knowing process [which are normally] denied access to attention" as the source of the frequently observed "mirth" of schizophrenics and of their "wisecracking level of cognition," which can give anyone who interacts with them the feeling of being laughed at.[67] Such alienated angles of perception certainly help to explain many instances of what looks to the observer like a kind of "inappropriate affect," most obviously in the case of the oddly affectless laughter that Eugen Bleuler considered to be one of schizophrenia's most distinctive signs.[68] Sullivan, generally an advocate of the primitivity hypothesis, assumed that these peculiar cognitive slants were consequences of regression, of "the inclusion in attention of primitive, diffuse processes" deriving from a "failure to restrict the contents of consciousness to the higher referential processes that can be consensually validated";[69] but, in reality, the anomalies at issue are more suggestive of a condition of alienation, a homelessness of mind quite foreign to anything characteristic of childhood.

Kurt Goldstein offers an interpretation analogous to Sullivan's in his attempt to account for the vacillation or slippage of perspective that can occur in schizophrenia. The example he addresses involves a reversal of the normal figure-ground relationship between objects and surrounding space, described by one schizophrenic patient as follows: "The air is still here, the air between the things in the room, but the things themselves are not there any more."[70] To Goldstein, the anomalous experience suggested by these words implies concreteness and dedifferentiation; thus he attributes "the inversion, that is, the coming into the foreground of the ground instead of the figure, and the sudden and nearly permanent fluctuation between figure and ground," to *"deficient* figure-ground formation," an *"inability* to maintain adequate boundaries," and the *"vagueness"* of such boundaries.[71] Actually, neither this example nor others like it (focusing on the staircase's risers rather than its treads, for example) really justifies this sort of interpretation: for, while inversions or fluctuations certainly do occur, they may be less a matter of a dissolving of structure than of a readiness to shift into alternative *kinds* of structure.[72] The distinction is not merely academic, for each reading implies a rather different conception of the schizophrenic lived world: on the one hand, a state of quasi-mystical fusion or the "blooming, buzzing confusion" of infancy;[73] and on the other, a vacillation among perspectives, a shifting among worlds, each with its own form of articulation and separateness, and where the confusion, when it occurs, stems from a kind of vertigo, a continual collapsing of one frame of reference into the next.[74]

Heroism of Doubt

A young schizophrenic artist named Martin described a kaleidoscopic drifting in which perspective gives way to perspective: "When I am awake, I can look at a tree or a cat or a bird and see the air around it, sometimes it looks like water, so sometimes I paint water. Sometimes there is sound in the water so I paint sound. Sometimes the sound is silent like a fish swimming so I paint fish swimming." It is not, perhaps, surprising that Martin should have managed to exploit this slippage as a source of artistic inspiration—such techniques have in fact been central to the creative imagination in our time.[75]

"I ceaselessly ruminate upon what interests me; by dint of regarding it in
different positions of mind (âme) I end up by seeing something new in it, and
I make it change its aspect."[76] The words are those of the novelist Stendhal,
speaking of his own favored methods of composition; more generally, they
describe Schiller's "sentimental" or "reflective" poet, the kind—increasingly common in modern times—who is "self-divided because self-conscious,
and so composes in an awareness of multiple alternatives, and characteristically represents not the object in itself, but the object in the subject."[77] Such
techniques are bound up with the modern realization of the importance of
point of view or mode of awareness, a realization that might be traced back
to Kant's description, at the end of the eighteenth century, of the constituting role of consciousness, and also to his emphasis on the unsurpassable
limits of the actual. This has led to an interest in states of consciousness
themselves, often at the expense of the external object, and has had the
paradoxical result of inciting desires for a more radical mental freedom. In
a world where the fact of perspective has an almost palpable presence, it is
perhaps not surprising to find what one critic describes as an "incessant
casting about for an entity that one does not yet know."[78] And so the
post-Kantian awareness of the limitedness of perspective engenders contradictory urges and futile yearnings, cravings to explore unimaginable viewpoints, uninhabitable mental climes. A minimalist sculptor of the 1960s
dreams of the hypothetical possibility of shapes that would transcend all
known categories (and perhaps all possible ones)—"A form that's neither
geometric or organic would be a great discovery"[79]—while conceptual artists claim to have introduced "a new form of apperception . . . which allows
for perceiving phenomena that are abstract and/or invisible."[80]

There is also a desire to occupy, if only for a moment, as many points of
view as possible, an impulse clearly present in the multiperspectivism of
analytic cubist painting, in portraits by Picasso, as well as in poems like
T. S. Eliot's "The Wasteland" and Wallace Stevens's "Thirteen Ways of
Looking at a Blackbird"—works in which a multiplicity of perspectives
conveys the realization that reality includes our attempts to see it.[81] Rimbaud and subsequent poets and painters, particularly the surrealists, have
used a "crossfade technique" that is structurally identical to contamination
responses on the Rorschach: two objects or domains so interfused that they
seem to have merged, creating a single object that could exist nowhere but
in some mental or inner universe (in Rimbaud's poem "Seascape," for example, this happens with the land and the sea).[82] Finally one might mention that most influential innovation of early modernism (and a major inspiration of so-called postmodernism): the cubist and futurist collage. Here
there is an intermingling, self-referential and self-questioning, not just of
disparate objects but of the motley contexts from which they derive, and
an incorporation of planes that may obtrude either as figure or as ground—

creating heteroclites and perspectival fluctuations similar to what occurs with schizophrenia; Picasso's still life with violin and fruit is a good example (see figure 4.4).[83]

The consequence of such proliferation is, however, the loss of any single, overarching perspective, any selective principle or hierarchy of significance, which results in the conjuring of a world where anything can stand for anything—where the merest detail can loom up as the most momentous event, and a heroism of doubt can lead to a refusal, or incapacity, to make any choices at all.[84] "Most of the time conclusions seem to me acts of stupidity," said Gustave Flaubert. He was expressing an attitude that, in the

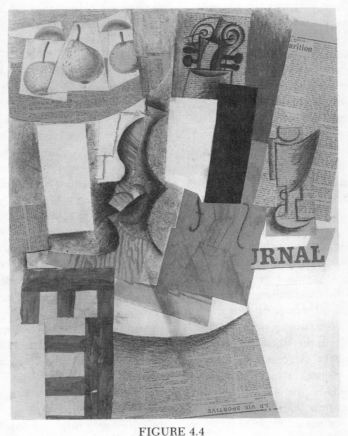

FIGURE 4.4

Pablo Picasso, *The Violin (Violin and Fruit)* (1913). Illustrates simultaneity of different perspectives. *Courtesy of Philadelphia Museum of Art, the A. E. Gallatin Collection*

view of some of modernism's critics (for example, Georg Lukács),[85] has led to a kind of political and ethical impotence, an inability to take a serious stand regarding the human condition. "Doubt in myself, doubt in everything, . . . never believing in truth": this was Marcel Duchamp's characterization of his own fundamental attitude.[86]

We find an analogous perspectivism in the thinking of many schizophrenics, where the simultaneity of or vacillation among perspectives is often associated with a particularly acute and in certain respects subjectivist awareness of the mind's role in constituting the world. Thus Anthony, a young schizophrenic patient who had referred to himself as an "old Buddhist," saw "embryonic warthogs" in a Rorschach card and, when asked what made the inkblot look like that, responded with the following reflection on the process of viewing the card: "Anthropomorphized. I take snapshots. Mind is a camera. On one of the takes they were anthropomorphized. Half human, half warthog." Like modernist uses of the crossfade technique, some of the contaminations and incongruous combinations in schizophrenic Rorschach records suggest a subjectivist focus on experience-as-such rather than some fundamental failure of reality testing.

The delusional system of another patient seems to have incorporated her confused sense of varying points of view, of perspectives contained within her that nevertheless retained some kind of quasi-independent status:

PATIENT: Yes, we all have perspectives, everyone does, and then you ask the perspective spirit to help you find a home you can live in, if you don't have one, and so . . .

INTERVIEWER: Where is this perspective spirit?

PATIENT: Yes, where is it? As a rule one has four perspectives, one in the head and one in each wrist, yes.

INTERVIEWER: And what happened to the fourth?

PATIENT: One in the head . . . no, I don't really know. Or two in the head. . . . There is at any rate, I don't really remember. But I, I don't rightly know it's arranged, I don't know how it's arranged.[87]

Many schizophrenics are quite aware, at least at moments, of their departures from the commonsense mode of life, and may experience this more as a rebellion than as an affliction overcoming them entirely against their will. "Everything I thought was weird. I used to change it round to look different," said one patient, echoing Stendhal's description of his technique of aesthetic rumination.[88] Often, the "pathological freedom" of their deviations serves as an inner, cognitive equivalent of the social defiance expressed more outwardly in the public persona of the dandy or the bohemian. For, as Manfred Bleuler has pointed out, many such individuals may feel the need to "separate themselves from the commonly accepted norms of intercourse and of thinking that have substance and validity in everyday life," as a way of establishing a strongly felt sense of individuality—in order, as Manfred Bleuler puts it, "to remain themselves."[89] The schizophrenic author of *I, Mary MacLane* describes herself in the following way:

> I am a fascinating creature. I move in no stultifying ruts. There's no real yoke of custom on my shoulders. . . . My mind goes in no grooves made by other minds. . . . When I look at a round gray stone by the roadside I look at it not as a young woman, not as a person, not as an artist, nor a geologist, nor an economist, but as Me—as Mary MacLane—and as if there had not before been a round gray stone by a roadside since the world began. . . . There may be equally egotistic viewpoints. . . . I don't know—I don't care. What is it to me? I know my own virile vision and that it thrills and informs and translates me as if crackling bright-jagged lightnings broke along my sky.[90]

The young schizophrenic man named Philip, whose letter I quoted from in the previous chapter, took an even more extreme position, asking why he should let himself be limited by "ideas of a normal metabolism"—given that "the importance of Reality is merely a social sanction (society inevitably ruled by those involved in reality), and the importance of control is merely a genus sanction. (Take porpoises, without arms and hands, perhaps higher IQs, and quite indifferent to control.) Why indeed should we be tied down by the ideal of reality? (Reality is a parameter—sort of relativity carried to the absurd.)" He said he wasn't trying to fool himself into thinking he could evade control—any more than he could evade guilt, but that he did "choose to consider both of them as illusions, because they should be. . . . Is the corollary to the things people joke about they take seriously, the things people talk about seriously are jokes? At any rate, I do want self-hypnosis, for other things. An orgy or two on the side can't hurt." Philip was a pure instance of a type described in a short story by the writer (and schizophrenic) Robert Walser: a "connoisseur and gourmet of freedom," "always bowing inwardly to the pure image of freedom."

This is a multifaceted and contradictory orientation, fraught with both exhilaration and fear, with both power and paralysis.[91] The utter and absolute skepticism to which it can lead seems to reach its apogee in schizophrenia, where (as Jaspers noted) it may not be "just blandly conceived but . . . experienced as a desperate affair."[92] To deepen our understanding of these modes of experience, and of their sources and repercussions, one might turn to any number of modernists, but especially to Friedrich Nietzsche and Robert Musil, perhaps the most penetrating and ambivalent analysts—as well as exemplars—of the psychological consequences of perspectivism to be found in modern Western thought.

Relativism and Perspectivism: "Vertigo of the Modern"

Nietzsche's own perspectivism is apparent in his persistent opposition to Platonism and all forms of essentialism, which he defined as the "idle hypothesis" that "things possess a constitution in themselves quite apart from interpretation and subjectivity."[93] It is hardly surprising that this view should have led him at times to favor "unbelief as an instinct"[94]—"an absolute skepticism toward all inherited concepts" and toward the "anthropomorphic error" whereby the mind identifies its own constructs with reality itself.[95] He claims, in fact, that "there is *only* a perspective seeing, *only* a perspective 'knowing,' " and therefore "the *more* eyes, different eyes, we can use to observe," the more complete our vision will be.[96] And in *The Gay Science* he glorifies the free spirit *par excellence*—the person who would "take leave of all faith and every wish for certainty, being practiced on maintaining himself on insubstantial ropes and possibilities and dancing even near abysses."[97] Yet despite these polemics and this hyperbole, Nietzsche was far from being a wholehearted proponent of such relativist tendencies, for he also recognized the sources of danger and weakness inherent in the skepticism and perspectival fluidity of modern times.

A "madly thoughtless fragmentation and fraying of all foundations, their dissolution into an ever flowing and dispersing becoming": these, for Nietzsche, were among the "remarkable symptoms of our age." He believed that new forms of historical and cultural awareness had exposed the modern individual to too many different views of existence. Modern man had been blinded by a "hypertrophic virtue": the presence of "much too bright, much too sudden, much too changeable light," which prevented him from distinguishing "what is clear and in full view from the dark and unilluminable." And as a result "the lines of his horizon restlessly shift again and again," rendering him incapable of "rude willing and desiring." For, as Nietzsche put it in one of his most powerful attacks on perspectivism, "the basic condition of all life" is to have a *single* perspective: "And this is a general law: every living thing can become healthy, strong and fruitful only within a horizon; if it is incapable of drawing a horizon around itself or, on the other hand, too selfish to restrict its vision to the limits of a horizon drawn by another, it will wither away feebly or overhastily to its early demise." He criticized those "given over to a restless cosmopolitan choosing and searching for novelty and ever more novelty," the people of an age in which "Knowledge, taken in excess without hunger, even contrary to need, no longer acts as a transforming motive impelling to action and remains hidden in a certain chaotic inner world which that modern man, with curious pride, calls his unique 'inwardness.' "[98] Such is the age of the "Don Juan of Cognition," the person who lacks sufficient love for the things he knows, yet nevertheless pursues knowledge relentlessly until, finally, "nothing remains to be hunted but the most agonizing effects of knowing" itself.[99]

One might contrast this condition, which the poet Louis Aragon called "the vertigo of the modern,"[100] with that of premodern, traditional, or (so-called) primitive societies, where one seldom (if ever) finds this kind of relativism, the sense of arbitrariness that accompanies the recognition that one's world view is but one possibility among many. Sir Edward Evans-Pritchard has written of the tight web of belief that he observed in the Zande culture of central Africa in the 1920s, where "every strand depends on every other strand, and a Zande cannot get out of its meshes because this is the only world he knows." For the Zande person, this web is not some arbitrary or "external structure in which he is enclosed. It is the texture of his thought and he cannot think that his thought is wrong."[101]

One of the clearest illustrations of modernist relativism, and of the weakening of personality it can cause, is Ulrich, the antihero protagonist of the novel *The Man Without Qualities*, a character whom Robert Musil (an avid reader of Nietzsche, from an early age) created both as an alter-ego figure and a sort of representative modern man.

Ulrich is plagued with excessive rationality and self-consciousness, and unusually open to alternative possibilities and modes of experience. A "possibilitarian," he has lived since childhood in a "subjunctive mood," once arguing in a schoolboy essay that "even God probably preferred to speak of His world in the subjunctive of potentiality . . . , for God makes the world and while doing so thinks that it could just as easily be some other way." Ulrich is so aware of "the leaps that the attention [takes], the exertion of the eye-muscles, the pendulum-movements of the psyche" occurring at every moment that even the act of keeping one's body vertical in the street seems to require tremendous energy. He cannot forget the importance of perspectives or horizons, and cannot trust his own, for, as another character in the novel points out, Ulrich knows too well that it is always "only a possible context that will decide what he thinks of a thing."[102]

It is therefore difficult for Ulrich to make decisions, whether in the matter of furnishing his house or choosing a career, for he so readily sees the arguments for all possible choices. Indeed, he can hardly summon up any sense of reality at all, since in his hyperreflexive state nothing seems to exist "in-itself" but only as a product of the mind that views it; he experiences only a "world going in and out, aspects of the world falling into shape inside a head." As a result,

> Nothing is stable for him. Everything is fluctuating, a part of a whole, among innumerable wholes that presumably are part of a super-whole, which, however, he doesn't know the slightest thing about. So every one

of his answers is a part-answer, every one of his feelings only a point of view, and whatever a thing is, it doesn't matter to him what it is, it's only some accompanying "way in which it is," some addition or other, that matters to him.[103]

It is understandable, then, that Ulrich should no longer experience commonsense reality, that "utopia of the status quo"[104] within which normal people go about their daily lives, as an inevitable terrain to which one simply opens one's eyes. On the contrary, as Musil explains in a passage that perfectly captures the sense of awe, uncanniness, absurdity, and paralysis so common in the early stages of schizophrenia, it is only by

exercising great and manifold skill [that] we manage to produce a dazzling deception by the aid of which we are capable of living alongside the most uncanny things and remaining perfectly calm about it, because we recognize these frozen grimaces of the universe as a table or a chair, a shout or an outstretched arm, a speed or a roast chicken. We are capable of living between one open chasm of the sky above our heads and one slightly camouflaged chasm of the sky beneath our feet, feeling ourselves as untroubled on the earth as in a room with the door locked. We know that life ebbs away both out into the inhuman distances of interstellar space and down into the inhuman construction of the atom-world; but in between there is a stratum of forms that we treat as the things that make up the world, without letting ourselves be in the least disturbed by the fact that this signifies nothing but a preference given to the sense-data received from a certain middle distance. Such an attitude lies considerably below the potentiality of our intellect, but precisely this proves that our feelings play a large part in all this. And in fact the most important intellectual devices produced by mankind serve the preservation of a constant state of mind, and all the emotions, all the passions in the world are a mere nothing compared to the vast but utterly unconscious effort that mankind makes in order to maintain its exalted peace of mind. It seems to be hardly worth while to speak of it, so perfectly does it function. But if one looks into it more closely one sees that it is nevertheless an extremely artificial state of mind that enables man to walk upright between the circling constellations and permits him, in the midst of the almost infinite *terra incognita* of the world around him, to place his hand with dignity between the second and third buttons of his coat.[105]

Schizophrenics often have a similar sense of the absurdity of things, which could so easily have been different (this may be one cause of the "empty smiling" and "meaningless hilarity" that are characteristic of schizophrenics, especially those of the hebephrenic, or so-called disorganized, subtype [patients characterized by seemingly incoherent thinking and incongruous affect, and by mannered or odd behavior]).[106] And, frequently, they will also experience an analogous feeling of being overwhelmed by endless possibilities. A patient mentioned earlier (the one who pondered how one differentiates the front from the back of a blouse) said that whenever she wrote something, she couldn't help but think about what she was not writing; and this, she explained, made her feel as if she were living inside some kind of endless hologram.[107] My patient Robert had prolonged phases of withdrawal when he would remain mute and nearly motionless for days at a time. After one of these periods he explained that he had felt unable to "exert his will-power" because, he told me, he had to deal with too many "echelons of reality"—there were "so many innuendos to take into account."[108] He had lost what Musil called the necessary "perspectival abridgement" of consciousness, that firm everyday grounding that allows the normal person to move through time at a steady pace, as on "a train that rolls down its own rails ahead of itself."[109] Robert once said that his awareness of where a conversation was heading, and of what the other person was likely to say next, would often prevent him from keeping his attention on what was being said in the present moment. I did have the impression that he would drift from the role of participant into that of self-conscious observer, such as on one occasion when he responded to a question not by answering but by asking if he was actually being asked that question; to another query he only said, as if musing to himself, "Sometimes I say yes, sometimes I say no."

This free-floating mode of cerebration can be expressed in an all-encompassing doubt, a doubt that gives rise to questions of a kind that seldom occur to normal individuals (or, for that matter, to the manic, depressed, or organic patient) since they concern phenomena usually seen as too random, or too trivial, to be explained at all (for example, asking why the pigeon alighted precisely on *that* part of the railing, or why a person one meets happens to be named Smith or Jones). People prone to such pervasive doubting may also wonder about issues that are generally assumed or accepted as utterly self-evident, such as questions about the existence of other minds and the possibility of believing in the past. One of Robert Walser's short stories, for example, consists almost entirely of one man's obsessive ruminations about whether the glass of wine he is looking at is really there and whether the door before his eyes is "really and truly closed."[110] One can well understand how such persons might come to feel disoriented. As some schizophrenics have said: "Everything I think of always gets away from me"; "Everything in me is changing continually"; "My thoughts are so confused, everything is wavering, nothing is fixed—one cannot hold fast to anything."[111]

Though such patients will usually have an intellectual awareness of where they are located, they may not *feel* as if they are in that place and time, for they lack that all-important source of orientation and stability: the sense of grounding in the lived body. (Perhaps Judge Schreber, the famous paranoid schizophrenic, was responding to this feeling of rootlessness when he complained that the "rays [he had delusions of being influenced and tormented by divine rays] did not seem to appreciate at all that a human being who actually exists *must be somewhere.*")[112] Another of Walser's short stories, "The Street," captures this dizzying turbulence and befuddlement extremely well:

A shiver passed through me; I hardly dared to walk on. One impression after another seized hold of me. I was swaying, everything was swaying. All the people here had plans in mind, business. A moment before, I too had had an end in view; but now, no plans at all. . . . I . . . sought some fixed point, but found none. In the midst of the unrelenting forward thrust I found the wish to stand still. The muchness and the motion were too much and too fast. Everyone withdrew from everyone. There was a running, as of something liquefied, a constant going forth, as of evaporation. . . . I told myself: "This hugger-mugger totality wants nothing and does nothing."[113]

The psychotic murderer Moosbrugger, the central figure in one of the major subplots of Musil's *The Man Without Qualities*, is an inarticulate character who is probably of subnormal intelligence. He experiences certain classic schizophrenic symptoms, and has been diagnosed as having *dementia praecox* (among other labels). This fictional character, crafted by one of the great masters of the prototypically modern "hovering life within," vividly illustrates the cognitive slippage and fraying of normal perspectives that have been the focus of this chapter; he also hints at some of the alternative orientations or visions of existence that can take their place—the nature of which will be my central concern in the following chapter.[114]

The normal citizens of Kakania, the fictional society of Musil's novel, imagine this murderer as a pure incarnation of all that is primitive and instinctual, a man whose violence supposedly attests to the utter immediacy and wholeness of his being. But Musil's description of Moosbrugger's inner life differs sharply from this image (suggesting, interestingly, that Musil may have had some inkling not only of the *parallels* between modernism and this kind of madness but also of the ironic error implicit in the standard Wildman image of the latter).[115] Consider, for example, the following passage, from the section "Moosbrugger does some thinking," which conveys Moosbrugger's sense of the absurd arbitrariness of human categories, specifically of words and concepts, while also showing how his attitude of defiance is bound up with his sense of relativism and alienation. In the last two sentences, there is even the suggestion that Moosbrugger experiences a kind of structuralism *avant la lettre:* a realization that human concepts depend for their meaning more on each other than on an objective reality, since the latter must remain always beyond their grasp ("scampering over the trees," as he puts it):

Now Moosbrugger has let his head sink and was looking down at the wood between his fingers. "In these parts they call a squirrel an oak-pussy" [a translation of a regional term for "squirrel"], it occurred to him. "But just let anyone try putting on a straight face and saying 'oak-tree cat'! They'd all prick their ears up, like when a real shot goes off in the middle of the quick popping of blanks on manoeuvres. In Hessia, now, they say 'tree-fox.' A much-traveled man knows that sort of thing."

And good heavens, how interested the psychiatrists made believe they were when they showed Moosbrugger a painted picture of a squirrel and he told them: "That'd be a fox or maybe a hare. Or it might be a cat, or some such." Every time then they would ask him as fast as anything: "What does fourteen and fourteen make?" And he would answer slow and thoughtfully: "Well, about twenty-eight to forty." That "about" caused them difficulties that made Moosbrugger smirk. For it was quite simple: he too knew that one gets to twenty-eight if one goes fourteen farther on from fourteen—but who's to say that one has got to stop there? Moosbrugger's gaze would always range a little further, like that of a man who has reached the top of a chain of hills outlined against the sky and now sees that beyond this again there are still more, similar chains of hills. And if an oak-pussy is not a cat and not a fox and not puss, the hare that the fox eats, one doesn't need to be so particular about the whole thing; somehow or other it's patched together out of all of it and goes scampering over the trees. Moosbrugger's experience and conviction was that one could not pick any one thing out all by itself, because each one hangs together with the next one.[116]

Moosbrugger is no intellectual, but his alienated, rather inchoate, insights into the nature of words and concepts are remarkably reminiscent of various modern forms of perspectivism. Thus at the end of this passage he seems to realize, at some level of awareness, that human concepts work through their relationships with each other (everything "hangs together") more than by any direct connection with the real (which, like the squirrel, goes about its business in supreme indifference to the human frameworks of understanding). Moosbrugger muses on the "changes [to which] things are unceasingly exposed, according to habit, mood and point of view," and on the inadequacy of all concepts and conventional understandings; for "life," he realizes, "forms a surface that pretends it has to be the way it is, [while] under its skin things are thrusting and jostling." And in this same section we get some insight into how this relates to his criminal behavior:

And it had even happened before now in his life that [Moosbrugger] had said to a girl: "Your sweet rose-lips," but suddenly the words gave way at the seams, and something came about that was very distressing: the face went grey, just like earth under the mist, and at the end of a long stem there was a rose. Then the temptation to take a knife and cut it off, or hit it to make it go back into the face, was enormous. True, Moosbrugger did not always at once get his knife out; he only did that when he could not manage any other way. Generally he just used all his gigantic strength to hold the world together.[117]

Even Moosbrugger's murderous violence, the most obvious expression of his supposedly bestial or Dionysian nature, actually takes place in an atmosphere of surrealistic alienation—motivated, it would seem, by a desire to erase his disconcerting sense of fragmentation, arbitrariness, and the absurd.

C H A P T E R 5

. . . .

Disturbances of Distance

What arbitrary assignments! . . . What arbitrary differentiations! What one-sided preferences, first for this, then for that property of a thing! . . . with words it is never a question of truth, never a question of adequate expression.

— Friedrich Nietzsche
"On Truth and Lies in a Nonmoral Sense" (1873)

The play with time was so uncanny . . . an alien time *seemed to dawn.*
— Schizophrenic patient
In Karl Jaspers, *General Psychopathology*

Complete understanding kills activity: indeed if it is directed inwards on the faculty of understanding, it kills itself. If one is fully aware of what is involved in moving a limb, one can no longer move it. But full awareness is impossible, *so activity remains possible. Consciousness is a screw with no end: at each moment it is applied, an infinity begins, so it can never be brought into action.*

— Friedrich Nietzsche
Unpublished note, 1870

With the wavering and slippage of traditional frameworks of thought, new possibilities come to light. When thinking is no longer restricted to the tracks laid down by convention and practical demands, objects and events may be seen or understood in strange and unexpected ways. We have found, in schizophrenia as well as in the culture of modernism, a tendency to adopt unusual or even bizarre standpoints, to fluctuate among radically diverse points of view, and to become aware of the fact of perspectives—thus demonstrating a certain reflexivity, a confusing and confused mode of self-awareness that nevertheless amounts to a kind of perspectiv*ism*. But what, more specifically, is the *nature* of the novel perspectives that such individuals tend to gravitate toward or adopt? What new horizons loom up as the conventional ones fade away?

Many peculiarities of schizophrenic thinking as well as many expressions of modernist idiosyncrasy may in fact be just plain weird, so variously unusual as to defy all generalizations. But, in addition to these, there are other anomalies that do suggest patterns—certain specific ways of deviating from our usual modes of conceptualizing or structuring the experiential world. Though no single term seems altogether satisfactory for labeling this diverse set of deviations, we might make do with a phrase derived from the psychologist David Rapaport: "disturbances of distance."[1]

Normal ways of perceiving and acting require what Robert Musil called a "perspectival abridgement."[2] It is important that the recognizable, middle-sized objects and familiar events that constitute the shared world of convention and practical activity be experienced not as arbitrary conventions but as the true furniture of reality, fully worthy of monopolizing our attention; for this to occur, all kinds of potential alternatives need to be blocked out of awareness. One needs, among other things, to maintain a certain optimal degree of distance in one's experiential stance— neither coming so close to the world of sensory or material particulars as to lose oneself in its sheer actuality, its infinite minutiae, or its endless mutability, nor moving so far away from particular objects or sensations as to lose touch with their conventional meanings or practical significance. In this chapter I will consider several characteristic ways in which schizophrenics appear to deviate from the complacency of this middle distance, examining, in particular, how this occurs in the formation of verbal concepts, in the structuring of narrative modes of understanding, and in the perception of visual form. In all three sections, we shall be concerned with semiotic issues, with the nature of symbol-referent relationships; but in dealing with the last two topics, issues of time and space will emerge as particularly central.

It makes sense to start with the topic that is closest to the issues of the previous chapter: the anomalies of verbal concept formation in schizophrenia. In introducing this topic, I turn again to the thought of Friedrich Nietzsche. Certain of the ideas of this exemplary and influential proto-modernist are of most obvious relevance to issues of categorization and concept formation, but they can also serve as a kind of blueprint for the other issues to be considered in this chapter.

VERBAL CONCEPTS AND NIETZSCHEAN
DUALISM

As I have already discussed, Nietzsche criticized the perspectivism, relativism, and cerebralism that he believed to be central to modern culture; but, in spite of his acute awareness of the practical advantages of resting within a single perspective, he was drawn toward pluralism and skepticism. A related aspect of Nietzsche's profoundly ambivalent, perhaps even contradictory philosophical position is of even more direct relevance here, as we attempt to specify some of the characteristically schizophrenic patterns or structures of thought.

Like many philosophers and artists of the late nineteenth and early twentieth centuries, Nietzsche accepted a kind of dualism, a view of experience that postulated, on the one hand, the categories and concepts brought to bear by human perspectives and, on the other, a raw immediacy of sensations or things, which was taken to consist of utterly unique components.[3] Nietzsche's attitude toward the latter, preconceptual domain was, however, as ambivalent or even contradictory as was his attitude toward perspectivism. Unlike many of the romantics, Nietzsche did not believe in the possibility of a "direct sensuous intuition of reality,"[4] of direct contact with this preconceptual level of experience, which he called "the formless unformulable world of the chaos of sensations"[5]; he thought that human consciousness was inevitably perspectival and concept-imbued. But, despite his conviction that consciousness is, as he said, always "arranged, simplified, schematized, interpreted through and through,"[6] he continued to yearn for some kind of direct, preconceptual contact and often tended, in his thinking, to presuppose and to glorify at least the possibility of approaching "the unique and entirely individual original experience[s]" from which (in his view) concepts ultimately derive.[7]

Thus Nietzsche would speak of the importance of escaping from instrumental convention and abstract ideas into the world of sensations, of immediacy, and of becoming—into a realm of "sudden impressions" not yet denatured into "less colorful" and "cooler" but somehow less real concepts.[8] He would fault abstract concepts for distorting the actual nature of the world, arguing that every concept—"leaf," for example—"arises from the equation of unequal things," and criticizing the tendency to ignore the unique features of the individual objects by assimilating them to the mere fiction of general concepts ("leaf" in general, for instance). Yet, in other moods, Nietzsche would take quite the opposite tack, glorifying the person who is able to detach himself from all concerns about what is real, actual, or authentic. Then he would suggest that seeking contact with formless immediacy was not in fact the proper response to recognizing the arbitrariness of all concepts, to realizing that the "infinitely complicated dome of concepts [is built] upon an unstable foundation and as it were on running water";[9]

one ought, rather, to abandon oneself to a kind of aesthetic and conceptual play—an "exuberant, floating, dancing, mocking, childish, and blissful" mode of creation, a surpassing freedom in which forbidden metaphors and strange combinations of concepts are manipulated without any of that "spirit of gravity" that seeks an ultimate reality or final truth.[10]

Both of these aspirations, the yearning for immediacy and a self-aware commitment to creative illusion, are prominent in modernism and postmodernism, as well as in many examples of schizophrenic-type consciousness—where they show up as a preference for the concrete sensation or the abstract concept at the expense of those more synthetic entities, percepts.[11] The first preference is illustrated by the essayist Roland Barthes's express desire to escape the "disease of thinking in essences" by adopting "ephemeral concepts, linked to limited contingencies"[12] (Borges's "having just broken the water pitcher" might be a good example of such a concept); as well as by the neodadaist John Cage's glorifying of the unique and the random (as when he professes fascination with mushrooms because of their unclassifiability: "the more you know them, the less sure you feel about identifying them. Each one is itself. Each mushroom is what it is—its own center").[13] This attitude harks back to the interest that Cage's master, Marcel Duchamp, took in the laws of exception, in single cases and unrepeatable events, and to Duchamp's desire to eradicate "the possibility of recognizing any two things as being like each other"[14]—all of which is in turn reminiscent of Alfred Jarry's "pataphysics," the mock-science of what Jarry called "the realm beyond metaphysics . . . the laws which govern exceptions . . . [and facts which] have the advantage of singularity."[15]

The other side of Nietzsche's position, willingness to engage in a kind of conceptual or aesthetic play, is no less common in modernism and postmodernism. One need only think of the surrealists' insistence on the imagination's ascendancy over the objective world; or, for a more recent instance, of that self-styled Nietzschean, Jacques Derrida, calling for a "joyous affirmation" of the play of the signifier, "the affirmation of a world of signs without fault, without truth, and without origin which is offered to an active interpretation."[16] This triumph of concept, perspective, or linguistic sign over object or thing is exemplified in a technique often used by the writers of the French *nouveau roman* school: describing two objects from a standpoint or in a vocabulary that renders them nearly indistinguishable from each other, though only in the world of the text; in Claude Simon's novel *Triptych* this occurs with a trout and a phallus.[17]

Both attitudes or orientations are also very common in schizophrenia. The first is present in many instances of what is too easily dismissed as a primitive or deficient "concreteness" in schizophrenic cognition—as when such patients take an abnormal interest in the immediate sensory presence or in seemingly trivial aspects of a perceptual object, or when they balk at defining things in terms that strike them as too general. A good example is the following set of responses that one schizophrenic, quoted by the psychiatrist Maria Lorenz, gave when asked to define various terms:

QUESTION: Book.
ANSWER: It depends what book you are referring to.
QUESTION: Table.
ANSWER: What kind of table? A wooden table, a porcelain table, a surgical table, or a table you want to have a meal on?
QUESTION: House.
ANSWER: There are all kinds of houses, nice houses, nice private houses.
QUESTION: Life.
ANSWER: I have to know what life you happen to be referring to. *Life Magazine* or to the sweetheart who can make another individual happy.[18]

As Dr. Lorenz rightly points out, there is no evidence here for the sort of incomprehension of the concept of kind or type that might be expected with a truly concretistic mentality—after all, this patient does ask in each case what *kind* of object is meant, as if acutely aware of, even preoccupied with, the existence of differing types.[19] What *is* suggested is a certain discomfort with common generalizations, with the extent to which immediate experiential reality (like the table one has a meal on) is likely to be forgotten in giving a more abstract, standard definition. (One might also note the fluidity of perspective suggested by this patient's move into a metaphoric level of interpretation in responding to the word *life*.)

The second Nietzschean attitude, a preference for conceptual play, seems to be present (though in a less euphoric and flamboyant way) in the following statement in which a psychotic patient is defining the word *parents:* "Parents are the people that raise you. Any thing that raises you can be a parent. Parents can be anything, material, vegetable, or mineral, that has taught you something. Parents would be the world of things that are alive, that are there. Rocks, a person can look at a rock and learn something from it, so that would be a parent."[20] This example comes from the most recent diagnostic manual of the American Psychiatric Association, where it is quoted as a supposedly proto-typical example of "illogical thinking"—defined in this official document as "thinking that contains obvious internal contradictions or in which conclusions are reached that are clearly erroneous, given the initial premises."[21] (Since the patient may seem to be making inaccurate equations, or to be subsuming virtually the entire universe under a single category, this passage is also a good illustration of the sort of speech that has given rise to the hypotheses of both paleologic and overinclusion.)

But contrary to what is claimed in DSM III-R, there is nothing really contradictory or erroneous in this statement. Nor does it seem right to say, in line with the paleologic hypothesis, that this patient has actually *equated* "parents" and "rocks," that is, that he cannot tell them apart; after all, he explains how he is choosing to define the word: "Parents can be anything . . . that has taught you something." (Note also that he is by no means ignorant of the conventional meaning of *parents*, since his definition takes off from this: "Parents are the people that raise you.") What his response does seem to indicate is a willingness to extend the use of a term in a quasi-metaphoric fashion without being concerned about staying with the conventional meaning of the word—which, as Nietzsche might have said, is itself ultimately no more than a social contract. This patient's extension of the meaning of *parents* can be read, then, as the sign of a certain conceptual freedom, a willingness to play with categories that results either from indifference or from hostility to conventions.[22] It is the latter propensity that may be the common element lying beneath the twin Nietzschean predilections for raw immediacy and for the free play of the concept or signifier. In both cases there is a failure, or a refusal, to inhabit the universe of common sense, that practical world of middle-sized objects that is bequeathed by one's culture and shared with one's fellow beings.

Nietzsche, of course, was well aware of the dangers of such a stance. Presumably, the Nietzschean hero would be a person who could hold all these rival perspectives in mind while still managing to act—a person who, while somehow remaining aware of the underlying flux in all its uncategorizable immediacy, as well as of the arbitrariness of all schemata or perspectives, could nevertheless, through force of will, draw about himself a firm horizon in which to live. But the constant, encroaching danger—one to which many schizophrenics bear testimony—is that these underlying awarenesses will steal the foreground, and that the split between bare concept and teeming flux will paralyze action, deaden emotion, and infect all meaning with a sense of absurdity and distortion.

The instances of schizophrenic thinking considered so far in this chapter as well as in the previous one are, for the most part, isolated responses to tasks of a purely cognitive or affectively neutral kind, such as the sorting of objects, the discernment of conceptual similarities, or the defining of words on vocabulary lists; this has allowed little scope for investigating the existential condition with which schizophrenic thinking might be bound up, either in aesthetic contexts or in everyday life. The data we shall look at next derive from projective tests, which encourage more complicated forms of self-expression and entail far more extensive and elaborate reactions to the world. And, since projective-test responses can be viewed as at least quasi-aesthetic productions, they will prompt us, in our seeking for modernist analogues, to consider not just general philosophical attitudes and cognitive tendencies in modern culture but also the specific formal characteristics of actual works of literature and visual art. Though the forms of eccentricity and vacillation already considered will still be present in many of these examples, I shall now be focusing more on other issues, including the structuring of time, of space, and of semiotic relationships (that is, relationships between symbols and their referents, or between a medium of representation and that which it represents).

In the projective test I will consider first, the Thematic Apperception Test, the individual is shown a series of pictures depicting people in psychologically charged but ambiguous situations of various kinds, and is asked to make up a story about what is going on in each scene. Since this test is designed to elicit narratives, responses to it can most appropriately be compared to works of literature, particularly fiction. The second test, which requires the organizing of spatial rather than temporal aspects of experience, is the well-known Rorschach, in which the subject describes what he or she sees in a set of ambiguous and symmetrical inkblot patterns. There is at least a rough analogy between this test and the art of painting, given that both activities involve an attempt to structure and give meaning to previously ambiguous visual material on a two-dimensional plane, and since a paradigmatic way of accomplishing this is through naturalistic or quasi-naturalistic representation of a three-dimensional space.

Needless to say, there are many ways in which projective tests and artworks are not analogous. Still, at an abstract level of description, all such acts of expression do call into play similar issues regarding the experience of reality and its relationship to the self. Both projective-test responses and artworks could be thought of as being objectifications, in sensuous form, of overall attitudes toward the universe; and, unlike the fleeting stream of experience, they have the advantage of holding still for our analysis. If we examine them carefully, and with an eye to general formal or structural qualities, we will find close resemblances in the dilemmas that beset consciousness in modernist art and in schizophrenia, and also in the formal devices that are evoked in response to these dilemmas.

NARRATIVE UNDERSTANDING

Narrative Form and Schizophrenia

The standard instructions for the Thematic Apperception Test (TAT) request that the subject look at each of a series of pictures and tell four things about it: (1) what activity is going on in the scene depicted; (2) what led up to this activity; (3) what the outcome will be; and (4) the thoughts and feelings of the characters. Obviously, these instructions pull very strongly for a narrative-type response, and the majority of subjects do comply broadly with these instructions by telling stories about fairly realistic people who engage in actions that have a comprehensible causal sequence and a normal narrative spread with a past, present, and future—what we might call the standard narrative form. Within these constraints there is, of course, room for enormous variability, and it is this that makes the TAT useful for the analysis of personality types and neurotic styles. Among patients without demonstrable brain disease, however, it is only the schizophrenics who deviate from this standard form of narration in a way that indicates a profound difference in the very structure of their experience (as opposed to suggesting, for example, only disinterest or defensiveness about revealing oneself to the examiner).

Consider the following story, which serves as the main illustration of a schizophrenic-type response in a major textbook on diagnostic psychological testing. It was told by a hospitalized eighteen-year-old male patient in response to a card that depicts two people shown facing each other and in close physical contact:

> Before this picture, these two people, ah, hated each other. . . . And then they were accidentally thrown together in some situation and just before this picture, a miraculous change took place which I can't describe. In the picture they—they feel as if they are a picture—a complete thing. And they're aware of their limits and they accept them and after the picture, they leave each other um—and the picture. [What are their limits? asks the testing psychologist.] The boundaries of the picture.[23]

In this story the past and future are described so perfunctorily that they seem barely to exist. Also, one is given a sense neither of understandable human intentions nor of deterministic events that might lend causal structure to the discourse by linking together past, present, and future. The story has a quality one might call presentism or, equally well, timelessness. Actually, it is in a sense more spatial than temporal. Notice, for example, the phrasing "before this picture" rather than the more usual "before this moment" or even "before this scene." Related to this is an oddity of a semiotic type. When asked by the examiner about the boundaries of the people described, the patient engages in one of those odd shifts of frame of reference that are characteristic of schizophrenics as of no other group: he says that the boundaries of the people are the boundaries of the picture. A question that would normally be understood to pertain to an imagined three-dimensional world of real people and events moving through time—

the depicted reality—is construed in terms of the literal and material realm of the medium of representation, a universe where only space, and a space of but two dimensions, exists. When interpreting the thoughts and feelings of the characters, the patient even says that "they feel as if they are a picture" and are "aware of their limits," which turn out to be the boundaries of the picture—almost as if he were ascribing to the characters represented an awareness of their existence *as* representations.

Schizophrenic discourse has often been observed to display similar characteristics: the lack of a cohesive theme or narrative line, of conventional space-time structure, of comprehensible causal relations, and of normal regulation of the symbol-referent relationship. It has been found, for example, that schizophrenics tend to use adverbs of a spatial type to replace those of a chronological type (*where* may replace *when,* for example)[24] and, more generally, to speak in ways that emphasize the static and deemphasize the dynamic and emotional aspects of the world, thereby evoking a universe more dominated by objects than by processes or actions (patients with affective psychoses do the opposite).[25] That these are not merely surface features of a particular linguistic style, but reflective of something about the actual experiences of such patients, is suggested by numerous self-reports in which schizophrenics speak, for example, of the immobility of time, of the loss of past and future, or of the difficulty of arranging remembered events in the correct order. As one schizophrenic named Lawrence put it, "I feel as if I've lost the continuity linking the events in my past. Instead of a series of events linked by continuity, my past just seems like disconnected fragments. I feel like I'm in the infinite present."[26]

The psychiatrist Silvano Arieti sees the loss of the ability or will to organize acts or thoughts into a causal sequence—what he calls the loss of "seriatim functions"—as a fundamental feature of schizophrenia, and he has pointed out the tendency, as the disease progresses, for the delusions of schizophrenics to relate to the present rather than to the future.[27] The psychoanalysts Rapaport, Gill, and Schafer state that shifts in frame of reference of the kind seen in the TAT example I gave are important indicators of potentially severe (presumably schizophrenic) disorders of thinking. And, interestingly enough, they single out those shifts on the TAT where the patient adopts a reflexive frame of reference when a nonreflexive response pertaining to the plot or content of the story would be expected—as when a patient asked to elaborate about the events in her story answers by referring to her own perceptual or thought processes involved in experiencing the picture or *devising* the story. A patient who had described a woman on a TAT card as "terrified," for example, was asked the standard inquiry question, "What led up to this?" and responded: "The expression on her face."[28]

These various distortions of normal time and space, of symbol-referent relations, and of frame of reference have nearly always been interpreted as indicators of cognitive incapacities or else of the collapse of all distinctions and structures brought on by regression. The tendency to focus on the *medium* of representation—on the TAT card itself, for instance—has often been seen as a sign of a concretistic mentality, as showing an inability to transcend the literal, physical presence of a stimulus-object by perceiving it as representative of some meaning or some hypothetical world existing beyond itself. (Shifts in frame of reference and distortions of temporal ordering have been viewed as indicating a return to earlier cognitive stages, stages preceding acquisition of the ability to stabilize perspectives or to sequence events in time.)[29] It is interesting to discover, therefore, that virtually the same characteristics can be found in some of what might be considered the most sophisticated narratives (or antinarratives) of our time.

Spatial Form in Modern Literature

"The Secret Room," first published in 1962, is a short story by Alain Robbe-Grillet, a writer of the French *nouveau roman* school. It consists of a series of static descriptions of what can be seen in a room in which, so to speak, there just happens to be the corpse of a woman. It is hard to imagine a piece of fiction that could better demonstrate the qualities described in Ortega y Gasset's famous essay, "The Dehumanization of Art." There Ortega interprets the distortions of naturalistic representation that occur in modernist art as resulting from a desire to escape the world of natural human feelings in favor of a less threatening, abstruse realm of purely aesthetic sentiments. But why, then, he asks, should there be anything of normal reality left in such art, which often does have some representational content, however distorted? Why is there not total abstraction in all cases? Ortega's answer is that the minimal presence of naturalistic subject matter serves the purpose of driving home a kind of victory over reality; it is a way, he says, of displaying the "strangled victim."[30]

In Robbe-Grillet's story, the realistic content actually does include a murdered victim—in this case not strangled but stabbed. And the corpse in question is described with an objectivity that goes beyond a merely clinical detachment: not only all emotion but all normal sense of meaning or even of reality is lacking.[31] There is, for example, no special emphasis on clues or on anything else connected with the crime as an act having human significance; it is as if the woman's body were no more or less important than the sofa or the wallpaper. This is clear from the very first paragraph, in which the dead woman's flesh and bloody wound are described as if they were objects for purely aesthetic contemplation or for a lesson in geometry: "The first thing to be seen is a red stain, of a deep, dark, shiny red, with almost black shadow. It is in the form of an irregular rosette, sharply outlined, extending in several directions in wide outflows of unequal length. . . . The whole stands out against a smooth, pale surface, round in shape, at once dull and pearly, a hemisphere joined by gentle curves to an expanse of the same pale color."[32]

The story is reminiscent of the presentism of the schizophrenic TAT story I discussed earlier, for it seems to be based on a detached, almost purposeless stare at a portion of time and space, with no attempt to construe this portion as fitting into a causal or purposive sequence. Although the scene does change slightly during the story, there is no sense of a coherent movement or transformation from one moment to another; we are, in effect, presented with a series of randomly chosen moments, each crystallized into immobility. The following passage, in which one schizophrenic patient remembers what it was like to watch the hands of a clock during his psychosis, captures this mood precisely: "The hand is constantly different: now it is here, then it jumps so to speak and turns. Isn't this a new hand every time? Maybe somebody is behind the wall and keeps replacing the hand with another one at a different place each time. You get absorbed in the observation of the clock and lose the thread that leads you to yourself."[33]

Another aspect of Robbe-Grillet's story recalls the semiotic aspect of the schizophrenic world. The sequence of static descriptions in "The Secret Room" eventually suggests that what is being described is not real but rather a series of stills from a film, run in reverse order: "The man has already moved several steps back. He is now on the first steps of the stairs, ready to go up." At other moments, there are hints that what is being described is a two-dimensional painting: "Farther on, these same colors are picked up again in the stone of the paving and the columns"; in the last line of the story, Robbe-Grillet refers to a column of smoke "rising vertically, toward the top of the canvas."

These suggestions involve a curious paradox typical of such fiction, a paradox reminiscent of Nietzsche's dual yearning for immediacy and illusion. On the one hand, such narratives seem objective in the extreme, as if the neutral and passive perspective were presenting us with reality in the raw, without those sentimental distortions of human judgment, the "prefabricated synopses" that Robbe-Grillet has deplored in his writings on the theory of the novel: "But the world is neither meaningful nor absurd, it quite simply *is* . . . all around us defying our pack of animistic or domesticated adjectives things *are there* . . . without false glamour, without transparency."[34] Yet at the same time this world of pure materiality can seem in danger of dissipation, of turning out to be as thin and unreal as a film or a painting.[35]

In *Triptych*, a novel by Claude Simon, another writer of the *nouveau roman* school, it frequently happens that what one thought was a real-world scene turns out to be the description of an image, as when a couple making love in a barn, described with uncanny precision, turns out to be only an element in the design of a poster on a wall. There are many such metamorphoses in Simon's novel, and they are like cinematic dissolves that lead not from one real-world scene to another but from one perspective to another—in a manner reminiscent of Borges's Chinese encyclopedia and the Foucault-ian heteroclite.[36] The emphasis of such fiction on the bedrock objectivity of an external world beyond human consciousness is thus contradicted on another level. For what one might call an omnipresent "coefficient of subjectivity" makes one aware that the fictions themselves are but representations of representations, indeed that everything is mere representation; and thus they implicitly suggest that all mental objects, whether real or depicted, have equal status. "There are no facts, only interpretations," asserted Nietzsche, who was wise enough to be worried about the leveling and weightlessness implicit in this subjectivization of all things.[37]

In this respect also such fictions are similar to the TAT response we have been considering—where the patient treated the card in one sense as a literal two-dimensional object in space, while in another sense describing the scene depicted as if, so to speak, it knew itself as mere representation (or even, perhaps, as an image in his, the viewer's, eye).[38] Actually, the characteristics that make schizophrenic stories unlike the standard narrative form are much the same as those that differentiate traditional from modernist literature in general, at least if one accepts a set of widely held critical interpretations. The classic statement of the relevant view regarding modernism is Joseph Frank's seminal essay of 1945, "Spatial Form in Modern Literature," which describes a widespread attempt in modern literature to deny time and thereby to achieve a sense of simultaneity at a deep level of response (this is not, incidentally, an either/or matter but a tendency present to some degree and in a variety of different modes). Such writers dwell, for example, on the description of static objects rather than on the recounting of processes or actions, or may engage in a reflexive turn ("a space-logic of reflexive reference," as Frank calls it), focusing attention not on the narrated events but on certain formal or structural aspects of the literary act and product—such as the act of writing itself, the sound or graphic appearance of the words, literary conventions, the merely fictional nature of the characters, or the presence of a perspective or standpoint that informs, even to a large extent creates, the story. Both tendencies have the effect of breaking down the reader's sense of the causal coherence and purposive thrust of the story as a sequence of real events in time.[39]

ESCAPE FROM TIME

At the end of a book on the turn-of-the-century origins of the twentieth century avant-garde, the literary scholar Roger Shattuck suggests that a time machine fantasized by the playwright Alfred Jarry could stand as a symbol for the consciousness of the modernist age. Jarry's time machine, a kind of gyroscope, achieves absolute immobility via controlled motion. By an elaborate pseudophysical (he called it "pataphysical") conceit, Jarry "proves" that if one could achieve such spinning immobility in space, one would also escape from the bounds of normal time. And since the imaginary machine, like a gyroscope, achieves its stasis-cum-motion by turning around its own center, its escape from chronology is achieved by means of a kind of involution or self-reference.[40]

This fantasy machine—conceived by a schizoid and typifying modernism—echoes with uncanny accuracy certain statements made by schizophrenics that have been collected by the psychiatrists Eugene Minkowski, Franz Fischer, and others. One patient, for example, described himself as "like a machine that runs but does not move from its place. It goes at full speed, but remains in place."[41] Another made explicit reference to the connection between introversion and his disturbed sense of time, describing an "intense cerebral activity in which inner experiences took place at greatly increased speed, so that much more than usual happened per minute of external time. The result," he said, "was to give an effect of slow motion. . . . The speeding up of my inner experiences provided in this way a slowing down of the external world."[42] A third patient's statement is richer still:

> I look for immobility. I tend toward repose and immobilization. I also have in me a tendency to immobilize life around me. . . . Stone is immobile. The earth, on the contrary, moves; it doesn't inspire any confidence in me. I attach importance only to solidity. A train passes by an embankment; the train does not exist for me; I wish only to construct the embankment. The past is the precipice. The future is the mountain. Thus I conceived of the idea of putting a buffer day between the past and the future. Throughout this day I will try to do nothing at all. I will go for forty-eight hours without urinating. I will try to revive my impressions of fifteen years ago, to make time flow backward, to die with the same impression with which I was born, to make circular movements so as to not move too far away from the base in order not to be uprooted. This is what I wish.[43]

The last statement, like Jarry's time machine, suggests that it would be wrong to interpret the time-space alterations as pure manifestations of some innate deficiency completely out of the purposive control of the subject. This is not to say that this turn toward the spatial dimension may not depend, to some extent, on losing the ability to experience standard narrative meanings or to maintain a single narrative frame of reference (issues treated in chapters 2 and 4); but we must also recognize that it serves important defensive functions. Schizophrenic spatialization is act, then, as well as affliction; and it seems reasonable to ask whether, as an act, its motivation might be akin to that of the spatial form found in modernism.[44]

Drawing on certain classic arguments made by the art historian William Worringer, Joseph Frank proposed that spatial form could be understood as a way of escaping what is felt by certain individuals or certain cultures to be the intolerably anxiety-provoking nature of external reality.[45] By rendering reality as a timeless present, its unpredictability, dynamism, and mystery— in fact, its very otherness—are denied. Frank also pointed out that flatness in painting is the equivalent of spatial form in literary art, and that together these stylistic features capture a great many of the important features of the modernist style. We have found similar characteristics to be central aspects of the space-time of schizophrenia; and the following quotation from a schizophrenic strikingly confirms the link between spatial form in narrative and visual flatness, while also suggesting a connection with reflexivity:

> I seemed to myself to be a timeless being, perfectly clear and limpid as far as the relations of the soul are concerned, as if it could see its own depths. . . . The past became restricted, shriveled, dislocated. It was formless. Can I say this? Or like when a wooden shack tumbles down. This formlessness, which came from that, then attacked me; or it was as if a picture with a spatial perspective of depth suddenly flattened and was then only on the surface.[46]

A more gradual progression toward flatness is clearly visible in the work of one schizophrenic man, Louis Wain, a commercial artist whose paintings of cats gradually lost the dimensions of both depth and time and, with the progression of his illness, increasingly took on the "morbid geometrism" that is particularly characteristic of chronic forms of schizophrenic psychosis (see figure 5.1 and, for another example of "morbid geometrism," figure 5.2).

Spatial form in literature and flatness in painting appear to involve a paradoxical combination of qualities, an equivocation between seeming contraries. (In this way they exemplify the tendency toward forms of both subjectivism and objectivism that is so characteristic of modernist thinkers, including Nietzsche.) In one sense the world is rendered more solid and dependable by such a mode of expression or experiential stance. The words and paint are tokens of a kind of materiality and otherness; and, to the extent that one focuses on these substantial aspects, one is aware of objects whose "thereness" is undeniable (unlike what is only represented) and which are unambiguous and unchanging (unlike the represented world of temporal flux and spatial depth).[47] But, at the same time, the focus on words or paint can also undercut the reality of the world: to the extent that one focuses on the *way* in which reality is rendered, reality's status as something independent and apart is denied. And, in this sense, the words or paint function not so

FIGURE 5.1

Louis Wain, cat paintings. Illustrate progression toward "morbid geometrism" during the course of a schizophrenic illness. *Photo by Derek Bayes, courtesy of* Life *Picture Service*

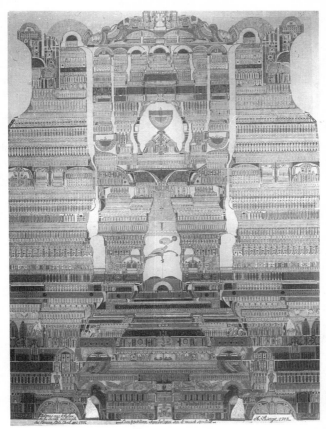

FIGURE 5.2
Augustin Lesage, *Composition Symbolique sur le Monde Spirituel* (1923). "Morbid geometrism" in a drawing by a schizophrenic. *Collection de l'Art Brut, Lausanne*

much as tokens of materiality as of the presence of mind, indeed, of the dependence of the world on the mind that represents it. External reality can thus be subjectivized, thereby neutralizing much of its potentially threatening nature.

These forms of reflexivity can, then, be a source of feelings of security of various kinds. The critic Clement Greenberg, who has identified modernism with "the intensification, almost the exacerbation, of [the] self-critical tendency that began with the philosopher Kant," sees modernist self-reflection as serving not to "subvert" the work of art but rather, as he says, "to entrench it more firmly in its area of competence."[48] But as Greenberg seems implicitly to acknowledge, subversion does remain an ever-present possibility: this kind of reflection is also capable of leading to the "fragmentation and fraying of all foundations," to that "dissolution into an ever flowing and dispersing becoming" that Nietzsche viewed as one of the symptoms of modern relativism (and which many "postmodernists" have embraced). (Such a development is, perhaps, suggested by the just-quoted patient's associating of timelessness and flattening with a "formlessness" that "attacked" him.)[49]

In the next section we shall examine some Rorschach responses typical of schizophrenic patients. These will provide further illustrations of a simultaneous yearning for both materiality and subjectivization, and will allow us to take a closer look at this second, more ominous possibility.

VISUAL FORM

Schizophrenia and the Rorschach Test

Sens: on peut voir regarder. Peut-on entendre écouter, sentir?
—Marcel Duchamp

The Rorschach subject is asked to look at a series of ten inkblots and, in each case, to tell the tester "everything you see in it that looks like something." The vast majority of people given these instructions automatically assume an orientation one might call standard representational realism. That is, they try to achieve a reasonably good match between the relatively unstructured visual forms of the blot and some known object that, whether real or imaginary, is three-dimensional. The Rorschach is a purely perceptual task, of course, yet the orientation most people assume is not unlike that adopted by the traditional representational painter—what Leone Battista Alberti, author of the first Renaissance treatise on painting, described in the fifteenth century as "to render with lines and colours, on a given panel or wall [in the Rorschach: on an ink-stained card], the visible surface of any body, so that at a certain distance and from a certain position it appears in relief and just like the body itself."[50] As with the TAT, there are many different ways to respond; but among non-brain-damaged patients, it is only certain schizophrenics and schizoids who do not seem capable of, or interested in, adopting this standard frame of reference.

One fairly common way in which schizophrenics and schizoids may deviate is by describing the literal characteristics of the inkblot rather than what it resembles. Here is an extreme example: "Thick disconnected dots on the peripheral flanges of the image, what could either happen from a dripping or a smearing effect. On the outer edge of the image, there seem to be some light dots, on the inner part of the image, some darker dots, indicating a build-up of ink. Right at the head of the image, it's more of a very delimited line, more of a descriptive stroke."

Responses of this kind have often been taken as evidence of the persistent notion of the primitivity or deficiency of schizophrenic cognition, since they seem to suggest a certain quality of concreteness. *Concreteness*, at least as Goldstein uses the term, implies being passively "bound by" or "too close to" stimuli; it implies a relative incapacity for the abstract experiences of shifting among a variety of different perspectives toward an object or of turning around upon one's thoughts in the sense of becoming aware of one's own cognitive acts. Such limitedness of point of view and subservience to the sensory world are characteristic of infants and young children and of many patients with organic brain damage. The literalness of this severely schizoid man's response might seem to suggest he is incapable of detaching himself from the blot itself, even to the extent of making a single representational interpretation of it.

Unfortunately for the concreteness thesis, however, there are certain characteristically schizophrenic Rorschach responses that are even more common; these suggest the very opposite quality, although they too involve deviation from standard representational realism. Sometimes the responses of such patients indicate little concern about the objective characteristics of the blot, which they seem to use as the stimulus to an impressionistic and symbolic interpretation of an "overly distant" and very abstract kind—as when a patient interprets an inkblot as looking, for example, like "motherhood," "democracy," or "the outside lookers, the onlookers of the outside." One patient responded as follows: "It's a symbolic volcano. It's like a volcano of thought. Thought comes from the spirit and goes through the mind, the body, and just comes out, emotionally."[51] Or, when asked to justify an interpretation of the blot, the patient may shift into an odd frame of reference. One schizophrenic who saw a blot as a "histological plate" was asked what made it look like that and, instead of responding, as most subjects do, with a description of how the appearance of the particular blot corresponded to the specific object he had seen, gave an oddly reflexive and abstract answer: "The sensation obtaining between light and one's eyes."[52] Finally, it should be noted that most schizophrenics who do manifest these anomalies of distance are not incapable of standard realism, since some of their responses will also be in this mode. And so we find, once again, that what is most characteristic of schizophrenic cognition is not any one type of response, but an extreme variability among widely divergent ways of perceiving or responding.[53]

This is a style that differs from the more truly concrete style of many organic patients, who may well be consistently stimulus-bound, and also from that of patients with affective illness, whose euphoric or depressive thought processes are generally more comprehensible even when they are psychotically disturbed. The thinking of affective patients—the antic, expansive flight of ideas of the manic or the impoverished and slowed-up associations of most depressed patients—seems to involve a change in the velocity of thought, and often a release from the constraints of logic or realism, and from any need to stick to the point.[54] The schizophrenic disorder, by contrast, often involves something like a shift of conceptual altitudes, as if the mental lives of such people were deprived of the vital ballast provided by engagement in the processes of life.[55] They are characterized by a certain inertia, involution, and self-preoccupation, and seem preoccupied with "the experience of experience."[56]

These typically schizophrenic qualities of experience—disengagement from the more usual conventions of time and space and orientation toward the literal or the abstract, along with a heightened preoccupation with experience itself—are vividly illustrated by the responses of one highly thought-disordered young schizophrenic man to whom I administered the Rorschach as well as other psychological tests. Several of Henry's responses were strikingly literalist: "Should I also see what looks like dirt as part of the picture? See, this is dirt or lint." Others were highly abstract: "Then what comes to me is an imaginary—I can't explain it—is an imaginary figment, a structural figment. . . . You can consider it anthropomorphic. It's a kinship, you can identify, it's a system, belief." Another of his responses managed simultaneously to manifest excessive and insufficient distance: "Blurring of orange and green. I think in the simple blurring there seems to be something archetypal, or an emblem. I don't really see any purpose in telling you this looks like this, this like this."[57]

This last sentence captures a couple of themes that recurred in a number of his responses. For one thing, there is an acute awareness of, and disdain for, conventionality ("Logic sounds clumsy to me—puritanical," he said to me in conversation; and once, after being shown several of the TAT cards, he asked, "Are these all clichés?"). In addition, there is a tendency to reflect on the very nature of the task or of his own mental processes. Unlike nearly all nonschizophrenic subjects, Henry did not readily and naturally adopt, then consciously forget, the ground rules of standard realism. In fact, he claimed to find them banal: "Like with the Rorschach, I thought it was dumb to see, for example, animals. Things were obvious, not important." At one point he even came close to stating spontaneously, in his odd language, the psychological principle of disturbances of distance. Asked to tell the tester what he saw that looked like something, he replied:

That's silly. I only could do this in one of two ways. I could tell you either what the thing is physically, or I could tell you how those things exist as spiritual embodiments. Now I might be confused. I don't know. I'm also reminded of [Rorschach], if he had specific ways of devising these inkblots which might explain why I seem to be able to respond in terms of shape or meaning, what I see is the form.

"What the thing is physically" or "shape," "spiritual embodiments" or "meaning": it is clear from his responses that these phrases refer, on the one hand, to the seemingly concrete, overly close descriptions of the look of the ink on the cardboard and, on the other, to his speculative, overly distant forays into a stratosphere of abstractions. Once again we find the tendencies so prominent in Nietzsche: dissatisfaction with conventional perspectives, and a turning instead either to conceptual speculation or toward the meaningless immediacy of substance or sensation.

Simply to call this patient's responses primitive, to ascribe them to the supposedly confused nature of a mind functioning on a lowered psychic level, or to wave the explanatory wand of the "primary process" over such instances of thought disorder, gives a very misleading picture of the structure of such a patient's experience.[58] Primitive or concrete modes of consciousness (whether conceived of as involving the primary process or early forms of secondary-process thinking) would presumably be relatively spontaneous and free of self-monitoring; whereas the disturbances of distance of the patient whose Rorschach we have been discussing seem to be a product of his reflexive self-awareness. Consider the following train of associations:

[Tester: You said you saw a man, but with a face like a penguin?] It didn't really make sense to me but . . . I noticed that his face looked like it could resemble a penguin. A penguin may have to do with sharply pressed black and white. Like the idea of cleanliness. Somehow the idea seems bland. Not so much bland, but blasé. [What's bland or blasé?] The contrast of black and white. And I think blasé fits better, because it's not bland. [How is it blasé?] Because black and white, white, sharply defined and socially accepted criteria of contrast, whether it be of race, morals, just because we're told one is a representation. [Why blasé?] Just because of all the colors I could think of, they're the most comfortable.

In this example the patient's train of thought leads him to ponder the concept of contrast, which seems to have been suggested to him by the black-and-white appearance of a penguin, one of his associations, and also by the Rorschach card itself, in this case an inkblot that *is* only black and white. Here the patient's thinking could be said to be simultaneously overly distant and overly close in Rapaport's sense, since it concerns both the literal reality of the card and something highly conceptual, the abstract idea of contrast.[59]

One way to understand these distinctively schizophrenic disturbances of distance is to recall that they involve features of experience that would normally be known in only an implicit sense. In the mind of the normal subject engaged in Rorschach perception, various psychological processes are going on, including the sensory-perceptual registering of stimulus information and the conceptual processes by which it is interpreted. In normal people, in fact in virtually all nonschizophrenics, these processes both happen and combine with each other without conscious awareness, whereas the above-quoted patient seems abnormally conscious of his own mental processing. It may even be the case, in fact, that his contemplation of the phenomenon of contrast is occurring in conjunction with explicit awareness of a feature of Rorschach perception that is usually experienced only tacitly: the fact that all that one sees is built upon this basic capacity to perceive contrast, in this instance between the blacker parts of the card, seen as figure, and the white, seen as ground.

The philosopher Michael Polanyi has built an entire philosophical edifice on the foundational idea he calls "the tacit dimension," the crucial distinction within experience between explicit and implicit knowing. As he has pointed out (using a famous example of how becoming too aware of the feel of a cane against one's hand disrupts one's ability to use it to explore the world), a certain disorganization and fragmentation of the coherence of experience occur as a result of excessive self-awareness.[60] Bearing this in mind, the fact that this patient's odd veerings into self-reflexivity are seldom sustained enough to be easy to understand, or to lead to a coherent synthesis of his response, is hardly an argument against the excessive self-consciousness interpretation. Indeed, as the following quote from Henry shows, the tendency to be excessively aware of awareness helps precipitate this man's perspectival fluctuations, thereby disrupting the coherence and clarity of his thinking. Asked what he had meant when he spoke about an archetype or emblem, he replied:

> I just felt that something is looking at the blurred combination, there seems to be something basic that has form. There seems to be something that offers, to my recollection of being an infant, to seeing confused colors, and acknowledging that the world consists of tools, and that everything that we glance at has some utilization, some use, purpose. It means something. We could also consider that to be paranoiac. But I'm not so sure. It's a fact that, I'm not so sure what I mean by a fact. . . . I'm trying to say something beyond a dichotomy between recognizing objects in the world and recognizing my own distortions, what I rather mean is my own hypothesized objects—there's a word to describe that. . . . I do think human beings

transform intelligence on the basis of being able to transform aesthetic—I can't explain what I'm talking about at this point.

Here there is a continual slippage from perspective to perspective, with explicit awareness of the fact of perspectives, endless consideration of other possibilities, and a recursive self-undermining and dissolution of prior possibilities. This, obviously, can be a major source of confusion, for the patient himself as well as for his listeners. Yet it has something in common with modernist attempts to incorporate our seeing of reality as part of reality itself—as in cubist painting, where, as one critic puts it, the "eye and its objects inhabit the same plane, the same field, and they influence each other mutually and reciprocally."[61] For Henry, as in many cubist works, there seem to be no stable objects; what he experiences is but a welter of experiences and points of view. (Thus he speaks not just of the "blurred combination" but of "something . . . *looking* at the blurred combination"; another schizophrenic patient's comment about an abstract drawing using geometrical forms gives a similar impression: "I think it's symbolic since it seems to be, it probably symbolizes a remembrance. It might be the distilled objective point of view of somebody who sailed a triangular sailboat.")[62]

As always, it is extremely difficult to assess the relative contribution of deficiencies as opposed to volitional or defensive factors in perceptions and experiences such as those conveyed in these Rorschach data. The kind of heightened reflexivity that occurs could largely reflect active psychological processes that have gotten out of control, and feed upon themselves in the manner of obsessional doubting; and this may well have a neurobiological basis, perhaps involving overactivation of certain parts of the brain. Alternatively, there could be neurophysiologically based deficits of, say, selective attention, maintenance of attention, or perceptual integration—which might then bring about, as a secondary consequence (secondary, that is, in the causal sequence, not in its degree of importance for the schizophrenic lived world), an exaggerated awareness of normally implicit fragments of experience and an anxious hyperintentionality that might not easily be inhibited.[63]

Though one or another of these factors may play a particularly important role with particular subgroups of schizophrenic patients, I am inclined to think that some complex and perhaps synergistic combination of several of them is likely to be most common of all. (In the domain of human personality, something like the opposite of Occam's razor may often be the best guide.) Interestingly, in trying to make sense of his own responses, Henry seems to be locked into just such an explanatory quandary, shifting among a variety of possible interpretations. "I'm not sure what to make of the symmetry," he said regarding Card #1. "I'm telling you that my own problems are impairing me. Whether it's this grandiose bullshit I'm giving you (referring, presumably, to his earlier response, 'an imaginary figment . . . a structural figment . . . a·kinship'), or that I'm finding it hard to concentrate." Speaking of his symptoms, another patient said: "It was partly my own choice, and partly it was repugnant to me."[64]

The Visual Arts

In closing I will touch upon the many ways in which visual art's intense reflection on itself in the twentieth century has engendered forms analogous to the schizophrenic disturbances of distance. Obvious examples of increase of distance could be taken from conceptual art, while equally obvious examples of decrease come from minimalism and other literalist trends. The famous quality of flatness—described by the critic Clement Greenberg as the goal of the progression of modern painting—is reminiscent of distortions of distance of both kinds. Writing in the 1940s and later, Greenberg described the loss of faith or interest in representing the three-dimensional world that occurred in the development of painting, and the growing preference for reflexively manifesting painting's own distinctive medium, the flat canvas.[65] This could be seen, in line with the views of William Worringer and Joseph Frank, as a retreat toward a kind of materially grounded security.

Basing his views on conversations with the artist, the critic Michael Fried interpreted certain paintings by Frank Stella as an even further progression (or retreat) toward such literalism. In an influential essay first published in 1966, he describes those works as foregrounding not just the flatness of the canvas (Greenberg's theme) but the surface qualities of the paint and canvas—so that one's experience of the "literalness of the picture-surface" is, as Fried puts it, "an experience of that literalness as an experience of the properties of different pigments, of foreign substance applied to the surface of the painting, of the weave of the canvas, above all of color." Fried also points to the exceptional literalness of Stella's treatment of visual shape or form. Previous kinds of abstract or nonrepresentational paintings were nevertheless representational in at least one sense: they did depict geometrical forms that stand out against the background provided by a neutral canvas, whose own literal shape (always rectangular, by convention) can be forgotten. Stella's paintings, by contrast, consist exclusively of hard-edged stripes that follow the external edge of a shaped, nonrectangular canvas; hence whatever shapes are depicted (by the stripes) are not independent of the literal shape of the actual physical canvas; indeed, they echo this literal shape and call attention to it. Fried offers an intriguingly anthropomorphic account of the travails of shape in the prior few years of avant-garde activity:

"[In] the development of Modernist painting during the past six years," he writes,

> it is as though depicted shape has become less and less capable of venturing on its own; of pursuing its own ends; as though unless, in a given painting, depicted shape manages to participate in—by helping to establish—the authority of the shape of the support, conviction is aborted and the painting fails. In this sense depicted shape may be said to have become dependent upon literal shape and indeed unable to make itself felt as shape except by acknowledging that dependence.[66]

As was the case with the literalism and presentism of the schizophrenic and *nouveau roman* narratives, such literalist visual work also reveals two seemingly contradictory tendencies. On the one hand there is the need to encounter some external object in an almost physical way—as if to ward off a sense of encroaching unreality. As Hans Richter, a former dada artist, wrote in a book published in 1964:

> It looks as if people today needed the instantly palpable material object to hold on to as a confirmation of their presence in the world. . . . An inner void seems to force [man] outward, an urge to convince him of his existence by way of the object, because the subject, man himself, got lost. . . . Our generation has become so greedy of presence that even the lid of a W.C. is holy to us, we are not satisfied with seeing it pictured, we want to *have* it altogether, bodily.[67]

On the other hand there is the subjectivization of reality. The sculptor Bruce Nauman, an important figure in the 1960s, said he felt dissatisfied with his own sculptures because "they seemed to have too much to do with sculpture and not enough to do with his own thought processes."[68] This expresses a widespread aesthetic attitude, one source of which is Marcel Duchamp's influential attempt to replace a merely "retinal" painting with something more purely conceptual, more directly an expression of the mind. But we find a similar attitude also in the formalist school of painting and criticism. For, surely, one implication of flatness in painting is to declare that the representation of some external object, scene, or event is not necessary in order to justify the existence of artist or artwork. In this sense we might say that the flat, formalist painting is a kind of symbol of mind, conceived of as a self-sufficient and reflexive entity.[69] Pervading many such works, it seems to me, is a distinctive combination of superiority and impotence, though sometimes one may also sense at least a hint of desperation.[70]

It is not difficult, incidentally, to find literary examples that manifest a similar duality. In the following passage from the Mexican writer Salvador

Elizondo's *The Graphographer*, for example, any connection with an actual context or real-world subject matter is lost via an extreme, vertiginous, and ultimately ludicrous involution:

> I write. I write that I am writing. Mentally I see myself writing that I am writing and I can also see myself seeing that I am writing. I remember writing and also seeing myself writing and I remember seeing myself remembering that I was writing and I write seeing myself writing that I remember having seen myself write that I saw myself writing that I was writing and that I was writing that I was writing that I was writing. I can also imagine myself writing that I had already written that I would imagine myself writing that I had written that I was imagining myself writing that I see myself writing that I am writing.[71]

Like the visual works we have been considering, this passage seems to involve both kinds of disturbances of distance: an increase of distance from any potential real-world subject matter, along with a loss of distance from the medium of creation, the writer's own thought processes and the act of writing itself.

The art historian Linda Nochlin has described modern art as involving a splitting apart of several elements that in the past were usually combined and integrated: the concerns with imagination, with natural reality, and with the material medium of the artwork. In 1867 Charles Blanc, she says, expressed the "traditional position in art," the theory of most Western artists from the Renaissance until the beginnings of modernism, when he wrote: "Painting is the art of expressing all the conceptions of the soul by means of all the realities of nature, represented on a single surface in their forms and in their colours."[72] This integrated, premodernist mode could be compared to David Rapaport's conception of the normal, adult Rorschach response process—in which perception of the stimulus characteristics of the blot (corresponding to the material medium), associations to memory images of real-world objects (corresponding to natural reality), and concept formation (corresponding to Blanc's "conceptions of the soul") all work together in a mutually dependent fashion to produce the normal perception of a well-seen and recognizable three-dimensional object, without the subject's ever being conscious of the highly integrated "cogwheeling" of these processes.[73]

In the modernist arts, there has been a tendency for particular artists or schools to focus on one of the elements of the traditional art process and to make that almost their sole concern, as in the case of "isms" like formalism, photorealism, or conceptual art. Similarly, schizophrenic projective responses often seem to be products of an intensely reflexive concern with some single aspect of the potential experience, such as the blot itself or one's own thoughts on contemplating it. Both seem akin to that Nietzschean view of things we considered at the beginning of this chapter—where the apparent world of familiar objects falls away to reveal the arbitrary concepts, or the chaos of unclassifiable sensations, out of which the world seems ultimately to be composed.

This is a problematic and a paradoxical vision and, as we shall see in the following chapter, one that can erode faith not only in normal forms of perception and action but in the very possibility of meaningful communication itself. These implications are beautifully captured in an essay on Nietzsche and Wittgenstein by Erich Heller, so I shall close with this literary scholar's reflections on these two philosophers who knew very well that too much consciousness could indeed be a thoroughgoing illness. Heller speaks of the predicament modern philosophy has entered, along with poetry and painting: "the stage where every act of creation is inseparable from the critique of its medium, and every work, intensely reflecting upon itself, looks like the embodied doubt of its own possibility." This is a quandary Nietzsche anticipated in "A Fragment from the History of Posterity," in his portrait of "The Last Philosopher": "Nothing speaks to him any more—except his own speech; and, deprived of any authority from a divinely ordered universe, it is only about his speech that his speech can speak with a measure of philosophical assurance."[74] Here is a person undermined from within: confounded by ambiguity and paralyzed by indecision, he finds himself shuttered inside his own self-consciousness and devoid of all belief in a communicable world.

C H A P T E R 6

Languages of Inwardness

MARIAN: I'm responsible for my own motives. I keep my mouth closed and my nose open.

NURSE: Can you say things a bit more clearly to let us know what's going on?

MARIAN: Just ask my autograph book who was signing it all the time. It's not my fault it's ripped up.

PSYCHIATRIST: Did you think we'd know what you meant when you said that?

MARIAN: I *know* you all know what I meant.

PSYCHIATRIST: I didn't.

MARIAN: It's not your fault.

NURSE: I suspect no one else in this room knew what you were talking about.

MARIAN: I said I could remember when my mother's hair was down her back and she kept cutting it off.

PSYCHIATRIST: I don't know what that means.

MARIAN: That's what I mean. There's been a pass over me. I've been passed over.

PSYCHIATRIST: I still don't know.

MARIAN: Look at the dark shadows. What do you see? Same old monkeys.

Talking with schizophrenic patients can be a profoundly disconcerting experience. Their speech, with its unexpected swerves and cryptic references, is likely to leave the listener feeling puzzled and adrift—and likely, too, to evoke the praecox feeling: that unnerving sense of encountering someone who seems inaccessible, uncanny, and remote. It may be extremely difficult to grasp the meaning of certain words or phrases, to follow the general drift of the patient's speech, or even to know whether one is included in the conversation in which the patient seems to be engaged.

The exchange that opened this chapter took place in a state hospital meeting room with a schizophrenic patient named Marian.[1] When she says, "Look at the dark shadows," and then asks, "What do you see?" how is one to know whether Marian is addressing herself, the people in the room, or some imaginary interlocutor? And when she speaks of the "same old monkeys," as if of some familiar thing whose meaning could be taken for granted, one can only wonder: Is she talking about real animals, about the look of the shadows, or perhaps about other people in the room? In addition to these specific doubts, general uncertainties are likely to arise, puzzlements that can erode the very framework of human understanding and cooperation. Is what I am hearing meaningful or pure nonsense? Is this person struggling to say something inexpressible, or perhaps to avoid something unspeakable? Is she aware of how strange she sounds? And finally, is she doing all this on purpose, or is it just that there is something wrong with her brain?

The oddities of schizophrenic language have been recognized since the classic works of Kraepelin and Eugen Bleuler, but, salient though they are, they have always been exceptionally difficult to characterize, let alone to explain. This is due partly to their daunting variety, which defies classification within any single category or explanation in terms of any single defect or tendency. Another complicating factor, too often forgotten, is the inconsistency and variability of the characteristic peculiarities: thus, some of the more striking and famous anomalies (such as the use of neologisms, or made-up words) are actually found in only a small percentage of schizophrenics; many schizophrenics never manifest *any* of the blatant deviances of speech or understanding, and those who do generally do so only *some* of the time. Manfred Bleuler remarks on the "old clinical observation that schizophrenic language (just like schizophrenic thinking and behavior) is not stable":

> One patient may speak in a very dissociated way that is difficult to understand, but the same patient may write letters as good as those of a healthy person. Another schizophrenic may speak in a clear and coherent way to me but in a very incoherent and peculiar way to his relatives. Another patient may not have uttered so much as an understandable phrase for several weeks but may suddenly give me in a coherent way (just as if he were healthy) the reasons for his wish to be discharged from the hospital.[2]

The interdependence of language with other psychological processes complicates matters still further, for this makes it difficult to know whether we are encountering a specifically linguistic disorder rather than, say, a more general cognitive or perceptual deficit, a certain social attitude or incapacity, a preoccupation with delusions or other abnormal ideas, or some combination of these. Given these ambiguities, it is not surprising that schizophrenic language should so often have been described in purely negative terms—as incomprehensible, unconventional, or idiosyncratic, for example; these, of course, are but ways of asserting the absence of something normal or expected without saying anything positive about the nature or sources of what *is* observed.

TRENDS IN SCHIZOPHRENIC LANGUAGE

Most linguists and psycholinguists who have studied the matter have concluded that, in most instances, the deviant quality of schizophrenic speech does not, in fact, reflect a disorder of language *per se;* not, that is, if one understands language in a strict sense: as pertaining to the presence or the nature of certain kinds of rules—specifically, phonological rules concerning the combining of sounds, grammatical rules governing word and sentence formation, or semantic rules determining the acceptability of individual sentences.[3] In this sense schizophrenic language differs markedly from that of the aphasic patient, whose more clearly linguistic deficits seem to result from focal brain damage, usually in the language centers of the brain. Marian's speech illustrates this basic linguistic intactness; despite the overall impression of strangeness, her words and sentences are quite well formed from a phonological as well as a syntactic standpoint, and the sentences she forms conform to basic semantic rules.[4] (In this chapter I will not deal with the small subset of schizophrenic patients—16 percent according to one estimate—who may have an aphasialike condition.)[5]

In recent years there has been a growing consensus that the distinctiveness of schizophrenic language is to be sought in qualities of another kind: in styles of speaking and interpreting language, and ways in which language ties in with its practical and interpersonal contexts. What schizophrenics seem to manifest, however, is not a single predominant style but a fairly diverse set of modes of language use;[6] and these, I would argue, can be reduced to three general trends: what I shall call the desocialization, autonomization, and impoverishment of schizophrenic language. (The trends are not mutually exclusive, incidentally, and a given patient may display two or even all three of them; indeed, they may also occur simultaneously, as different aspects of the same utterance.) Though not always linguistic in a strict sense, these diverse qualities are bound up intimately with particular ways of understanding words, sentences, and larger discourse structures, and with the use of these modes for the purpose of representing and communicating (and, perhaps, of disguising) meanings of various kinds.[7] All three contribute to the unconventionality and incomprehensibility of schizophrenic language; and, as I shall demonstrate, all three are related to the reflexivity or inwardness that is so characteristic of modernism.

Desocialization

Desocialization, the failure to monitor one's speech in accordance with social requirements of conversation, can occur at various levels and in various styles of speaking—for instance, in an extreme terseness and the use of cryptic words, but also in the use of sentences that seem endless, never coming to the point. Schizophrenics often fail to provide clear transitions in moving from topic to topic, which gives their speech a disorganized, irrelevant, or even incoherent quality. Their language may also sound telegraphic, as if a great deal of meaning were being condensed into words or phrases that remain obscure because the speaker does not provide the background information and sense of context the listener needs to understand.

The meaning of the schizophrenic's communication also tends to be obscure at those (relatively rare) moments when schizophrenics use neologisms, or, what is more frequent, when they employ common words in personalized and idiosyncratic ways without bothering to explain what they mean or even to indicate that they are using them in some special or metaphorical sense. The intended meaning will sometimes be easy enough to guess—as when a patient speaks, for instance, of being tormented by "insinuendos," "elbow people," or "side voices," or of being "botanized"—but more often the effect is baffling.[8] When one schizophrenic man talked about "superskeletonization," for instance, his listeners could have no way of guessing that he was referring to the state of being higher than the vast, skeletonlike suspension bridge that could be seen from a floor high up in the mental institution where he lived.[9] A related characteristic is the failure of the deictic aspect of speech. *Deixis* is a technical term that derives from the Greek word for "pointing" or "indicating," and it refers to aspects of speech that are relative to the practical and social context of the sentence or utterance—to its time or place and to the identity of its participants, for instance. Most speech contains some deictic ambiguities, but these are especially pronounced in the speech of many schizophrenics. "We are already standing in the spiral under a hammer"; "Death will be awakened by the golden dagger"; or "I don't know what I am to do here, it must be the aim, that means to steal with the gentlemen," such a patient may say, leaving a listener completely in the dark about who is being addressed, what the intended time frame is, and what is being referred to by these phrases.[10]

It is hard to know whether, or to what extent, such obscurity is willful. It is clear, however, that schizophrenics frequently ignore the pragmatic rules of conversation, failing to orient the listener by providing the necessary background or contextual cues or to establish the kinds of logical connections that make for a coherent and readily grasped utterance.

Autonomization

A second characteristic of schizophrenic language involves tendencies for language to lose its transparent and subordinate status, to shed its function as a communicative tool and to emerge instead as an independent focus of attention or autonomous source of control over speech and understanding. In what is known as *glossomania*, for instance, the flow of speech will be channeled largely by acoustic qualities, or by irrelevant semantic connotations of one's words. When asked to identify the hue of a color chip, one patient responded, "Looks like clay. Sounds like gray. Take you on a roll in the hay. Hay day. May day. Help."[11] Such discourse is led as least as much by rhyme or alliteration as by any overarching theme or meaning. The flow of discourse may also be determined by potential meanings generated by individual syllables or component parts of words, as when another schizophrenic (Philip) referred in a letter to his father's "demise," and then began writing of his father's "dim eyes."

We find the same tendencies in the reception as in the production of language. Instead of grasping the overall meaning of something read or heard, schizophrenics will often attend to material qualities of the signifier, to the sounds of words or their graphic appearance on the page, or they will become aware of a large number of the potential, but normally irrelevant, meanings of words. Unlike patients with diffuse organic brain damage, who often resist the notion that a single word can have more than one meaning, schizophrenics often seem hypersensitive to the polysemous nature of language; as a result, they may be prone to making puns or, in listening and reading, to feeling overwhelmed by the plethora of possible meanings.[12] "I try to read even a paragraph in a book," one patient said, "but it takes me ages because each bit I read starts me thinking in ten different directions at once."[13] Another schizophrenic, asked to define the word *contentment*, responded to normally unnoticed meanings that could be found in isolated syllables or letters:

Contentment? Well uh, contentment, well the word contentment, having a book perhaps, perhaps your having a subject, perhaps you have a chapter of reading, but when you come to the word "men" you wonder if you should be content with men in your life and then you get to the letter T and you wonder if you should be content having tea by yourself or be content with having it with a group and so forth.[14]

In these glossomanic ways of speaking and understanding, a certain disengagement or abdication of responsibility seems to occur. Instead of being guided by an overall sense of intended meaning, the flow and sense of the message is determined largely by intrinsic and normally irrelevant features of the linguistic system. One consequence is that, when reflecting upon their own writing or speech, such individuals may come to find their words just as opaque and ambiguous as their listeners do.[15] A patient who is asked to explain particular phrases or sentences may adopt the quizzical attitude of an observer deciphering a code, as if he were in no better position than the listener to interpret the meaning of the words he himself has uttered.

A sense of meaning may, in fact, be absent at the very moment such words are spoken, or there may be a loss of the feeling of initiating or intending one's utterances. One schizophrenic patient explained that her words sounded like tape recordings to her; another said, "I often repeat the same words but they do not mean the same thing. . . . I understand absolutely nothing of what I say. . . . When I stop it is because the sentence has just finished."[16] Such persons seem prone to a form of disengagement in which they experience their own speech or writing as some kind of alien substance rather than as a medium they inhabit and imbue with meaning. "I become confused by the idea that I write," said a third schizophrenic, "and I cannot distinguish between writing as an author and the mere act of creating letters. If I see something I have written, I become more confused and seeing my name in print makes me feel crazy and drives me further into my insane persona."[17] This autonomy of language can also be reflected in visual hallucinations or illusions, as in the case of one schizophrenic who saw "words flashing like ticker tape," or another who saw words coming out of the top of someone's head.[18]

This ceding of responsibility need not occur in so anxiety-laden or so extreme a fashion, however; nor, paradoxically enough, need the patient necessarily feel that the loss of meaning and control is entirely beyond the sphere of his will. This is apparent in the following, rather pompous and abstract-sounding passage, which is a good example of subtle glossomania. Individual words do seem to have been chosen less for sense than for sound, because they begin with syllables like *sub, mis, un,* or *con;* yet as the last line coyly suggests, this very fact is something of which the speaker seems to be quite aware—and something he may well have intended: "The subterfuge and the mistaken planned substitutions for that demanded American action can produce nothing but the general results of negative contention and the impractical results of careless applications, the natural results of misplacement, of mistaken purpose and of unrighteous position, the impractical serviceabilities of unnecessary contradictions. For answers to this dilemma, consult Webster."[19]

Impoverishment

Impoverishment of schizophrenic language is the most heterogeneous of the three features, for it brings together several phenomena that may not actually have a great deal in common. The first of these is poverty of speech, which refers to a simple restriction in the *amount* of spontaneous speech—as when patients become extremely laconic or even mute, a condition that may be transitory or may last for years.[20] The second is called poverty of *content* of speech, and refers to utterances that are adequate in amount, in sheer number of words emitted, yet that seem to convey little information because the language is "vague, often overabstract or overconcrete, repetitive, and stereotyped." This latter quality, which some studies have found to be the single most distinctive feature of schizophrenic language, often manifests itself in utterances that sound, to many listeners, like "empty philosophizing," "fruitless intellectualizing," or "pseudo-abstract reasoning."[21] Such speech is often taken to reflect a quality of "vague wooliness" in the thinking that underlies it, or the presence of a murky, undifferentiated, and homogenizing mode of cognition.[22] As the following passage illustrates, such language can easily leave the listener, especially the impatient or unsympathetic one, with a sense of great vagueness or even emptiness:

> Chirps in a box. If you abstract yourself far enough from a given context you seem somehow to create a new kind of concretion. It isn't something you have or see but yet somehow. It's being fascinated by the generative process of the mind. The thing is to be caught in it, yet abstract from it. Both be in it and out of it—revolving everything around me. You explode like when stars explode. In the sky a plate which burned bright. Symbol of all light and energy with me contracted into this plate.[23]

A couple of other features of schizophrenic discourse are especially difficult to classify, though they appear to have at least some affinities with impoverishment. *Blocking* refers to occasions when thinking, and speech along with it, seems to halt in the middle of a train of thought, or even to cease altogether, usually at moments when the patient is trying to move from one idea to another.[24] Another feature is a strikingly bombastic or precious quality of language. Some schizophrenics, as Eugen Bleuler has pointed out, are inclined to express trivialities "in the most lofty, affected phrases, as if they were dealing with the highest interests of mankind"; one patient, for instance, would fill his letters with phrases such as: "The undersigned writer of these lines takes the liberty of sending you this by mail."[25] The repetitive and stereotyped use of such pretentious figures of speech or other stylistic anomalies usually conveys a quality of emptiness, as if semantic content were being sacrificed in favor of verbal mannerism; but often these "pathological whimsies" will also seem to have some ironic, joking, or mystifying intent. One schizophrenic described *coitus* as "to perform holy vaccination"; and, rather than speaking directly of death, another would say, "We shall long have been guests of the crematorium."[26]

TRADITIONAL THEORIES OF SCHIZOPHRENIC LANGUAGE

There have been a great many attempts to account for the oddities of schizophrenic language over the past eighty years or so, few of which have faded away entirely (as one scholar remarks, this is a field where "hypothesis struggles with hypothesis in a conflict in which new contenders enter the field but the defeated never retire").[27] The most influential interpretations can be divided into two broad groupings: the psychoanalytic and certain like-minded cognitive-developmental approaches, and the cognitivist or information-processing perspectives of experimental psychology (the latter have usually been allied with medical-model psychiatry).

The various psychoanalytic theories share a by now familiar emphasis on the supposedly primitive or regressive nature of schizophrenic language patterns, but differ according to what kind of primitivity is emphasized. Some psychoanalytic writers emphasize the supposedly childlike egocentricity of schizophrenic consciousness, which is said to prevent schizophrenics from adopting the perspective of their interlocutors. Other psychoanalysts stress the inherent nature of the experiences or meanings that preoccupy such individuals, arguing that these are too primitive in nature—too imbued with a sense of primal fusion or with the Dionysian "alogic" of the instincts—to be captured in the conventional categories of adult language. Still others focus on the infantile nature of the schizophrenic's experience of language itself, seeing the thinglike or opaque quality that words so often take on in this condition as reflecting a profound regression to an early stage in the development of language—to a time when the sound of the word was still fused with its referent and the signifier's materiality and emotional resonance were not yet effaced in favor of pure meaning.

In contemporary cognitive and experimental psychology, we find schizophrenia being conceived in largely mechanistic rather than developmental terms, and described in vocabularies of deficiency, deficit, or dysfunction. Usually this involves assuming models (rather speculative ones, I hasten to add) that divide psychological processes into a hypothesized set of component subfunctions, with explanation then being understood as a matter of specifying the phase or subfunction, or the relationship among subfunctions, whose failure can account for the symptom. (Though such failures are generally assumed to have some biological substrate, the nature of this substrate often remains unspecified.) The postulated dysfunction may involve some general disturbance of cognition—such as an "inability to integrate perceptual and cognitive processes," a failure of some aspect of selective attention, or a disturbance of "central feedback of information about willed intentions."[28] It may bear more specifically on social knowledge, as in the case of one theory that postulates an inability to construct the "second-order representations" necessary for inferring the consciousness of others, for example.[29] It may also pertain to language *per se*, as when the theory hypothesizes a disturbance of the "unconscious planning mechanism for the production of discourse" or "disruption in the ability" to find conventional words appropriate to the meanings the patient wishes to convey.[30]

Apart from a few perfunctory speculations about the confusion and anxiety likely to result from the malfunction in question, the cognitivist theories have not had a great deal to say about the lived-world or existential condition that may underlie and motivate these anomalies of expression. And, since these cognitivist theories generally understand schizophrenic abnormalities of speech and understanding as a causal by-product of a malfunctioning brain or cognitive mechanism, they tend to downplay or even to deny the intentional and meaningful aspects of such language.[31] This is not to say, however, that one could not incorporate elements of the cognitivist theories into a more encompassing model that does account for these aspects. But, though certain cognitive disturbances may well play an important role, they alone do not help us to understand the *experience* of language, nor the various uses to which these abnormal tendencies can be put.

That schizophrenics have less control over the processes of speaking and understanding language than do either creative writers or average speakers has, in fact, been widely assumed, in mainstream psychiatry and cognitive psychology as well as in psychoanalysis. And the usual corollary (at least in psychiatry and cognitive psychology) has been that their language is less worthy of interpretation, since its oddities are largely the products of malfunctions rather than of purposeful attempts to convey meaning. Implicit in this view is what has been called a "principle of asymmetry" in modes of explanation,[32] a principle that holds that normal behavior should be understood teleologically, through the ascribing of purpose, while breakdowns or instances of non-natural functioning need to be explained in a causal-deterministic manner.[33]

The powerful influence such presuppositions can have is particularly well illustrated by the varying responses that literary scholars and other writers have had to the late poetry of Friedrich Hölderlin, poetry written during the long schizophrenic period of his life. Specialists given to more traditional literary and psychiatric assumptions have tended to see these works as consisting of "odd words, lumped together without plan, and of an awful unintelligibility"—indeed, as signs of "a catatonic form of idiocy" that show "failure of linguistic expression" and "helpless banality," and as filled with "empty words" that cannot conceal a profound incapacity to grasp or to express abstract concepts.[34] (Eugen Bleuler described them as examples of "emptiness and obscurity of ideas with preservation of a certain formal technical skill.")[35] Yet other critics have seen these very same poems as pregnant with meaning, and as constituting this great poet's finest work. "Signs of apparent helplessness prove to be calculated operations, and apparent slips in the flow of [Hölderlin's] language [turn out] to be a deliberate control of the system," writes one scholar, who discovers in these works processes of the most "profound artistic understanding."[36] In a study co-authored by Roman Jakobson of Hölderlin's language in the period of his madness, there is a detailed analysis of the morphological variations, rhythms, syntactic complexities, and semantic layering to be found in the eight lines of the following poem, *Die Aussicht* ("The Perspective"), probably the last poem Hölderlin ever wrote.

The Perspective

When into the distance fades the mortal life of human beings,
Where into the distance gleams the season of the ripening vines,
There too are the summer's empty fields,
The wood appears with its dark image.

That Nature completes the image of the seasons,
That while it lingers, they pass by quickly,
Is something of perfection, the heights of heaven glow
Upon human beings then, as blossoms wreathe the trees.[37]

This and other late works have been described as monotonous and stereotyped; but, as Jakobson shows, they can also be seen as manifesting an impressive "architectonic cohesiveness," "complex and purposeful design," and "a tension between the strictest canon and an amazing richness of creative shadings and variations."[38]

It is obvious, perhaps, that neither pole of the affliction-versus-act dichotomy can really capture the whole truth about schizophrenic language. In the following pages I would like to suggest some alternative perspectives on schizophrenic language—perspectives that, in my view, can better account for its variety, its variability, and its distinctive linguistic qualities, and that can offer richer insights into the various attitudes and experiences that may underlie it. For this we shall again look to the poets and novelists of the modernist age, a period marked by a widespread crisis of language and by a literature of difficulty that, both in structure and intent, has profound affinities with the language of schizophrenia.

PARALLELS WITH MODERNISM

It is widely acknowledged that the last decades of the nineteenth century saw a major shift in prevailing attitudes toward language. This crisis in the intellectual and literary worlds, like the literature it spawned, was a highly complex and multifaceted event, not easily summed up in a sentence or a phrase. It may, in fact, seem difficult to characterize it at all except in negative terms: namely, as a rejection of conventional forms and uses of language or as a turning to literary styles united only by a certain incomprehensibility.[39] As with the language of schizophrenia, however, several central underlying tendencies can be identified. Each of these has special prominence in one or another theory of literary modernism, and, as it turns out, each can provide a most illuminating analogy for the desocialization, autonomization, or impoverishment trends in schizophrenic language just discussed. (I will, however, present them in a different order, one more convenient for purposes of exposition.)

The first tendency is a new preoccupation with the uniqueness and particularity of unverbalized experience, and with the sense of ineffability this invariably evokes. The second is a move toward a kind of inner speech that is felt to be more authentic than conventional language. And the third is a new recognition of the independent nature of language, an acknowledgment of its existence as a system imbued with its own inherent mysteries and forms of productiveness—what I call the apotheosis of the word. Though each trend can occur in isolation, one also finds them combined (as, for instance, in the poetics of Rimbaud, Mallarmé, and André Breton). Still, each tendency does represent a potentially independent orientation toward language, and each merits separate consideration for the special light it can shed on the language of schizophrenia.

An investigation of these parallels should expose the inadequacy of certain popular notions regarding differences between creativity and madness—notably, the oft-expressed view that whereas "the poet is a master of language, the schizophrenic is a slave to it."[40] Such views generally presuppose a rather simplistic version of the act/affliction distinction, and one consequence of this is a failure to capture the complexity of either madness or art. For, in reality, more than a few modern poets and other writers *have* felt unable to master language, and some have even made this experience into a central theme of their work. Many such writers have believed that the poet must cede initiative to words, which would suggest that the true master of language is the one who knows precisely how to enslave himself to it. Investigating the complexities of these modernist (and postmodernist) phenomena should help to illuminate the no less complex motives and modes with which schizophrenics can approach language; also it should cure us of certain overly simple dichotomies, such as the assumption that the unusual speech of schizophrenics must necessarily be either empty nonsense or utterly saturated with meaning, or the tendency to see such people either as Machiavellian schemers or overwhelmed victims.

Impoverishment and Ineffability

I shall call modern the art which devotes its "little technical expertise"
. . . to present the fact that the unpresentable exists.
—Jean-François Lyotard
The Postmodern Condition

To some important critics, the principle turning point in the history of Western literature occurred in the last decades of the nineteenth century and the beginning of the twentieth; these were the years when, for many writers, language ceased to feel like a natural organ of expression and came instead to be experienced as a constraining force, a devitalizing or banalizing medium incapable of capturing the unique nuances and particularities, or the deepest truths, of either the internal or the external world. This loss of faith in words was, perhaps, inevitable, once the arts became imbued with what Baudelaire saw as the essence of "modernity"—fascination with "the transitory, the fugitive, the contingent" aspects of reality—and once writers began to be seduced by the self-contradictory ambition of Rimbaud: "to write of silences and of night, to note down the inexpressible."[41] By the early twentieth century these attitudes were widespread indeed: it was as if the very ineffability of an experience had come to be the true sign of its significance.[42]

A classic statement of this preoccupation with the indescribable is a work I considered in an earlier chapter: Hugo von Hofmannsthal's "Letter of Lord Chandos," whose central theme is the narrator's utter loss of faith in language. To Hofmannsthal's alter ego, Lord Chandos, words and concepts have come to seem like banal abstractions, utterly inadequate for capturing the heart-wrenching and unspeakable thereness, tangibility, and individuality that he now finds everywhere he looks, even in things as humble as a waterbug in a bucket or a wheelbarrow in a shed.[43] Similar themes emerge in Wittgenstein's famous, and famously complex, meditation on the impossibility of what he called a "private language," in which he argues that any conceivable language must refer to categories that are public in nature, tied in with shared and observable criteria; it follows that language, by its very nature, is incapable of referring to the private and unique sensations of a single individual.

Whereas Hofmannsthal concentrated on the unspeakable actuality and presence of external objects, Wittgenstein was concerned with the ineffable uniqueness of inner experiences, and thus with the question of the private versus public nature of language.[44] But more important is what the two writers share: an acute awareness of the abstract or categorical nature of language, and of the consequent impossibility of describing the individual objects or immanent moments of our experience. This concern has precursors in romanticism as well as in the tradition of mysticism, but only in the modernist period did it come to dominance—permeating the work of Rilke, Musil, T. S. Eliot, and many other writers, all of whom shared the malaise and frustration expressed in Eugène Ionesco's lament: "There are no words for the deepest experience. . . . Of course, not everything is unsayable in words, only the living truth."[45] A passage from Sartre's *Nausea* (1938) offers what is perhaps the most vivid and revealing portrayal of this modernist experience of ineffability and alienation.

In this famous climactic scene, the protagonist and narrator, Roquentin, is sitting in a park, staring fixedly at the root of a chestnut tree and feeling overwhelmed by the individuality and sheer actuality of what he sees before him. In this moment the categorical and functional concepts of language feel utterly irrelevant and even deceptive to him: all words—*root, tree, leaf*—seem to have "vanished and with them the significance of things, their methods of use, and the feeble points of reference which men have traced on their surface," he writes. As Roquentin sits, plunged in a kind of "horrible ecstasy," he struggles vainly to regain his normal sense of orientation in a meaningful and categorizable world by repeating words to himself, yet finds himself only sinking further into the infinite uniqueness of this object before his eyes:

> Knotty, inert, nameless, it fascinated me, filled my eyes, brought me back unceasingly to its own existence. In vain to repeat: "This is a root"—it didn't work any more. I saw clearly that you could not pass from its function as a root, as a breathing pump, *to that*, to this hard and compact

skin of a sea lion, to this oily, callous, headstrong look. The function explained nothing: it allowed you to understand generally that it was a root, but not *that one* at all. This root, with its colour, shape, its congealed movement, was . . . below all explanation.[46]

It is not uncommon for schizophrenics to experience a similar sense of the inadequacy of language. In *Autobiography of a Schizophrenic Girl*, in fact, we find an almost identical scene—a moment when Renee, caught up in her truth-taking stare and overwhelmed by the sheer presence and actuality of physical objects, tries to escape their hold by calling out their names: "I said, 'chair, jug, table, it is a chair.'" She, however, is no more successful than Roquentin: as she says, words feel "deprived of all meaning," like mere "envelope[s] emptied of content"; they seem to echo hollowly and are no longer capable of subduing the defiant and mocking presence of the objects with which they were once connected.[47] Another schizophrenic felt that words were objects bearing no real relationship to what they labeled, and he seems to have experienced something very like Roquentin's and Chandos's sense of the unspeakable actuality of the object world: "None of my words have any meaning, so what can I tell you?" he said. "There is a difference between thinking and expressing. I can't express my thoughts." "But what is a train?" he asked in his first therapy session; "It's a word. The word has nothing to do with a solid thing like a train."[48]

Many schizophrenic persons will also become preoccupied with the impossibility of describing experiences that are felt to be inner and private. The writer and actor Antonin Artaud, for example, a man diagnosed as schizophrenic and hospitalized for most of the last ten years of his life, felt anguished by his feeling that words couldn't capture the particularities of his inner feelings and sensations. He yearned desperately for the impossible goal of a private language: "If it is cold I can still say that it is cold, but there are also times when I am incapable of saying it: this is a fact, for there is in me something damaged from an emotional point of view, and if someone asked me why I could not say it, I would answer that *my inner feeling on this slight and neutral point did not correspond* to the three single words I would have to pronounce." "What I lack," he wrote, "is words that correspond to each minute of my state of mind."[49] It is hardly necessary to assume that such a person's feelings or perceptions are especially primitive or concretistic in nature (as Kurt Goldstein, Harry Stack Sullivan, and various other psychoanalysts have claimed),[50] or even that they are in any intrinsic way different from those of other people. The mere fact of being oriented toward private inner sensations or toward focusing on unique particulars is likely to make one aware of an inexpressible specificity that is actually present in all human experience, though this specificity, and the sense of aloneness it may imply, will be *noticed* only in those moments of detached scrutiny or introversion that are so familiar, and so compelling, to a person disengaged from participation in practical activity or interaction with fellow beings.[51] (In fact, focusing on experiences in this way may even *create* the sensations in question.)

Also, of course, there often enough *will* be something unusual about certain perceptions or modes of thought in schizophrenia (above and beyond the introversion itself); this too would draw attention toward experience itself, toward the kind of "inner" phenomena (for example, one's *mode* of experience) for which language tends to be inadequate. These several sources of ineffability are suggested by Patricia Ruocchio, a schizophrenic woman who describes the "agony in not being able to communicate one's mind": "My own inadequacy to use language to express what lies buried so deeply inside me, even when I am lucid, makes words a curse. . . . There are things that happen to me that I have never found words for." She speaks of wishing "to visualize the inner mind that has claimed me as its own" and of yearning to show "the totality of my mind" to someone else: "I want to infuse my mind into his, to *show* him what is happening in there, but I am blocked by the limitations of inadequate words, a brain that scrambles thoughts, and a bony structure that will not let me pass beyond its boundaries."[52]

Such preoccupation with inner sensations, as described by Wittgenstein and exemplified by Artaud, presupposes a self-conscious concern with individuality and inwardness that is hardly characteristic of earlier stages of either individual or cultural evolution. Close empirical investigation of the language of schizophrenic adults also fails to support the traditional primitivity, Dionysian, or deficit views: there is not in fact much evidence of the animism, emotionality, focus on bodily needs, or relative lack of reflective self-awareness that are characteristic of the young child; nor is there evidence of the prototypic organic patient's incapacity for abstraction, symbolic thought, or self-reflection. Indeed, empirical studies suggest quite an opposite picture: unlike that of aphasic patients, the speech of schizophrenics tends to be characterized by a dearth of references to issues crucial for adaptation in everyday life, such as work and community, by a predominance of "universal themes" (religion, science, politics, and so on), and by other preoccupations of a symbolic or coldly intellectual kind. Also characteristic of the content of schizophrenics' speech is a great number of reflexive or self-scrutinizing references to their own cognitive processes, often with expressions of inner confusion and doubt about their own senses and thoughts.[53]

Acute experiences of the inadequacy of language might elicit a variety of responses, and several of these seem to correspond to schizophrenic "impoverishment." One possible reaction is simple refusal, a (sometimes ostentatious) lapsing into silence in order to escape entirely the contaminating or diluting forms of speech or writing.[54] Robert, a patient I saw for some months in psychotherapy, had remained silent during a week of semi-catatonic torpor; as I mentioned in an earlier chapter, he explained this long period of muteness ("poverty of speech") as resulting from his sense of the unutterable complexity and profundity of existence: he had been unable to talk, he said, because there were just "so many echelons of reality . . . so many innuendos to take into account." Another possible response to the discrepancy between language and reality is to speak in an approximate or quasi-metaphoric way, continually using phrases such as "it seemed as though" or "it feels like"—locutions, common in schizophrenia, that are unlikely to leave most listeners with a very distinct sense of meaning.[55]

A third reaction is to abdicate any attempt to express meaning and to give oneself over entirely to the repetition of nonsense and cliché, a central element in Ionesco's play *The Bald Soprano* and other works of the absurdist tradition. Something close to this type of response may also occur in schizophrenics, in those cases where patients adopt, in what sometimes seems a faintly mocking way, an extremely formal or high-flown language, or where they mouth, in repetitive or even echolalic fashion, highly conventionalized or clichéd phrases, which may begin to take on the quality of meaningless sounds. The *ne plus ultra* of this in modern literature may well be the famous word-salad monologue delivered by Lucky toward the end of Act I of Beckett's *Waiting for Godot*—a simulacrum of schizophrenic speech so filled with vagueness, empty repetition, and stereotyped or obscure phrases that it achieves nearly total incoherence. Here is a brief extract:

> Given the existence as uttered forth in the public works of Puncher and Wattmann of a personal God quaquaquaqua with white beard quaquaquaqua outside time without extension who from the heights of divine apathia divine athambia divine aphasia loves us dearly with some exceptions for reasons unknown but time will tell . . . but not so fast and considering what is more that as a result of the labors left unfinished crowned by the Acacacacademy of Anthropopopometry of Essy-in-Possy of Testew and Cunard it is established beyond all doubt all other doubt than that which clings to the labors of men that as a result of the labors unfinished of Testew and Cunard it is established as hereinafter but not so fast for reasons unknown . . .[56]

It is unlikely, of course, that *all* instances of "poverty of speech" would be related to the experience or the fact of ineffability. A person may, after all, be silent or laconic for many reasons, willful and otherwise.[57] And so-called poverty of *content* of speech (which is a highly judgmental, hence potentially subjective, assessment, and one that can involve a variety of different styles of speech) can also result from several different underlying processes—including simple indifference to one's audience, the wish not to be understood too precisely, pretentiousness (motivating the use of unnecessarily fancy and abstract-sounding words), as well as an unfocused or vacillating cognitive style that can prevent topics from being carried through to closure. Still, the phenomenon of ineffability does seem a particularly central issue, as indicated by how frequently schizophrenics themselves complain of the inadequacy of language.

But the ineffable concreteness, uniqueness, or particularity of objects and sensations are not the only aspects of reality that can pose a challenge to language's capacity to represent or to express. A rather different source of ineffability also emerges in the same climactic scene of *Nausea*, and it may also be implicated in some forms of schizophrenic "impoverishment."

In his visit to the park, Roquentin's sense of unspeakable particularity alternates with an overwhelming experience of the utmost generality: his realization of the fact or the meaning of existence itself, which is something too general, in a sense too abstract, to be easily perceived or expressed. "Never, until these last few days," he says, "had I understood the meaning of 'existence.' I was like the others . . . I said, like them, 'The ocean *is* green; that white speck up there *is* a seagull,' but I didn't feel that it existed or that the seagull was an 'existing seagull'; usually existence hides itself. . . . And then all of a sudden, there it was, clear as day: existence had suddenly unveiled itself." The object of this vision—the sheer fact of Being itself—is in one sense about as abstract and general as anything can be: Being, after all, is not an object among objects or a fact among other facts; if it is difficult to describe in words, this is because it is so all-encompassing that any particular way of describing it is likely to mislead us about its real nature. The two major philosophers of the twentieth century, Wittgenstein and Heidegger, have written of this second kind of ineffability, arguing that some issues are of such great generality and foundational significance that they cannot be spoken about, at least not in anything like normal modes of speech. As they point out in their very different ways, such issues—which pertain to metaphysical or ontological questions concerning the ultimate nature of Being and the relationship between mind and world or language and world—are already embedded in or presupposed by our forms of experience and of speech; and this makes it extremely difficult to detach ourselves from these all-encompassing matters in order either to describe them or to call them into question.[58]

Many schizophrenics do seem to be highly preoccupied with experiences involving revelations of such cosmic or totalistic proportions—about the nature of existence in general or its fundamental relationship to the self. The experiential transformations they experience often have an all-encompassing quality, affecting not just this or that object but the look or feel of the entire experiential world. And, as schizophrenics disengage from the social and pragmatic world, any focused, practical concerns they may have had tend to be replaced by preoccupations of a highly abstract or universal nature. "Tell me what was on your mind," prodded one interviewer. "Well, a little bit of everything, I guess," responded the patient, "the present, the past, the future, everything I could think about."[59] One schizophrenic responded as follows to a Rorschach inkblot (Card #5): "The two ends look like the tail and rear end of something diving into something, diving into eternity, coming out of this world and going into nothing."[60] A quality of hypergenerality or apparent vagueness is present in the following passage by Antonin Artaud, which is an excellent example of the sort of statement that tends to be dismissed as an instance of pseudo-philosophizing and poverty of content: "Like life, like nature, thought goes from the inside out before going from the outside in. I begin to think in the void and from the void I move toward the plenum; and when I have reached the plenum I can fall back into the void. I go from the abstract to the concrete and not from the concrete toward the abstract."[61]

The preoccupation with general ontological or epistemological concerns, with issues pertaining to the nature of reality in general and to the general structure of self-world relations, is evident here; and it has resulted in speech unlikely to seem meaningful to the person not attuned to such issues. Statements like these seem to be attempts to express things whose intrinsic nature renders them close to ineffable, experiences that are so total as to pervade the whole universe, yet so subtle as to seem at times like nothing at all—experiences of such things as the being of Being or the unreality of Unreality, or, perhaps, of what it is like to feel oneself existing both inside one's own mind and outside in the objects of one's knowing.

As Jaspers has said, many schizophrenic patients "delightedly believe that they have grasped the profoundest of meanings; concepts such as timelessness, world, god and death become enormous revelations which when the state has subsided cannot be reproduced or described in any way—they were after all nothing but feelings."[62] It is understandable that such concerns might often reduce a person either to silence or to oblique and vague attempts at description—as when schizophrenics caught up in a truth-taking stare can say only that everything seems "different," "somehow wrong," "unreal," or perhaps *more* real" than usual. At least some of the statements that strike observers as woolly or empty philosophizing (poverty of *content* of speech) may thus be attempts—sometimes inept but sometimes not— to express concerns that are just too all-encompassing or too abstract to be stated in clear and specific terms, even by the most clear-minded of speakers.[63]

I would argue, in fact, that the famous obscurity of Heidegger's own highly abstract prose—which, it has been said, is "untranslatable, even into

German"—derives largely from the same source; for, in using phrases like "the world worlds" and "the nothing itself nothings," he was attempting to express the ontological without resorting to what he saw as the distorting vocabulary appropriate for describing identifiable objects *within* the world.[64] One might, in fact, compare the hostile or contemptuous responses to Heidegger of such empirically oriented analytic philosophers as A. J. Ayer and Rudolph Carnap, who claimed that most of Heidegger was devoid of cognitive significance, to the way many psychiatrists dismiss what they see as the poverty of content in some schizophrenic speech. In both cases we note a similar impatience, verging sometimes on revulsion and contempt, for an attitude of mind that turns away from the noonday world of social and practical reality toward the elusive one of ontological speculation. But anyone who has indulged in such musings, whether during adolescence or since, will know that anything said on such ultimate and totalistic topics can easily seem, even to the speaker, to waver between profundity and utter meaninglessness. Is this, perhaps, what is being alluded to in the following words, spoken by a schizophrenic patient who had complained of feeling dead, of the world seeming unreal, and of being unable to express his thoughts?: "One talks and it seems one says nothing and then one finds one has been talking about the whole of one's existence and one can't remember what one said."[65]

I have been describing the two sources of ineffability—the particularity-vision and that involving abstract or totalistic concerns—as if they were opposites. But, although in one sense opposites, they are actually very closely related, a point that is implicit in the chestnut tree passage in *Nausea* and that may be one source of the curious combination of hyperabstraction and apparent concreteness in schizophrenia. With the vanishing of familiar meanings and distinctions, one can easily become engrossed in the particularity of individual things or sensations; yet, precisely *because* of this vanishing, the sheer fact of the existence or the presence of these phenomena is what is likely to become most salient (all else being categorical in nature)—and this is the very quality they share with *all* objects.

This peculiar combination of hyperabstraction and apparent concreteness that can accompany a loss of pragmatic perception may in fact actually be described in a passage I quoted earlier (page 180) to illustrate so-called poverty of content of speech. This, at least, would be one plausible reading of what follows the passage's first elusive phrase, "Chirps in a box": when the patient says, "If you abstract yourself far enough from a given context you seem somehow to create a new kind of concretion," he may be alluding to the awareness of particulars that can follow the loss of pragmatic or categorical modes of awareness. And as he continues, he seems to be turning to reflexive concerns of a most general or hyperabstract nature: "It isn't something you have or see but yet somehow. It's being fascinated by the generative process of the mind. The thing is to be caught in it, yet abstract from it. Both be in it and out of it—revolving everything around me."[66]

Inner Speech

Put your trust in the inexhaustible character of the murmur.
—André Breton

Disillusionment with language need not, however, be as uncompromising or all-encompassing an experience as it was for Hofmannsthal and Ionesco and for the schizophrenics just considered. It need not be felt to apply to language in general but only to certain of its manifestations, which leaves open the possibility of discovering a language of a different and more authentic kind. The advent of literary modernism has sometimes been identified with the inhabiting of just such a language—an inner speech that is markedly similar to the desocialized schizophrenic language discussed earlier.

A second feature of the new literature emerging around the turn of the century was its reliance on juxtaposition rather than transition, on the technique of setting elements beside each other without explicit causal, logical, or narrative connectives. In *The Banquet Years*, a study of the origins of the twentieth-century avant-garde, the critic Roger Shattuck argues that this stems from an essential reflexivity, a focusing of awareness onto the inner processes of consciousness itself—where disparate sensations, thoughts, words, and feelings seem to be conjoined in the manner of collage or cinematic montage. To illustrate the "carefully detonated" art that results from this reflexive turn, Shattuck offers "Lundi Rue Christine," a poem by Guillaume Apollinaire, the first impresario of the twentieth-century French avant-garde:

> *Three lit gas jets*
> *The proprietor has lung trouble*
> *When you've finished we'll have a game of*
>   *backgammon*
> *A conductor who has a sore throat*
> *When you come to Tunis I'll have you smoke*
>   *some kiff*
> *It seems to rhyme.*[67]

It is important to realize that the literary artists associated with this second line of modernist aesthetics did not assume that the inner or unconscious experiences they wished to evoke were, in any essential sense, *non-verbal in nature*. Rimbaud was the first great master of this poetics of fragmentation, alogicality, and innerness; and, far from insisting on the essential ineffability of experience, he sometimes spoke of exploring truer and more vibrant levels of existence precisely through what he called an "alchemy of the word."[68] Similarly, in his surrealist manifesto of 1924, André Breton rejected the view that thought is somehow too subtle or too rapid to be captured in language. The technique of automatic writing that he advocated would be (or, at least, would give the *impression* of being) "a monologue spoken as rapidly as possible, on which the subject's critical spirit brings no judgement to bear, which is subsequently unhampered by reticence, and which is, as exactly as possible, *spoken thought*"; it would thereby provide "a true photograph of thought."[69] The crucial requirement would not be a wariness toward the inevitably distorting or contaminating powers of words, as it would be for Ionesco and for Sartre, but a freeing of words from the constraints of rationality and public communication. For language—at least *inner* language—could be the medium of the most authentic mode of human consciousness; and so Breton called on his readers to have faith in "the inexhaustible character of the murmur."[70]

The linguistic characteristics of this inner murmuring are presented in *Thought and Language* (1934), a classic study by the Russian psychologist Lev Vygotsky, who had close ties with the literary avant-garde of his day. Vygotsky asserts that the structure or skeleton of normal adult thought is provided by a kind of "inner speech." As he explains, the form of this speech derives from its function, its role as a medium of expression rather than communication, a way of symbolizing thoughts for oneself. It follows that all that is obvious to the speaker can be omitted. And so, in inner speech, language becomes abbreviated or telegraphic: syntax is simplified, explicit causal and logical connections are omitted, and there is an absence of framing devices such as those normally used to distinguish metaphorical from literal meanings of verbal images. Also, the topic is presupposed rather than asserted directly; and few explicit references are made to speaker or addressee, or to temporal and spatial contexts, for all of these can simply be taken for granted.[71]

The features of inner speech that Vygotsky describes are also found in much of the literature of the twentieth-century avante-garde and are central, too, in the desocialized speech so characteristic of schizophrenia. Consider, for example, the following two illustrations: a poem by the proto-surrealist writer Blaise Cendrars and a sample of spontaneous speech from an unnamed schizophrenic (which I have reproduced in versified form):

> *It's raining electric lightbulbs*
> *Montrouge Gare de l'Est subway North-South*
> *river boats world*

Everything is halo
Profundity
In the Rue de Buci they're hawking l'Intransigeant
 and Paris-Sports
The airdrome of the sky is on fire, a painting
 by Cimabue.

Regret. Where is Rita. Rio Rita.
Pas regrette. Regrette. No Rita.
The infanta. Same as Rita.
L'Infanta and Rita, the same.
Velasquez. Line is.
You said us, I believe.
No. Why is. Gold leaf.
English maple. In a breeze.
Have another cookie. The children get two.
The children get into.
Difficultés des vieux.
Difficultés des jeunes.
Day and noo-it. Noo-it and day.
Compact powder. Caron, Contraction . . .
I thought New York too small to hold.
One expands from tree to tree
Dryads. Seven Druids.
Celts. The Celts of 5th Avenue.
Wall Street, the street of kings.
C Street. The stand is the sea.
Eva. That is Siva. S-E-A.[72]

   It would obviously be absurd to understand Cendrar's style (the first of
the above quotations) as resulting from the kind of incapacity that is postulated by experimental psychologists who study schizophrenic language—
from something like a "pragmatic deficit" or a failure of the "unconscious
planning mechanism" that would prevent the poet from following the rules
of normal conversation or writing, or from a certain egocentricity or inability to create "second-order representations" of the listener's point of view
(see page 182). We all know, after all, that poets, at least modern poets,
are aiming for something other than the efficient communication of clear-
cut and conventional meanings; indeed, since the late nineteenth century,
obscurity has come to be not just a by-product but a value in itself, almost
a required mark of the seriousness and aesthetic worth of a poetic effort.
The sources for these literary developments are manifold—including, in
addition to the simple desire for self-exploration, the wishes to mystify, to

intimidate, to antagonize, and to impress; what has occurred, in any case, is a turning away from communal themes and modes of expression and toward the concerns and processes of the inner life, which have come to seem, at least in many circles, more authentic, more powerful, and more real. ("The writer expresses. He does not communicate. The plain reader be damned," declared one writer in a manifesto published in the avant-garde review *transition*.)[73]

Given the variability of schizophrenic obscurity, which often disappears abruptly when patients really want to make themselves understood, it seems plausible that the desocialization of schizophrenics' speech might have some of the same sources and motives. Many such patients do seem inclined to report on whatever crosses their minds, in the manner of the disjointed automatic monologues of the surrealists or of poets like Rimbaud, who was far more interested in observing the "flowering" of his own thought than in communing with any audience.[74] Consider, for example, the following couplet, which was written by a schizophrenic who had been asked to complete the sentence, "I get warm when I run because . . .": "Quickness, blood, heart of deer, length, / Driven power, motorized cylinder, strength."[75]

These verbal fragments are not irrelevant to the incomplete stimulus sentence (the associations are not particularly loose, we might say); yet they lack the explicit logical connectives, and the editing out of excess alternates, that would be necessary to communicate rather than simply to express a flow of inner associations. Empirical research indicates that this is generally the case: when schizophrenics are engaged in a particular task, such as describing a picture, their discourse shows no particular evidence of being interrupted by thematically inappropriate intrusions.[76] When speaking freely, however, they often sound disjointed or thematically incoherent,[77] as if (one might argue) they were letting their words follow the drift of their inner thoughts and associations, without sticking to a single focus *or* being concerned about the needs of the listener.

It is difficult to say whether the obscurity common in much schizophrenic discourse is a simple by-product of an introverted orientation or whether, as so often in modernism,[78] obscurity has become a goal in itself—perhaps serving as a method of intimidation or of severing the social bond. But such obscurity does seem, at least in many instances, to be less a matter of some fundamental cognitive or linguistic dysfunction than of a shift of attitude,[79] a turning of attention inward, accompanied by loss of interest in, or refusal of, the conventions of social discourse.

It would be a mistake to assume that rejecting the social domain necessarily means immersing onseself in a realm of irrationality, instinct, or the passions—as if the only alternative to conventional, secondary-process thought and language were a regression to the primary process. Inner speech, or the language that approximates its condition, need not involve the exuberant cacophonies of Apollinaire and Cendrars, let alone the impassioned ecstasies of Rimbaud, with his radical juxtapositions of fragmentary and incompatible desires. Any such lingering romantic belief in a necessary linkage between inwardness and the Dionysian is certainly refuted in the fiction of Samuel Beckett. In reading Beckett, we find ourselves inside a head, listening to a kind of inner speech, but the thoughts we encounter could hardly be more repetitive or devitalized. In this passage from "Imagination Dead Imagine," a short prose piece, the inner voice is an obsessional one, preoccupied with the death of the very faculty—imagination—that inwardness was supposed to potentiate, at least according to many in the romantic tradition:

> No trace anywhere of life, you say, pah, no difficulty there, imagination not dead yet, yes, dead, good, imagination dead imagine. Islands, waters, azure, verdure, one glimpse and vanished, endlessly, omit. Till all white in the whiteness the rotunda. No way in, go in, measure. Diameter three feet, three feet from ground to summit of the vault. Two diameters at right angles AB CD divide the white ground into two semicircles ACB BDA. Lying on the ground two white bodies, each in its semicircle.[80]

A passage similar in its self-absorbed obliviousness, its hesitating obsessionality, its mood of isolation, and its emphasis on loss was spoken by the patient who was quoted in versified form two pages earlier:

> How many seconds on a thousand islands is another question I was asked. Equal the two. I think I am playing regret. There was a walk, a brick walk. I don't know where it is gone. Well, there was a step of white marble and a magenta walk and that is all. It led to no palace. Well, that is regret. Danger field. . . . Chitchat. You can chitchat, you think. All right, whenever you chitchat, you think. All right, you have shown me. Contraction. . . .[81]

Recent empirical studies of speech protocols suggest that schizophrenics do tend to intermingle associations into their speech without clearly indicating their relevance; their speech does not, however, show the prominence of sexual and aggressive themes, or the disordered logic, that psychoanalytic theory would lead one to expect. (It is also noteworthy that the patients, when interviewed, are generally able to explain the relevance of their associations quite satisfactorily.)[82] This suggests that the desocialization of schizophrenic speech is not—at least not primarily—the consequence of a move backward to childhood or downward toward the instincts and emotions. Like modernism, it seems to involve a turning away from the human community, and a focus instead on expressing the inner life.

The Apotheosis of the Word

I have a disease, I see language.   —Roland Barthes

The search for a more authentic language, one closer to the spontaneous, inner life of the mind, is not the only alternative to the despair that was felt by writers like Hofmannsthal and Ionesco. In addition to a glorifying of inner speech, modernism contains another positive attitude toward language, one that glorifies the being of language itself rather than its presumed connection to something inward, personal, or primal. This vision might be called the apotheosis of the word. It has inspired literary developments that closely resemble the autonomization of language found in schizophrenia.

In *Writing Degree Zero* (parts of which appeared as early as 1947), the critic Roland Barthes articulated a view that was to become orthodox in the poststructuralist movement: the notion that modern literature originates when the Word sheds its transparency and begins to shine forth as an independent object of attention and source of meaning. He contrasts this type of literature with the "Classical language" of earlier periods, when the Word was "guided in advance by the general intention of a socialized discourse."[83] In these periods literary language had only a secondary status, as a way of coding, communicating, and beautifying meanings that were assumed to have a prior existence and to guide the writer's subsequent choice of words. The radical transformation implicit in modernism was sounded in the 1880s by Mallarmé, in his call for a poetry whose impetus would come not from thoughts, emotions, or authorial intentions but from the inner resources of language itself:

> The work of art in its complete purity implies the disappearance of the poet's oratorical presence. The poet leaves the initiative to the words, to the clash of their mobilized diversities. The words ignite through mutual reflexes like a flash of fire over jewels. Such reflexes replace that respiration [of the poet] perceptible in the old lyrical aspiration or the enthusiastic personal direction of the sentence.[84]

Though he was not the first to write of thought's determination by language (the German writers Novalis and Heinrich von Kleist had both articulated similar positions around 1800),[85] in his poetry and theorizing Mallarmé gave this view its most influential expression. And ever since, this language-centered vision has been a major source of literary innovation, achieving what is perhaps its purest expression in twentieth-century writers like Gertrude Stein, the Russian futurists, and the Parisian *Tel Quel* group, as well as in members of the American "language poetry" movement of the last decade or two (the latter explicitly reject both the trace of individual ownership characteristic of many variants of inner speech literature and what they have called the "illusory" concept of the incommunicable, the core of the ineffability aesthetic).[86]

This Mallarméan withdrawal, this ceding of initiative to words, effects a profound transformation in one's experience of language. The very possibility (and the worth) of referring to stable meanings or to realities external to language comes into question; and, at the same time, two aspects of the linguistic medium come into prominence, aspects usually ignored in everyday language as well as in more traditional literature: the sensory presence of a signifying vehicle (phonological in speech, graphological in writing) and the elusive multivalence of meaning.

Mallarmé advocated a poetry that would approach the condition of music, in which pure sound would nearly eclipse all reference; and he drew attention to the graphic appearance of a poem—not only to the positive markings of the letters but even to the negative spaces between them, which he compared to a "luminescent alphabet of stars" written across the "dim field" of the heavens. He also called for an art of ephemerality, a poetry of infinite ambiguity and suggestiveness that would depict "not the thing but the effect it produces."[87] A physical object was not to be described in terms of its standard function or obvious physical features but by means of all the associations—metaphoric, acoustic, and otherwise—that might be evoked by the object itself or even by the sound of its name. The resulting descriptions would be so indirect and evanescent, would lead down so many alternative paths of association, that the object would be virtually unrecognizable, dissolving into its own evocations.

It is the poststructuralist philosopher Jacques Derrida who has stated this language-centered position most explicitly and taken it to its furthest limits, universalizing what was essentially a vision of the poetic function of language into a much more dogmatic conception of language in general.[88] Derrida (who might be called a kind of "warmed-over Mallarmé" and who can be viewed as a theorist of both modernism and postmodernism)[89] is constantly calling our attention to the actual look of written letters on a ground—saying, for example, that what should be remarked about some words on a blackboard "will always be a certain way of writing in white."[90] Also, he frequently focuses on the acoustic qualities of words, hearing in them not only puns of all kinds (for example, the fact that, in French, *Hegel* sounds virtually the same as *l'aigle*, or "eagle") but also the half-absent/half-present vestiges—he calls them "traces"—of meanings that the signifier might have had in other contexts. These latter meanings are themselves equally elusive, leading always toward still other meanings in a (glossomanic) series whose endpoint recedes as steadily as the horizon. Derrida maintains that the opacity and multivalence of the Mallarméan poetic word are actually the true condition of all words, a view that undermines traditional conceptions of language as either specifying particular referents or expressing an author's intent.

This linguistic vision is well illustrated by Derrida's own reading of Plato's *Phaedrus*, a work that happens to contain one of the earliest philosophical discussions of speech and writing. In this Platonic dialogue, the figure of Socrates describes writing with the Greek term *pharmakon*, which means both "remedy" and "poison." (Socrates was suggesting that writing is a gift to mankind that was intended to be a remedy—for failure of memory—but that turned out to have certain contaminating and corrupting effects.) Despite the absence of any textual evidence that certain additional meanings were part of what Plato intended the dialogue to say, Derrida brings in these other notions, which he hears as traces within the similar-sounding *pharmakon*—among them *pharmakeus*, which means "magician" or "prisoner," and *pharmakos*, which means "scapegoat"; and he offers a reading that assigns these meanings a central importance. The "intentions of an author who goes by the name of Plato" are not his concern, Derrida explains; what interests him are the infinitely ramifying associations occasioned by "the play of language"—and these links "go on working of themselves," regardless of the author's intent or awareness. "Like any text, the text of 'Plato' couldn't not be involved, at least in a virtual, dynamic, lateral manner, with all the words that composed the system of the Greek language," he writes in justification of his language-centered approach. "Certain forces of association unite . . . the words 'actually present' in a discourse with all the other words in the lexical system, whether or not they appear as 'words.' . . . They communicate with the totality of the lexicon through their syntactic play and at least through the subunits that compose what we call a word."[91]

Derrida's approach to a philosophical text is thus very similar to Mallarmé's pronouncements on poetry. Both exemplify Roland Barthes's description of modern literature as dominated not by the intention of the speaker but by a monolithic Word (for example, *pharmakon*), a Word that "shines with an infinite freedom and prepares to radiate towards innumerable uncertain and possible connections . . . plung[ing] into a totality of meanings, reflexes and recollections."[92] We can see some of the consequences of this vision of language in a passage where Derrida describes speaking as an anguished yet exhilarating experience of losing control—the speaker passively watching as "all possible meanings push each other" within "the necessarily restricted passageway of speech," thus "preventing each other's emergence," yet all the while "calling upon each other, provoking each other too, unforeseeably and as if despite oneself, in a kind of autonomous overassemblage of meanings, a power of pure equivocality that makes the creativity of the classical God appear all too poor."[93]

The parallels between this hyperbolic Mallarméan vision and the autonomization of language in schizophrenia are fairly obvious. Schizophrenic people also pay inordinate attention to the graphic appearance or sound of words ("Looks like clay. Sounds like gray"), and they too are highly sensitive to puns ("demise"/"dim eyes"). They are also inclined to have a heightened awareness of ambiguities; to feel overwhelmed and confused by the multiplicity of potential meanings in language ("each bit I read starts me thinking in ten different directions at once"); and to cede responsibility to words— allowing their discourse to be led by traces within words (schizophrenic glossomania) and sometimes even feeling that the sentences emanating from their mouths or pens don't really belong to them at all (various passivization experiences). (One such patient, in fact, described what may seem a classic Derridean obsession: he said he felt "compelled to give things a second meaning, *especially if they were spoken by other people.*")[94] Such individuals experience an "autonomous overassemblage of meanings," to use Derrida's term. And one can understand how this could lead to two very different, but nevertheless related disturbances in speech production that Eugen Bleuler saw as being "peculiar to schizophrenia": a "pathologically increased flow of ideas, and the particularly characteristic 'blocking' "[95]—the latter occurring because (in Derrida's words) the presence of "all possible meanings" within "the necessarily restricted passageway of speech" can prevent any of them from emerging. Antonin Artaud describes this very explicitly when he speaks of a

> contraction that shuts off my thought from within, [that] makes it rigid as in a spasm; the thought, the expression stops because the flow is too violent, because the brain wants to say too many things which it thinks of all at once, ten thoughts instead of one rush toward the exit, the brain sees the whole thought at once with all its circumstances, and it also sees all the points of view it could take.[96]

Derrida is of interest not only for his vision of language but also because of the existential stance or attitude that seems to underlie this vision—a stance that is most clearly visible in the master metaphor he uses to promote his own vision of autonomization: his special notion of writing.

Most previous theories of language, Derrida points out, have held that the essence of language lies in speech, and they have relegated the written word to a secondary status, merely an encoding of the more fundamental, face-to-face acts that occur in oral communication. Derrida himself, however, prefers a conception of language that would put writing at the center; for this brings out the two features of language that he considers so important: the independence and the ambiguity of the signifying medium. After all, written marks exist apart from their author or their reader in a most literal way: at a distance and in a physical space distinct from any intention to signify. And, instead of dying out along with an accompanying inner experience, written marks obviously persist in time and space, and can be transported far away from the locus of the original signifying act. Also, writing, in contrast with speech, is less likely to be directed toward a specific individual in a specific time and place. For these reasons, Derrida says, written language makes us aware of both the materiality of the signifying medium and its potential for ambiguity, its nonidentity with an original intention-to-signify. He argues, however, that these aspects of written language are, on reflection, the essential features of *any* usage of language, *including* speech, since even oral communication uses conventional and arbitrary signifiers. To capture this essential truth about language, Derrida therefore postulates a more inclusive notion of writing, one no longer *opposed* to speech since it *includes* speech as one of its (somewhat less perspicuous) subtypes; and this he calls "arche-writing."

Taken on one level, Derrida's conception of language as arche-writing is hard to fault. How, after all, could one deny that linguistic communication always *does* employ differential distinctions based on conventions and carried by a sensory medium, or that any given string of signifiers can be shown to contain potential ambiguities, traces pointing toward more than one potential meaning? Yet we must recognize that these near-truisms have, in a sense, a purely theoretical significance: they refer to the abstract system of language, to what Saussure called *langue* rather than to linguistic communication as normally experienced (*parole*).[97] The usual nature of linguistic understanding, at least as it is consciously lived by human beings most of the time (and Derrida presents no evidence that the experience of *parole* is any different on some hypothetical unconscious level), is, in fact, very different from what Derrida describes. Generally, meaning is communicated fairly effectively, and we do not find ourselves staggered, paralyzed, or thrilled by the materiality or the infinite ambiguity of the linguistic medium. Indeed, "the wonderful thing about language," as the phenomenologist Maurice Merleau-Ponty points out, "is that it promotes its own oblivion"; and this is as true in reading or writing as it is in hearing or speaking: "my eyes follow the lines on the paper, and from the moment I am caught up in their meaning, I lose sight of them. The paper, the letters on it, my eyes and body are there only as the minimum setting of some invisible operation. Expression fades out before what is expressed, and this is why its mediating role may pass unnoticed."[98]

My primary concern here, however, is not with the (rather dubious) validity of Derrida's vision as a general philosophy of language but with the kind of relationship with language that this vision tends to foster. For, to insist on conceiving language on the analogy of "writing" (as Derrida uses the term) certainly does sanction a particular attitude toward language; and this attitude is the opposite of the one Merleau-Ponty describes: it involves maximum disengagement from the lived intention to signify, be this one's own (if speaking or writing) or what might have been ascribed to the other (in listening or reading). This Derridean vision of arche-writing encourages one to react to any linguistic message, indeed to each part of it, as one would to a scrap of paper found on the street—as something that could be authored by and addressed to anyone or no one, and referring to anything under the sun or to nothing at all. Thus one treats the signifiers as if they were alien and mysterious objects, noting first the opaque particularities of their physical presence (as if one were not at first sure they were signifiers at all), then considering all possible meanings each part of the message might possibly have. Such an attitude is obviously depersonalized, divorced from any feeling of shared social context, and devoid of any sense of, or any seeking after, empathic union with a human interlocutor.

Various aspects of what I have called schizophrenic autonomization are more consistent with this kind of disengagement or alienation than with the regressive processes or cognitive defects so often postulated. The primitivity view assumes, for example, that patients who show the tendency to focus on the sensory qualities of words have regressed to a stage prior to a realization of the arbitrariness of the signifier, to a time when the word is felt to be an intrinsic property of its object rather than to have a purely conventional connection with it.[99] But the schizophrenic's focus on the word's sound or graphic appearance often involves, in reality, something closer to a Derridean attitude. This was expressed by one schizophrenic patient whom I saw in psychotherapy, a young man who was particularly preoccupied with words and language, and who said it was strange that "words have their own textures, which may not be the same as the texture of the things they represent." Renee, the author of *Autobiography of a Schizophrenic Girl*, describes a similar linguistic alienation: where each word "echoed hollowly, deprived of all meaning," and seemed to be only "an envelope emptied of content," "divorced" from its object.[100] Such descriptions suggest not an inability to distinguish the word from the object it represents, which various psychoanalysts and other developmental theorists have postulated,[101] but something more like a profound distanciation—an experiential attitude that would sever the word from any intention-to-signify.

Even something like focusing on the meaning of the syllable *men* in the word *contentment* (an example discussed earlier), which has been interpreted as indicating a primitive fusion between symbol and meaning,[102] need not be understood in these terms. To separate a word into syllables in this way is certainly abnormal; but, once this fissioning had taken place, the signifier *men* was then interpreted in perfect accord with the standard lexicon, *not* according to onomatopoetic principles (and only the latter would really suggest a primitive fusion of signifier with signified). Nor is there any evidence that, in responding to *men*, this schizophrenic patient was any less conscious of the arbitrary nature of signifiers than the person who responds to *contentment* as a whole would be. What *is* undeniable is the presence of a fragmenting kind of awareness, a tendency to respond to phenomena, in this case syllables, in isolation from their normal contexts.

That there is a connection between this sort of fragmenting awareness and an attitude of disengagement is made particularly apparent in many passages in which Derrida insists on the illegitimacy of restricting the meaning of any part of a signifying chain—of a sentence, phrase, word, or even syllable—to the particular meaning that may seem most obvious or appropriate in its actual linguistic setting. Since it is always *possible* to bring out other potential meanings by inscribing or grafting the signifying element onto other chains of signifiers, it follows, Derrida argues, that "no context can enclose it"—and that we ought to open ourselves to all the other meanings this element could have.[103] What Derrida is recommending here is a peculiar mode of linguistic consciousness—first narrowing, as it focuses in on isolated parts, then expanding as it incites an unchecked proliferation from the "traces" that seem to be discovered in each part (thereby precipitating us into a kind of cognitive slippage). Underlying these responses to language is the adoption of a peculiarly hypothetical and disengaged stance: rather than directing our awareness toward what a speaker might *actually* have intended to convey, Derrida would have our awareness drift toward the things that *could* have been meant by certain isolated words or phrases *if* the context were different.

Similar processes seem to be involved in the schizophrenic's tendency to be acutely conscious of alternative meanings of words, meanings that are normally ignored due to their contextual irrelevance.[104] On word association tests, such individuals, as compared to normal people, show less influence from the prior semantic context (in associating to the ambiguous word *pen*, for example, they might well say *farm* rather than *ink* even though the stimulus word has been preceded by references to desks and writing).[105] And in everyday life they often perceive ambiguities and alternative meanings that would normally go unnoticed. Out on a walk together, one schizophrenic patient and a colleague of mine passed a Pedestrian Crossing sign that read "Ped Xing"; turning to his therapist, the patient said, in a voice laden with irony, "Now we are entering the Chinese village." Noticing this kind of potential meaning in the sign suggests a particularly fluid and speculative mode of perception, and this would seem to require a certain disengagement from the conventional context of practical reality (in this case, the traffic and streets).

Derrida's own propensity for detachment is perhaps most evident in an essay called "Signature Event Context," where he puts special emphasis on one particular way in which signs can escape a given context and engender an infinity of new ones—this by virtue of being "*cited*, put between quotation marks."[106] (As he notes, even a seemingly meaningless string—"green is or," for instance—might be cited as an example of agrammaticality, thereby gaining a certain significance.) This emphasis on the possibility of citing a signifier, or perceiving it as already being a citation, goes beyond a simple disjoining from an original setting; it means putting the signifier in a particular type of alternative context, one in which language is mentioned rather than used, where it is seen *as* a signifying medium rather than being inhabited, and rendered transparent, in the act of attending to some extra-linguistic referent. This particular type of meta-move resembles an aspect of schizophrenic language use that traditional theories rarely address: the tendency of some schizophrenics to mouth banal or pompous phrases, or to speak with an exaggerated formality—perhaps as a way of calling attention, often in an ambiguously ironic way, to phrases or sentences that, at the same time, they seem to be disowning as hopelessly clichéd or predictable. At times one almost has the sense that such patients, like certain deconstruc-tionists, are experiencing words, both their own and those of others, as if they were perpetually surrounded by quotation marks.[107]

INTENTION AND MEANING IN SCHIZOPHRENIC SPEECH

Two general issues that have been touched upon repeatedly in this investiga-tion of language and schizophrenia need to be addressed more explicitly: the closely interconnected questions of the degree of intentionality and the degree (or kind) of meaningfulness present in schizophrenic speech. Are we to understand these linguistic anomalies as caused or willed, as conse-quences of breakdowns of the cognitive or linguistic apparatus or activities meant to achieve some purpose? And do these peculiarities suggest a relative absence of meaning or, perhaps, attempts to convey meaning in some special way or of some special type?[108]

Any extreme claim about the nonintentional nature of schizophrenic lan-guage deviances runs up against the important fact that this supposed defect or deficit is highly variable, and variable in a most selective way. The patient mentioned earlier who had a singular interpretation of the word *content-ment* tended, for example, to ignore conventional contextual meaning in very specific circumstances, primarily with words whose highly personal tone may have been felt as threatening—words such as *contentment, happy, lonely,* or *grief.* For another patient, described by the psychiatrist Maria Lorenz, such shifts of focus also seemed to serve a purpose, in this case as part of a determined strategy to avoid dialogic meaning or shared reference;

interestingly enough, the strategy was once used with regard to the word *refer* itself:

> INTERVIEWER: What does it mean . . . Don't cry over spilt milk?
> PATIENT: I did today.
> INTERVIEWER: What happened today?
> PATIENT: Today happened today.
> INTERVIEWER: To what aim do you refer?
> PATIENT: I do not refer; fur is . . . fur is a cover for the animal kingdom.[109]

As Dr. Lorenz points out, this patient obviously understands the concept "refer"; indeed, her shift to a punning sound association—which in this instance seems to be part of a general retreat from shared reference—is in the service of a denial or refusal of just this meaning. It may well be that the ease of such shifting reflects some anomaly or deficiency of cognitive functioning (a deficit of selective attention, perhaps), but we must also acknowledge how very selective this deficit seems to be—given that it is elicited, or perhaps deployed, only in certain specific situations.[110]

The willful or intentional element in schizophrenic language is also suggested by the content of some of the deviances, for these often seem to involve more than mere errors or slips. To shift from *demise* to *dim eyes* in writing about one's father's death is not to make a merely random sound association but to suggest something thematically sensible and rich—and this, according to some of the linguists who have studied the matter, is very often the case with schizophrenic glossomania. Unlike aphasics, many such patients demonstrate a "verbal keenness," even a "magnificent control" over their ability to match meanings to words; also, unlike aphasics, they are often aware of their deviances, sometimes being able to give convincing and comprehensible justifications for why they spoke as they did.[111] In a letter written by the patient who referred to his father's dim eyes, for example, the young man (Philip) uses a neologism in talking about a woman he'd been seeing, which he then comments on: "My *imego* would like to think it's because such purity and innocence offends me. . . . But somehow I suspect that despite all my rational ideas as to the equality of woman and my desire for a liberated mate, she, medieval woman, is what my *libego* wants (the word has great psychological hedging potential)."[112] It is possible that some disturbance or abnormality of information processing may have allowed peripheral associations to come more readily to this man's mind, but if so he has certainly exploited this condition in meaningful ways.

This is not to say, of course, that *all* anomalies of schizophrenic speech are meaningful and worthy of extensive semantic interpretation. Schizophrenic language is heterogeneous above all else; and, whereas an instance of inner speech may well express certain of the speaker's experiences, an instance of, say, the apotheosis of the word may involve random sound association with no further semantic significance. It is also the case that a speaker may be willfully obscure even when no deep meaning is being hidden in the words.

One critic of modern literature and art sees a progressive development over the last century and a half: from a period when art simply found itself *becoming* mysterious because it had begun to treat mysteries, through a period when art deliberately *chose* to be mysterious in order to protect its mysteries from comprehension by the many, and leading finally to a period when art actually strives for mysteriousness for its own sake—because its ability to attract attention has come to depend so heavily on this quality.[113] ("There is a certain glory in not being understood," Baudelaire once said.)[114] The enigmas of some schizophrenics may be equally blank and equally deliberate. Thus one schizophrenic (Lawrence) explained to his therapist that he would go into his "schizy" way of talking—speaking in a highly abstract way and employing exceedingly complicated words that might or might not be used meaningfully—when he was either upset or angry with someone. Baffling others with language they could not understand was his way of intimidating them and proving to himself that he had not lost his intelligence. As R. D. Laing has suggested, a large part of schizophrenic speech may be "simply nonsense, red-herring speech, prolonged filibustering to throw dangerous people off the scent, to create boredom and futility in others." "We schizophrenics say and do a lot of stuff that is unimportant," explained one of his patients, "and then we mix important things in with all this to see if the doctor cares enough to see them and feel them."[115]

Laing's point about the willfulness of schizophrenic obscurity is well taken, though we should once again be wary of overgeneralization. One might also speak confusingly because of a simple indifference, a total lack of concern for the social environment or one's impact on it (as in the case of a patient who blithely used "self-invented" words—*wuttas* to mean "doves," for example—simply because he couldn't immediately remember the correct word).[116] Or there might be certain internal motives or factors, such as a tendency to perceive the world in a multifaceted or ironic fashion, a desire to express preoccupations or experiences that are inherently ineffable, or a need to avoid too direct a confrontation with the reality of upsetting themes.

It would be just as mistaken to overgeneralize about the question of intentionality as about the issue of meaning—to assume, for instance, that the peculiarities of schizophrenic speech are entirely intentional and under conscious control, or else that they are always or completely a matter of what one psychologist (somewhat with tongue in cheek) called "the art of being schizophrenic."[117] At times the obscurity may be largely intentional, but in other cases, organic deficits, fatigue, anxiety, or hyperarousal might play a major role (perhaps by leading to dysfunctions of automatic attentional processes; hyperarousal, for example, has been shown to lead to a loss of a sense of the *meaning* of speech).[118] No less significant is the fact that most single instances of deviant speech probably involve some complex combination of both kinds of factors, a combination not easy to define or describe. The orientation to the linguistic medium of a Mallarmé or a Derrida illustrates the point: while a certain passivity may be inherent in desisting from the attempt to meld language to one's will, there is also something inherently active about the stance of scrutinizing objectification that replaces such attempts (even though *this* stance may be experienced as a kind of compulsion). Moreover, there may be times when the paradoxical state of desisting from active control over speech just seems to happen, to come over one like a mood or a dream, and other times when it might be quite purposeful (indeed, one might well have to exercise a kind of self-control to achieve a state of will-lessness, of giving oneself over to the flow of language). I see no reason to assume that the situation in schizophrenia is any less complicated or variable. That the patient's own experience of linguistic abnormalities can shift between the passively determined and the active or deliberate is suggested by one patient who would say of his speaking that "someone is controlling me," that "it goes out all by itself," or that "I am being forced to talk," yet who would speak his special "languages" on request and who once complained that he could not *practice* these languages for fear that those witnessing him would think him mad.[119]

I have considered three different styles of schizophrenic language in this chapter, each with its analogues in modernist and postmodernist literature and each involving a distinct attitude toward words. Each one of the orientations seems to contain an intrinsic logic that, if taken to its extreme, would exclude the possibility of any of the others; yet it would be misleading to overemphasize this heterogeneity. Rimbaud is one modern writer who can be claimed as a forerunner of all of the major modernist orientations, and a passage like Lucky's monologue in *Waiting for Godot* can easily be seen as manifesting all three. Many schizophrenics are no less varied, sometimes shifting among all three types of deviant speech even within a single discourse or speech. What, then, we may ask, do the three modes have in common? The only possible answer, it seems to me, is a tendency to reject or ignore the social imperatives and realistic concerns so prominent both in everyday language and in earlier periods of literature and, going along with this, a shift toward more inner concerns. As with modernism, so in the case of schizophrenia, we can speak of a "discovery and colonisation of inwardness," of "a little cosmos of inwardness salvaged from the devaluation of the world."[120]

This is most obvious in the case of inner speech, a form of language that ignores other human beings in preference for expressing private concerns.

Another mode, the preoccupation with the ineffable, entails a focus on idiosyncratic or hyperabstract realities—which is to say, on phenomena too unique or all-encompassing to be easily stated or to be of immediate interest to a listener who takes social conventions or external reality for granted. At first the impersonality of the third mode, the apotheosis of the word, may seem to set it apart from these other two, but not, I think, in a way that makes it any the less involutional and asocial. After all, in the apotheosis of the word, it is not only the poet who disappears but also external reality and the human other. The old ideal of a relationship with the world or with others that is mediated *by* words is replaced by an isolating relationship with language alone—and with a language that, in its emphatic self-sufficiency, has itself come to stand as an epitome of isolation and self-involvement.[121]

Jacques Villon, *Le Scribe* (1949). *Musée National d'Art Moderne, Paris. Giraudon*

PART THREE

SELF AND WORLD IN THE FULL-BLOWN PSYCHOSIS

Loss of Self

The poet disappears (this is absolutely the discovery of our time).
—Stéphane Mallarmé
Propos sur la Poésie

It talks out of me.   —Schizophrenic patient

*The instinct for knowledge is malicious (something murderous, opposed to
the happiness of mankind). . . . the will to knowledge . . . dissolves the unity
of the subject; it releases those elements of itself that are devoted to its
subversion and destruction. . . . its development is not tied to the constitution
and affirmation of a free subject; rather, it creates a progressive enslavement
to its instinctive violence. Where religions once demanded the sacrifice of
bodies, knowledge now calls for experimentation on ourselves, calls us to the
sacrifice of the subject of knowledge.*
—Michel Foucault
"Nietzsche, Genealogy, History"

n his *Meditations on First Philosophy*, first published in 1641, René
Descartes sets himself the task of questioning every possible assumption,
every unexamined certitude that human beings have always taken for
granted. On this, the famous journey of doubt that launched so much of
modern thought, Descartes is led to concede that the entire material world—
"the sky, the air, the earth, colours, figures, sounds, and all external
things"—might in fact be nonexistent: "nothing better than the illusions of
dreams." Even his own body—"hands, eyes, flesh [and] blood"—might be

nothing more than a figment of a deluded imagination. But through all of this, he asserts, there is one thing that remains unshakably certain, that cannot possibly be questioned: his own existence as a mind or conscious being. Doubting, after all, is *itself* an act of the mind; it follows that to doubt the reality of one's consciousness is, paradoxically, to furnish yet another proof of its existence. Indeed, Descartes points out that this particular kind of doubt would be an especially clear exercise of that perfect freedom that (along with a fundamental indivisibility) he considered to be an axiomatic feature of the very idea of consciousness or the mind: "It is so self-evident that it is I who doubts, understands, and desires," Descartes concludes, "that there seems no way in which it can be more clearly explained. Further, it is also I who imagines; for even if (as I supposed) none of the things that I imagine is true, yet this power of imagination really exists and forms part of my thought. Finally, it is I who have sensations, that is to say, who is aware of objects as though by the senses, since indeed I see light, I hear noise, I feel heat."[1]

This sense of utter certitude about one's own subjectivity is within easy grasp, at least for most denizens of modern Western culture. Normally, one does have the sense of living one's perceptions, thoughts, and actions as if from within, with an implicit or semiconscious sense of intention and control; one generally feels that one's own consciousness belongs to oneself, and that unless one communicates the inner life through word or gesture, it will remain private. These presuppositions are, in fact, so deeply embedded in our general outlook and mode of existence that to state them has the ring of tautology—as if any alternative were simply impossible to conceive. ("It would make no sense to think or say: *This* inner experience is occurring, but is it occurring to *me?*" writes the contemporary philosopher P. F. Strawson.)[2] But, strangely enough, with the development of a schizophrenic psychosis, these very assumptions can no longer be relied upon—and, in the wake of their collapse, the nearly unimaginable holds sway.

A schizophrenic person may, for example, actually lose the sense of initiating his own actions: "When I reach my hand for a comb it is my hand and arm which move, and my fingers pick up the pen, but I don't control them. . . . I sit there watching them move, and they are quite independent, what they do is nothing to do with me. . . . I am just a puppet that is manipulated by cosmic strings. When the strings are pulled my body moves and I cannot prevent it." Such a person may lose the feeling that the thoughts in his own mind really belong to him, and may conclude that what he experiences is actually the consciousness of someone else: "I look out of the window and I think the garden looks nice and the grass looks cool, but the thoughts of Eamonn Andrews come into my mind. There are no other thoughts there, only his. . . . He treats my mind like a screen and flashes his thoughts on to it like you flash a picture." A schizophrenic may even have the feeling that his own thoughts are being extracted from his head in some weird manner—"sucked out of my mind by a phrenological vacuum cleaner extractor," as one patient said, leaving "nothing in my mind, it is empty."[3]

For Descartes, the sense of possessing one's own consciousness and inhabiting one's acts (the essence of the Cartesian *cogito*) served as an Archimedean point, a fulcrum of certitude so absolute that he actually used it to deduce the existence of God and the reality of external things, thereby reinstating faith in all that he had just conjured away. But, far from providing a solid base, in schizophrenia the *cogito* may come to seem the most dubious or evanescent of phenomena, and, with this loss of the awareness of one's own subjectivity and capacity to will, there may occur a more general fragmentation, a dissolution of all sense of one's own cohesiveness, separateness, or continuity over time. One schizophrenic spoke, for example, of "no longer [being] able to distinguish how much of myself is in me and how much is already in others. I am a conglomeration, a monstrosity, modelled anew each day." Another said, "I am a cannibal, I am falling to bits"; and a third said she felt as if someone had taken a hammer and split her, "like a drop of quicksilver," into a thousand quivering pieces.[4] "Something has happened to me—I do not know what," wrote the schizophrenic Lara Jefferson. "All that was my former self has crumbled and fallen together and a creature has emerged of whom I know nothing. She is a stranger to me. . . . She is not real—she is not I . . . she is I—and because I still have myself on my hands, even if I am a maniac, I must deal with me somehow."[5] Given such profound experiences of ontological insecurity, of uncertainty about the very existence of the ego or the self, it is understandable that many schizophrenics will manifest the so-called "I am" sign—the habit of repeating over and over to themselves some desperate litany such as "I am"; "I am me, I am me"; "I am the one present in everything"; or "I am the mind, not the body."[6]

Clearly, such peculiar experiences are at odds with some of the most fundamental assumptions of our culture—described by the cultural anthropologist Clifford Geertz as our "Western conception of the person as a bounded, unique, more or less integrated motivational and cognitive universe, a dynamic center of awareness, emotion, judgment, and action organized into a distinctive whole and set contrastively both against other such wholes and against its social and natural background."[7] It is understandable, then, that Karl Jaspers should have considered such experiences to be beyond the pale of any normal person's empathic capacity, and in his influential *General Psychopathology* should offer these symptoms as the primary illustrations of schizophrenia's unsurpassable alienness and incomprehensibility.[8] But, though the view sketched out by Geertz has certainly been the dominant one in mainstream Western culture over the last several centuries, in philosophy as well as in everyday life, it is not in fact the only one. Other views—and, possibly, other modes of being—contradict the universality and perhaps even the validity of this Cartesian vision of a controlling or inner self, and may provide insight into the privations of agency and self-possession experienced in schizophrenia. "What gives me the right to speak of an 'I,' and even of an 'I' as cause, and finally of an 'I' as cause of thought?" asked Friedrich Nietzsche. "A thought comes when 'it' wants, not when 'I' want. . . . *It* thinks: but that this 'it' is precisely that famous old 'I' is, to put it mildly, only an assumption, an assertion, above all not an 'immediate certainty.' "[9] Related ideas can also be found in the soberer realms of the philosophy of science—where the influential physicist and philosopher Ernst Mach, writing in the 1880s, criticized the standard Cartesian distinction between subject and object, arguing that the usual notion of the ego is misleading because the individual is really only a "relatively stable complex of sensational elements."[10]

Such statements have become increasingly common in the course of the twentieth century; indeed, in the postmodernist art and poststructuralist thought of the last couple of decades, they came to be accepted almost as a kind of orthodoxy. In this chapter, I shall explore the illuminating affinities between such doctrines and what might be called the self-disturbances or I-disorders of schizophrenia.[11] But first let us look at the views of these schizophrenic phenomena that have been dominant in psychiatry and psychoanalysis as well as in the literary avant-garde.

PSYCHIATRIC, PSYCHOANALYTIC, AND AVANT-GARDIST VIEWS

The importance of self-disturbances in the diagnosis of schizophrenia is largely due to the work of the German psychiatrist Kurt Schneider, an important follower of Jaspers who proposed a list of what he called First Rank Symptoms—delusions, hallucinations, and other anomalous experiences he considered to be definitive indicators of a schizophrenic disorder (if observed in the absence of evidence of coarse brain disease).[12] All these symptoms are quite specific, and all involve passivization or other fundamental distortions of the normal sense of volition, inwardness, or privacy. The patient may feel, for instance, that his emotions, actions, perceptions, or bodily sensations are imposed on him, or are experienced or controlled by some external being or force. He may hear his thoughts aloud, as if spoken outside him; he may feel that his thoughts are broadcast throughout the world; or he may have certain specific kinds of auditory hallucinations (to be described later). The processes of thought itself may seem alien and out of control—as, for example, in the case of a patient whose mind felt to her like a dry beach onto which thoughts would break like waves; or one's thoughts may seem foreign, the "workings of another psyche"[13] inserted into one's brain or flashed like pictures onto the screen of one's mind. Schneider's list has long been influential in British, German, and Scandinavian psychiatry, and its items have recently been incorporated into the current diagnostic system of the American Psychiatric Association—which now lists "loss of ego boundaries," "extreme perplexity about one's own identity," and various "bizarre" delusions (all of them Schneiderian First Rank Symptoms) as characteristic features of schizophrenia.[14]

Schneider was extremely wary of all speculative tendencies, and refused to offer any hypothesis to explain these striking experiential aberrations. With few exceptions (a notable one is the British psychologist C. D. Frith, whose views are discussed on pages 497–98), most of those influenced by Schneider's system have been equally atheoretical, offering no causal hypotheses or explanatory generalizations to account for the schizophrenic self-disorders. These symptoms have, however, been equally important for psychoanalytic conceptualizations of schizophrenia, and in that tradition theoretical interpretation has been allowed to play a far more prominent role.

The psychoanalytic view of such self-disturbances was originally worked out in a famous paper by Victor Tausk, a member of Freud's original circle who first introduced the phrase "loss of ego boundaries." The particular delusion Tausk focused on in his article, "On the Origin of the 'Influencing Machine' in Schizophrenia" (1919), incorporates most of the Schneiderian First Rank Symptoms, and certainly evokes the praecox feeling:

> The patient is Miss Natalija A., thirty-one years old, formerly a student of philosophy. She declares that for six and a half years she has been under the influence of an electrical machine made in Berlin. . . . It has the form of a human body, indeed, the patient's own form, though not in all details . . . The trunk has the shape of a lid, resembling the lid of a coffin and is lined with silk or velvet. . . . She cannot see the head—she says that she is not sure about it and she does not know whether the machine bears her own head. . . . The outstanding fact about the machine is that it is being manipulated by someone in a certain manner, and everything that occurs to it happens also to her. When someone strikes this machine, she feels the blow in the corresponding part of her own body. . . . The inner parts of the machine consist of electric batteries, which are supposed to represent the internal organs of the human body. Those who handle the machine produce a slimy substance in her nose, disgusting smells, dreams, thoughts, feelings, and disturb her while she is thinking, reading or writing. At an earlier stage, sexual sensations were produced in her through manipulation of the genitalia of the machine.[15]

To Natalija, all that would normally be felt to be purposive or purposeful—the movement of an arm or the semi-controlled play of attention across a set of thoughts—feels imposed upon her. And imposed in a manner far more absolute than coercion: it is as if her own actions and experiences are but epiphenomena—only the automatic, immediate, and passive reflection of what happens to the machine, whose exact location can only be said to be "elsewhere."[16] (A drawing of the human body by another schizophrenic, Katharina, may evoke something of what Natalija experienced; see figure 7.1.)

Tausk interpreted Natalija's feelings of having her movements, sensations, and desires controlled by an external force, as well as her sense of her body as something separate and apart (the Natalija machine lying elsewhere), as revivals of the fetal and nursing stages. He reasoned that, since these developmental stages preceded the acquisition of self/world boundaries or of a sense of competence and control over one's physical being, it would be a time when the body would feel to the infant like part of a foreign environment. To the infant, bodily sensations and impulses would seem to come "as if from an alien outer world."[17] Freud, in attendance at Tausk's original presentation of his paper, agreed with this regression interpretation of the loss of ego boundaries, and suggested some additional nuances.[18] Since that time psychoanalytic writers of virtually all persuasions have interpreted these profound distortions of the normal sense of self as primary indications of the schizophrenic's characteristically deep regression to an "original undifferentiated state"[19]—an early, usually Dionysian mode of experience dominated by primary-process thinking, by hallucinatory wish fulfillment, by the absence of an "observing ego" ("little capacity to reflect on the self and on immediate experience"),[20] and by what Anna Freud called "those primitive levels of mental life where the distinction between the self and the environment is lacking."[21]

It is not only in psychiatry and psychoanalysis that these self-disturbances of schizophrenia have been a topic of central concern; they have played an equally important role in the imagination of the twentieth-century literary avant-garde, serving there as the objective correlative for what one critic has called "the persistent contemporary rhetoric of a fragmentation of the subject."[22] In this world (and to a considerable extent in the antipsychiatry movement) schizophrenic persons have usually been viewed in accord with Nietzsche's vision of a "Dionysian madness" of "self-abnegation" and "self-forgetfulness," where the "collapse of the *principium individuationis*" makes way for the "endemic ecstasies" of primal unity.[23] Over the last fifteen or twenty years, the influence of poststructuralism has intensified interest in notions of a decentered existence, which is often viewed as a more authentic and vital mode of being than is the integrated self—which Nietzsche described as a fiction, "something added and invented and projected

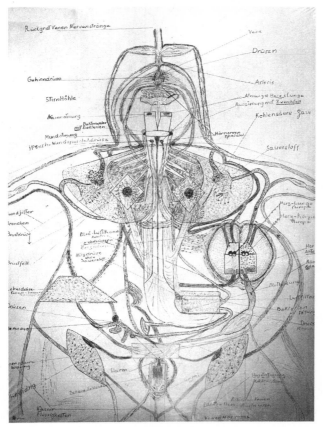

FIGURE 7.1

Katharina, *Corps Humain* (1965). Drawing of a human body, showing internal organs and apparently without a head. A drawing by a schizophrenic that is reminiscent of Natalija's "influencing machine." *Collection de l'Art Brut, Lausanne*

behind what there is."[24] In a book published in 1976, for example, one literary scholar compares the schizophrenic's loss of self to the ecstatic surrender of self ("the delights of self-scattering") that he finds in the writings of Rimbaud, Lautréamont, Genet, and Artaud, and which he contrasts with traditional literature, where the self exists as "an ordered and ordering presence." In the former cases, he tells us, the coherence and boundedness of identity are burst asunder by the heterogeneity of desublimated pre-oedipal desire, with its polymorphous yearnings and its urges toward fusion with the desired object.[25]

COMING APART: MODERN CULTURE AND THE SELF

In this chapter I shall be proposing a very different view of the mutations of the sense of subjectivity and selfhood that occur in schizophrenia as well as in many central experiences of modernist art and thought. And to do this I shall need to trace an alternative route or genealogy leading toward the progressive fragmentation and dissolution of the self—a route that is certainly prominent enough in modern art and thought, though it seems to be all too readily forgotten by those who are inclined to denigrate selfhood as a false transcendence or to glorify loss of self as if it were necessarily a more authentic and liberated expression of the free play of desire.[26]

I begin by examining one of the clearest examples of this alternative genealogy: the meditation on selfhood offered by William James, the greatest of philosophical psychologists and a figure poised at the threshold of the modernist age. Though this was not his purpose, James lucidly illustrated what one might call a central paradox of the reflexive: that seemingly contradictory yet widespread process by which acute *self*-consciousness actually contributes to an *effacing* of the self, while simultaneously obscuring its own role in this effacement.

William James: Searching for the Self

In his chapter on "The Consciousness of Self" in *The Principles of Psychology*, William James begins his discussion by asserting (in rather Cartesian fashion) that the feeling of a "central nucleus of the Self," something that gives one's thoughts and sensations the sense of being unified rather than of "flying about loose," is virtually a defining feature of any consciousness we might call human. Compared to this unifying core, the other elements of the stream of subjective life seem "transient external possessions, of which each in turn can be disowned, whilst that which disowns them remains." James then asks about this feeling of an "innermost centre within the circle." Of what does this "sanctuary within the citadel" really consist?[27] If we choose to become aware of this feeling and to direct our attention to it, what, he wants to know, will we then discover?

First James gives one answer. He argues that the feelings of control over and of identity with one's stream of experience are related: the part or aspect of one's stream of experience that seems most intimately allied to the self—that which one feels one *is*—tends to be the part from which one's sense of activity emanates. This "active element in all consciousness" is, he says, a spiritual something that "seems to *go out* to meet these qualities and contents, whilst [the qualities] seem to *come in* to be received by it. It is what welcomes or rejects. It presides over the perception of sensations" and "is the source of effort and attention, and the place from which appear to emanate the fiats of the will." The two aspects of selfhood—unity and a sense of active intentionality—appear to be inseparable and interdependent.

But, having given this account of the spiritual self, James immediately finds it unsatisfactory, too general and vague. Such descriptions—the findings of what I shall call "casual" rather than "exigent" introspection—do not for James have the feeling that comes of hitting bottom. And so, he takes a harder and more careful look, hoping to "grapple with particulars [and come] to the closest possible quarters with the facts"—now trying to seize a given moment of experience and to regard it more intently, to be a keener observer and thus to ferret out the microscopic but concrete details of which the lived event is really composed.

What James then finds, adopting this "exigent" mode, is that there *is* no purely spiritual element at all: "whenever my introspective glance succeeds in turning round quickly enough to catch one of these manifestations of spontaneity in the act, all it can ever feel distinctively is some bodily process, for the most part taking place within the head." Among the acts James analyzes are willing, reflecting, consenting, and negating. He finds, for example, that the sense of volitional control he has when attending to visually represented thoughts turns out, on close scrutiny, to be based on "a fluctuating play of pressures, convergences, divergences, and accommodations in my eyeballs." When trying to remember or reflect, there is a feeling of inwardness, of withdrawing from the external world, and this is "due to an actual rolling outwards and upwards of the eyeballs." Similarly, the feelings of consenting and negating seem to involve the opening and closing of the glottis, while the feeling of air passing freely through his nose and throat is "one strong ingredient of the feeling of assent." All these examples demonstrate an important feature of the exigent observational stance: the setting up of a radical separation between the introspecting ego, which seems passive, a mere watcher, and the watched self, the distant place where all movement seems to be taking place.

Once it is carefully examined, James finds that the "Self of selves," the "citadel within the sanctuary," is reducible to "a collection of these peculiar motions in the head or between the head and throat." It appears, then, that "all that is experienced is, strictly considered, *objective*," even including that "imaginary being denoted by the pronoun 'I.'" When we scrutinize our experience, we discover nothing inner or active, only a variety of kinesthetic or physiological processes happening all by themselves. This, however, is tantamount to saying that the "I," the inner sanctuary of identity and intentionality, does not exist, since the criteria that had appeared to define its presence—a sense of relative innerness, activity, and unity—seem on more careful examination to be revealed as illusory. "At present, then," writes James, "the only conclusion I come to is the following: That (in some persons at least) the part of the innermost Self which is most vividly felt turns out to consist for the most part of a collection of cephalic movements or 'adjustments' which, for want of attention and reflection, usually fail to be perceived and classed as what they are."

The ever wise, ever reasonable James did retain a degree of tentativeness about this seeming discovery, however, even though he did not follow his doubts to their logical conclusion;[28] and elsewhere in his *Principles of Psychology* he provides all the necessary elements for a self-critique. Thus, in his chapter on "The Stream of Thought," James points out that the process of introspection seems inherently to contain a potentially misleading prejudice in favor of the definite and the distinct.[29] As a result, introspection, especially in its exigent form, is naturally prone to the error of overemphasizing the "substantive" parts of the stream of experience and neglecting what James calls the "transitive" aspects (the latter would include such phenomena as feelings of relationship, of processes, and of activity). He compares trying to see and specify transitive phenomena to the futile attempt to grasp motion by seizing a spinning top, or to see darkness by turning up a lamp very quickly: the phenomenon is effaced in the very act of looking for it. As soon as one tries to introspect about a transitive aspect, one's glance is likely either to settle upon some substantive part of the stream or else to distort the lived reality of the stream by rendering the transitive part into a substantive one.

It is not difficult to see how this illusion, born of observational method, might dissolve the experience of the active and integral ego or self, given that the latter is an experience likely to be carried by transitive rather than substantive parts of the stream of consciousness. Indeed, James's own exigent analysis of the consciousness of self is a perfect *illustration*, just as his discussion of observation's bias for substantive over transitive aspects of the stream of experience is a perfect *explanation*, of how this loss can come about—not from a weakening of the observing ego or a lowering of the conscious level but, to the contrary, from a hypertrophy of attentive, self-reflexive awareness.

Oddly enough, James does not turn his analysis around upon himself in the way one might expect; he does not contextualize his own "discovery" of the nonexistence of the inner and active self by seeing *its* dependence on the attitude, and the corresponding lived world, of exigent introspection. But we do find criticism of such failures to contextualize in the works of Ludwig Wittgenstein, who saw them as leading to all kinds of unjustified "metaphysical" assertions and unnecessary quandaries. "To get clear about philosophical problems," Wittgenstein writes in the *Blue Book*, "it is useful to become conscious of the apparently unimportant details of the particular situation in which we are inclined to make a certain metaphysical assertion."[30] He suggests that staring often played a particularly important role in what we might call the phenomenology of philosophical illusion (he claims, for example, that solipsistic assertions are more likely to seem true when one is passively watching than when one is walking about, active and involved in life).[31] In the *Philosophical Investigations*, Wittgenstein actually addresses William James's claim that the self consists mainly of "peculiar motions in the head and between the head and throat," suggesting that this "discovery" is a function of the introspector's attitude: "And James' introspection showed, not the meaning of the word 'self' (so far as it means something like 'person,' 'human being,' 'he himself,' 'I myself'), nor any analysis of such a thing, but the state of a philosopher's attention when he says the word 'self' to himself and tries to analyze its meaning. (And a good deal could be learned from this.)"[32]

Wittgenstein wrote of the unnaturalness of a mode of expression or thought that would put states of consciousness or of willing at a remove, as if these were things that, in the normal case, we had to contemplate or to will (that is, as if one had to *perceive* that one was conscious or, by a second act, had to will to will). It is not that such an inner division is impossible but that, when it does occur, it sets up an aberrant state of mind. After all, notes Wittgenstein, "I cannot observe myself unobserved"; hence a sentence like "I *perceive* I am conscious" describes an abnormal way of disposing one's attention, one likely to undermine the usual sense of engagement in one's activity and awareness and therefore to make "my actions, my movements, uncertain," depriving me of a sense of intending my behavior.[33] The form of self-generated illusion that Wittgenstein is warning us about in these passages can be particularly difficult to overcome, for its source is the very thing that is so often a prerequisite of clear understanding: withdrawal from activity into dispassionate, disengaged contemplation. What underlies such forms of illusion is a paradoxical condition: a failure to be sufficiently self-conscious about the effects of one's own self-consciousness, to distance oneself adequately from distanciation itself.[34]

Literary Developments: "Imagination Imagining Itself Imagine"

Though precedents for this loss of self associated with exigent introspection can certainly be found in earlier eras, they have become especially common in modernist culture, where art and philosophy so largely involve a scrutinizing either of experience-as-such or of the medium of language. In a well-known essay called "The Age of Suspicion," the French novelist Nathalie

Sarraute discusses the disappearance from the modernist novel of the foundations of traditional narrative—consistent characters engaged in coherent actions and an integrated and understandable author/narrator—and explicitly denies that this development, which her own fiction exemplifies, can be understood as a regression to some infantile form of consciousness. Rather, she claims, it shows "an unusually sophisticated state of mind" and illustrates Stendhal's statement about the modern age: "The genius of suspicion has appeared on the scene."[35]

Sarraute's own novels evoke the mode of experience that results when everyday life comes to be pervaded by inwardness and an associated kind of exigent introspection. They describe not public actions but infinitesimal interior stirrings that seem to occur with an almost vegetable automaticity, the subtle driftings of an inner life that usually go unnoticed yet for her constitute the true essence of human existence. According to a view that has come to seem almost orthodox in some circles, the truth about human experience is veiled by the deceptive sense of unity and control, those illusions underlying the "bourgeois" notions of identity and willpower. Human consciousness is in fact constituted by tiny and virtually autonomous events that are at once exterior *and* interior—the fleeting memories, half-remembered phrases, and semiconscious urges and sensations that move independently across one's field of awareness like waterbugs across a pond.

In Sarraute's estimation, developments in modern fiction are dominated by a trend toward an objectifying kind of introspection. Whereas earlier explorations of the inner life treated the "formless, soft matter that yields and disintegrates under the scalpel of analysis" (the stuff of casual introspection, perhaps), the universe of the contemporary novel, though mental, is hard and opaque. The typical protagonist/narrator is someone whose "relation to himself is as though someone else were observing and speaking of him" (but from within).[36] Rather like a man in a cartoon, he examines his thoughts and actions as if they existed apart from him, in a bubble that threatens to fill the world. Thus in Sarraute's *Between Life and Death*, Alain sits alone, watching words and sensations that seem to traverse his field of awareness of their own accord. And to this modernist Everyman, even his own "self"—if one can even use this term in such a context—is something he contemplates from a remove:

The little drops of words mount in a thin jet, they shove one another, then fall down again. Others mount, and others still. . . . That must absolutely happen again. To let oneself drift once more . . . to let oneself float, curled up to oneself, subject to the slightest eddy. . . . To wait until there are outlined in the thickness of the ooze those halting progressions, those retractions, until, once more, something transpires.

For this latter-day Mallarméan observer, it is words that are "sovereign":

> They play, answer, echo one another. They reverberate. They reflect one
> another, they sparkle. . . . And he is caught in the labyrinth of their mirrors,
> imprisoned in the interlacings of their reflections. . . . He turns, mirrored
> from one to the other. . . . This is the moment when we must become two
> persons. One-half of me becomes detached from the other: a witness.[37]

The harder the protagonist/narrator looks, the more the objects of his awareness come to seem like reified external things that encompass all of existence; and the more any sense of a self transcending this flux disappears. The
externalization is so extreme, in fact, that one might even be inclined to
question the very term *intro*spection, were it not that the observed phenomena do retain a certain subjective quality: they are sense data, not things.[38]

This phenomenalism, which is bound up with a kind of exigent introspection or hyperreflexive involution, thus leads to a dispersal. By a process Paul
Valéry once termed "a centrifuging of the self," all the phenomena of
awareness are, as it were, spun outward and away.[39] And Sarraute ends
another novel, *The Planetarium*, by asserting the truth revealed by this
centrifuging: "Everything in him, everything about him is coming apart.
. . . I think we're all of us, really, a bit like that."[40]

Sometimes a peculiar duality can be inherent in this kind of hyperreflexivity—when, along with an *ex*ternalization of what would normally be felt
to be inner or subjective, there is also a characteristic *in*ternalization, a
subjectivization of what is usually external and objective. This occurs when
the object of the reflexive gaze is a *representing* entity; and we see it most
clearly in certain literary works of the contemporary postmodernist avant-
garde, works in which the dizzying tendency toward self-consciousness and
self-reference is a characteristic not so much of the characters with*in* the
work as of the artwork itself. Many such works undermine or dismantle
themselves by concentrating attention upon their own status as novels or
paintings—or even on their ephemeral existence as acts of writing or painting (or reading or looking, in cases where the self-conscious focus is on
audience rather than creator). And under these circumstances, the world
depicted seems to be subordinated to the consciousness by which it is constituted. This is the condition of "imagination imagining itself imagine,"[41] a
state captured by the prominent literary notion of the "aporia" or "mise en
abyme"—the infinite involution or vertiginously self-referential abyss that
occurs when two mirrors are placed face to face or when a photograph shows
a photograph in which the first photograph appears, thus depicting another
photograph depicting itself, and so on, endlessly.[42] In the presence of such
artistic and linguistic self-awareness, subject matter and external reality are
drained of all sense of importance and substantiality, but, at the same time,

the distinct selfhood and felt actuality of both author and character are likely to dissolve; we are left with a peculiar contradiction: a subjectivism without a subject, a narcissism without Narcissus.[43]

It would be a mistake, it seems to me, to equate this tradition of hyper-reflexivity with the tradition of aesthetic antirationalism alluded to earlier. True, the self as an "ordered and ordering presence" disappears for both James and Sarraute, as it does in the works of Lautréamont, Rimbaud, and Genet. And the experiential world depicted by writers like Sarraute may also be reduced to a series of discontinuous, fragmentary scenes that lack the solidity and constancy of real objects and dissolve one into another with all the fluidity of images. But there are also important differences between a phantasmagoria of the desiring imagination and the kind of *mise en abyme* just discussed. In the former tradition, at least as some critics have conceived it, the poet "coerce[s] the world into becoming an excited version of his desires"; "the person is dismembered by the very fertility of its resources," dissolved in "exuberant fusion with those scenes which offer themselves, literally, as the theatre of our desires."[44] In such a "triumph of desiring fantasy," the inner self dissolves outward into the objects of its yearnings. In the latter forms of self-fragmentation, by contrast, there is a turning *away* from a world of desired objects and *toward* inner experiences and an increasingly devitalized self; further, it is not desire or emotion that dominates, but the relentless impulse to *know*. It is not impossible for these two tendencies to be included, perhaps even synthesized, in the same work; but the fact remains that the two trends are, if not exactly incompatible, at least in fundamental tension with each other.[45]

Given the widespread acceptance of regression notions of schizophrenia, it should not be surprising that the schizophrenic loss of self has so often been assimilated to the former, Dionysian tradition.[46] But let us turn to the realm of madness to see which of these examples—"exuberant fusion" and the "delights of self-scattering," or the exigent introspection of James and Sarraute—might provide a better model for understanding what really occurs in schizophrenia. We shall begin by considering the experiences of Natalija.

SELF-DISORDERS IN SCHIZOPHRENIA

The Influencing Machine

As we saw in our discussion of William James, the person who stares intently at his own stream of experience is unlikely to discover any concrete evidence of his own identity, innerness, or volition. Even his own bodily sensations will seem separate from him, since the very fact of scrutinizing will make them seem out there, apart. To experience one's own sensations as having their original locus in another version of one's own body, in an influencing machine not under one's own control, would seem an appropriate way of symbolizing such an experience (and of providing a subjective explanation for it). We might think of the velvet that lines the lid of Natalija's machine as a symbolic representation of her tactile awareness of her own body as it is lived in the mode of intense introspection: were it not for the presence of the exigently introspective attitude, her kinesthetic sensations might retain a more transitive or implicit character—more processlike than objectlike; but in the presence of this introspective mode, these sensations take on an increasingly static and substantive form and hence come to be symbolized as a thing, a piece of velvet. Also consistent with this analysis is Natalija's inability to say what the machine's face looks like, though she knows it has a head and senses it is her own: for, though casual introspection will recall, in a loose sort of way, the vague totality of the normal field of meaning, a field likely to include some sense of how one might look to others, in exigent introspection one's head and face will likely fall away, to be replaced by a vague cloud of nothingness sitting over the shoulders, or perhaps by a set of kinesthetic sensations located vaguely on top.

I am suggesting that we might see the influencing machine as a late-stage symptom of a certain introversion, a crystallization of a phenomenological world in which explicit attention fixes on the inner sensations and body-image experiences that would usually be transparent and unthematized, that would normally remain latent while the external world occupies the focus of awareness. According to this interpretation, the influencing machine would be a projected image not of the physical body but of the subjective body—a lived body that is, so to speak, turned inside out and solidified, reified by the intensity of a self-directed gaze. And this inside-out body nearly fills the universe, reducing the world to a room located in some vague elsewhere and other people to phantoms whose only function is to manipulate and discuss the Natalija machine lying before them.

In many cases, the progression of the disease is quite consistent with such an interpretation. As we know, the most common premorbid personality of schizophrenics is the schizoid type, usually characterized by intense social alienation and extreme self-consciousness. In one autobiographical account, a schizophrenic who eventually developed delusions of influence describes himself as having been from "very early in life an observer of my own mental peculiarities, to a degree which I think must be a very rare exception."[47] As Tausk himself pointed out, the illness of patients like Natalija often begins with mild experiences of estrangement. At first, the alterations of the perceptual world characteristic of the *Stimmung* may appear; but as attention turns inward, the patient begins to notice, and to feel distanced from, phenomena previously identified with the self. The saliva in his mouth, the set of his neck, or the movement of his eyelids begins to feel odd, and bodily sensations or thoughts start to seem somehow at a remove.[48] Such experiences tend to feed upon themselves. As the patient's own strange sensations and thoughts attract his attention, this attention itself makes the sensations seem all the more distant, external, and concrete. There is a loss of tacit forms of knowing; and instead of inhabiting the body and being immersed in the sensory world, there is a kind of disengagement, a detachment that may be akin to certain forms of phenomenological "reflection"—the contemplative stance that, in Merleau-Ponty's words, "slackens the intentional threads which attach us to the world and thus brings them to our notice."[49]

The mode of exigent introspection often has a hyperintentional quality to it, but, as we know, this does not mean that the mode itself is entirely or essentially volitional in nature; its sources can in fact be understood in various ways. To some extent, this form of awareness might reflect exacerbation of an introverted temperamental disposition (schizoid personality) or of an overfocused cognitive style. It could also reflect some more specific cognitive factor rooted in neurobiological abnormalities, such as an incapacity (or a disinclination) to synthesize larger Gestalts or, perhaps, an inability to desist from paying attention to stimuli that are habitually experienced and that would not normally be focused on (kinesthetic and other "inner" sensations would be one important subset of such sensations).[50] In these latter cases, fragmentation of the self would be not just a consequence but, in a sense, also a cause of a certain kind of hyperfocused introspection (and in this respect, it should be noted, the parallel with William James may not be entirely apt, since James's exigent introspection *is* an essentially willful phenomenon). Whatever its sources, a relentless kind of introspection is clearly a central element of schizophrenic experience (we shall see more evidence for this shortly), and it seems to make a profound contribution to schizophrenics' sense of detachment from their own actions and experience. This, perhaps, is what a patient quoted in the introduction may have meant when she spoke of her sense of subjectivity or selfhood (what she calls "the most sacred monument that is erected by the human spirit, i.e., its ability to think and decide and will to do") as being "torn apart by itself."

We can understand, then, how a person who steps back from his own experience might begin to feel as if his sensations and thoughts originated somehow outside his own body or mind, how he could begin to hear his own thoughts as words spoken outside his head, or even to feel his actions, sensations, or emotions as being imposed upon him from without. (Some catatonic patients actually feel guilty about stopping their ongoing actions, since they experience their own movements as independent things with which they have no right to interfere.) This absence of a unifying intentionality can readily lead to a sense of dispersal, as if the "Self of selves" were breaking into particles that spin outward and away:

> I get shaky in the knees and my chest is like a mountain in front of me, and my body actions are different. The arms and legs are apart and away from me and they go on their own. That's when I feel I am the other person and copy their movements, or else stop and stand like a statue. I have to stop to find out whether my hand is in my pocket or not.

Another schizophrenic patient described

> my body breaking up into bits. I get all mixed up so that I don't know myself. I feel like more than one person when this happens. I'm falling apart into bits. . . . I'm frightened to say a word in case everything goes fleeing from me so that there's nothing in my mind. It puts me into a trance that's worse than death. There's a kind of hypnotism going on.[51]

This progression of simultaneous involution and externalization may end in the formation of a systematized delusion that can alleviate a frightening sense of chaos and disintegration. Thus the notion of some kind of influencing machine, one of the classic delusions of schizophrenia, may stabilize the world by filling it with a quasi-external symbol of the subject's own hyper-reflexive consciousness, and by providing some way of accounting for the distorted, passivized experiences being undergone. (See figure 7.2 for one patient's depiction of his influencing-machine delusion.)

According to the traditional primitivity view, the attenuation of "reflective thinking" or "observing ego" (the self-monitoring capacity of the psyche) and the loss of "self" (of the sense of the reality, discreteness, and cohesiveness of one's being) are complementary—interdependent characteristics of primitive and pathological forms of consciousness.[52] Accordingly, many psychoanalysts have recommended psychotherapeutic approaches whose main purpose is actually to encourage introspection and the development of an observing ego.[53] This assumption of the interdependence of ego boundaries and of reflective awareness, and of the weakening of both in schizophrenia, is, in fact, made by virtually all those who have attempted to interpret these aspects of the schizophrenic condition—including nonpsychoanalytic psychologists as well as members of the literary avant-garde.[54] A good example is the academic psychologist Julian Jaynes, who sees the schizophrenic loss of selfhood—he calls it the "erosion of the analog 'I' "—as a consequence of an inability to introspect, to think about thinking, or to recognize an inner "Mind-Space." Jaynes argues that the famous auditory hallucinations so characteristic of schizophrenics are throwbacks to the

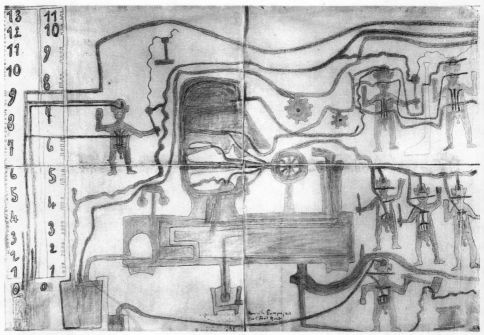

FIGURE 7.2

Robert Gie, *Distribution d'Effluves avec Machine Centrale et Tableau Métrique*
(Distribution of Emanations with Central Machine and Metric Table) (c. 1916).
Illustration by a schizophrenic of his influencing-machine delusion. *Collection de*
l'Art Brut, Lausanne

neurological commands of an earlier period of human evolution (the "bicameral" period, prior to 3000 B.C.), when they served to orient and direct individuals too unevolved to exercise conscious deliberation or personal control over themselves.[55]

But by now we have seen that an alternative interpretation of this erosion is possible: rather than *sustaining* a sense of self, certain forms of self-observing may actually serve to undermine it. But why, we may ask, should the latter be preferred? What reason is there to choose the model of hyper-reflexive awareness over the more usual ones—regression to infancy or the emergence of unrestrained desire—if both are able to account for the anomalies of schizophreniform thought and action? In answering this question, it will help to look more closely at the specific nature of some of Schneider's First Rank Symptoms, and then to reflect more generally on the overall mood and structure of the schizophrenic world.

"Thoughts-Out-Loud"

Like some other advocates of the primitivity interpretation, Julian Jaynes suggests that the quintessential example of auditory hallucination in schizophrenia is the "command hallucination," obeyed without hesitation or conscious reflection. In fact, however, the auditory hallucinations most characteristic of schizophrenia, those listed by Schneider as First Rank Symptoms, do not fit this description at all. Schneider lists three specific types, and in two of them the role of hesitation or self-monitoring is particularly obvious: first, a voice mocking, criticizing, or commenting on what the schizophrenic person is doing or thinking ("Now he's walking down the road, now he's reached the corner and he's wondering which way to turn; now he's looking at that girl's legs, the filthy so and so"); and second, two or more voices discussing or arguing about the individual's ongoing activities. In the third type the person hears his or her own thoughts being spoken aloud, either just before or just after having them.[56] A schizophrenic with paranoid and catatonic features named Jonathan Lang recounts his experience of these symptoms in the following passage, quoted at length to convey the characteristic style of this man's experience as well as his manner of expressing himself. The voices Lang describes are of two types, both of which he calls "thoughts-out-loud" and both of which, according to his own report, "the conscious self neither initiates nor anticipates":

> These two respective styles correlate fairly highly with various orientations of the ego. When the ego has an overt orientation, as in reading or writing, or in observation of the environment, the verbal productions of the thoughts-out-loud take the form of a running presentation of verbals suited to the activity holding the interest of the ego, adding an occasional side remark addressed to the ego. For example, if the individual is reading, the thoughts-out-loud reproduce the words of the book the individual is reading, sometimes making a comment on a passage. When the orientation of the ego is more strictly introvert, as for example in reflection, the verbal productions often take the form of an imaginary conversation between the individual and some person with whom the individual is acquainted.[57]

When Jonathan Lang's consciousness is extroverted, his voices represent a consciousness of consciousness, a level of meta-awareness that usually shadows but occasionally disrupts the ongoing intentional act:

> the thoughts-out-loud [tended] to provide verbalization of the thought trends of the ego whenever the ego develops a strong orientation. However, sometimes the thoughts-out-loud continued to present foreign ideas despite the fact the ego is trying to engage in activities which demand words.

And when he is more reflective or introverted, the voices engage in an inner dialogue of deliberation, hesitancy, and argument:

> In connection with the expression of foreign ideas, the verbal productions of the thoughts-out-loud usually take the form of monologues attempting to persuade the ego to adopt a belief in the authority of the agent behind the thoughts-out-loud and to accept a Messianic fixation. Attached to these monologues are expressions of the thoughts of the ego concerning the arguments. Another variant is the presentation of arguments seeking to persuade the individual to specific acts.[58]

It is common for schizophrenics to hear their own thoughts aloud, or to hear voices commenting on their current thoughts and actions.[59] Often their verbal hallucinations will have a contradictory quality, with voices taking the roles of pro and con, or with one voice commanding the patient to do something but then criticizing or jeering when he or she obeys (or, for that matter, doesn't obey).[60] A thirty-two-year-old woman would hear a male voice repeating her goal-directed thinking in an intense whisper. "I must put the kettle on," the patient would think, and after a second or so the voice would say, "I must put the kettle on," or the opposite, "Don't put the kettle on." A twenty-four-year-old man repeatedly heard a couple of voices discussing him. A deep, rough voice would say, "G. T. is a bloody paradox"; then a higher-pitched one would chime in, "He is that, he should be locked up"; and a female voice would occasionally interrupt, saying, "He is not, he is a lovely man."[61] A schizophrenic nurse named Clare Wallace described a "critical self who gave me no peace": a kind of "outside agency" that gave "the feeling of being an observer of myself: of seeing everything I did, as though I were someone else." "I lie down and try to think," she wrote, "but the voices interrupt, pass comment and criticize. Everything is criticized. Every thought—almost before it has come into my mind—is criticized."[62]

Auditory hallucinations have often been thought to express primitive urges or archaic memories that have somehow pushed their way upward, bursting suddenly into the more rational chambers of the mind.[63] As we see, however, the most typical schizophrenic examples are hardly consistent with this traditional portrait. One might better think of the hyperrationalism Nietzsche criticizes in *The Birth of Tragedy*: what he describes as the condition of that "monstrosity," the *"non-mystic,* in whom the logical side has become, through superfetation, as overdeveloped as has the instinctual side in the mystic," and where consciousness, the "dissuader and critic," replaces instinct as the dominant motivating force. (In *The Birth of Tragedy*, Socrates epitomizes this aberrant condition that Nietzsche believed was increasingly becoming the norm in Western civilization; and Socrates is described as hearing a quasi-divine voice that speaks to him as if from without—a voice that, as so often in schizophrenia, is a "purely inhibitory agent": it "always spoke to *dissuade*.")[64] For such a person, command hallucinations, if they do occur, might actually serve as a way of *escaping* a dominant mood of anxious self-awareness and paralyzing ambivalence, a way of catapulting oneself out of more characteristically schizophrenic states of endless deliberation, self-criticism, and doubt.

Obviously, we are a far cry from the lived world portrayed by Julian Jaynes—a nonconscious, automatized world devoid of inner mind-space. One might more accurately characterize these voices as an "externalization of involution," a way in which the patient's closely watched (and closely watching) inner life fills the external world, virtually crowding out everything else. (The voices schizophrenics hear tend to emanate not from any particular person or object in external space but from inside the body or from the sky, as if permeating the entire universe.)[65] The thoughts-out-loud seem, in fact, to represent a bringing to explicit awareness of the essential but usually implicit structures of human consciousness itself—structures that are experienced as primarily linguistic, a realm of inner dialogue. By far the most frequent kind of hallucination in schizophrenia is, in fact, of highly intelligible voices; and these voices (unlike the auditory hallucinations of patients with alcoholic hallucinosis, the other group that very commonly hears voices) generally have more of a conceptual or cognitive than a sensory or perceptual taint, as if heard with the mind rather than the ear.[66]

Like Natalija's influencing-machine delusion, such auditory hallucinations do appear to be the product of a gradual development, one that seems to involve increasing withdrawal from practical activity and the social world. Thus the voices heard by schizophrenics, unlike those in alcoholic hallucinosis, seldom occur early in the course of the illness; and they tend to escalate during circumstances of passivity[67] and social isolation, and to diminish when patients interact with other people,[68] listen to an interesting conversation,[69] or engage in repetitive physical activities like shoveling snow[70] (thus losing themselves in something external, and acting without deliberation and conscious choice). The quality of mild self-alienation that can occur at the earlier stages, before the progression of self-consciousness has reified thoughts into external voices, is illustrated by the following lines, which are a description of the mind written by a schizophrenic patient named Frank (a physicist by profession): "Mind is here defined as an organ of thought, and thinking has meant to me the meaningful production of words, *but so softly that only I could hear them*. I experience these silent words as *freely arising inside my head out of nothing*, but they are sufficiently under my control that I feel that I am thinking them."[71]

One of the articles by Jonathan Lang seems to provide an account of the entire process of externalizing involution. He describes his own consciousness as being divided into three selves—or perhaps one should say three nonselves, since each of these realms of being (even the one he calls the "quasinormaloid stratum") is felt to exist at a remove, as if it neither belonged to him nor was the expression of his will (each realm is reified, and described as an "it"). Lang describes himself as largely withdrawn from "sensorimotor activity," and as dominated, during all his waking hours, by "ideological activity—that is, central-symbolic, particularly verbal" forms of thought. Not unlike one of Sarraute's protagonists, Lang seems to experience himself as passive, a mere observer of a process in which, as he puts it, "concepts sometimes shift from one stratum to another" in what seems usually to be a process of increasing alienation, with mental contents migrating ever outward, away from a center that shrinks toward a point of nonexistence. Thus, Lang describes "concepts" that have moved out of the "quasinormaloid stratum" or the "self-defense stratum," to be taken over by the more alien "hallucinoid ideological stratum" (where the sense of disengagement is strongest). The shift into the "hallucinoid stratum" does seem to originate in some kind of centrifuging of the self, for Lang states that his "hallucinoid ideological stratum has its origin in the foreign content of the thoughts-out-loud experienced by the writer. That is, it is that part of ideas expressed by the hallucinary allied phenomenon of minimal, involuntary, subvocal speech which the writer's self classifies as being foreign."[72]

Lang's whole discussion, in fact, closely resembles William James's exigent analysis of the self, with its concentration on substantive elements of the stream of experience rather than on more processlike or "transitive" features, its "discovery" of the nonexistence of any inner core to the self, and, finally, its oddly unself-critical use of introspection (that is, the acceptance of what are to some extent the products of exigent introspection as discoveries rather than inventions). In one passage, for instance, Lang seems to recognize that the quality of externality that his voices can take on—what he calls the "hallucinatory factor"—is related to the focal awareness of substantialized sensations ("the sensation of proprioceptive pressure"). This recalls William James's "finding" that the self is nothing more than some "bodily process taking place within the head," and it also illustrates the difficulty of knowing whether the objects observed (what James calls the "substantive" sensations) are discovered or created by the observing attitude: "In addition to the verbal productions, a minimal tonus of vocal muscles and a sensation of proprioceptive pressure also are present," Lang writes with regard to his "thoughts-out-loud." "In so far as there is any hallucinatory factor in the experience, the sensation of proprioceptive pressure probably provides it."[73]

We have traced how William James was led by his method to deny the reality of the inner and active "citadel within the sanctuary"—the "Self of selves"—to conclude that, contrary to what appeared to be the case in casual introspection, "all that is experienced is, strictly considered, *objective*," even including that "imaginary being denoted by the pronoun 'I.' " Lang seems to have been led by a similar process to a form of life in which everything, even "the writer's self" and the "quasinormaloid stratum," seems to exist apart and to be watched from afar. If Natalija's influencing-machine delusion represents the lived body turned inside out and contemplated at a remove, Lang's "strata" involve an analogous externalization—a projection outward of the usually implicit phenomena of inner speech and dialogue. In the apt vocabulary of the philosopher Samuel Alexander, each tends to "contemplate" experiences or psychological processes that would normally be inhabited (lived through) or "enjoyed."[74] And such tendencies are hardly likely to confirm a sense of self: the formula of exigent introspection is not "I think therefore I am" but "It thinks and therefore I am not."[75]

"Dispossession" and "Furtive Abductions"

Schizophrenic individuals often believe or sense that they are being watched. In his diary, a young artist named Martin, who had had several schizophrenic episodes, wrote of "being examined throughout my life—secret cameras and microphones the whole James Bond Ian Fleming trip is whirring in my head," and another schizophrenic patient described being monitored by a "Watcher-Machine" that protectively oversaw her daily activities.[76] In psychoanalysis such experiences have often been interpreted as manifestations of a primitive grandiosity and egocentricity that are akin to the infant's feeling of being the center of the universe; in fact, however, the schizophrenic's sense of being watched usually involves characteristics that suggest a level of cognitive development well beyond that of the infant or young child.[77]

When emerging from a quasi-catatonic state, a patient of mine said, "I feel like a man in a cartoon. My thoughts and actions are outside my body, as if in a bubble."[78] Though his world was "subjectivized" in some sense of the word, this was hardly the *kind* of subjectivization that is characteristic of infancy. Presumably, infantile "subjectivization" is relatively *lacking* in self-consciousness: subjective projections may transform the external world, but they change it into a magical universe largely devoid of any *sense* of subjectivity.[79] This patient's complaint of his thoughts feeling outside himself suggests, however, that he is very self-conscious of his own consciousness; indeed, he seems to have been taking subjectivity-as-such as his object, thereby turning inner processes into external things. A similar passivization and sense of alienation from one's own mental processes (linguistic ones, in this instance), along with intense self-consciousness, seem to be implicit in a visual hallucination mentioned in the previous chapter: "A second face within a face, with a second pair of eyes; words coming out of the top of his head."[80] Also, the feeling of being watched typically involves an acute awareness of the presence of *other* consciousnesses, and this too is foreign to any current conception of infantile experience. Consider this passage from Thomas Hennell's autobiographical account of schizophrenia, whose title, significantly enough, is *The Witnesses:*

> I thought that a powerful cine-camera took a photographic record of this scene, for some such instrument was focused on me, and its effects remained for some weeks afterward. At any rate I was in this gallery and in this horrible presence, and my part was the miserable one of a feeble, half-paralyzed victim. . . . A voice whispered: "They have taken a photograph of your mind, *Thomas.*"[81]

Such manifestations of hypertrophied self-consciousness are not likely to facilitate normal forms of pragmatic and social activity, which may help to explain why some schizophrenics seem to move in such a stiff or awkward way. One schizophrenic patient complained, "None of my movements come automatically to me now. I've been thinking too much about them, even walking properly, talking properly and smoking—doing anything. Before they would be able to come automatically."[82] "I am not sure of my movements any more," said another patient:

> It's very hard to describe this. . . . It's not so much thinking out what to do, it's the doing of it that sticks me. . . . I found recently that I was thinking of myself doing things before I would do them. If I am going to sit down, for example, I have got to think of myself and almost see myself sitting down before I do it. . . . It takes more time to do things because I am always conscious of what I am doing. If I could just stop noticing what I am doing, I would get things done a lot faster.[83]

Silvano Arieti describes a patient, John, whose catatonic paralysis evolved out of this kind of alienating hyperconsciousness. At camp John became possessed by uncertainties: he couldn't chop down a tree because, as he put it, he was "doubting and doubting his doubts, and doubting the doubting of his doubts." Soon this became an overwhelming anxiety that affected his every action. He became aware of a discrepancy between intentions and behavior: the words he uttered did not seem precisely the ones he wanted to say, but only related to them. Then he began to feel more disconnected: while remaining perfectly lucid, he would feel he couldn't control his actions at all, and he feared he might commit some crime or do something that would cause disaster to the whole camp. The terror soon became intense enough to inhibit all movement, causing a petrification; in his own words, he saw himself "solidifying, assuming statuesque positions."[84]

Not surprisingly, the self-objectifying tendencies so often associated with schizophrenic self-disorders are often accompanied by a diminution of instinctual desires and strong affect states (other than a profound, all-encompassing, yet somehow abstract anxiety). Jonathan Lang's chillingly precise and depersonalized descriptions of his psychotic experiences could hardly be less Dionysian; they read, in fact, almost like a parody of a scientific monograph, with the rigorous stance and the academic tone of introspectionist psychology. To be sure, this exaggeratedly distanced and impersonal tone, with its reliance on the passive voice, was appropriate to the occasion: Lang's articles appeared in publications like the *American Journal of Psychiatry*. Yet it is hard to dismiss the feeling that there is more to it than this, that such a tone is uncannily well suited to this patient's actual and spontaneous form of experience. It is ironic, then, that the schizophrenic loss of self should have been taken, in antipsychiatry and in the artistic avant-garde, as some sign of liberation into the free play of desire. Actually, some such patients gradually cease to have any sexual feelings at all—a development that, in Natalija's case, was mirrored by the fact that all traces of genitalia gradually disappeared from her influencing machine.[85]

We have considered how the reification and rigidity pervading the worlds of both Natalija (with her influencing machine) and Lang (with his "strata") give to their experience a certain stability. But it is also important to understand how hyperreflexivity can be involved in certain experiences of dissolution and chaos that are more characteristic of the "acute" phases of schizophrenia, for these are even more readily assumed to involve regression of the ego or the ascendancy of the id.

As we have seen, the schizophrenic often seems to be caught in an insoluble dilemma, driven to search for the self yet likely to destroy it in the act of searching. One patient was afraid of forgetting herself: "When I suddenly realized I hadn't been thinking about myself I was frightened to death. The unreality feeling came. I must never forget myself for a single instant. I watch the clock and keep busy or I won't know who I am."[86] Another patient sought the experiential center of her own consciousness but became confused when, like an infinitely receding horizon, it continually eluded her attempts to grasp it; she ended by not being able to be sure that her thoughts were really her own:

These thoughts go on and on. I'm going over the border. My real self is away down—it used to be just at my throat, but now it's gone further down. I'm losing myself. It's getting deeper and deeper. I want to tell you things, but I'm scared. My head's full of thoughts, fears, hates, jealousies. My head can't grip them; I can't hold on to them. I'm behind the bridge of my nose—I mean, my consciousness is there. They're splitting open my head, oh, that's schizophrenic, isn't it? I don't know whether I have these thoughts or not. I think I just made them up last time in order to get treated.[87]

The literary *mise en abyme* has been described as a paradoxical combination of self-constitution and self-cancellation, a process in which categories are "torn apart" by their own self-referentiality.[88] The patient just quoted seems trapped in an analogous dilemma: her frantic attempt to constitute the self actually undermines it—as if the exigent searching, the desperate attempt to locate a self as solid as a thing, were part of what tears it apart.[89]

Finally, let us consider the fragmentation and self-dissolution experienced by a figure of singular importance for modern conceptions of madness who has been alluded to earlier: the poet, playwright, and general visionary of the theater Antonin Artaud. Both a diagnosed schizophrenic (hospitalized for most of the last ten years of his life) and an artist of great significance, Artaud was perhaps the major influence on experimental theater in our century. Of particular relevance, however, is his emblematic status for devotees of an extreme antirationalism. In the literary and antipsychiatric avant-garde, he has been presented as the supreme example of a Dionysian madness—a sort of Wildman figure whose literary productions have been said to display the "uncontrollable, polymorphous movement of desire" or "libido unbound," and to show that "emotion released from all restraint of logic . . . can result in a glorious rhetoric of unbridled passion." Artaud's aesthetic project has been said to display an "exuberant" self-dissolution comparable to Rimbaud's *Illuminations*, itself a "triumph of desiring fantasy."[90] To consider Artaud's own writings is, however, to suspect the superficiality or, at least, the radical incompleteness of this common portrayal.

Artaud's most famous work, *The Theatre and Its Double* (written between 1931 and 1936), does call for a Dionysiac "theatre of cruelty" that would burst the bounds of normal selfhood through an excess of passion and pain. In fact, however, the most constant theme of Artaud's writings is something very different: what he himself describes as "an absence of mental fire, a failure of the circulation of life," or "a disembodiment of reality."[91] Artaud well knew that "there is in me something damaged from an emotional point of view." "In matters of feeling," he wrote, "I can't even find anything that would correspond to feelings." It in no way diminishes the unique and uncanny brilliance of his writings to suggest that the sensual excesses of his "theatre of cruelty" may be better understood not as expressions of a naturally overflowing vitality but as defenses *against* the devitalization and derealization that pervaded his being. Indeed, Artaud himself practically tells us as much: "I wanted a theatre that would be like a shock treatment, galvanize, shock people into feeling," he said.[92] In the preface to

The Theatre and Its Double, this author, who would have liked to identify with the murderous sensualist of his imagination, the Roman emperor Heliogabalus, speaks of "the unprecedented number of crimes whose perverse gratuitousness is explained only by our powerlessness to take complete possession of life."[93] (There is an analogy here to the acts of self-mutilation and the risk taking in which schizoid and schizophrenic individuals may engage as a way of trying to regain a feeling of their own physical existence.)

Artaud did desire to eclipse the mind through ecstatic sensation and fusion with the ambient world; yet, far from being his primordial condition, this was an escape he never achieved—not through drugs, not through the theatre of cruelty, not even through his own quest for the primitive, his famous voyage to the land of the Tarahumara Indians of Mexico (where he expected to find the world "in perpetual exaltation"). One might say, in fact, that Artaud's persistent misery, and the most powerful motivation for the extreme antimentalism of his aesthetic philosophy, lay in the fact that the loss of self he actually experienced—he called it a "constant leakage of the normal level of reality," a "fundamental slackening of my being," or "dispossession of my vital substance"—had a far more cerebral character, one closer to the *mise en abyme* of self-alienating introspection. As he puts it in *The Theatre and Its Double*, "If our life lacks brimstone, i.e., a constant magic, it is because we choose to observe our acts and lose ourselves in consideration of their imagined form instead of being impelled by their force."[94] And in texts such as *The Umbilicus of Limbo* and *The Nerve Meter* he writes, "We are of the inside of the mind, of the interior of the head"; "I suffer because the Mind is not in life and life is not the Mind; I suffer from the Mind as organ, the Mind as interpreter, the Mind as intimidator of things to force them to enter the Mind."

In 1925 Artaud described a sense of bodily fragmentation, a physical state "presenting to the brain only images of limbs that are threadlike and woolly, images of limbs that are far away and not where they should be." He speaks in the same year of the "pitfalls" and "furtive abductions" of his thought processes, writing, "I am the witness, I am the only witness of myself." It seems that Artaud was never able to shake this vitiation of the sense of controlled mental activity and bodily self-presence or the disturbing self-consciousness that accompanied it. When, a dozen years later, he returns from his voyage to Mexico, he is profoundly disillusioned with his experiment in primitivism, his attempt to "liberate" his body by participating in the peyote rituals of the Tarahumara Indians. Now he can only marvel at "what false presentiment, what illusory and artificial intuition" could ever have given him these hopes; for, rather than infusing him with vitality and a feeling of physical integrity, the experience seems only to have exacerbated his self-preoccupation and sense of fragmentation. Thus he describes having experienced his physical being as a sort of vast and fragile body-universe disintegrating beneath his watchful eye: "This cataclysm which was my body . . . this dislocated assemblage, this piece of damaged geology. . . . Twenty-eight days of this heavy captivity . . . this dislocated assemblage . . . this ill-assembled heap of organs which I was *and which I had the impression of witnessing* like a vast landscape on the point of breaking up."[95]

CONCLUSION

To stress the role of hyperreflexivity in schizophrenic self-disturbances is not, as we know, to suggest that these developments are essentially volitional in nature, as if the fragmentation and dislocation in question were purely the result of some perverse strategy engaged in willfully. The very processes of introspection that *dissolve* the sense of volition or active engagement can seem, in fact, to be imposed upon the schizophrenic individual—who may well feel victimized by an "irresistible seeing," a kind of inwardly directed truth-taking stare. This is apparent in the case of one schizophrenic woman who described what she called "the splitting 'dialectic' and the splitting 'egos which inspect each other' "; these were processes of self-monitoring that occurred when she was participating in a conversation and that seemed to have a kind of mechanical inertia of their own and to lead to painful and unwanted consequences: "then I, through this combination of myself projecting into the other person, and the other person in itself, am monitored to react as expected," she said, "and that happens so rapidly that I, even if I had wanted to, am unable to stop myself. And after that, I am left by myself and very lonely."[96]

One wonders whether this lack of a sense of willing one's own introspectiveness might itself be, to some extent, self-imposed—with the process of externalizing introspection contributing even to its *own* self-alienation. In any case, various kinds of neurobiological factors or cognitive abnormalities could well be involved—whether by constituting the more or less immediate neurophysiological substrate of these hyperreflexive processes or by creating conditions that might elicit the analytic scrutiny in some more indirect manner. A proper understanding of these I-disorders demands, then, that we go beyond the standard polarities of act/affliction or defense/deficiency that have channeled so much thinking about madness. We clearly need to explode the received distinctions—to recognize, for instance, that it is both true and not true that such patients lack awareness of and control over themselves. What patients like those we have been considering cannot seem to control is self-control itself; what they cannot get distance from is their own endless need for distancing; what they cannot be conscious of is their own hypertrophied self-consciousness and its effect on their world. Schizophrenics may well become perplexed and confused, lost in the endless recursions of an isolated and abstract journey into the interior; but what entraps them there is a condition of hyperintentionality, with exaggerated willfulness and self-reference. What prevents them from returning to a more normal existence is no simple failure of will but, in a sense, an inability to *desist* from willing—an inability to let themselves be caught up in and carried along by the ongoing flow of practical activity in which normal existence is grounded. Thomas Hennell seems to have understood these paradoxes: "The introverted mind believes itself busy, yet produces nothing," he wrote; "Its self-torture is partly involuntary, but partly willful: for that which ambitiously directs it increases its painful labor."[97]

The importance of disengagement and self-consciousness in the schizophrenic I-disorders also casts a new light on the praecox feeling—that essential strangeness that, in Jaspers's view, is so closely bound up with fundamental mutations of selfhood and volition. It suggests that what is alienating to the external observer about such individuals is not *just* their sheer differentness. Encountering such a patient is *not*, for example, like encountering someone from a radically different culture or someone who is in any highly different state or stage of consciousness—as with, say, a delirious alcoholic, a euphoric manic, or a young child; what seems to be alienating about schizophrenics like Natalija and Jonathan Lang cannot be separated from the self-alienation felt by the patients themselves. But if this is so, it has the odd implication that the observer's alienation may not, in fact, indicate a total failure of empathy: it may be a *shared* alienation, a feeling evoked by accurate intuitions of what the patient is actually going through. Could it be, then, that the dizzying abyss we feel in the presence of certain schizophrenic patients is connected with the *mise en abyme* into which they themselves are falling?

CHAPTER 8
· ·

Memoirs of a Nervous Illness

*I have decided to apply for my release from the Asylum in the near future
in order to live once again among civilised people and at home with my wife.
It is therefore necessary to give those persons who will then constitute the
circle of my acquaintances an approximate idea at least of my religious
conceptions, so that they may have some understanding of the necessity
which forces me to various oddities of behaviour, even if they do not fully
understand these apparent oddities.*

*This is the purpose of this manuscript. . . . I cannot of course count upon
being fully understood because things are dealt with which cannot be expressed in human language; they exceed human understanding. Nor can I
maintain that everything is irrefutably certain even for me; much remains
only presumption and probability. After all I too am only a human being and
therefore limited by the confines of human understanding; but one thing I
am certain of, namely that I have come infinitely closer to the truth than
human beings who have not received divine revelation.* [41]°

So begins *Memoirs of My Nervous Illness*, the most influential account of
a psychotic disorder ever produced by a psychiatric patient. This book,
published in 1903, is the work of one Daniel Paul Schreber, a highly intelligent, articulate man who suffered his first psychotic break in 1894, the year
after he was appointed to the position of presiding judge (*Senatspräsident*)
in the Superior State Court in Dresden, in what was then the kingdom of
Saxony. He developed symptoms of paranoid schizophrenia and was to

°Numbers in parentheses in this chapter refer to page citations in Daniel Paul Schreber,
Memoirs of My Nervous Illness.[1]

spend thirteen years of his life in insane asylums. It was toward the end of a long period of hospitalization (1893 to 1902, spent mostly at Sonnenstein Asylum) that Schreber wrote the weird, eerily precise memoir that drew the attention of most of the luminaries of early-twentieth-century psychiatry and made its author perhaps the most famous mental patient who ever lived.

Schreber's manuscript is a complex and fantastic document whose content is impossible to summarize and whose tone is exceptionally difficult to convey: an odd mix of certainty and tentativeness, of the literal and the abstract, of the lucid and the utterly bizarre. Though his symptoms cover virtually the entire range of psychiatric abnormality, the most striking involve profound transformations of selfhood, including an exaggerated sense of his own centrality in the universe, a loss of the normal sense of volitional control, and feelings of the fragmentation, dissolution, or multiplication of the self. Schreber describes the most astonishing experiences and beliefs, often involving an otherworldly, private cosmos inhabited by strange beings—"nerves," "rays," and "souls" who are capable of taking over his consciousness, thinking his thoughts, and looking out through his very eyes. He speaks, for example, of "a time when souls in nerve-contact with me talked of a plurality of heads (that is several individuals in one and the same skull) which they encountered in me and from which they shrank in alarm crying 'For heaven's sake—that is a human being with several heads' " (86). While these strange symptoms have been seen in psychoanalysis as illustrative of regressive, infantile experiences, and in psychiatry as quintessential examples of incomprehensibility, a careful reading of the *Memoirs* suggests that Schreber was hardly devoid of the kinds of reflexive thinking and self-consciousness usually associated with the most advanced and sophisticated forms of adult mental life. In fact, many of his themes and concerns coincide remarkably closely with what the philosopher/historian Michel Foucault (in his influential *Discipline and Punish*) describes as the central and defining features of the modern self.

Schreber's book has been of profound importance both in psychoanalysis and in medical psychology generally. Freud, much taken with it, made it the subject of the most extensive paper he ever wrote on psychosis, the famous "Psychoanalytic Notes upon an Autobiographical Account of a Case of Paranoia (Dementia Paranoides)"; and since that time Schreber has provided psychoanalysis with its classic case of both paranoid and schizophrenic illness, serving as a prime example of that profound regression to "infantile autoerotism" and egolessness that schizophrenia is assumed to entail.[2] Schreber's words were also read by most of the classic early writers on schizophrenia, including Eugen Bleuler, Adolf Meyer, Carl Jung, and Karl Jaspers, among others, and he was frequently cited as an example of schizophrenia in major psychiatric monographs and textbooks. Several passages from the *Memoirs* appear in Jaspers's *General Psychopathology*—as illustrations of the passivity experiences Jaspers considered to be the epitome of schizophrenic bizarreness and incomprehensibility.[3]

Schreber's memoirs are, in fact, so filled with descriptions of boundary confusion and passivization that they read almost like a manual of Schneider's First Rank Symptoms of schizophrenia—though seen from within. At times Schreber believed he was as wide as all space, that his boundaries were coextensive with the universe.[4] Yet he would sometimes maintain that his actions, both physical and mental, were entirely out of his control, sometimes under that of other beings or minds who imprisoned his "will power," thereby committing what he called "soul murder" on him. With his "mind's eye" he saw "rays," looking like "long drawn out filaments [that] approach[ed] my head from some vast distant spot on the horizon . . . stretching sometimes towards my head, sometimes withdrawing from it" (227); he saw alien souls (later these too became "rays") who had taken the form of little men and were now occupying themselves with the task of pulling his eyelids up and down with filaments as fine as cobwebs (138). Even the direction of his gaze or the attitudes of his mind would be manipulated through the "cursed creation of a false feeling." A "frame of mind" might be falsely imposed on him by "miracles," and he sometimes maintained that some external force was creating the objects before his eyes (insects in a garden, for example) and directing his gaze toward them just after the moment they were brought into being. Schreber's passivization was also expressed in a delusion that Freud particularly emphasized: a feeling that his body was losing its masculine characteristics and taking on the character of "feminine voluptuousness."

This bizarre universe of nerves and rays, of miracles and acts of soul murder, may at first seem beyond the pale of any rational understanding. *Memoirs of My Nervous Illness* is a book of nearly overwhelming complexity, written in a convoluted, at times Byzantine style, and larded with a wealth of what seem to be almost arbitrary details. One may be tempted to think that the delusions and near-hallucinations it describes are little more than the almost random products of a state of pure irrationality, perhaps of some kind of near-dementia, or of a delirium in which virtually any random fancy passing before the mind can be extracted and treated as real. Yet the more closely one reads, the more difficult it becomes to dismiss the hope for achieving some kind of interpretive or empathic understanding of Schreber's experiences. The whole structure of his lived world seems to have such specificity and precision; one cannot help but wonder whether it is possible to discover a coherent system lying behind it all. As Schreber himself remarks, it seems difficult to believe that a man could have just

> sucked from his fingers so to speak the whole complicated structure of ideas with its enormous mass of factual detail (for instance, about the soul-language, soul-conception . . . etc., etc.). Does not rather the thought

impose itself that a human being who is able to write on such matters and attain such singular ideas . . . must in fact have had some particular experiences and particular impressions from which other human beings are excluded? [296]

But what, one may ask, could these particular impressions be? What sort of existence could give rise to an experience of these "foundation" nerves that are like filaments vibrating with language, or of rays that course like arrows of curiosity through infinite (or is it interior) space? And finally, do the particular experiences that underlie Schreber's cosmos lie outside all normal or comprehensible human experience?

Freud's interpretation of the Schreber case focused on symptoms with an obvious sexual content. He postulated that Schreber felt a threatening erotic desire for his powerful father, "an outburst of homosexual libido," and that this was the essential underlying meaning both disguised and expressed in his various delusions.[5] Even to most psychoanalysts, however, this explanation has seemed insufficient; the radical transformations in the very *structure* of Schreber's existence—that is, the passivization and boundary confusion, what one might call the schizophrenic as opposed to merely paranoid features—have seemed far too extensive and profound to be accounted for on the basis of homosexual *content* alone.[6] Most psychoanalytic writers have therefore felt the need to emphasize regression of a more profound type.

The psychiatrists who translated the *Memoirs* argue, for example, that the core of the illness is something more primitive than homosexual libido, namely, "a reactivation of unconscious, archaic procreation fantasies concerning life, death, immortality, rebirth, creation," fantasies dating back to the oral or earliest stage of individual development (395). Other eminent psychoanalysts discover in the *Memoirs* abundant evidence of "conflict over voracious, primitive oral impulses," "unfulfilled yearning for infantile gratifications," and regression into "primitive perceptions," "oral greed," and "infantile clinging." Still others have spoken of a return to a virtually prepsychological stage, the "earliest beginning of ego development when various body parts assume an independent, autonomous role . . . representing the world and reality for the patient," as well as to archaic forms of "magical thinking" characteristic of infancy.[7]

Certainly there were moments when Schreber's behavior did seem to confirm conceptions of him as psychologically primitive. When, as often happened, he would break into a loud, incomprehensible, and seemingly uncontrollable bellowing, he must surely have looked and sounded like some Wildman; and when, as also happened, he would be incontinent, apparently losing control of his bowels, he must have seemed very like an infant.[8] I would not deny that his actions and experiences may, in certain respects, echo and evoke aspects of early childhood and that they may express instinctual needs. This, however, is true of nearly all of human behavior; and it hardly accounts for the distinctively *schizophrenic* features of Schreber's lived world. Far from demonstrating an enslavement to impulse and stimulus or an incapacity for self-monitoring awareness, Schreber is in fact a fanatic of self-consciousness, a self-victimizing victim whose relentless awareness is both his defense and his prison. Indeed, the very symptoms that seem most obviously primitive—such as his incontinence and his bellowing—turn out to derive from just this hyperreflexivity, a condition that is closely akin, as we shall see, to the configuration of knowledge and power in modern society described in Foucault's *Discipline and Punish*, a work that purports to offer a "genealogy of the modern 'soul.' " Obviously, it would be absurd to view Schreber as being in any sense a *typical* man of modern civilization, but there are nevertheless certain respects in which he could be considered an *exemplary* one. For as I shall demonstrate, Schreber does manifest, in a most exaggerated fashion, certain qualities that are central to the modern mind and self. (Incidentally, Foucault's book is not specifically concerned with modernism but with general developments in the nature of social existence over the last two centuries or so; the modes of being and forms of consciousness implied by his analysis seem, however, to emerge with particular prominence and clarity in the culture of modernism.)

The delusional schizophrenic has often been viewed as someone who has reverted to a precivil condition—a kind of Aristotelian beast ruled by the language of the heart, indifferent to "the knowledge, language, and assumptions of civil society and rationality."[9] In his early book on notions of insanity, *Madness and Civilization,* even Foucault took the view that psychosis was a "sovereign enterprise of unreason," a wild state of an "inaccessible primitive purity" that might provide inspiration for a "total contestation" of modern Western civilization.[10] The truth, as we shall see, can be very different: the most autistic delusional system may be uncannily reminiscent of the public world, mirroring social practices and mores in the innermost chambers of the self.

But before we can investigate this modern self, before we can discern the conditions of an age in the solitary reaches of one man's being, we must first learn more about Schreber's illness and about the structure of his inner world.

SCHREBER'S DELUSIONAL COSMOS

Schreber, who would be considered a case of "late-onset schizophrenia,"[11] did not suffer his first mental breakdown until 1884, when, at age forty-two, he came down with a variety of symptoms, including speech impediments, hypochondria of near-delusional proportions, and an extreme oversensitivity to noise. He was admitted to a psychiatric clinic in a "very unstable state of mind" (xi), but was discharged six months later, apparently cured—the illness having passed, as he himself put it, "without any occurrences bordering on the supernatural" (62).

It was some eight years later, not long after being named *Senatspräsident* of the Dresden court, that Schreber suffered a second mental collapse, this time a true psychotic break that would cause him to be hospitalized, sometimes against his will, for thirteen of his next twenty-seven years. His troubles began with the hearing of strange noises in the walls, noises he attributed to the existence of a "more or less definite intention . . . to prevent my sleep." Soon these noises turned into "inner voices," and Schreber's illness took on a "menacing" character; for the next seven years, the voices would speak to him incessantly, persisting undeterred even when he was engaged in conversation or physical activity (68–69, 225). Though discharged in 1902, after eight years of hospitalization, Schreber relapsed in 1907 and was admitted to the asylum at Leipzig-Dosen, where he died four years later in what is said to have been "a state of physical deterioration and total madness."[12]

Schreber's actions during his psychotic periods could certainly be described as bizarre. Without explaining what he meant, he might complain of a "loss of rays," or would say that the doctor had "negligently emitted rays" (268). At mealtimes he would stare rigidly or move restlessly with strange grimaces, while loudly clearing his throat and touching his face in attempts to push open his eyelids, which he believed were "closed by miracles." His excitement sometimes resulted in bursts of loud and persistent laughter or bellowing, or he would pound heavily on a piano in what his doctor and attendants found "a most disturbing manner" (269). Occasionally he would be incontinent, defecating in bed or in his pants. But when matters other than his delusions were discussed—law, politics, state administration, or art—he was generally lucid, cogent, and correct in his judgment; according to one doctor's report, "Equally he was well-behaved and amiable during light conversation with the ladies present and his humor was always tasteful and decent" (280).

A similar duality characterizes the pages of the *Memoirs*. Sometimes Schreber reports the most peculiar or impossible experiences, or makes the most grandiose claims: "On one occasion 240 Benedictine Monks under the leadership of a Father whose name sounded like Starkiewicz, suddenly moved into my head to perish therein" (71); "I am absolutely certain that . . . I command experiences which—when generally acknowledged as valid—will act fruitfully to the highest possible degree among the rest of mankind" (33). But alongside such statements, which might seem to imply total breakdown of accurate reality testing, he displays a remarkable reasonableness and ability to assess the point of view of his audience. Indeed, Schreber himself was well aware of the intractability of his subject matter, which he called "the most difficult subject ever to exercise the human mind," and seemed to anticipate the praecox feeling his book would elicit. To Schreber, the "order of the World itself was out of joint," and he was aware that an audience of normal readers, having no familiarity with these transformations, would inevitably have difficulty imagining his experiences: "Again it is extremely difficult to describe these changes in words because matters are dealt with which lack all analogies in human experience and which I appreciated directly only in part with my mind's eye, in part only by their effects so that I may have formed but an approximate picture" (117).

Schreber does, however, give a detailed account of the nature and course of his illness. In his estimation, the central element of his "nervous illness" was that his reason was under attack. His first symptoms involved a torturing insomnia, an uncontrollable *heightening* of awareness. At first he became acutely aware of happenings around him, such as odd crackling noises in the wall of his bedroom. But soon his attention turned inward, as he was afflicted with what he called the "mental torture" of "compulsive thinking." This meant having to think incessantly, never to give what he called the "nerves" of the mind their needed rest (70).

In Schreber's opinion, the circumstances of this compulsive thinking were "infinitely difficult" to describe since they lay "outside all human experience" and would therefore be impossible for normal readers to imagine. Nevertheless, he did write a fair amount about this phenomenon. In one passage he likens the experience of "compulsive thinking" to that of a person trying to memorize a passage or repeat to himself a silent prayer; but he also points out an important respect in which this analogy is *not* accurate: whereas in the normal case the use of language "depends only on the will of the person whose nerves are concerned," in his case, Schreber explains, the "nerves are set in motion *from without*" (69, 70). Schreber also describes compulsive thinking as taking place in a special "nerve-language" or "basic-language" that differs in certain linguistic respects from normal human language.

To understand the experience of compulsive thinking and the nerve-language, it is necessary to understand the nerves and rays, for these, along with God, constitute the fundamental ontological forms of what he calls his "out-of-joint" world. Consider Schreber's own characterization of this "miraculous structure"—which, he says, has recently suffered a "rent" that is intimately connected with his own personal fate (54):

> The human soul is contained in the nerves of the body; about their physical nature I, as a layman, cannot say more than that they are extraordinarily delicate structures—comparable to the finest filaments—and the total

mental life of a human being rests on their excitability by external impressions. Vibrations are thereby caused in the nerves which produce the sensations of pleasure and pain in a manner which cannot be further explained; they are able to retain the memory of impressions received (the human memory) and have also the power of moving the muscles of the body which they inhabit into any manifest activity by exertion of their will power. [45]

Nerves, it seems, are the "foundation" of all human experience (70n), since their activity, in the form of "vibrations," corresponds to the events occurring in a human being's consciousness. This, clearly, is a metaphysical vision that imputes a profound passivity, and a quality of materiality, to the human mind: in fact, the very term *nerves* has mechanistic or physicalistic connotations. Like an aeolian harp, the nerves vibrate in automatic response to passing influences. Even volition, or what might more accurately be called the *illusion* of volition, is but a function of these mechanistically determined nerve-filaments; for, as Schreber explains, "other nerves (the nerves of intellect) receive and retain mental impressions and as the organs of will, give to the whole human organism the impulse to manifest those of its powers designed to act on the outside world" (45). All nerves, then, appear to be the determined recipients of influences from outside themselves, influences that come either in the form of the external impressions mentioned earlier or in the form of rays.

The rays, actually, are nerves themselves, though of a somewhat different sort than the foundation nerves of the human mind. As Schreber explains, they are transformations of the "infinite and eternal" nerves of God, who is "only nerve, not body, and akin therefore to the human soul" (46). At times these rays influence the nerves to think their compulsive thoughts in the nerve-language, thus forcing the nerves to be a conduit for the rays' thoughts. And in addition to influencing the nerves, the rays also watch the activities of the nerves. "What are you thinking of now?" they ask incessantly, refusing to believe, or to allow, that a human mind (the foundation nerves) might sometimes be thinking nothing at all (70). (Incidentally, Schreber is not entirely consistent in his terminology; sometimes he uses both *nerves* and *rays* in a generic sense that includes both types of beings or "souls.")[13]

Obviously, the relationship of rays to nerves is in some sense antagonistic, analogous to that of master and slave or spy and victim. But it also involves a certain interdependence: like a pair of lovers, the nerves and rays are dependent on maintaining contact with each other while also requiring a precise degree of distance. Much of the *Memoirs* is taken up with their problematic relationship, a relationship described in the most concrete or spatialized terms, almost as if it involved physical entities in a kind of delusional solar system. The rays' interest in the nerves, for instance, is frequently represented as a physical moving of the rays toward the nerves—not unlike a magnetic attraction. And Schreber explains that when the foundation nerves are overly excited, vibrating (that is, thinking or experiencing) too intensely, they attract the rays down toward them with too much force, threatening a dissolution of their separateness.

Frequently this anticipated fusion of nerves and rays seems to be experienced as a desirable state, inspiring feelings of "soul-voluptuousness." But more often it seems dangerous, since it threatens annihilation of the rays. Then the rays resort to extreme measures in order to save their integrity. And in his "mind's eye," Schreber sees the fight against this attraction in quite vivid and physicalistic terms—as, for instance, when the rays use the defense of "tieing-to-celestial-bodies," attaching themselves to the stars far above them in order to avoid being sucked down and dissolved in the nerves (118). Yet there is also the danger of too *little* attraction between nerves and rays. This occurs when the thought in the nerves is one that has already been observed and written down by the rays; for then, says Schreber, "the approaching rays [may be] sent down with the phrase 'We have already got this,' *scil* written-down; in a manner hard to describe the rays were thereby made unreceptive to the power of attraction of such a thought" (122). (One of the special characteristics of the nerve-language is the incompleteness of its sentences; Schreber uses *scil*, standing for the Latin *scilicet*, to indicate that a phrase—in this case "written-down"—was omitted from what he heard.)

And if the thoughts carried by the nerves should be incapable of attracting the contemplative attention of the rays, then God, the source of the rays, will assume that Schreber's mental powers are extinct, his reason destroyed. No longer attracted by the gravitylike force of the nerve-language, both the rays and God himself will withdraw from Schreber. And this is a traumatic separation, which brings on a mini-apocalypse (165–66). Noises seem to well up and Schreber finds himself bellowing (or, as he puts it, the "bellowing-miracle" is set in motion); meanwhile, cries of "help" can be heard from the rays, which now feel separated from the nerves, and from God himself, from which they are withdrawing. (These "cries of help" are, incidentally, always instantly followed by a phrase that has been learned by rote: "If only the cursed cries of help would stop.")

Here, then, are the basic elements of Schreber's delusional cosmos: a world of nerves and rays, of compulsive thinking and bellowing-miracles, of tieing-to-celestial-bodies and foundation nerves vibrating with language. In a moment we will see that these curious entities and processes can be understood as the expressions of a quintessentially modern frame of mind—a condition depicted in Foucault's *Discipline and Punish*.

One of the major objectives of Foucault's work, as he himself has noted, is to explore the nature and development of modern forms of experience and modes of subjectivity; he wants to grasp how "the self is not merely given but is constituted in relationship to itself as subject"—and, in certain of his works, to understand how "the subject is objectified by a process of division either within himself or from others."[14] Foucault, however, is not a phenomenologist; what he focuses on is not individual experience itself but, rather, the surrounding social forms—the institutions, technologies, social practices, and ideological orientations that shape and echo this inner realm. Thus in *Discipline and Punish* one finds descriptions of penal practices and prison architecture, of disciplinary methods and judicial systems; and one must read between the lines in order to grasp the relevance of all of this for what is our main concern: the nature of modern subjectivity. (Also, Foucault's book includes at least a quasi-causal thesis—or a "genealogical" one, as he would call it. He seems to imply that forms of subjectivity are, in the main, consequences of certain social and political arrangements. Here I am concerned only with the nature or structure of modern subjectivity, not with its sources or external conditions, so I will actually be applying only a limited aspect of Foucault's overall argument.)

PANOPTICISM

The organizing metaphor of *Discipline and Punish*, its central image for describing the modern social order (and, ultimately, for characterizing modern subjectivity), is the Panopticon—an architectural design conceived by Jeremy Bentham in 1791, at the height of the Enlightenment enthusiasm for technical rationality. Though originally designed for prison buildings, the Panopticon could also be used for other kinds of institutions requiring observation or discipline, such as schools, hospitals, or military barracks. Its essential point was to effect a radical separation between observer and observed, and to keep the latter under constant surveillance. The Panopticon consists of two elements: a central observation tower and an encircling building containing numerous small cells. Because of the thinness of the encircling building, each cell would to be open on two sides, with bars on the outer wall allowing light to flood the cell and bars on the inner wall exposing the occupant to the gaze of the watcher in the central tower. In this way, those in the cells would always be within sight of the implacable tower, which itself was darkened and fitted with narrow slits so that those within could peer out without being seen.

Foucault describes the Panopticon as "a machine for dissociating the see/being seen dyad: in the peripheric ring, one is totally seen, without ever seeing; in the central tower one sees everything without ever being seen."[15] In Foucault's view, this little-known architectural fantasy cannot be dismissed as some "bizarre little utopia" or "perverse dream," for it captures the grim essence of the modern age—pervasive characteristics of modern life that prevail even in the absence of any literal Panopticon. Whereas premodern society had been the era of the "principle of the dungeon," with the powerless hidden away in dark places and the powerful highly visible (for instance, in the spectacles of the royal court), in the modern world it is the principle of "panopticism" that dominates: now the powerless are exposed, and power lies in the relentless, invisible gaze that studies them.

For our purposes, the significance of this panoptic system has less to do with the synoptic knowledge it offers to those in the tower than with the effect it has on those observed, who are brought to internalize, and to act in accordance with, the standards and expectations of the system in which they are caught. If we imagine the situation of the prisoner in the Panopticon, we realize he must remain constantly aware of the observation tower looming before him; further, since the prisoner cannot know whether he is *in fact* being watched, he is never able to let down his guard. As Foucault points out, if vigilance is able to replace the severity and drama of punishment, this is because the eternal vigilance that supplants the circus of torture is ultimately an inner vigilance, an observing of the self *by* the self. Paradoxically enough, this situation may even give rise to a sense of freedom in the prisoner—the freedom of a self bent on scrutinizing and subduing a "lower" or more objectified part of its own being.

Though Foucault does not detail just *how* the experience of such an individual prisoner would be shaped, it is not difficult to imagine some of the paradoxical consequences. Such a system will force one to experience oneself *both* as the body that feels itself observed (without ever knowing for sure when this is the case) and also as the watcher who feels like a pure and omniscient consciousness. But oddly enough, while the prisoner is in one sense both observer and observed, in another sense he cannot truly identify with either of these polarized roles (that is, either with a bodily self-presence or with an observing consciousness). One cannot experience one's own *bodily* being from within but only from without, from the imaginary position of an observer in the tower. And, insofar as one identifies oneself with the mind, one will be identifying with a being whose essence is always elsewhere—an imagined, alien consciousness, perpetually watching from a remove.

A second paradox is that these two selves are characterized by both an absolute separation and an absolute interdependence, an interdependence amounting to a kind of symbiosis. In this variant of the master/slave dialectic, each self—observer and observed—comes to be defined almost completely by its relationship with the other, a relationship whose essence is distance and difference: thus, the prisoner's body would have to be experienced *by* the prisoner as a body-as-perceived, a body *for* the distant observer; while the observer's being would be reduced to a single function, the-being-who-observes-*me*-from-afar. The Panopticon also brings about a peculiar kind of isolation, in which one never feels alone. Though deprived of all "horizontal" relationships—all possibility of interacting with one's equals or of shedding individuality by, say, ecstatic merging with a crowd—one is nevertheless forced to experience, and ultimately to internalize, a "vertical" relationship with an always superior, always invisible Other. According to Foucault, this entire system culminates in the nineteenth-century penitentiary colony of Mettray, where the principal punishment was solitary confinement in one's cell, on whose walls were written these words: "God sees you."[16]

Foucault considers the Panopticon and Mettray to be only the most concrete and blatant manifestations of a new regime of power/knowledge whose reach extends far beyond penal systems. In his view, all the many techniques that have developed in the modern world for the observation, analysis, quantification, and control of the behavior of human beings participate in a pervasive new "regime of truth"—present not merely in the development of psychiatry, psychology, and the social sciences but also in practices like psychotherapy and in the insidious psychologization of everyday life. Innocent and well-intentioned as these methods may seem, they cannot deny their association with a regime for which the "ideal point of penality . . . would be an indefinite discipline: an interrogation without end, an investigation that would be extended without limit to a meticulous and ever more analytical observation, a judgment that would at the same time be the constitution of a file that was never closed, the calculated leniency of a penalty that would be interlaced with the ruthless curiosity of an examination."[17]

As we have seen, the central elements of Schreber's delusional world are the nerves, the rays, and God, while his central preoccupation is the relationship among these various types of beings. I now want to show how these strange, quasi-cosmological entities—which suggest a kind of weird planetary system existing in a reified, external space—must be read as symbolic representations of aspects of Schreber's own consciousness, a consciousness both rent and joined by an inner panopticism. Whereas the nerves represent the part of the mind that is observed—self-as-object—the rays represent the part that *does* the observing—self-as-subject. Further, the God who lies behind the rays (for rays, as the reader will recall, are the nerves of God) corresponds to that invisible, potentially omniscient, only half-internalized Other who is the source and grounding of Schreber's particular kind of introversion. We shall see how uncannily close is the correspondence between these ontological entities and the fundamental elements of the Panopticon—with its prisoner, its imagined Other watching from the dark tower, and the internalized gaze that forges an infernal marriage between two distant beings.[18]

"Rays" and "God"

The association of rays with reflective meta-awareness is implied in many parts of the memoirs. In one passage, Schreber distinguishes human nature from that of plants according to the criterion of *self*-consciousness, which he associates with rays: "it is incomprehensible, at least for human beings, that divine rays could enter into *plants* which, even if considered in a way as living, yet lack all self-awareness" (192). In another passage he speaks of "self-awareness" being returned to corpses "through the influence of the rays" (48–49).

Further, the *kind* of self-awareness associated with rays seems to involve a characteristic combination of internality with externality, of intimacy with alienness, that is reminiscent of the prisoner of panopticism. The main characteristics of Schreber's "God" are the same as those of the observer in Bentham's tower: first, distance or hiddenness and, second, omniscience or, more precisely, a *potential* omniscience. Thus, among the voices Schreber hears is the voice of God calling himself "I who am distant" and that of the rays referring to God as "the one who retires to an enormous distance" (160, 191). At the same time Schreber experiences God as having ready access to his own innermost thoughts: for, as he puts it, it is "always *possible* for God to get to know the inner person through nerve-contact, whenever the need arose" (54). Schreber's feeling that the rays are both outside and inside the self—visible, as he says, to the "*bodily* eye when I keep my eyes open" and to the "*mind's* eye when my eyes are closed" (227)—also seems to be an expression of the feeling of being scrutinized by a gaze that exists both outside and within, belonging to the self as well as to some distant Other. On the one hand, rays are those beings who, as Schreber puts it, "are able to read my thoughts" or "to partake of my thoughts" (187, 50). While in this sense internal to the self, the rays are also antagonistic and alien; the questions and statements they address to him are nearly always those of an endlessly suspicious, incessantly demanding external observer and critic. The rays ask, "What are you thinking of now?" or "Are you not ashamed then?"—and often demand, "Why do you not say it aloud?" Sometimes they sneer, "Fancy such a person as a *Senatspräsident*," or badger with the remark "has been recorded" each time they encounter, in the nerves, a thought they have already observed (70, 199).

Schreber's vulnerability is, however, even more profound than that of Bentham's ever-visible prisoner, for Schreber's is an *inner* panopticism; and not even the boundaries of the body provide protection against these rays that exist in a dimension beyond the physical and can penetrate to the core of his being:

> I will mention the idea which is bound up with the phrase that the *devil can crawl through a keyhole.* In my opinion this belief is correctly based on the fact that no mechanical obstacle made by man can prevent the entry of the rays. I experience at every moment on my own body that this is so; no wall however thick, no closed window can prevent the ray filaments penetrating in a way incomprehensible to man and so reaching any part of my body, particularly my head. [242]

Typically, Schreber expresses this vulnerability in quite concrete terms—speaking, for example, of "flights of rays" that "ploughed through" or "temporarily thinned" his skull by "pulverizing" the "bony material" (131, 136).

"Nerves" and "Nerve-Language"

One of the unusual characteristics of the "nerve-language" is that its expressions would often be grammatically incomplete, at first leaving out a few key words, later leaving out most of a sentence. Schreber explains that, by what he calls an "abominable abuse of me," he was forced to think through each of these incomplete expressions to completion—as if there were a demand, emanating from some unknown source, to check whether he really knew the full sense of each sentence (70). Also, as time passed, the language Schreber heard in his hallucinatory world would sometimes take on another odd characteristic: he would lose any sense of meaning and hear the words only as sounds.

As I mentioned, Schreber believed that the average person would have great difficulty understanding his descriptions of "compulsive thinking," as of other aspects of his "out-of-joint" world. As he says, "matters are dealt with which lack all analogies in human experience and which I appreciated directly only in part with my mind's eye" (117). Yet there is a perfectly normal aspect of human consciousness that closely corresponds to what Schreber finds so odd: what psychologists call inner speech. The very characteristics he considers unique to his own compulsive thinking can be understood either as *usual* aspects of inner speech or as consequences of the *unusual* act of bringing inner speech into explicit awareness (for this is normally an implicit or tacit process).

According to Vygotsky's classic *Thought and Language*, the structure or skeleton of normal adult thought is largely provided by an "inner speech" that initially derives from and mimics overt, vocalized speech.[19] Through a lengthy process of internalization and transformation in the course of maturation, inner speech increasingly develops linguistic characteristics that differentiate it from most overt speech. Language becomes condensed, its syntax simplified, the number of words reduced. Since, in one's own mind, one is always already implicitly aware of the subject matter and context of one's own thoughts, it is not necessary, Vygotsky argues, for the inner process of symbolization to be explicit and complete; indeed, it is in the interest of efficiency that it *not* be.

The expressions Schreber heard in his compulsive thinking have precisely the same syntactic oddities as are found in inner speech, with its lacunae and its condensations. At first a word or two would be left out, as when Schreber (or rather, the "nerves") had the thought, "He should ——— about the order of the World," with the word *think* omitted. Later what Schreber calls "the system of not finishing a sentence" became more prevalent and more extreme. He began to hear phrases such as "why not . . . ," "why if . . . ," "why, because I . . . ," or "lacking now is . . ." and "I shall . . ." (172). Schreber explains that since the phrases had earlier been expressed more completely, he always knew their fuller sense and could make this sense explicit. "I shall . . . ," for example, meant "I shall have to think about that first."

There are several points in his memoirs where Schreber seems close to a conscious realization that the nerve-language is in fact a kind of inner speech. In one footnote, for example, he writes that "the souls were in the habit . . . of giving their thoughts (when communicating with one another) grammatically incomplete expression; that is to say they omitted certain words which were not essential for the sense" (70). Here he seems just on the verge of understanding the reason why expression in the nerve-language is incomplete—that is, because the same person, he himself, is both the speaker and listener of the thoughts. This, by the way, may be the psychological reality lying behind Schreber's experience, mentioned earlier, of being "a plurality of heads (that is several individuals in one and the same skull)" (86).

The prominence of compulsive thinking in Schreber's experience shows the extent to which his is an *inner* panopticism, an involuted existence whose main object of scrutiny is not the bodily but the inner self, the silent and private realm of thinking. But it is important to recognize that the exigent introspection of his panoptical gaze does not just reveal or illuminate certain phenomena; what Foucault calls the "power that insidiously objectifies all those on whom it is applied" also transforms its objects. To see this we might look once again to Schreber's compulsive thinking—now, however, by considering not similarities but differences between Schreber's nerve-language and normal inner speech.

In normal inner speech, the thinker generally experiences himself as active and in control of his thought.[20] Also, thoughts are not experienced as incomplete or meanings as unknown. Further, as Vygotsky points out, the thinker generally pays focal attention to meanings—seeming, as it were, to dwell *in* his words and therefore to be almost unaware of their presence *as* words. While providing a kind of structure or skeleton for the ongoing flow of thoughts, words will have a certain experiential transparency, akin to that of a hammer, which seems to merge with one's hand and arm, forgotten as all attention is directed to the nail or board that is being worked on. Thus, in normal (that is, non-hyper-self-conscious) thinking, meaning stays in the foreground while characteristics of the linguistic medium, such as syntactic structure and sound, tend to recede from awareness.[21] But Schreber's compulsive thinking is permeated by a scrutinizing objectification, and, in the artificial glare of his self-consciousness, the "outward appearance" and "bodily presence" of the linguistic medium do show up.[22] Language is experienced not as a transparent medium in which one dwells but as an opaque and mysterious nerve-language, existing at a psychological remove and independent of one's own efforts.

Thus, while Schreber immediately knew the full meaning of a sentence in the nerve-language, he still remained acutely aware of the syntactic incompleteness of the sentence. Further, he always felt obliged to prove to the rays and to God that he knew the full meaning, as if he were communicating not with himself or an intimate but with alien voices who repeatedly demanded, "Why do you not say it aloud?" (70). As time passed, Schreber became explicitly aware even of the sound characteristics of the words in his thoughts. For instance, a certain quality of externality and opacity was characteristic of the speech of certain "miraculously created" rays that took the form of birds that sometimes seemed inside, sometimes outside, of Schreber's mind. As Schreber explains, these bird-rays (which seem to represent projections of his own mind) "do not understand the *meaning* of the words they speak, but apparently they have a natural sensitivity for *similarity of sounds*" (thus "it matters little to the birds whether one speaks of 'Santiago' or 'Carthago,' 'Chinesenthum' or 'Jesum Christum' ") (168–69).

This last symptom—the tendency to respond more to the sound quality than to the semantic meaning of words (or to let the latter be determined by the former)—is common in schizophrenia, as is the experience of a loss of the sense of control over one's thoughts.[23] Virtually all psychoanalytic writers have seen these symptoms as indicating regression to an early stage in the development of language and thought, a stage when the symbol/referent distinction has not yet been acquired and the acoustic image of the word still compels the child's attention, and when the infant does not yet realize that his thoughts are not part of the outer world.[24] Yet the linguistic experience of the young child is vibrant and magical, with meanings proliferating wildly and sound and sense bleeding into each other. In Schreber's experience, by contrast, language is progressively *stripped* of significance: words stand forth with a quasi-materiality nearly devoid of all emotional or semantic charge. It seems more accurate, and more consistent with the overall character of his panoptical world, to understand this linguistic opacity (and also the passivization) as resulting from an intense and disengaged introspection, from an alienated mode in which language is not inhabited but contemplated as a thing apart.[25]

What is remarkable about Schreber's "compulsive thinking," then, is not so much *what* he sees or hears as *that* he sees or hears it—for *what* he sees is largely dependent on the fact of his looking. The peculiar elements of the nerve-language (syntactic incompleteness, passivity, semantic opacity) turn out to be the perfectly mundane and *normal* phenomena of inner speech, but in the perfectly *abnormal* situation of an exaggerated or panoptical self-consciousness.

AN ALLEGORY OF INNERNESS

When the mind is left to commune with itself and no longer has to come to terms with objects, it is in a sense reduced to imitating itself as object.
—Claude Lévi-Strauss
The Raw and the Cooked

By now it should be clear that Schreber's whole world of nerves and rays virtually demands to be read as a psychological rather than a cosmological vision, as a kind of allegory of the divided state of Schreber's own hyper-aware, acutely reflexive mind. As we have seen, the nerves constitute a kind of foundational level of experience in which are expressed the relatively "spontaneous" thoughts that are the *object* of scrutiny. Over these nerve-thoughts hover the rays, the part of the mind that actively monitors what takes place below, in the realm of inner speech. In this dichotomous ontology we discern the same vexed schism that is brought about by the Panopticon. (For a visual evocation of the preoccupation with the observing eye that can occur in schizophrenia, see figure 8.1.)

In another of those tantalizing footnotes that come so close to providing an exegesis yet never quite do, Schreber himself suggests the appropriateness of such a psychological rather than physical reading of nerves and rays:

FIGURE 8.1

Adolf Wölfli, *Saint Adolf Portant des Lunettes, entre les 2 Villes Géantes Niess et Mia (Saint Adolf Wearing Glasses, Between the 2 Giant Cities Niess and Mia)* (1924). Illustrates preoccupation with the observing eye in a painting by a schizophrenic. *Collection de l'Art Brut, Lausanne*

he says that the force of attraction exerted by the nerves on the rays ought not to be understood "in terms of natural forces acting purely mechanically" but as "something like a psychological motive power: the rays too find that 'attractive' which is of interest to them" (48). Since rays and nerves evidently stand for different parts of his own mind, it seems apparent that what interests Schreber is primarily his own endless involutions, which always seem to be taking place in some distant elsewhere.[26]

In this inner cosmos, which is neither incomprehensible nor primitive, the rays and nerves have the same interdependence, the same qualities of activity and passivity, and the same emptiness and plenitude, as would be expected of a self split into observing subject and object observed. The nerves and rays are, in fact, more than a little reminiscent of the polarized philosophy of Jean-Paul Sartre, where the Nothingness of consciousness and the passive plenitude of Being play out their endless and antagonistic symbiosis.[27] Thus, though the rays are generally in the active role, they also possess a quality of emptiness. Schreber explains that rays moving toward human beings are "essentially without thoughts" (234), and, as mentioned earlier, one of the compulsive, incomplete thoughts he reports is, "Lacking now is . . . "; when rendered explicit and complete, this means, "Lacking now is only the leading idea, that is—we the rays have no thoughts." The rays, it seems, have no life of their own; their whole existence is taken up with attending to what goes on in the nerves. Like a pure, disembodied Consciousness—essence of freedom and emptiness, a Being Without Qualities—they batten off the definiteness and plenitude of the nerves, whose own existence increasingly takes on the solidity and opacity of the physical world. The strange medium of the nerve-language might perhaps stand as a metaphor for modern subjectivity in general. For, though the most intimate and familiar part of the self, this ghostly product of self-scrutiny nevertheless exists as a quasi-external object, an alien, mysterious realm that must constantly be examined and decoded by the very being who creates and lives it.

The voluminous writings of the French man of letters Paul Valéry, whom T. S. Eliot once described as the exemplary poet of the twentieth century, at times recall, with eerie precision, Schreber's fretfully divided existence. In Valéry's alter-ego character, Monsieur Teste, the parallels are particularly obvious; Valéry's portrayal of this figure offers a far more direct account of the kind of experience that Schreber's *Memoirs* reveals in a more idiosyncratic and quasi-allegorical fashion. (Some differences between Schreber and Monsieur Teste will be discussed in the next chapter.)

Valéry describes this curious individual—whose name is an archaic spelling of *tête,* the French word for "head"—as "a Head: a formidable closed Implex" and as "the home of the Selves, the island of the Selves."[28] Valéry clearly identifies with this "monster of isolation and peculiar knowledge," this "severed head" or "mystic and . . . physicist of self-awareness, pure and applied," who—Valéry tells us—was conceived during a period of "strange excesses of consciousness of my *self,*" when the poet was himself "suffering from the acute ailment called precision." In Teste, Mind fights against Life; for, like the author of *Memoirs of My Nervous Illness,* he is a man "observed, watched, spied on by his 'ideas,' " who cannot sleep because when he dreams, he realizes that he is dreaming. Valéry's notes on Teste's state of mind could in fact stand as a description of Schreber's universe, of that mind's-eye world where mental entities (nerves and rays) consort in a kind of quasi-space:

> Monsieur Teste. . . . The internal becomes external (objective). The external become internal, and the *visible* or perceptible or external world becomes *rarefied.* . . .

If we could close the eyes of the mind, withdraw from the *inside*, the so-called inner world would be external, like the other.

Both are fabrications.

Teste is an "eternal observer" who denies the existence of external things, a being who feels the whole to be entirely contained within himself. But, as with the exigent introspection of William James, discussed in the previous chapter, the self was also objectlike: located in "cephalic, or cephalopsychic, sensations" in the head or behind the face, or positioned as a *"Thing* between the crease at the left corner of my mouth and the pressure of the eye-lids and the torsion of the eye-muscles."

Though both Schreber and Teste yearn for unity within the self and communion with the world, in the end they seem doomed by self-consciousness to a disturbing inner rift and a sense of isolation. A passage from Valéry's notebooks entitled "Teste and Narcissus" reads as follows:

On the Consequences of Self-seeing.
  (a) Study of duplication. Possibility.
  . (b) Unbearable diminution
       Surrounded by images of one's self.[29]

And here are some thoughts Valéry ascribes to Madame Teste: these questions, of a fictional wife thinking about her fictional husband, apply very well to Schreber—and perhaps also to Valéry and many another devotee of the hyperreflexive quest: "Is he not aiming beyond the world? Will he find life or death, at the extremity of his attentive will? Will it be God, or some frightful sense of encountering, at the deepest point of thought, nothing but the pale ray of his own miserable substance?"

BODY AND SOUL

One must not eye oneself having an experience, lest the eye become an evil eye.

—Friedrich Nietzsche
Twilight of the Idols

If Schreber's relentless hyperreflexivity divides consciousness, it also ranges more widely through his entire being, disrupting the sensual and resulting in strange behaviors that have, somewhat understandably, been understood almost exclusively on the analogy of the infant or the Wildman.[30] Yet these very behaviors—the outbursts of loud bellowing, the seemingly mindless recitation of irrelevant or nonsensical speech, even Schreber's incontinence—turn out to be but further ramifications of an implacable, highly cerebral, and panoptical form of consciousness.

Schreber describes his experience of the human condition as consisting of two different states, "compulsive thinking" and "soul-voluptuousness." These two states are fundamentally opposed to each other, for, as Schreber puts it, "every mental activity . . . is always accompanied by a considerable decrease in bodily well-being" (210). It seems he cannot rest comfortably in *either* of the states. As Schreber explains, human beings are "not born for voluptuous pleasure," but it is also true that "continued thinking, uninterrupted activity of the *nerves of intellect* without any respite, such as the rays impose on me through compulsive thinking, is equally incompatible with human nature." Though he states that "the art of conducting my life in the mad position I find myself . . . consists in finding a fitting middle course" between the two, such a course always eludes him, and instead he finds himself swinging back and forth between the extremes (209). Let us try to understand the reasons for this dis-ease that plagues him everywhere and always.[31]

As we have seen, the state of compulsive thinking involves the intense self-consciousness of a mind compelled to watch its own functioning. Most of the time, Schreber finds himself in a panoptical state of heightened awareness and reflexivity, as if this rather unnatural state were what came most naturally to him. Indeed, he is generally so incapable of spontaneity or absorption that he cannot perform the most trivial act—such as watching a butterfly flutter by—without obsessively monitoring his own experience and checking on whether he is really doing what he thinks he is doing:

> Whenever a butterfly appears my gaze is first directed to it as to a being newly created that very moment, and secondly the word "butterfly—has been recorded" is spoken into my nerves by the voices; this shows that one thought I could possibly no longer recognize a butterfly and one therefore examines me to find out whether I still know the meaning of the word "butterfly." [188]

In Schreber's cosmological-psychological world (which I have argued is an allegory of innerness), psychological division, introversion, and self-alienation are represented as a physical kind of distance, a spatial separation between the observing rays (or God) and the observed nerves (not unlike the distance between tower and cells in the Panopticon). Thus Schreber himself speaks of "the spatial conditions of God's existence, if I may so put it" (229).

In soul-voluptuousness, by contrast, there is an *absence* of such self-monitoring, which in turn is experienced as a collapsing or diminishing of the distance between rays and nerves—as when the nerves exert too much attraction and the rays disappear into them. Such an effacement of self-consciousness seems to occur at times of absorption, whether in intense physical pleasure or in perceptual experience; while at the theater or a church service, for example, Schreber would lose himself momentarily, since "the rays, always inquisitive, were so absorbed in watching the spectacle that their tendency to withdraw [that is, to retreat to the proper distance for panoptical self-consciousness] was minimal" (222).

Schreber both yearns for and fears what he calls this "voluptuousness" or "union of all rays" (a phrase that refers to the union of rays with nerves). On the one hand, such a state offers escape from the "mental torture" of compulsive thinking, from that state of self-torturing reflexivity that, according to Schreber, can be pictured as "the rays of a whole world—somehow mechanically fastened at their point of issue—which travel around one single head and attempt to tear it asunder and pull it apart in a fashion comparable to quartering" (136). But voluptuousness also has its dangers, not of separation or fragmentation but of annihilation. After all, as the passage about seeing the butterfly suggests, Schreber often requires the presence of some watcher to confirm for himself his own existence; and the state of voluptuousness, with its absence of self-division, precludes such confirmation. To be enjoyed, or even tolerated, a nonreflexive state of awareness would need to be able to assume and accept its own existence without constantly checking on itself, and Schreber seems to be incapable of such faith. For, as he explains, "every time my thinking activity ceases God instantly regards my mental powers as extinct" (166).

Such a condition of not-thinking threatens the existence not only of the nerves but also of the rays, the self-regarding part of his mind. To continue to exist, the rays must stay at an appropriate distance from the nerves. Too *little* attraction by the nerves, the consequence of a state of thoughtlessness in Schreber, seems to threaten the rays—as if the rays, whose very essence is to watch, knew they would be annihilated if they drifted into a space beyond the gravitational field of their object, the nerve-vibrations. (This, incidentally, is what brings on the mini-apocalypse mentioned previously—an experience in which "short blasts of wind coinciding with pauses in my thinking" occur, and the "cries of 'help' of those of God's nerves [which are here functioning as "rays"] separated from the total mass sound the more woeful the further away God has withdrawn from me" [165].) But too *much* attraction is also dangerous to the rays, since this causes them to dissolve *into* the foundation nerves. It follows that Schreber must also avoid thought that is too intense and absorbing, for this, like sensual experience, could make him forget to watch himself, thereby threatening the separate existence of the rays. (This danger Schreber refers to as the "Achilles' heel" of the "Order of the World" [140].)

Interestingly enough, the only rays that were *not* concerned to maintain this scrutinizing and parasitic autonomy were those associated with his wife. "These soul parts," Schreber says, "were filled with the devoted love which my wife has always shown me; they were the only souls who showed willingness to renounce their own further existence and find their end in my body" (116). The wife's rays expressed this willingness in the basic nerve-language as the incomplete expression "let me," a phrase Schreber explains in the following strange and touching footnote: "This expression could be rendered, grammatically complete, in the following words: 'Let me—you rays that are trying to pull me back—do let me follow the power of attraction of my husband's nerves: I am prepared to dissolve in my husband's body.' "[32]

We see, then, that Schreber yearned at times for a voluptuousness that could serve as an antidote to his incessant self-monitoring, though he seldom felt at home with the absence of self-consciousness this would require. Playing the piano was one technique he used to overcome his self-aware-ness. By absorbing himself in the actions and the sounds emanating from the instrument, Schreber could lose himself—and, for a few moments at least, the self-regarding eye would close, the voices fall silent. But it seems that Schreber couldn't bear this, couldn't stand to feel so at one with himself. In one passage he describes how, while at the piano, he would "picture" himself elsewhere. While still sitting there and playing, he would imagine himself right out of his actual situation, by picturing himself in another place, another time. In his imagination ("my mind's eye") he saw himself not at the piano but standing in front of a mirror, wearing female attire (181). Rather than allowing himself just to *be* the Schreber at the piano, he had catapulted himself out of himself by invoking another Schreber—this one a quintessen-tially self-conscious being who confronts his own reflection, thus watching himself watching himself watching himself watch.

But this hyperreflexive mode of being contains a fatal flaw: after all, a certain loss of self-consciousness is required for carrying out certain essential human activities—for falling asleep, say, or for engaging in sex or performing excretory functions. Schreber is quite explicit about this aspect of bodily experience, though he expresses it in his quasi-allegorical way as a "union of all rays." Such a union occurs in sleep, and also in the process of moving his bowels or urinating: "Liberation from the pressure of faeces present in the guts creates an intense feeling of well-being, particularly for the nerves of voluptuousness; the same happens when I pass water. For this reason all rays have always and without exception been united during evacuation and passing water" (178).

But Schreber's compulsive thinking and purposefulness were likely to preclude such a state. By his own account, Schreber "needs always to be guided by a purposeful thought. I must ask myself every moment: Do you now want to go to sleep or rest or follow some intellectual occupation or carry out some bodily function, for instance empty yourself, etc.?" (228). He declares that for seven years he has had hardly a moment free of such voices emanating from the rays, which, of course, are largely the expression of self-monitoring (225). As we have seen, the self-conscious part of his mind strives always to preserve itself, and this means preventing "the union of all rays" from occurring; we saw how he resisted absorption in the piano music. He also felt a conflict "whenever the need to defecate is produced by miracle" (178): for, as he explains, "despite talking a great deal about 'Sh . . . ,' one always tried to force back the need to empty myself by means of miracles, as if its satisfaction causes soul-voluptuousness" (228).

In his famous case study, Freud viewed Schreber's rays as symbols of erotic energies or charges (Schreber's "rays of God" are "in reality nothing else than a concrete representation and external projection of libidinal cathexes," Freud writes);[33] but, as we have seen, these inquisitive filaments actually have a restraining or antilibidinal effect that is hardly captured by this reading. The physical inhibition they bring about is, in fact, a very clear illustration of Foucault's generalization about the modern, panoptical age: here, quite literally, "the soul is the prison of the body."[34]

Schreber was often the victim of such self-inflicted "forces" that paralyzed his physical functioning. For days at a time he would feel as if he were not allowed to defecate (or would not allow himself to defecate; it is difficult to say which phrasing is more apt). It is not surprising, therefore, that long periods of this kind of inhibition should conclude with incontinence—the body in the end will relieve itself. But it seems clear, despite appearances, that such incontinence has nothing in common with—in fact is the polar opposite of—that of the young child who is not yet able to monitor or inhibit the spontaneous functioning of the excretory system. Nor does Schreber's experience resemble that archaic consciousness so often attributed to schizophrenia, with its supposed "more immediate and absolute involvement with [the] physical environment," its "greater in-the-worldness," and its diminished "capacity to reflect on the self and on immediate experience."[35] Indeed, it is one of the great ironies of modern thought that the madness of patients like Schreber should so often have been viewed as a regression to wildness or innocence—even, at times, as an enviable escape from the "rationalist repression" of the modern world (as with André Breton).[36] The real process, at least in his case, is more like a hypertrophy of alienating self-consciousness, and this may have more in common with what Schreber himself diagnoses as "a general spread of nervous excitement in consequence of overcivilization" (140).

Certain of the other, seemingly infantile or bizarre actions Schreber engaged in can also be understood in the light of his panopticism—not, as with the incontinence, as direct consequences of the self-consciousness but as ways of coping with or defending *against* such a mode of being. As Schreber explains, one of his bizarre habits actually functioned as a way of overcoming the constipating effect of his self-consciousness, a state allegorized in the separation of rays from nerves:

> I must therefore put up temporarily with such evils as bellowing when I want to go to sleep, empty myself, etc., to be able to do *in concrete* what is indispensable for one's bodily well-being: emptying in particular which one [that nebulous being, sometimes associated with God] tries to prevent by miracles, I now achieve best when I sit on a bucket in front of the piano and play until I can first piss and then—usually after some straining— empty my bowels. However incredible this may sound it is true; for by playing the piano I force the rays trying to withdraw from me to approach, and so overcome the opposition put up against my effort to empty my bowels. [228]

Schreber's bellowing and muttering served a similar purpose. As he explains, speaking aloud, yelling, and the endless repeating of random sentences he had memorized (recited "in silence and on the quiet verbatim") were actions he engaged in "in order to drown the senseless and shameless twaddle of the voices and so procure temporary rest for my nerves" (176, 123).[37] In the case of bellowing, he speaks of "allowing" something to happen rather than of a transparently intentional act (227), but like the muttering, this clearly served a purpose, one of which he was quite well aware.

Schreber was also mindful of how he must have looked to others at these times; indeed, he laments that his behavior "might have appeared as raving madness to the physicians who did not know the true reason, and so might have caused the corresponding treatment which indeed was meted out to me for years" (123).[38] As Schreber tells us at the outset of his book, in the passage quoted at the beginning of this chapter, his motive in writing the *Memoirs* was to give "an approximate idea at least of my religious conceptions, so that [others] may have some understanding of the necessity which forces me to various oddities of behaviour" (41). To judge from prevailing views of madness, and of Schreber in particular, one may doubt how successful he was in achieving his purpose. It is true that he craved a "union of all rays," a dissolution of self-consciousness and self-control that might well be termed "primitive." But such a mode of being was less the core of Schreber's madness than its potential antidote:

> Naturally I consider it beneath my dignity to have to bellow like a wild animal. . . . Nevertheless at certain times I have to allow the bellowing as

long as it is not excessive, particularly at night when other defensive measures like talking aloud, playing the piano, etc. are hardly practicable. In such circumstances, bellowing has the advantage of drowning with its noise everything the voices speak into my head, so that soon all rays are again united. [227–28]

His union of all rays plays a role akin to primitivism in modernist culture: not the expression of an inner essence but a yearned for, and always elusive, escape from a more fundamental division and self-alienation.

·················

The Morbid Dreamer

Am I in the sun? Who am I?
> —Schizophrenic patient
> In Karl Jaspers, *General Psychopathology*

For me the substance has become spirit.
> —Schizophrenic patient
> In Manfred Bleuler, *The Schizophrenic Disorders*

Le fou "déraisonne" bien moins souvent qu'on ne le croit, peut-être même ne déraisonne-t-il jamais. —Eugene Minkowski, *La Schizophrénie*

D isturbances of self and world have been at issue throughout this book, but it is only in the preceding two chapters that we encountered the more extreme distortions. There we saw how the sense of being a unified center of intentional activity could dissolve, how one could come to experience one's consciousness as under the control of alien forces or could feel oneself disappearing or fragmenting into parts. In this and the following chapter, the focus shifts from such distortions of selfhood to equally profound mutations in the experience of the world, mutations that frequently defy both the patient's capacity for description and the psychologist's for understanding. For, along with the fragmentation and evanescence of ego or self, an antithetical attitude may rise up: the feeling that the conscious self is no mere pawn of alien forces but the necessary and omnipotent foundation of the entire universe, and that it is the *external* world that is ephemeral and illusory.

"Reality, as it was formerly, no longer exists. Real life has suffered a decline," said one schizophrenic patient. Another such individual experienced all other human beings as mere images or representations, while at the same time insisting on the greater existential certainty of the subjective, inner domain of mind or spirit: "It seems as if all people were *one* picture and only an *illusion* which is perceived in the scattered *multitude*," he said; "There is no reality but only the *spirit*. For what is material reality no one knows, but what spirit is no one doubts who has experienced it." A third patient spoke of "the belief I share with many schizophrenics that I am real and the rest of the world unreal."[1]

Statements like these recall the subjective idealism of Bishop Berkeley as well as elements of post-Kantian idealism; they touch, in fact, on what has sometimes been seen as the very essence of the modern era. According to the philosopher Martin Heidegger, we have lived for some time in what he terms the "Age of the World View" or "World Picture"—a period when the world has come to be experienced *as* a view, as a kind of subjectivized picture. With this fateful development—initiated by Descartes, realized by the Kantians, and now reaching a curious and in some ways self-contradictory apotheosis in contemporary postmodernism and poststructuralism— human consciousness sets itself up as the foundation of all existence; one of the important consequences is that the encompassing universe tends to suffer what Heidegger terms "a loss of Being."[2]

Here and in the following chapter, I shall explore these parallels in some detail. Let me begin by sketching the several aspects of the schizophrenic worldhood that will be of concern.

SCHIZOPHRENIC WORLDHOOD

Major Symptoms

The signs and symptoms to be discussed in this and the next chapter have traditionally fallen under three somewhat overlapping rubrics which, taken together, map the fundamental status of the schizophrenic experience of external reality. The first of these pertains to certain apparent distortions in the patient's judgments concerning the consensual world, the quality known as "poor reality testing"; the second, often termed "loss of ego boundaries," refers to the loss or attenuation of the basic sense of the separateness of the world; the third involves delusions or hallucinations of what is called "world catastrophe" or "world destruction."

The first is perhaps the most important symptomatic concept in clinical psychology and psychiatry, since it is generally used to distinguish actual madness—psychosis—from all lesser forms of psychological disturbance. Thus, in DSM III-R, *psychotic* is defined as a term indicating "gross impairment in reality testing," a condition in which the individual "incorrectly evaluates the accuracy of his or her perceptions and thoughts and makes incorrect inferences about external reality, even in the face of contrary evidence." Psychotic patients are defined as those with "true" delusions or hallucinations—that is, those who supposedly believe in the literal truth of idiosyncratic ideas that, in actuality, are "false" and grossly "incorrect," and who experience their perceptions of nonexistent things as having "the immediate sense of reality of a true perception."[3] Essentially the same view is orthodox in psychoanalysis, where "poor reality testing" is used to delineate the boundary between the psychotic and the borderline and neurotic disorders.[4] This equation of madness with error, the received view in contemporary psychopathology, crystallized during the 1800s, but it has important sources in the two previous centuries[5]—for example, in Dr. William Battie's influential *Treatise on Madness* of 1758, in which "deluded imagination" is taken to be the essence of insanity: "That man and that man alone is properly mad," wrote Battie, "who is fully and unalterably persuaded of the existence or the appearance of any thing, which either does not actually exist or does not actually appear to him, and who behaves according to such erroneous persuasion."[6]

There are certain instances of "poor reality testing" that are especially characteristic of schizophrenia (as opposed to manic-depressive or pure paranoid psychoses). These include delusions where the beliefs in question are "bizarre," not simply unrealistic but flagrantly impossible, contradicting the laws of logic and the most fundamental structures of the human condition (where, as DSM III puts it, the "content is patently absurd and has *no* possible basis in fact").[7] One of Eugen Bleuler's patients claimed, for instance, to have been dead three times even as he prophesied his imminent demise and continued to make suicide attempts; another said of herself that she could "be switched around; at times, she is a virgin maid, at other times a married woman."[8] Unlike the "mood-congruent" delusions of patients with manic or depressive psychoses, the most typical schizophrenic delusions are difficult to understand as the products of heightened emotions, whether positive or negative. Whereas the affective patient may believe himself to be widely loved, hated, or disdained, or to be terrifically strong or afflicted with disease, the schizophrenic will claim to be a machine, will equate himself with the sun, or will say he is only a character in a book. Particularly characteristic of schizophrenia are certain grandiose, nihilistic, or religious delusions that focus on highly general or universal issues rather than on more personalized or worldly concerns like jealousy or persecution—delusions that have what one patient called a "metaphysical" or "cosmic" character, a "character of the infinite."[9] Many thousands of persons and "everything from the largest to the smallest is contained in me!" declared one schizophrenic; another believed the whole world would become pervaded with the "magnetism" from his head, thus signaling the moment of his death throughout the world and marking the beginning of "a new era from which to reckon time."[10]

In these last two examples of "disturbed reality testing," we see, in addition, the second kind of alteration in the patient's experience of reality: the loss of ego boundaries separating self from world. Boundary loss, of an extreme degree, is also apparent in an autobiographical account by the patient Morag Coate; she describes how, "In my mental illness I had been, as a person, enlarged and stretched beyond all reasonable limits. I was a part of everything, and the whole world, sometimes the whole universe, was in a sense a part of me." A second patient signed himself "The Beginning and End of the World"; and a third refused to swallow because each time she did, she swallowed the entire world.[11]

When a schizophrenic experiences this kind of loss of separateness, he may come to feel at the mercy of external forces; as we saw in chapter 7, experiences or actions can seem the effects, or even the epiphenomenal reflections, of outer events or of the thoughts of other sentient beings.[12] But equally likely is a sense of the self's limitless power. One patient believed his gaze was a kind of radar beam that moved people about or made them become pale and frightened; a second felt he could control the weather by shifts in his inner mood; a third sensed that, by means of an electromagnetic fluid, she was causing all the deaths, illnesses, and catastrophes in the world, and was stealing the minds of those who went insane.[13] One patient experienced physical objects and human beings as somehow emanating from her own eyes: "Many things come out of my lovely blue eyes, e.g., bed sheets, smoothly ironed pillows and quilts of soft feathers (white or colored), bedsteads, commodes, baskets, thread, stockings of all colors, clothes from the plainest to the most elegant; and finally, people fly out, fortunately not naked but completely dressed."[14]

The third aspect of the schizophrenic world, to be treated in the following chapter, is the nearly indescribable "world catastrophe," the fantastical experience in which the entire universe seems to have been, or to be about to be, destroyed. External reality seems to die, to collapse into utter chaos, or to lose all substance and be transformed into passing images.[15] Schreber, for example, believed that the whole of mankind had perished and that the people around him were only appearances—"fleeting-improvised-men," he called them. Another patient reported that everyone around him seemed like a cadaver when he was psychotic, while a third saw only "animated fakes."[16] "You can question me about everything and I will be able to answer you," said one patient, "but I have the impression that nothing exists."[17] Schizophrenics will sometimes concoct delusional explanations for these experiences of world catastrophe—"I hear the world blowing up," said one schizophrenic; "I've got to go, the world is being overrun . . . I think there's a nuclear explosion," said another[18]—but often this sense of cosmic destruction will leave patients feeling shell-shocked and dumbstruck, unable to find any words to convey the earth-shaking alterations in their experiential world. Glimmerings of apocalypse may still appear, however, in projective tests such as the Rorschach, where an inkblot might, for example, be described as looking "not so strong as an explosion—expanding, coming apart of what was once all together, smoke curling up, essences of the original center."[19]

Traditional Interpretations

It should come as no surprise that, in psychoanalysis, these three aspects of schizophrenic worldhood have generally been understood as manifestations of profound forms of regression. "Poor reality testing" has usually been interpreted as a consequence of returning to a condition in which instinctual wish-fulfillment fantasies overwhelm the personality, or in which a weakened ego regresses to the infantile illogicality of the primary process. "Loss of ego boundaries" has usually been viewed as a reversion to the infant's state of fusion or near-fusion with the world.[20] (Often this supposedly infantile condition of nondifferentiation is considered the basis of poor reality testing, which is said to result from an inability to distinguish fantasies existing "inside" the self from what lies "outside"—the real objects of veridical perception.) World catastrophe has been ascribed to several factors: projection of the infant's powerful destructive urges onto the world; libidinal regression, whereby erotic attachments abandon the external world and return to their original narcissistic or "autoerotic" object, the self; and, finally, the loss of a distinct object world that occurs with a loss of boundaries.[21] Although these theories of schizophrenic worldhood are fairly diverse, they do share certain underlying assumptions, and these are worth spelling out in detail.

First—an obvious point—all the schools assume that patients are essentially in a state of confusion, that they cannot or will not differentiate among domains of existence such as subjective and objective, inner and outer, fantasy and reality, or metaphoric and literal.[22] A second, widely held assumption is that this confusion of realms has a certain directionality—that it involves, in most instances, an assimilation of fantasy *to* reality, of subjective *to* objective, of the metaphorical *to* the literal, rather than the reverse. Like infants or savage men who, supposedly, can "sense no difference between fact and fiction, but treat all stories as real reports,"[23] schizophrenics are generally assumed to believe in the objective existence of anything that affects them, including their most subjective fantasies and fears. They are assumed to manifest that unquestioning "animal faith" that George Santayana once described, in another context, as "a sort of expectation and open-mouthedness [that is] more than ready to swallow any suggestion of sense or fancy," a kind of "primitive credulity, as in a dream, [that] makes no bones of any contradiction or incongruity in successive convictions, but yields its whole soul to every image."[24]

The third assumption is perhaps already implicit in the previous two, and this is that the schizophrenic's confusion of realms involves an attenuation or absence of reflexive self-awareness, especially of the ability to appreciate the role of the mind in shaping or constituting experience.[25] Various psychoanalytic writers have considered "the absence of reflective awareness," diminished "capacity to reflect on the self and on immediate experience," as perhaps the central feature of schizophrenic illness; and the consciousness of the chronic schizophrenic, like that of the dreamer, has often been assumed to involve what Piaget calls a "radical egocentrism," with "complete lack of differentiation between the ego and the external world" and "suppression of consciousness of the ego by complete absorption in, and identification with, the external world."[26] Marguerite Sechehaye believes, for example, that Renee's world-catastrophe fears result from a projecting of "inner components like suffering, fear and aggression" onto the outer and public world, and that Renee's experience of these negative affects as literally "out there" occurs because Renee "no longer retains awareness of her subjectivity."[27] (A final assumption—widely though not so universally held as the previous three—is that the delusional world is infused with affect and desire, since it represents the domination of consciousness by the id and the primary process.)

Unlike the psychoanalysts, mainstream medical-model psychiatrists have not understood the distortions in the schizophrenic experience of the world as consequences of regression to a primitive condition (nor have they necessarily viewed hallucinations and delusions as expressions of instinctual, wish-fulfillment fantasies). Often they have contented themselves simply with describing and noting the diagnostic relevance of such symptoms (as in DSM III-R and the Schneiderian system of First Rank Symptoms), or else they have viewed these symptoms as epiphenomena of, or reactions to, neurological or physiological abnormalities of various kinds. But as the DSM III-R definitions of the words *delusion, hallucination,* and *psychotic* make very clear, such psychiatrists are, in general, no less committed to the three main assumptions just outlined. These assumptions (of the confused, literalist, and nonreflexive nature of schizophrenic consciousness) are, in fact, so deeply rooted in Western conceptualizations of mind and madness as to be nearly inseparable from all modern notions of insanity.

Here, then, are the typical modes of schizophrenic world disturbance and the standard interpretations of these phenomena. But what of the actual experiences and characteristic behavior patterns of schizophrenic patients: Are these truly consistent with the traditional assumptions that for so long have fixed the image of insanity in the modern mind?

Anomalous Features of Schizophrenic Delusion

One of the most curious features of schizophrenic delusions is a characteristic combination of utter certitude and indifference—what Karl Jaspers, sketching the criteria for what he calls the "true" delusions of schizophrenia, describes as an "extraordinary conviction with an incomparable subjective certainty" and an absolute "imperviousness to any counterarguments." The schizophrenic's delusional beliefs are, in the typical case, unshakable; and no logical argument or empirical evidence is capable of undermining the patient's commitment to them. (Interestingly enough, Jaspers states that a belief that has these qualities may be considered delusional *even if its content turns out to be true*.)[28] As both Jaspers and Eugen Bleuler have emphasized, however, schizophrenic patients seldom respond as if these delusional convictions or beliefs were of relevance to the practical and consensual world. Rarely do they act on their grandiose or paranoid beliefs, and, in general, they behave far more normally and competently than these beliefs might lead one to expect: "those actions which would follow on the basis of logic from the delusional premises are the very ones which are met with rather infrequently. . . . They curse us in the strongest terms as their poisoners, only to ask us in the very next moment to examine them for some minor ailment, or to ask for a cigarette."[29]

Thus the patient whose moods control the weather still worries about getting his grounds pass; the patient who insists her coffee is poisoned with sperm still drinks it without concern; the Virgin Mary or the Queen of England continues, without protest or any apparent feeling of incongruity, to perform the same menial tasks as other patients. And the contradictoriness of such coexisting positions does not, it turns out, entirely escape the attention of the schizophrenic patients themselves. A patient who declared, "I am God in Heaven," would immediately reverse himself, saying, "Don't write that down; it is a damned lie that I am God."[30] Martin (the young artist who had been hospitalized for schizophrenia) once explained to me that when he was psychotic his delusions seemed both absolutely "real" and impeccably "logical" to him—indeed, he felt sure at those times that he could defend them with the tightest and most rigorous reasoning; yet, as he explained, the word *convinced* did not accurately reflect the attitude he had had toward these delusions (delusions of a kind that, for instance, called into question the "reality" of his perceptions: "Oh, for example, I might have believed that this table next to us wasn't really there").

Instead of confusing the realms of the delusional and the real, then, such patients frequently manifest a quality of "double" or "multiple bookkeeping," whereby the delusional is kept separate from the rest of experience.[31] Thus Renee sensed that her own delusion of world catastrophe was somehow private, relating exclusively to herself: "Nevertheless I did not believe the world would be destroyed as I believed in real facts. Vaguely I had some misgivings that this belief was linked to my own personal fear, that it was specific and not generally held."[32] But the presence of double bookkeeping seldom makes the schizophrenic any more likely to give up the delusions; and a patient who senses the privacy of her catastrophe fears or who laughs heartily about his delusions of persecution will nevertheless hold firmly to these very same beliefs.[33]

Also striking is the profound apathy or indifference such patients evince toward the delusions that obsess them and which they cling to so tenaciously—a phenomenon found not only in the "burnt-out" later phases of the illness but also in its earlier moments. Whereas a patient with a manic psychosis or a querulous paranoid personality disorder is typically filled with passionate conviction—he may, for example, try to seduce everyone in sight, spend all his money on some harebrained scheme, or devote himself to endless litigation[34]—the schizophrenic's delusions generally seem to exist in some special domain, sealed off from real-world action or any sort of normal emotional response. Indeed, it is common for the inner life of a deluded schizophrenic to be devoid of worldly emotions like fear, sadness, and joy—even though it may be infused with uncanny, objectless, and somehow cosmic forms of euphoria, anxiety, or ironic detachment. The patient may describe the most horrifying persecutions or catastrophes with utter indifference or even a trace of a smile.[35]

Schizophrenic hallucinations are often imbued with a similar unreality. For, despite what feels like the sensory actuality and, at times, vividness of these experiences—a point on which many schizophrenics insist—such patients seldom relate to their hallucinations as if these were objective perceptions with real-world referents or sources. Renee, for example, would hallucinate various noises and voices, but, as she explained, she "readily distinguished them from the noises of reality. I heard them without hearing them, and recognized that they arose within me."[36] When queried, most patients will describe their hallucinatory voices as something heard in the mind or head rather than with the ears.[37] Eugen Bleuler talks of one catatonic who claimed to have "seen everything filled with green snakes" but who also said she had not really seen the snakes—it was only "as if they were there." Another patient explained the origin of his hallucinatory voices as analogous to the rustle one hears on putting a seashell to one's ear. Bleuler believed, in fact, that what may seem to be visual hallucinations in schizophrenia are usually only "pseudo-hallucinations" or "illusions," experiences recognized by the patient as involving "pictures" or "images" rather than real objects.[38] This was clearly the case with the schizophrenic Morag Coate's vision of an intruder kneeling in her bedroom: "I saw the man only abstractly with my inner eye," she explains. "I was aware of his attitude and general build, but we were apart in time and on different planes of existence."[39] Many hallucinations and delusions that at first seem to involve entirely objective claims turn out, on careful probing, to have some kind of as-if or metaphorical quality.[40]

But even in those exceptional cases when schizophrenics do act on their delusional beliefs, we should not necessarily assume they are taking these beliefs as literal or objective truth. In the following passage, a patient treated by the psychotherapist August Forel, Miss L. S., describes how a sense of unreality would infuse her delusional ideas and identity even while she acted them out:

> Bordering on the true delusional idea yet definitely distinct from it, there existed another condition throughout the entire course: half-driven by an inspiration, half-aware and half-willing, I created for myself a role which I carried on playing and reciting. I became so enwrapped in, so completely absorbed by, this role that I acted in accordance with it, without precisely believing that I was identical with the persons portrayed. Sure enough in all this, there were many gradations from the borderline of the delusional idea, perhaps from the delusion itself, to the merely exuberant or excited mood; all this happened while I was completely clear as to myself and to my surroundings or, at least, so it seemed to me.[41]

Once, under the influence of a delusional notion that, as he put it, "the Chinese had invaded and taken over almost everything," Martin walked into a lake and nearly drowned. Nevertheless, he did not exactly *believe* in this invasion; it all felt, he said, as if he were "living out a story I was telling myself." Despite their absorption in these delusional identities and actions, we cannot say that either Miss L. S. or Martin took the reality of these phenomena for granted. It was not, it seems, a question of belief, nor, for that matter, of disbelief; we might do better to borrow a term from aesthetics: the suspension of disbelief.

In an earlier chapter I described how, for many patients in the schizophrenia spectrum, even objective reality may seem to lack a solid ontological grounding and therefore may be perceived as having a devitalized, inauthentic, or ghostly presence. Often, a too-acute awareness of the role of their own consciousness seems to lend a subjective coloring to all the objects of perception: "I don't see things as I used to," said one patient, referring to the actual external world. "I see things devoid of substance. . . . They must be hallucinations and not real objects. . . . Things act only on my eyes, not on my brain. Doubtless I see everything, without doubt nothing is changed, except that things are not real. . . . what I see is only a play, a Punch and Judy show; it is clumsy, vulgar, unpleasant and, above all, false; it doesn't really exist." Another patient complained that he could not have intercourse with his wife but only with his image of her.[42]

A schizophrenic patient named F. Peters offers a particularly revealing description of one such world, where reality is reduced to appearances and there is no longer any sense of an encompassing external universe:

> Whenever I took my eyes off them [the hospital guards], they disappeared. In fact, everything at which I did not direct my entire attention seemed not to exist. There was some curious consistency in the working of my eyes. Instead of being able to focus on one object and retain a visual awareness of being in a room, a visual consciousness of the number of objects and people in that room, all that existed was what was directly in my line of vision.[43]

Schreber often had similar experiences: certain things—what he called the "miracled-up" insects or the "fleeting-improvised-men"—would seem to exist only in his immediate vicinity, while he was looking at them, but would seem to disappear as soon as he looked away.[44]

At least on a superficial level, such experiences are certainly reminiscent of the lack of "object constancy" that is characteristic of the infant or young child (to whom a toy placed out of sight will seem to have gone quite out of existence). In both cases, what is not immediately perceived may seem not to exist, and reality is equated with what is momentarily present to one's consciousness. Yet there are also certain crucial differences that must not be ignored: for one thing, the child lacks reflexive awareness of the role of his own consciousness; for another, what the child does perceive is usually felt to have an actual or objective kind of existence. "The primitive impulse is to affirm immediately the reality of all that is conceived," remarks William James in the *Principles of Psychology*, making a point with which most subsequent psychologists have agreed. (James imagines the situation of a newborn perceiving an image of a lighted candle against a dark background; whether real or imaginary, this image will be experienced as objectively real: "whilst [it] lasts it constitutes the entire universe known to the mind in question," James writes. "That candle is its all, its absolute. Its entire faculty of attention is absorbed by it. It *is*, it is *that*; it is *there*; no other possible candle, or quality of this candle, no other possible place, or possible object in the place, no alternative, in short, suggests itself as even conceivable; so how can the mind help believing the candle real?")[45] The world of schizophrenia seems to have a rather different cast, one more reminiscent, in fact, of philosophical idealism or solipsism. This may not always be as explicit as in the cases of Schreber and F. Peters; still, the objects of schizophrenic perception *are* often felt to have a subjectivized status—to be somehow unreal or to depend for their existence on the subject who observes them.

Also, the patient's sense of living in a subjectivized world may well involve an awareness of other such worlds existing side by side with, but in isolation from, his own ("each one created a world after his own fashion," as Renee puts it); and this, of course, differs from primitive "egocentricity," where there is a failure to appreciate that other consciousnesses exist, separate from and unlike one's own. Even when a schizophrenic forgets or loses this awareness of other conscious beings, thereby manifesting a *kind* of egocentricity, a residual perspectivism or subjectivism may still operate. F. Peters's reference to "the working of my eyes" suggests an acute awareness of the role played by consciousness or the perceptual apparatus in constituting the world; and the same could be said of the claims of other patients who sense the world's dependence on the direction of their own gaze or on the "radar beam" or "electromagnetic fluid" controlled by their eyes. "[I]t is by no means impossible," Schreber once reflected, "that seeing . . . is confined to my person and immediate surroundings"—which suggests that he suspected his own consciousness might be the real center, and sole source, of the ambient universe.[46]

This way of experiencing the world must be distinguished from a childish egocentrism, from the concrete literalism of the classically brain-damaged patient, from the manic's passionate intensity or the fanatic's conviction, as well as from the spontaneous credulity of tribal man.[47] Once again, the closest analogies are to be found in the era of modernism and postmodernism, the culminating moment of the Age of the World as View.

THE AGE OF THE WORLD AS VIEW

Various anthropologists and cultural historians have argued that in primitive, nonliterate cultures and, to a lesser extent, in European culture prior to the modern age, human existence was permeated by what the scholar Walter Ong has called "world presence"—an experiential orientation in which the existence and value of the external world were taken for granted, and the world was felt to encompass, rather than to be encompassed by, the human beings within it. It was in the late sixteenth and the seventeenth centuries that the earlier sense of an inclusive, meaningful cosmos began its decline, coming eventually to be replaced by a mode of experience in which both Being and truth are felt to be grounded in the human subject's capacity to represent or conceive them. This shift from world presence to world as view involves various forms of what might be called "subjectivism" or "aestheticism"—subtle but profound transformations whereby Being itself is felt to be subordinated to the consciousness or the modes of representation by which it is known or depicted. These trends reach one particularly explicit type of culmination in the "phenomenologist's attitude" of the philosopher Edmund Husserl, whose fundamental technique was to "bracket" all belief in the "pregivenness" of the world (that strongest and most universal of bonds), thereby transforming the world into a "correlate" of the "gaze" of subjectivity. Husserl describes this as an "interruption" of "natural existence" which effects "a complete personal transformation, comparable in the beginning to a religious conversion [and bearing] within itself the significance of the greatest existential transformation" of mankind.[48]

Some scholars have argued that the shift in attitude or orientation at issue was first apparent in the new treatment of landscape that became widespread in seventeenth-century painting.[49] In these new forms of "realism," the natural world was, for the first time, depicted strictly from the standpoint of a single human spectator, thereby according the human observer an almost godlike status as the organizing center of the perceptual universe, and replacing the earlier sense of an encompassing universe imbued with its own intrinsic value (that is, a value that does not depend on its role as object-of-vision).[50] Preoccupation with the role of the observing consciousness has, in any case, led since the nineteenth century to more obvious and thoroughgoing forms of subjectivism or aestheticism—which, in painting, can be illustrated by various movements *away* from representational realism. In the work of a romantic artist like William Turner, the external world increasingly serves to express the mood or sensibility of the artist or observer; in impressionism and cubism it is reduced to subjective sensations or formal structures of perception; and in the "tachism" of an action painter like Jackson Pollock, it dissolves altogether into the movements of the painter's hand and brush. It is as if, in modernism, each artwork were aspiring to constitute an entire new universe on the basis of some unique way of seeing or representing; often the visual world is depicted not as a true three-dimensional universe but as a single, uninterrupted continuum where objects occur as inflections of a subjectivized and, in some sense, two-dimensional universe.[51] And this has led to what might be thought of as two alternative forms of aestheticism: one in which the artwork functions as a haven of subjectivity, freedom, or order amid the darkness and chaos of a surrounding material world, and another in which the artwork serves to declare that there *is* no reality apart from what exists in our minds.[52]

Obviously, these subjectivist or aestheticist trends constitute an extremely broad and heterogeneous current—encompassing numerous stylistic movements, reflecting various sensibilities, and affecting personal experience in a variety of different, though not wholly unrelated, ways. One such effect, the exacerbation of human solitude, was brought out in a passage written by the subjective idealist philosopher F. H. Bradley in 1893, and which was later quoted in the notes to that anti-epic of modern life, T. S. Eliot's "The Wasteland" (1922):

> My external sensations are no less private to myself than are my thoughts or my feelings. In either case my experience falls within my own circle, a circle closed on the outside; and, with all its elements alike, every sphere is opaque to the others which surround it. . . . In brief, regarded as an existence which appears in a soul, the whole world for each is peculiar and private to that soul.[53]

A somewhat different aspect of subjectivism, the sense of separation from objects rather than from other subjectivities, is captured in Marcel Proust's description of consciousness as intruding between himself and the external world, thereby "enclosing [the object] in a slender, incorporeal outline which prevented me from ever coming directly in contact with the material form."[54] But experiencing the world as view may also be associated with something more severe than mere distanciation: an actual disappearance of the external world. In one passage, Paul Valéry captures very well the feel of these moments of ontological mutation, when the world sheds its independence and comes to seem but an emanation of the self: " 'Solitude' I call this closed form where everything is alive . . . all that surrounds me shared in my presence. The walls of my room seem the shells of a structure of my will."[55]

A related but even more extreme view—one raised nearly to the status of sacred dogma by certain postmodernists and poststructuralists—is forcefully stated in Jacques Derrida's call for a revision of Plato's myth of the cave. In Plato's well-known myth, human beings, imprisoned within a cave, are blocked from seeing objective reality and are able to perceive only the shadows or reflections of this reality that happen to be visible through the cave's mouth. The skepticism inherent in this classic statement of a fundamental rift between human consciousness and reality-in-itself is, however, far from all-encompassing: Plato does at least assume that the prisoners in the cave really exist, and that there *is* an objective reality somewhere beyond the human ken (assumptions shared by Bradley, Proust, and Valéry). Derrida, by contrast, postulates a completely subjectivized or aestheticized universe, where all entities—including the human beings, the cave itself, and the entire world outside—are, without exception, composed merely of images or reflections:

> Imagine that mirrors would not be *in* the world, simply, included in the totality of all *onta* and their images, but that things "present," on the contrary, would be in *them*. Imagine that mirrors (shadows, reflections, phantasms, etc.) would no longer be *comprehended* within the structure of the ontology and myth of the cave—which also situates the screen and the mirror—but would rather envelop it in its entirety.[56]

It is not only the individual ego or self that Derrida is calling into question. He also undermines the commonsensical polarities and hierarchies still present in Plato and Bradley—such as real versus unreal, objective versus subjective, original versus representational, and actual versus imaginal; or else he transmutes these into distinctions lying entirely within the domain of the second term, that of the unreal, the subjective, the representational. A philosopher could certainly challenge the logical coherence of such a position (can we really speak of mirrors, shadows, or reflections while simultaneously denying any contrasting realm, any domain of the real or the original?), but this issue is not of concern to us here. For, whatever its logical adequacy, such a vision of a radical and depersonalized subjectivism or aestheticism does have its psychological analogues, in madness as well as in modernism.

SUBJECTIVISM AND THE SCHIZOPHRENIC WORLD

I have already considered several descriptions of subjectivism in schizophrenia, but it is worth showing how very close the affinities with modernism and postmodernism can be. One aspect of subjectivism, the Bradleyan theme of a scattering of private worlds, is stated explicitly in the following lines from Renee's memoirs:

> As an instance, one of [the doctors] had asked me how I liked the hangings in my room. "Awful," I said. In saying this, I didn't have the least intention of being disagreeable. But at that time, according to my concept of the world, things didn't exist in and of themselves, but each [person] created

a world after his own fashion. Therefore it seemed natural that the doctor should find the hangings pretty, the nurse find them interesting, and I find them awful. The question of social relationships did not touch my spirit in the slightest degree.[57]

A different though related aspect, the sense of being cut off from any substantial world of external objects, is emphasized by a patient named Frank, a physicist by profession and a schizophrenic who would eventually identify himself with Rasputin, Julius Caesar, and Jesus Christ, claiming that through telepathic communication he was controlling events throughout the universe. During the initial phase of his illness, Frank composed what he called a "scientific paper" on "the nature of words and reality" that contained the following line: "There is no reason for believing in the existence of an unobservable like an external world, and therefore my mind, cluttered with surprisingly uncooperative images, is my only reality." At least at this point in his illness, Frank was well aware of both the advantages and disadvantages of this solitary mode: "This view may have its compensations but it is a lonely one," he writes. "It is clear that avoiding the idea of an external world is desirable. . . . one lives in a world of mere images, shared with no one and connected with some colorless, rushing reality." The "rushing reality" that Frank refers to here is that of his inner thoughts, whose pallid yet compelling presence, he says, "seriously reduces one's interest in one's surroundings."[58]

It is evident that this patient did retain, at least while writing these lines, some residual awareness of the standard distinction between reality and the merely imaginary, for he clearly senses the innerness and the unreality of his realm of "mere images." Only when this sense of distinction disappears is a condition of maximum confusion likely to ensue. There is no reason to assume, however, that when this does occur, the confusion is necessarily of the type assumed in the traditional concept of poor reality testing—where the inner or imaginary is assimilated to the domain of the objective or the literal. Patients may in fact do just the opposite, losing the ability to distinguish real from imaginary precisely because everything, actual beings and events as well as imaginary ones, is now felt to be only an evanescent image or an animated fake. The very possibility of distinguishing real from imaginary will have disappeared upon entering this kind of Derridean world, where "shadows, reflections, phantasms" have enveloped the universe in its entirety. Thus one schizophrenic experienced *actual* encounters with other people as if these were inner or subjective events, and he was troubled because such events had come to seem confused in a turbulence of purely subjectivized states. "I don't know, when I talk to you," he said to his therapist, "whether I'm having an hallucination, or a fantasy about a memory, or a memory about a fantasy."[59] To this patient, the only issue seems to have been what *kind* of subjectivized event was happening, as if the occurrence of real events were quite out of the realm of possibility.

The Realm of the Imaginary

What is lost in such moments is some quality of actuality or reality, but it is no easy task to define this quality with any precision. Perhaps "belief, the sense of reality," just "feels like itself [and] that is about as much as we can say" about it, as William James suggests in "The Perception of Reality," a chapter of his *Principles of Psychology*.[60] Actually, James does not leave it at that, but goes on to describe several qualities of experience that, if not exactly definitive, are at least closely allied with what might be called the reality-sense.[61]

The first of the qualities James mentions, the capacity to arouse vivid and interesting sensations, does in fact characterize certain schizophrenic hallucinations—which is one reason such patients will often claim that their voices or tactile hallucinations are more "real" to them than anything else. There are other schizophrenic hallucinations, however, that lack the vivid and concrete quality of a real sensory perception, and these seem to have more of a conceptual than a sensory taint.[62] Rarely, in any case, do their hallucinations and delusions manifest either of the other two aspects of the reality-sense discussed by James: the tendencies to "incite our motor impulses" and to arouse normal and full-bodied emotions. A fourth quality, not mentioned by James, is consensuality: the feeling that the objectively real is also present to other human beings. Several of the statements just quoted show that schizophrenic delusions and hallucinations are not necessarily felt to be objective or actual in this sense; and the general disinterest schizophrenics have in convincing others of their delusions, or in getting others to share their hallucinations, suggests that this is probably true of most such patients.

In *The Psychology of Imagination* Jean-Paul Sartre distinguishes between experiences of the "real" and of the "imaginary," pointing out that only in the former is a given experiential object implicitly felt to transcend its momentary appearance—that is to say, to contain an endless number of aspects apart from those visible at the present moment, aspects that can evoke curiosity or arouse suspense. Unlike a merely imaginary house, a real house is composed of an infinity of unknown but nevertheless distinct aspects or facts, so that one might sensibly ask how many steps lead down to its basement, how it was built, whether it has a back porch, and so forth. But as Sartre points out, the attitude that most schizophrenics and other "morbid dreamers" (as he calls them) take toward their hallucinated and delusional objects suggests that they experience these objects as imaginary rather than real.[63] It has been noted that schizophrenic hallucinations generally lack certain qualities of surprisingness and independence; for example, they occur under particular circumstances: when the patient is in a listening attitude, in some sense *expecting* to hear them.[64] And, usually, the delusions of such patients do not evoke in them the kind of curiosity or sense of suspense that would be appropriate to an actual, objective world that is inexhaustibly rich and transcends its momentary appearance. Such individuals, as Emil Kraepelin once observed, "do not try to give any account of the reliability of their observations and conclusions, do not search for explanations of their remarkable experiences, their persecutions, their good fortune"; often their delusions "are either not at all, or only in a very superficial way, worked up mentally and are scarcely brought into inner connection with one another."[65] Typically, for example, such persons are not concerned to identify exactly where their voices come from,[66] nor do they fear that the speaker behind the voices might one day appear in the flesh. And a patient who believes in an influencing machine is unlikely to begin wondering about the mechanics of how it was built, or about the exact appearances of the mysterious men who manipulate it. An interviewer who brings such issues up quickly senses that his or her questions are somehow beside the point—as if these delusional objects simply *had* no qualities beyond those present in the image or representation already being experienced by the patient.[67]

Obviously this is a far cry from the state of "primitive credulity" or simple erroneousness that has so often been assumed. Instead of taking everything literally, losing awareness of the mind's role in constituting reality and reifying even the ghostly shapes of inner fancy, schizophrenics seem more often to experience a world whose mental, representational, or subjective nature is foregrounded. It is, in fact, almost as if they were living out some form of transcendental idealism, as if the world existed for them not as an independent substance but as a pure idea, a product or emanation of consciousness itself.[68]

The subjectivist aspect of the schizophrenic lived world helps to explain many of the strange or anomalous features of schizophrenic delusions mentioned earlier—their impossible, bizarre, and cosmic qualities, as well as the curious combination of certainty and indifference.

Thus it seems clear that none of the usual logical or realistic constraints need apply in a universe of pure idea. A man may die and yet be alive; virginity may be lost and regained; a person may be in two places at once, frozen in the bathtub yet still here[69]—without any of these fantastical events occasioning shock or amazement. If the patient realizes, perhaps only in some implicit or half-conscious way, that the events in question are only mental transformations, akin to thought experiments occurring in some unreal or imaginary domain, then such contradictory claims—which even the most intelligent and, on other topics, logical schizophrenics may assert with blithe unconcern—need not imply any logical incompetence. The patient who claims to change sexes ("now I can have a man's sexual organs, now organs like a boy's, and I can even feel a woman's organs," one schizophrenic asserted)[70] would not really be contradicting the laws of biological reality, given at least a dim awareness that he is really describing the realm of his own passing fancies—an unconstrained, imaginary realm where such strange transformations really can occur, though only as thoughts.

Other claims that seem to involve failures of logic may result not from the lack of constraints natural to the imaginary but from the duality of double bookkeeping. One of Storch's patients maintained that he had all the objects in the world within him but also agreed readily that these objects existed outside: "Even this room here, or the table?" asked the interviewer. "Yes!" "But that's outside you!" "Yes, that too," agreed the patient, not hesitating to affirm the validity of the "real." A patient may say, "I am Dr. H.; I am not Dr. H.," or, "I am a human being like yourself, even though I am not a human being."[71] When one patient's claim to contain thousands of persons was challenged, he replied, "Oh, it really doesn't matter. I stay just one person, even though I contain them all."[72] Diagnosticians sometimes view such statements as evidence of disordered logic or the indifference to contradiction characteristic of primary-process thought (where something is allowed to be x and not-x at the same time). But patients may simply be shifting their references between two modes or realms of experience: between the real, where they acknowledge the normal facts of the human condition, and the imaginary, where they can indulge the most grandiose and unrealistic of fantasies without taking these as literally true.[73] If such an awareness of different modes *is* present, usually in some implicit or unthematized way, then the fantastical nature of such statements can hardly be taken as evidence of a fundamental irrationality, at least not in the strict sense of showing a tolerance of logical contradiction. Indeed, if we take a closer look at some of the most grandiose and nihilistic of schizophrenic delusions, we will see that even the content of these delusions may not be as unrealistic as it first sounds—or, at least, may not be fallacious in quite the way the poor-reality-testing formula implies.

We have already seen that schizophrenics can tacitly ascribe a subjective status to many of their experiences—to their hallucinations and delusions, as well as to actual perceptions. The quality of subjectivization does not, however, always remain in the background, as a pervasive, atmospheric feature of the delusional world; it may also appear in the overt content of the delusion itself, as an explicit theme that expresses the pervasive but difficult-to-specify ontological status of their lived world.

Epistemological Delusions

Paranoid delusions are common in nearly all types of psychosis (including affective and pure paranoid psychoses), but certain *kinds* of paranoid delusions seem to be specifically characteristic of schizophrenia; these are not primarily concerned with the *content* of reality—with issues existing *within* the world that would be likely to evoke heightened fears or feelings of persecution (such as thinking that a burglar is lurking somewhere in real space, spying and poised to attack). Here it is a matter not of some intruder who threatens one's calm and safety but of a profound transformation in the coordinates of experience itself—an ontological unhinging that nullifies reality by reducing everything to a troubling and insistent process of "seeing." In such moments the world can come to seem unnervingly unreal, dependent for its existence on being an object of knowledge for some consciousness or representational device that records or represents events. "Then it started in the living room," said one patient. "I kept thinking I was being watched by videocameras. . . . I had a tremendous feeling of claustrophobia. I felt trapped. . . . It was all like a story."[74] Two other patients recounted remarkably similar experiences of what might be called epistemological delusions. A schizophrenic nurse described "a most disturbing experience. I saw everything I did like a film camera"; and Morag Coate wrote: "I was myself a camera. The views of people that I obtained through my own eyes were being recorded elsewhere to make some kind of three-dimensional film."[75]

The significance of this kind of epistemological delusion is missed when, as so often occurs, the patient's claims are interpreted as essentially analogous, except for the fact of their erroneousness, to everyday statements about objects in the real world—as if, for example, the patient just quoted were imagining that a real videocamera trained on him existed somewhere in actual space, or even in the same space that contains the *un*real objects being filmed. My point here is somewhat more subtle than the earlier one about the aestheticized or subjectivized nature of the experiential world of schizophrenia, for now I am suggesting that phenomena like the videocamera or Natalija machine do not even exist in the same *subjectivized* domain as do other delusional objects. I would argue, rather, that these delusional phenomena function as something like symbols for subjectivity itself, for the self-as-subject, and thus that they are not objects *within* the world, whether real or delusional, so much as expressions of the felt, ongoing process of knowing or experiencing by which this world is constituted. If this is true, such phenomena would be expected to be doubly ephemeral and unreal—difficult to locate not only because they have no existence in the objective world independent of the subject's consciousness but also because, like the eyeball that sees, they are unlikely to appear even as immanent objects within their own (subjectivized) fields of vision.

And, in fact, the knowing, representing, or recording devices or persons in the epistemological delusions of schizophrenia often do have an especially shadowy mode of being. There is a videocamera "somewhere," but the patient doesn't actually see it in the mind's eye and cannot tell you where it is. (This also seems to be true of Natalija's influencing machine.) Other types of imaginary or delusional objects may not be felt by the subject to have a substantial presence or to comprise an inexhaustible set of definite facets or features, but they do have at least one defined and locatable aspect—whereas devices like videocameras are often felt to be everywhere and nowhere, existing only as unspecifiable, almost atmospheric presences that pervade the universe like a miasma of unreality. (After all, if such a phenomenon did have a more specific, objectlike kind of existence, how could it also serve as a symbol of the consciousness *by which* such objects are seen? For such a constituting entity to appear as an immanent object-of-awareness would seem to imply some kind of profound contradiction. But this is not to say that such contradictions cannot occur in schizophrenic experience, sometimes with disconcerting results—an issue to be elaborated in chapter 11.)

We might say that such delusions are concerned with *ontological* questions—with the general metaphysical status of the entire universe or the most fundamental issues involving the relationship of knower and known, rather than with objects or events existing *within* such a universe. Blindness to this fact—which is enshrined in the widely accepted poor-reality-testing formula—has, in my view, been one of the most important sources of misunderstanding between schizophrenics and those who treat them. A patient who says that "everything from the largest to the smallest is contained within me" should not be taken literally, as though he means that things exist within him the way furniture exists within a room or pencils inside a drawer. A patient who says "my eyes and the sun are the same" is unlikely to mean that the sun has been removed from the sky and inserted into his skull.[76] Although such statements may at first seem to involve the most egregious mistakenness about material reality, they are better understood as having an ontological or epistemological import—for example, as being ways of claiming to be the consciousness for which all objects exist, of saying that one's own perceiving (symbolized by the eyes) does not simply reflect but somehow vivifies or makes possible the perceptual universe (as does the sun).

The same point can be made about the patient who spoke of objects and people coming out of her "lovely blue eyes." Such delusions probably amount to a sort of epistemological claim, akin to that of the philosophical solipsist who draws back into an acute awareness of his experience-as-such and, as a result, feels and declares the world to be his own idea. This seems less a reversion to the infant's ignorance of ego boundaries than the consequence of an exaggerated awareness or sense of the role of consciousness in constituting its world. (This implies that, when the patient speaks of her eyes, we should understand her to be referring not to an anatomical part so much as to a locus of awareness; and that the flying out of people and objects would refer to a sense of things coming into being rather than to a movement through space).[77] This is not to say, of course, that there is nothing abnormal or pathological about this living out of a kind of solipsism. But to speak of poor reality testing is to equate this ontological mutation with the *kind* of mistake that occurs within the commonsense world. And this is not only to overestimate schizophrenics' proneness to error but, even more important, to underestimate how profoundly their form of life differs from the normal.

TWO OBJECTIONS

I have argued that schizophrenic delusions are implicitly felt to have only a subjective status, and that, in many instances, the objects of these delusions have an epistemological import, pertaining not to particulars within the world so much as to the overall ontological status of the world itself. And as we have seen, these hypotheses seem able to account for a number of aspects of schizophrenia that are inconsistent with the more usual poor-reality-testing formula. Before proceeding with my analysis, however, there are a couple of potential objections to these claims that ought to be considered. It is only by taking these into account that one can arrive at a proper understanding of the schizophrenic world, one that acknowledges the very real element of unreasonableness that the poor-reality-testing formula does bring out, however misleadingly.

A defender of the traditional view might call attention to two features of schizophrenic delusion that so far I seem to have ignored: the factual or literal-sounding *way* in which many schizophrenic patients describe their delusions, and the specific, thinglike, or substantial-sounding nature of many of their delusional *objects*. Both of these features contribute to the impression of a "lack of insight" that is so characteristic of this illness;[78] and both may well seem inconsistent with my emphasis on felt subjectivization and hyperreflexivity. Let us take up these important objections one at a time.

The Question of the "Real"

In the preceding pages I have quoted a number of patients who specifically mentioned the subjectivized or unreal quality of their delusional worlds, but it must be acknowledged that this is far from always the case. The patient who talked of objects coming out of her eyes, for example, did not say it was *as if* these things were flying out; nor do patients concerned about world catastrophe generally say that it is only *as if* the world were coming to an end. True, when confronted tactfully, many schizophrenics will back down somewhat from their delusional statements, admitting that these might be taken in some kind of metaphorical way; it is noteworthy, however, that they may need to be pressed to do this, and one may doubt whether the relevant insight was present all along. Certainly there are many schizophrenics who do not spontaneously describe their delusions in qualified or tentative terms. And, though such patients will seldom attempt to convince others of the truth of these delusions, they clearly accord their beliefs a singular importance. Is any of this suggestive of a person who can be said to be aware of experiencing mere images or fantasies, mere figments in the mind's eye?

This aspect of schizophrenia can be illustrated by returning to Judge Schreber and Monsieur Teste. In the previous chapter I considered the striking similarities between these two intensely self-conscious individuals, both of whom were fixated by a kind of exigent introspection that fragments being into a series of separate and externalized selves; but I neglected a significant difference between the famous madman and the fictional aesthete of Valéry's imagination. When, in his notes on Monsieur Teste, Valéry writes such things as that "the mind's aim is the mind," we assume that the implied insight into the self-referential and subjective relevance of Teste's preoccupations is as available to Valéry's alter ego, Monsieur Teste, as it is to Valéry himself. With Judge Schreber, however, the situation seems rather different: he appears to describe the phenomena that obsess *him*—the nerves and rays—as the constituents of a metaphysical or cosmic vision, one composed not so much of inner or mental events as of entities that have an objectlike, externalized, even quasi-physical mode of being. It is true that Schreber may not always treat the entities of his nerve-ray cosmos as entirely objective beings (as I mentioned earlier, he does speak of them as existing "in the mind's eye,"[79] and in at least one footnote he suggests a nonliteral or psychological reading of the attraction of rays to nerves); but this does not belie the strikingly physicalistic and somehow external quality of these entities, which he repeatedly compares to filaments and anatomical structures and characterizes as components of a kind of mysterious solar system waiting to be explored.[80] It is this that accounts for the aura of craziness hovering about the *Memoirs*, whereas the writings of the imaginary Monsieur Teste remain those of a highly eccentric, but not insane, mystic or philosopher. It seems that, while Schreber can recognize that his is a mind's-eye world, he nevertheless treats it as having a kind of objectivity and an exceptional importance, indeed, as containing the key to the universe—a kind of "religious and metaphysical truth." "I must state therefore," he wrote in a legal brief appealing his involuntary commitment, *"the certainty of my knowledge of God and the absolute conviction that I am dealing with God and divine miracles tower high above all empirical science."*[81]

Given that Schreber is such an intensely introspective person, and so obviously endowed with the intellectual capacity for sophisticated understanding, this failure does seem rather odd. How, we might ask, does this most self-conscious of men fail to realize the most central fact of his own existence: that the entities he experiences are but projections of his own mind—indeed, his own mind projected outward? What accounts for his tendency to experience the nerves and rays as quasi-external objects rather than as parts of himself—as manifestations, if you will, of his own miserable substance?

Traditionally, this question would be answered by invoking concepts such as an incapacity for accurate reality testing or for reflective self-awareness—deficiencies that supposedly prevent a patient from recognizing the merely imaginary and projected nature of his or her delusional objects. In Schreber's case, however, such answers hardly seem apt.[82] Schreber's fundamental ability to engage in careful and logical argument, and to reflect on his own experience, is just too much in evidence for one to believe that some basic intellectual inferiority could account for his apparent lack of insight.[83] (Schreber indicates, for example, that he is quite aware of the incredulity others are likely to feel and that he can understand this reaction, even as he continues to insist on the revelatory significance of his experiences.)[84] The issue, it seems to me, is less likely one of cognitive capacity than of experiential attitude, of what one might call Schreber's overall existential stance.

A more normal person might conceivably experience phenomena roughly akin to the nerves and rays of Schreber's *Memoirs*—at least if that person were to engage in a similar kind of isolated introspection for a long enough time. If so, however, he or she would be unlikely to experience (or to describe) these phenomena in as reified a fashion, or to take them quite as seriously, as Schreber does; and this would have something to do with that person's basic commitment to the everyday form of life. The world we normally take for granted, and credit as being a kind of unquestionable foundation of being, is the world of social engagement and practical activity, a shared realm where objects are not felt to exist in some mind's eye but, rather, to occupy an independent domain that is equally open to the experience of anyone. ("When I consider my perception itself, before any objectifying reflection, at no moment am I aware of being shut up within my own sensations," writes Maurice Merleau-Ponty. "Paul and I 'together' see this landscape, we are jointly present in it, it is the same for both of us, not only as an intelligible significance, but as a certain accent of the world's style, down to its very thisness.")[85] To the person who takes such a world as fundamental, the objects of a private, contemplative awareness can only have a diminished ontological status. Instead of being experienced as the basic building blocks of reality, phenomena like the nerves and rays, the self and other of a private universe, will seem somehow trivial and unreal—as if the person senses, "It is only me, introspecting."

It may be tempting to view this normal, deflating kind of realization as the product of some higher level of self-awareness, of some further act of reflection that is able to grasp and transcend the illusions of a kind of exigent introspection. But as we have seen by now, schizophrenic patients do not seem to lack the capacity for another move of the same type, another recursion added to a sequence of "I know that I know that I know," and so forth. What Schreber seems to have lost touch with is the usual social and pragmatic world, the sense of living in a shared horizon of practical activity. A person given to solitary contemplation, and who lacks a primary commitment to the shared, practical universe, might be expected to take the products of isolated, introspective contemplation rather seriously.[86] Indeed, if he had arrived at a truly solipsistic position, where all phenomena were felt to depend on his consciousness, then, to him, the reified objects of solitary self-contemplation would be as real as anything could possibly be. ("Illusion is no longer possible, because the real is no longer possible," as Jean Baudrillard says of a somewhat parallel situation in the postmodern world.)[87]

The distinctive feature of Schreber's lived world might then be described as his failure to accept this premise or this organizing horizon; the mark of what we might call his autism is the fact that (like a solipsistic philosopher) he puts his ultimate faith in his own immediate experience, and in particular in the experiences he has while in a passive, detached, and isolated position.[88]

As we see, then, the schizophrenic's experience of his own subjectivism will be rather different from that of the normal person's—either because he accords so little importance to the shared, objective world (he suspends his fundamental commitment to it) or because the latter world comes itself to be incorporated into a subjectivized vision (thereby coming to seem no more real than the delusional one). It is this absence of a sense of an encompassing objective reality that accounts for the schizophrenic patient's tendency to take his delusional objects so seriously, and to accord them such ontological weight.

The Ontic and the Ontological

Even after accepting this way of accounting for the curious combination of insignificance and significance that schizophrenics' delusions seem to have, one might still raise another objection to what I have been saying, this time to my emphasis on the ontological import. This second objection bears more specifically on the notion of epistemological delusions, delusions that pertain (as I have argued) to highly general aspects of the lived world rather than primarily to the specific objects, events, or processes contained within it. A critic of my view might wish to remind me of the strikingly specific or thinglike nature of the vocabulary that such patients often employ: Is it likely, my critic might ask, that a schizophrenic would speak of, say, objects and people "flying out" of her eyes if she were really talking about an epistemological relationship or an ontological event, and if her real concerns pertained to quasi-philosophical issues of an abstract and highly general nature? Would a patient speak of "containing" all things if he really meant to express not a spatial but an epistemological relationship? Would he speak of a videocamera if he really wanted to express a more cosmic sense of things being constituted by a consciousness? After all, if their concerns really have this more general, philosophical import, then why don't they just say so?

As I shall discuss a bit later, such a criticism does have a certain validity: there may well be some respects in which this physicalistic vocabulary may accurately reflect qualities of the actual lived event. But to assume that this argument vindicates the traditional poor-reality-testing view, or refutes the ontological readings, would require one to ignore certain subtle but crucial facts about language and its relationship to the human condition, to ignore the inherent difficulty (indeed, the near-impossibility) of describing or conceptualizing experiences or insights of an ontological kind *without* resorting to a vocabulary or repertoire of concepts derived from the physical and everyday world. This, incidentally, is an issue to which both Heidegger and Wittgenstein have devoted considerable attention. In their different ways, each has argued that many of the major errors, obscurities, and controversies in Western philosophy derive from the tendency, even on the part of the greatest thinkers, to adopt language and conceptual imagery applicable to objects *within* the world when attempting to characterize the world in its totality or in its fundamental relationship with consciousness. Here I shall borrow primarily from Heidegger.[89]

Perhaps the most important criticism that Heidegger (and others) has directed at Descartes, for example, is that his philosophy makes the category mistake of treating the experiential subject as if it had the same ontological status as its objects, as if it were an entity *within* the world rather than the transcendental ground *of* the world. Both Kant and Husserl also made this criticism of Descartes, yet—at least in Heidegger's view—neither was really able to liberate himself from the same misleading way of thinking, which their own philosophies only reproduced in subtler forms. Thus Heidegger argues that the Kantian and Husserlian tendency to conceive of the transcendental subject as if it could, at least in principle, exist prior to or in the absence of its world stems from conceiving of subject and world on the analogy of two objects existing side by side *within* the world. Such a way of thinking obscures the essential inseparability of consciousness and its objects, and can lead to the error of conceiving the mind's epistemological constituting of experiential objects on the model of some kind of actual generation or production of one object by another.[90] Heidegger considers this tendency to interpret, understand, or express ontological issues concerning the fundamental nature of existence or the world on the analogy of empirical facts within the world (the latter being what he calls merely "ontic" issues) to be the deepest and most treacherous source of confusion in the entire history of Western thought.[91] (It is for this reason, he says, that the study of Being as such has been either forgotten or else confused with thought about particular—that is, "ontic"—beings.)

If Heidegger's analysis has any truth to it, we ought not to be surprised that schizophrenic patients, who can hardly be expected to be more subtle or careful than most philosophers of the Western tradition, should also succumb to this same temptation—a temptation that is irresistible because it is unseen, and unseen because it is irresistible. We should not, then, be surprised that they should speak of spatial and physical relationships such as "containing" the universe, or of objects "flying out" of their eyes, when they are, in some sense, responding to ontological experiences of their own epistemological role, their centrality as knowers, in the (which is to say, in their own) experiential world.

It would be simplistic, however, to think of such an ontic way of speaking as a mere metaphorical choice—one used, in complete self-knowledge, to make points whose essentially ontological import the patient fully recognizes. The confusion of ontic with ontological is not, after all, some trivial error of translation that can easily be corrected, but one that stems from a deep truth about the human condition: the extreme difficulty not only of describing but also of conceptualizing, reflecting upon, or in any way fixing in one's mind aspects of experience that have such a totalistic, horizonal, or all-encompassing nature. These are the aspects that Heidegger describes as being so close to oneself and so ubiquitous as to remain largely hidden, nearly impossible to see. We must not think of this ontic/ontological confusion as applying only to those laymen and mental health professionals who, in attempting to understand such patients, readily adopt conceptualizations like the notion of poor reality testing. The patient himself is also likely to suffer under a kind of ambiguity and confusion, as he too lacks the necessary conceptual and linguistic tools to thematize or formulate it on its own terms. In his own attempt to comprehend the transformation of his world, he too will tend to fall back on those more readily available modes of understanding that construe what are, in fact, totalistic mutations on the analogy of discernible events that occur *within* the world.[92]

Before proceeding, some qualification of my emphasis on the only pseudo-ontic nature of schizophrenic experiences is in order, for otherwise we might be left with an oversimplified image of the phenomenology of these schizophrenic worlds. In some cases it may not be merely a question, as I have been implying, of an ineffable form of experience—of which the patient is, somehow, inwardly aware—and a misleading (that is, an ontic) mode of expression or conceptualization, each of these being entirely independent of the other. It is true that there may sometimes be a level of what might be called "prereflective" awareness in which the sense of a purely ontological mutation is registered by the patient, however dimly. But as Heidegger has emphasized, experience can also be transformed by how it is interpreted—so that, for example, certain conceptual models of human existence, like the Cartesian, may not just disguise but also distort their objects. Heidegger clearly believes that not just philosophy but human experience itself has been affected by the errors of philosophy that began with Plato and reached a culmination in Descartes.[93] How such metaphysical or explanatory models, the products of reflective thought and articulation, might insinuate themselves into the prereflective domain and affect lived experience is, perhaps understandably, one of the more obscure issues in Heidegger's masterwork, *Being and Time*.

I would argue, in any case, that it is possible for what is in some sense a fundamentally ontological experience actually to be transformed into one that is at least quasi-ontic in nature. This might be expected to happen whenever a person transfers certain kinds of ontological insights back into a more everyday context—as may occur, for example, when a solipsistic insight concerning my own experiential centrality is felt to be not just a fact *for me* but one of relevance to the consensual world, or when the dependence on consciousness of the table-as-seen-by-me (which is in fact a pure tautology) is taken to imply that the table is somehow flimsy in a material way, as if, say, it were made of tissue paper. Actually, total avoidance of such tendencies to revert to an everyday context would require an individual to have escaped almost entirely the normal conditions of human action and speech, which include the presupposition of a physical and shareable world, and this may well be close to impossible for anyone, schizophrenic or not. (Wittgenstein has argued, in fact, that the very use of any language whatsoever necessarily assumes just such a context.)[94] The dominating presence of the everyday mode of being thus seems to exert an almost gravitational pull on both language and experience ("When I perceive my body, I feel obligated to be around those others," as one schizophrenic patient acknowledged),[95] a pull that will be resisted only by those most introverted and cerebralized patients whose journey into the interior has somehow taken them beyond its field of force.

As a result of this near-inescapability of the everyday mode, a schizophrenic who has the largely ontological (and tautological) experience of being the constituting center of the experiential universe (the universe *for him*) may not only describe but also come to experience or perceive himself as doing something akin to producing or containing the universe in a literal or ontic sense, as if he had some kind of empirical power. Or the patient who has the reflexive and solipsistic experience of noticing that only what he focuses his gaze on is visible may, at least at moments, actually experience the disappearance of the rest of the universe as if this were somehow akin to such ontic events as the evaporation of clouds after a rainstorm or of people after a parade. The psychologist Heinz Werner describes one patient who adopted a curiously literal vocabulary to characterize the peculiarly intimate connection that, for her, existed between the external world and her own consciousness: "She 'transmits' her visual and auditory senses to things, and in this way penetrates into them. Her eyes are directed outward and touch things directly. Upon looking at a landscape, for example, she carries away with her some of the actual material of which it is constituted."[96] Such reports suggest the existence of what is in effect a hybrid or (at least from the standpoint of logical description) contradictory kind of experience, or one that wavers back and forth between two different modes. And this is the sense in which my critic would be correct in insisting that the schizophrenic's rather literal (ontic) mode of expression must in fact reflect something of his underlying experience (even though it would be a vast oversimplification to maintain that the latter is *simply* ontic, as the poor-reality-testing formula implies).

It is this curious ambiguity that can make the nature of some schizophrenic delusions so very elusive: clearly they are not empirical claims meant to apply directly to the consensual, objective world; yet, at the same time, they are something other than purely philosophical claims, transparently abstract and utterly devoid of all reference to the domain of the concrete or the particular. As a result, the patient himself may be confused not only in expressing but even, odd though it may sound, in *experiencing* his own experience; and, not unlike the solipsistic or idealistic philosophers criticized by Heidegger and Wittgenstein, both his experiences and his assertions may waver back and forth between having an empirical-ontic and an ontological significance. (In the conclusion I discuss a closely related duality in schizophrenic experience, in connection with Michel Foucault's notion of the "epistemological doublet.")

SCHIZOPHRENIC SOLIPSISM

Now that we have clarified the (quasi-)subjectivized quality of the schizophrenic's delusional realm, it should be possible to understand the curious paradox noted by Jaspers and Bleuler—the fact that, despite an absolute certitude, many patients are nevertheless curiously apathetic about their delusions and seldom take action on the basis of these "beliefs" to which they devote so much attention.

If the patients' claims are completely intransitive, referring to inner experiences alone, then the subjectivized world they refer to would have to be immune to any normal test of validity. If I claim that someone is in two places at once, this would amount, in such a universe, merely to the circular and nearly self-validating claim that I have had this thought or feeling; so long as I remain within such a context, there is nothing you could say, no evidence or logic you could muster, that would have any chance of dislodging my certitude—for it is the incontrovertible certitude of a person attending to his own mental state.[97] Yet at the same time, this certitude will in many ways be irrelevant. My own implicit sense of the subjective or private nature of my experiential object—toward which my posture is less one of belief than of suspension of disbelief—will, in many instances, keep me from acting upon it, or from being concerned in quite the way I am about a world that is both actual and felt-as-actual. The more general, ontological delusions or quasi-delusions—those pertaining to the unreal or merely subjective nature of the world, for instance—will also be pervaded by a certain quality of irrelevance and unreality, a feeling of the unreality of unreality, if you will. Hence, like a philosopher of solipsism who continues to move his pencil as if it were an objective thing and to address his colleagues as if "other minds" really did exist, such a patient may well carry on a semblance of normal life in spite of his own belief in the supposed nonexistence of reality.[98]

The curious disengagement and affectlessness of schizophrenia, so different from the attitude of most delusional manic-depressives,[99] are also understandable if the patient is experiencing a purely private, subjectivized, and cerebral realm, for such a realm would be irretrievably cut off from the wellsprings of normal emotion, action, and desire. This is not to say that there are no moods of any kind associated with schizophrenic subjectivization—such patients can, in fact, experience at these moments the most intense forms of nihilistic despair and blissful revelation.[100] It is interesting, however, that their moods so often have a curiously nonphysical, cosmic, almost abstract quality; this, I would argue, is because the patient is concerned not with normal ambitions, fears, and griefs existing *within* the human condition but with the existential status of the universe itself. The associated moods (*emotion* may not be an appropriate term for experiences so very cerebral and abstract) will therefore be of a particularly cosmic sort—the bliss, for example, of feeling one is actually centering the universe.[101]

Presumably such a world would be devoid of all sense of worldly restraint, and this is why, as one patient put it, "it sometimes suits my purpose to have the privilege of being mad. . . . The life of a mental patient means being a prince, with all its freedoms and thoughts." Another schizophrenic patient stated this still more succinctly: "In my world I am omnipotent; in yours I practice diplomacy."[102] But as Jean-Paul Sartre points out, what this kind of morbid dreamer escapes is not so much the *content* of reality—poverty, failure, or frustration in love—as the *form* of the real, that is, its unpredictability and independence. Without these qualities there can be no possibility of surprise (but also no suspense: for what suspense can there be in a story one tells *oneself?*), nor the slightest need to adapt one's actions to external demands. (One woman, recalling her schizophrenic experiences, described "the world of insanity" as a realm "where everything is predictable, all is the same, and nothing changes.")[103] Hence the power and responsibility in question are of a curiously abstract or ontological sort, suggestive more of a constituting deity than of a worldly king. It is also a peculiarly passive kind of power, exercised not by acting *in* the world but by standing back from experience until the world in its totality seems to depend on oneself as a kind of universal constituting ego. It is significant in this context that many hallucinations and delusions, in particular, delusions of unreality, tend to occur when schizophrenics are inactive and to disappear when they interact with the external or physical world—for instance, by cooking a meal or combing their hair.[104] "When I lie still, everything comes back again and again," said one schizophrenic patient of his hallucinations of half-human, half-animal creatures;[105] and another patient described the link between inaction and subjectivization in more detail:

> I was lying on my bed and reality somehow passed inwards as if my brain turned round. . . . I then became more interested in memory than perceiving reality around me. . . . At the beginning I had a sense of despair almost amounting to terror, later replaced by flattening. . . . I became the opposite of spontaneous, as a result of which I became very diffident, very laboured.[106]

In modernism, passivity and hyperconcentration have often been used as a way of replacing the natural attitude with something akin to subjective idealism or solipsism. Thus in *La Femme Visible* (1930), Salvador Dali speaks of the scrutinizing perceptual attitude of his "paranoid-critical method," which he describes not just as a method for creating fantastic juxtapositions and transformations but also as a way to make a kind of ontological claim—"to contribute to the total discrediting of the world of reality," as he put it, and to assure that the "reality of the external world serves as an illustration and a proof, and is put in the service of the reality of our mind."[107] Some schizophrenics seem to adopt similar techniques, behaving at times like Murphy, a character in a Beckett novel who ties himself to a chair in order to live more purely in the mind; and this may account, in part, for the willful element so often present in chronic states of schizophrenic withdrawal. One such patient, for example, would intentionally induce a contemplative state by standing still and staring at the sky for

FIGURE 9.1

René Magritte, *The False Mirror* (1928). A painting evocative of the schizophrenic experience of a solipsistic universe. *Oil on canvas, 21 1/4" × 31 7/8". Collection, The Museum of Modern Art, New York; Purchase*

hours, thereby identifying his feelings with different cloud formations until he brought about what his analyst called "inner sensations of bliss and spacious freedom."[108] The inner dimension of what would seem to be an almost identical experience is illustrated in a TAT story that one schizophrenic patient (Carl) offered in response to an expressionistic drawing of a deserted snow scene dominated by swirling clouds (Card #19). The mood of the story is somehow uncanny—cosmic and grandiose, yet static and devitalized all at the same time: "The sky is filled with dark foreboding as someone's electric fantasy unravels itself and distorts the landscape. Unmindful of the now, he waits until all the objects in the sky are marshaled and ranked." When asked, "What is the feeling?" the patient replied: "An impression of grandeur."

This story well illustrates the ontic/ontological hybrid so characteristic of the schizophrenic delusional world: in it, the totality of the world—represented by sky and landscape—can be read as an equivalent of the all-encompassing mind, while the objects contained within this totality, about to be "marshaled and ranked," seem to represent something like the thought-things of a solipsistic universe. Such a universe attests to the ontological power of the "he" who waits, passively watching as the universe becomes suffused with his own subjectivity. (For a visual evocation of this kind of experience, see figure 9.1, of René Magritte's *The False Mirror*.) Since the feelings of omniscience and omnipotence are the result of experiencing the self as the transcendental foundation of all of existence, it should not be surprising that these feelings can be so absolute and so unqualified, so utterly free of all worldly anxieties and constraints. By identifying the entirety of Being with their own mental essence, such patients may, in fact, have achieved what Paul Ricoeur once called the threefold wish of absolute consciousness: the wish to be *total*, encompassing all points of view; to be *transparent*, with all elements of the self and the world appearing as objects of awareness; and to be entirely *self-sufficient*, without dependence on either the body or the social milieu.[109] Ever since Descartes's tactical retreat into the seeming self-certainty of the *cogito*, this has also been a central ambition of the modern mind—and it is in the various expressions of modernist aestheticism that we find the ambition most fully realized.[110]

It need hardly be repeated that the sense of omnipotence thereby achieved is not that of Dionysian passion or infantile fusion. Whether in modernism or in madness, the experience is closer to that of Monsieur Teste, that " 'eternal' observer" or "severed Head" who, instead of acting, watches himself live, and whose thought, Valéry tells us, "is equally free (when [Teste] is HIMSELF) of its similarities and confusions with the *World*, and, on the other hand, of its affective values." Like Teste, such a person has become the "most complete psychic transformer . . . that ever was," a being to whom "everything seemed . . . a special case of his mental functioning, and the functioning itself now conscious, identical with the idea or sense he had of it." And as Valéry notes, the awareness of one's own ultimate omnipotence now becomes inevitable, for one realizes: "God is not far. He is what is nearest."[111]

CHAPTER 10

. . . .

World Catastrophe

Le maximum de la conscience, fin de monde.

—Paul Valéry
Cahiers

The sum total of the spirit is constant, and the crazy thing about it is that it adds up to zero.

—Schizophrenic patient
In Manfred Bleuler, *The Schizophrenic Disorders*

The object of knowledge is the annihilation of the world.

—Friedrich Nietzsche
Unpublished note, 1870

The previous chapter concluded on a note of triumph: the spectacle of consciousness declaring its omniscience and boundless power. It would be wrong, however, to end this analysis of worldhood on this point—as if to imply that schizophrenic solipsism were some kind of pure apotheosis of subjectivity, an absolute omnipotence and omniscience freed from all anxiety, confusion, and fear. This is not to retract all I have just been saying—there is indeed a sense in which schizophrenic experience may fulfill the threefold wish of absolute consciousness (the wish to be total, transparent, and self-sufficient), and there are moments when such patients may attain this wish in virtually unadulterated form. But frequently, and probably in the majority of cases, schizophrenic subjectivization also undermines or contradicts the solipsistic sense of power and security; indeed, it may deplete the sense of subjectivity itself. This is not to say that schizophrenics are not solipsistic but that their solipsism is intrinsically paradoxical or self-vitiating.

It is the same with modernism—the period when Hegel's prediction that reality would come to be experienced as "a mere appearance due to the I" has been most fully realized;[1] and also with postmodernism—where appearances, it is said, may break free even of any grounding in an experiential subject. One kind of anxiety that can pervade such a world is evoked in the following lines from "Auroras of Autumn," a poem by Wallace Stevens: "The scholar of one candle sees / An Artic effulgence flaring on the frame / Of everything he is. And he feels afraid."[2] Something a bit different is captured by Jean Baudrillard, the social theorist of the postmodern age, who speaks of a cold ecstasy of *self*-dissolution that can accompany the loss of all sense of the real. Baudrillard describes a "forced extroversion of all interiority [and a] forced injection of all exteriority," developments that destroy all sense of boundaries or limits and dissipate any halo of privacy, leaving one open to a total instantaneity and an obscene proximity of all things.[3]

I shall be treating various paradoxes in this chapter, paradoxes that are highly interdependent and overlapping but that can be divided for the sake of exposition into two types. Both types can be understood as unexpected consequences, natural but unintended outcomes of an exacerbated subjectivism, and both are as characteristic of modernism as of the schizophrenic type of psychosis. The first involves a tendency for solipsistic grandiosity to flip over at a certain point into a disconcerting sense of responsibility, a profound ontological insecurity, and a devitalization of both self and world; the second, a tendency for subjectivism to efface the very distinctions on which it depends, thereby bringing on states of confusion and fusion that, at their limit, can cause subjectivity itself to dissolve. If the first could be said to invoke a feeling, or a fear, of nothingness—of death and the void—the second eventuates in something more like chaos, in a kind of ultimate metaphysical collapse.

RAMPANT SUBJECTIVISM

Ontological Insecurity

The most obvious impulse of solipsism is its grandiose declaration of power and security, the imperialistic gesture by which the universe is claimed to be subordinate to the conscious ego, or even to *be* a part of the self, externalized and somehow disguised. The Western thinker who comes closest to espousing a thoroughgoing solipsism is the German Johann Gottlieb Fichte (1762–1814), the first major philosopher to register the profound influence of Kant and, in certain respects, the high-water mark of rampant subjectivism in modern philosophy.

Kant initiated the transcendental turn whereby the structures of reality came to be seen as subordinate to those of the knowing subject, and it is this that makes him the true source of modernism in both art and thought. The subjectivist implications of Kant's philosophy were, however, muted by two factors: his continued postulation of a reality beyond human knowing, a *noumenon* or thing-in-itself, which, though unknowable, was assumed to be the source of all our experiences; and his assumption that there could be only one possible set of categories of understanding. Fichte, who had been liberated by Kant's writings from a materialist and determinist world view, considered these two restraining assumptions to be entirely unjustified—indeed, to contradict the fundamental insight of Kantian thought; in repudiating them he initiated a metaphysics of utter freedom that could stand as the prototype for the modernist aggrandizement of the self. In his most influential work, *The Vocation of Man* (published in 1800), Fichte radicalized certain of Kant's insights, dramatized the hyperbolic subjectivism that results, and carried it all to a point that can seem tantamount, as Bertrand Russell once remarked, to "a kind of insanity."[4]

All knowledge is "but pictures, representations," Fichte declared; in fact, there *is* no material world since it "arises only through knowledge." And to realize these truths is "no longer [to] tremble at a necessity which exists only in thine own thought [or] fear to be crushed by things which are the product of thine own mind."[5] Fichte tended to characterize this ascendancy of the mind in rather ontic-sounding terms—as if it were a matter of exercising some form of worldly or political power: "Then shall my powers, determined by, and subject to the dominion of, my will, invade the external world. I will be the lord of Nature, and she shall be my servant. I will influence her according to the measure of my capacity, but she shall have no influence on me."[6] But it seems that this liberation from worldly necessity and fear can be accompanied by a new kind of anxiety whose implications Fichte may not fully have grasped: a cosmic, somehow abstract anxiety that pertains not to events in the world so much as to the ontological status of existence itself.

If it is the case that (to steal a phrase) in dreams begin responsibilities, then, surely, the ultimate responsibility falls, with all its weight, on the one whose dream the world is. I have suggested that many schizophrenics are indeed solipsists, "scholars of one candle" who experience themselves as the quasi-divine center and foundation of the All. What I have not yet considered is how their reflexive sense of the self's role in constituting the world can, in fact, often be linked with the possibility of the fading away or dying out of objects or people, or even with an absolute obliteration of the entire universe. Here are several patients who express this in a variety of ways: "If you do not keep in touch with me, you will perish." "Once I am dead, you will all lose your minds." "If you can't find a substitute for me, everything is lost."[7]

One schizophrenic claimed that he, his wife, and his son were the first and, apparently, the foundational "seers and listeners"—for, he said, "the warmer we are, the more productive the sun becomes." But it was his own person who truly anchored the universe, it seems; and this realization appears to have been linked to fear of an ultimate ontological catastrophe, a world disappearance:

> Only one peasant in the whole of Europe can support himself, and that man is I. . . . if I look at or walk over a piece of wasteland, it becomes good land . . . my body bears fruit . . . it is a world body. . . . No state can support itself. If the world grows poor, they must come and fetch me; they have to have someone to support the world; *the world must be represented or the world will disappear.*[8]

Not all schizophrenics progress to such an extreme kind of solipsism. It should not be surprising, however, that those who do can as easily feel constrained or paralyzed by a sense of awesome responsibility and apocalyptic terror as reassured by feelings of power and security. Thus one catatonic patient felt that he was obliged to keep the "wheel of the world" in motion by making circular movements with his body; another stood in an uncomfortable position for hours, up on her toes with one arm upraised, for fear of upsetting the universe: "If I succeed in remaining in a perfect state of suspension," she explained, "I will suspend the movement of the earth and stop the march of the world to destruction."[9] To experience the world as an emanation from one's mind, a private or purely mental object, is to forfeit the anchoring stability, and the sources of vitality, that are inherent in consensual experience, practical activity, and the lived body. Whatever strategy one adopts, any sense of security and omnipotence must necessarily remain vulnerable to the possibility of a total reversal or collapse. "I thought that if I thought quickly my body should move more quickly," said Rachel Rosser's patient; but "sometimes I am high on a thought, holding it up in my head, then it collapses in the emptiness inside."[10]

Concern about such consequences has long been an important sub- or countertheme in nineteenth- and twentieth-century culture, and it is one that comes increasingly to the fore in the wake of the triumphalist subjectivism of the high modernist age.[11] In the bleak universe of Samuel Beckett, everything seems to occur inside the "ivory dungeon" of an "abandoned" or "imaginary head."[12] Thus the climactic and most horrible moment of the novel *How It Is* occurs when the narrator is forced to acknowledge what he has probably known implicitly all along: the voices he has been hearing exist only inside his own head, and therefore he, and he alone, is the source of his world. In an earlier chapter I quoted Beckett's short prose piece "Imagination Dead Imagine," in which a total disappearance of the natural world is linked with the death of imagination, as if existence itself were dependent on the vitality of the mind: "No trace anywhere of life, you say, pah, no difficulty there, imagination not dead yet, yes, dead, good, imagination dead imagine. Islands, water, azure, verdure, one glimpse and vanished, endlessly, omit."[13] We should not think of this vanishing as an independent event that, so to speak, just happens to be observed: it is the subjectivizing glance itself that annihilates the object before it, and does so precisely by transforming the object into a mere object perceived. Indeed, this negating can also be exploited, as a way of flaunting a kind of godlike epistemic control. One patient, for example, said that she could "kill" any object through thought alone; and another spoke of "purging" his visual field, making the "ghostly forms crumple up, become as dry as bone, and helpless."[14]

But it is not only the world and its objects that may be ontologically dubious in a solipsistic universe; the self too can come to seem ephemeral and unreal. We have seen in earlier chapters how subjectivity itself can be extruded, mutating at times into a kind of quasi-object; now we must recognize that subjectivity can be derealized as well as alienated, thus leading to the prospect of a subjectivized universe that is nevertheless devoid of any sense of subjectivity by which it might be anchored or constituted.

The ontological vulnerability of the self is clearly suggested in Fichte's subjective idealism, where the self is described as the product of what can only be called a kind of metaphysical bootstrapping operation, a process by which: "I create myself:—my being by my thought, my thought by thought itself."[15] For Fichte, such self-creation is a testimony to the power of consciousness—and so it is, so long as it succeeds. But what if one loses confidence in one's ability to constitute entities, including oneself? "I am my experience, but nobody knows about it so I am not," said Rosser's patient; "I used to cope with all this internally but my intellectual parts became the whole of me." This patient believed that because he himself had no memory, and no one else knew all the events of his past, it followed that he simply had no past at all.[16] Another schizophrenic patient grounded her being totally in herself—"She's self-sufficient, she's the self-possessed," she would declare of herself—but eventually she came to feel insubstantial and devitalized, like "the ghost of the weed garden" or a "ruined city," or like some dead thing lying under "a black sun." A third patient was afraid of losing all selfhood once the ties with external reality were cut: "I think so deep that I almost get out of this world. Then you get frightened that you are going to get into a jam and lose yourself. That's when I get worried and excited."[17]

In the following lines from a poem called "In Clear Things," the young schizophrenic artist Martin very effectively evokes these feelings of ontological vulnerability. His poem offers a vision of a subjectivized world, a universe flattened into a two-dimensional image and bounded by the signs of consciousness ("eye slits, the blurred edge of a lash"), which then undergoes a kind of ontological collapse, as both self and world plummet down into nothingness:[18]

> Eye slits, the blurred edge of a lash
> Borders of a flattened world,
> We fall off the edge.
> Beyond floats a white-washed wall.
> The truth lies inside the square of atoms.
> I worry about the stream plunging from the edge.

The processes I have been considering involve a form of abstraction, a separation from what Merleau-Ponty would call the flesh of the world—the realm of vivid, constant, full-blooded objects that might compel one to feel and to act. But there is a danger that this abstracting process will itself be understood too abstractly or too much in isolation—as if it were only some kind of controlled intellectual exercise, like the armchair speculations of a skeptic who would never allow his thoughts to disrupt the pleasures and duties of his daily routine. We need to appreciate the peculiar mixtures of activity and passivity and of pain and numbness (of pain becoming numbness, of numbness felt as pain) that are inherent in these acts of subjectivization, acts that can afflict one like a curse. And we need to appreciate how pervasive and insidious schizophrenic subjectivization can be—how it can seduce with the prospect of unbounded power and security while at the same time corroding one's confidence with intimations of some ultimate calamity: a banishment, a starvation, an asphyxiation, and, finally, a horrible vanishing. Although these experiences may be close to indescribable, we do get glimmerings from patients' references to deadness, to ruin, and to their sense of catastrophe.

For a fuller evocation of such a world, of its logic as well as its mood, I turn next to *The Invention of Morel*, a novella by the Argentine writer Adolfo Bioy Casares, who was a close friend and sometime collaborator of Jorge Luis Borges.[19] Though not well known in the English-speaking world, Casares's novella, first published in 1940, has had a major influence on the school of the *nouveau roman* and is said to have inspired Alain Robbe-Grillet and Alain Resnais's important film *Last Year at Marienbad*. It is a work we can read as an allegory of both the schizophrenic and the modernist mind.

Casares's novella takes the form of the diary of a man who wakes up to find himself on a mysterious island where two suns and two moons are visible; apparently he has traveled there in order to escape prosecution for some unidentified crime. On the island this nameless man, who is both protagonist and narrator, soon discovers a group of elegant people who remind him of visitors to a summer resort like Marienbad. Spying on them as they dance, stroll about, and converse, all the while listening to phonograph records of "Tea for Two" and "Valencia," the narrator eventually notices certain oddities in their behavior. For one thing, these men and women seem incapable of noticing the protagonist's presence—Is he invisible? Are they blind? he wonders. Also, strangely enough, they tend to repeat themselves, playing out more than once exactly the same interaction or conversation.

It is only after some time that the protagonist grasps the reasons for the peculiarities. The people he is seeing are only illusions: talking, three-dimensional images somehow projected into the space before him. It turns out, in fact, that virtually everything around him—not only the people but also the walls, the fish in an aquarium, and even one of the suns and one of the moons—are also but illusions, images projected and moved about by mysterious, light-producing machinery that he later discovers hidden underneath the island. (A book he handles is, for example, but a "ghost-copy," and, holding it beside a real version of the book, he finds that he is seeing "not two copies of the same book, but the same copy twice.")[20]

Eventually he learns that the process by which these images were made and are now projected was invented and employed by one Morel, a person who actually appears in his own film sequences, where he (or, rather, his image) explains how he used his process to record the actions of his friends and acquaintances. The purpose of the technique was to give a kind of eternal life to the people and the moments captured on film, but the price of this gift was that those filmed would thereby be deprived of their actual lives. Later it becomes apparent that many of the scenes of the film never actually took place at all: we realize that Morel may have altered the scenes—for example, by walking next to one of these images and then rerecording it, thereby placing himself for all eternity by the side of Faustine, the young woman he apparently loves.

Throughout the story, but especially at its later stages, there are hints (nothing, it should be said, is entirely certain in this phantom universe) that the protagonist may, in fact, be Morel himself, and thus that these films—images that discuss their own making and that are, to an extent, copies without an original—were created by the very person who now views them. How else could we account for the protagonist's immediate and uncanny familiarity with the machinery; for the coincidence that he too is an inventor; or for his reference to the "case of the inventor who is duped by his own invention"?[21] (Indeed, one has to wonder: Could the protagonist's crime, the one that made him flee from his familiar world to this strange island, actually be the same as Morel's: inventing and using a machine that murders to preserve?) Thus the protagonist describes the feeling of playing a dual role, both actor and spectator, and he asks himself whether "the hell I ascribe to Morel is really my own?" "I am the one who is in love with Faustine, who is capable of murder and suicide; I am the monster," he says, now admitting that he sometimes sees Morel's act "as something sublime."[22] In the last pages of the novella, the narrator, like Morel before him, turns on the receivers in order to record himself beside the moving image of his beloved Faustine, and the diary ends with the hint that his very soul may be about to pass over completely to the realm of the image.

The Invention of Morel demands to be read as a kind of allegory about living in a world as view, a universe dependent on some consciousness or representational device—symbolized by the mysterious machinery that records and projects, as well as murders—and felt to consist not of real presences but of images, illusions, representations, or other subjectified phenomena that threaten to incorporate even the perceiver into their unreal domain.[23] (We might think of it, in fact, as an evocation of the lived world of the classic influencing-machine delusion, where all that one experiences feels somehow unreal, mere illusions generated by a mysterious machine—a machine that is at the same time a manifestation of one's own mind and an alien, mysterious device that can influence one from afar.) But, obviously, the story of Morel, a man in an ineluctable predicament of his own making, is no celebration of subjectivization. In one passage the narrator speaks of himself as an "ex-corpse" and as "a dead man who suffered from insomnia," thus describing a hyperconsciousness amid devitalization and decay.[24] If the narrator's crime is in fact identical to Morel's—murdering to possess and to preserve—we might in fact read his arrival on the island of phantasms not as his escape but as the reaping of a well-deserved punishment, a punishment that exactly coincides with the crime itself. For such subjectivizing preservation exacts the price of death, a death that first surrounds, then infects, the narrator. Indeed, when the narrator imagines an improved and more complete version of Morel's machine, he says it would make of life itself "a repository for death." At times the narrator finds such an existence appealing—"So I was dead! The thought delighted me. (I felt proud. I felt as if I were a character in a novel.)"—but elsewhere he criticizes his own "'no hope' therapy" (that is: "never hope, to avoid disappointment; consider myself dead, to keep from dying"), describing its result as a "frightening, disconcerting apathy."[25]

At the end of the diary, the narrator hopes against hope that all this unreality is itself unreal, only some horrible dream; he is "plagued by the hope that my illness is pure autosuggestion; that the machines are harmless; that Faustine is alive." But by then it is apparent that everyone is already caught up in an inexorable "collective death." And though the narrator may try to convince himself to be satisfied with the prospect of a life in "seraphic contemplation" of mere images, now he cannot forget that even this "happiness, like everything human, is insecure." After all, he realizes, it is always possible that the machines could break down, that some doubt could enter and ruin his paradise, or, indeed, that *he* could die. And, in the last pages, it is clear that the vitality of the narrator (who has placed first his left hand and later his whole body in front of the recording machine, thereby turning himself into an image) is itself beginning to leak away: "I have scarcely felt the progression of my death," he writes; "it began in the tissues of my left hand. . . . I am losing my sight. My sense of touch is gone; my skin is falling off; my sensations are ambiguous, painful." He describes the "absurd impression" of a pain that seems to be increasing even though he feels it less and less—as if even this were fading into unreality.[26] As in Derrida's dreamcave, no substantial presences seem to remain; indeed, at one point the narrator even hints that the projecting machines themselves may have been recorded by Morel, which would suggest that even the image-producing devices have been turned into images themselves.[27]

In several passages Casares suggests that the world of his novella is equivalent to that of the writer or artist, the "fugitive," "recluse," or "misanthrope" who retreats to a sovereign but inevitably impoverished world. Thus the protagonist refers to "the books that I hope to write as a kind of justification for my shadowy life on this earth," and he suggests the diary itself is just such a work, an analogue of the mysterious machines that derealize and preserve ("My aim is to save [the images] by writing the diary," he says). He also admits that "a recluse can make machines or invest his visions with reality only imperfectly, by writing about them or depicting them to others who are more fortunate than he."[28] Such a portrait is particularly well suited to the condition of the modernist and postmodernist artist or writer, for whom subjectivism and derealization are such central preoccupations—a writer who must ask himself the question that Wallace Stevens poses in one of his late poems: "have I lived a skeleton's life, / As a disbeliever in reality, / A countryman of all the bones in the world?"[29]

But the artist is not the only human type to whom the narrator of *The Invention of Morel* is compared; for, on several occasions, the narrator wonders whether the island might actually be an asylum, with the other people either inmates or hallucinations and he himself either a mental patient or the hospital's director. (Incidentally, there was in fact a French alienist named Benedict-Augustin Morel who, in 1860, used the term *démence précoce* for the first time. This may be Casares's way of hinting that his story should be read as, among other things, an allegory about madness.) Though it may be obvious that this novella conveys something of the nature of the schizophrenic world, the closeness of the parallel may come as a surprise. The following delusion, shared by two actual paranoid schizophrenics, sisters engaged in a *folie à deux,* could, for example, have come straight from the mouth of one of Morel's victims:

> We were never born. My sister and I were made by a machine. She is not my sister, but she is nearer than a sister and we belong together by machine rules. We cannot tell why. We were made by a machine. A lot of these things were taken out of my memory by a professor. . . . The machine is called the "invisible." We do not know how it works. . . . We do not see the machine. Sometimes it changes to a person and then back again. Sometimes it becomes a light and we see the light sometimes. . . . We are always happy.[30]

This machine's transformations into a person or a light, and the fact of its invisibility, suggest that the patient identifies this constituting mechanism with a consciousness and experiences it as having an epistemological form of power.[31] And the effects of this mechanism are much the same as those of Morel's recorder and projector, which bring about what the narrator of *The Invention of Morel* describes as a "rotating eternity [that] may seem atrocious to an observer, but . . . is quite acceptable to those who dwell there. Free from bad news and disease, they live forever as if each thing were happening for the first time; they have no memory of anything that happened before."[32]

The words of another schizophrenic patient might have come from Morel himself, and they indicate that the patient's epistemological delusion may well serve a purpose identical to that of Morel's recordings: "There's no reason for anybody in the world to be unhappy or miserable in the world today," she said, because "they have antidotes for everything." "People don't die," the patient claimed; they are simply "changed," "moved about from place to place," made the unwitting subjects of motion pictures, or the like. (It was only later, when the psychosis began to abate, that she admitted the limits of this subjectivizing power: "*I* can't turn those leaves into sheep, for instance," she then acknowledged.)[33]

Not all schizophrenics have delusions that offer such explicit parallels to the subjectivist derealization and alienation of *The Invention of Morel.* But as we saw in the last chapter, such patients do commonly experience their delusional objects (or, sometimes, their real objects as well as their delusional ones) as having the quality of illusions or representations rather than realities; and they often have epistemological delusions concerning mysterious cameras, machines, or living beings that steal, preserve, or project their inner experiences, or that insert thoughts or perceptions into their minds. Like Casares's narrator, they may feel they are the observers or creators of the images, or else as if they were *among* these images (one schizophrenic even spoke of her own perceptions as being recorded elsewhere to make "some kind of three-dimensional film").[34] And very frequently, this derealization or subjectification is associated with a depletion of the sense of vitality and of reality. A schizophrenic named Joan speaks of her own existence with virtually the same phrasing that Casares's narrator uses to describe his "no-hope therapy":

> I felt as though I were in a bottle. I could feel that everything was outside and couldn't touch me.
> *I had to die to keep from dying:* I know that sounds crazy but one time a boy hurt my feelings very much and I wanted to jump in front of a subway. Instead I went a little catatonic so I wouldn't feel anything.[35]

Similar images crop up repeatedly in schizophrenic delusions and self-descriptions. One patient claimed to be "dead and yet living"; while another said, "I am only an automaton, a machine; it is not I who senses, speaks, eats, suffers, sleeps; I exist no longer; I do not exist, I am dead; I feel I am absolutely nothing."[36] "I can't feel or relate," said Rosser's patient:

> I used to feel emotions like physical pain and I couldn't stand it. So I blocked off. I can't empathize with people. . . . I can't work because there is nothing in me. Perhaps my nervous tissue has been destroyed. . . . I used to think everyone else was an automaton. Then I saw them relating to one another and I realized I was the automaton.[37]

Hölderlin, the great German poet who became schizophrenic in his early thirties and who is often viewed as a major proto-modernist figure, lamented his inability to charge the deadened world with life. As he put it in a letter from 1799: "a wondrous horror then overcomes me, and silently I remind myself of the terrible truth: a living corpse!"[38]

This kind of deadening may serve as a defense against the fear of overwhelming emotion. However, it can itself become so frightening that the patient may desperately attempt to bring back some feeling of substantiality or aliveness—"to recapture reality," as one patient said,[39] by imitating other people's behavior, or by extreme actions like burning oneself with cigarettes or terrorizing oneself with risky acts such as walking on high ledges.

DISSOLUTION OF EGO BOUNDARIES

Despite qualities of bizarreness, in most of the instances of boundary confusion discussed in previous chapters, at least a rudimentary differentiation between self and object was preserved. Thus, in Natalija's influencing-machine experience, there was still some vestige of an outside world, an "elsewhere" separate from her own presence—indeed, the Natalija machine itself lay in just such a space (as did the illusory objects projected before her gaze). Similarly, the protagonist of *The Invention of Morel* does not actually merge with Morel but contemplates his alter ego as an image appearing before him. Certainly these solipsists may *identify* with the Other; still, instead of fusing with the self, that Other maintains its place at the far point of the arc of consciousness—subjectivized by, but not totally merged with, the observing subject. *Nihilation* is Sartre's term for the fundamental feature of human consciousness that is retained in these symptoms— the implicit awareness that I, the self-as-experiencing-subject, am not-that-thing, not-that-thought, or not-that-image, that there is something constituting my consciousness that lies here, behind the eyeballs as it were, rather than out there in whatever experiential object currently occupies the field of awareness. Sartre found it simply inconceivable that human consciousness could ever be devoid of this kind of differentiation: the self may be only an absence or a sense of nothingness, something that cannot be located or specified in the manner of an object, but he insists nevertheless that it is always real enough to prevent a collapse into the objects of its perceiving.

There are times, however, when schizophrenic patients do seem to have this supposedly impossible experience, moments when all vestiges of the self/world distinction appear to be effaced, and when, instead of Sartrian nihilation, there is a true annihilation of boundaries, a flooding in of Being that obliterates all the distances or distinctions hitherto maintained. At these moments the connection between what happens within the self (whether in body or mind) and in the world outside seems absolute and instantaneous, amounting to a virtual equivalence.

"All the clocks of the world feel my pulse," says one schizophrenic. "When my eyes are bright blue, the sky gets blue," says another. "My eyes and the sun are the same," says a third.[40] When a nurse let the bathwater rush in, one schizophrenic cried out, "You are making my urine run and nothing will be left in my body." Another patient said, "That's the rain. I could be the rain." "That chair . . . that wall. I could be that wall. It's a terrible thing for a girl to be a wall."[41]

At first such a total loss of boundaries may not seem amenable to the interpretation I have been offering: for this degree of fusion or confusion might seem to preclude the existence of a hyperreflexive ego and of the hyperacute and alienated modes of attention I have been emphasizing. This kind of merging may, in fact, seem more consistent with the primitivity and Dionysian models I have been at such pains to criticize, for it does recall the infantile experience that precedes formation of firm boundaries between self and world and between reality and fantasy,[42] and perhaps also that Dionysianism described in Nietzsche's *The Birth of Tragedy*—a "shattering of the *principium individuationis*" where "feverish excesses" and "paroxysm[s] of lust and cruelty" cause us to "sink back into the original oneness with nature." Further, such a total identification with the objective world—with a wall or with the rain—may seem inconsistent with the model of solipsism. After all, such experiences surely lack a feeling of subjectivized mastery or invulnerability—and, with the disappearance of "nihilation," even the most basic sense of subjectivity must disappear.[43]

Some instances of schizophrenic boundary dissolution are, in fact, exceptions to the general picture of hyperreflexivity and alienation presented in this book—though not, I think, in a way that truly contradicts the general portrait I have been offering. For, rather than representing the bursting forth of some core or essential schizophrenic element, self-dissolution in intense physical sensation may actually be more of a defense: a way of escaping a more characteristic sense of division, deadness, and derealization or of avoiding the terror of solipsistic responsibility for the world. As Nietzsche pointed out, Apollonianism itself, the propensity for "drawing boundary lines, and . . . enjoining again and again the practice of self-knowledge," may bring on a periodic need for release, a yearning for a primitive "Dionysiac flood tide" that breaks up the rigidity and destroys "all the little circles" of the Apollonian will and self.[44] We discussed how Schreber used piano playing and bellowing to restore "soul-voluptuousness" and overcome the self-consciousness that paralyzed his physical functioning; and we considered Artaud's attempts (usually unavailing) to find redemption, relief from what he called "dispossession of my vital substance," in the ecstasies of primitive ritual and the frenzies of a "theatre of cruelty."[45] This hankering for blood consciousness as an antidote to disembodiment and alienation is far from uncommon, either in madness or in modernism, but it should not be mistaken for a purer and less motivated primitivity.

The Dionysian escape is not, in any case, the only kind of boundary dissolution that comes about in schizophrenia, and the true world catastrophe is likely, I think, to have a different, more awesome cast. As the German psychiatrist A. Wetzel noted in 1922, the "end of the world" experience tends to occur as an ultimate "realisation" of a sinister and uncanny mood-state. It emerges against a backdrop of preoccupation with cosmic events and grand themes, is associated with the sense of being somehow at the center of these dreadful happenings, and occurs in an atmosphere of impending doom dominated by euphoria, dysphoria, or a curious mixture of both.[46] This, I would argue, is the outcome of a hyperreflexive progression, the culmination of a process that, at the extreme point in its development, undermines itself and thereby erases the very conditions of reflexivity and alienation that made it possible in the first place.[47] For clues to how this may come about, we might look to the philosophy of Fichte, the modern philosophical thinker who comes closest to explicit solipsism. Fichte's argument may seem rather abstract (later we shall take up more concrete examples), but for this very reason it can reveal the underlying logic in this progression, thus helping us to grasp the powerful impulsion toward catastrophe that can exist in schizophrenia.

Fichte and the Subjectivization of the All

I have already mentioned the major theme of the early sections of Fichte's *The Vocation of Man*: the denial of the reality of an external or objective world and the consequent declaration of consciousness's sovereignty over its objects. One particularly condensed and representative sentence captures the hyperreflexive presuppositions and solipsistic implications of his position: "My consciousness of the object is only a yet unrecognized *consciousness of my creation of a presentation of an object*," he writes.[48] To achieve this "yet unrecognized consciousness" is, presumably, to realize the truth: namely, that there *is* no external world, that only the "presentations" experienced—indeed, created—by consciousness actually exist. We have seen how the lived world of schizophrenia can involve something very like this kind of Fichtean solipsism, with its attendant isolation, omnipotence, and ontological vulnerability. But for clues to understanding the experience of boundary dissolution, we must look to later stages of Fichte's argument, when the unreality or nonexistence of an external world can already be assumed.[49]

Having previously argued that the world is *subordinate* to the self, Fichte now stresses how the world also *resembles* the self. If, as he has said, there is never consciousness of the world but only a consciousness of a *consciousness* of the world, then self and that which the self knows (the world of immanent objects, of "pictures" or "representations") would seem to be equivalent in some essential sense—both having the nature of consciousness or mind, not physical things. Thus for Fichte the subjectivity of the experiential object resides not just in its insubstantial or projected quality but also in its being an experienc*ing* entity:

And the objective, that which is contemplated and of which I am conscious, is also myself—the same self which contemplates, but now floating as an objective presentation before the subjective. . . . I see (*consciousness*) my own vision (*the thing of which I am conscious.*)

Hence this object is also thoroughly transparent to thy mind's eye, because it is the mind itself.[50]

That which is experienc*ed* as object turns out, in the final analysis, to be nothing other than the experienc*ing* subject, which has been projected outward before itself. But slightly later in the development of his position, Fichte stresses an opposite kind of homogenization of the field of awareness: not reduction or assimilation of the experiential world to the self but, rather, the reverse.

It is true that, at least at first, a reflexive turn may discover the self or "I" to be more immediate, indubitable, and foundational than are its objects of awareness (says Fichte, "I have immediate knowledge of myself alone: whatever I may know more than this, I know only by inference"). But if one follows through solipsism's central premise—namely, that only immediate experience, and nothing lying behind it, is to be accepted as fundamental— then it may well seem that only the *experience* of the self or ego, and not the ego itself, can be accepted as truly real. "[S]trictly speaking," Fichte writes, "I ought to say 'the thought appears that I feel, perceive, think'—but by no means 'that I feel, perceive, think.' " Now it will seem that it is the world, the world of "presentations," that is the most indubitable and fundamental type of entity; for the self turns out to be nothing more than one of those pictures or representations that only *seem* to refer to something beyond themselves and only *seem* to appear before an independent ego:

> There is nothing enduring, either out of me, or in me, but only a ceaseless change. I know of no being, not even of my own. There is no being. I myself absolutely know not, and am not. Pictures are:—they are the only things which exist, and they know of themselves after the fashion of pictures:—pictures which float past without there being anything past which they float: . . .—pictures without anything which is pictured in them, without significance and without aim.

Instead of stabilizing the representations, holding them in place like spokes around a hub, the self now collapses outward into its world—turning out to be, if anything, even more evanescent than other representations:

> I myself am one of these pictures;—nay, I am not even this, but merely a confused picture of the pictures. All reality is transformed into a strange dream, without a life which is dreamed of, and without a mind which dreams it;—into a dream which is woven together in a dream of itself.[51]

And so, Fichte comes to postulate a universe like that of Derrida's mirror-cave, a universe composed only of shadows, reflections, and phantasms.

Fichte's vision is lived out, with both of its homogenizing tendencies, by Valéry's Monsieur Teste—that now familiar modernist Everyman to whom everything seemed "a special case of his mental functioning, and the functioning itself now conscious, identical with the idea or sense he had of it."[52] And in the "nerves" and "rays" of Daniel Paul Schreber's universe, we find an even more blatant example of this transformation of the object into a manifestation of the subject. As we saw in the discussion of Schreber's panopticism, the rays are a quasi-projection of the self-regarding element of his own divided consciousness ("What are you thinking of now?" they say to him), and thus they provide an example of how the object may be not only derealized (for these entities are seen, as Schreber puts it, in the mind's eye) but also transformed into a simulacrum of the self-as-subject—in this case, in fact, of the self-as-subject in its most self-conscious or hyperreflexive mode. The rays are thus a perfect exemplification of Fichte's description of the "objective" as being "also myself"—the same self that contemplates.

The other trend leading toward homogenization of the arc of experience is the transformation of self into mere image. As we have already seen, some patients come to feel that the self exists only as a perception, perhaps in their own or perhaps in someone else's consciousness. One patient insisted that she was not really herself but merely a reflection of herself; another said that he used to be a drawing in a book, until he got away and came to the hospital; and a third spoke of feeling "like a moving picture projected on the wall. I only existed because you [the therapist] wanted me to and I could only be what you wanted to see."[53] Here the self is expelled from its central location, dispersed into an outer realm where it floats among pictures from which it is virtually indistinguishable. This, in fact, seems to have been Renee's experience during a time of "torpor and mutism," when, as she said, "everything had become so irrelevant, so devoid of emotion and sensibility . . . I simply could not react, the essential motor force had broken down. Images with whom I had nothing to do, from whom I was remote, moved toward and away from my bed. I was, myself, a lifeless image."[54] (Recall Fichte's "pictures which float past without there being anything past which they float.") Thus the solipsistic patient can come to experience the world as a manifestation of himself while also experiencing the self as utterly ungrounded and illusory. And with these developments the patient enters a domain of unreality where there is little chance of distinguishing the self from its objects. "Who can prove to me that this blanket on my legs is really a blanket and that I am I?" asked one patient, pointing out—quite rightly, given this kind of world—that "there is nothing to prove that I am not the blanket."[55]

The disappearance of anything that would contrast with either the "object" or the "subject" gives rise to a new domain that is neither "objective" nor "subjective" in any usual sense but, rather, a twilight realm that normal language can barely describe. What comes to exist is a kind of mono-domain, something like a volatile and filmy gauze of representations lacking any objective referent or substantial subject by which they might be stabilized or anchored—what one patient referred to as "a two-dimensional hyperplane of reality."[56] The feel of this mono-domain, its insubstantiality, transparency, and mutability, is very effectively evoked in the following lines from Martin's poem "In Clear Things," with their peculiar mingling, in a single realm of substance and consciousness, of "membrane" and "molecules" with "a protean eye":

> Our insight has evaporated, dehydration has occurred.
> Only formal structures E's axiom thus and therefore . . .
> Lapses of lingering transparencies
> Celluloid was metamorphic
> Light passes through membrane
> Flagellate proto-zoa bumping molecules
> A protean eye, the blur of life
> In lights and darkness

The poem continues with a reference to a distant world of physical sensation and external substance, which may represent memories of the commonsense realm ("sediments left behind" and thirst-quenching soda pop), but this is followed by the image of solipsistic world catastrophe I quoted earlier:

> Ripples, the feeling of soda pop
> From a plastic vacuform bottle.
> The floor beneath the clarity
> Sediments left behind.
> Only the purity of bubbling water
> And caffein colored carmel
> Quench the thirst.
>
> Eyes slits, the blurred edge of a lash
> Borders of a flattened world,
> We fall off the edge.

Antonin Artaud's own involutional journey was suffused with a similar kind of cerebral devitalization. He too was propelled toward that catastrophe zone—sometimes tinged, for him, with euphoria—where self and world are undone. In "Fragments from a Diary in Hell" (1925), he describes "the metaphysics which I have created for myself as a result of this emptiness I carry within." Like so many of Artaud's texts, this one is a litany of despair over the feelings of coldness, abstinence, castration, and asphyxiation that pervade his alienated and self-conscious existence, which he describes as a "living death." It ends by describing how a purely cerebral consciousness seeks itself in the unreal space of its own being and merges with the All: "When I think about myself, my thought seeks itself in the ether of a new space. I am on the moon as others are on their balconies. I participate in planetary gravitation in the fissures of my mind."[57]

Dissolution of the *principium individuationis* need not, then, be associated with Nietzsche's Dionysian floodtide or the infantile regression postulated by psychoanalysts; it may stem from those introversive movements whereby consciousness separates itself from material reality and the vital bodily instincts and instead turns inward, there to discover, or to found, an entire world. But so far my primary illustrations of boundary dissolution in schizophrenia have concerned only the culminating moment when the cataclysm actually occurs. Ideally one would like a single example that illustrates each phase of this Fichtean progression—the entire course whereby milder symptoms of hyperreflexivity and solipsism actually progress toward world catastrophe. But when one considers the difficulty of describing such experiences—which are so radically at variance with the presuppositions of ordinary language and life—it should not be surprising that few autobiographical accounts by actual patients are complete, specific, or lucid enough to serve this purpose.

I propose instead another literary example: "Description of a Struggle," an early short story by Franz Kafka that offers what is perhaps the most vivid evocation of schizophrenic experience in all of Western literature. Kafka's story, which he began writing in 1904, is, of course, a product of the literary imagination, yet it seems to offer a semi-autobiographical account of the experiences undergone by its author—a distinctly schizoid man who felt himself to be close to madness and who on at least one occasion approached a world-catastrophe experience of his own.[58] This story has managed to repel many of Kafka's most ardent admirers; their complaints—about its supposed qualities of uncanny arbitrariness, absurd exaggeration, confusion, and sheer perversity—seem to betray something very like the praecox feeling.[59]

Kafka's "Description of a Struggle"

The critical scene of Kafka's story is its penultimate one, to be discussed shortly. Of special interest in the present context, however, are the earlier scenes in the story, for it is these that allow us to trace the process leading up to the closing moments of cataclysmic apocalypse.

Kafka's story, which can be described as having "assimilated every sense of the Modern [as well as the postmodern] spirit,"[60] contains nearly every feature of modernism discussed in earlier chapters, including derealization, dehumanization (disappearance of the active self), giddy perspectivism or relativism, and detachment. The recurrent plot structure of this antistory—which is organized not linearly but in something like a series of concentric circles—also reveals (though less obviously) qualities of spatial form as well as a kind of aesthetic self-referentiality. In addition, virtually every aspect of schizophrenia is described in this story, from relatively mild schizoid phenomena to the most extreme forms of solipsistic experience. Whereas *The Invention of Morel* can be read as an *allegory* of the schizoid and schizophrenic condition, "Description of a Struggle" seems almost to give us the experience itself: it is an extremely raw and direct, at times almost unbearable, presentation of those central schizoid themes that make Kafka one of the most representative of twentieth-century writers—a sort of Dante of modern times.

The story, which is divided into a number of sections, opens with its narrator, a young man, sitting alone at a wedding party, sipping a glass of benedictine and surveying the other guests in the room. Quickly one senses the alienation and self-consciousness of this protagonist, who is one of those diffident antiheroes with transparently false bravado who have haunted the European imagination ever since Dostoevsky's *Notes from the Underground*. Abruptly, Kafka's narrator finds himself engaged in a strange string of nonsequiturs with another young man whom he has met for the first time that evening. When the two go out for a walk in the mountains, it soon becomes apparent that this new acquaintance is some peculiar kind of alter ego—a man whose social ease makes him an envied opposite but whose inner thoughts the narrator assumes he can read (though the reader may well doubt whether the narrator is really just projecting, perhaps even imagining, the whole thing).

During the walk, the young narrator's estrangement from social interaction and from his own body and emotions becomes obvious: "Hardly were we outside, when I *evidently* began to feel very gay," he writes, speaking of his own feelings as if they could only be surmised (11; emphasis added).* A few moments later, a failed attempt at friendliness toward the acquaintance leaves him feeling detached from his own hand: "No sooner had I given him an encouraging slap on the back than I suddenly no longer understood his mood, and withdrew my hand. Since I had no use for it, I stuck it in the pocket of my coat." Now and at later moments the narrator also engages in

---

*Numbers in parentheses in this chapter refer to page citations in "Description of a Struggle."[61]

a truth-taking stare, scrutinizing the world with an intensity that can transform any innocuous event into something portentous, threatening, or simply odd: a melody hummed by his acquaintance begins to seem insulting; words lose their connection to the objects they depict and stand forth in their arbitrariness (11, 33).[62]

After the two men have been walking in the mountains for a while, the story turns blatantly surreal, mutating into what we might call a psychotic mode. The narrator leaps onto the shoulders of the other man and goads him forward like a horse until, finally, the acquaintance injures his knee and collapses. The landscape now begins to change, losing its quality of objective reality (it is described as "a vast but as yet unfinished landscape") and then responding to the narrator's wishes as if it were but a figment of his imagination: "I walked on, unperturbed. But since, as a pedestrian, I dreaded the effort of climbing the mountainous road, I let it become gradually flatter, let it slope down into a valley in the distance. The stones vanished at my will and the wind disappeared" (21–22). The narrator seems to have entered some kind of solipsistic universe in which he is the central point or axis around which the world turns: when he climbs a tree, it is the tree trunk rather than his own body that seems to be moving—"sliding quickly down the rings formed by my arms and legs."[63] While falling asleep in the tree, he spies "a squirrel of my whim" poised at the end of a trembling branch (23).

In the next section the young man, who by now has abandoned his injured acquaintance, encounters another mysterious double—a monstrously fat man who is sitting, Oriental fashion, on a wooden litter borne by four naked men. Despite his exotic appearance, the fat man, like the acquaintance before him, also turns out to be some kind of *doppelgänger* for the narrator, though in this case less an envied opposite than a twin. The fat man first describes feeling overwhelmed and threatened by the sheer objectivity of the world about him—the landscape, he says, "makes my reflections sway like suspension bridges in a furious current" (26)—but then, after imploring the world about him to give him some breathing room, he pulls off a solipsistic victory by making the surrounding mountains "shift in hasty obedience" to his wishes (27). The section ends with a bizarre little demonstration of the unreality of everything, including the solipsist himself: "A tiny mosquito with stretched wings flew straight through [the fat man's] belly without losing its speed" (29).

The following section is narrated by the fat man, who tells his story of meeting the supplicant, this being another young man whom the fat man accosted after seeing him praying and moaning during a church service. Much of the rest of Kafka's story is a recounting, by the fat man, of his conversations with the supplicant; but in the midst of this section there is a lengthy monologue in which the supplicant in turn takes on the role of narrator, now telling of further encounters that *he* has had, first with a young lady at a party and later with a drunk in the street. In this part the ontological vulnerability of both self and world, already a recurring theme in the story, becomes an overwhelming preoccupation, and the fragile solipsistic grandiosity of the earlier sections gives way to a focus on the fraudulence, fragility, or unreality of both self and world. The supplicant, it turns out, is so filled with trepidation about the stability of his own self and the world around him that he clasps his hands together "to give his body unity" and never takes a step without first testing the ground with his toe (34, 31).[64] At one point he crouches down before the fat man to explain himself:

> Now I can also tell you at last why I let you accost me. Out of curiosity, from hope. Your stare has been comforting me for a long time. And I hope to learn from you how things really are, why it is that around me things sink away like fallen snow, whereas for other people even a little liqueur glass stands on the table steady as a statue. . . . Why, after all, should I feel ashamed of not walking upright and taking normal steps, of not tapping the pavement with my stick . . . ? Am I not rather entitled to complain bitterly at having to skip along the houses like a shadow without a clear outline, sometimes disappearing in the panes of the shopwindows? [34–35]

In this description of the self as but an amorphous shadow disappearing in the panes of the shopwindows, one of the outcomes of Fichtean solipsism is perfectly realized: no longer a privileged or substantial center, the self of the supplicant has become just another "mere presentation"—only "a dream which is woven together in a dream of itself."[65]

Here, then, are the overt themes of Kafka's story: experiences of alienation from the world and from oneself, followed by moments of brief-lived solipsistic triumph and a more pervasive ontological collapse. Even more central to the story's profoundly disconcerting effect, however, is the way these themes are paralleled and sometimes prefigured by its narrative structure or form.

All the speakers—young man, fat man, and supplicant—have much the same voice and nearly identical experiences: feelings of dissolution and social alienation, and obvious but unavailing attempts to overcome or deny such feelings. It is, in fact, as if each narrator were incapable of imagining any story other than his own, as if the only Other he could encounter were but a projection of himself.[66] And with few clues to frame the reported speech and to remind the reader of just whose perspective is being presented at a given moment, the reader can easily lose awareness of who is speaking: the narrator's point of view becomes obscure or ambiguous, as it merges with that of the supposed interlocutor or the person being described. As a result, the reader, in the immediate act of reading, undergoes something closely akin to the experience of merger that the fat man finally makes explicit at a certain point in his encounter with the supplicant: " 'But why do you pray in church every evening?' I asked then, while everything between him and me, which until then I had been holding together as though in my sleep, collapsed" (44).

Along with this confusion or merging of perspectives, there is another, closely related development: a progressive subjectivization or derealization. Even at the outset the reader cannot help but be aware of seeing the world through the lens of a particular, and rather peculiar, consciousness—that of the self-conscious young man who is the first narrator. (One wonders, for example, whether the stranger met at the party really said what is reported or whether the narrator just imagined it.) This feeling of subjectivization can only increase as one enters into the fat man's narrative, for his story has, presumably, been refracted not only through his own mind but also through that of the original narrator. By the time one reaches the supplicant's monologue, one is inhabiting a triply subjectivized perspective, a story within a story within a story. (The supplicant's tale exists within the mind of the supplicant, but the supplicant himself exists only within the mind of the fat man, who in turn exists only within the mind of the original narrator.) As a result, the reader, too, is likely to have a sense of derealization: just as the supplicant's world seems to him to "sink away like fallen snow," so the characters described by each narrator, as well as the narrators themselves, will be felt by the reader to be but airy and unreal projections or fantasies, as evanescent as those shadows in the passing windowpanes.[67]

The structure of Kafka's narrative seems, in fact, to be in perfect accord with the two sides of Fichte's solipsism described earlier. The world is assimilated to the self—since, as we have seen, every other person who is encountered turns out to be (in Fichte's words) "myself, the same self which contemplates, but now floating as an objective presentation before the subjective." And at the same time, the self is assimilated to the world—alienated outward where it floats as a kind of externalized yet unreal picture or mere representation. What we have in Kafka's story is a solipsistic hypertrophy of the conscious mind and the mind's self-consciousness, a Fichtean universe where everything is felt to be constituted *by* the mind or self—or even, in the case of the alter egos (the acquaintance, the fat man, and the supplicant), to *be* the self, now present to itself as its own representation. It is easy to imagine how ego boundaries could become fragile under circumstances such as these: for what principle of differentiation could there possibly be once everything is subjectivized and unreal? In the pages of Kafka's story just preceding the final catastrophe, this predicament becomes eminently clear.

Here the supplicant alludes to the solipsistic feeling that the world will cease to exist if one does not attend to it: he refers to a moment between night and day "when everything stands still without our knowing it, since we are not looking, and then disappears; we remain alone, our bodies bent, then look around but no longer see anything" (43). A moment later the supplicant (who might as well be speaking for any of the narrators) gives voice to a number of his fears: "that one's body could vanish, that human beings may really be what they appear to be at twilight, that one might not be allowed to walk without a stick, that it might be a good idea to go to church and pray at the top of one's voice in order to be looked at and acquire a body" (44).

At this point the experience of ontological insecurity is approaching a kind of crescendo, and the supplicant (or is it the fat man, or perhaps the original narrator?) makes a last desperate attempt to shore himself up against the oncoming convulsion; this, however, he does in a most curious, characteristic, and ultimately self-defeating way. "For we are like tree trunks in the snow," he says. "They lie there apparently flat on the ground and it looks as though one could push them away with a slight push. But no, one can't, for they are firmly stuck to the ground. So you see, even this is only apparent" (45). Here the speaker is trying to reassure himself against fears of his own fragility—by assuring himself that even his sense of fragility is unreal: "only apparent" since, like the appearance of a tree that only *seems* to balance on top of the snow (yet is really rooted), it is but an impression, no more than an image in the mind. We might say, then, that the supplicant is trying to derealize the experience of derealization—by negating negation to achieve some kind of affirmation, as if in the hope that a further turn of the screw of doubt could somehow return him to a more primal orientation and hold off the looming absence.

But this strategy only heightens the instability, for in the next section, "Drowning of the Fat Man," there is a decisive collapse of all boundaries and a virtual evaporation of the world. The ensuing experiences are virtually indistinguishable from schizophrenic world catastrophe—where the self can change size (one such patient felt she would expand to many times her normal dimensions, like an immense balloon, then would shrink to become a tiny self inside the vastness);[68] where self and world can become indistinguishable ("Who can prove to me that this blanket on my legs is really a blanket and that I am I?"); and where the world may seem to explode or to disappear ("I hear the world blowing up"; "I have the impression that nothing exists").[69] Here are Kafka's words:

> And now everything was seized by speed and fell into the distance. The water of the river was dragged toward a precipice, tried to resist, whirled about a little at the crumbling edge, but then crashed in foaming smoke.
>
> The fat man could not go on talking, he was forced to turn and disappear in the loud roar of the waterfall.

I, who had experienced so many pleasant diversions, stood on the bank and watched. . . .

Meanwhile the banks of the river stretched beyond all bounds, and yet with the palm of my hand I touched the metal of a signpost which gleamed minutely in the far distance. This I really couldn't quite understand. After all I was small, almost smaller than usual, and a bush of white hips shaking itself very fast towered over me. This I saw, for a moment ago it had been close to me.

Nevertheless I was mistaken, for my arms were as huge as the clouds of a steady country rain, save that they were more hasty. I don't know why they were trying to crush my poor head. It was no larger than an ant's egg, but slightly damaged, and as a result no longer quite round. I made some beseeching, twisting movements with it, for the expression of my eyes could not have noticed, they were so small.

But my legs, my impossible legs lay over the wooded mountains and gave shade to the village-studded valleys. They grew and grew! They already reached into the space that no longer owned any landscape, for some time their length had gone beyond my field of vision.

But no, it isn't like that—after all, I'm small, small for the time being— I'm rolling—I'm rolling—I'm an avalanche in the mountains! Please, pass-ers-by, be so kind as to tell me how tall I am—just measure these arms, these legs. [46–47]

In Kafka's story, we have the entire progression of a schizophrenic illness: from schizoid self-consciousness and hyperscrutiny through self-alienation and solipsism, and on to the dissolution of both self and world. It is as if the entire story were carried along by some forceful momentum, the action moving inexorably toward its culmination: an annihilation of all differences that is barely held off by the most desperate of remedies—remedies that aggravate the very condition they oppose, thus triggering the final cataclysm.

Conclusion: Paradoxes of the Reflexive

Our knowledge will take its revenge on us, just as ignorance exacted its revenge during the Middle Ages.

—Friedrich Nietzsche
In Karl Jaspers, *Nietzsche*

In the introduction to this book I stressed two features of schizophrenia that pose a special challenge to the search for empathic understanding or explanatory generalization: the extreme alienness and the baffling heterogeneity of the representative symptoms. By now we have seen that many of these mysteries can in fact be comprehended, that it is possible to empathize with the characteristic deviations from normal human existence and to discover underlying affinities in what can be understood to be various expressions of schizophrenic reflexivity and detachment. Yet we have still not considered one of the strangest and, perhaps, most revealing of the many paradoxes that lie coiled at the heart of the schizophrenic condition—a paradox that can emerge only from a gathering together of the themes of the last four chapters.

As we have seen, many schizophrenic patients tend to lose their sense of active and integrated intentionality. Instead of serving as a kind of anchoring center, the self may be dispersed outward, where it fragments into parts that float among the things of the world; even the most intimate thoughts and inclinations may appear to emanate from some external source or mysterious foreign soul, as if they were "the workings of another psyche."[1] But we also know that the self can come to seem preeminent and all-powerful: rather than drifting somewhere in space, like the detritus of some forgotten explosion, one's own consciousness may seem poised at the epicenter of the universe—with all the strata of Being arrayed about it, as around some constituting solipsistic deity. On the one hand: "I feel that it is not me who is thinking"; "feelings are not felt by me, things are not seen by me, only by my eyes"; "I have been programmed . . . I am the beeps of the computer." On the other hand: "My thoughts can influence things"; "this event happens because I think it"; "to keep the world going, I must not stop thinking."[2] Rosser's patient recalled that, during an intense period of his psychosis, common objects like tables and chairs had seemed to be only "projections in my mind," yet he had also found himself uncertain of the very existence of his mind, doubting that "it is me thinking, myself."[3] This kind of duality may be the most dramatic illustration of that paradoxical or contradictory quality so characteristic of schizophrenia—whereby, as Vygotsky put it, every major symptom seems to be matched by a "countersymptom, its negative double, its opposite," a sort of antiworld where everything appears in reverse.[4]

In part three, I considered each side of this duality and examined some of the paradoxes and reversals each side can entail: how searching for the self can dissolve it, for example, and how the sense of awesome ontological power can devolve into a kind of abject metaphysical terror. What remains to be investigated is the intimate interconnection—indeed, the deep interdependence—that seems to exist *between* these apparently contradictory modes of experience, between the loss of self and its apotheosis in moments of unrestrained solipsistic grandeur.

Although evidence for this peculiar duality is widespread, it has not been accorded as much attention as it deserves. As both Eugen Bleuler and Karl Jaspers have noted, however, there is a tendency for the megalomania of such individuals to be mixed with feelings of persecution, powerlessness, and inferiority:[5] the same patient who declares himself to be omnipotent will also say that he doesn't exist, or that his body or his thoughts are under alien control; the schizophrenic who claims to be all-knowing also complains of being mystified by the workings of either real or delusional phenomena; the person who claims she can conjure whole worlds into or out of existence nevertheless complains that mysterious machines, lasers, or electrical forces are controlling her thoughts, actions, or field of awareness. The patient is "sometimes an automaton moved by the agency of persons, . . . at others, the Emperor of the whole world," as John Haslam wrote in 1810, in what is widely regarded as the first psychiatric description of a schizophrenic person.[6] But it is not merely that such patients tend to shift readily between what seem to be opposite claims; they may even maintain both positions at the same moment, often without being troubled by the apparent inconsistency. Thus, while a person suffering from schizophrenia is as likely to identify with God as with a machine, perhaps the most emblematic delusion of this illness is of being a sort of God machine, an all-seeing, all-constituting camera eye.

The metaphors schizophrenics use to characterize their own moods or modes of experience frequently bring out this peculiar combination of omnipotence and passivity, of omniscience and utter ignorance. On emerging from one of his recurrent periods of catatonic withdrawal, for example, a patient of mine (Robert) would say that the external world had seemed to him like a two-dimensional transparency, something like an architect's drawing or plan, and (as mentioned before) he would also describe his own mind as having felt to him like a photocopy machine. This suggests that he (or his mind) had somehow *produced* the two-dimensional transparencies, thus that the world felt like an unreal or replicated copy made by himself but also that the entity making these representations was mechanical, automatistic. One might suppose that a person who constitutes the universe could never be surprised and could not, therefore, experience the paranoia of the unknown: of necessity, nothing could lie outside his awareness or control. Yet many schizophrenics *are* preoccupied with just this kind of pervasive fear: though subjectivized, their worlds are shot through with a curious anxiety and suspiciousness—as if they experienced their actual thoughts and perceptions against the backdrop of an unspecifiable and threatening unknown. It seems that the all-knowing can feel ignorant or blind; the all-powerful can feel passive or afraid.

Here it is easy to feel that one is confronted with the very paradigm of strangeness and irrationality. These examples may well seem not just deviations from normal human life but profound forms of *self*-contradiction—a flouting of what, since Aristotle, has been considered the fundamental rule of reason, the identity principle or law of contradiction that states the impossibility of affirming both p and not-p. For Freudians such tolerance of contradiction might suggest regression to the primitive alogic of primary-process thinking, that unself-conscious state that ignores the principle of contradiction and all the other canons of rationality; for cognitivists it might seem a simple collapse of the higher faculties of mind. But we can also view these incongruities in a rather different light, as the consequences of a hyperreflexive attitude or condition.

Indeed, it turns out that these dualities so basic to schizophrenia come very close to a set of contradictions and paradoxes that are no less basic to modern thought—to the era of Western intellectual history when consciousness first comes to know itself as such, to appreciate its own subjective being and recognize its own contribution to the world it knows. Indeed, if "rationality" can be *defined* as "reflexivity"—as "the capacity to make problematic what had hitherto been treated as given; to bring to reflection what had only been used; . . . to think about our thinking," as one contemporary scholar puts it[7]—then we might even say that these forms of incongruity are actually products of a kind of hyperrationality: forms of irrationality generated by rationality itself.

The various paradoxes, oscillations, and interdependencies that are at issue have received their most extensive discussion in an early book by Michel Foucault, *The Order of Things*—his famous and forbidding study of the taken-for-granted modes or structures of knowing (*epistemes,* he calls them) that have channeled thought in the major epochs of Western history since the Renaissance. Foucault is the greatest contemporary chronicler and analyst of the nightmare side of modern times, and the prime critic of its myths of emancipation and enlightenment through self-knowledge; in the final two chapters of this dense, at times almost cryptic work, he describes the modern mode of thought as riven by deep contradictions, by tensions, paradoxes, and other dilemmas so varied and convoluted as nearly to defy summary. All these dilemmas do, however, have something in common, for they all derive from a certain duality in the status of human consciousness—a duality bound up with the hyperreflexivity of modern life, with what Foucault sees as our ultimately self-deceiving preoccupation with, and overvaluing of, the phenomenon of our own consciousness.[8]

Foucault, like many others, singles out as the origin and prime exemplar of modern thought the philosophy of Kant and the neo-Kantians—ideas that have been described as "the portal to the dwelling of modern philosophy" and as the true source of the modernist project of self-reflection. Let us consider Foucault's discussion of that tradition.[9]

THE DOUBLET OF MODERN THOUGHT

At the close of the eighteenth century Kant offered his immensely influential reflection on the "categories of understanding," those forms of temporal, spatial, and causal organization to which the world of human experience, the realm of "phenomena," must necessarily conform.[10] The profound effect of the new mode of philosophical awareness that Kant initiated was to foreground the role of the human mind in the constitution of the world. Perhaps for the first time in the history of Western thought, people came to conceive, and to be profoundly interested in, an object whose essence was understood to be its role as a constituting or epistemological subject. Previously we had, as it were, looked right *through* the lens of consciousness at the objects it revealed; now, with Kant's new, transcendental forms of reflection, that lens seemed to be clouding over and calling attention to itself, thereby withdrawing cognition from an interest in the world and directing it back upon its own intrinsic structure.[11] But the withdrawal and involution inherent in this new "philosophy of reflection"[12] had two implications—one tending to elevate the status of consciousness, the other to lower it.

In his analysis of the fundamental structures of knowing to which all possible experience must necessarily conform, Kant seemed to have shown that it was the world that had to arrange itself in accordance with the conditions of human consciousness rather than the reverse. Since, for all practical purposes, only what the human mind was capable of conceiving could exist, the world seemed to take on an existence that was secondary or subordinate to that of consciousness. Being, we might say, was shown to depend on Knowing—almost as if the external reality we experience were but a projection of the sovereign mind.[13] Bound up with this notion of the primacy of consciousness as the constituting center were three closely related notions, three elements of what Foucault would later refer to as "transcendental narcissism":[14] the freedom of consciousness, its self-creating nature, and its status as a complete and lucid source of truth.[15]

If the world is dependent on consciousness rather than vice versa, it would seem impossible to imagine how consciousness could be anything but a free spontaneity, operating in a self-generated sphere of total freedom. How, after all, could the causal forces of the natural world constrain or determine consciousness if this very world were itself dependent on consciousness for its own existence? Also, consciousness would seem, by such an account, to have arisen from itself—for how could something be the causal product of the very world of which it is itself the source? Finally, if all that exists presents itself *to* consciousness, it would seem that an exhaustive investigation of the contents of consciousness would have to reveal the whole of Being, including the nature of consciousness itself—for how could any existing thing avoid presenting itself before the clear gaze of the very mind by which the All, of which it is inevitably a part, is constituted?[16] Hence reflection on the self seemed to contain the key to understanding the entire universe.[17]

These insights—consciousness's discovery of its freedom, of its self-sufficiency, and of its omniscience and self-transparency (corresponding to the threefold wish of absolute consciousness discussed at the end of chapter 9)—seem to be implicit in the human being's discovery of his unique role as constitutor of the world. All three insights would feel like incontestable, self-evident truths to the (post-Kantian) person who, so to speak, looked out from *within* consciousness and saw the world glowing with its dependence on him.[18]

But an opposing perspective has been simultaneously present in that broad and varied current of modern self-reflection that began with Kant. In addition to being felt as the ultimate subjective center, the constitutor of the All (or, at least, of all that *we* can know), consciousness beginning with Kant also became a prime *object* of study[19]—and this development had various problematic consequences. For one thing, consciousness itself tended to be placed by the human sciences (the sciences of subjectivity) into the empirical order of objectifiable entities, and this conflicted with its status as a *transcendental* being to which and for which all entities must appear. (Consciousness as conceived in the modern age can therefore be described as, in Foucault's words, "a strange empirico-transcendental doublet.")[20] Consciousness was also assimilated into the natural order of cause and effect, which conflicted with the notion of its ultimate power and freedom. Thus the Kantian categories—from one standpoint the transcendental foundation of the relevant universe—were also facts *in* this universe, sometimes understood as the product of natural forces, and existing (in some sense) side by side with other objects of knowledge, on the same plane with other empirical phenomena such as atomic structures, pancreases, and bird migration patterns. "The world is entirely idea, and as such demands the knowing subject as the supporter of its existence. . . . on the other hand, this conscious being [is] just as necessarily entirely dependent upon a long chain of causes and effects which have preceded it, and in which it itself appears as a small link": thus Schopenhauer stated one of the fundamental antinomies or contradictions of post-Kantian thought.[21]

There is another form of contradiction to which such reflection can lead, this time involving a recognition of the constraints on the known that are imposed by consciousness itself and that are, in a sense, felt from within.

The very awareness of the nature of the Kantian categories implies certain limitations on knowledge, because it implies the indescribable existence of unknowable realities that, presumably, do *not* conform to the demands of the human mind. To be aware of the categories is, after all, to be aware that, at least on principle, there could be other realities to which one is necessarily blind—that is, other possible worlds that do not conform to the categories of human understanding (the latter being understood as reflections of the empirical, and therefore in some sense arbitrary, facts about the human mind).[22] There is also the fact that the categories themselves (or other structures of consciousness, however these may be conceived) are not something that naive consciousness readily grasps—it does, after all, require a sophisticated "reflection" in order to recognize the very existence of these structures (Kant's Transcendental Analytic and Deduction, for example). To become aware of the categories, to bring them to light, as it were, is therefore also to become aware that, at least much of the time, consciousness is not in fact transparent to itself.[23]

And so we see that in the modern era, consciousness, that seemingly self-aware foundation and transparent medium of representation, is also found to be surrounded by and imbued with a kind of obscurity. Foucault speaks of consciousness discovering, "both in itself and outside itself, at its borders yet also in its very warp and woof, an element of darkness, an apparently inert density in which it is embedded, an unthought which it contains entirely, yet in which it is also caught."[24] This realization clearly contradicts the other side of the modern doublet, the notion, which can seem equally self-evident, that all of reality—including the mind itself—must necessarily expose itself before the clear gaze of the mind by which it is constituted. This dual image and experience of consciousness may give rise to a kind of tunnel-vision solipsism: an experience in which consciousness is felt to be both an ultimate constituting source and a limiting and mysterious channel—omniscient and omnipotent, but only within a sphere whose boundaries are acutely felt from within. In Foucault's view this dual image also dooms the human sciences—the sciences of human experience—to various forms of instability, internal contradiction, and self-cancellation, an issue I will return to shortly.

In *The Order of Things* Foucault is concerned with explicitly theoretical modes of thought, with fields like linguistics, economics, and their academic predecessors; and he gives little indication of the implications these post-Kantian forms of reflection might have at the more immediate level of individual human experience. Some sense of the concrete existential consequences is, however, conveyed by a work like Kafka's "Description of a Struggle," with its febrile waverings between grandiosity and abjection, between the euphoria of solipsism and the nausea or terror of world dissolution. The narrative viewpoint of this quintessentially modernist work does seem to exemplify both sides of the "empirico-transcendental doublet" that Foucault sees at the core of the modern mind. Thus we find ourselves, much of the time, occupying a transcendental position, in fact an almost solipsistic one—identifying with a narrator who experiences himself as the center of the universe (remember: the narrator does not move; the tree trunk slips past him). Yet we also experience the self as alienated and passive: for, instead of owning his own experience, the narrator is continually discovering his thoughts and feelings outside himself, as the experiences of an Other who is, in fact, only a simulacrum of himself; thus what *was* primarily a godlike entity—the narrator's constituting ego—is continually being transformed into (empirical) objects *within* his own (and our) field of awareness. Further, though the events in the story generally have a quality of unreality, of being mere subjective illusions, they seldom appear to be anticipated or willed. They are like dream images that roll across the horizon without warning.

'Description of a Struggle" evokes all the dizzying shifts of modern thought: a veering between a bracing sense of epistemic omnipotence and an equally compelling awareness of blindness and constraint. And these parallel quite precisely the dualities in schizophrenia—where patients can experience themselves both as ultimate solipsistic centers and as mechanical and fragmented beings (as some kind of transcendental photocopy machine, camera recording the world, or deified corpse-with-insomnia); and where they will often claim to know or to control everything, yet will fear unknown dangers lurking about them and feel confronted by some colossal riddle.

THE CONSCIOUSNESS MACHINE

Both sides of this duality—the solipsistic grandiosity as well as the felt impotence and ignorance—are best exemplified by Natalija's influencing machine, the subject of Victor Tausk's famous essay of 1919. One implication of this classic delusion is that it places Natalija's own person or mind at the very center of the universe, in a position of great epistemic importance.[25] For, given the implications of her delusion, the persons and things of which she was aware must not have seemed truly independent beings, solid objects existing apart from her, but mere images existing for her alone—indeed, actually *constituted* by the fact of her perceiving them. (She claimed, after all, that what she saw were but pseudo-objects, slides displayed before the eyes of the Natalija machine. In some sense these images seem to be described as "ontic" phenomena, as things existing *within* the horizons of Natalija's experience. Clearly, however, they can be read as having an *ontological* import: as suggesting the insubstantial or subjectivized quality that all of reality could have for her; and, interestingly enough, Natalija did in fact come to perceive the world as a kind of two-dimensional image, existing in a single plane.) At the same time the very notion of a mysterious influencing device, a mechanism with invisible parts and obscure functions, controlled by unidentified men who display only certain images before her sense organs, suggests that Natalija did not feel wholly identified with or in control of her experiencing, and, in addition, that there were other, unknown realities beyond those that happened to appear before her own, carefully manipulated field of awareness.[26]

In these paradoxes of Natalija's delusion, there is the suggestion that her experience may have suffered from certain forms of "essential instability" and "precariousness" that Foucault (and others) have discerned in the human sciences of the modern episteme.

According to Foucault, the Kantian and post-Kantian project of (self-) reflection, in which consciousness attempts to turn around upon itself and know the foundational conditions of its own being, is doomed to engage in a series of "warped and twisted forms of reflection."[27] Because of the epistemological configuration they place themselves in, the post-Kantian sciences of "Man" are subject to the doublet's ever-present potential for equivocation and self-cancellation. We can see this by beginning on either side of the doublet—by concentrating on the objectlike realities of mind or on the subjective nature of the world. In either case we encounter aporias or contradictions that undermine the project of self-knowledge.

Thus if we emphasize the determined or empirical nature of mind, thinking of consciousness as merely a thing among things, it then becomes impossible to understand how such an entity could possibly know the truth about its own nature. But things will not be any more coherent if we think of mind as a truly constituting entity. After all, if the categories or forms of understanding really define the limits of what can be known, then it should not be possible to know these limits or conditions. For what would one contrast them with? How could one know them *as* limits? How, indeed, could the conditions themselves be able to show up as knowable entities within the very field they themselves define?[28]

In Foucault's view it is the failure to recognize these impossibilities that is the key blind spot at the core of the modern episteme; it is this that dooms modern thought to a fundamental instability, a constant shuttling between incompatible alternatives. Modern man nevertheless remains obsessed with the prospect of a kind of absolute self-knowledge, a self-knowledge that promises to unriddle the universe; yet all the while this prospect of perfect enlightenment, of utter awakening to the truth about the self, is the source of greatest self-delusion. Foucault compares it to a sleep—a sleep "so deep that thought experiences it paradoxically as vigilance."[29]

A similar instability and precariousness haunt the universe of the influencing machine. For, according to the "logic" of a delusion like Natalija's, the very things that cause or bring about all the images of her subjectivized world—namely, the mysterious men and the influencing machine itself—would themselves have to be mere images or representations. After all, if *everything* Natalija experiences is an illusion, merely a slide image or the like, shouldn't this apply to the Natalija machine also, since she is aware of it? (And in fact the components of her machine did begin, over time, to take on a two-dimensional quality, as if they too were entering the realm of images!)[30] But how, then, could a mere vision, an insubstantial figment in her mind, actually have the causal powers of an influencing mechanism, the capacity to *produce* consciousness? The situation is no less paradoxical, however, if we start on the other side of the doublet, with the supposed objectivity and causal power of the machine: given such an arrangement, we would have to ask how Natalija could possibly *know* these very facts about the finitude or limitedness of her own mind. If she sees only the images, has only the thoughts, that the machine and its manipulators allow her to "see" or to "think," how, then—short of being shown slide images of the machine itself, and of the entire system that includes the machine[31]—would it be possible for Natalija to know the limits of her own finitude? Doesn't her knowledge *of* these facts suggest that she must somehow be able to catapult herself out of the condition these facts describe? (That Martin, the young schizophrenic artist, may have been sensing some of these spiraling para-doxes is suggested by the following lines from his diary: "What is the intellect? Probably the force which asked the question 'What is the intel-lect?' If the intellect asked itself what itself is, can it answer itself?")

At least on a logical level, then, the universe of the influencing machine is fraught with irresolvable contradictions. Though well-nigh impossible, it was nonetheless quite actual; it did exist, at least as some sort of experiential claim and mode of existence. And this suggests that Natalija must have lived in a condition of perpetual oscillation—in one moment feeling the entire universe, influencing machine and all, to be a figment of her own, all-constituting ego, but in the next, experiencing her own consciousness, repre-sented by the mysterious machine, as a mere object among objects, an objectified, partially unknown thing that is subject to the effects of external causes.

"A METAPHYSICAL ILLNESS"

If my interpretation of Natalija seems overelaborate, even fanciful—espe-cially given the lack of direct quotations from her and the (admittedly) rather limited information about her delusions in Tausk's article—remember that many of these themes do preoccupy other schizophrenics, some of whom have been much more explicit in describing the nature of their problems. An especially clear account was given by Lawrence, a schizophrenic man in his early thirties (the one who remarked on the Ped Xing sign; see chapter 6) who captured the two sides of the doublet in a distinction he made between two different types of thinkers or ways of thinking. This patient's level of intelligence and articulateness was far above the average, and he was more focused on explicitly philosophical topics than is common even among schizo-phrenics. But while he may not, for these reasons, be the most *typical* schizophrenic person, he does in some sense epitomize the condition: his descriptions bring out the fundamentally ontological nature of experiences and preoccupations that many other such patients might describe in a more "ontic" manner. A consideration of his central concerns shows that he, like Natalija, shared the fate of the modern episteme, that he too existed in a kind of fitful equivocation between objectivism and subjectivism, between self-abnegation and self-deification, between finitude and the infinite.

This young man had suffered from schizophrenia for many years and had been in mental asylums over a dozen times before. On his most recent admission, he offered the following as his chief complaint: "I have a meta-physical illness; my mind is rapidly deteriorating." Somewhat later in this period of hospitalization, he complained of being misunderstood by the staff on the ward: "Just because they don't understand me they think [I'm speaking] word salad." "I'm not crazy: mad, perhaps, but not crazy," he said, explaining that to be "mad" was to be driven "to the extremes of experience, to experience ideas at the extreme; but [the ideas I had were] all true so I wasn't crazy."[32]

The notions that preoccupied Lawrence centered around his distinction between what he referred to as "intuitive" and merely "mechanical" or "empirical" types of thinkers. In his opinion the vast majority of human beings were of the latter sort—not truly living minds but only "organic machines" or "mental vegetables" who lacked a real soul; he claimed that what appeared to be thinking on their part was, in fact, only the mechanical retrieval and processing of facts and memories from a memory bank. (In Lawrence's view, psychiatry, as he explained to his therapist, is a particularly egregious example of merely empirical thinking: "I feel psychiatry is a lot of empirical nonsense, no offense. I object to empiricism—it's all based in facts—the logos is absent.") In the past Lawrence had generally counted himself among the other group, the intuitive thinkers, those capable of conceiving abstractions and having truly original thoughts. His conception of the intuitive thinker was clearly bound up with the capacity for experiencing the ascendancy and self-sufficiency of one's mental essence: as Lawrence put it in one therapy session, "the intuitive thinker knows his mind because he *is* his mind. You are it and it's you. It's not an asset; it's total identification there"; and he described any kind of compromise as "a sin for the intuitive thinker. I just never compromised; I was in search of mental purity." He even specifically cautioned against assuming that innocence could be a route to wisdom or grace: "Christ was wrong in thinking achieving a childlike state of innocence would allow you to receive god. Only intuitive thinkers are in a grace state. Only they are enlightened people."

Lawrence's identification with his own consciousness has, in fact, much in common with the Kantian trend of modern thought, of which he seems to have had some knowledge (indeed, he even spoke of intuitive people as living by the "synthetic a priori," something that merely empirical thinkers were unable to recognize). In the condition of Lawrence's "intuitive thinker" we can find all the characteristics of transcendental narcissism (the first side of Foucault's doublet), with consciousness declaring its freedom, its self-creating nature, and its indubitable lucidity as an ultimate source of truth.

The sense of solipsistic power, along with its attendant anxieties, is clear in the following statements that Lawrence made to his therapist:

You can't imagine how terrifying it is to realize that you're in a world of organic machines with the intuitions that enable you to create truths, to make synthetic a priori. Where ideas and thoughts permeate all that you are—where all you need to do is to be able to conceive of something for it to come true. I could create the events of my universe by just thinking them, believing them to be true. . . . What really terrified me was when I realized that I could conceive of wrenching the world from its axis. Do you know how it would feel to have that kind of power? You see, you're protected from that kind of power . . . that is, not being a true intuitive thinker you're incapable of creating truths. For you, death could only come through interventions in your physiology. For me, all I would have to do would have been to think in certain ways in order to achieve physical death. It would not have had to involve physiological damage. One time I was sitting in a chair and I felt myself capable of thinking myself to death—I felt an incredible sense of calm come over me.

The sense of having special knowledge, a kind of divine insight, pertained especially to what Lawrence called the realm of "abstraction," in particular, to the workings of the mind and its fundamental relationship to the world. He spoke, for example, of having discovered the science of "psychomathematics," which concerned the abstract principles of mental functioning and which constituted "a discrete mathematical theory of the intuitive and non-intuitive mind" (mathematics being, as he said, "the logos of the mind"); and he claimed to have "come to understand the mind more completely than, and please pardon what may seem to you my grandiosity, more completely than anyone possibly in the history of mankind. I never did figure out the soul, but in coming to understand the mind in its relationship to the physical, I came to resolve the mind-body problem."[33] Since, to him, abstractions were "the only reality," and "the most concrete thing there is," psychomathematics could be said to have "had substance, it was real." Not surprisingly, given its essentially reflexive nature, psychomathematics was a peculiarly intransitive science; as Lawrence explained, this intuitive science of the mind "required no research whatsoever" and had no purpose beyond its own, self-generated coming into being: "I applied it as soon as I discovered it; the discovery was the application."

This essential intransitivity accounts for the quality of grandiosity along with limitation that was characteristic of his solipsistic claims, which, in many instances, applied only within a self-referential or subjectivized domain.[34] Thus it was clear that Lawrence did not experience his own godlike control as affecting objective or intersubjectively recognizable events (he explained to his therapist that she need have no fear—his wrenching of the world's axis would have no effect on her); also, the self-engendered death he refers to lacked the finality of a *real* death (he claimed to believe "I've already been dead once," and that his redemption lay in this kind of death, which would eventually lead to enlightenment—in his opinion, "Heaven is eternal enlightenment"). The same holds for his claims of special insight—which, in reality, pertained only to a certain range of phenomena: what he called "truth" as opposed to mere "facts." "Facts are nothing; it's truth that's important"; "I've never been wrong though I may have been mistaken"—he would say, thereby acknowledging that he had no special expertise regarding the concrete, arbitrary, purely objective—and, for him, ultimately trivial—real-world phenomena that are the standard preoccupation of merely "empirical" minds. In true Kantian fashion, he was concerned with more general, formal, seemingly necessary features of experience, with truths about the nature of mind that can presumably be uncovered by a kind of transcendental reflection or introspection.

In the past, Lawrence said, he had experienced himself mostly as an intuitive thinker, though the sense of quasi-solipsistic power and insight had never been the sole theme of his experience. But with the passage of time, he seemed to be veering more and more often into an antithetical mood; as he put it, there had been "a change in the configuration of the void." These experiences recall the other side of Foucault's empirico-transcendental doublet. Before, he explained, "I used to live my ideas; they surrounded me; I lived in the plasma of my ideas." But now Lawrence began to feel as if the realm of truth had been closed off to him and he were being presented only with illusions. "My intelligence is my portal to reality and the glass is clouding over," he said. And on other occasions: "I am like the person in Plato's cave. All I see is the images reflected from reality; all I see is the verisimilitude of reality, not reality itself. I've lost access to reality, it's really horrendous"; and "my memories are just memories of themselves . . . memories of memories of memories. . . . I no longer have the original." At moments, in fact, he felt that he was becoming even more mechanical and ignorant than the organic machines he so despised—"My truths were reduced to facts, and now I'm starting to forget the facts"—and he even went so far as to maintain that he had completely lost his intelligence: "Sometimes I can become deluded into thinking I still do have intelligence, although the reality is that I've lost my mind completely"; "I am devolving into a mental vegetable."

It is natural to wonder whether Lawrence's sense of mental degeneration might reflect some actual decline of cognitive capacity, perhaps secondary to actual neurophysiological deterioration (such as cell loss in his brain); but, though one cannot entirely exclude such a possibility, upon reflection this hardly seems an adequate interpretation. For one thing, the deterioration Lawrence experienced did not follow anything like a progressive course. There were many shifts back and forth between the "intuitive" and the "mechanical" condition, sometimes from day to day but also from hour to hour.[35] Even more telling is the lack of any real evidence of lowered cognitive capacity during those periods when he complained of mental debility. We must remember that at the very moments of claiming to *be* in some kind of severely deteriorated state, Lawrence was simultaneously *describing* this condition in an articulate, even eloquent fashion. Sometimes he would say he had lost all ability to understand written and spoken language, to grasp "the formal aspects of the language, the grammatical structures of the sentences" ("This morning I couldn't even understand *Life* magazine, and that's written for morons"). But if asked to explain what he had just read or heard, he was perfectly capable of doing so—though he would all the while insist that he was carrying out some merely "syntactic" or purely "mechanical" processing rather than displaying the true understanding of a "living mind."

It seems, then, that the capacity of his mind had not actually deteriorated, at least according to any conventional standards. How, then, can we account for Lawrence's *sense* of mental decline? What was it that caused this individual to lose a feeling of understanding things, or of owning or identifying with his own conscious processes?

Various factors seemed able to undermine Lawrence's sense of mental vitality; it was vulnerable, for instance, to mood shifts and also to changes in his psychiatric medications (he spoke, for example, of having once "lost his soul" when he was given psychotropic medications that, as he put it, were "spiritually contraindicated"). The sense of decline seems, at times, to have reflected his own disdain for what were in fact perfectly normal processes of everyday practical thinking, processes that struck him as lifeless and banal in comparison with the more abstract, transcendental reflections of his "intuitive" periods. (Ironically, what Lawrence experienced as deterioration seems to have impressed others as an improvement—presumably because, by their standards, his thinking, now focused on mere empirical facts, had become more relevant and clear: "People kept thinking I was regaining my brilliance, but what I was really doing was retreating to simpler and simpler levels of thought. But to the empiricists I was recovering.")

The factor that Lawrence himself emphasized as the source of his supposed mental decline was his own at least partly willful mental activity. In this reflexive or intransitive realm, to believe something was tantamount to making it true, especially if the mind's object were itself; and so, Lawrence explained, "I *believed* that I could destroy my mind. I could conceive of [this destruction], and I made it into my own truth—a synthetic a priori—in my own global system, and so it became true."[36] Particularly important, according to his own account, was the process of introspection itself. "My downfall was insight," he explained, ". . . too much insight can be very dangerous, because you can tear your mind apart." "Well, look at the word 'analysis,'" he said on another occasion. "That means to break apart. When it turns in upon itself the mind would rip itself apart." Lawrence spoke of "doing six self-analyses simultaneously" and of how he needed to change his living environment often, because he knew that, once everything around him had been scrutinized, his mind would then turn inward and begin undoing itself, leading him eventually to the feeling of having no real mind at all: "Once I started destroying [my mind], I couldn't stop."

In the following statement, made in response to a question from his therapist, we can see how this man's relentless self-scrutiny could fix upon certain routine mental operations, thereby seeming to confirm his sense of being nothing more than some kind of data-processing machine:

> . . . because there's nothing there, no cognition at all. I'm actually deluding myself into thinking I could think. I was trying to think of an answer to that question, but I'm incapable of thinking. Because I was actually searching my memory bank and generalizing slightly from the dialectical juxtaposition of a couple of memories. . . . non-mechanical thinking? I can't conceive of that any more. I can give you labels that have lost their meaning to me.

Here Lawrence seems to have been experiencing the second kind of reflective self-awareness inherent in the doublet—not the subjectivizing kind, the transcendental narcissism that experiences the world as if it were pulsating with the mind's constituting power (as in "intuitive thinking"), but the objectifying sort, where the mind turns more directly upon itself, coming to experience itself as just another empirical object, constrained by all the determinisms of the natural order.

Foucault's discussion of the modern episteme suggests a way of understanding the profound interdependence of these two ways of experiencing one's mind—these two visions that function like the systole and diastole of the same reflexive process. It seems that the reflexive move, the turning inward, has the potential of bringing on the condition and contradictions of the doublet: insofar as I focus on the world, it will seem like *my* world; but insofar as I focus more directly on thoughts or feelings, these will seem to exist out there and apart.[37] And so, in the realm of madness, as in modernism, we find, tightly intertwined, a solipsism that would elevate the mind and derealize the world and a self-objectification that would rob the subject of its transcendental role as a center of power and knowledge. This parallelism of paradoxes is no mere coincidence; what we are discovering in both domains are the characteristic paradoxes of the reflexive—contradictions generated by the alienation and hyper-self-consciousness that are central both to schizophrenia and to the modern episteme.

Recognition of epistemological centrality is, then, the obverse of the objectification or reification of the mind; and reflective consciousness is likely to be doomed to perpetual oscillation or irresolvable contradiction. Perhaps this can account for the close association between Lawrence's affinity for abstract or intuitive thinking and his experience of mental deterioration. He himself maintained that his propensity for abstraction, his seeking of intuitive "truths," was what actually brought about this deterioration, this devolution from being an intuitive to a merely mechanical mind. He even viewed this decline as an inevitable punishment that was somehow contained in the very act of abstract thinking itself (but that, significantly, he had previously been able to arrest by feeling strong emotions—love or hate). As he explained, "the punishment for the sin was in the act of committing it"; "with every brilliant thought a piece of your mind dies." The death in question lacked finality, however, since beyond it lay the prospect of yet another reversal, and of a distant reward (which, however, was seldom able to overcome his anguish, since he often assumed that some unforeseeable complication would surely bring about his worst fears): "The punishment from God was that my mind deteriorate," Lawrence explained, "but the reward for this suffering was that when I die I will have eternal Enlightenment, I will be all-knowing."[38]

✿　✿　✿　✿　✿

My approach throughout this book has been largely descriptive and interpretative. I have not been seeking causal explanations for the remarkable similarities between madness and modernism, and, for the most part, I have tried to avoid making value judgments about the worth or the validity of the phenomena I have examined. But, of course, these *are* important issues, and one cannot help but wonder about them; and so, in the remainder of the book I would like to take them up.

What, to begin with, does it *say* about modernism that it should display such remarkable affinities with this most severe of mental illnesses, which some have called the cancer of the mind? What does this parallelism suggest about how we should judge the relevant aspects of the modern sensibility? Can we view the alienation and self-consciousness of the modern mind as the inevitable signs of increasing degrees of complexity, subtlety, or insight, or must we see them as something far less benign—signs of deep pathology, perhaps, of a disease or spiritual decadence corroding the style and sensibility of our age?

We might ask as well how these parallels should affect our evaluation of schizophrenia. I have been disputing the condescending and derogatory implications of traditional views of this illness, with their tendency to equate the unintelligible with the unintelligent—but how far in this opposite direction should we go? Do the affinities with modern thought and expression suggest that there is something especially sophisticated, insightful, or self-aware about this condition—or that, perhaps in some tragic sense, such persons are more in touch with the true human condition than is the normal or average individual?

Questions of a different order also arise. How, after all, should we *account* for the parallels between madness and modernism? Is it all some kind of fortuitous coincidence, or are there causal links or influences between the two? And what of the relationship between brain and mind: What connection, if any, is there between the aspects of schizophrenic experience and expression I have been discussing and underlying abnormalities that may exist in the structure or functioning of the brain?

Here, in the second half of this concluding chapter, I shall take up the evaluative questions; other issues, concerning the possible role of modern culture or society in the etiology of schizophrenia and also the significance of neurobiological abnormalities in its pathogenesis, will be dealt with in the epilogue and the appendix, respectively.

ROMANTICISM, MODERNISM, POSTMODERNISM

Is the artist sick? Is the madman creative, authentic, or wise? Such questions are hardly new, having been raised again and again since ancient times (in Plato's *Phaedrus*, for instance). Indeed, in the twentieth century, the resemblance of madness to specifically modern forms of art and literature has frequently been asserted, usually in connection with comparisons of artworks produced in the asylum and by the avant-garde. Generally, however, those making such comparisons have assumed the shared element to be something either atavistic or primal, and their evaluative judgments have naturally been determined by their attitude toward this shared primitive core—which may be admired as a source of passionate vitality or deplored as some kind of decline into bestiality and perversion. My analysis of both modernism and madness clearly differs markedly from these, and it suggests that any evaluations would have to be based on a different set of issues: namely, on judgments about the forms of hyperreflexivity and detachment that I have been emphasizing. We might ask whether *these* qualities should be viewed as a source of insight or of illusion, of life or of deadness. Do they express or do they betray the deepest truths of the human spirit?

By posing these questions, I am not suggesting that there are any real answers, or at least any direct or easy ones. The forms of experience and expression at issue are simply too varied, too multifaceted, and too colored by the differing contexts in which they can occur to allow for any sweeping judgments or grand generalizations. Still, it is worth raising these issues, if only as a way of leading us toward consideration of certain larger, philosophical positions, an awareness of which would allow more nuanced and qualified judgments to be made.

The best place to begin our exploration of the evaluative issue is with the aesthetic philosophy and ethos of the romantic period, for this is the era when the essential criticisms of hyperreflexivity were initially formulated.

Later we shall see that a range of different positions toward the problem of self-consciousness has developed in twentieth-century thought, including an essentially critical view that tends to deplore hyperreflexivity as a source of error and malaise and a celebratory one that praises it as a fulfillment of the human essence. Whereas the first position retains certain elements of the romantic view and is therefore in some sense *post*romantic, the second rejects romanticism almost entirely and might therefore be described as hypermodernist.

The Romantic Critique

Living at a time of rapid industrialization and urbanization, and in the immediate wake of the Kantian revolution in human self-understanding, the romantics were the first generation to confront "the depressions of unbelief, the starvations of feeling, [and] the anemia of the doubting intelligence"[39] that seem to occur at the higher, or later, stages of cultural development in the West. What these German and English writers of the early nineteenth century perceived as a widespread malaise and sense of dereliction was, in their view, the consequence of a growing fragmentation and overintellectualization of human existence. It resulted from the progression of self-consciousness—a process of division and detachment whereby the developing ego divided itself into observing and observed parts, and ultimately came to be separated from itself as well as from others and the natural world.[40]

In his famous sixth letter on the aesthetic education of mankind, Friedrich von Schiller (1759–1805) described how the mental faculties came to be separated from the heat and vigor of the emotions, and how, once detached, the "all-dividing intellect" tends to effect divisions and dissociations all its own. In an obvious reference to Kant, he speaks of the "speculative spirit" becoming a stranger in the material world and the realm of fact, wrenching itself loose from matter for the sake of concept and form, sacrificing "fullness and warmth" for the sake of clarity, and, ultimately, succumbing to the temptation "to fashion the actual according to the conceivable, and to exalt the subjective conditions of its imagination into laws constituting the existence of things." In Schiller's even more famous essay "On Naive and Sentimental Poetry," he speaks of the rise of the "sentimental" or reflective type of artist—the one who no longer feels connected to an external world, who is ever aware of multiple alternatives, and who, rather than expressing his spontaneous reactions, "*reflects* upon the impression that objects make upon him," therefore representing in his work not the object in itself but "the object in the subject."[41]

Though Schiller stressed the subjectivism of modern self-consciousness (which corresponds to the first side of the doublet of modern thought), other romantics were more concerned about a concomitant objectivism. Thus in 1806 the philosopher F. W. J. von Schelling equated the true "fall of man" with the detached vision of modern, mechanistic science, which he characterized as the condition of a man "who holds that the world, which he conceives to be dead, absolutely manifold, and separated, is in fact the true and actual world."[42] In similar fashion Samuel Taylor Coleridge (1772–1834) lamented how "all the products of the mere *reflective* faculty partook of DEATH" and suggested that too exclusive a devotion to such an attitude could bring "death into our own souls," leading us to experience our own minds as purely passive and receptive—mere mechanisms rather than the active, organic forces they are meant to be (and this would correspond to the second side of the doublet of modern thought).[43] For the romantics, Life was the central organizing principle and highest good. Qualities of unity and vitality were, at the same time, essence and aim, defining features of reality, and the goal toward which to strive.

It is understandable that the romantics' acute awareness of fragmentation, estrangement, and devitalization should have led at times, by way of reaction, to a yearning for something antithetical—for instance, to primitivist, Dionysian, or mystical longings for self-dissolution. More typically, however, they conceived of the proper antidote in a manner less regressive and less extreme, not as an obliteration of all individuating self-consciousness but as the overcoming of its excesses that is to be attained from a higher kind of self-consciousness that is, at the same time, a higher self-forgetfulness.[44] The classic statement of this ambition is to be found in Heinrich von Kleist's famous dialogue-essay of 1810–11, "On the Puppet Theater." Here Kleist discusses the discoordinating effects of self-awareness, describing the physical awkwardness, the destruction of natural grace, that occurs when acts become separated from intentions and contrasting this with the fluid ease of lower animals, which are spared the curse of self-awareness. But his essay does not end with any simple call for a return to nature; instead, Kleist asks whether it might be possible to escape self-consciousness *through* self-consciousness—whether, by means of a further act of reflexivity, an additional meta-move, one might achieve a state like that which existed *before* the first fatal move was taken:

"We see how, in the organic world, as reflection grows darker and weaker, grace emerges ever more radiant and supreme [explains the wise interlocutor of Kleist's essay]. But . . . just as our image, as we approach a concave mirror, vanishes to infinity only to reappear before our very eyes, so will grace, having likewise traversed the infinite, return to us once more, and so appear most purely in that bodily form that has either no consciousness at all or an infinite one, which is to say, either in the puppet or a god."

"That means," said I, somewhat amused, "that we would have to eat of the tree of knowledge a second time to fall back into the state of innocence."

"Of course," he answered, "and that is the final chapter in the history of the world."[45]

What Kleist imagines in this passage is, presumably, a state of higher innocence in which alienating self-consciousness would be transcended rather than banished altogether. How this goal was to be obtained is not easily stated,[46] but it is clear that the romantics generally conceived it not as a primal fusion (of human with nature or subject with object) but as some kind of integration that would preserve the independence of each part.[47] Thus Schiller imagined an ideal synthesis of reflectiveness with a kind of naïveté, an "intimate union" in which the dangers of detachment and uncertainty would be balanced by a robust faith and spontaneity of action.[48] If the romantics held art and imagination in such high esteem, it was precisely because they considered the aesthetic realm to be the privileged domain for achieving such an integration.[49]

Two Modernisms: Postromantic and Hypermodernist

In treating modernism in this book, I have been primarily interested in manifestations of alienation and hyperreflexivity, and this, obviously, has had the effect of emphasizing the gap between modernism and romanticism, the ways in which modernist art and literature fall short of the romantic ideal. Certainly modernism often does reject the aspirations of romanticism—replacing the goal of a reconciliation or higher integration (of mind with nature, subject with object, or form with content) with willful veerings into states of extreme inwardness or radical objectivism. From the standpoint of a Schiller or a Schelling, this might be grounds for condemnation, suggesting as it does capitulation to the alienation, unanchoring, and spiritual dessication of modern life (brought on by the unchecked and untranscended fragmentation and cerebralization of the self). From this standpoint the striking parallels between modernism and schizophrenia would simply be further proof, if such were needed, of the essential fallenness of the modern mind, its severance from that vital organic unity that is the heart and goal of the human spirit.

As with all neighboring periods of cultural history, however, it is possible to discern continuities as well as discontinuities; given a different set of purposes and interests, one might have chosen to emphasize the former rather than the latter. Romantic or quasi-romantic elements are, in fact, rather prominent in many classic works of the "high modernist" period—

both in the implicitly critical attitude they take toward the depredations of self-consciousness and in their persistent ambition to achieve some kind of fulfillment, some sense of meaning, order, or blissful stasis through contemplation of a unified aesthetic object.[50]

The critical edge is evident in works such as T. S. Eliot's "The Hollow Men," "The Love Song of J. Alfred Prufrock," and "The Wasteland," with their rueful mockery of the timorous hesitations and paralyses of self-consciousness, and their lamenting of the dessication and disarticulation of modern existence.[51] We find it also in Robert Musil's portrayal of the absurdly self-conscious Ulrich, the vacillating antihero of *The Man Without Qualities* who experiences reality as fragmentary and merely subjective while at the same time losing a sense of his own subjective being. (Ulrich experiences "the world going in and out, aspects of the world falling into shape inside a head," and loses "the belief that the most important thing about experience is the experiencing of it, and about deeds the doing of them.")[52]

Vestiges of the positive side of romanticism are also apparent in modernism's persistent desire for a kind of aesthetic bliss, a lyrical moment that might redeem the disorder and banality of modern life. Yeats spoke of a form that would be "full, sphere-like, single," Eliot of the "aura around a bright clear centre," and Joyce of the aesthetic image that is apprehended "as *one* thing . . . self-bounded and self-contained . . . [in a] luminous silent stasis of esthetic pleasure."[53] The romantic impulse toward communion with nature and fellow humans may have given way to a sense that personal isolation is the inevitable condition of artistic creation and perception; yet something of the romantic aspiration toward unity does persist in this idea of the wholly absorbing, wholly unitary image—the emblem of an existence immune from all possibility of self-estrangement.

But if we turn to many of the aesthetic works and ideologies associated with the term *postmodernism,* the situation is very different, for here the lingering vestiges of romanticism seem to have been banished almost entirely—leading, in effect, to a kind of hypermodernism. In place of the critical portrayals of self-consciousness and subjectivism to be found in Eliot or Musil, for example, there is often a glorifying of self-referentiality—as in one postmodernist novelist's call for a kind of self-deconstructive "metafiction": "a kind of writing, a kind of discourse whose shape will be an interrogation, an endless interrogation of what it is doing while doing it, an endless denunciation of its fraudulence, of what *it* really is: an illusion (a fiction), just as life is an illusion (a fiction)."[54]

This difference can also be seen from a comparison of Samuel Beckett's protagonists—those emblems of modern detachment and despair—with the entirely deadpan manifestation of a similar condition by Andy Warhol, perhaps the central figure in the postmodern visual arts. Beckett's solipsistic and devitalized protagonists manifest both sides of the doublet: the loss not only of the sense of encountering a vibrant or solid external reality, a world outside the head, but also of any feeling of volition or personal integrity. Although Beckett is no moralist—at least not overtly—we hardly feel he is condoning what he so obsessively portrays. He may despair regarding the possibility of a fulfilled, vibrant existence; he may anticipate the world whimpering to an ignominious end—but we do not find uncritical acquiescence, still less glorification, of these states of deadness and estrangement.

With Warhol, by contrast, all critical distance collapses; he cannot hold himself aloof from such modes of experience, for he incarnates them in his very being—presenting them to us less as an aberration than as an actualization of some higher sophistication.[55] Thus he seems to have striven to experience his own mind as a mechanism ("I want to be a machine," he said),[56] whose function is to transform the surrounding universe into pure image—like those silkscreen Marilyns, Jackies, and Elvises, images made of images of people who, in a sense, already exist more as media caricatures than as real beings in their own right, yet who seem to declare the universality of their nonbeing. Warhol thereby seems to encapsulate, and in some sense to foster, the condition of the doublet that is so characteristic both of schizophrenia and of the modern age. (He is, in fact, almost the embodiment of a delusion—rather as if the Natalija machine had been tilted upright and set moving in the world.)

Philosophical Positions: Postromantic and Postmodernist

A clearer sense of how we might evaluate these phenomena can be obtained from a related comparison, one that operates on a more explicit or theoretical plane. This is the contrast between the approach taken by three great philosophers of the early and middle twentieth century (Heidegger, Wittgenstein, and Merleau-Ponty), as opposed to that adopted by certain more recent thinkers of a "poststructuralist" or "postmodernist" persuasion (Jacques Derrida and Paul de Man). If we consider Heidegger's attacks on the legacy of Cartesianism, Wittgenstein's critique of metaphysical thinking, and Merleau-Ponty's persistent quest for the inarticulable immediacies of prereflective experience, we find they have at least a couple of things in common: at bottom, all three are critics of reflection, of the ultimately misleading or even corrupting consequences that can result from placing too much reliance on the posture of detached contemplation and introspection; further, they seem to share the dream of a higher innocence, a way of transcending the deluding and life-denying effects of reflexive awareness.

As we know, Heidegger considered the age of the world view, which involves subjectivizing as well as objectifying tendencies, to result from new forms of reflexivity that focus on the self as the *subjectum* before which and for which the world seems to be represented; this he associated with an overreliance on the insights afforded by detached contemplation in preference for those grounded in practical activity (such as hammering a nail). Wittgenstein has been mentioned only in passing in these pages, but we did note his dissatisfaction with William James's externalization and volatilization of the self, brought on by an attitude of exigent introspection; the seductive illusions of solipsism and subjective idealism were of even greater interest to Wittgenstein—and these he also associated with an overreliance on detached perspectives and a failure to keep in touch with the practical and communal realities that ground common sense and everyday language. But it is in Merleau-Ponty's unfinished work, *The Visible and the Invisible*, that we find the most explicit statement of the dream of a higher innocence—a level of reflection that might transcend, and ultimately heal, the products of "all-dividing" intellect.

Merleau-Ponty had always been drawn to what he described as "a philosophy for which the world is always 'already there' before reflection begins—as an inalienable presence," a philosophy that would concentrate all its efforts "upon reachieving a direct and primitive contact with the world, and endowing that contact with a philosophical status."[57] He was well aware of how compelling the act of reflection could be and of how necessary to any attempt at philosophizing it was (the "movement of reflection will always at first sight be convincing," he writes; "in a sense it is imperative, it is truth itself, and one does not see how philosophy could dispense with it"); but he did not believe reflection alone was capable of bringing philosophy "to harbor," since it seemed always to lead into "a labyrinth of difficulties and contradictions." As he noted, reflection always seems to subjectivize the world, to transform the brute actuality of perceived entities into mere thoughts existing "for me" and, in addition, to cerebralize the experiential self—by understanding it as a constituting intellect rather than a worldly entity in active interaction with a physical universe that is shared with one's fellow beings.[58]

To avoid such errors Merleau-Ponty calls for something very reminiscent of Kleist's higher innocence, something that would correct the errors of reflection and put in its place a kind of sophisticated phenomenological naïveté. This is an operation beyond reflection but more fundamental than it: what he calls a *sur-réflexion* that would help us "learn again to see the world."[59] This *sur-réflexion* would transcend the usual forms of reflection by understanding the total situation in which reflection occurs, and by recognizing how the light of reflection tends to alter the spectacle of experience in the very process of illuminating it. Accordingly, it would not efface the brute perception and the brute thing by transforming them into "perception-reflected-on and thing-perceived-within-a-perception-reflected-on"; nor would it "cut the organic bonds between the perception and the thing perceived with a hypothesis of inexistence."[60] *Sur-réflexion* would not forget its own dependence on a more fundamental, prereflective level of experience; and so it would not be taken in by extreme subjectivism and extreme objectivism, nor by any of the other illusions of philosophies that are insufficiently self-aware to recognize their own projections and reifications.

All three of these philosophers are participants in the general project of modernist thought (both Heidegger and Merleau-Ponty are, in fact, discussed by Foucault as examples of the doublet),[61] and each is clearly engaged in the difficult, post-Kantian enterprise of reflecting upon the subject of experience. But, though they certainly *reflect* on subjectivity, they understand subjectivity itself to be—in some fundamental sense—*non*reflective or *pre*reflective in nature, as Merleau-Ponty would put it. From their standpoint, many of the modernist and schizophrenic modes of hyperreflexivity discussed in this book would involve transformations or even perversions of authentic human existence—an existence that, at its most fundamental or essential level, would be characterized by a sense of contact, by active engagement and participation in meaningful social action rather than by doubt, distance, and unreality.

I have discussed various forms of consciousness in this book, including perceptual alienation, unanchoring, and doubt, a splitting of (abstract) form from (concrete) sensation, retreat from shared reference, loss of the objective world, and the various reifications, aggrandizements, and dissolutions of selfhood; these can be seen in some sense as analogous to the philosophical attitudes—to the extreme skepticism, solipsism, subjective idealism, radical materialism, and so on—that are criticized by Heidegger, Wittgenstein, and Merleau-Ponty. Many modernist artists, and particularly postmodernists, might be viewed as expressing—and many schizoid and schizophrenic individuals as living out—something akin to the philosophical abberrations or distortions that emerge when one loses contact with the prereflective world that is the normal dwelling place of human existence.

A very different assessment is likely to emerge, however, if one shifts to a perspective that has been popular over the last couple of decades: the so-called deconstructionist philosophy of Jacques Derrida and certain of his followers, notably the literary theorist Paul de Man. Derrida has been described as the postmodernist thinker par excellence,[62] and so he is, though his complete refusal of the legacy of romanticism also qualifies him as a hypermodernist.

Unlike Heidegger, Merleau-Ponty, and Wittgenstein, these deconstructionist thinkers do not attempt to put us back in touch with ourselves by recalling us to some deep sense of groundedness and unity; they try instead to make us face up to a (supposedly) more fundamental alienation, divided-ness, and inauthenticity that, they say, are normally suppressed or ignored. They are critics not primarily of reflection but of the supposed illusions of "presence" and "authenticity"—which they refer to as "logocentrism" and the "metaphysics of presence," or as "recovered unity" and "the nostalgia and the desire to coincide."[63] (Thus Derrida criticizes Heidegger for "the dominance [in his work] of an entire metaphorics of proximity, of simple and immediate presence, a metaphorics associating the proximity of Being with the values of neighboring, shelter, house, service, guard, voice, and listen-ing.")[64] This seems to have definite implications for our evaluation of both madness and modernism, for it suggests we might view these hyperreflexive aspects not as distortions of human experience but as its fulfillment—as a rendering explicit of its true, if generally unrecognized, basis.

Derrida's primary focus is on the problematic status of language, but, starting from these reflections, he develops positions that touch upon nearly every aspect of experience discussed in this book. Indeed, if one *were* to take this hypermodernist philosophy literally, imagining an actual living out of its claims, the existence one would arrive at might well resemble the schizo-phrenic condition I have been describing in this book. Derrida's language-based philosophy has already been glimpsed in chapter 6; as we saw there, he puts forward a vision of language that is at odds with one's normal, prereflective sense of shared meaning. Through the notion of arche-writing, Derrida would alienate us from what he considers the self-delusory moment of *"s'entendre parler"*—that moment of hearing oneself speak in which one has the sense of maximum unity with one's own intentions and meanings and of direct contact with the world.[65] We have already discussed the parallels between Derrida's concept of arche-writing and the schizophrenic autonom-ization of language, with its focus either on the concrete materiality of the signifying medium (sound, or black marks on a page) or on an uncontrolled proliferation of possible meanings. On a more general level, this concept illustrates a profound philosophical faith in, and preference for, what might be termed an alienated, in some sense schizoid, mode of being—in which one stands back from one's (linguistic) tools and watches their independent functioning. And, as we saw, this can lead to a falling away, or a falling apart, of standard forms of meaning.

Perhaps the most peculiar feature of Derrida's philosophy is, however, the striking way in which he manifests the contradictions of the modern doublet. On one side we have his ideas about the syntactic play of signifiers, communicating as if on their own with the "totality of the lexicon"[66]—which certainly suggests a dissolution or fragmentation of active intentionality or selfhood. But on the other side are his tendency to deny objective reference ("perception does not exist"; "there is nothing outside of the text")[67] and his doctrine of undecidability, which have given rise to a vision of untrammeled interpretive freedom that has been taken to its limit by many of his American followers—what, in a famous passage, Derrida describes as the sport of a kind of Nietzschean superman: "joyous affirmation of the play of the world and of the innocence of becoming, the affirmation of a world of signs without fault, without truth, and without origin which is offered to an *active* interpretation."[68] This, by now, is a familiar vacillation: if in one moment we feel insignificant (but flickering shadows of distant semiotic events), in the next we claim a nearly godlike power—the ability to determine meanings, and thus reality itself, in accord with our own passing whims.[69]

One of the more confusing features of Derrida's rhetoric, evoked in the previous quotation, is the way he lays claim to a certain Dionysianism— suggesting that his doctrines of undecidability and infinite deferral of meaning differ from more conventional views in the way that "ardor" differs from "structure," or Dionysus from Apollo.[70] This conception is very reminiscent of antipsychiatry's glorification of schizophrenia as an ex- hilarated irrationality, a form of mysticism or of triumphant sensuality; and it may be equally misleading. Derrida's alternative to the usual (ratio- nal) understanding of language and communication is, in fact, hardly a product of passion or regression: it derives from a reflective standing back from experience, a removal from engaged interaction, and it is motivated less by any plumbing of the unconscious or the instincts than by the recol- lection of abstract theories (notions of *langue*) and by the endless postula- tion of hypothetical possibilities (imagined graftings onto other possible contexts).[71]

To understand the real nature of this postmodernist vision, and its impli- cations for our reading of schizophrenia, it makes sense to turn to Paul de Man, whose writings are not beclouded by this kind of misleading Dionysian rhetoric. In his most famous essay, "The Rhetoric of Temporality," de Man sets himself explicitly against the (in his view) self-mystifying aspirations toward organic unity and reconciliation that are characteristic of romanti- cism (and of the postromantic strains of modernism), and he pulls no punches about the dryly rational and distanciating nature of the "philosophy of necessary separation" to which he subscribed.[72]

De Man (who in this part of his essay was closely following certain passages from Baudelaire) describes self-consciousness as the act of self- duplication or self-multiplication by which one divides oneself in two (into an empirical self and a disinterested spectator) and differentiates oneself from the external world. He associates this explicitly with the "reflective activity" of the philosopher (or the poet who is self-conscious about lan- guage—Schiller's "sentimental" type, presumably), in contrast with "the activity of the ordinary self caught in everyday concerns." But, unlike Mer- leau-Ponty or Heidegger, de Man treats the latter, prereflective mode as a "self-mystification," while praising the much rarer philosophical attitude for its "lucidity"—its ability "authentically" to capture the "inauthenticity" at our core.[73]

Dividedness, in his view, is the insurpassable predicament of the human being (the subject is, in fact, always separated from its object, the self from its roles, the signifier from the signified). As he writes in a passage that would dismiss all hope for any kind of Kleistian higher innocence or Merleau-Pontyan *sur-réflexion*, it is an error to think that higher levels of self-consciousness can lead to a synthesis or "recovered unity"—a "cure for a self lost in the alienation of its melancholy."[74] Higher degrees of self-consciousness can lead, he maintains, only to a further distancing, to endless recurrences of "a self-escalating act of consciousness"; they result not in any synthesis or reconciliation but only in heightened awareness of duplicity and dissimulation, in a fuller realization of the purely fictional nature of all one's knowledge, and in a more acute awareness of the inevitability of one's stiltedness and alienation.

This, obviously, is a very different conception of human reality from what we find in romanticism (or in the more romantic elements of modernism). It is not that de Man would deny the malaise or the sense of upheaval and psychic unraveling that can be engendered by this kind of hyperreflexivity and alienation, but he prefers to see these as the by-products of true insight into human reality; hence the ability to tolerate such experiences comes to be viewed as a kind of paradigm of heroism. Clearly this can lead to a very different, far more positive evaluation of many of the phenomena at issue in this book, in modernism as well as in schizophrenia.

De Man considers the valorizing of organic unity inherent in the notion of the symbol (described by James Joyce as the image "luminously apprehended as self-bounded and self-contained upon the immeasurable background of space or time which is not it . . . wholeness . . . *integritas*")[75] to be a form of mystification, and he would replace such vestiges of romanticism with an aesthetic based on the trope of allegory—a rhetorical figure criticized by the romantics for its mechanical, arbitrary, and divided nature, but which the postmodernists have taken up and made into one of the central elements of their style.[76] He also endorses a form of irony that Baudelaire associated with the higher forms of comedy: the *comique absolu*. Like the meta-irony of Duchamp and the black humor of Alfred Jarry and Jacques Vaché, this Baudelairean humor must be distinguished from the vulgar or empirical kind that would join one in convivial laughter with others. It is a self-conscious humor, founded not upon a bringing together of equals but on acts of distancing whereby a person distinguishes himself from a world perceived as nonhuman; and it inevitably engenders the "irony of irony," or irony to the second power, that recognizes that no recursion of ironic acts can ever lead to synthesis or a sense of totality—that there is in fact no such thing as a higher innocence.[77]

Interestingly enough, Baudelaire, and de Man along with him, wished to associate the capacity for true insight implicit in the *comique absolu* with the condition of madness. In *On the Essence of Laughter* Baudelaire noted the commonness of laughter among madmen, and he ascribed this to the attitude of superiority that is inherent in the absolute irony that they turn upon the most fundamental conditions of life. Adopting this view, de Man suggests that the sanity of the normal individual depends on one's ability to ignore, or one's inability to see, the fundamental duplicities of social existence and the forms of alienation that are the essence of our condition. To recognize these facts is to risk losing a conventional sense of grounding in the empirical self, and to be precipitated into a free-fall that is akin to insanity. Hence absolute irony, according to de Man, can be said to be "a consciousness of madness . . . a reflection on madness from the inside of madness itself."[78] By these lights insanity becomes something more interesting than any mere collapse or devolution of the mind: it comes to be seen as a dizzying, self-canceling, but heroic mode of "terrifyingly lucid irony" and "absolute skepticism," an "unrelieved vertigo" before the prospect of endless acts of self-alienation—beyond hope of reconciliation or relief.[79]

Here, then, are two ways of understanding and evaluating hyperreflexivity and alienation, the postromantic and the hypermodernist. In closing, I would like to return to schizophrenia, asking just how well each of these visions seems to accord with the actuality of the condition and, in particular, how well each seems to capture the patient's own experience of his or her problematic mode of being.

ANGUISH AND OMNIPOTENCE

There are moments, certainly, when schizophrenics do seem to see more sharply or more deeply than individuals more engaged in the activities of daily life. Of course, if we understand *insight* as this word is conventionally defined in psychiatry—as "a correct attitude to morbid change in oneself" (this implies agreeing with the medical view that one suffers from a mental illness, that this essentially accounts for one's unusual perceptions and preoccupations, that one's delusions are incorrect, that one requires psychiatric care, and so on)—then we must acknowledge that schizophrenics are indeed lacking in this quality.[80] But many schizophrenics do have a special aptitude for apprehending certain facets of reality that generally go unnoticed, facets that can hardly be dismissed as trivial. Often they seem to have a special capacity for perceiving what Hegel called the "self-apprehending vanity of all reality," the way "everything [is] estranged from itself,"[81] and also for noticing the background assumptions that constitute the horizons or foundations of human activity; hence they can be acutely aware of the inauthenticities and compromises of normal social existence, and of the usually unremarked presuppositions of their own trains of thought. In this sense there may be some truth to a remark that Martin, the schizophrenic artist, once made to me: "our insight into schizophrenia is insight into insight." And, as his statement suggests, it is not uncommon for schizophrenics themselves to have a *feeling* of possessing some special awareness, some sense of having seen more deeply into the essence of death or eternity, of God, consciousness, or the world.[82] Lawrence claimed to have a greater knowledge of the human mind that any human being who had ever lived; and Schreber said he had come "infinitely closer to the truth than human beings who have not received divine revelation."[83]

There are moments, too, when schizophrenics feel a great sense of security and of freedom, something akin, perhaps, to the exhilaration that, according to Derrida, is a reward that lies beyond belief in the "metaphysics of presence" (belief in the existence of objective realities and determinable meanings), when they experience the thrilling affirmation of the play of the signifier, or the freedom of a world without truth or limits. Recall the following statements, all from schizophrenic individuals:

> I'm enjoying so much wonderful freedom in my mental illness. . . . The life of a mental patient means being a prince, with all its freedoms and thoughts.

> I used some words in order to express a concept entirely different from the usual one. Thus, I blithely employed the word *mangy* to mean *gallant*. . . . I would seek release in self-invented [words], as for example, *wuttas* for *doves*.

> In my world I am omnipotent, in yours I practice diplomacy.[84]

Of course, it would be far too simple to leave it at this, as if the schizophrenic could be viewed as some kind of postmodernist hero—fully conscious of the inauthenticity and arbitrariness of human existence, infinitely self-aware, and generally able to enjoy a state of unanchoredness and isolation. Schizophrenics are, in fact, often lacking in many forms of practical and commonsense judgment (as Lawrence admitted: "I have this problem translating things into the concrete"), and their reflexivity and detachment can often lead as much to a sense of confusion as to one of insight. Also they seldom seem to have a great deal of what we might call insight into their own insight, of awareness of the pathological role played by their own hyperreflexivity (Lawrence may be something of an exception here); and in this sense we could say that they know both too much and too little. Martin once remarked to me that schizophrenia is "like Aladdin's lamp: it can do wonderful things, but you don't know how to handle it." Moreover, even while schizophrenics have a sense of omniscience and grandiosity, frightening possibilities seem always to be hovering at the periphery of their being; and, instead of feeling the pleasures of freedom and unreality, they will often be overcome by a nagging sense of dissatisfaction, by a sense of rootlessness, incompetence, or ignorance, or even by a fear of imminent world catastrophe. Again, we might recall the words of several schizophrenic patients:

> Reality recedes from me. Everything I touch, everything I think, everyone I meet, becomes unreal as soon as I approach.

> I . . . sought some fixed point, but found none. . . . The muchness and the motion were too much and too fast. Everyone withdrew from everyone. There was a running as of something liquefied, a constant going forth, as of evaporation. Everything was schematic, ghostlike, even myself.

> The most sacred monument that is erected by the human spirit, i.e., its ability to think and decide and will to do, is torn apart by itself. . . . Instead of wishing to do things, they are done by something that seems mechanical and frightening. . . . The feeling that should dwell within the person is outside longing to come back and yet having taken with it the power to return.[85]

Hölderlin wrote, "So short my life, / Yet comes my cold evening. / I am here like the shadows." And some years later: "I am no longer party to this world's delight, / . . . Now I no longer live and have no joy."[86] It is likely that such feelings contribute to the high suicide rate among schizophrenics.[87]

It is understandable, then, that those schizophrenics who do emerge from their psychoses should look back on these periods with various attitudes—sometimes with regret for the sense of intensity, superiority, or safety they have lost, but probably more often with feelings of relief for having come through reasonably intact and with a sense of continuing vitality and connection. In the case of Renee, the first patient I discussed at length in this book, the latter feelings were clearly dominant; and in this sense her own attitude was far closer to the postromantic than to the postmodernist (or hypermodernist) point of view. When she found herself engaged once again with the everyday, prereflective world, she rejoiced, looking back on the Land of Madness—that eerie realm of phantoms and machines revolving in an unearthly glare—as a place of utter misery and dereliction:

> Instead of infinite space, unreal, where everything was cut off, naked and isolated, I saw Reality, marvelous Reality, for the first time. The people

whom we encountered were no longer automatons, phantoms, revolving around, gesticulating without meaning; they were men and women with their own individual characteristics, their own individuality. It was the same with things. They were useful things, having sense, capable of giving pleasure. Here was an automobile to take me to the hospital, cushions I could rest on. With the astonishment that one views a miracle, I devoured with my eyes everything that happened. "This is it, this is it," I kept repeating, and I was actually saying, "This is it—Reality."[88]

It is now the world of the natural attitude, the world of practical activity, shared communal meanings, and real physical presences—a world where, as Renee says, "the oneness of my body and myself was conclusively accomplished"—that feels most real and authentic to her, so "warm, magnificent, vibrant, palpitating" after the "stage setting of arid desert" from which she finally emerged. "If I can put it that way, reality became more real, more rich, and I more social and independent," she says on the last page of her memoir. Madness she associates with unreality, confusion, and anxiety; it is a realm of electric immobility and unbearable vastness, of cardboard scenery and meaningless substances—"without warmth or color."

Still, the realm of madness is not to be entirely despised, for, as she goes on to observe, in her final line: "Only those who have lost reality and lived for years in the Land of cruel, inhuman Enlightenment, can truly taste the joy in living and prize the transcendent significance of being a part of humanity."[89] Even this recognition owes something to the blinding revelations of Unreality that Renee has suffered, as if only by wandering in the Land of Light could she have found her way to this wiser kind of innocence.

Schizophrenia and Modern Culture

A s I have already stressed, the arguments in this book have been directed toward understanding rather than explanation. My purpose has been to describe the texture and to elucidate the structure of schizophrenic experience and expression, rather than to account for these phenomena in a causal sense. Thus in pointing out the parallels of madness with modernism, I have not been proposing an etiological hypothesis—about, say, the influence of culture on psychopathology—and in criticizing psychoanalytic and psychiatric theories I have been disputing not hypotheses about schizophrenia's origins or physical substrate but only notions about its nature as a psychological condition. My particular concern has been with the phenomenological dimension, and I have tried to treat this aspect in relative isolation, unprejudiced by assumptions or speculations about origins. To pose questions about etiology or pathogenesis is to engage in a very different type of enterprise, one that, at least in our present state of knowledge, has to be even more speculative in nature.

But this is not to say that these two sets of issues are entirely independent and devoid of mutual implications. What one says about the phenomenology of the illness should not, of course, actually be contradicted by what is said about its causes (though if it is, it is not immediately obvious that it is the phenomenological interpretation rather than the causal theory that must yield); ultimately a complete theory of schizophrenia would have to take both perspectives into account. In any event, one can hardly help but be curious about questions that transcend issues of phenomenological description and interpretation. One set of such questions, taken up in this epilogue, concerns the nature of the influences or causal connections that may exist between modern society and schizophrenia. Can schizophrenia be said to be, in any sense, a disease of modern civilization, and, if so, how can we account for this relationship? A second set of questions, to be taken up in the appendix, concerns how schizophrenic consciousness might relate to the underlying neurophysiological disorders and certain related cognitive abnormalities emphasized by contemporary biological psychiatry and experimental psychology. Are the modes of consciousness I have described compatible with these theories? And if the biological theories are true, what implications might they have for the significance of the modes of experience I have described? These issues, bracketed until now, will take us beyond the patient's immediate experience, leading us first outward or upward to the level of social forces and cultural meanings, then downward to the level of brain tissue and nervous impulse. (In Aristotelian terms, this epilogue and the appendix deal primarily with issues of "efficient" and "material" causality, whereas the bulk of the book has been concerned with "formal" and perhaps—to a lesser extent—with "final" causality.)

Both sets of issues are immensely complex. Not only is there a vast amount of empirical research of potential relevance but in each case a panoply of theoretical and philosophical issues are implicated—including all the complexities inherent in trying to relate social, cultural, and psychological levels of reality (for example, the vexing issue of the relationship between modern*ity* and modern*ism,* between socioeconomic and cultural-psychological phenomena) as well as all the classical dilemmas associated with the mind-body problem. To cover either of these topics in a reasonably comprehensive way would take a great many pages, and my purpose in this epilogue, as in the appendix, is necessarily far more modest.

I would like, first, to expose certain widespread assumptions and prejudices. If not opposed, these prejudices tend to constrain speculation about the relationship between individual experience and either the sociocultural or the physical domain; and in some instances they may undermine or else trivialize the phenomenological account I have been offering. On a more positive note, I will discuss some etiological models, both sociocultural and neurobiological, that *are* compatible with the experiential tendencies I have described. I hasten to add, however, that these latter models are offered in a spirit of skepticism and speculation. After nearly a century of research, schizophrenia can still be said to be "a condition of obscure origins and no established aetiology, pathogenesis and pathology," without even any clear disease marker or laboratory test by which it can readily be identified.[1] Currently available evidence is insufficient to allow us to do more than endorse, with a sense of real certainty, a few very general statements: for example, that *some* structural or physiological abnormalities of the brain are probably implicated in the pathogenesis of many (perhaps most) cases of schizophrenia (though not necessarily as a primary or sufficient cause); that many cases have a significant genetic component; and that some as yet unspecified psychological or social factors are important in the maintenance and shaping, and perhaps also in the etiology, of most—if not all—such illnesses.

It should not be thought, then, that any one of the etiological hypotheses to be suggested here and in the appendix is inevitably linked with the phenomenological and hermeneutical arguments that constitute the core of this book. As should soon become apparent, the portrait of schizophrenia presented in this book is in fact compatible with a wide variety of causal models, and does not stand or fall with any one of them.

T. S. Eliot diagnosed the modern condition as a "dissociation of sensibility": a widening rift between thought and emotion, intellect and sensation, and a general failure to achieve "unification of sensibility."[2] This is remarkably close to Emil Kraepelin's and Erwin Stransky's classic definitions of *dementia praecox*—as "a loss of inner unity of intellect, emotion and volition, in themselves and among one another," or as "disturbances of the smooth interplay" between the ideational and emotional layers of the psyche.[3]

It is entirely possible that this sort of close parallel is largely fortuitous; for example, that certain independently existing psychological tendencies, possibly neurobiologically based, just *happen* to mimic central features of the modern sensibility. (Various neurobiological hypotheses discussed in the appendix could account for many of the relevant aspects of schizophrenia.) But one must certainly wonder whether there might be something more than mere elective affinities here, whether actual influences or causal processes of some kind might link the two domains. Might insanity be, in some sense, a disease of certain highly advanced forms of cultural organization, perhaps "part of the price we pay for civilization"—as was occasionally suggested in the nineteenth century?[4] And if so, is this because modern culture creates the conditions for the genesis of schizophrenia, or at least for the introversive and reflexive forms discussed in this book? Or might it be more the other way around, the schizophrenia spectrum of illnesses—in the form of influential schizoids and schizophrenics such as Hölderlin, Strindberg, Kafka, and Artaud—having a decisive influence on central aspects of modern culture? Yet another possibility is that both madness and modernism are consequences or reflections of a third factor determining both culture and the psyche from another level of being, such as the economic or political conditions underlying the economic and social order—the level of what might be called moder*nity*.[5]

Before we can speculate fruitfully about these questions of causality, we must first consider the issue of prevalence. Is schizophrenia, or the related spectrum of illnesses, especially common in modern Western civilization—either in comparison with other cultures in the contemporary world or with earlier epochs in the West?

THE PREVALENCE OF SCHIZOPHRENIA

The Cross-Cultural Dimension

Most contemporary psychiatric textbooks state, and most psychiatrists seem to believe, that schizophrenia has approximately the same prevalence in all contemporary societies, slightly under 1 percent.[6] Such a fact, if true, would obviously undermine claims that schizophrenia has a particular association with either the culture of modernism or the society of modernity; and, perhaps not surprisingly, those committed to essentially biological accounts of its etiology often cite this as evidence in their favor (although, as the psychiatrists E. Fuller Torrey and Assen Jablensky have pointed out, it is questionable whether a uniform frequency would be any more consistent with theories of biological etiology, given that hardly any *physical* diseases are equally common in all population groups).[7] Theorists wedded to an exclusively biological account generally acknowledge the rather obvious fact that culture can affect the *content* of symptoms, making it, for instance, more likely that the delusions of schizophrenics in industrialized societies will concern television sets and X rays rather than ghosts and spirits; and many such theorists are willing to accept that the way a given society responds to deviance might affect the illness's course and outcome. Aspects such as these are, however, often considered to be of secondary importance, as they are presumed to have little or nothing to do with the illness's genesis or essential form.

According to a distinction that has been widely accepted in medical-model psychiatry, the truly "pathogenic" factors are those that pertain to "the actual cause of the illness"; they are what endow a disease "with a specific character, its quality of being 'thus and no other.' "[8] Sociocultural factors, by contrast, are assumed to be merely "pathoplastic"—able only to give "content, colouring and contour to individual illnesses whose basic form and character have already been biologically established." And this means, in the words of one psychiatrist, that "cultural relativism is of no value in explaining the psychosis"; for the "culture of a group can determine the content but not the forms of a psychosis."[9]

This standard view turns out to be questionable, however, on theoretical as well as on empirical grounds, as some of the more culturally oriented psychiatrists have noted.[10] For one thing, the distinction between the pathogenic and the pathoplastic (or between essential form and incidental content) is not always easy to make, since it in turn depends on what should *count* as the essential as opposed to merely incidental features of schizophrenia—a question by no means easy to settle.[11] (Indeed, one cannot assume that it will ever be settled once and for all, since there may not *be* any single correct definition of schizophrenia.) In addition, the empirical claim that schizophrenia is equally common across different cultures is far from established. Both these points are best approached through a consideration of the major international research projects that have dominated discussion of sociocultural influences in the last decade or so: the International Pilot Study of Schizophrenia and the Determinants of Outcome Study, both sponsored by the World Health Organization (WHO).

The International Pilot Study investigated psychotic individuals who were admitted to psychiatric centers in nine cities: Aarhus (Denmark), Agra (India), Cali (Colombia), Ibadan (Nigeria), Taipei (Taiwan), Prague, London, Moscow, and Washington, D.C. It was found that patients who manifested schizophrenic symptoms—in particular, a "nuclear" set of features that included Schneider's First Rank Symptoms—showed up in all the locales and did not seem to be especially rare in any of them. Since the International Pilot Study offered no way of estimating the overall frequency of schizophrenia in its various settings (it simply studied the characteristics of patients who *had* schizophrenialike symptoms), this objective was attempted in the subsequent Determinants of Outcome Study, which found that patients with certain clinical features of schizophrenia did in fact seem to be as common in the developing as in the developed societies.[12] Although these findings, the most widely disseminated results of the WHO studies, have often been taken to undermine the significance of sociocultural factors in the etiology of schizophrenia, such a conclusion is unwarranted, for at least three reasons.

First, it must be realized that the WHO studies came up with an equally important result that has just the opposite implication: schizophrenic patients in Third World as opposed to Western settings showed a marked difference in course and outcome (as evidenced on two-year follow-up), tending more often to have an acute rather than a gradual or an insidious onset of their symptoms and showing a striking tendency to recover more quickly and more completely. A more benign outcome was especially characteristic of the Nigerians and Indians, who came to the hospital from rural and agricultural communities.[13] Though it is impossible to state with certainty, it is widely assumed (even by many biological psychiatrists) that these discrepancies must be due to one or more of a variety of social factors, such as the effect of extended families and small communities, which are more supportive of deviant members; the lack of specialized work roles and competitive expectations; the absence of stigmatization of mental illness in many traditional societies (which lack or deemphasize the disease concept, ascribing many mental—as well as physical—disorders to supernatural forces rather than to attributes of the individual); the practice of healing rituals and ceremonies designed to reintegrate the disturbed individual back into the group;[14] or (on a more general level) the absence of the "complex, conflicting, and potentially disorienting cognitive requirements" characteristic of more technologically sophisticated societies.[15] Since most medical-model psychiatrists have conceptualized such factors in the light of the pathogenicity/pathoplasticity distinction, however, it is often assumed that such factors modify only incidental aspects of the illness (course and outcome) without affecting its incidence or fundamental form. But these findings reveal a crucial ambiguity in this distinction, which brings me to the second point.

It is important to realize that the diagnostic criteria for schizophrenia used in the International Pilot Study do not take into account the chronicity of the illness;[16] and that the existence of a chronic, deteriorating course of illness is in fact central to at least some definitions of schizophrenia—Kraepelin's, for instance, as well as that of the most recent diagnostic systems of the American Psychiatric Association. Whether course of illness should be considered a critical element in the "schizophrenia" diagnosis remains uncertain (indeed, there is a genuine dilemma here, for to impose the criterion of chronicity would necessarily obscure potential findings about cross-cultural differences in *course* of illness). But if course of illness *were* to be considered, quite possibly some of the International Pilot Study "schizophrenics" would better be described as having certain of the (nonschizophrenic) acute transient psychotic illnesses that seem to be especially common in Third World settings and that can sometimes be difficult to distinguish from true schizophrenia (a point acknowledged by Jablensky, one of the principal investigators of the WHO study).[17] The fact that more patients in the developing countries (in both WHO studies) had a relatively abrupt onset of their illness (emergence of symptoms and progression to florid psychosis in less than a week) rather than a slow and insidious onset (development over more than a month, sometimes with no clear demarcation between traits of the premorbid personality and the gradually emerging psychosis)[18] is consistent with this speculation, since a sudden outbreak is more characteristic of the transient psychoses.

Even more intriguing are the subtype diagnoses reported in the later WHO study. Consider, for example, the fact that 40 percent of the "schizophrenics" in the developing countries versus only 11 percent of those in the developed countries were given the subtype label "acute schizophrenic episode." According to the international diagnostic system used in this WHO study, an acute schizophrenic episode (also called "oneirophrenia" and "schizophreniform attack" or "schizophreniform psychosis, confusional type") is characterized by "a dream-like state with slight clouding of consciousness and perplexity"; remission of symptoms often "occurs within a few weeks or months, even without treatment."[19] This is certainly not one of the core or prototypical forms of schizophrenia. Indeed, in DSM III and

DSM III-R most such patients would not be considered schizophrenics at all but would instead be said to have "schizophreniform disorder," "brief reactive psychosis," or "atypical psychosis." Inclusion of these brief psychoses in the so-called schizophrenia group could easily have inflated the statistics on prevalence, as well as improved the indices of prognosis of "schizophrenia" in the developing world.[20] It is also significant that the opposite pattern was found in the case of "hebephrenic schizophrenia" (13 percent of developed-world schizophrenics versus 4.3 percent of those in the developing world), because this is a more prototypical subtype of schizophrenia, with a stranger and more off-putting and autistic quality. (The International Classification of Diseases describes hebephrenia as involving a "mood [that] is shallow and inappropriate, accompanied by giggling or self-satisfied smiling, or by a lofty manner, grimaces, mannerism, pranks," disorganized thinking, "a tendency to remain solitary," and "behavior [that] seems empty of purpose and feeling," as well as an onset relatively early in life, between the ages of fifteen and twenty-five.)[21] Various studies have indicated also that Schneiderian First Rank Symptoms are less commonly found in schizophrenics from developing countries than in those from Western cultures.[22]

Anyone who pays serious attention to these facts about differences in characteristic course, type of onset, and subtype diagnosis in different cultures and who acknowledges the irresolvable uncertainties about what the *essential* criteria for schizophrenia ought to be[23] must recognize that the implications of the WHO studies are ambiguous to say the least. Do the findings indicate that schizophrenia simply has a more benign course in the developing world (the standard, mainstream interpretation) or that it has a somewhat lower incidence or prevalence there?[24] Clearly it would be naive to think there has to be one right answer to this question; or that there is necessarily a sharp boundary rather than a gradual transition between brief psychoses and what most experts would view as the core types of schizophrenia. But what the WHO studies do suggest, in any event, is that the more persistent and—at least according to most definitions—more prototypical forms of this illness (these being the forms I have concentrated on in this book) may well be more common in the more modern and developed sociocultural settings.

The third point to be noted about the WHO studies is that the Third World settings that were examined were all in *developing* societies, where the allied forces of modernization, Westernization, and industrialization had already been able to have a significant degree of influence.[25] A full analysis of the issue of cross-cultural prevalence would require the examination of societies that are more radically different from our own, namely, preliterate, tribal, hunter-gatherer, or other so-called primitive societies that have had a minimum of contact with the modern, industrialized world.[26]

Evidence from such cultures is very sparse and not entirely consistent, but in the main it seems to indicate that schizophrenia, at least as we know it, is in fact more rare in such contexts.[27] Certainly this was the view of most anthropologists who worked with so-called primitive cultures during the first half of this century, before Western influence had become widespread. "We seldom meet with insanity among the savage tribes of men; not one of our African travelers remark having seen a single madman," wrote Sir Andrew Halliday in 1828.[28] In a 1929 article on "Temperament, Conflict, and Psychosis in a Stone-Age Population" of highland New Guinea, the anthropologist Curt Seligman wrote that he could find "no evidence of the occurrence of mental derangement, other than brief outbursts of maniacal excitement, among natives who have not been associated with White Civilization."[29] And in 1939 the anthropologist and psychoanalyst George Devereux stated that the rarity or absence of schizophrenia in authentically primitive societies is "a point on which all students of comparative society and of anthropology agree"—and that the illness seems to appear very quickly once such societies are subjected to acculturation.[30]

A particularly interesting report comes from the anthropologist Meyer Fortes and his wife, the psychiatrist Doris Mayer.[31] Fortes first lived among the Tallensi of northern Ghana for two and a half years in the mid-1930s, when they were still a traditional, farming people, hardly touched by technology, Western education, or a money economy; at that time Fortes encountered only one clearly psychotic person in a population of five thousand. When he returned with his wife in 1963, the society had changed considerably, largely due to the fact that many of the young men now spent long periods of time in southern Ghana, where they could earn wages. They had brought back with them a money economy that was now firmly fixed atop the communal, subsistence patterns of the traditional Tallensi way of life. This time Fortes and Mayer found at least thirteen obviously psychotic people, of whom ten appeared to be schizophrenic—a rise far greater than the modest population increase in the intervening years, and involving blatantly psychotic cases of a kind Fortes could not have missed during his earlier stay. Fortes and Mayer attributed the rise to the economic and social changes that had taken place, noting that most of the psychotics had become ill while in the south. ("They travel South and are brought back mad," as the tribal elders of some of the northern tribes would say.)[32]

Psychiatric epidemiologists have often discounted the reports of cultural anthropologists, on the grounds that they are merely anecdotal; but as it turns out, much of the quantitative research done subsequently is reasonably supportive of the anthropologists' claim that schizophrenia is in fact uncommon in such cultures (though not, in all likelihood, entirely absent).[33] Studies carried out since the 1970s in New Guinea have found the rate of schizophrenia in the coastal districts, areas with more extensive Western contact, to be five to ten (or even twenty) times higher than that in the more isolated highland areas.[34] Similarly low rates of schizophrenia have been found in other non-Westernized groups, such as among Formosan aborigines, in northern Sumatra, on several Pacific islands, and in various African societies, as well as in traditional Hutterite and Amish communities in North America.[35] (Also, there is evidence that, in the United States, insanity/schizophrenia is considerably less prevalent in less urbanized settings.)[36]

This is not to say that psychotic illnesses *in general* are rare in tradition-directed, preindustrial, nonurbanized cultures. Significantly, schizophrenia's rarity in many such cultures seems to be counterbalanced by a higher prevalence of *other* forms of severe mental disorder that present a different symptomatic picture—especially what are known as the transient, atypical, hysterical, or acute delirious psychoses (the French term is *bouffée déli-rante;* according to one expert it accounts for 30 to 40 percent of the psychotic conditions in Africa but only 5 percent in France).[37] The psychiatrist John Carothers wrote in 1951 of the "primitive psychoses" he encountered very frequently during his many years in Kenya and which he found to be "undiagnosable" in standard Western terms; these patients were marked by excitability and confusion and tended to be highly active and dominated by intense (but syntonic) emotion.[38] Other investigators have described the typical psychotic in Africa as lacking the marked thought disorder, the personality disintegration, the social withdrawal, and the organized delusions found in many Western schizophrenics, and as showing emotional lability rather than the kind of flat or inappropriate affect that can evoke the praecox feeling. It is possible that some of these psychotic illnesses may be secondary to infectious diseases like malaria, which are common in the Third World and can mimic some aspects of schizophrenia, though they may be quickly overcome by people with the high immunity that comes from residing since infancy in unsanitary environments.[39] One exploratory study did suggest, however, that a common precipitant of these brief psychoses was some untoward event, often followed by a trip to the traditional healer or shaman and coupled with "a strong belief in and fear of easily angered spirits or bewitchment." (Such states were not uncommon in Europe at the end of the last century, incidentally, and have occurred at times in epidemic proportions among ethnic groups facing massive cultural change.)[40]

As do Western patients with so-called hysterical psychoses (an informally used, unofficial diagnostic term), psychotic individuals in a number of tribal cultures tend to manifest more readily comprehensible dynamics than do schizophrenics, and they remain in better contact with the environment and with other people, sometimes manifesting a propensity for histrionic dramatization.[41] Hysterical reactions such as amnesia, fugue states, brief fits of frenzy, and paroxysmal behavioral outbursts seem to have become rare in the industrialized world, yet they remain hallmarks of mental disorder in Africa and perhaps elsewhere in the Third World, occurring far more frequently than do the internalizing states that have a comparable importance in the West.[42] George Devereux goes so far as to describe hysteria as *"the ethnic disorder of many primitive societies,"* a view he shares with various other experts. He remarks on the extroverted and exhibitionistic nature of these syndromes, contrasting them with the "ethnic personality of modern man," whom he describes as "basically schizoid" and inclined to an "asocial turning inward."[43]

These transient or hysterical psychotic conditions have been ascribed to a fragility of inhibitory mechanisms that allows "facility of emotional outbursts" and "libido invasion," as well as to weakness or idleness of the higher psychic functions ("frontal idleness"), which results in a liberation of automatic psychomotor centers.[44] Such interpretations are very similar to traditional views of schizophrenia in the West, views I have been disputing throughout this book; it is possible, however, that they are more applicable to the transient psychoses common in Africa and elsewhere in the Third World (as well as to hysterical and perhaps some manic psychoses in the West), given that the latter do tend to be marked by heightened emotionality, impulsivity, and extroversion, and a lack of off-putting bizarreness.

Estimates of the prevalence of schizophrenia in various cultures will obviously vary depending on how one categorizes such psychoses—whether as benign forms of schizophrenia or as other forms of psychosis that may fall outside the schizophrenia spectrum altogether.[45] But given the absence of any absolute or unquestioned criterion for schizophrenia, this must remain in part a semantic issue (though it should be noted that the contemporary fashion in diagnostic practice is to narrow the category, which would result in the exclusion of many such short-lived psychoses as at most only schizophreni*form*). Nevertheless, the evidence does seem to indicate that the most clear-cut cases of schizophrenia—those characterized by the core symptoms of chronicity and social withdrawal, by flat and inappropriate affect, by Schneiderian First Rank Symptoms, and by unusual and abstract styles of thinking—may well be less common in cultural settings where traditional or premodern forms of social organization prevail.[46]

The Historical Dimension

A look at the historical dimension reinforces the impression of an association between schizophrenia and the social and cultural forms of modernity. Because of the absence of reliable epidemiological statistics before the nineteenth century, only indirect evidence can be used to assess the prevalence of schizophrenia in the West across time. What evidence there is suggests that schizophrenic illnesses did not even appear, at least in any significant quantity, before the end of the eighteenth century or the beginning of the nineteenth.[47] If so, their increasing frequency would have occurred just after the most intense period of change toward industrialization in Europe, a time of profound transition when traditional rural modes of communal life were giving way to the more impersonal and atomized forms of modern social organization (this has been considered the second of two great transitions in the history of the human species, comparable in depth and scope to the first—the prehistoric shift from hunter-gatherer to settled, agrarian societies).[48] This would also mean that schizophrenia's emergence coincided with the birth of the modern episteme (identified, by Foucault among others, with the Kantian revolution at the turn of the nineteenth century).

As I discussed at the beginning of the book, the several syndromes of what we now call schizophrenia were not brought together under a single rubric, *dementia praecox*, until the last decade of the nineteenth century. It might be argued, however, that this is simply a consequence of the extreme heterogeneity of the symptoms, which could have obscured their shared features. But even the various subtypes—Hecker's "hebephrenia" and Kahlbaum's "catatonia," for instance—were not described until after 1850. Even more telling is the absence or extreme rarity of descriptions of clear instances of individual cases of schizophrenia, at least of the chronic, autistic form, in either medical books or general literature prior to the nineteenth century. The first clinical descriptions are those of John Haslam and Philippe Pinel, both in 1809; the first literary descriptions that definitely qualify are those of the main characters in Georg Büchner's story "Lenz" and Honoré de Balzac's "Louis Lambert," both written in the 1830s—and this despite the fact that easily recognizable descriptions of all other major mental diseases, including the affective psychoses, can be found in ancient as well as Renaissance and eighteenth-century texts.[49] Many writers in the eighteenth century made systematic attempts to describe the known forms of mental illness, which resulted in works like Haslam's *Observations on Insanity* (1798) and Pinel's diagnostic system (1801). But despite the striking clinical picture that schizophrenia presents (at least in its acute and florid forms), one can find no account of it in these or any earlier works.[50]

Also significant is the perception, widespread in Europe and America throughout the nineteenth century, of a striking increase in the incidence of insanity. By the time Henry Maudsley read his paper "Is Insanity on the Increase?" to the Medico-Psychological Association in 1871, this issue had come to be of profound concern in England, where for decades there had been a need to build new asylums to accommodate a burgeoning population of the insane. (Between 1869 and 1900, there was a tripling of first admissions to asylums, counted as a proportion of the general population.)[51] In recent decades there has been a tendency (fueled, no doubt, by the animus of biological determinism) to discount these reports and to dismiss this apparent increase as an illusion or an artifact, resulting either from a growing awareness of insanity or else from a shift toward lengthier stays in the asylum. After carrying out a meticulous examination of the evidence, however, the medical historian Edward Hare concluded that these factors, though real, cannot explain away the apparent increase. Hare argues, in fact, not only that there was a significant rise in the incidence of insanity or lunacy in the nineteenth century but that this increase consisted largely of patients with the illness we now call schizophrenia (a condition that the president of the Medico-Psychological Association of Great Britain and Ireland described in 1906 as "then apparently so rare, but now so common").[52] As we approach modern times, we find more and more evidence of patients manifesting a symptomatic picture involving withdrawal, highly idiosyncratic and abstract patterns of thinking, and a preoccupation with hidden meanings. Interestingly, this increase appears to have been accompanied, in the past century, by a decline in the number of patients with the more socially engaged and less bizarre forms of transient psychosis that are so common in the developing world.[53]

Neither the historical nor the cross-cultural evidence is beyond dispute, and in both instances any conclusions must certainly be tempered by an acknowledgment of significant methodological problems and inconsistent findings. Nevertheless, the bulk of the evidence is suggestive: whether considered from a historical or a cross-cultural standpoint, modern Western civilization does seem to have a statistical association with schizophrenia, or at least with its severely chronic or autistic forms. Having arrived at this (admittedly somewhat tentative) conclusion, I turn next to the still more difficult question of how one might account for this intriguing association. The various causal hypotheses that might be proposed are not mutually exclusive, but for purposes of discussion I will take them up one at a time.

ETIOLOGICAL HYPOTHESES

I begin with what is likely to seem the least plausible of the hypotheses mentioned earlier: the possibility that schizophrenia could in some sense be a cause of modern culture. On its face such a theory may well seem absurd: How could so debilitating a condition, one characterized by withdrawal and passivization and affecting no more than 1 percent of the population, have a significant effect on the customs and sensibility of society as a whole? On the other hand, as Karl Jaspers has pointed out, the number of schizophrenics who have been of profound cultural importance in European society since 1800 is quite remarkable; Jaspers also notes that he cannot find any such persons who were of importance before 1800 (which is not to deny the cultural importance of individuals manifesting *other* types of psychosis in earlier centuries).[54]

If one considers the cultural significance of the works of actual schizophrenic individuals such as Hölderlin, Nijinsky, and Artaud, and of probable or near-schizophrenics such as Gérard de Nerval, Alfred Jarry, Raymond Roussel, and August Strindberg, not to mention the more indirect influence of schizophrenic eccentrics like Jean-Pierre Brisset and Louis Wolfson (who inspired various surrealists, poststructuralists, and postmodernists),[55] it may not seem absurd to attribute a degree of influence to this condition. (Consider that Nerval and Hölderlin might reasonably be described as the most influential precursors of modernist poetry in French and German.)[56] If one were to include markedly schizoid persons like Baudelaire, Nietzsche, van Gogh, de Chirico, Dali, Wittgenstein, Kafka, and Beckett (whose own central characters so often resemble schizophrenics), this thesis might even begin to seem rather plausible.[57]

Avant-garde theater in the twentieth century provides a very striking instance, since its course has been so profoundly affected by the innovations of three individuals with very prominent schizophrenialike traits: the absurdism and rebelliousness of Jarry, Strindberg's explosion of the unified ego, and Artaud's rejection of narrativity and realism. Each of these aesthetic predilections obviously has an intrinsic logic of its own and cannot be reduced to a mere reflex of a temperament or mental affliction, yet it would be naive to divorce these artistic attitudes entirely from the writer's personal mode of being, which they obviously reflect. Who can say to what extent the schizophrenia of such artists may have inspired, or at least reinforced, the antinomianism and inwardness that are so pervasive in modern culture?

Having suggested this hypothesis, however, I must immediately qualify it: for such individuals to have much impact, it would seem that the culture would already need to be imbued with something like a modernist orientation—that is, with a peculiar openness to all that is idiosyncratic, inward, and enigmatic (not just any culture will attend carefully to those paradoxical creatures, Kierkegaard's "town criers of inwardness"). Schizoid and schizophrenic productions and ways of being might well foster such a taste, but surely they would also depend on it for any influence they might have. Of course, there is also the possibility that these personal modes of being are not in fact wholly independent factors, that the traits of such persons have already been molded, at least to some extent, by the culture in which they are found. This brings us to the second causal hypothesis—that modern culture contributes to the rise of schizophrenia rather than the other way around.

This fairly popular hypothesis has been asserted in a variety of different ways, not all of them assigning the same degree of importance to sociocultural factors as such. At least a few of the psychiatrists who believe schizophrenia to be more common in the modern industrialized West argue that this effect is mediated by biological rather than social or psychological factors. Torrey suggests, for example, that the rise in schizophrenia is a consequence of a slow viral epidemic beginning in the West some two hundred years ago; the incubation and spread of this hypothetical virus was supposedly fostered by the demographic circumstances and social conditions associated with urbanism and industrialization—conditions that are now gradually being spread, along with the virus, throughout the developing world.[58]

There is another approach that does grant importance to the psychological aspect of culture and society, while assigning to these factors only a negative function. In this view schizophrenia continues to be understood as, in essence, a consequence of intellectual deficiencies or emotional vulnerabilities, such as defective filtering of attention, sluggish information processing, or generalized ego defects (of the kind, for example, postulated by Daniel Weinberger's version of the hypofrontality notion, discussed in the appendix); and it is assumed that these deficits are rooted in biology (or perhaps, for psychoanalysts, in the traumas of early childhood). Modern social settings are, however, assumed to be particularly troublesome for persons with these defects—perhaps because it is difficult for such people to muster the individual initiative, self-reliance, and exercise of judgment that these settings demand; perhaps because such cultures encourage such persons to blame themselves (rather than supernatural forces) for their behavior; or perhaps because modernity's belief in integral and discrete selfhood causes the self-disorganization of schizophrenia to be experienced as more pathological.[59] According to these views, then, the conditions of modern life—its "complex, conflicting and potentially disorienting cognitive requirements," its harrowing assignment of individual responsibility[60]—are able to precipitate the occurrence of the psychosis, or to exert a detrimental effect on acute schizophrenic episodes that occur independently (thereby encouraging the development of more severe and chronic forms of the illness); but it is assumed that these conditions do not affect the illness's essential form.[61]

Modern culture can, however, also be assigned a more positive role in the production of schizophrenia or in the shaping of its definitive characteristics. Elsewhere in this book (pages 444 and 501) I have suggested that arrival at the stage of adolescence might not just represent a particular challenge for certain vulnerable individuals (due to the new degree of autonomy it requires); it might also be a precondition for the development of certain kinds of (reflexive) symptoms—since these symptoms would require the capacity for thinking about thinking, which is not achieved before the advent of the cognitive-developmental stage of formal operations. A similar point might be made on the level of cultural rather than individual development, by suggesting that the ways of thinking, believing, and feeling characteristic of modern Western society are prerequisites for the development of the reflexivity and detachment characteristic of both the schizoid and the schizophrenic condition. Some kind of biological vulnerability (for instance, in the form of a temperamental disposition, such as schizoid personality [broadly defined, as in chapter 3], or in the form of a cognitive abnormality) might well be necessary for developing such forms of schizophrenia, but culture might be another necessary (or nearly necessary) factor—affecting the form and not just the content of these illnesses. (And if social factors can largely determine whether a psychotic breakdown will have a long-term, deteriorating course, and whether bizarre and withdrawn symptomatology will be present, then such factors cannot be dismissed as merely "pathoplastic," as they could be playing a critical role in both the pathogenesis and maintenance of the specifically schizophrenic forms of madness.)

This, however, raises the question of just which specific *aspects* of modern culture are likely to be causally relevant. It would be impossible to enumerate them all here,[62] but in these final pages I can touch upon a few central features, focusing in particular on the development of the modern self.

Consider, first, the emphasis on disengagement and self-consciousness that was fostered by the ideas of philosophers like Descartes, Locke, and Kant (as well as by patterns of socialization in daily life) and that played such an important role in later centuries, culminating in aspects of modernism. One contemporary scholar has described how this turned modern human beings away from the search for an objective external order, enjoining us instead "to turn inward and become aware of our own activity and of the processes that form us . . . to take charge of constructing our own representation of the world, which otherwise goes on without order." Central to these tendencies is a pervasive detachment, a "disengagement" that "demands that we stop simply living in the body or within our traditions and habits, and by making them objects for us, subject them to radical scrutiny and remaking."[63]

Related currents, more closely associated with romanticism and its aftermath, have tended to glorify the inner self, by implying that human fulfillment lies in discovering one's own uniqueness and recognizing the central role of one's own subjectivity. (It is only with romanticism that autobiographies come to be filled with forms of self-reflection focused on the drama and idiosyncrasies of one's own inner life.)[64] One effect of this was to foster the sense of inwardness so eloquently lamented in Rilke's Seventh Duino Elegy:

> Nowhere, Beloved, will world be but within us. Our life
> passes in transformation. And the external
> shrinks into less and less. Where once an enduring house was,
> now a cerebral structure crosses our path, completely

> belonging to the realm of concepts, as though it
> still stood in the brain.
>
> . . .
>
> a Thing that was formerly prayed to, worshipped, knelt before—
> just as it is, it passes into the invisible world.[65]

European culture over the last three centuries or so has been increasingly dominated by individualism and subjectivism, by rationalism and relativism, and a new character type has come into dominance in the twentieth century: "psychological man," who is "intent upon the conquest of his inner life" and embraces the ideal of "salvation through self-contemplative manipulation."[66] It is easy to see how such attitudes might foster the state of permanent reflectiveness and subjectivization that the sociologists Helmut Schelsky and Arnold Gehlen see as endemic to modern consciousness—a condition in which intuitiveness and a sense of unproblematic accessibility are replaced by intellectuality and cautious deliberation.[67] If schizoids and schizophrenics, like other human beings, are subject to the influences of their social milieu, it is not hard to see how a number of their core traits (the asocial turning inward, the lack of spontaneity, the detachment from emotion, the hyperabstractness, the anxious deliberation and cognitive slippage, and the exquisitely vulnerable sense of self-esteem, for example)[68] might be exaggerations of tendencies fostered by this civilization. Such traits might also be rooted in neurobiology, of course, in which case biology and culture would be mutually reinforcing.[69]

This interiorizing culture is certainly very different from what is found in traditional tribal societies, the kind where transient or hysterical psychoses are more common and where privacy, inwardness, and individualistic striving are not emphasized. The contrast is illustrated by certain difficulties that arose in one cross-cultural psychiatric study involving the Xhosa-speaking people of South Africa, people to whom the concerns of Rilke's elegy would be likely to seem alien indeed. The British investigators describe a number of problems they had in attempting to ask questions from a standardized interview format for psychiatric research (the "Present State Examination"). They note the inappropriateness in this African context of the Cartesian assumption, standard in the West and implicit in a number of the interview questions, that the self can be imagined as a kind of physical space inside of which one's thoughts move about. The British authors state that the English word *worry* was difficult for the Xhosa to grasp; as they explain, "in Xhosa one worries with one's heart." It was also virtually impossible to find close translations into Xhosa for the notion of higher mental functions—"concentration" or "thoughts drifting" or "states of mind," for instance—as well as for concepts like "derealization" and "delusional mood" (concepts that focus on states of mind of a particular, alienated sort).[70] The modes of experience suggested by these difficulties of translation can help us understand why psychopathology in such a culture would differ from what is common in the West, why psychotics in such settings might have a more extroverted, emotional, and action-oriented quality, without the isolation and introversion, the affective flatness, and the bizarreness so typical of the schizophrenic in the modern West.

A comprehensive model of the social origins both of schizophrenia and of the modernist sensibility would need to go beyond this discussion of abstract ideas and *mentalité,* and to acknowledge as well how each of these conditions is intricated with the modern social order—with the patterns of political and bureaucratic organization, family structures, economic practices, and technological developments of modern*ity*. The most influential descriptions of these aspects of modernity come from the founding fathers of sociology: Karl Marx—on the alienating consequences of certain economic structures and relationships; Max Weber—on the growing rationalization, technologization, secularization, and bureaucratization of modern life; and Emile Durkheim—on the juggernaut of industrialization and the growing reflectiveness that cause traditional values to lose their quasi-natural status. These changes, occurring over the last three centuries, have been as great—in scope, in intensity, and in rapidity—as any that have previously occurred; indeed it has been argued that they constitute the most profound discontinuity in all of recorded history.[71] (Changes in the realm of philosophical ideas—like the doctrines of possessive individualism and of mind-body dualism—have developed in tandem with these more concrete transformations in political organization and economic production, sometimes facilitating and encouraging the societal changes, at other times serving to justify or explain what was already taking place.)

In *The Homeless Mind: Modernization and Consciousness,* the sociologists Peter Berger, Brigitte Berger, and Hansfried Kellner (adopting a perspective closest to that of Weber) play out in some detail the effect these social, economic, and political developments have had at the level of individual experience. Among the consequences they see are the following: the development of a certain anonymity and impersonality in social relationships, a heightened demand for rational planning and reflectiveness in everyday life, a rising sense of separation between one's social identity and a segregated sphere of individual consciousness, and the replacement of synthetic-intuitive by more abstract modes of thought and perception, largely as a result of administrative demands to separate means from ends and of the componential nature both of actual machinery and of bureaucratic mechanisms (which require interchangeable parts).[72]

Another contemporary sociologist, Anthony Giddens, stresses the unsettling quality of modernity's "wholesale reflexivity"—which is turned not only on all traditions but even on the nature of reflection itself, resulting in the dissolving of anchored vantage points and a universal "institutionalization of doubt."[73] It is not hard to conceive the role such transformations might play in fostering schizoid and schizophrenic pathology—by encouraging (or exacerbating) the social withdrawnness, the cognitive wavering and incertitude, the sense of being a divided self, and the predilection for overly abstract modes of thought that are characteristic of such persons. Certain theorists who see Western societies as having moved into a stage of *post*modernity emphasize a somewhat different set of developments, among them: the waning of affect, the dissolution of the sense of separate selfhood, the loss of any sense of the real, and the saturation by images and simulacra detached from all grounding outside themselves; these, obviously, are more than a little reminiscent of certain schizoid and schizophrenic tendencies, and it is not difficult to imagine that such general cultural developments might also influence the modes of experience characteristic of such individuals.[74]

This is not to say, of course, that such forms of pathology are likely to be simple reflections of the objective circumstances of the social order. The domain of personality (like that of culture) is not, after all, a mere consequence or effect, but also an at least potentially independent factor in reciprocal interaction with social practices and institutions (Weber has pointed out, most famously in his discussion of the Protestant temperament, how psychological traits and cultural values can facilitate changes in the economic sphere). In addition, we must acknowledge the highly problematic and dialectical nature of the relationship schizoid and schizophrenic individuals tend to have with modern society—a relationship that may not be unlike that of the modernist artist. Like those bards of inwardness, the town criers of modern consciousness, schizophrenics are in a dual relationship with modernity, existing not just as a product *of* but also as a reaction *against* the prevailing social order. Both their antinomianism and their withdrawal bear witness to an unwillingness, or incapacity, to conform to the standard expectations of modernity, and to a yearning instead for some kind of subversion or escape.

But in saying this, one must be sure not to adopt too simplistic an understanding, as if either the subversion or the escape (whether in its modernist or its schizoid form) could spring from some domain entirely separate from the social order that is being fled or opposed. This, I believe, is the mistake commonly made by those who adopt primitivist models. They see madness— or modernism, for that matter—as a spontaneous, natural, and precivil mode of being, a simple bursting forth of primitive, presocial energies that escape the constraining forces of society and self-control. In reality both the oppositional stance and the mode of escape (the inward turn) may to a certain extent already be inscribed, at least as potentialities, within the modern sociocultural order itself.

This curious but distinctive symbiosis is perhaps best illustrated in Foucault's image of the Panopticon, which so clearly combines objectifying with interiorizing trends. In our discussion of Schreber's panoptical universe, that "mind's-eye" world of "nerves" and "rays," we saw how the bizarre and seemingly chaotic inner world of madness could mirror the rationalized and alienating social order without.[75] Far from being a "sovereign enterprise of unreason" or the source of a "total contestation" of modern Western civilization,[76] madness, at least in Schreber's case, turned out to be one of the most extreme exemplars *of* this civilization—a simulacrum of the modern world in the most private recesses of the soul.

A P P E N D I X

· ·

Neurobiological Considerations

The study of schizophrenic consciousness and expression can, and indeed to a certain extent *must*, be carried out independently of the
study of accompanying neurophysiological processes. Schizophrenia,
after all, is something we define and recognize by the presence of certain
forms of experience and action, forms that can be neither described nor
conceptualized in purely physicalistic terms. In an important sense, in fact,
the study of these psychological phenomena must logically precede a physiological investigation of them, since any hypothesis that purports to *account*
for "schizophrenia" must necessarily be consistent with forms of experience
and action that are recognized independently of biological factors with
which they may then be found to correlate. This does not imply that the
psychological and the physiological planes are unrelated; nor does it detract
from the importance of examining apparent correlations or from speculating
on possible causal interactions (or other forms of relationship) that may link
the two domains, with a view toward ultimately achieving a comprehensive
understanding of this condition. In this book, in fact, there is a special reason
to address the possible relationships among mind, human action, and the
nervous system: all too frequently, acknowledgment of the neurophysiological aspects of schizophrenia is assumed to be somehow incompatible with the
kind of approach to this illness that I have been offering in these pages.

A common assumption is that the discovery of biological correlates for
psychopathology, or at least for psychotic illnesses, is likely to diminish the
importance of the experiential dimension (and also that of cultural factors)
and in particular to undermine any conception that—like mine—would attribute a significant degree of meaningfulness, intentionality, or rationality
to the patient's experience. Such an assumption is not, in fact, supported by
a careful analysis of recent neurobiological research on schizophrenia; nor,

I think, would such a view be espoused by most of the more philosophically sophisticated psychiatrists, neuropsychologists, and other neuroscientists.[1] But it is nevertheless deeply embedded in much of the most influential thinking about madness, not only currently but over the last one hundred and fifty years or more—and so it will require some examination before we can rid ourselves of its constraining prejudices.

In this appendix I outline the nature of the assumptions implicit in this reductionistic view, trace their sources in the nineteenth century, and then discuss their contemporary manifestations. Later I offer some criticisms of such views, first on general grounds and then through discussing a variety of specific neurobiological findings and hypotheses (including several hypotheses that seem particularly congruent with the phenomenological portrait offered in this book).

BIOLOGICAL REDUCTIONISM: ASSUMPTIONS AND SOURCES

Implicit in a great deal of biological psychiatry is an asymmetry of explanatory principles. Normal (or healthy) forms of consciousness are assumed to be, to a great extent, under one's intentional control and, in addition, to operate according to rational principles and to be oriented toward the objective world. While these normal mental processes are certainly assumed to be *correlated* with physical events occurring in the brain, seldom are they viewed as being *mere* causal by-products of such events, since the meaningfulness and directedness they exhibit seem intrinsic to the psyche, to the realm of meaning rather than of physical event. But *ab*normal modes of consciousness, at least those characterizing the insane, have often been seen very differently: as involving a "fall into determinism,"[2] a lapse from dualism whereby the malfunctioning physical processes (in brain and nervous system) disrupt the mental or psychic stream, depriving it of its intrinsic rationality and meaningfulness.[3] Two related assumptions are inherent in this traditional conception of mental abnormality and will continually recur in the following discussion. Though seldom stated in explicit or categorical fashion, these presuppositions are widely held.

The first, more general assumption is that the physical plane has causal primacy, namely that, at least in the domain of the psychoses, it is primarily brain events that cause mind events rather than the reverse. The second assumption concerns the particular *kind* of mental events or processes that are supposedly brought into being by such physical causes. It is assumed that, when the brain invades the mind, the result is inevitably a lowering of the mental level (to use Pierre Janet's phrase); this implies a diminution of one or more of the qualities that have traditionally been considered the defining features of higher or human modes of consciousness: rationality, volition, and self-conscious awareness. Let us call these the assumptions of "physicalism" and of "lowered mental level." Together they constitute what I shall term the reductionistic model of insanity.

As mentioned in the prologue, this talk of "lowering" has very deep roots in Western thought and has held special prominence since the seventeenth-century Enlightenment. The other assumption is, by contrast, largely the product of nineteenth-century forms of physicalism, which replaced the, in some respects, more complex dynamics of mind-body relations that had prevailed in the eighteenth century.[4] The way the two are related should be fairly easy to see: to ascribe significant rationality, volition, or self-awareness to the abnormal mind suggests a certain capacity for independence or self-transcendence on the part of this mind; and this would hardly be consistent with a determinism that treats such a mind as the purely passive product of physical events.[5]

Both of these basic grounding assumptions are deeply flawed, however— the first largely for philosophical reasons and the second because it is contradicted by numerous counterexamples from neurology and neuropsychology. Indeed it is quite possible to accept the undeniable fact that mind is, *in some sense,* located in the brain without accepting either of these presuppositions—a point that (as I have indicated) is unlikely to be disputed by the more philosophically informed of contemporary experts on the brain.[6] Nonetheless these assumptions have dominated thought about madness and the brain for over a hundred years, in neurology and psychiatry as well as among the lay public. (I would argue, in fact, that something like these assumptions tends, in practice, to imbue the thinking even of many persons who do not overtly subscribe to them, and who might disagree with the assumptions if they were explicitly stated.)

Recent developments in the neurobiology of schizophrenia are unquestionably valuable and exciting; unfortunately, however, one of their effects has been to revive inclinations toward reductionism, at least in many quarters.[7] Particularly among many organic psychiatrists, there is now a renewed tendency to ignore the psychological interpretation or empathic understanding of mental symptoms, to accord importance to these phenomena only insofar as they may be reliable signs of underlying biological disorders or tendencies. In addition, there has been a rediscovery of "the dementia in dementia praecox"[8]—a return to the idea that schizophrenia is essentially to be understood as a defect state, a "more or less well-marked mental enfeeblement" (as Kraepelin called it)[9] involving the diminished rationality and lowered mental level traditionally associated with the classic organic brain syndromes. To gain a better understanding of these trends, we need to embark on a brief "history of the present"—a quick survey of some of their sources in the nineteenth century, the period when this combination of assumptions, and the associated denial of the project of psychological understanding, received its classical formulation.

A particularly important figure of the late nineteenth century is J. Hughlings Jackson, a British neurologist whose influence on both neurology and psychiatry continues to the present day. Jackson, inspired by the evolutionism of his time, postulated a variety of different levels in the nervous system, ranging from the less to the more volitionally controlled and from the less to the more organized. He viewed the insane individual as having "a lower consciousness and a shallower nervous system than the former person, his sane self"[10] and saw mental illnesses, both neurologic and psychiatric, as being, in essence, consequences of a disintegration of the higher or more volitionally controlled mental processes. The effects of this disintegration, he argued, could show up in one of two ways: either directly, as "negative" mental symptoms, involving deficiencies of higher mental processes such as volition, control, consciousness, and reasoning, or more indirectly, in the form of "positive" symptoms such as hallucinations, delusions, or impulsive and automatic behavior patterns. Jackson viewed the positive symptoms as regressive phenomena, as automatisms emerging from "lower" or more primitive levels of the nervous system that had been released due to the failure of the higher levels to exert their normal inhibitory control. In his view such positive symptoms were only "indirectly caused, or rather permitted," by the disease process; they were important only insofar as they suggested the failure of "higher" inhibitory functions to which they owed their release.[11]

This conception, which has received widespread acceptance, discourages serious search for meaning or intentionality in psychopathological experience, for it implies that the central feature of all mental symptoms is simple defect or deficiency. To Jackson, the important thing to understand was always the failure or dysfunction of higher mental processes. Charles Mercier, his disciple and friend, could not have been more explicit: "In every case of insanity the essential feature is defect," he wrote. "In no case does disease make a real, fruitful addition to function. The affection of function is always in the direction of loss, of deficit, or diminution. . . . in all cases of insanity, the real and important aberration is not necessarily the most conspicuous feature—the over-action— . . . but the degradation of action to a lower plane." It follows that "defect" is "the underlying disorder upon which the other [symptoms] are superimposed, and around which they are clustered."[12]

Both positive and negative symptoms were thus only deficit products, devoid of purpose or significance of their own and closed to any but a physicalistic mode of understanding. Jackson never viewed abnormal states of consciousness as legitimate objects of study in their own right: "strictly speaking," he wrote, these "mental symptoms" were "only signs to physicians of what is not going on or what is going on wrongly in part of a patient's material organization." By the end of the nineteenth century this had become practically an official dogma. As Henry Maudsley, perhaps the most important British psychiatrist of his time, wrote in 1874: "It is not our business, it is not in our power, to explain *psychologically* the origin and nature of any of [the] depraved instincts [manifested in typical cases of insanity]." The alienist's purpose was only to observe and classify, since the "explanation, when it comes, will come not from the mental, but from the physical side."[13] In this view, "tangles and twists in the mind" are relatively unimportant; all attention is to be directed instead at "blots and spots in the brain."[14]

The legacy of the Enlightenment focus on rational processes as the definitive human essence can be seen in the fact that dementia, the decline and disintegration of the mental faculties, was considered by many late-nineteenth-century psychiatrists to be the essential feature of all types of insanity, the end state toward which all such diseases were progressing. One doctor, Sir Thomas Clouston, actually *defined* mental disease as "a tendency to dementia." But dementia, or the profound defect states that approach this condition, is, by definition, deprived of organized thought and rational activity, and of both objective awareness and self-consciousness. In the extreme this condition, which was often assumed to result from atrophy of the brain, undermined the very possibility of meaning itself and implied the actual extinction of mind. It is understandable, then, that those who held such views would consider the experiences and expressions of the insane to be unintelligible—beyond, or rather beneath, the possibility of empathic understanding. Thus Mercier concluded that "we cannot dive into the illogical processes of the insane," and Maudsley spoke of the surprising "mindlessness" that, he believed, exists even "at the back of what looks like very partial mental disorder."[15] There can, of course, be something self-fulfilling about such views, since the assumption of a dementing process and an underlying neurological disorder may lead one to expect nonsense and thus to refrain from putting real effort into the task of empathic comprehension. (The obverse also occurs: the perception of a patient's incomprehensibility causes people to assume the existence of a purely biological explanation.)[16]

This prevailing image of mental illness as a form of irrationality also guided nineteenth-century attempts to localize insanity in particular parts of the brain. Though the actual anatomical locus that was postulated would differ according to which of the three major axes of brain functioning was considered most important (the vertical, anterior-posterior, or lateral axis), nearly always it involved a weakening of the areas serving advanced, intellectual processes, sometimes combined with a hypertrophy of lower and more archaic psychic processes involving instinct and emotion.

Thus, in the view of some theorists, it was the upper or outer layer of the brain, the cortex, a late evolutionary development, whose functioning was impaired, thereby allowing more primitive activity from the lower, subcortical parts of the brain to overwhelm the controlling aspects of intelligence. Others focused more on the frontal-posterior dimension, arguing that schizophrenic patients had deficiencies of the frontal lobes, supposedly the "flower of the brain" and the seat of human reason and intelligence (by contrast, the posterior lobes of the brain, located behind the Rolandic fissure, were said to be the site of passions and the instincts).[17] Still others concentrated on the lateral dimension, viewing madness as a dominance of the supposedly more primitive right hemisphere (what Maudsley called the "brute brain within the man's") or a weakness of the more evolved and voluntary left hemisphere, which had been discovered to be specialized for language, that uniquely human capacity.[18] In retrospect it is fairly easy to see that prevailing conceptions of these three axes were by no means based solely on empirical findings but were themselves imbued with many of the same rationalist notions that were guiding the understanding of insanity itself.[19]

Such conceptions of insanity held sway in much of Europe throughout the Victorian era, reaching a culmination in the 1890s with the work of Emil Kraepelin, who, as I discussed earlier, coined the term *dementia praecox* for much of what had been called insanity or lunacy and who viewed "a tangible morbid process occurring in the brain" as the only plausible explanation for what he described as this "acquired mental debility."[20] This highly antipsychological, deficit-based approach was not, in fact, seriously challenged until the early years of the twentieth century, when psychoanalytic notions about unconscious significance and intentionality began to exert their influence. It was then that Eugen Bleuler, who was influenced by Freud, rejected the term *dementia praecox* and began to take a greater interest in the inner life and psyche of what he preferred to call the "schizophrenic" patient. With the publication in 1911 of Bleuler's *Dementia Praecox and the Group of Schizophrenias,* the way was opened for many other attempts at psychological understanding—not only for various psychoanalytic interpretations based on the regression-fixation model but also for more innovative phenomenological studies that would take a closer look at the subtleties of the experiential world.[21] (It should be noted, however, that neither Freud nor Bleuler seriously questioned the Jacksonian tendency to see "positive" pathological symptoms as indicating regression to lower evolutionary planes, and as largely devoid of rationality, though not of meaning. Freud, incidentally, was very directly influenced by Jackson, who introduced him to the concept of regression. And the Freudian distinction between primary and secondary processes stems directly from Jackson's notions about higher and lower cerebral centers.)[22]

But the reductionistic views of Jackson, Kraepelin, and like-minded thinkers have never ceased to have a very substantial following. Throughout the twentieth century, a great many psychiatrists have always believed that the essentially (and almost entirely) somatic nature of schizophrenia can be assumed with what one expert, writing in the 1930s, spoke of as "a priori certainty" (the assumption of "physicalism").[23] There has also been a continuing tendency to read schizophrenic symptoms as deficits involving lower and less volitional modes of psychological functioning. Schizophrenia has often been understood according to the predominant models of organic brain disorder, which derive from diseases like senile dementia, Korsakoff's syndrome, and general paralysis of the insane.[24] This "lowered-mental-level" assumption is perhaps best exemplified in the work of Kurt Goldstein, whose notions of concrete versus abstract modes of functioning have been so important in psychology, psychiatry, and neurology since the 1920s. Goldstein, too, was influenced by Jackson, and he shared the earlier neurologist's tendency to assimilate insanity to the classic organic brain syndromes and to view both these forms of illness as involving the loss of higher, and the emergence of lower, psychological processes.[25]

The last ten or fifteen years have seen a tremendous resurgence (particularly in Anglo-American psychiatry, which is profoundly influential throughout much of the world) of biologism, of self-styled "neo-Kraepelinian" theories, of the ideas of Jackson, and of notions reminiscent of Kurt Goldstein. And the views of some contemporary biological psychiatrists—regarding both schizophrenia in particular and brain functioning in general—are strikingly close to those of their influential predecessors. Nancy Andreasen, one of the more prominent researchers in biological psychiatry, writes, for instance, that "Kraepelin and his fellow psychiatrist-neuroscientists of the early twentieth century were on the right track." Her own reductionism is patent in her recent book, *The Broken Brain: The Biological Revolution in Psychiatry*, in which she informs her readers of what she sees as the message of contemporary neuroscience: "we need not look to theoretical constructs of the 'mind' or to influences from the external environment in order to understand how people feel, why they behave as they do, or what becomes disturbed when people develop mental illness. Instead we can look directly to the brain," she writes, for all the symptoms of mental illness "must be understood in terms of the interaction of neural systems and neural circuits."[26]

Jackson has also gained new prominence through the revival of his concept of positive and negative symptoms, which has become the most popular way of categorizing symptoms or subtyping schizophrenic patients in contemporary biological psychiatry.[27] Current knowledge about the brain and nervous system is far more sophisticated than it was in the late nineteenth and early twentieth centuries, yet many of the theoretical models remain remarkably unchanged. Nor is it clear that we are that much closer to understanding the truly distinctive elements of the neurobiology of schizophrenia (indeed, one contemporary neuroscientist remarks, perhaps too pessimistically, that as the neurosciences become more complicated with each passing year, they may also be becoming less useful for explaining mental illness, since it now seems virtually inconceivable to map or interrelate the known neuromodulatory pathways.)[28]

The resurgence of biological psychiatry was initially fueled by the discovery of neuroleptic drugs in the 1950s, which led to theorizing about the effects of neurotoxins and of abnormalities of neurotransmission, particularly the well-known hypothesis postulating excessive activity of the neurotransmitter dopamine. In recent years, however, these theories have been on the wane, with some former advocates concluding that the dopamine hypothesis is no longer tenable as a primary explanation of schizophrenia.[29] More recently, attention has focused on neuroanatomy and neurophysiology of the brain, largely as a result of dramatic developments in computerized imaging techniques, which vastly increase our capacity for direct study of the brain.[30] Not unlike X rays, yet able to show soft tissues, some of these imaging methods make it possible to assess the size, density, and other structural aspects of the parts of the living brain. Other techniques can picture the brain's ongoing functioning by displaying the relative activation of its different regions, which is indexed by the amount of blood flow or of glucose metabolism in its various regions. These techniques, in conjunction with older ones like postmortem brain examination and neuropsychological testing, have led to renewed speculation about the precise anatomical locus of neurological dysfunctions in schizophrenia. It is striking to discover how close some of the best-known contemporary hypotheses are to their nineteenth-century predecessors, not only in their overall conception of the schizophrenic disorder itself but in where they locate the underlying neurological dysfunctions—which they, too, place in the left, the upper, or the forward part of the brain.

Thus the so-called negative symptoms are frequently understood as involving intellectual impairments of various kinds and as being rather direct consequences of structural or functional changes in the brain. Sometimes these changes are said to involve atrophy of the cortex (the upper or outer part of the brain), or perhaps a deactivation or dysfunction of the prefrontal cortex—this being the (anterior) part of the brain often assumed to be the "higher" cortical locus par excellence, subserving self-awareness and self-control as well as the capacities for judgment and abstraction.[31] The laterality dimension has also been invoked, with the most popular theories hypothesizing dysfunction of the left hemisphere, which is often conceptualized as being the more rational, volitional, and self-conscious, and the more dominant side of the brain. (According to one researcher of the laterality dimension, left-hemisphere dysfunction is suggested by disturbance of the schizophrenic's ability to conceptualize, to use abstractions, to draw logical inferences, and to make appropriate judgments.)[32]

"Positive" symptoms, including hallucinations, delusions, and certain kinds of thought disorder, on the other hand, are not infrequently viewed as consequences of failures of control or inhibition that result in "intrusions of memories and experiences from a lower [and more archaic] level of functioning." Andreasen, who expressly follows a Jacksonian model, thus suggests that auditory hallucinations may occur when auditory memories— "perhaps heard long ago and now forgotten," but "stored" in parts of the more "primitive" and subcortical limbic system (the amygdala and hippocampus)—are intermittently released due to "lack of regulatory input from another brain region such as the frontal cortex."[33] (The limbic system is housed deep inside the brain, underneath the cortical covering, and it subserves, among other things, arousal, attention, and appetitive and aversive functions. It was once called the "nose brain," because it was believed to have an especially intimate connection with the sense of smell; and it is still sometimes referred to as the "paleocortex," because its organization is supposed to be simpler and more primitive than that of the cortex. More recently it has been seen in a somewhat different light, largely due to a new understanding of the hippocampus and related systems—an issue I will return to shortly.)

Another prominent biological psychiatrist, Daniel Weinberger, presents a similar theory, also specifying a failure to activate parts of the frontal cortex, which he describes as the most highly evolved part of the brain (from both a phylogenetic and an ontogenetic standpoint). In a formulation consistent with Jackson's, he theorizes that this failure is related, at least in part, to a lack or hypofunction of the neurotransmitter dopamine in the prefrontal cortex, which in turn causes a failure of inhibitory processes, thereby permitting hyperactivation of dopamine-mediated processes in subcortical parts of the brain. And in a formulation reminiscent of Kurt Goldstein, Weinberger has described the prefrontal hypofunction as resulting in an incapacity for abstract functions analogous to what is seen in young children and in the elderly (he specifies a loss of the ability to form abstract concepts, to shift mental sets, to use hypothetical deductive reasoning, and to exercise independent judgment). In one article he even goes so far as to speculate that this neurobiological model might provide a physiological explanation for the classical psychodynamic model of schizophrenia, with "inadequate ego defenses" reflecting hypofunction of part of the prefrontal cortex and "overwhelming instinctual forces" reflecting subcortical dopamine disinhibition."[34]

The neurophysiological approach to schizophrenia, at least as presented by Nancy Andreasen and Daniel Weinberger, may well seem to be at odds with my approach in this book. First, there is a certain physicalistic reductionism, blatant in Andreasen but considerably muted in the more subtle formulations of Weinberger; this has had the effect of downgrading the importance of a phenomenological perspective, so that descriptions of the patient's mode of experience are often accorded a merely diagnostic importance. Second, the underlying neurophysiological conditions that are postulated are assumed to produce psychological conditions of a certain kind, namely, states of diminished reflectiveness, intentionality, and self-control that at least approach the mindlessness, dementia, or regression postulated in the Victorian age. Persons holding such views are likely to deny, or at least to downplay, the significance of intentional, meaningful, and rational aspects to the central symptoms of such patients. It may well appear, then, that the recent discoveries in the field of neurobiology tend to trivialize the significance of phenomenological approaches and, in particular, to undermine the validity of the kinds of interpretations offered in this book.

In the following pages, the assumptions underlying this kind of neurobiological position will be subjected to critical scrutiny. My point, however, is not to *deny* that biological abnormalities are important in schizophrenia—it is obvious, in fact, that such factors very likely play an important role (at least in a great many such patients). One need not be opposed to the idea of a biological contribution in order to find fault with the reductionistic conceptions that have come once again to dominate the zeitgeist of Anglo-American psychiatry. Indeed it is only by detaching oneself from such an approach that one can appreciate the potential complexity of the possible interactions or interweavings that can exist between the psychological and biological planes; only thus can one imagine the intricate syntheses that can occur between acts and afflictions, between meanings and causes, between reason and madness.

Before proceeding to my discussion of general issues concerning neurobiological approaches, I would like to mention a number of specific problems that pertain to most of the findings about neurostructural, biochemical, and neuropsychological abnormalities in schizophrenia, which I will not dwell on in the next section. First, and perhaps most important, one should be aware that most of these abnormalities are nonspecific, since they may be equally characteristic (or nearly as characteristic) of certain other chronic or severe mental patients with quite different symptomatology (enlarged cerebral ventricles, poor eye tracking, and poor performance on certain tests of cognitive functioning are also common in patients with affective psychoses, for instance).[35] Second, most of the abnormalities only seem to be present (or prominent) in *subgroups* of the schizophrenic population; according to one estimate, for example, only 20 to 35 percent of schizophrenics show significant evidence of brain impairment.[36] Third, some of the abnormalities seem not to be stable characteristics but to shift over time (this seems true of "hypofrontality"—to be explained shortly—but probably not of enlarged ventricles). Fourth, the abnormalities often have little prognostic value and dubious correlation with symptomatology or with behavioral patterns or cognitive capacities.[37] And fifth, rather than being causes, at least some of these phenomena (for instance, the number of dopamine receptors) may be consequences of treatment with neuroleptic medications or of long-term hospitalization; or they may be associated with factors other than psychiatric status or diagnosis (such as socioeconomic status or educational level, in the case of claims that the brain or the frontal lobes of schizophrenics are slightly diminished in size).[38]

Neuropsychological findings suffer from other problems as well. In studies of cognition it can be difficult to know whether one is observing fundamental incapacities or only the by-products of, say, anxiety, disinterest, lack of motivation, unwillingness to comply with testing, or the distracting effects of delusions and hallucinations.[39] It should also be noted that many of the recent neuropsychological "demonstrations" of the "dementia" of schizophrenic patients have focused only on quantitative scores, without much analysis of the underlying processes that account for the apparent deficits.[40]

The following critique has two parts, roughly corresponding to the two assumptions mentioned at the outset of this appendix. First I consider certain general problems with biological determinism; then I address some specific neurophysiological models and findings, considering their relevance to the notion that schizophrenia involves some kind of lowering of the intellectual or mental level.

GENERAL CRITIQUE OF NEUROBIOLOGICAL REDUCTIONISM

One obvious problem with the traditional reductionistic approach is its dubious practice of dichotomizing modes of understanding: attributing meaning and intentionality to the normal person's experiences while denying them to the schizophrenic's. The notion of a "broken brain" evokes the image of a machine whose damaged state prevents it from serving its intended functions. It is much more likely, in fact, that schizophrenia involves exaggerations or diminutions of normal processes rather than anything so radically distinct.[41] After all, comparisons between schizophrenics and nonschizophrenics—on both psychological and physiological measures—usually show considerable overlapping;[42] indeed, on some tasks the performance of schizophrenics, or of certain subgroups of these patients, can actually surpass that of normal individuals.[43] On what grounds, then, can one justify a stark asymmetry of explanatory principles that tends to ignore the continuity between normal and schizophrenic modes of experience while consigning the latter to an entirely different universe of explanation (a deterministic one)?[44]

A related problem concerns the general assumption of unidirectionality in brain-mind relationships in the psychiatric patient. Most of the empirical findings document only correlations, such as the co-occurrence of certain mental symptoms with over- or underactivation of particular lobes of the brain. This, however, is not the same as demonstrating a linear sequence of events, and often there is no reason (save an a priori assumption of complete biological determinism) to assume that it is always the physiological changes that bring about the mental events rather than the reverse.[45] To be sure, brain-to-mind causal sequences do occur, and probably play an important role in the etiology of many aspects of schizophrenia. But functional changes in patterns of brain activity can also be consequences of mental states, including willful or habitual mental activity of various kinds (known as "downward causation").[46] This has been demonstrated, for instance, by *in vivo* studies of cerebral blood flow,[47] and there is even reason to believe that such functional changes can have long-term structural effects. (It is possible, for example, that inactivity and social withdrawal can result in cerebral atrophy; and it has been demonstrated that neural pathways in the limbic system, for example, in the hippocampus, can be potentiated or enhanced as a result of repeated activation by stressful events.)[48] In this sense one would have to acknowledge that certain attitudes and patterns of behavior—phenomena that must be understood *psychologically* (and that may be socially or culturally determined to a significant extent)—may play an important causal role in determining even some of the *biological* aspects of this multi-faceted illness. The well-known work of the neuroscientist Eric Kandel has shown, for example, how experience—involving something akin to anxiety—can modify patterns of brain functioning even in lower organisms like the snail. Kandel takes this finding to show that discoveries in neurophysiology, if properly understood, are "unlikely to diminish the interest in mentation or to make mentation trivial by reduction"[49]—a statement radically at odds with the reductionistic physicalism espoused by Nancy Andreasen.

Another prejudice inherent in Jacksonian and Kraepelinian approaches is less overt in contemporary psychiatric theory, though it still plays a role in the thought of some biological reductionists. This is the assumption that the significant feature of a disease—"the real and important aberration," as Charles Mercier termed it—is the physiological disorder itself and its direct causal consequences, not the organism's active modes of response *to* this disorder.[50] But we know, of course, that organisms do not just *suffer* organic insults or defects, they always also respond to them—for example, by attempting to compensate for deficiencies and preserve their perhaps fragile identities in changed and difficult circumstances. (This is true even of organic brain syndromes, where the neurological substrate is far more clear-cut and well recognized than is ever likely to be the case with schizophrenia.)[51]

The defensive responses that are evoked may involve various forms of introversion and withdrawal from the environment—motivated by a patient's wish to retreat to a position of safety where various cognitive demands can be avoided; but they may also involve consciously undertaken efforts at coping and problem solving (for instance, concentrating visual attention on a physical object that has special personal significance, muttering or yelling to drown out auditory hallucinations, or avoiding anxiety in interpersonal interaction by reminding oneself that, as one patient said, "it is only a matter of playing a role").[52] Such responses often become habitual and quasi-automatic, and they may eventually come to be tightly interwoven or even interfused with the defects themselves.

The characteristic signs and symptoms associated with the disease entity may, then, be composed as much of certain defensive acts and ingrained reaction patterns as of the underlying biological disorder, even if the latter is, in a linear-causal sense, prior; and so it may be impossible to distinguish what is act (or, at least, what has its origin in intentional or quasi-intentional activity) from what is mere affliction.[53] The cognitive abnormalities so often manifested by schizophrenic patients might well result, for example, from some combination of neurophysiological dysfunctions and introversive withdrawal elicited as a defense. Thus it may be the case that structural or functional disorders of the brain make it difficult to screen out irrelevant stimuli, to direct focal attention toward novel stimuli, to process information in a rapid manner, readily to constitute perceptual Gestalts, or to change principles, mental sets, or frameworks of understanding in a fluent way—to mention but a few hypotheses of cognitive defect proposed in recent years.

It seems plausible that such deficiencies could make a person turn inward toward thought, fantasy, or self-analysis as a way of replacing a wealth and chaos of external stimuli with a more predictable, less anxiety-provoking inner world. (And such inward-turning modes of defensive reaction might be especially likely to occur in persons of schizoid temperament, or perhaps in cultural settings like that of the modern West, which, far from stigmatizing self-involvement, actually provides a rather elaborate technology of inwardness and individual selfhood.) Given that many of the neurophysiological abnormalities and cognitive deficits found in schizophrenia are nonspecific, it could well be the case that it is these secondary or defensive reactions that constitute the more distinctive features of the specifically *schizophrenic* type of psychosis.

It is crucial to realize, however, that such defensive reactions can bring on problems of their own.[54] For example, they can have certain consequences for perceptual and cognitive functioning, consequences suggestive of defect states that may end up by eroding any real sense of psychological security. A passive orientation, for instance, can make one oversensitive to external stimuli, transforming the organized perceptual world of pragmatic appercepion into a welter of meaningless and therefore confusing sensory impingements;[55] it can also make particular stimuli seem to stand out with a peculiar clarity and salience, thus encouraging delusional or quasi-delusional interpretations (of the kind discussed in chapter 2). Even hallucinations have been found more likely to occur in an individual who lapses from an attitude of goal-directed activity (which is why many schizophrenics will busy themselves with routine tasks as a way of controlling their hallucinations and delusions);[56] and cognitive errors of all kinds, as well as a general slowing of reaction time, appear to be associated with higher degrees of introverted reflection.[57]

Some underlying neurophysiological abnormality may well be a *necessary* causal factor in most cases of schizophrenia. It seems, however, that prominent clinical features of many schizophrenic patients (including their inactivity and cognitive errors—so-called negative symptoms—as well as positive symptoms like hallucinations and delusions) may be profoundly affected, at least in their incidence and intensity, by defensive acts involving withdrawal, introversion, and other coping mechanisms.[58] Further, the sudden disappearance of symptoms that can occur even with what seem to be the most dilapidated of schizophrenic patients suggests that irreversible physiological deterioration may be less important than a kind of apathy syndrome.[59]

SPECIFIC CRITIQUE OF NEUROBIOLOGICAL APPROACHES

I have so far been criticizing the general assumption of unidirectional brain-to-mind determinism. But what of the specific neurobiological models that have been offered to account for schizophrenia? Let us suppose that the central signs and symptoms *are* rather direct consequences of neurophysiological abnormalities: Would this necessarily commit one to envisioning the disorder in the traditional way—as involving diminution of rationality, volition, or self-conscious awareness?

I have shown how a number of the best-known neurobiological theories of recent years are in fact very consistent with this traditional (irrationalist) conception of the disorder. These approaches claim to base themselves on the most up-to-date evidence, and they postulate a lowering of the intellectual or mental level—whether through decline into quasi-dementia and concreteness or through release of more primitive neural mechanisms. I would now like to examine these theories more closely, and to do so I need to address both the empirical issue of whether schizophrenic patients really do manifest the brain abnormalities in question and the theoretical or interpretive issue of what, in any event, it would mean for these structural characteristics or functional patterns of brain activation to be present. As we shall see, my emphasis on hyperconsciousness, reflexivity, and alienation is not, in fact, contradicted by the available biological evidence. Indeed there are a number of alternative neurobiological formulations or models—models that are somewhat less well known and that I have not yet mentioned—that actually suggest that the schizophrenic's hyperreflexivity and disengagement could be fairly direct reflections of, rather than reactions to, an underlying neurophysiological abnormality. These alternative hypotheses provide possible solutions to a dilemma articulated early in this century by Karl Jaspers: how to account for a mental disorder that seems likely to have some organic basis, yet that (as he, unlike many others, always remembered) fails to resemble closely any of the paradigmatic cases of organically based mental disorder—with their focal deficiencies of particular cognitive functions (such as memory or aspects of speech) or their general decline of such higher mental capacities as abstraction, reasoning, and volition.[60]

The following discussion of specific neurobiological hypotheses is organized according to the three major axes of brain functioning.

The Anterior-Posterior Dimension

Several studies done in the 1970s found a tendency toward lower levels of cerebral blood flow in the frontal lobes of some schizophrenic patients.[61] Given prevailing assumptions about the prefrontal cortex (its role in subserving the higher faculties of mind), it may seem reasonable to suppose that this functional abnormality, termed *hypofrontality*, might be a key factor in the disease—but this notion can be criticized on both empirical and theoretical grounds.

First, the empirical issues: the original studies found hypofrontality in a sample of older, deteriorated chronic schizophrenics, and this finding has not been consistently replicated with other types of schizophrenic patients. Most investigators have, in fact, found an absence of hypofrontality or even a heightened activation of the frontal lobes in schizophrenics who are unmedicated or in early stages of their illness (within the first two years) or who are manifesting more florid symptoms.[62] Even in more chronic patients the hypofrontal pattern is reversible, and, interestingly enough, seems to disappear during exacerbation of their psychotic experience.[63] While such findings certainly do not rule out the importance of hypofrontality in at least some schizophrenic patients, some phases of the illness, or some situations, they do suggest that this factor is unlikely to play the very general role in schizophrenia it has sometimes been accorded.[64]

Equally important is the question of what psychological significance this neurophysiological pattern would have in those instances where it *is* present. The exact nature of frontal lobe function remains something of a riddle, but many students of the brain would now dispute the traditional understanding of the frontal cortex as the locus of all the higher intellectual and central executive functions.[65] The more sophisticated models in contemporary neuroscience do not envision the anterior-posterior axis as corresponding to a dimension of abstractness versus concreteness, or to a distinction of intellectual versus instinctual and appetitive functions, as was widely held in the nineteenth century.[66] It is now recognized that certain forms of abstract reasoning and logical problem solving tend, in normal individuals, to activate not the frontal but the posterior lobes;[67] and that among the most obvious functions of the frontal lobes are the control of motor responses and the organization, direction, and monitoring of complex action sequences (particularly in connection with the use of external cues). Patients with organic disorders known to involve lesions in the frontal lobes often manifest "a curious dissociation between knowing and doing": though they have the relevant knowledge and understanding, and may even be able to give a verbal definition of the actions that are required, they are unable to *apply* what they know in modifying their behavior.[68] A more accurate characterization of the anterior-posterior axis might therefore emphasize the role of the frontal lobes in the control and monitoring of goal-directed action and that of the posterior lobes in subserving sensory reception and knowing.

Given this conceptualization of the anterior-posterior dimension, a hypofrontal tendency would not best be understood as involving a general lowering of the mental level or the global absence of abstract cognitive processing that Goldstein associated with immersion in practical activity and a concretistic focus on things of use. Instead it would involve some kind of withdrawal from intentional activity or from orientation to the external world, perhaps secondary to a specific defect affecting the control of motor programs[69] (this is consistent with the finding that the patients who manifest the highest degree of hypofrontality also seem to be especially indifferent, mute, and withdrawn).[70] Thus it has been suggested that the pattern of a relative increase of posterior and decrease of anterior activation or metabolism, which is sometimes found in schizophrenic brains, is a sign of *hypo*intentionality and *hyper*gnosia, the latter term implying exaggeration of the perceptual or "knowing" functions.[71] (The important findings of Daniel Weinberger, who has refined the hypofrontality hypothesis by studying performance on particular cognitive tasks, might be understood in this way; see pages 554–56 for a discussion of his work.)[72]

A British psychiatrist writing in 1909 gave a related but more colorful description, speaking of "the contemporaneous existence in one brain of morbid apathy and active, though misguided cerebration."[73] Such a formulation is very consistent with my discussion of how passivization combined with hyperconsciousness may underlie some of the transformations of self and world that occur in this illness. (The schizophrenic patient Jonathan Lang describes this condition exactly, speaking of how "schizophrenes" such as himself tend to withdraw from "sensorimotor activity" and to be dominated, during all their waking hours, by "central-symbolic, particularly verbal activity"; he acknowledges difficulty with "sensory discrimination" and "neuro-muscular coordination" but goes on to criticize studies of concept formation that attempt to describe "the *general* mental level of the schizophrene" on the basis of sensorimotor tests only, arguing that one must also consider the "ideological level" [the level of inner symbolic thought], which "is the most highly developed level in the ideocentric schizophrene.")[74]

The Cortical-Subcortical Dimension

As we have seen, both Nancy Andreasen and Daniel Weinberger adopt a Jacksonian approach to the positive symptoms, hypothesizing a diminution of higher (cortical) and a relative dominance of lower or more primitive neural centers associated with affect and instinct (the subcortical limbic system). But if one considers the full range of available evidence and the most plausible current conceptualizations of brain functioning, this traditional interpretation of the role of cortical and subcortical factors in schizophrenia seems dubious at best.

For one thing, the empirical claim of a decline of cortical activation in schizophrenia is far from established. Indeed there is reason to suspect that schizophrenia, at least in its florid phases, may often be accompanied by an *over*activation of the cortical area (a fact consistent with the apparent hyperactivity of thinking in certain phases of the illness).[75] Evidence concerning structural abnormalities of the brain also fails to be consistent with the Jacksonian model, which predicts that such lesions would be concentrated in the "higher," or cortical, areas. In fact, both postmortem and *in vivo* brain-imaging studies of schizophrenia indicate that structural alterations of the brain are most common not in cortical but in subcortical areas, primarily in the part of the limbic system that includes the hippocampal formation (part of the medial temporal lobe).[76] (Many schizophrenics appear to have smaller hippocampi or disordered hippocampal neurons.)[77] And patients with organic brain disorders who are known to have lesions in the limbic system do not, in most instances, tend to embody the irrationalist model of insanity, that is, to manifest prominent intellectual deficits or predominance of primitive and automatic modes of functioning; more striking are qualities of depersonalization and various distortions of perception and emotion (and, at times, certain behavioral automatisms, for example, with temporal-lobe epilepsy patients). This is illustrated by one patient from whom part of the limbic system, including most of the hippocampus, had been removed: he seemed to have lost the capacity for the spontaneous experience and expression of emotion, and as a consequence would address his parents as "sir" and "madam."[78]

Structural abnormalities of the limbic system, especially of the hippocampus and closely related structures in the temporal lobe, are, in fact, the most robust of recent findings on the neurobiology of schizophrenia. In addition, there are indications of increased activation of these areas, at least at certain early or symptomatically productive phases of the illness.[79] What implications these physiological characteristics might have for lived experience or psychological functioning are rather unclear, however, partly because of the exceptionally mysterious nature of the hippocampus—a part of the brain that could, at least until very recently, be described as a "riddle inside an enigma" and as the "black hole" of neurology.[80] The limbic system is now widely recognized as serving a variety of functions that transcend previous conceptualizations of it as a "nose brain" involved primarily in primitive or lower processes.[81]

It now seems likely that parts of the limbic system, such as the hippocampus, actually play an important—though hard-to-specify—role in sophisticated cognitive functions, even when these are not emotionally colored.[82] (The temporal-hippocampal system is frequently linked to memory functions.[83] Some recent models are more specific, ascribing to the hippocampus and related structures a so-called comparator function, which involves the building up of internalized models of expected environmental inputs—a process that, in all likelihood, would involve a complex interplay of action plans, perception, and decision-making processes, and that would allow for the registering of novel or unexpected perceptual stimuli as well as for the inhibiting of attention to very common stimuli. The hippocampus is sometimes also viewed as carrying out "internal monitoring of willed intentions.")[84] A recent article on the neurobiology and psychology of schizophrenia suggests, for example, that dysfunction of this system could lead to a kind of "over-attention" or hypervigilance (probably mediated by heightened effect of dopamine transmission) in which even familiar stimuli are treated as significant, or could result in a failure to "mediate the transition from controlled to automatic processing"; as a consequence cognitive activity would have to "proceed at the level of consciously controlled sequential processing." This could lead to the development of a kind of delusional mood (akin to the Apophany described in chapter 2) or to the dysfunctional hyper-awareness and deliberateness sometimes found in schizophrenic patients.[85]

In the light of such functions, it is obvious that the limbic system cannot be thought of as a kind of neurobiological equivalent of the Freudian id. And it follows that an overactivation (or other dysfunction) of this system need not necessarily be imagined (as Andreasen and Weinberger are inclined to do, following Jackson) as causing a welling up of forgotten memories and uncontrolled emotions or an overflow of primitive urges from the lower depths. Various neurobiologists suggest, rather, that activation of the hippocampal system might have, as its primary effect, the generation of anxiety in the face of pragmatic uncertainty and a consequent inhibition of motor activity. Indeed one neuroscientist describes the hippocampus as "an organ of hesitation and doubt."[86] It is therefore possible that the limbic hyperactivation that often occurs in early stages of schizophrenia should be conceived of as the neurological correlate not of overwhelming instinctual forces but of the anxiety-ridden vacillation and paralysis described in earlier chapters.[87]

The Laterality Hypothesis

The third dimension of relevance in the study of the schizophrenic brain is the lateral axis, and here the most common position is the hypothesis of weakness or dysfunction of the left hemisphere.[88]

Until fairly recently the left hemisphere, which is specialized for language, abstract symbolic thinking, and detailed and analytic modes of cognition, received virtually the entire attention of neurologists and neuropsychologists.[89] It is usually described as the dominant hemisphere, its particular specialization being considered a more recent development in the evolution of the brain. Ever since the discovery of brain lateralization in the nineteenth century, it has tended to be viewed as the true seat of consciousness and rationality, of "the executive conscious self" (it is the *cogito* of Descartes's famous *Cogito ergo sum*, as one psychiatrist puts it).[90] This is apparent in the contemporary neuroscientist Michael Gazzaniga's conception of what he calls the "interpreter," a function he locates on the left side of the brain. Gazzaniga describes this "interpreter" function as constituting the true uniqueness of the human brain and as the source of self-consciousness, freedom, and rationality—the capacities that have defined human nature since the Enlightenment.[91] (The "minor" hemisphere, by contrast, is often assumed to be capable only of consciousness of the environment, not of that superior function: *self*-consciousness.)[92] The hypothesis of left-hemisphere dysfunction is, then, in perfect accord with traditional conceptions of schizophrenia as a form of irrationality, for it postulates deficits in the higher and more advanced faculties of mind.[93]

In recent years this hypothesis has been subjected to a number of telling criticisms by theorists who argue that it is not in fact the most plausible way of accounting for the most characteristic features of schizophrenic pathology. Instead of a primary dysfunction of the left hemisphere, these theorists hypothesize one of three possibilities: a dysfunction (or state of underactivation) primarily located in the *right* brain; an overactivation of the left hemisphere or a propensity to overrely on this hemisphere in cognitive processing; or some combination of the two.

The strongest evidence for the first hypothesis is the pattern of cognitive abnormalities typically found in schizophrenia, as these most closely resemble those manifested by organic patients known to have right-brain damage.[94] The right hemisphere is specialized for imagistic, holistic, synthetic, and visual-spatial modes of knowing, and thus for Gestalt or intuitive processing; it is dominant in the recognition of the human face, in processing emotional cues, and in the maintenance of involuntary attention (preattentive processing)—all functions that tend to be compromised in schizophrenia. In children neurological and neuropsychological evidence of right-hemisphere deficits has been found to be associated with solitariness, "weirdness," and with difficulties in emotional expression and interpersonal relationships.[95] The effect of right-hemisphere damage on linguistic functions presents a particularly striking parallel: like schizophrenics, patients with such lesions generally retain the basic skills pertaining to phonological, syntactic, and semantic aspects of language (which seem to be localized primarily in the left brain), yet they show disturbance of pragmatic or discourse elements—that is, of the ability to understand context, tone, and presuppositions, and thus to grasp the overall interpersonal intent of a conversation.[96]

Like schizophrenics, patients with known right-hemisphere damage often have delusions that seem to be based on the loss of a sense of the reality or uniqueness of an event (an organic patient who had served in World War I remarked: "It is not a real war, but merely an experimental war [*une guerre d'expérience*]").[97] Such patients also resemble schizophrenics in their tendency to lack a capacity best described as common sense, and they often fail to register the farfetched nature of certain possibilities, treating these no differently than far more plausible possibilities.[98] They also seem to have in common a general inability to take context into account or to deal with larger synthetic wholes.[99] One neuroscientist suggests that the most basic function of the right hemisphere is to perceive context and thereby to provide a framework or grounding within which the more focal (and consciously intentional) left-hemisphere processing can take place; hence he speaks of the right hemisphere's "stabilizing, coherence-giving, framework-building role."[100]

If understood in these terms, a dysfunction (or underactivation) of the right hemisphere would certainly be consistent with the absence of an enduring sense of context or a guiding framework of reference in many schizo-phrenic patients. (Recall the cognitive phenomena discussed in chapter 4 and the linguistic anomalies discussed in chapter 6, which I compared to Derridean deconstructionist doctrines about infinite ambiguity and to Derrida's inciting of an uncontrolled proliferation of contexts of understanding.) Whereas left-hemisphere syndromes often involve disturbances of fairly circumscribed cognitive capacities that are fairly easy to imagine or describe, those of the right seem more diffuse and in some sense more basic; to the normal person the inner state of such patients may therefore seem unimag-inably remote and alien.[101]

We see, then, that a right-hemisphere hypothesis can account for many distinctive qualities of schizophrenic consciousness and expression. How-ever, it is by no means obvious that it can explain *all* of them—especially certain abnormalities that have figured prominently as evidence in favor of the left-hemisphere hypothesis (such as a certain inefficiency or slowness in processing information presented to the perceptual fields controlled by the left hemisphere, and certain abnormalities of language and thought that do seem suggestive of left-brain dysfunction). But postulating a primary and predominant dysfunction on the left side is not the only possible—and per-haps not the most plausible—way of accounting for these latter findings.[102]

It has been suggested that these errors might result not from *primary* dysfunction of the left hemisphere but from abnormalities of cognitive pro-cessing that are secondary to *overactivation* of this side of the brain (the second hypothesis).[103] Such overactivation could load the left hemisphere beyond its normal capacity, thereby filling up all the available "cerebral space" and leading to disturbed performance on the tasks for which this hemisphere is usually dominant. Research on cerebral metabolism has in fact shown, with a fair degree of consistency, that schizophrenics (and also schiz-oids)[104] do tend to overactivate the left hemisphere and to rely on it in circumstances in which it would be more usual to activate the right. (Inter-estingly, symptom severity has been found to correlate with left-hemisphere activation, and one of the effects of neuroleptic drugs is to correct this imbalance or bias.)[105] Though explanations for this imbalance are necessar-ily speculative, it is possible that the left-hemisphere overactivation is a secondary consequence of a dysfunction in the right hemisphere, since such a dysfunction could lead to compensatory overactivation of the contralateral area of the brain (a well-recognized tendency).[106] The left-hemisphere bias could also be an independent phenomenon.

The cognitive style of many schizophrenics is consistent with the hypothe-sis of an overly dominant left and/or a weak right hemisphere. They will often adopt a particularistic, overintellectualized, and deliberate approach, relying on piecemeal, decontextualized analysis rather than intuitive, spon-taneous, or global modes of response.[107] "My intellectual parts became the whole of me," said one schizophrenic man (Rosser's patient).[108] Another schizophrenic (Carl) attempted to understand how to interact socially by scrutinizing the details of other people's behavior, as if he were some kind of anthropologist; he wanted to encode the steps involved in making friends and to devise "new schemata" for relationships on his hospital ward, and he spoke of becoming a more efficient "communications machine." Eugene Minkowski describes one schizophrenic man who " 'parades' each word before his principles to make sure that he says only useful things" (he soon comes to the point of saying nothing at all), and another patient who claims that "everything in life, even sexual sensations, are reducible to mathematics."[109] Such examples may well exemplify what the authors of one article describe as a typically schizophrenic tendency to "use the cerebral hemisphere specialized for deductive and logical modes of thought (i.e., the left) when initiating thought that normally requires holistic and spatial processing (i.e., the right)."[110] Another feature of schizophrenia consistent with this hypothesis is the prominence in such patients of delusions involving self-reference (given that it is the left hemisphere that is capable of self-awareness).[111]

The hypothesis of an overactive left hemisphere certainly has very different implications than does the hypothesis of a simple left-hemisphere dysfunction or weakness, for it postulates an exaggeration of the very forms of cognition—intellectual, abstract, and reflexive modes—whose diminution was once taken to be virtually definitive of insanity. The surprising implications of such a neurobiological hypothesis emerge with special clarity when we recall Gazzaniga's concept of the interpreter in the context of Jacksonian neurology. In Jackson's view, there is something lawlike about the effect of lesions of the cerebral nervous system; and this law (which applies to insanity) is "that parts suffer more as they serve in voluntary, and less as they serve in automatic operations." He defines voluntary actions as involving greater self-awareness, since they are "preconceived" or "represented in consciousness."[112] But if left-hemisphere overactivation results in greater activation of those functions that constitute the "interpreter," wouldn't this imply an increase of all that is volitional and self-aware in human functioning? And doesn't this suggest a possibility almost unthinkable within the classical framework: that brain abnormalities could be associated with *exaggeration* of the higher mental functions and, in particular, with exacerbation of rational tendencies and of self-consciousness—even perhaps of freedom itself?

Having made this suggestion, however, I must immediately acknowledge the ways it may be misleading. To state, at least without serious qualification and elaboration, that schizophrenics are more rational, free, or self-aware than normal people would, after all, require that one ignore all the paradoxes discussed in this book—all the ways schizophrenic hyperreflexivity can undermine itself, leading to paralysis or confusion. It would also mean forgetting that the true exercise of freedom and rationality (at least as we normally use these terms) relies on the smooth operation of many forms of nonconscious mentation and of spontaneous or automatic behavior, all of which are likely to be disrupted in schizophrenia. (This disruption could be understood as resulting from the failure of right-brain processes to provide a normal sense of grounding or context—whether because of defects intrinsic to that hemisphere or because of an inappropriate reliance on the hyperconscious, hyperintentional left hemisphere; it could also be understood in other ways—for instance, as a disturbance of the "comparator" function located in the hippocampus and related structures.) Still, such a hypothesis is heuristically useful, because it opens to us a possibility that is too often ignored: that neurophysiological abnormalities might be associated less with deficits of "higher" and volitional processes than with overreliance on them, or with disturbance of those "lower" and more automatic processes that normally allow for spontaneity while providing a sense of natural embeddedness in the practical and social world. Perhaps these latter disturbances can account for the lack of a sense of syntony, the disharmony in the relationship both to self and world that is central to the schizoid disposition and that (according to Kretschmer and Eugen Bleuler, among others) may lie at the root of many cases of schizophrenic psychosis. (For other ways of understanding this characteristic lack of syntony, consider the views of C. D. Frith and Philip Holzman; see pages 473–76.)

In conclusion, then, we see that recent neurobiological research does not necessarily indicate regression, instinct domination, or a decline of rational factors. The evidence is at least as compatible with models postulating hyperconsciousness, a loss of the normal sense of spontaneity or embeddedness, or even a kind of hypertrophied rationality. Even if one were to accept something closer to the traditional models of the neurophysiology of schizophrenia (Weinberger's, for instance), it would still not follow that the entire disease, including its psychological aspects, has to be seen as a mere deficit or epiphenomenon of brain events.

It should not be thought, of course, that the key to explaining schizophrenia must necessarily be contained in but one such explanatory theory. Indeed it is likely that schizophrenia is a heterogeneous illness, and in at least two different ways. First, it is probably not a disease entity in which all cases have the same etiology, but more of a final common pathway to which a variety of different causal factors may lead; in this sense, two or more of the above-mentioned theories could be true, each applying to a different subgroup of patients. For example, the salient symptoms of some schizophrenic patients could be, in large part, direct manifestations of underlying brain dysfunctions, whereas those of other schizophrenics might be composed largely of psychological reactions of various kinds; and, of course, many other permutations are also possible.[113] Second, the various biological pathways are not incompatible with one another: that is, a given patient could well have, say, *both* a left-hemisphere bias and a dysfunction of the septohippocampal system or, perhaps, some combination of hypofrontal tendencies and hippocampal abnormalities. The brain, after all, is a complex of interacting systems. We must remember that our models are really only artificial abstractions, likely to give the misleading impression that what exists is a set of clearly demarcated and separable modules.[114]

The causal picture would, of course, become even more complicated if one were to take up an issue I have not even attempted to broach here: what *brings about* the purported biological abnormalities—whether, for example, they derive from genetic predispositions, from trauma or infection, or perhaps from developmental anomalies of various kinds.[115] Things would become still more complicated if one attempted to factor in the possible role in the causation of schizophrenia of the social or cultural phenomena discussed in the epilogue. Not only could the sociocultural factors operate in numerous ways; they could also interact variously with neurophysiological factors, both functional and structural, of many different kinds.

We are far from having a full understanding of the neurobiology of schizophrenia, or of its interconnections with either consciousness or culture. But two general implications are clear: the projects of neurobiological explanation and phenomenological interpretation are by no means incompatible; and brain abnormalities need not be associated with a lowering of mental level, a decline of those fundamental tendencies of mind that have long been considered to define the human essence.

NOTES

. . . .

Prologue: The Sleep of Reason

1. John Haslam, *Observations on Madness and Melancholy,* 1810; excerpt in V. Skultans, *Madness and Morals: Ideas on Insanity in the Nineteenth Century* (London and Boston: Routledge and Kegan Paul, 1975), p. 31.
2. In his book *Rationality* ([London: Routledge and Kegan Paul, 1964], p. 5), the philosopher J. Bennett uses *rationality* to mean "whatever it is that humans possess which marks them off, in respect of intellectual capacities, sharply and importantly from all other known species."
3. The words are those of the physician John Monro, 1758; quoted in A. Scull, "Moral treatment reconsidered," in A. Scull, ed., *Madhouses, Mad-Doctors, and Madmen: The Social History of Psychiatry in the Victorian Era* (Philadelphia: University of Pennsylvania Press, 1981), p. 109.
4. See C. H. Kahn, *The Art and Thought of Heraclitus* (Cambridge: Cambridge University Press, 1979), p. 77; and P. Edwards, ed., *Encyclopedia of Philosophy,* vol. 7 (New York: Macmillan, 1967), p. 479.
5. W. F. Bynum describes the medical literature before the nineteenth century as putting "almost exclusive emphasis on disturbances of *reason,* or the highest intellectual faculties of man. Insanity was conceived as a derangement of those very faculties that were widely assumed to be unique to man" ("Rationales for therapy in British psychiatry, 1780–1835," in Scull, *Madhouses, Mad-Doctors, and Madmen,* p. 39). As the alienist Joseph Cox wrote in 1813: "If the possession of reason be the proud attribute of humanity, its diseases must be ranked among our greatest afflictions, since they sink us from our preeminence to a level with the animal creatures" (quoted in A. Scull, *Museums of Madness* [London: Allen Lane, 1979], p. 64). The equation of the unreasonable with the irrational is made explicit by the authors of *Chronic Schizophrenia,* a psychoanalytic study, who equate "reality-break" with "dementia": " . . . of course there is an inverse relationship between the degree of dementia or reality-break and the degree of secondary process thought available" (T. Freeman, J. L. Cameron, A. McGhie,

onic Schizophrenia [New York: International Universities Press, 1958], p. 1).

The change in the definition of a so-called bizarre delusion, which occurred between the two most recent versions (3rd ed. and 3rd ed., rev.) of the American Psychiatric Association's *Diagnostic and Statistical Manual of Mental Disorders* (Washington, DC: American Psychiatric Press, 1980, 1987), could be described as a shift from a concept of irrationality to one of mere unreasonableness. Whereas DSM III spoke of "content which is patently absurd and has no possible basis in fact" (p. 356), DSM III-R refers to "a phenomenon that the person's culture would regard as totally implausible" (p. 395). This change in definition was motivated primarily by a recognition of difficulties in operationalizing the earlier concept; see K. S. Kendler, R. L. Spitzer, and J. B. W. Williams, "Psychotic disorders in DSM-III-R," *American Journal of Psychiatry, 146,* 1989, 953–62. But it does not, I think, indicate any major change in the mainstream conception of schizophrenia as a form of irrationality.

6. K. Jaspers, *General Psychopathology,* trans. J. Hoenig and M. W. Hamilton (Chicago: University of Chicago Press, 1963), p. 8.

7. L. Wittgenstein, *Philosophical Investigations,* trans. G. E. M. Anscombe (Oxford: Basil Blackwell, 1953), p. 48.

8. Quoted in M. Foucault, *Madness and Civilization: A History of Insanity in the Age of Reason* (New York and Toronto: New American Library, 1965), p. 40.

9. Quoted in G. Rosen, *Madness in Society* (New York and Evanston: Harper and Row, 1968), pp. 89–90. In the ancient world the insane person was considered to be "blind to the 'logos' " and unable to "administrate himself"; and to be "always a man who does not know, an ignorant" (quoted in G. Roccatagliata, *A History of Ancient Psychiatry* [New York: Greenwood Press, 1986], pp. 230, 53).

10. Quoted in Foucault, *Madness and Civilization,* p. 77.

11. Plato imagines how "lusts, amid clouds of incense and perfume and garlands and wines, and all the pleasures of a dissolute life, now let loose, come buzzing around," dissolving any sense of shame and "nourishing to the utmost the sting of desire" (*The Republic,* Book 9, in *The Dialogues of Plato,* vol. 1, trans. B. Jowett [New York: Random House, 1937], pp. 830–31). Re ancient psychiatry in general, see Roccatagliata, *A History of Ancient Psychiatry.*

12. Nineteenth-century views are discussed in M. J. Clark, "The rejection of psychological approaches to mental disorder in late nineteenth-century British psychiatry," in Scull, *Madhouses, Mad-Doctors, and Madmen,* 271–312. See the appendix for further discussion.

13. H. Deutsch, "Some forms of emotional disturbance and their relationship to schizophrenia," *Psychoanalytic Quarterly, 11,* 1942, 321.

14. "Find out all about dreams and you will have found out all about insanity," wrote Hughlings Jackson (quoted in S. Freud, *The Interpretation of Dreams,* trans. J. Strachey [New York: Avon Books, 1965; first published in 1900], p. 608n). Freud called dreams "our normal psychosis"—having "all the absurdities, delusions and illusions of a psychosis" (*An Outline of Psychoanalysis* [New York: Norton, 1949], p. 61). See *The Interpretation of Dreams,* pp. 606–8, re the similarity of dreams, psychosis, and infantile mental life; pp. 119–124 re the literature on "The relations between dreams and mental diseases."

15. Coleridge is one of many who have expressed this idea; he spoke of madness as

"the sleep of the spirit with certain conditions of wakefulness . . . lower or bestial states rise up into action or prominence" (in Skultans, *Madness and Morals*, p. 17). Some of the most influential of recent neurobiological accounts offer an analogous interpretation, viewing schizophrenia as resulting from defects of the (higher) prefrontal cortex, which allow release of the more emotional and archaic processes characteristic of the normally suppressed limbic system; see appendix.

16. Nietzsche bemoaned the state of normal human beings, those semianimals unhinged from instinct and "no longer (able to) count on the guidance of their unconscious drives," being forced instead "to think, deduce, calculate, weigh cause and effect—unhappy people, reduced to their weakest, most fallible organ, their consciousness!" (*The Genealogy of Morals* [and *The Birth of Tragedy*], trans. F. Golffing [Garden City, NY: Doubleday, 1956], p. 217). The epigraph from Nietzsche that appears at the beginning of this book is quoted in E. Kahler, *The Disintegration of Form in the Arts* (New York: Braziller, 1968), p. 34.

17. Norman O. Brown, *Love's Body* (New York: Vintage Books, 1966), p. 142.

18. I am quoting from my memory of the filmed version of *Suddenly Last Summer*.

19. Nietzsche, *Birth of Tragedy*, p. 23.

20. F. Dostoevsky, *Notes from Underground* and *The Grand Inquisitor*, trans. R. E. Matlaw (New York: Dutton, 1960), p. 6.

21. If the madman is thought of as wise, his wisdom will be conceived either as naive or as feral: the innocence of the child who sees without the blinders of prejudice and convention, or the almost preternatural acuteness of lower creatures still at one with the rhythms of nature.

22. See T. Ziolkowski, *German Romanticism and Its Institutions* (Princeton, NJ: Princeton University Press, 1990), pp. 167, 176, 184, 187, 193, 201, 205, 210–12; T. Ziolkowski, *Dimensions of the Modern Novel* (Princeton, NJ: Princeton University Press, 1969), pp. 346–47; D. Gascoyne, *Hölderlin's Madness* (London: Dent, 1938), pp. 8–13; E. Faas, *Retreat into the Mind: Victorian Poetry and the Rise of Psychiatry* (Princeton, NJ: Princeton University Press, 1988), pp. 60–61. Re Baudelaire's view of madness as a "folie lucide," see P. de Man, *Blindness and Insight* (Minneapolis: University of Minnesota Press, 1983), p. 216.

It should be noted, however, that while overcivilization and excessive cerebration were sometimes seen as *causing* madness, in many instances the madness that supposedly resulted was still viewed as a lowering of the mental level (resulting, for example, from fatigue or deterioration of cognitive-intellectual faculties subjected to too much wear and tear); see M. Altschule, "The concept of civilization as a social evil in the writings of mid-nineteenth-century psychiatrists," *Roots of Modern Psychiatry*, 2nd ed. (New York and London: Grune and Stratton, 1965), pp. 119–39. See also H. Maudsley, "The growth of civilization and insanity," (1879), excerpt in V. Skultans, *Madness and Morals*, 64–70; and Rosen, *Madness in Society*, pp. 182–94.

See also M. J. Clark, " 'Morbid introspection,' unsoundness of mind, and British psychological medicine, c. 1830–c. 1900," in W. F. Bynum, R. Porter, and M. Shepherd, eds., *The Anatomy of Madness: Essays in the History of Psychiatry*, vol. 3, *The Asylum and Its Psychiatry* (London and New York: Routledge, 1988), pp. 71–101. Clark discusses mid- and late-nineteenth-century views of madness as related to "morbid introspection" ("the too frequent and earnest direction of the mind inwards upon itself," as Sir Henry Holland put it in 1839 [p. 71]) and to "absorption in purely 'subjective' states of consciousness" [p. 72]). These notions did not necessarily contradict the traditional association of madness with loss of reason and self-control and with dominance by the passions, however (see pp. 72, 74–75; the self-absorption was often conceived of as a kind of excessive indulgence in imagination (as opposed to reason), and as a giving oneself over to dominant and automatized trains of thought (pp. 76–77), and as being allied with "undue prominence of feelings as uncontrolled by intellect" (p. 82, re hysteria) or with indulgence in "drink, sex and drugs" or the "solitary" and "injurious vice" of masturbation (pp. 84, 87). The movement inward, away from society and the objective world, was assumed to be "evolutionarily regressive"—a movement backward to an unsocialized state and downward toward instinct and the body (pp. 90, 84, 74–75). Also of interest, however, are the views of Henry Maudsley, who (along with other writers of the time) came to adopt a view of healthy psychological functioning as an acting "from instinct without need of reason" and as a return to the paradise preceding the "forbidden fruit" of consciousness (pp. 91–92) (a view reminiscent of Heinrich Kleist's essay "On the puppet theatre," quoted on pp. 342–43 of this book).

It should also be noted that the ancient Greeks believed that *excluding* the Dionysian could sometimes cause madness; however, the madness that was supposed to result from this exclusion presumably took the form of possession *by* Dionysus; see B. Simon, *Mind and Madness in Ancient Greece* (Ithaca and London: Cornell University Press, 1978), p. 149.

23. See E. Minkowski, *La Schizophrénie* (Paris: Payot, 1927); and R. D. Laing, *The Divided Self* (Harmondsworth, UK: Penguin Books, 1965).

24. It is interesting to note that R. D. Laing, whose first and best book, *The Divided Self*, developed such a thesis (under the influence of E. Minkowski and J.-P. Sartre), soon lapsed back, in *The Politics of Experience* ([New York: Ballantine Books, 1967], see pp. 126, 167), into a variant of the more popular romantic vision.

25. I am referring to the diffuse brain syndromes and those affecting primarily the left hemisphere. Re the past tendency to focus on these conditions, and for discussions of other forms of brain damage or disease, see J. Cutting, *The Right Cerebral Hemisphere and Psychiatric Disorders* (Oxford: Oxford University Press, 1990); and O. Sacks, *The Man Who Mistook His Wife for a Hat* (New York: Summit Books, 1985), pp. 1–5.

26. D. P. Schreber, *Memoirs of My Nervous Illness*, trans. I. Macalpine and R. A. Hunter (Cambridge: Harvard University Press, 1988; originally published in German in 1903), p. 117n. Nerval quoted in Jaspers, *General Psychopathology*, p. 115. Jaspers considers Nerval to have been schizophrenic. Given the presence of some significant affective symptoms, however, Nerval might have been "schizoaffective"—which would still put him in the "schizophrenia spectrum."

27. See Foucault, *Madness and Civilization*, pp. 90–98.

28. Jaspers, *General Psychopathology*, pp. 284, 115. Also see E. Bleuler (*Dementia Praecox, or the Group of Schizophrenias*, trans. J. Zinkin [New York: International Universities Press, 1950], p. 67) re the "very common preoccupation of young hebephrenics (a subtype of schizophrenia) with the 'deepest questions' "; Bleuler characterizes this—rather dismissively—as "nothing but an autistic manifestation." Because of the profound threats to the very sense of being that they experience, schizophrenics, according to one biological psychiatrist, are "the

world's experts on the existential crises of humanity," and their utterances are "laden to overflowing with profound philosophical queries" (S. Snyder, *Madness and the Brain* [New York: McGraw-Hill, 1974], p. 5).

29. Jaspers, *General Psychopathology*, p. 116. "Explanation of chaos": said by the patient Henry.

30. Claude Lévi-Strauss has written of the scholar who tries to make the people he studies as different as possible, "as though he were seeking, consciously or unconsciously, and under the guise of scientific objectivity, to make the latter—whether mental patients or so-called 'primitives'—more *different* than they really are" (*Totemism*, trans. R. Needham [Boston: Beacon Press, 1963], p. 1).

31. Patient quoted in Jaspers, *General Psychopathology*, pp. 579–80.

32. Freud, *Interpretation of Dreams*, see pp. 87–89, 607.

33. Hans Sedlmayr, *Art in Crisis: The Lost Center* (Chicago: Henry Regnery, 1958), p. 180. This is a characteristic not found in earlier periods, according to Sedlmayr.

34. I recognize that there is diversity among the types of art that have been called "modernist." Though I consider the themes and works I mention to be exemplary of the major, if not the only, general stylistic trends of "modernism," it is not really crucial to my interpretation of schizophrenia that this should be the case. What is important is that the modernist examples I *have* chosen *do* manifest the qualities I describe, and that they can therefore be used to illuminate the schizophrenic and schizoid phenomena in the way that I claim.

35. H. Rosenberg, *Act and the Actor: Making the Self* (Chicago: University of Chicago Press, 1970/1983), p. 9.

36. Kafka's diary, January 16, 1922, quoted in A. Heidsieck, "Kafka's narrative ontology," *Philosophy and Literature*, 11, 1987, 250.

37. Quoted in R. Monk, *Ludwig Wittgenstein: The Duty of Genius* (New York: Free Press, 1990), p. 451.

38. It should perhaps be said that I use the term *phenomenology* in the Continental sense, to refer to the study of experience or the lived world; not in the sense of Anglo-American psychiatry, where it refers to the study of observable or readily identifiable signs and symptoms of mental disorders.

39. Schizophrenia is a fairly common form of psychosis, and it has come to be considered the quintessential manifestation of insanity—the "madness par excellence" or "madness proper" of our age. Far from being neglected, it has been psychiatry's primary preoccupation since around the turn of the twentieth century. Given these facts, would one not expect that more psychologists and psychiatrists would have become dissatisfied with the traditional models? If my alternative portrait of this illness is even approximately correct, why haven't more of them tried to offer some kind of radically different picture?

The best answer, it seems to me, is to recognize the tremendous influence on theorizing likely to be exerted by a conjunction of certain general propensities of human understanding and certain facts of language and intellectual history. I am thinking, first, of the deep-seated human tendency to think in terms of essences and antitheses, and second, of the traditional, rationalist vision of human nature that has been so dominant in the West. Some of the things insane people do or say are liable (virtually by definition) to seem strange and unreasonable to us, and to strain our ability to understand, empathize, or feel we share a common humanity. It is natural enough to assume that such a person somehow lacks that quality we accept as most definitive of our own nature—rationality; for, whenever we find something unreasonable, we are prone to assume it must be based on something other than reason—hence our theories postulating a decline or an overwhelming of volition, logic, and self-consciousness, qualities that are assumed to constitute the human essence.

I offer a second answer only very tentatively, since it depends on an unproven, perhaps unprovable hypothesis: namely, that schizophrenia may in fact be a modern illness in some actual historical sense—something quite rare before, say, around 1800 (re this possibility, see the epilogue). If this were the case, it might help to explain why we have been slow to develop an accurate grasp of this condition: the main forms of psychosis that existed prior to 1800 may have conformed more readily to the traditional models of irrationality and excessive passion; as a result, these models may have sunk deeply into our collective modes of understanding, and a certain intellectual inertia could then explain why a new form of illness should continue to be understood in accordance with models that *were* fairly adequate and accurate for most of the past two and a half millennia.

40. Dr. Basil Reeve, paraphrased in Monk, *Ludwig Wittgenstein*, p. 451.
41. Quoted in C. Geertz, *Local Knowledge* (New York: Basic Books, 1983), p. 24.
42. Nietzsche speaks of Dionysian "paroxysm[s] of lust and cruelty" in which "all the . . . walls . . . between men are shattered" and there is a "sink[ing] back into original oneness with nature." In the Dionysian festivals of ancient Greece, he writes, it was "as though nature were bemoaning the fact of her fragmentation, her decomposition into separate individuals" (*The Birth of Tragedy*, pp. 23–27). By contrast, Apollo—the god of higher civilization, and of brightness, form, clarity, contemplation, and restraint—is "the apotheosis of the *principium individuationis*," who, as "a moral deity . . . demands self-control from his people and, in order to observe such self-control, a knowledge of self" (pp. 33–34). The "brand-new daemon called Socrates" (p. 77) seems to represent for Nietzsche an exaggeration and perversion of the Apollonian tendency, which "now appears disguised as logical schematism" (p. 88). Socrates is portrayed as the bringer of "dubious enlightenment" (p. 82) to what had been a healthier and more spontaneous Greek civilization. Socrates is thus the "great exemplar of . . . *theoretical man*" (p. 92), who is sustained by the "deep-seated illusion . . . that thought . . . might plumb the farthest abysses of being and even *correct* it" (p. 93); he is the "perfect pattern of the *non-mystic*" (p. 85), whose "great Cyclops' eye . . . never glowed with the artist's divine frenzy" (p. 86) since he always preferred "logical schematism" to either beauty or passion. For discussion of these issues, see M. S. Silk and J. P. Stern, *Nietzsche on Tragedy* (Cambridge: Cambridge University Press, 1981); and A. Megill, *Prophets of Extremity: Nietzsche, Heidegger, Foucault, Derrida* (Berkeley: University of California Press, 1985), pp. 38–42, 54–58, 213–19, and passim.
43. C. Geertz, *The Interpretation of Cultures* (New York: Basic Books, 1973), p. 145.
44. As Jaspers notes, "Phenomenology has nothing to do with the genesis of psychic phenomena. Though its practice is a prerequisite for any causal investigation [one must know *what* one is seeking the cause *of*] it leaves genetic issues aside, and they can neither refute nor further its findings" ("The phenomenological approach in psychopathology," *British Journal of Psychiatry*, 114, 1968, 1322).

I would dispute only certain *reductionistic* interpretations of biological factors, those that would minimize or deny the role of intentional factors or the importance or possibility of phenomenological investigation; see the appendix for a discussion of these issues.

45. E. Heller, *The Disinherited Mind* (New York and London: Harcourt Brace Jovanovich, 1975), p. 188.

46. To deny that schizophrenic consciousness is childlike in nature is not, however, to deny that early experiences or events might play a significant causal role in the *etiology* of this condition. Psychological trauma could, for example, initiate abnormalities of psychological structure or orientation, or could elicit patterns of psychological defense (such as withdrawal from what is felt to be a threatening environment) that become transformed and compounded over the subsequent course of development; or else neurological insult or hormonal imbalance suffered in infancy could introduce neuropsychological abnormalities that may become evident only much later in life.

47. That schizophrenia is a heterogeneous disease is a widely, but not universally, accepted view today, though there is little consensus on how to divide it up into subtypes. Irving Gottesman is one expert who views schizophrenia as "at its core, *essentially* one entity, one clearly definable mental disorder that must be studied in unity along the whole continuum of its manifestations" (*Schizophrenia Genesis: The Origins of Madness* [New York: Freeman, 1991], p. 20).

48. Weber was well aware of the idealized nature of the ideal type—which he described as being "formed by the one-sided accentuation of one or more points of view and by the synthesis of a great many diffuse, discrete, more or less present, and occasionally absent concrete individual phenomena, which are arranged according to those one-sidedly emphasized viewpoints into a unified thought-construct" (M. Weber, *The Methodology of the Social Sciences* [New York: Free Press, 1949], p. 90). In his opinion, any attempt to grasp as complex and ambiguous a phenomenon as, say, the "spirit of Capitalism" would best succeed if it depicted only a selected portion of the phenomenon, and if it regarded its object from a single point of view. Re the relevance of Weber's ideal-type notion for psychiatric diagnosis and the understanding of psychopathology, see O. P. Wiggins and M. A. Schwartz, "Research into personality disorders: The alternatives of dimensions and ideal types," *Journal of Personality Disorders*, 5, 1991, 69–81.

To describe an ideal type is, of course, not just to characterize but also to define, at least implicitly, what is being described. Therefore, I should say a word about how my conception of schizophrenia compares to traditional definitions of this illness.

As I see it, the core features of this condition are best captured not by the Kraepelinian conceptualization but by those of Jaspers, Schneider, and Bleuler; my analysis is therefore most applicable to patients who manifest First Rank Symptoms and a syndrome including autistic withdrawal, affective incongruity or flattening, and ambivalence. It probably also applies best to those patients who were premorbidly "schizoid" (using the latter term in its traditional broad sense, which includes traits termed "schizotypal" and "avoidant" as well as "schizoid" in DSM III-R).

(It should be noted that there is no single, universally accepted definition of schizophrenia at this time, and in all likelihood, there never will be; one reason for this is that a variety of different *kinds* of criteria could be used—including outcome and course of illness, drug response, and symptomatic picture—and these seem unlikely ever to correspond very precisely with each other. Re the inherent ambiguities of the schizophrenic concept, and the inappropriateness of seeking a single "correct" definition, see the comments of W. Janzarik, quoted in J. Hoenig, "The concept of schizophrenia: Kraepelin–Bleuler–Schneider," *British Journal of Psychiatry, 142,* 1983, 555; see also K. S. Kendler's discussion of the unavoidable complexities of psychiatric diagnostic concepts, and the *"fundamentally* nonempirical" nature of many nosological issues; "Toward a scientific psychiatric nosology: Strengths and limitations," *Archives of General Psychiatry, 47,* 1990, 969–72. The highly conventional nature of the schizophrenia diagnosis is very apparent in discussions of proposed diagnostic criteria for DSM IV and for the International Classification of Diseases (ICD) system; see, for example, N. Andreasen and M. Flaum, "Schizophrenia: The characteristic symptoms," *Schizophrenia Bulletin, 17,* 1991, 27–49. Re the acceptability of defining a disease according to symptomatic features rather than purported etiology, see J. G. Scadding, "The semantic problems of psychiatry," *Psychological Medicine, 20,* 1990, 243–48.

As I suggested in the text, much of what I have to say is also applicable to patients who may not merit the diagnosis of schizophrenia per se but who are in the schizophrenia spectrum—for example, to persons who, in DSM III-R terms, would be said to have schizoaffective disorders, or, to a lesser extent, schizophreniform disorder (especially those with poor prognostic features; other schizophreniform patients probably have more in common with cycloid psychoses or with *"bouffée délirante,"* a form of psychosis especially common in non-Western, nonindustrialized settings; see epilogue), and also, in attenuated form, to persons with schizoid personality disorders (broadly defined—as just explained). (Re the affinities of schizoaffective and schizophreniform disorders with schizophrenia, see Kendler, Spitzer, and Williams, "Psychotic disorders in DSM-III-R," p. 958; M. E. Shenton, M. R. Solovay, and P. Holzman, "Comparative studies of thought disorders, II: Schizoaffective disorder," *Archives of General Psychiatry, 44,* 1987, 21–30. Re the relationship between schizophrenia, schizophreniform illness, and *bouffée délirante,* and re the schizoid-schizotypal and schizophrenia association, see the discussion and references in M. Maj, "Nosology of schizophrenia and 'schizophrenic spectrum': Return to Bleuler?" in M. Casacchia and A. Rossi, eds., *Schizophrenia: A Psychological View* (Dordrecht, The Netherlands: Kluwer Academic Publishers, 1989), pp. 17–30. Re "avoidant personality" as a precursor to schizophrenia, see K. S. Kendler and P. Hays, "Schizophrenia with premorbid inferiority feelings," *Archives of General Psychiatry, 39,* 1982, 643–47.

My characterization becomes less and less applicable, however, as typically affective, rather than schizophrenic, features begin to predominate (re the existence of a continuum between schizophrenic and affective disorders, see M. Stone, *The Borderline Syndromes* [New York: McGraw-Hill, 1980]). It is also likely to be less applicable to schizophrenics who have prominent signs of brain damage and whose symptomatic picture is closer to that of true dementia.

Incidentally, it may seem at first glance that my analysis is only relevant to what have recently been called "positive" symptoms, rather than to so-called negative symptoms, and also, perhaps, to the more acute and paranoid patients, but I don't think this is really true. In this book I discuss affective flattening, poverty of speech and poverty of content of speech, anhedonia and associality, disturbances of attention and emotional withdrawal—which comprise most of what has recently been included under the rubric "negative symptoms." It is important to realize that many of these symptoms are more active and goal-directed than may at first seem to be the case (see J. S. Strauss, J. Rakfeldt, C. M. Harding, and P. Lieberman, "Psychological and social aspects of negative symptoms," *British Journal of Psychiatry*, 155 [suppl. 7], 1989, 128–32); often, mute, seemingly deteriorated patients will suddenly show themselves to be more aware of their surroundings, more mentally alive, and more intellectually capable than one might have thought. And as we shall see, much of what may appear to be obviously regressed, deteriorated, or meaningless turns out to be amenable to very different kinds of interpretation.

49. As an organizing principle, "hyperreflexivity" is on a par with such traditional concepts as "primary process," "primitivity," and "looseness of associations," though it obviously contrasts with them in other respects.

50. It is sometimes claimed that there is something profoundly reductive and objectifying about referring to *a* schizophrenic, and that one should always speak instead of "a *person with* schizophrenia." The latter phraseology implies that schizophrenia is a disease that, as it were, just *happens* to afflict an individual; and it tends to obscure the sense in which schizophrenia constitutes an entire *mode* of being, one that may be related to fundamental qualities of character and sensibility. The recommended terminology—persons *with* schizophrenia—is certainly more wordy and awkward, and, in addition, it has the irritating ring of euphemism. We do speak very readily and naturally of athletes, of redheads, and of Frenchmen, after all—so why not of schizophrenics, whose shared characteristics are at least as central? But it should go without saying that the use of the nominative form is not meant to imply that the individual so designated is *nothing but* a schizophrenic—as if he or she were somehow less complex or human than other people.

Chapter 1: Introduction

1. See I. Macalpine and R. A. Hunter, "Translators' introduction," in D. P. Schreber, *Memoirs of My Nervous Illness*, trans. Macalpine and Hunter (Cambridge and London: Harvard University Press, 1988), p. 14. As J. Frosch and others have noted, there has been a tendency, in psychoanalysis as well as in psychiatry, to equate schizophrenia with psychosis in general; see Frosch, *The Psychotic Process* (New York: International Universities Press, 1983), p. 13.

2. See I. I. Gottesman, *Schizophrenia Genesis: The Origins of Madness* (New York: W. H. Freeman, 1991), pp. xi, 4, 68–75.

3. E. Kraepelin, *Dementia Praecox and Paraphrenia*, trans. R. M. Barclay (Huntington, NY: Robert E. Krieger, 1971; first English ed. 1919), p. 3; I have used the translation in M. Bleuler, *The Schizophrenic Disorders*, trans. S. M. Clemens (New Haven and London: Yale University Press, 1978), p. 491; E. Bleuler, *Dementia Praecox, or the Group of Schizophrenias*, trans. J. Zinkin (New York: International Universities Press, 1950), p. 9.

4. Karl Jaspers, *General Psychopathology*, trans. J. Hoenig and M. W. Hamilton (Chicago: University of Chicago Press, 1963), p. 447.

5. M. Bleuler, *Schizophrenic Disorders*, p. 15.
6. E. Minkowski, *Lived Time*, trans. N. Metzel (Evanston, IL: Northwestern University Press, 1970), pp. 287–88.
7. "Renee," in M. Sechehaye, ed., *Autobiography of a Schizophrenic Girl*, trans. G. Rubin-Rabson (New York: New American Library, 1970); M. Bleuler, *The Schizophrenic Disorders*, p. 490. Trachea example is from Robert, one of my patients.
8. A schizophrenic patient quoted in P. Schilder, *The Image and Appearance of the Human Body* (London: Kegan Paul, Trench, Trubner, 1935), p. 159.
9. Jaspers quoted in M. Sechehaye, *A New Psychotherapy in Schizophrenia*, trans. G. Rubin-Rabson (New York and London: Grune and Stratton, 1956), p. 149.
10. Patient quoted in E. Meyer and L. Covi, "The experience of depersonalization: A written report by a patient," *Psychiatry*, 23, 1960, 215.
11. R. Musil, *The Man Without Qualities*, vol. 1 (New York: Capricorn Books, 1965), p. 175. I have used the translation from D. Luft, *Robert Musil and the Crisis of European Culture, 1880–1942* (Berkeley: University of California Press, 1980), p. 217.
12. Jaspers, *General Psychopathology*, p. 577; see also pp. 447, 578–83. See also H. C. Rümke (1941), "The nuclear symptom of schizophrenia and the praecoxfeeling," *History of Psychiatry*, 1, 1990, 331–41.
13. R. Nijinsky, ed., *The Diary of Vaslav Nijinsky* (Berkeley: University of California Press, 1968), p. 168.

According to Jaspers, patients with mania or depressive psychosis could be "comprehend[ed] vividly enough as an exaggeration or diminution of known phenomena and as an appearance of such phenomena without the usual causes or motives"; but schizophrenics, he thought, were "entirely inaccessible to us," and any attempt to bridge this gap through empathic understanding or comparison with normal experience could only be a fool's errand (*General Psychopathology*, pp. 577, 580). Even schizophrenics are not able to understand each other, in Jaspers' view, for, he believed, there *is* no single schizophrenic world, but only a multiplicity of uniquely bizarre and mutually incomprehensible universes (ibid., pp. 282–83).

For a recent study that supports the validity of "understandability" as a criterion for diagnosis, see F. T. Varghese, "Schizoaffective states: Understandability and outcome," *British Journal of Psychiatry*, 159 (suppl. 14), 1991, 29–35.

14. Quoted in E. Kahn, "Emil Kraepelin: February 15, 1856—October 7, 1926—February 15, 1956," *American Journal of Psychiatry*, 113, 1956, 290. Kraepelin spoke of a "weakening or annihilation of the influence which general conception, higher emotion, and the trend of volition have on thought, feeling, and acting," and of "a loss of inner unity . . . [in summary] an orchestra without a conductor" (quoted in J. Cutting, *Psychology of Schizophrenia* [Edinburgh: Churchill Livingstone, 1985], p. 23).
15. E. Kraepelin, *Dementia Praecox*, pp. 1, 75 (comma added); see also p. 3 and passim. Kraepelin, "Dementia praecox" (excerpt from *Psychiatrie*, 5th ed. 1896), in J. Cutting and M. Shepherd, eds., *The Clinical Roots of the Schizophrenia Concept* (Cambridge: Cambridge University Press, 1987), p. 14. Kraepelin once said in a lecture that the schizophrenic has no ego left: *"Da ist ein ich einfach nicht mehr da"*; see Kraepelin, *Dementia Praecox*, p. xvi.

16. The phrase is that of Pierre Janet (*"abaissement du niveau mentale"*); see E. Bleuler, *Dementia Praecox,* p. 380.
17. J. Berze, in M. Hamilton, ed., *Fish's Schizophrenia,* 3rd ed. (Bristol: John Wright, 1984), pp. 177–78.
18. J. E. Gedo and A. Goldberg, *Models of the Mind: A Psychoanalytic Theory* (Chicago and London: University of Chicago Press, 1973), p. 161. *Automatism* is defined by Pierre Janet; see P. Nayrac, "Mental automatism," in S. R. Hirsch and M. Shepherd, eds., *Themes and Variations in European Psychiatry* (Bristol: John Wright, 1974), pp. 405–29. M. Bleuler has described the widespread view that schizophrenia involves "a final, irrevocable loss of one's mental existence" (*Schizophrenic Disorders,* p. 417; see also p. 218).
19. Instead of "a person like ourselves, beset by universal human problems," we see "merely a cerebral machine thrown out of gear," as Carl Jung put it (quoted in A. Harrington, *Medicine, Mind, and the Double Brain: A Study in Nineteenth-Century Thought* [Princeton, NJ: Princeton University Press, 1987], p. 254).
20. The idea of the ununderstandable essence of existence was central to the existentialist philosophy Jaspers was later to develop; see L. Kolakowski, *Metaphysical Horror* (Oxford: Basil Blackwell, 1988), p. 9. Perhaps Jaspers's concept of schizophrenia was an avatar of this view, a premature objective correlative for his later philosophy of the ineffable and the incomprehensible.
21. Kraepelin, "Dementia praecox," p. 23.
22. K. Jaspers, *Strindberg and Van Gogh,* trans. O. Grunow and D. Woloshin (Tucson, AZ: University of Arizona Press, 1977; originally published in 1922), p. 83. Jaspers does not deny that some of the *content* of schizophrenic experience may be understandable (paranoid fantasies, e.g., may symbolize a generally fearful orientation, and their particular themes may derive understandably from current or previous life circumstances); the *formal* aspects of schizophrenic experience are what remain incomprehensible (e.g., the loss of the sense of intentionality or volition).

    As I shall stress, particularly in the appendix, there is no *necessary* link between a belief in biological causation of schizophrenia and a belief in its inaccessibility to empathic comprehension; nevertheless, the connection has often been assumed. Re this issue, see M. Bleuler, *Schizophrenic Disorders,* p. 448.
23. See R. D. Laing, *The Divided Self* (Harmondsworth, UK: Penguin Books, 1965), p. 28.
24. E. Bleuler, "Autistic thinking" (1913), in D. Rapaport, ed., *Organization and Pathology of Thought: Selected Sources* (New York: Columbia University Press, 1951), pp. 401–2.
25. For a fine summary of the views of Kraepelin, Bleuler, Jaspers, and Jaspers's follower, Kurt Schneider, see J. Hoenig, "The concept of schizophrenia: Kraepelin—Bleuler—Schneider," *British Journal of Psychiatry, 142,* 1983, 547–56. Re Eugen Bleuler as a mediator between these two traditions, see H. Stierlin, "Bleuler's concept of schizophrenia: A confusing heritage," *American Journal of Psychiatry, 123,* 1967, 996–1001.
26. S. Freud, "Psychoanalytic notes upon an autobiographical account of a case of paranoia (dementia paranoides)" (1911), in *Three Case Histories* (New York: Collier Books, 1963), p. 180. In *The Interpretation of Dreams* (trans. J. Strachey

[New York: Avon Books, 1965; originally published in 1900]), Freud had already made this point re psychosis: "What once dominated waking life, while the mind was still young and incompetent . . . these methods of working on the part of the psychical apparatus . . . become current once more in psychosis" (p. 606). Later Freud went so far as to state that "each individual somehow recapitulates in an abbreviated form the entire development of the human race." Therefore, in the presence of patients "it is as though we were in a prehistoric landscape—for instance in the Jurassic; the great saurians are still running around; the horsetails grow as high as palms" (Freud in 1916 and 1938, quoted in S. J. Gould, "Freud's phylogenetic fantasy," *Natural History, 12,* 1987, 10–19).

27. S. Ferenczi and O. Rank, *The Development of Psychoanalysis* (published with Ferenczi, *Sex in Psychoanalysis*) (New York: Dover Publications, 1956; originally published in German in 1923, in English in 1925), p. 31.

28. According to one psychoanalytic study, a knowledge of infantile forms of consciousness "aids us in attempting to cross the gap which separates us from the schizophrenic patient" (T. Freeman, J. L. Cameron, and A. McGhie, *Chronic Schizophrenia* [New York: International Universities Press, 1958], p. 103).

29. The conflict between defense and defect models (or between act and affliction models, as they might also be called) is the central psychoanalytic controversy concerning the nature of schizophrenia, and it cuts across the traditional schools of thought. Thus the classical analysts Arlow and Brenner (with their notion of a "regressive instinctualization" of functions), the ego-oriented analyst S. Arieti (with his notion of "progressive teleologic regression"), and most of the members of the British object-relations school tend to view schizophrenic modes of being as goal-directed phenomena, ways of retreating from those forms of experience that threaten to elicit intolerable anxiety (thus D. W. Winnicott maintains that we are wrong to "think of psychosis as a breakdown, it is a defence organization relative to a primitive agony, and it is usually successful" ["Fear of breakdown," *International Review of Psychoanalysis, 1,* 1974, 104]).

Other analysts—including the ego psychologists Paul Federn and Heinz Hartmann, the eclectic theorist Otto Kernberg, the self psychologist Heinz Kohut, and ego-psychology–object-relations theorists like Sidney Blatt and Cynthia Wild or Thomas Freeman and his coauthors—tend to emphasize instead the role of innate or acquired deficiencies; and generally they see these factors as resulting in developmental deviations from, or failures to progress along, normal developmental pathways. For Federn, for example, "the psychosis itself is no defense but a defect"—"a defect of an ego (unable) to defend itself against the impact of instinctual demands, the requirements of external reality, and the conflicts which derive from them" (*Ego Psychology and the Psychoses* [London: Maresfield Reprints, 1977], pp. 188–89).

Still other psychoanalysts—including H. F. Searles, Ping-Nie Pao, and John Frosch—emphasize the need to synthesize deficiency and defense models. But despite these (and other) sources of variability within psychoanalysis, virtually all such theorists place the greatest emphasis on the primitive (and, often, the Dionysian) aspects of schizophrenic psychoses. This is perhaps most straightforward and obvious with the defense model, which postulates a defensively motivated regression to forms of consciousness that are very like those of (normal) infancy and early childhood, and with those versions of the deficiency model that emphasize developmental arrests at early stages of development (re the latter, see the discussion in M. Eagle, *Recent Developments in Psychoanalysis* [Cambridge and London: Harvard University Press, 1987], pp. 127–43). However, even where there is a focus on defects or abnormalities of psychological functioning, or on deviations from normal developmental lines, the schizophrenic condition is viewed as, in large part, a primitive condition involving a failure to develop the control over instinctual forces or the forms of rationality that are characteristic of mature consciousness. Thus Hartmann speaks of the schizophrenic's inability to "neutralize" instinctual energies, to harness and transform the passions—especially aggression—for the purposes of cognition and adaptation; others have stressed the inability to sustain memory traces or internalize a constant image of other human beings, to use an "observing ego," or to maintain "ego boundaries" (e.g., Federn, Freeman, and McGhie). These weaknesses of ego or self are shared by the infant or young child, and, as with the child, they are usually seen as permitting the emergence into conscious awareness of primitive or instinct-dominated mental contents.

The psychoanalyst Melanie Klein emphasizes "that, in so far as the psychotic regresses to the earliest months of infancy, he regresses to a phase in development which already possessed pathological features in his infancy" (H. Segal, *Introduction to the Work of Melanie Klein*, 2nd ed. [London: Hogarth Press and the Institute of Psychoanalysis, 1973], p. 54). An abnormal infant is, however, still an infant, with infantile cognitive capacities—and these would include, for example, a lack of "reflective distance from oneself," of the ability to experience oneself as being the "observer and creator of one's own thoughts, feelings, and perceptions," in the words of the Kleinian analyst T. H. Ogden (*The Matrix of the Mind* [Northvale, NJ: Aronson, 1986], p. 128; see also pp. 25–31, 104–12, 128, including sections re "the infant's mental capacities" and "acute regression to the paranoid-schizoid position"). (For further remarks on the British object-relations school, see note 71, chapter 3).

Sometimes psychoanalytic theorists (especially those with an ego-psychological bent) do acknowledge that, along with a shift to lower developmental levels, schizophrenic consciousness can also involve a disorganization of adult mental activity that is not intrinsically primitive or regressive in nature; see, for example, T. Freeman, J. L. Cameron, and A. McGhie, *Studies on Psychosis* (New York: International Universities Press, 1966), p. 15. This aspect of such models is less distinctively *psychoanalytic*, however; it amounts to a borrowing of elements of the cognitivist approaches that are prominent in academic psychology and medical-model psychiatry (and which are discussed and, in certain respects, criticized in various places in this book).

30. T. Freeman, *Psychopathology of the Psychoses* (New York: International Universities Press, 1969), pp. 137, 163; Anna Freud, "Introduction" to Freeman, Cameron, and McGhie, *Chronic Schizophrenia*, p. viii. See also Freeman, Cameron, and McGhie, ibid., pp. 84, 86, where schizophrenia is explicitly associated with Piaget's descriptions of infantile consciousness; for example, "We assume an egocentrism in which there is no differentiation between ego and external world, and therefore no capacity for reflective thinking through which the subject could comprehend his own symbolism" (p. 84).

No one speaks, of course, of a *literal* regression or a total fixation, for obviously, a literal return to childhood is impossible, and the schizophrenic condition must in some sense involve a new adaptation to the world; in this sense the concept of primitivity is "freed from its bondage to time" (B. Kaplan, "The study of language in psychiatry," in S. Arieti, ed., *American Handbook of Psychiatry*, 2nd ed., vol. I [New York: Basic Books, 1974], p. 663). But it is widely assumed that one can discover or invoke modes of experience that, in a formal or structural sense, are closely akin to those that once prevailed. (In *The Interpretation of Dreams*, p. 587, Freud speaks of both "temporal" and "formal" regression, arguing, however, that they are really "one at bottom and occur together as a rule; for what is older in time is more primitive in form.")

It should also be noted that psychoanalysts would not deny that schizophrenics sometimes engage in higher-level modes of thinking. This does not contradict their fundamental equation of the pathological with the primitive, however, since these instances of mature or rational thinking tend to be seen as islands of relative normalcy while the characteristically *schizophrenic* aspects of the patient continue to be viewed as involving regression to infantile cognition. See, for example, J. Frosch, who argues that there are "irregular developmental movements, with facets of ego functioning (and of libidinal attachment) moving ahead and others lagging behind" (*Psychotic Process* [New York: International Universities Press, 1983], p. 344). Gedo and Goldberg make essentially the same point, criticizing a monolithic version of the fixation/regression hypothesis while continuing to view schizophrenic pathology as highly primitive in nature (*Models of the Mind*, pp. 153–59).

31. See Freud, *The Interpretation of Dreams*, p. 607, for a discussion of psychosis that echoes Plato very closely.

32. T. McGlashan sums up the situation very well in a fairly recent review article:

No writer (on the psychotherapy of schizophrenia) considers the schizophrenic patient's mental structure and functioning equivalent to that of the infant. The patient, unlike the infant, has undergone subsequent phases of growth and development, making his mind far more complex. Nevertheless, most writers maintain that in regression, states of mind more primitive chronologically and developmentally gain ascendancy and that these states resemble, in structure and function, those postulated to be operative during infancy and early childhood." [McGlashan, "Intensive individual psychotherapy of schizophrenia," *Archives of General Psychiatry*, 40, 1983, 911]

33. A. Koyré, *From the Closed World to the Infinite Universe* (Baltimore and London: Johns Hopkins University Press, 1957), p. 2. According to the ego psychologist Robert Holt, "as we go higher . . . originally raw, blind urges are increasingly tamed by controlling structures" ("Gauging primary and secondary processes in Rorschach responses, in his *Methods in Clinical Psychology*, vol. 2: *Projective Assessment* [New York and London: Plenum, 1978], p. 213). Also see the schematic chart (called "the fulcrum of development") that G. Blanck and R. Blanck offer to illustrate the transition from "living in the body," "undifferentiated self-object," and "direct impulse charge" to "living in the mind (structure)" and "ego as mediator" (*Ego Psychology Two: Developmental Psychology* [New York: Columbia University Press, 1979], p. 72).

For other statements of the primitivity or regression view, see O. Fenichel,

The Psychoanalytic Theory of Neurosis (New York: Norton, 1945), pp. 421–23 (Fenichel speaks of the ego dropping back to "infantile," even "intrauterine" types of adaptation); C. G. Jung, "On the psychogenesis of schizophrenia," *The Psychogenesis of Mental Disease*, trans. R. F. C. Hull (*The Collected Works of C. G. Jung*, vol. 3) (New York: Pantheon Books, 1960), pp. 233–49; H. S. Sullivan, *The Psychiatric Interview* (New York: Norton, 1954), p. 206; W. S. Pollack, "Schizophrenia and the self: Contributions of psychoanalytic self-psychology," *Schizophrenia Bulletin*, 15, 1989, 311–21.

34. L. Wittgenstein, *Lectures and Conversations* (Berkeley: University of California Press, 1967), p. 43.

35. A. Freud, "Preface" to Freeman, Cameron, and McGhie, *Chronic Schizophrenia*, p. viii.

36. R. D. Laing, *The Politics of Experience* (New York: Ballantine Books, 1967), pp. 126, 167.

37. G. Deleuze and F. Guattari, *Anti-Oedipus: Capitalism and Schizophrenia*, trans. R. Hurley, M. Seem, and H. Lane (New York: Viking, 1977), pp. 87–88. See also F. Jameson, "Imaginary and symbolic in Lacan," *Yale French Studies*, 55/56, 1977, 338–95. "Emblem of creative insurrection": Jean Broustra, quoted in J. H. Matthews, *Surrealism, Insanity, and Poetry* (Syracuse, NY: Syracuse University Press, 1982), pp. 4–5. According to J. H. Matthews: "Surrealists regard mental disorder as restoring the mind to productive activity. . . . All forms of censorship are lifted . . . and word pictures are painted with admirable freedom from reason's unwelcome restraint" (*Surrealism, Insanity, and Poetry*, p. 88). A similar view was expressed by Jean Dubuffet, the great champion of "Art Brut"; see, for example, Dubuffet's talk on "Anticultural positions," reproduced in part as an appendix to W. Sypher, *Loss of the Self in Modern Literature and Art* (New York: Vintage Books, 1962), pp. 170–76. André Breton wrote that "I could spend my life provoking the confidences of madmen: they are people of scrupulous honesty, whose innocence is equalled only by my own" (quoted in M. Nadeau, *The History of Surrealism* [Harmondsworth, UK: Penguin Books, 1978], p. 96). In *Love's Body* (New York: Vintage Books, 1966), Norman O. Brown writes: "The reality-principle is based on desexualization; in symbolic consciousness thought and speech become resexualized. As in schizophrenia" (p. 250). In *Madness and Civilization* (p. 223), Foucault refers to madness as a "sovereign enterprise of unreason," a "wild state" of an "inaccessible purity."

38. E. Cassirer, *Mythical Thought*, vol. 2 of *The Philosophy of Symbolic Forms*, trans. R. Manheim (New Haven, CT: Yale University Press, 1955), p. 13.

39. C. Lévi-Strauss, *The Savage Mind* (Chicago: University of Chicago Press, 1966), p. 42. According to Lucien Lévy-Bruhl, for example, primitive man does not apprehend himself as a subject, nor as differentiated from objects not himself: "In the vague idea which the primitive has of himself, elements arising out of individual self-reflection count, as we know, for very little" (*The "Soul" of the Primitive* [London: George Allen and Unwin, 1928], p. 15). See also G. Stocking, "The dark-skinned savage: The image of primitive man in evolutionary anthropology," *Race, Culture, and Evolution: Essays in the History of Anthropology* (Chicago: University of Chicago Press, 1982), pp. 110–32.

40. M. Sechehaye, *A New Psychotherapy in Schizophrenia*, trans. G. Rubin-Rabson (New York and London: Grune and Stratton, 1956), p. 155. The deficiency,

primitivity, and Dionysian models of schizophrenic pathology should not, incidentally, be assumed to be mutually exclusive. It is true that many academic psychologists and some medical-model psychiatrists have held a relatively pure version of the deficiency view (without assuming that schizophrenia is either regressive or Dionysian), and that some antipsychiatrists have emphasized the impassioned and mystical impulses of the schizophrenic without asserting any associated impairment of the ego. In many cases, however, the models overlap to a considerable extent. Thus it is generally assumed that primitive modes of experience are dominated by instinct and emotion, as well as being deficient in cognitive capacities. "Classical psychoanalytic" theories of psychosexual regression (such as Freud's notion of regression to the "autoerotic" stage) are fairly congruent with the Dionysian image favored by the avant-garde and the antipsychiatric radicals. Psychoanalytic "ego psychology," with its emphasis on cognitive disturbances, has significant affinities with the cognitivist-deficiency approach.

41. Michel Foucault states the upshot of this skein of assumptions very succinctly: "While *man* can always go mad, *thought* . . . cannot be mad"; "madness is precisely the condition in which thought is impossible" (quoted in A. Glucksmann, *The Master Thinkers*, trans. B. Pearce [New York: Harper and Row, 1980], p. 96).

42. Hegel, for example, defines subjectivity as the presence of reflection and freedom; see J. Habermas, *The Philosophical Discourse of Modernity*, trans. F. Lawrence (Cambridge: MIT Press, 1990), p. 16.

43. In a Rorschach study, J. E. Exner reports that, in contrast with patients with Borderline Personality Disorder, schizophrenic and schizotypal individuals did not display an "affectively influenced intuitive approach" but, rather, an "introversive coping style, which involves a strong commitment to delay and ideation in formulating decisions and behavior" ("Some Rorschach data comparing schizophrenics with borderline and schizotypal personality disorders," *Journal of Personality Assessment*, 50, 1986, 465). See also, for example, J. Cutting, *Psychology of Schizophrenia*, pp. 305–8, 345–48, and passim.

44. Quoted in P. Koestenbaum, *The New Image of the Person* (Westport, CT: Greenwood Press, 1978), p. 448.

45. E. Kraepelin, *Lectures on Clinical Psychiatry*, 2nd ed., rev. and ed. T. Johnstone (New York: William Wood, 1906), p. 22.

46. See Kraepelin, *Dementia Praecox*, p. 33; E. Bleuler, *Textbook of Psychiatry*, trans. A. A. Brill (New York: Macmillan, 1929), p. 410; D. E. Raskin, "Bleuler and schizophrenia," *British Journal of Psychiatry*, 127, 1975, 232. Even the dreams of schizophrenics are not especially likely to involve raw sexual or aggressive themes, as the primitivity model would predict; the only differentiating feature seems to be a difficult-to-define quality of uncanniness or bizarreness; see Arieti, *Interpretation of Schizophrenia*, p. 594.

47. P. Holzman, "Cognitive impairment and cognitive stability," in G. Serban, ed., *Cognitive Defects in the Development of Mental Illness* (New York: Brunner/ Mazel, 1978), p. 364; also, personal communication, Dr. P. Holzman, February 10, 1992. For similar reports, see J. Cutting, *Psychology of Schizophrenia* (Edinburgh: Churchill Livingstone, 1985), p. 39 (re observations by Kraepelin and Pavlov); M. Bleuler, *Schizophrenic Disorders*, p. 480; E. Minkowski, *La Schizophrénie* (Paris: Payot, 1927), p. 259.

48. E. Bleuler, *Dementia Praecox*, p. 72. There is also some experimental evidence suggesting that schizophrenics may be *more* efficient and accurate on certain kinds of cognitive tasks; see J. Cutting, *The Right Cerebral Hemisphere and Psychiatric Disorders* (Oxford: Oxford University Press, 1990), pp. 285–86; see also discussion in chapters 2 and 4, pages 72 and 127, and in appendix, pages 384–85. Some schizophrenics may be better than normal subjects at discriminating between genuine and sham expressions of emotions in other people; and it has been suggested that "the underlying quality of schizophrenia is not a defect at all, but an exquisite sensitivity of the nervous system, which . . . gets translated into an *appearance* of deficit as the individual progresses into a state that we recognize, quite rightly, as illness" (G. Claridge, "Schizophrenia and human individuality," in C. Blakemore and S. Greenfield, eds., *Mindwaves: Thoughts on Intelligence, Identity, and Consciousness* [Oxford and New York: Blackwell, 1987], p. 40; see also pp. 38–39).

49. E. Bleuler, *Dementia Praecox*, p. 77. The mere fact of variability of functioning does not, of course, rule out the existence of some cognitive deficiency or an underlying organic anomaly; it is well known, after all, that fluctuations occur in patients with well-recognized organic brain syndromes, sometimes as a function of motivation (though seldom are these as dramatic, or as apparently willful and directed in nature as what occurs in schizophrenia). My point is that the role of intentionality in schizophrenic functioning is especially important and should not be neglected or downplayed. Bleuler also gives the example of a patient who seems incapable of understanding that antisocial behavior will keep him from being discharged from the hospital, yet who is capable

of presenting a well-reasoned, hour-long lecture in which he convinces most of his audience that he is of sound mind, in which he very deliberately omits everything that is contrary to his argument and embroiders, or even changes, whatever favours his theme. He can carry out complicated tasks, can show scholastic knowledge which his doctor might well envy, can understand that knowledge and make correct use of it. He can make refined plans for flight, or for hoodwinking and deceiving clever people . . . [yet] at a certain point he may become blocked and seem demented. The schizophrenic, however, is no simple dement; he is demented in respect of certain issues, certain periods of time, or certain complexes only. [E. Bleuler, "The prognosis of dementia praecox," in Cutting and Shepherd, *Clinical Roots*, pp. 63–64]

Also see M. Bleuler, *Schizophrenic Disorders*, pp. 481–82, re the fact that schizophrenics who may seem totally withdrawn and barren of interest in the environment will often "pick up an astounding amount of information from snatches of conversation about the personal lives of their doctors and care personnel, and about tensions among them."

50. Sinclair, quoted in D. Gascoyne, *Hölderlin's Madness* (London: Dent, 1938), p. 6 (emphasis added).

51. R. Rosser, "The psychopathology of feeling and thinking in a schizophrenic," *International Journal of Psychoanalysis, 60,* 1979, p. 184.

52. Cutting, *Psychology of Schizophrenia*, p. 239.

53. P. Barham, *Schizophrenia and Human Value* (Oxford: Blackwell, 1984), pp. 4–5.

54. E. Bleuler, *Dementia Praecox*, p. 14.

55. Phrase is from E. Minkowski, *Lived Time*, trans. N. Metzel (Evanston, IL: Northwestern University Press, 1970), p. 277.

56. E. Bleuler mentions the "mixture of megalomania with delusions of persecution and inferiority . . . the patient is especially powerful and at the same time powerless" (ibid., p. 54). See also Jaspers (*General Psychopathology*, p. 413): "Delusion always *encompasses both poles*, so that honour and humiliation of the self, delusions of grandeur and delusions of persecution go together."

57. Quoted in E. Canetti, *Crowds and Power* (New York: Continuum, 1962/1973), p. 322. See also L. Binswanger, "Extravagance, perverseness, manneristic behavior and schizophrenia," in Cutting and Shepherd, eds., *Clinical Roots*, pp. 83–88.

58. Jaspers, *General Psychopathology*, p. 563.

59. Ibid., pp. 581–82. The theories mentioned include those of Janet, Stransky, Berze, and E. Bleuler. "Intrapsychic ataxia" is a term Erwin Stransky used to refer to what he considered the central feature of schizophrenia: dissociation between intellectual and emotional functions of the brain ("Toward an understanding of certain symptoms of dementia praecox" [1904], in Cutting and Shepherd, *Clinical Roots*, pp. 37–41).

60. R. D. Laing once confessed that schizophrenics seemed so little alien to him that he had difficulty in discovering the signs and symptoms of this psychosis in patients he interviewed (*Divided Self*, p. 28). By contrast, Sigmund Freud was emotionally repulsed even by descriptions of such patients: "Ultimately I had to confess to myself," he wrote to a colleague, "that I do not care for these patients [psychotics], that they annoy me, and that I find them alien to me and to everything human. A peculiar kind of intolerance which undoubtedly disqualifies me as a psychiatrist" (quoted in T. McGlashan, "Intensive individual psychotherapy of schizophrenia," *Archives of General Psychiatry, 40*, 1983, 911). Freud himself speculated as to whether his dislike was due to "preference for the primacy of the intellect, the expression of animosity toward the id" (quoted in J. Frosch, *The Psychotic Process* [New York: International Universities Press, 1983], p. 3).

61. See, for example, H. M. van Praag, "About the impossible concept of schizophrenia," *Comprehensive Psychiatry, 17*, 1976, 481–97.

62. Jaspers, *General Psychopathology*, pp. 567–68. "In the formation of these two groupings," Jaspers wrote, speaking of Kraepelin's distinction between dementia praecox and manic-depressive insanity, "there must be some kernel of lasting truth not present with previous groupings" (p. 568); therefore, he believed, it was both legitimate and necessary to accept some notion of these illnesses, ill-defined though it may be, in order to make any progress in psychopathology.

63. The quoted phrase is Harold Rosenberg's: *The Tradition of the New*, 2nd ed. (New York: McGraw-Hill, 1965).

64. Quoted in M. Bradbury and J. McFarlane, "The name and nature of modernism," *Modernism: 1890–1930* (Harmondsworth, UK: Penguin Books, 1976), p. 20.

65. Irving Howe, "The idea of the modern," in *The Idea of the Modern in Literature and the Arts* (New York: Horizon Press, 1967), p. 13. H. Read quoted in Bradbury and McFarlane, "Name and nature of modernism," p. 20. A leading German authority on modernist literature describes the post-1910 literary revolution as "a chaotic maze of antagonistic currents, emotions, ideas and forms of expression. There appears to be no unitary, mutual element, unless it be in the negation: in the break with tradition. But even that is not very accurate. There were

also ties being established with traditions" (W. Emrich, quoted in A. Eysteinsson, *The Concept of Modernism* [Ithaca and London: Cornell University Press, 1990], pp. 52–53).

66. The relationship between modernism and postmodernism is a controversial issue in contemporary studies of literature and art; and it seems fairly obvious that there is no one answer to the question of whether postmodernism constitutes a decisive break from modernism. Clearly, hypothetical entities like artistic styles and cultural sensibilities—not unlike many psychiatric diagnoses—can be imagined in various ways, and compared along many different dimensions; and there is no reason to assume that one of these dimensions should have priority for all purposes. (Max Weber's wise remarks about the necessarily tentative and perspectival nature of historical and cultural constructs, such as his own notion of "the spirit of capitalism," are very apropos here; see *The Protestant Ethic and the Spirit of Capitalism* [London: Unwin Hyman, 1930/1990], pp. 47–48). But given my interests, the similarities seem far more impressive than the differences.

I am, then, adopting the more inclusive definition of modernism that polemicists for the "postmodern" have put somewhat out of favor—though it was quite widely accepted until fairly recently. I have chosen to concentrate on the aspects of postmodernism that face toward (earlier) modernism rather than on, say, its affinities with popular culture. And in my treatment of modernism I have emphasized the aspects that face away from, rather than toward, romanticism. This latter is the more prominent view of the modernism-romanticism relationship, though there are scholars who emphasize the traces of romanticism to be found in modernist literature; see F. R. Karl, *Modern and Modernism* (New York: Atheneum, 1985), p. 418, for discussion. (I do treat the romantic side of modernism at greater length in the conclusion.) I should also mention that I do not oppose modernism to what is sometimes called the avant-garde, comprising (usually) dadaism, surrealism, and Russian futurism—movements sometimes seen as proto-postmodern.

The continuity of modernism and postmodernism is argued by Frederick Karl, and also by Gerald Graff, Frank Kermode, Julia Kristeva, and Jean-François Lyotard, among others; see A. Eysteinsson, *The Concept of Modernism*, p. 107. Eysteinsson convincingly surveys the essential bankruptcy of many of the attempts to distinguish postmodernism from modernism (chap. 3); as he notes (p. 40), much of literary and philosophical poststructuralism, often considered an expression of postmodernism, can easily be seen as a theory of *modernist* artforms. A similar point is made by A. Huyssen; see "Mapping the postmodern," *New German Critique*, 33, 1984, 5–52.

A few more words about the problematic and controversial distinction between modernist and postmodernist art may be helpful for those readers not familiar with these arguments.

In literary and cultural studies, "modernism" is sometimes understood in a more restrictive sense than I adopt in this book (i.e., as being *exclusive* of postmodernism); then it is usually assumed to encompass the period between the turn of the century and the beginning of World War II, with its heyday, the period of "high modernism," occurring before and just after World War I in the work of writers and artists like Eliot, Pound, Virginia Woolf, Valéry, Rilke, Kafka, Picasso, and Matisse. Postmodernism, by contrast, is often said to begin some time after World War II, perhaps as late as the 1960s. Major figures identified with the postmodernist style, sensibility, or mood would be the writers Jorge Luis

Borges, Alain Robbe-Grillet, Thomas Pynchon, and Donald Barthelme; the poet John Ashbery; the artists Robert Rauschenberg, Jasper Johns, and Andy Warhol; and the composer–conceptual artist John Cage. Increasingly, however, this temporal distinction—first modernism, then postmodernism—has come into question; for it is noted that the stylistic features and aesthetic attitudes identified as postmodern (e.g., an emphatic self-referentiality, profound relativism and uncertainty, extreme irony, and tendencies toward fragmentation) have in fact been with us throughout the twentieth century. (It has even been alleged that art goes through a postmodernist phase before it can become modern!: "A work can become modern only if it is first postmodern," writes J.-F. Lyotard in *The Postmodern Condition: A Report on Knowledge*, trans. G. Bennington and B. Massumi [Minneapolis: University of Minnesota Press, 1984], p. 79.)

The latter realization has led in two directions. Some writers would locate the distinctive postmodern characteristics only in certain (in a sense, proto-postmodernist) movements of the early twentieth century—usually in dadaism, futurism, and in aspects of surrealism and cubism (see, e.g., M. Perloff, *The Futurist Moment* [Chicago and London: University of Chicago Press, 1986]), with Marcel Duchamp often being cited as a major postmodernist (or, *proto*-postmodernist) of the first half of the twentieth century. But others note that the supposedly distinctive features of this postmodernist style are in fact present in the canonical works of high modernism; and they would deny that postmodernism has any real distinctiveness either in a stylistic or a temporal sense.

The term *modernism* is sometimes used in yet another way: to refer to the whole trend of rationalistic-scientific thought that begins with Galileo, Newton, and the seventeenth-century Enlightenment. *Postmodernism* then comes to be associated with the adversarial, relativistic, antifoundationalist reactions against this trend that occur in twentieth-century art, thought, and culture. On this usage of the term (which I do not adopt in this book), so-called postmodernism would obviously have to subsume a great deal of what literary and art historians have traditionally called "modernism" (including even so-called high modernism).

67. See R. Poggiolli, *The Theory of the Avant-Garde* (Cambridge and London: Harvard University Press, 1968), p. 230.

68. *Lettres du Voyant,* quoted in ibid., p. 215 ("inspecter l'invisible et entendre l'inouï").

69. See G. Steiner, "On difficulty," in *On Difficulty and Other Essays* (New York: Oxford University Press, 1978), pp. 18–47; S. Sontag, "The aesthetics of silence," *Styles of Radical Will* (New York: Dell, 1969), pp. 3–34; E. Heller, "The poet in the age of prose," *In the Age of Prose* (Cambridge: Cambridge University Press, 1984), pp. 1–19.

70. Quoted in C. Russell, *Poets, Prophets, and Revolutionaries: The Literary Avant-Garde from Rimbaud through Postmodernism* (New York and Oxford: Oxford University Press, 1985), p. 105; and in Eysteinsson, *Concept of Modernism*, p. 157.

71. Leverkuhn, the hero of Thomas Mann's novel *Doctor Faustus*, asks, "Why does almost everything seem to me like its own parody? Why must I think that almost all, no, all the methods and conventions of art today *are good for parody only?*" (*Doctor Faustus*, trans. H. T. Lowe-Porter [New York: Vintage Books, 1971], p. 134).

72. F. Jameson characterizes this as a "homeopathic expropriation" and co-optation of cliché and of the machine; see *Fables of Aggression: Wyndham Lewis, the Modernist as Fascist* (Berkeley: University of California Press, 1979), pp. 70–82.

73. Phrases from Lionel Trilling, *Beyond Culture* (New York: Viking, 1965), pp. xv–xviii; Harold Rosenberg, *Tradition of the New*, 2nd ed. (New York: McGraw-Hill, 1965); and Ezra Pound.

74. Paz, *Children of the Mire: Modern Poetry from Romanticism to the Avant-Garde* (Cambridge and London: Harvard University Press, 1974), pp. 1–2.

75. C. Greenberg, "Modernist painting," in G. Battcock, ed., *The New Art: A Critical Anthology*, rev. ed. (New York: Dutton, 1973), p. 67: "Because he was the first to criticize the means itself of criticism, I conceive of Kant as the first real Modernist."

76. F. Nietzsche, *The Will to Power*, trans. W. Kaufmann and R. J. Hollingdale (New York: Vintage Books, 1968), pp. 14–15.

77. F. Nietzsche, *Beyond Good and Evil*, trans. R. J. Hollingdale (Harmondsworth, UK: Penguin Books, 1973), p. 120.

78. Such a combination of extremely vivid sensations with an inability to act accounts for the presence in many modernist works of the motif of the "corpse with insomnia," a disembodied consciousness that cannot control but only helplessly endure all that it perceives. One finds it, for example, in T. S. Eliot's "The Wasteland" and in Samuel Beckett's *Endgame;* re Eliot, see M. H. Levenson, *A Genealogy of Modernism* (Cambridge: Cambridge University Press, 1984), pp. 165–76.

79. Quoted in Jameson, *Fables of Aggression,* p. 97.

80. E. Heller, *The Disinherited Mind* (New York and London: Harcourt Brace Jovanovich, 1975), p. 172.

81. M. Schapiro, "Abstract art," in *Modern Art* (New York: Braziller, 1978), p. 198.

82. M. Heidegger, "The age of the world picture," *The Question Concerning Technology and Other Essays*, trans. W. Lovitt (New York: Harper and Row, 1977), pp. 128–31.

83. Quoted in R. Shattuck, *The Banquet Years: The Origins of the Avant-Garde in France 1885 to World War I*, rev. ed. (New York: Vintage Books, 1968), p. 327. "Ma pensée se pense" was Mallarmé's more succinct statement of this sentiment, which has played so central a role in the development of modernism; see ibid., p. 327.

84. Phrases are from Jean-Paul Sartre and Roland Barthes, respectively. Some critics view the tradition emanating from Ezra Pound in this light. Thus, D. S. Carne-Ross writes that in Pound's poetry "the whole reverberating dimension of inwardness is missing. There is no murmurous echo chamber where deeps supposedly answer to deeps. Not merely does the thing, in Pound's best verse, not point beyond itself: *it doesn't point to us*" (quoted in M. Perloff, *The Dance of the Intellect: Studies in the Poetry of the Pound Tradition* [Cambridge: Cambridge University Press, 1985).

85. A. Robbe-Grillet, *For a New Novel*, trans. R. Howard (New York: Grove Press, 1965); I have used the translation in C. Butler, *After the Wake: An Essay on the Contemporary Avant-Garde* (Oxford: Clarendon Press, 1980), pp. 166–67.

86. Re these issues, see G. Graff, *Literature Against Itself: Literary Ideas in Modern Society* (Chicago and London: University of Chicago Press, 1979), pp. 49–50.

87. Heidegger, "The age of the world picture," p. 128. Heidegger's argument is reminiscent of Hegel's view that the essence of the modern age is its assumption of the "principle of subjectivity or self-consciousness," whose two facets are objectifying science and the absolute inwardness of modern and romantic art; see Habermas, *Philosophical Discourse of Modernity*, pp. 16–18, 133 (re Heidegger on Cartesianism, the latter being a major source of objectifying concepts that nevertheless construes truth as subjective certainty). This rather abstract point can be illustrated by thinking of novels like Hemingway's *The Sun Also Rises*, Camus's *The Stranger*, and various works by Alain Robbe-Grillet. On one level, these are highly objectivist fictions, describing objects with a nearly scientific detachment; yet they also make one aware of an almost claustrophobic subjectivism: the very rigor and purity of the mode of observation and description alert us to the fact that everything is always seen from a certain standpoint, usually, that of a single human subject, a detached (often rather schizoid) individual who concentrates on reporting his or her visual perceptions in a neutral manner. In an essay in *For a New Novel* (pp. 138–39) Robbe-Grillet is explicit about the profoundly subjectivist nature of his own seemingly "objectivist" books. In contrast with the omniscient, godlike view of the novels of Balzac, he says, his fictions report only what a single, neutral human observer would see: "The New Novel aims only at a total subjectivity. . . . It is God alone who can claim to be objective. While in our books, on the contrary, it is *a man* who sees."
88. Quoted in J. Frank, "Spatial form in modern literature," *The Widening Gyre: Crisis and Mastery in Modern Literature* (Bloomington and London: Indiana University Press, 1968), p. 9.
89. Hegel had predicted that art would come to "desire to find its satisfaction solely in its own in-dwelling as the true abode of truth" (quoted in E. Heller, *The Artist's Journey into the Interior and Other Essays* [San Diego and New York: Harcourt Brace Jovanovich, 1976], p. 117).
90. See discussion in M. H. Abrams, "Coleridge, Baudelaire, and modernist poetics," *The Correspondent Breeze* (New York: Norton, 1984), pp. 109–44.
91. M. Foucault, *The Order of Things* (New York: Vintage Books, 1970), p. 300.
92. See F. Jameson, *The Prison-House of Language: A Critical Account of Structuralism and Russian Formalism* (Princeton, NJ: Princeton University Press, 1972), pp. 89–91.
93. This kind of work "neither brackets nor suspends the referent but works instead to problematize the activity of reference" (C. Owens, "The allegorical impulse: Toward a theory of postmodernism, Part 2," *October, 13*, 1980, 79–80). The claim that this constitutes a sharp difference between modernism and postmodernism is cogently disputed by Eysteinsson, *Concept of Modernism*, p. 125.
94. C. Greenberg, "Modernist painting," in G. Battcock, ed., *The New Art: A Critical Anthology*, rev. ed. (New York: Dutton, 1973), p. 67.
95. Valéry paraphrased in W. Sypher, *Loss of the Self in Modern Literature and Art* (New York: Vintage Books, 1962), p. 123. Cummings quoted in Shattuck, *Banquet Years*, p. 343.
96. J. Ortega y Gasset, *The Dehumanization of Art and Other Essays* (Princeton, NJ: Princeton University Press, 1968), pp. 47, 21, 22. As T. S. Eliot wrote, "Poetry is not a turning loose of emotion, but an escape from emotion; it is not

the expression of personality, but an escape from personality" ("Tradition and the individual talent," *Selected Essays, 1917–1932* [New York: Harcourt Brace, 1932], p. 10).

97. Ortega y Gasset, *Dehumanization of Art*, pp. 46–47.

98. Re the disappearance of emotion and pathos in postmodernism, see F. Jameson, "Baudelaire as modernist and postmodernist: The dissolution of the referent and the artificial sublime," in C. Hosek and P. Parker, eds., *Lyric Poetry: Beyond New Criticism* (Ithaca, NY: Cornell University Press, 1986), p. 260.

99. Re these issues, see M. H. Abrams, *Natural Supernaturalism* (New York: Norton, 1971), pp. 445–48 and passim.; see also T. Rajan, *Dark Interpreter: The Discourse of Romanticism* (Ithaca, NY: Cornell University Press, 1980), pp. 20–21, 30–31, 265–66, and passim.

100. L. Trilling, *Sincerity and Authenticity* (Cambridge: Harvard University Press, 1972), p. 131.

101. Quoted in Sontag, "Aesthetics of silence," p. 8. The central role that such extreme detachment and irony have played since the beginning of modernism is apparent in the influence exerted by figures like Alfred Jarry, inspirer of the Theatre of the Absurd, who engaged in an all-encompassing and profoundly off-putting form of black humor, which Maurice Nadeau has characterized as "the answer of superior minds to this world in which they feel themselves alien." Similar tendencies are apparent in Jacques Vaché's notion of *"umour,"* which, he said, "must not produce"; it is that feeling or sense "of the theatrical uselessness (and no joy there) of everything. *When you know"* (M. Nadeau, *The History of Surrealism* [Harmondsworth, UK: Penguin Books, 1973], pp. 25, 63, 78).

102. Thus *avant-gardism* clearly involves a heightened awareness of one's own place in the history of styles, while *ironic detachment* presupposes a critical distance from one's own emotions as well as from the audience. *Perspectivism* and (subjectivist) *derealization* stem from an intensified awareness of the role of the observing subject—of the uniqueness and limitedness of any particular stand-point and of the subjective contribution to the constitution of reality; while *aesthetic reflexivity*, as well as many devices of *spatial form*, imply a self-conscious focus on the means by which an aesthetic world is structured. (Claude Lévi-Strauss has an interesting description of nonrepresentational painting as "a school of academic painting in which each artist strives to represent the manner in which he would execute his pictures if by chance he were to paint any" [*The Savage Mind*, p. 30].) Disengagement and devitalization are obviously central elements of the objectivist *unworlding* and of objectivist *dehumanization;* while subjectivist *dehumanization* involves an intense inwardness and self-detachment whereby the mind takes itself as its own, and sole, object.

That alienation and self-consciousness are no less present in postmodernism than in (narrowly defined) modernism is apparent from the work of John Ashbery, perhaps the most prominent of contemporary postmodern poets. In the words of one critic, he is "a poet of the mind very far off inside itself, dependent on the quality of intensity of its own responses for its final sense of reality, and therefore—a conclusion from which Ashbery does not flinch—ultimately isolated." Ashbery manifests an "extreme self-consciousness about style," evoking a world in which "endless self-consciousness makes every gesture the possible occasion for endless self-knowledge" (A. Williamson, *Introspection and Contemporary Poetry* [Cambridge: Harvard University Press, 1984], pp. 117, 119).

103. In *The Banquet Years*, Roger Shattuck describes acute self-consciousness as the major departure of modernist from romanticist aesthetics: "Not self-forgetful, the artist of the twentieth century seeks the means to become totally *self-remembering*, self-reflexive, without conventions of location and of logical consistency. This is the still-emergent unity of his work" (p. 332). For another argument concerning the Apollonian essence of modernism, see Maurice Beebe, "What modernism was," *Journal of Modern Literature*, 3, 1974, 1065–84.

104. See M. H. Levenson, *A Genealogy of Modernism: A Study of English Literary Doctrine 1908–1922* (Cambridge: Cambridge University Press, 1984) for discussion of these issues. Re the bifurcation of literature after romanticism into subjectivist and objectivist variants, see Erich Heller's essays, "The romantic expectation," and "The realistic fallacy," both in *Artist's Journey into the Interior*, 73–98, esp. pp. 84, 94–98.

105. Re the subjectivism, see, for example, L. Hutcheon, *Narcissistic Narrative* (New York and London: Methuen, 1984); re the hyperobjectivism, see Susan Sontag's comment on the importance of the "pure, untranslatable, sensuous immediacy" of the images in the movie *Last Year at Marienbad* (*Against Interpretation* [New York: Dell, 1969], p. 19).

In literary criticism there has been considerable debate concerning whether there is a radical break between modernism and romanticism. Gerald Graff is one who argues for an essential continuity between romanticism and modernism. He also mentions those critics—J. Hillis Miller, Harold Bloom, and Morse Peckham—who emphasize the skeptical, ironical, or nihilistic side of romanticism (*Literature Against Itself*, p. 39). The view I adopt here is close to that of M. H. Abrams, perhaps our foremost critic of romanticism; see his essay, "Coleridge, Baudelaire, and modernist poetics."

106. See, for example, D. Bell, *Cultural Contradictions of Capitalism* (New York: Basic Books, 1976), pp. 46–51; M. K. Spears, *Dionysus and the City: Modernism in Twentieth-Century Poetry* (London: Oxford University Press, 1970).

107. Various analysts, including Carl Jung and Franz Alexander, have in fact argued that both the modern artist *and* the psychotic show a propensity to be readily overcome by a "Dionysian exuberance" involving "elemental breakthrough, from the unconscious, of the primitive disorganizing impulses of the id," and a regressive immersion in the sensory surround (F. Alexander, "A psychoanalyst looks at contemporary art," in William Phillips, ed., *Art and Psychoanalysis* [Cleveland, OH: World Publishing, 1957], p. 357; C. Jung, " 'Ulysses,' a monologue," in *The Spirit in Man, Art, and Literature* [Princeton, NJ: Princeton University Press, 1971], p. 119).

108. See prologue, note 42, re Nietzsche's conception of Dionysus, Apollo, and Socrates.

109. See, for example, Beebe, "What modernism was."

110. Ortega y Gasset, *Dehumanization of Art*, pp. 182–83.

111. Friedrich von Schiller, *Naive and Sentimental Poetry* (published with *On the Sublime*), trans. J. A. Elias (New York: Ungar, 1966), p. 105; see also pp. 85, 110. I am suggesting that this modern primitivism is akin to that of the "senti-

mental" poet described by Schiller—the one who self-consciously "seeks" nature, unlike the "naive" poet who just "is" nature. Re this aspect of Gauguin and of surrealism, see R. Goldwater, *Primitivism in Modern Art*, rev. ed. (New York: Vintage/Random House, 1966), pp. 64–65, 221–22. In one of his poems, the German writer Gottfried Benn, who considered nihilism and a devitalizing cerebralism to be the central features of modern life, stated this yearning for regression to the very earliest forms of being: "Oh that we were our primal ancestors, small lumps of plasma in hot, sultry swamps; . . . A dragonfly or gull's wing—already these would signify excessive suffering" (quoted in George Lukács, *Realism in Our Time*, trans. J. and N. Mander [New York: Harper Torchbooks, 1971], p. 32). Raymond Williams has described the romantic critique of Enlightenment rationalism as having collapsed into an "alienation of the irrational, which has become complete only in our century" (quoted in R. W. Noland, "The Apocalypse of Norman O. Brown," *American Scholar*, 38, 1968–1969, 62).

112. Poggiolli, *Theory of the Avant-Garde*, p. 153.
113. The sequence of symptoms treated in the following chapters should not be taken too literally. I am not suggesting that every schizophrenic will necessarily manifest all the phenomena I discuss. Nor is it the case that the phenomena treated in different chapters do not overlap: they can and often do occur simultaneously. I have simply tried to capture, in a rough sort of way, the progression of features that tend to emerge as most salient over the course of a schizophrenic episode. It should also be noted that it is possible (and common) for a given person to go through such a sequence many different times.

Chapter 2: The Truth-Taking Stare

1. See M. Hamilton, ed., *Fish's Schizophrenia*, 2nd ed. (Bristol, UK: John Wright, 1976), p. 117.
2. Re the perplexity that occurs when patients realize they are becoming detached from the world of normal perception, see G. Störring, "Perplexity," in J. Cutting and M. Shepherd, eds., *The Clinical Roots of the Schizophrenia Concept* (Cambridge: Cambridge University Press, 1987), pp. 79–82.
3. See K. Jaspers, *General Psychopathology*, trans. J. Hoenig and M. W. Hamilton (Chicago: University of Chicago Press, 1963), pp. 93–107.
4. J. H. Plokker, *Art from the Mentally Disturbed*, trans. I. Finlay (Boston: Little Brown, 1964), p. 56. *Wahrnehmungstarre* refers to a rigidity or stiffness of perception. *Wahrnehmung* means "perception" or "observation" in German; I have chosen to translate this in an unusually literal way—as "truth-taking"—because this seems better to capture the schizophrenic experience in question.
5. Paul Abély, "Le signe du miroir dans les psychoses et plus spécialement dans la démence précoce," *Annales Médico-Psychologiques*, 88, 1930, 28–36.
6. M. Hamilton, ed., *Fish's Schizophrenia*, 3rd ed. (Bristol, UK: John Wright, 1984), p. 180.
7. See Hamilton, *Fish's Schizophrenia*, 2nd ed., pp. 41–45. Delusional percept is one of Schneider's First Rank Symptoms of schizophrenia.

8. J. Cutting, *Psychology of Schizophrenia* (Edinburgh: Churchill Livingstone, 1985), p. 318.

9. J. Cutting and F. Dunne, "Subjective experience of schizophrenia," *Schizophrenia Bulletin, 15*, 1989, 229.

10. Jaspers, *General Psychopathology*, pp. 115–16.

11. As I use the term, then, the *anti-epiphany* includes epiphanic aspects. The Italian artist-critic Soffici, who knew de Chirico and set forth the principles of de Chirico's aesthetic in his essays, captured this paradox when he wrote that "the Sense of Senses, is nothing other than . . . Nonsense" (J. M. Lukach, "De Chirico and Italian art theory," in W. Rubin, ed., *De Chirico* [New York: Museum of Modern Art, 1982], p. 39).

12. De Chirico was a shy and isolated man who was excused from military duty in World War I because of mental instability. James Soby describes de Chirico's childhood as "marked by extreme introspection" and states that "in compensation for his isolation from the life around him, he developed an extraordinary reverence for inanimate objects" (*Giorgio de Chirico* [New York: Museum of Modern Art, n.d.], p. 5; see also pp. 7, 20, 58). Epigraph to chapter from de Chirico's manuscripts in M. Jean, ed., *The Autobiography of Surrealism*, trans. L. Bourgeois and R. Goldwater (New York: Viking Press, 1980), pp. 5–9.

13. See M. Nadeau, *The History of Surrealism* (New York: Penguin Books, 1973).

14. Quoted in Jean, *Autobiography of Surrealism*, p. 6.

15. E. Kahler, *The Tower and the Abyss: An Inquiry into the Transformation of Man* (New York: Viking, 1957), p. 182. After a discussion of Sartre's descriptions of such experiences, the exceptionally well read Kahler writes, "I do not know of any document relating such a consciously sustained and far-reaching existential experience before the beginning of our century, whereas since 1900 it has been expressed by more authors than could be quoted here, before and independent of explicit existentialism" (p. 182).

16. G. Picon, *Surrealists and Surrealism* (New York: Rizzoli, 1977), p. 59.

17. See Kahler, *Tower and Abyss*.

18. De Chirico declared that his own experience of the *Stimmung* "belongs to a class of sensations which I have observed in only one man: Nietzsche" (quoted in Jean, *Autobiography of Surrealism*, pp. 4–5). De Chirico mentions in particular the famous revelatory experience during which Nietzsche was inspired to write *Thus Spake Zarathustra*. This, interestingly enough, is the very moment in the philosopher's life when, according to Karl Jaspers, Nietzsche develops "a strangeness that places him at an unbridgeable distance" (*Nietzsche* [South Bend, IN: Regnery/Gateway, 1979], p. 92).

19. Klaus Conrad states that *all* forms of schizophrenia begin with the *Trema* and that some such illnesses never develop beyond this phase (in Hamilton, *Fish's Schizophrenia*, 3rd ed., pp. 183–84). Whether this is strictly true is no doubt debatable, but it is clearly the case that such experiences are especially characteristic of patients traditionally considered to be in the schizophrenia *spectrum* of disorders.

20. She was diagnosed, by various psychiatrists, as schizophrenic, as hebephrenic schizophrenic, and as having dementia praecox of a paranoid type; see M. Sechehaye, *Symbolic Realization* (New York: International Universities Press, 1951), pp. 18–19. "Hebephrenia" is a form of schizophrenia characterized by apparently incoherent speech, by incongruous, flat, or silly affect, and by mannerisms or other oddities of behavior.

21. M. Sechehaye, ed., *Autobiography of a Schizophrenic Girl* (New York: New American Library, 1970), p. 19.
22. Ibid., p. 33; see also p. 22 and passim.
23. Ibid., p. 28.
24. Ibid., pp. 28–29.
25. E. Bleuler, *Dementia Praecox or the Group of Schizophrenias*, trans. J. Zinkin (New York: International Universities Press, 1950), pp. 125, 141.
26. Patient quoted in J. Cutting, *The Right Cerebral Hemisphere and Psychiatric Disorders* (Oxford: Oxford University Press, 1990), p. 266.

It is possible that the phenomena I refer to (following Renee) as Unreality actually constitute a somewhat heterogeneous grouping. My usage of the term *Unreality* certainly seems to be more inclusive, in any case, than that which was understood in an important retrospective interview study conducted by J. Cutting and F. Dunne, where "a sense of unreality" seems to have referred primarily to a dreamlike quality ("Subjective experience of schizophrenia," *Schizophrenia Bulletin*, 15, 1989, 217–31). In the Cutting and Dunne study, experiences of unreality were *not* found to be highly characteristic of the early psychotic experiences of the schizophrenic patients. Their schizophrenic subjects did, however, describe the quality of reality as having changed in some indefinably strange way, and they particularly emphasized changes of visual perception. The changes they had experienced did not primarily involve an emotional tainting. Some aspects of the environment had altered, while others remained the same (things and people remained recognizable though they were distorted in shape or expression, perhaps exemplified by a patient who spoke of "fascination about waxworks, surreal imagery"). There was often a sense of distance between perceiver and perceived: for example, "I was here and they were there, and I was perceiving things away from me"; "I felt detached"; "It was like looking out the window and seeing things happen." Also, these schizophrenic subjects sometimes *did* use the word "unreal," if only to qualify it afterwards: for example, "Things were unreal, only from a mental viewpoint, not through my eyes"; "It wasn't really unreal; it was just strange, funny, different; I can't explain" (pp. 221, 227, 229–30). Clearly, there is considerable overlap between these phenomena and the sorts of experiences referred to as Unreality by Renee and by myself in the present chapter.
27. Cutting, *Right Cerebral Hemisphere*, p. 267.
28. Sechehaye, *Autobiography of a Schizophrenic Girl*, pp. 40–41.
29. Ibid., p. 41; see also p. 57: "And I said, 'The chair is making fun of me, it is playing tricks on me.' This was not quite exact, but I did not command the words to express the fear and this keen awareness that the chair was alive and had no other significance."
30. Ibid., p. 37. At another time Renee describes the world as appearing "in parts, divided, torn, a piece here, a piece there . . . an immense puzzle, a mosaic; each part is independent and has nothing to do with the next" (in M. Sechehaye, *A New Psychotherapy in Schizophrenia* [New York and London: Grune and Stratton, 1956], p. 62). This fragmentation was sometimes reflected in her drawings (p. 62)—as is often the case with drawing and other visual artwork by schizophrenics; see F. Reitmann, "Facial expression in schizophrenic drawings," *Journal of Mental Science*, 85, 1939, 264–72, quoted in Cutting, *Right Cerebral Hemisphere*, p. 290.

31. P. Matussek, "Studies in delusional perception," in Cutting and Shepherd, *Clinical Roots of Schizophrenia Concept*, p. 92.

32. J. Chapman, "The early symptoms of schizophrenia," *British Journal of Psychiatry, 112*, 1966, 229.

33. R. Rosser, "The psychopathology of feeling and thinking in a schizophrenic," *International Journal of Psychoanalysis, 60*, 1979, 184.

34. Term used by K. Conrad in 1958; see M. Hamilton, *Fish's Schizophrenia*, 3rd ed., p. 50.

35. See Cutting, *Right Cerebral Hemisphere*, pp. 142–43, for discussion of possible neurobiological underpinnings of this experience.

36. This particular experience does not seem to have been prominent in Renee's experience; but see *Autobiography of Schizophrenic Girl*, p. 76.

37. Jaspers, *General Psychopathology*, p. 100.

38. B. E. Brundage, "First person account: What I wanted to know but was afraid to ask," *Schizophrenia Bulletin, 9*, 1983, 583–85. See also R. Anscombe, "The disorder of consciousness in schizophrenia," *Schizophrenia Bulletin, 13*, 1987, 249.

39. Gérard de Nerval (1808–1854), whose psychotic illness seems to have been at least in the schizophrenic spectrum (he seems to have had a schizoaffective quality) and who is a major influence on modernism by way of his influence on symbolist poetry, expresses this experience very well in *Le Rêve et la Vie* (originally published in 1855), the narrative of his madness that Nerval was working on at the time of his suicide: "I then saw, vaguely drifting into form, plastic images of antiquity, which outlived themselves, became definite, and seemed to *represent symbols*, of which I only seized the idea with difficulty" (quoted in A. Symons, *The Symbolist Movement in Literature* [New York: Dutton, 1958], p. 18 [emphasis added]).

    A passage from *The Witnesses* (New Hyde Park, NY: University Books, 1967, p. 171), an autobiography by the schizophrenic Thomas Hennell, captures this peculiar mood, in which the feeling of significance is so omnipresent and powerful that even neutral or nondescript qualities can seem fraught with meaning, as if they too must surely *indicate* something: "Stray cats were presently discerned to be familiar spirits, whose movements tokened distant malice or misfortune, or most convincingly, indifference."

40. G. E. Berrios and J. Cutting have both remarked on this neglect; Berrios, "Delusions as 'wrong beliefs': A conceptual history," *British Journal of Psychiatry, 159* (suppl. 14), 1991, 12; Cutting, "Gestalt theory and psychiatry: Discussion paper," *Journal of the Royal Society of Medicine, 82*, 1989, 430.

41. A. McGhie and J. Chapman, "Disorders of attention and perception in early schizophrenia, *British Journal of Medical Psychology, 34*, 1961, 103–16. See also J. Chapman, "The early symptoms of schizophrenia," pp. 225–51; Cutting, *Psychology of Schizophrenia*, pp. 212–13.

42. McGhie and Chapman, "Attention and perception," pp. 112, 110. This information-processing conception is based on D. E. Broadbent's "filter" mechanism model of attention; see A. McGhie, *Pathology of Attention* (Harmondsworth, UK: Penguin, 1969), pp. 9, 16–19.

43. See P. Matussek, "Studies in delusional perception," in Cutting and Shepherd, *Clinical Roots*, pp. 89–103; Cutting, "Gestalt theory and psychiatry"; Hamilton, *Fish's Schizophrenia*, 3rd ed., pp. 51–52, 128, 180–84. My discussion in this

chapter has much in common with the views of Conrad and Matussek. I disagree, however, with their tendency to neglect elements of active intentionality (as discussed at the end of this chapter).

44. Actually, not only McGhie and Chapman but also both Matussek and Conrad considered the cognitive disturbances which they described to be manifestations of some kind of regression to ontogenetically or phylogenetically earlier modes of perceptual awareness. See McGhie and Chapman, "Attention and perception," pp. 103, 107, 110–12; Matussek, "Studies in delusional perception," p. 99 (where Matussek suggests a primitivity interpretation but without offering any real argument for it). Re Conrad, see P. Berner, "Delusional atmosphere," *British Journal of Psychiatry, 159* (suppl. 14), 1991, 89. These primitivity interpretations can, however, easily be detached from the (far less speculative) accounts that these writers offer of the perceptual changes; so I (like most other commentators on the theories in question) have chosen to ignore this aspect. Arguments against the psychoanalytic primitivity model offered later in this chapter would, however, also apply to this (nonessential) feature of these cognitively oriented theories.

45. Sechehaye, *Autobiography of Schizophrenic Girl*, pp. xiv, 123, 118. Says Sechehaye: "Approaching adulthood, a too-demanding environmental complexity drove her back to a lower, infantile level of development. The first sign of ego regression consisted in the strange perception of the real, giving rise to severe anxiety" (p. 117).

46. P. Federn, *Ego Psychology and the Psychoses* (London: Maresfield Reprints, 1953).

47. S. Arieti, *The Interpretation of Schizophrenia*, 2nd ed. (New York: Basic Books, 1974), p. 121. For a regression interpretation of the fragmentation experience, see idem, "The microgeny of thought and perception," *AMA Archives of General Psychiatry, 6*, 1962, 463–66.

48. S. Freud, "The uncanny," in *Studies in Parapsychology*, ed. P. Rieff (New York: Collier Books, 1963; originally published in 1919), pp. 20, 42–47, 58.

49. The combination of strangeness with recognition is clearly present in de Chirico's Apophany: "Everything looked at me with a strange and questioning glance. . . . At that moment it seemed to me that I had already seen this palace, or that this palace had once, somewhere, already existed. Why are these round windows an enigma?" De Chirico, in Jean, *Autobiography of Surrealism*, pp. 8–9.

50. Freud, "The uncanny," p. 20.

51. H. von Hofmannsthal, *Selected Prose* (New York: Pantheon, 1952), pp. 142–44.

52. Ibid., p. 147.

53. Ibid., pp. 133–34.

54. Ibid., pp. 134–35.

55. Ibid., p. 138. A mood of exaltation can occur in the schizophrenic *Stimmung;* see Schneider, *Clinical Psychopathology*, p. 109. This mood does not seem to have been characteristic of Renee, however; but see *Autobiography of Schizophrenic Girl*, p. 24.

56. R. Musil, *The Man Without Qualities*, vol. 2, trans. E. Wilkins and E. Kaiser (London: Pan Books, 1979), p. 275.

57. S. Beckett, *Watt* (New York: Grove Press, 1959), p. 81.

58. R. Musil, *Young Torless*, trans. E. Wilkins and E. Kaiser (New York: New American Library, 1955), p. 136. There is an interesting description of an Apo-

phany experience in Musil's *The Man Without Qualities* (vol. 3), suggestive of the linkage to that sense of personal centrality conducive to delusions of reference: "The mute emphasis of life itself outweighed all natural chance, randomness, the accidental. . . . [Clarisse] found a meaning in almost insubstantial correspondences, such as the fact that one man stopped under her window and another was a carpenter. . . . [This experience] entitled Clarisse to assert that it was she herself who attracted whatever it might be" (trans. E. Wilkins and E. Kaiser [London: Picador, 1979], p. 308). See also R. Barthes, *Writing Degree Zero* (published with *Elements of Semiology*), trans. A. Lavers and C. Smith (Boston: Beacon Press, 1967), p. 50: In modern poetry, Barthes writes, "nature becomes a fragmented space, made of objects solitary and terrible, because the links between them are only potential. . . . Nature becomes a succession of verticalities, of objects, suddenly standing erect, and filled with all their possibilities." Encroaching Unreality is described in Rilke's autobiographical *The Notebooks of Malte Laurids Brigge* ([London: Hogarth, 1930; originally published in 1910], p. 49), which is a harbinger of themes of alienation that were to become almost commonplace as the century proceeded. The narrator tells of his fear that he is withdrawing not only from human beings but from everything: "A moment more and everything will have lost its meaning, and that table and the cup, and the chair to which he clings, all the near and commonplace things around him, will have become unintelligible, strange, and burdensome."

59. See E. Heller, *The Disinherited Mind* (New York and London: Harcourt Brace Jovanovich, 1977), p. 172; also, *In the Age of Prose* (Cambridge: Cambridge University Press, 1984), pp. 15, 19.

60. See J. Piaget and B. Inhelder, *The Child's Conception of Space,* trans. F. J. Langdon and J. L. Lunzer, in H. E. Gruber and J. J. Vonèche, eds., *The Essential Piaget* (New York: Basic Books, 1977), pp. 635–38.

61. Lively discussions of the perceptual world of the child can be found in: E. Schachtel, *Metamorphosis* (New York: Basic Books, 1959); J. Church, *Language and the Discovery of Reality* (New York: Vintage Books, 1966). See also Merleau-Ponty, *The Structure of Behavior*, trans. A. L. Fisher (Boston: Beacon Press, 1963), pp. 166–71; and, of course, the works of Heinz Werner and Jean Piaget.

The dynamism, sensory aliveness, and pervasiveness of appetite and visceral involvement characteristic of the child's world, have never more effectively been evoked than in the first paragraphs of James Joyce's *A Portrait of the Artist as a Young Man* ([New York: Viking, 1964; originally published in 1916], p. 7):

Once upon a time and a very good time it was there was a moocow coming down along the road and this moocow that was coming down along the road met a nicens little boy named baby tuckoo . . .

His father told him that story: his father looked at him through a glass: he had a hairy face.

He was baby tuckoo. The moocow came down the road where Betty Byrne lived: she sold lemon platt.

Oh, the wild rose blossoms
On the little green place. . . .

When you wet the bed first it is warm then it gets cold. His mother put on the oilsheet. That had the queer smell.

His mother had a nicer smell than his father. She played on the piano the sailor's hornpipe for him to dance. He danced.

62. In 1912 de Chirico, for example, spoke of the aim of future painting as "once and for all to free itself from the anthropomorphism that always shackles sculpture; to see everything, even man, in its quality of *thing*. . . . This is what I try to demonstrate in my pictures" ("Meditations of a painter," in H. B. Chipp, ed., *Theories of Modern Art* [Berkeley: University of California Press, 1968], p. 397). See V. Erlich, *Russian Formalism* (New Haven and London: Yale University Press, 1981), pp. 182–83, re the Russian formalists' rejection of the emotivist theory of poetic language.

63. Kahler, *Tower and Abyss,* pp. 182, 90, 159.

64. See M. Nadeau, *The History of Surrealism,* trans. R. Howard (Harmondsworth, UK: Penguin Books, 1973), p. 114.

65. Kahler, *Tower and Abyss,* pp. 154, 98.

66. Sechehaye, *Autobiography of Schizophrenic Girl,* pp. 33, 25, x.

67. Ibid., p. 97. See also J. Frosch, *The Psychotic Process* (New York: International Universities Press, 1983), p. 289; H. Werner and B. Kaplan, *Symbol Formation* (New York: Wiley, 1963), p. 256.

68. Sechehaye, *Autobiography of Schizophrenic Girl,* p. 37. Schizophrenics commonly see both other human beings and themselves as somehow mechanical—"a cross between robots and people," as one patient said (Cutting, *Right Cerebral Hemisphere,* p. 256). A study by Norman Cameron showed that the explanations given by schizophrenics are much more likely to refer to cause-and-effect relationships than to psychological motivations, in contrast with those favored by young children ("Reasoning, regression, and communication in schizophrenia," *Psychological Monographs, 50* [whole no. 221], 1938).

69. Sechehaye interprets certain difficulties Renee had with adopting a normal sense of perspective in time and space as manifestations of a primitive egocentricity that allowed her to relate things only to herself in a manner characteristic of young children (*Autobiography of Schizophrenic Girl,* p. 114). But one can also understand this difficulty as resulting from a sense of alienation and detachment so profound that it robs Renee of any *sense* of situatedness in time or space, and thus of any anchoring point from which to organize the world. This would, of course, be almost the opposite of the experiential world of the infant or young child, who is too embedded in or limited to a single perspective. Thus, in Renee's Land of Illumination, all parts of the visual field seem to be of equal importance, as if Renee herself were everywhere and nowhere. (This quality is also characteristic of de Chirico's paintings, which simultaneously offer several different, mutually contradictory sets of converging perspective lines, thus defying the viewer's sense of being situated at a single point in space; see W. Rubin, "De Chirico and modernism," *De Chirico.*) And, although Renee does perceive motion and action—people scurrying about like ants, for instance—at the same moment she also has the sense of a sort of cosmic paralysis. Even the movement all around her somehow seems still and unchanging—as if her own profound sense of disengagement from any possible action or involvement had somehow caused time itself to come to a halt, to collapse into a single, unchanging present moment. (Renee's sense of unsituatedness may also be reflected in her prefer-

ence for being referred to in the third person.) For a philosophical reading of Renee's lived world, see my essay "The truth-taking stare: A Heideggerian interpretation of a schizophrenic world," *Journal of Phenomenological Psychology, 21,* 1990, 121–49.

70. Most psychoanalytic interpretations of the *Stimmung* involve fairly straightforward regression theories of the sort I have criticized above. There are, however, two psychoanalytic interpretations of schizophrenia that seem more compatible with the phenomenological realities of the *Stimmung* than are the theories I have criticized.

According to the first of these theories, the schizophrenic condition involves a profoundly narcissistic return of cathexes (mental energies) onto the self and a concomitant withdrawal of these cathexes from the external world—an argument put forward by Freud, among others. (See Freud, "On narcissim: An introduction" and "The unconscious," both in *General Psychological Theory* [New York: Collier Books, 1963; originally published in 1914, 1915].) This shift is presumed to be motivated by the overwhelming anxiety aroused by external reality. If applied to one aspect of the *Stimmung*—Unreality—such an interpretation seems apt enough, for one could argue that the devitalization of the external world characteristic of the Unreality vision is a phenomenological consequence of this decathecting of the world. But it is more difficult to see how it could account for the visions of Mere Being and Fragmentation or for the Apophanous mood, since these involve an exaggerated focus *on* the external world (and on an external world that is *not*, via projection or fusion, imbued with emotive, or in any sense "inner" qualities). The notion of a removal of psychological interest from what is "outside" and a return to what is "inner" hardly seems consistent with the transfixing fascination with the perceptual world felt by patients in such a state.

The second theory postulates that the Stimmung is a manifestation not of regression itself but of defense *against* regression—a defense that involves not introversion of cathexis but a nearly total shutting down of all emotional responsivity. (See, e.g., T. H. McGlashan, "Aphanasis: The syndrome of pseudo-depression in schizophrenia," *Schizophrenia Bulletin, 8,* 1982, 118–34; and K. R. Eissler, "Notes upon the emotionality of a schizophrenic patient," *Psychoanalytic Study of the Child, 8,* 1953, 199–251.) This shutting down has been seen as a defensive response to an anticipated and feared regression to a (primitive) mode of experience characterized by chaotic affect states. Here again, the Unreality experience seems compatible with such a model of the intrapsychic dynamics of schizophrenia: presumably, Unreality would be the inner, symptomatic counterpart to the schizophrenic sign of "flatness of affect," understood as being a defensive reaction. Further, since this theory does not imply lack of all *interest* in the external world, but specifically an absence of *affective* interest, it may not be contradicted by the appalled fascination with external reality that is characteristic of the *Stimmung*. It should be noted, however, that those who take such a position have generally considered the later phenomena of full-blown schizophrenic illness to be manifestations of primitivity, even if this presumably brief moment of defense against regression (the prodromal *Stimmung*) is not.

I cannot claim to have offered any convincing refutation of this latter interpretation in this chapter. Indeed, in some respects such a view, with its emphasis on the severe diminishment of emotional responsivity and engagement, is quite consistent with my phenomenological account. In any case, a phenomenological examination such as I have offered could not on principle refute such a theory— which, by postulating experiences hidden from the subjects themselves, operates more at a metapsychological than a phenomenological level. But I would disagree with a psychoanalytic theorist who, in adopting such an interpretation, wished to dismiss the importance of the phenomena I have been discussing on the grounds that they are short-lived and of a "merely" defensive significance. One way of countering such a dismissal would be to demonstrate that later phases of schizophrenia involve a further exacerbation of such states of hyperconsciousness, not a lapsing *out* of such states (the latter being the usual psychoanalytic view of full-blown stages of psychosis). In the remaining chapters of this book I go on to make just such an argument.

I should add that I would disagree with any attempt to distinguish *"merely defensive"* from truly constitutive elements of psychopathology, if this were meant to imply that the defensive withdrawal or affective shutting down is somehow less central to the true essence of schizophrenia. For, even if the *Stimmung*-as-defense-against-regression interpretation were accurate, it would still be the case that the patient's mode of experience is largely determined by "defensive" aspects of schizophrenia; it is these, I would argue, that give the illness its characteristically *schizophrenic* stamp.

71. Jaspers, *General Psychopathology*, p. 100. See also K. Schneider, *Clinical Psychopathology*, 5th ed., trans. M. W. Hamilton (New York: Grune and Stratton, 1959), pp. 104–10, re the "preparatory field" of "delusional atmosphere" that often precedes delusional perception.

72. I think Schneider is wrong to say (*Clinical Psychopathology*, p. 109) that the delusional atmosphere offers no hint as to the content of the delusional perceptions that arise out of it. Paranoid themes, and also concerns regarding the falseness, inauthenticity, or repetitiousness of objects or events, can be understood as deriving from the particular perceptual qualities of the delusional atmosphere.

73. Delusions need not always develop out of the apophanous phase (which seems most likely to engender paranoid delusions of reference). They may also, for example, develop out of the Unreality or Mere Being experiences—as seemed to be the case with one patient I interviewed whose primary delusional idea was the preoccupying thought that no one but himself really had consciousness, that what seemed to be other human beings were really just illusions or else elaborate automatons.

Re the experiential progression of schizophrenic symptoms, see Matussek, "Studies in delusional perception"; Hamilton, *Fish's Schizophrenia*, 3rd ed., pp. 180–84; and M. Bowers, *Retreat from Sanity: The Structure of Emerging Psychosis* (Baltimore: Penguin Books, 1974), pp. 175–92.

Some of the possible neurobiological and cognitive underpinnings of such processes of delusion formation are ingeniously described in two papers that came to my attention very recently: D. R. Hemsley, "Cognitive abnormalities and the symptoms of schizophrenia," and H. M. Emrich, "Subjectivity, error correction capacity, and the pathogenesis of delusions of reference," both to appear in M. Spitzer, F. A. Uehlein, M. A. Schwartz, and C. Mundt, eds., *Phenomenology, Language, and Schizophrenia* (New York: Springer, 1992).

74. Matussek, "Studies in delusional perception," p. 96.

75. Sechehaye, *Autobiography of Schizophrenic Girl*, pp. 57–58.
76. R. Poggioli, *The Theory of the Avant-Garde*, trans. G. Fitzgerald (Cambridge: Harvard University Press, 1968), p. 191.
77. Actually, this is true to some extent even of von Hofmannsthal and Rilke, who, after all, took the loss-of-meaning experience as a major theme for their art.
78. Erlich, *Russian Formalism*; G. M. Hyde, "Russian futurism," in M. Bradbury and J. McFarlane, eds., *Modernism* (Harmondsworth, UK: Penguin, 1976), pp. 259–73.
79. In one of his (proto-surrealist) descriptions of the creative state of mind, de Chirico focuses on this aspect of memory, describing its loss as a kind of madness that, he says, is "an inherent phenomenon in all profound artistic manifestations":

Schopenhauer defines the madman as a person who has lost his memory. It is an apt definition because, in fact, that which constitutes the logic of our normal acts and our normal life is a continuous rosary of recollections of relationships between things and ourselves and vice versa.
. . . But let us suppose that for a moment, for reasons that remain unexplainable and quite beyond my will, the thread of this series is broken. Who knows how I might see the seated man, the cage, the paintings, the bookcase! Who knows with what astonishment, what terror and possibly also with what pleasure and consolation I might view the scene.
The scene, however, would not be changed; it is I who would see it from a different angle. Here we meet the metaphysical aspect of things . . . which can be seen only by rare individuals in moments of clairvoyance or metaphysical abstraction, just as certain bodies that exist within matter which cannot be penetrated by the sun's rays, appear only under the power of artificial light, under X-ray for example. [in Chipp, *Theories of Modern Art*, p. 450]

This description, interestingly enough, is precisely congruent with certain recently proposed interpretations of schizophrenic experience that emphasize disturbances in hippocampus-based "comparator systems" and consequent disruption of the role of stored regularities of previous perception and the guiding "world-models" of expected new perceptual input that they generate; see D. R. Hemsley, "Cognitive abnormalities and symptoms of schizophrenia," and H. M. Emrich, "Subjectivity, error correction capacity," both to appear in M. Spitzer, et al., *Phenomenology, Language, and Schizophrenia*.
80. F. Jameson, *The Prison-House of Language* (Princeton, NJ: Princeton University Press, 1972), p. 60. Jakobson, another member of the formalist school, defined the function of poetry as: "to point out that the sign is not identical with its referent"; for without this awareness, "the connection between the sign and the object becomes automatized and the perception of reality withers away" (quoted in Erlich, *Russian Formalism*, p. 181).
81. Nadeau, *History of Surrealism*, p. 22.
82. A. Breton, *Nadja* (New York: Grove Press, 1960), pp. 59, 16.
83. A. Breton, "Crise de l'objet," *Cahiers d'Art*, 1, 1936, 21–26.
84. Breton, *Nadja*, pp. 19–20. This surrealist mood could be called *pseudo*-allegorical, for there is a feeling of meaning without any real, specific meaning to be

discovered. As Breton says, the surrealist image or analogy "does not presuppose, beyond the visible world, an invisible world which is striving to manifest itself"; and this, according to Leopold Senghor, is what distinguishes it from the images and fetish objects of African surrealism, which is truly mystical or metaphysical in nature (Senghor, "Speech and image: An African tradition of the surreal," in J. Rothenberg and D. Rothenberg, eds., *Symposium of the Whole* [Berkeley: University of California Press, 1983], pp. 119–20; Breton quoted on p. 120). Incidentally, the surrealists often did profess to adhere to a primitivist aesthetic; and both they and the Russian formalists would sometimes compare the renewal of vision they were seeking to that available to the child; see, for example, Erlich, *Russian Formalism,* p. 76. The self-consciousness and sophistication of their methods, and the qualities of alienation and de-animation that they achieved, tend to belie this claim and this comparison; re this, see discussion in R. Goldwater, *Primitivism in Modern Art* (Cambridge: Harvard University Press, 1986), p. 222.

85. S. Sontag, "The aesthetics of silence," *Styles of Radical Will* (New York: Dell, 1978), pp. 15–16.

86. A fixed stare can also result in a reversal of normal figure-ground relations—not just of an isolated perceptual Gestalt but of those figure-ground relationships that define the horizons of our very being. This seems to have occurred with one patient who stared at a swinging light cord until it began to seem stable while the rest of the world was in motion (Matussek, "Studies in delusional perception," p. 93). To interpret such a perception as indicating that the end of the world has come, as this patient did, is certainly far-fetched, yet it cannot be said to be completely beyond the pale of empathic comprehension.

This kind of perceptual experience would seem to require a disconnection from the lived body, which usually keeps us anchored in a particular standpoint and meaningful context. For normally, as Merleau-Ponty has written, our "own body is in the world as the heart is in the organism: it keeps the visible spectacle constantly alive, it breathes life into it and sustains it inwardly, and with it forms a system" (*Phenomenology of Perception,* trans. C. Smith [London: Routledge and Kegan Paul, 1962], p. 203).

In some fairly recent work, the British artist David Hockney was attempting to replace this kind of "stare" with something closer to "the look." In a published interview, he discusses such ideas as that "one-point perspective robs the viewer of his body" and "how photography paves the way to madness." He speaks of wanting instead to develop a photographic technique that captures the fact that (in normal modes of experience) "a human eye never stares but is always darting about" and that "we can't separate ourselves from the world" (quoted in D. McGill, "David Hockney's journey to the new cubism," *New York Times,* November 21, 1984, p. H29).

87. Quoted in Kahler, *Tower and Abyss,* p. 177 (first page of *Nausea*).

88. At one point this happens when Roquentin examines his own face in the mirror: I can understand nothing of this face. . . . My glance slowly and wearily travels over my forehead, my cheeks: it finds nothing firm, it is stranded. Obviously there are a nose, two eyes and a mouth, but none of it makes sense, there is not even a human expression. . . . Brown wrinkles show on each side of the feverish swelled lips . . . it is a geological embossed map. And, in spite of everything this

lunar world is familiar to me. I cannot say I *recognize* the details. But the whole thing gives me an impression of something seen before which stupefies me (*Nausea,* trans. L. Alexander [New York: New Directions, 1969], pp. 16–17).

89. Kahler, *Tower and Abyss,* pp. 138, 182, 177.

90. Ibid., p. 170.

91. Sechehaye, *Autobiography of Schizophrenic Girl,* p. 57 (emphasis added).

92. Jaspers, *General Psychopathology,* p. 122 (emphasis added).

93. Cutting, *Right Cerebral Hemisphere,* p. 259. Renee, too, said she was sometimes "held motionless by a blade of grass or a ray of light (*Autobiography of Schizophrenic Girl,* p. 65). Renee would usually focus on small things, a tiny spot, a drop of coffee, a shadow, or a ray of light—"the boundless world of the infinitely small," as she called it (pp. 55–56).

94. D. Shapiro, describing paranoid cognitive style: *Neurotic Styles* (New York: Basic Books, 1965), p. 74. See also P. F. Gjerde, "Attentional capacity dysfunction and arousal in schizophrenia," *Psychological Bulletin,* 93, 1983, 57–72, re anxiety and arousal as possible explanations of schizophrenic cognitive aberrations.

95. D. P. Schreber, *Memoirs of My Nervous Illness,* trans I. Macalpine and R. A. Hunter (Cambridge: Harvard University Press, 1988; originally published in German in 1903), p. 64. See also McGhie and Chapman, "Attention and perception," p. 104.

96. Patients quoted in Chapman, "Early symptoms of schizophrenia," p. 239; Cutting and Dunne, "Subjective experience," pp. 221–22.

97. Beckett, *Watt,* pp. 85–86.

98. See, for example, J. A. Gray, J. Feldon, J. N. P. Rawlins, et al., "The neuropsychology of schizophrenia, *Behavioral and Brain Sciences,* 1991, 18. See also D. R. Hemsley, "An experimental psychological model for schizophrenia," in H. Häfner, W. F. Gattaz, and W. Janzarik, eds., *Search for the Causes of Schizophrenia* (Berlin and Heidelberg: Springer, 1987), pp. 179–88.

99. See, for example, Cutting, *Right Cerebral Hemisphere,* pp. 77, 327, 409–10, and passim. The phrase "almost obsessed with parts" is quoted from J. Levy, "Cerebral asymmetries as manifested in split-brain man," in M. Kinsbourne and W. L. Smith, eds., *Hemisphere Disconnection and Cerebral Function* (Springfield, IL: Charles Thomas, 1974), pp. 165–83.

100. Gjerde and others have proposed that we should see schizophrenia as an arousal disorder rather than as an information-processing disorder; see Gjerde, "Attentional capacity dysfunction," esp. pp. 64–67, 70; see also Cutting, *Psychology of Schizophrenia,* pp. 215, 366–67. An increase in arousal (i.e., in the activity level of psychophysiological systems reflecting the state of the sympathetic nervous system or the reticular activating system) or of anxiety can have the effect, among others, of narrowing the width of the beam of attention, so that less attention is paid to cues in the visual periphery, which would cut down on the usual sense of context. It may also result in a bias toward noticing physical characteristics of a stimulus rather than semantic ones (which could be related to the experience of Mere Being). Interestingly enough, higher levels of arousal seem to be characteristic of introverted, as opposed to extraverted, personalities—and this would include the schizoid type (the most common "premorbid" personality type for schizophrenia). A state of high arousal is also consistent with the curious combination of activity and passivity that can characterize schizophrenic attention: thus, high arousal tends to impair the ability to be selective in the information one attends to, and also the ability to use

active, organizational processes. Yet high arousal also leads to a reliance on serial modes of processing, which are more deliberate, where parallel or simultaneous processing would previously have been used. While hyperarousal is not very widely accepted as a general explanation of schizophrenic symptomatology, it is certainly plausible that such processes could play an important role in the early phases of the *Stimmung*.

101. Re eye-tracking, see P. Holzman, "Cognitive impairment and cognitive stability," in G. Serban, ed., *Cognitive Defects in the Development of Mental Illness* (New York: Brunner/Mazel, 1978), pp. 365–67; but for evidence *against* maintenance of attention as an essential feature of schizophrenia, see Cutting, *Psychology of Schizophrenia*, pp. 211–12.

102. Still another neurobiological-cognitive hypothesis of potential relevance is the one offered by C. D. Frith and D. J. Done, who postulate a degradation of the feedback from willed intentions ("Toward a neuropsychology of schizophrenia," *British Journal of Psychiatry, 153*, 1988). If one bears in mind the probable dependence of normal modes of perception on a sense of rootedness in the lived body (which obviously presupposes having a sense of intentionality, of *inhabiting* one's actions), it seems quite possible that this hypothesis could account for many of the perceptual changes of the *Stimmung*. Re the relationship of lived-body and perception, see M. Merleau-Ponty, *Phenomenology of Perception*, esp. part 2, pp. 203–345.

103. C. Lamb, "Sanity of true genius," in T. N. Talfourd, ed., *The Works of Charles Lamb*, vol. 2 (New York: Harper and Bros., 1858), pp. 204–7; E. Kris, *Psychoanalytic Explorations in Art* (New York: Schocken Books, 1964), pp. 103–5 (see also pp. 25, 60, 253–54, 292–93, 302, 311–13). In the essay mentioned, Carl Jung compared avant-garde artists with psychotic people on the grounds that in each case intellect or ego is readily overcome by an exuberant flood of ungovernable Dionysian forces and immersion in the sensory surround. Jung maintained that James Joyce's *Ulysses*, often considered the quintessential modernist novel, is devoid of an ego or self, an "acutely conscious human center," and therefore manifests the "abaissement du niveau mentale" to be found in schizophrenics and the brain-damaged: "If worms were gifted with literary powers, they would write with the sympathetic nervous system for lack of a brain. I suspect that something of this kind has happened to Joyce, that we have here a case of visceral thinking with severe restriction of cerebral activity and its confinement to the perceptual processes" ("'Ulysses,' a monologue," in *The Spirit in Man, Art, and Literature* [Princeton, NJ: Princeton University Press, 1971], pp. 119, 125, 112). Also see my introduction.

104. R. Ellman, *James Joyce* (New York: Oxford University Press, 1959), p. 692. R. Ellman, *James Joyce*, rev. ed. (New York: Oxford University Press, 1982), p. 679. Line re "all his creative forces" is from a letter Jung wrote in 1955 (G. Adler, ed., *C. G. Jung: Letters* [Princeton, NJ: Princeton University Press, 1973], p. 266).

105. For example, see A. F. Fontana and E. B. Klein, "Self-presentation and the schizophrenic 'deficit,'" *Journal of Consulting and Clinical Psychology, 32,* 1968, 250–56; H. D. Brenner, W. Böker, J. Müller, L. Spichtig, and S. Würgler, "On autoprotective efforts of schizophrenics, neurotics, and controls," *Acta Psychiatrica Scandinavica, 75,* 1987, 405–14; V. Carr, "Patient's techniques for coping with schizophrenia: An exploratory study," *British Journal of Medical Psychology, 61,* 1988, 339–52; J. S. Strauss, "Subjective experiences of schizophrenia: Toward a new dynamic psychiatry—II," *Schizophre-*

nia Bulletin, 15, 1989, 179–87. See also M. Bleuler, *Schizophrenic Disorders,* pp. 480–81, 488–89.

106. M. H. Johnston and P. Holzman, *Assessing Schizophrenic Thinking* (San Francisco: Jossey-Bass, 1979), p. 17. Another of many possible examples: "Mais l'automatisme de l'Art est bien différent et s'oppose à celui de la folie. L'artiste en cultive son esprit, en apprenant son métier, prépare volontairement son automatisme. . . . Le fou subit l'automatisme imposé par la folie" (Jean Vinchon, *L'Art et la Folie* [Paris: Librairie Stock, 1924], p. 120).

107. See S. J. Schneider, "Selective attention in schizophrenia," *Journal of Abnormal Psychology, 85,* 1976, 167–73; C. D. Frith, "Consciousness, information processing, and schizophrenia," *British Journal of Psychiatry, 134,* 1979, 225–35. Re these and other problems with the selective attention hypothesis, at least as traditionally formulated, see Cutting, *Psychology of Schizophrenia,* pp. 212–13, and pp. 208 and 216 re the fact that distractibility or disturbance of concentration is at least as common in depression and in psychotic disorders more generally. See also D. R. Hemsley, "Attention and information processing in schizophrenia," *British Journal of Social and Clinical Psychology, 15,* 1976, 199–209; and the references in C. D. Frith and H. Allen, "Language disorders in schizophrenia and their implications for neuropsychology," in P. Bebbington and P. McGuffin, eds., *Schizophrenia: The Major Issues* (Oxford: Heinemann, 1988), p. 176. Re abnormalities of schizophrenic attention as due not to distractibility or a general broadening (à la McGhie and Chapman), but, rather, to the loss of an ongoing sense of context (of "the influence of stored regularities on current perception"), see Hemsley, "Cognitive abnormalities"; also S. H. Jones, D. R. Hemsley, and J. A. Gray, "Contextual effects on choice reaction time and accuracy in acute and chronic schizophrenics: Impairment in selective attention or in the influence of prior learning?" *British Journal of Psychiatry, 159,* 1991, 415–21.

108. J. Cutting has made this point; *Right Cerebral Hemisphere,* p. 258.

109. See Cutting, *Psychology of Schizophrenia,* pp. 299, 308. Re ideational rather than intuitive style, see J. Exner, "Some Rorschach data comparing schizophrenics with borderline and schizotypal personality disorders, *Journal of Personality Assessment, 50,* 1986. See also J. Zubin, "Problem of attention in schizophrenia," in M. L. Kietzman, S. Sutton, and J. Zubin, eds., *Experimental Approaches to Psychopathology* (New York: Academic Press, 1975, 139–66), pp. 146, 160. Zubin argues that what may seem to be indications of disturbed selective attention, maintenance of attention, and reaction time (slowness) in schizophrenia may in fact be a function of "the goalless uniquely idiosyncratic life" or the unusual "culture" and past experience of the typical schizophrenic person.

110. See Matussek, "Studies in delusional perception," pp. 93–94.

111. Cutting, *Right Cerebral Hemisphere,* p. 286; Cutting, *Psychology of Schizophrenia,* p. 299. See also J. Baruch, D. R. Hemsley, and J. A. Gray, "Differential performance of acute and chronic schizophrenics in a latent inhibition task," *Journal of Nervous and Mental Disease, 176,* 1988, 598–606.

112. Sechehaye, *Autobiography of Schizophrenic Girl,* p. 22.

113. There is suggestive evidence of this difference in findings reported by A. Breier and J. S. Strauss: "Self-control in psychotic disorders," *Archives of General Psychiatry, 40,* 1983, 1141–45. See also Jaspers, *General Psychopathology,* p. 141.

114. Quoted in Sechehaye, *A New Psychotherapy*, p. 32. Renee would do the same thing, Sechehaye notes.
115. See, for example, Sechehaye, *Autobiography of Schizophrenic Girl*, pp. 33, 34.
116. Ibid., p. 22. Renee herself was surprised to discover what madness really was (submersion in the "electric light") and that it could not provide an escape from her "consuming fear" (pp. 32–33).
117. O. Paz, *The Labyrinth of Solitude*, trans. L. Kemp (New York: Grove Press, 1961), pp. 62–63.

Chapter 3: The Separated Self

1. See, for example, J.-P. Sartre's *Being and Nothingness*, trans. H. Barnes (New York: Philosophical Library, 1956). See also the notebooks of Paul Valéry (section re "conscience" in particular).
2. P. Valéry, *Cahiers*, vol. 2, ed. J. Robinson (Paris: Gallimard, 1974), p. 224; idem, *Monsieur Teste*, trans. J. Matthews (Princeton, NJ: Princeton University Press, 1973), p. 107.
3. R. D. Laing, *The Divided Self* (Harmondsworth, UK: Penguin Books, 1965), p. 17.
4. Manfred Bleuler reports studies finding 52 percent and 58 percent of schizophrenics to have been premorbidly schizoid (*The Schizophrenic Disorders*, trans. S. M. Clemens (New Haven and London: Yale University Press, 1977), p. 163. This would be in contrast to an incidence of 1 to 2 percent in the general population (p. 164); re first usage of term *schizoid*, see pp. 129 and 434. One recent study found 39 percent of a sample of DSM III-R schizophrenic patients to have had premorbid personality disorders of the schizoid-schizotypal kind; 44 percent seem to have had normal personalities (V. Peralta, M. J. Cuesta, and J. de Leon, "Premorbid personality and positive and negative symptoms in schizophrenia," *Acta Psychiatrica Scandinavica*, 84, 1991, 336–39). See also J. J. Nannarello, "Schizoid," *Journal of Nervous and Mental Disease, 118*, 1953, 242; and E. Bleuler (*Dementia Praecox or the Group of Schizophrenias*, trans. J. Zinkin [New York: International Universities Press, 1950], pp. 251–52), who reports finding premorbid schizoidlike traits in over half his schizophrenic patients.
5. R. Gittelman-Klein and D. F. Klein, "Premorbid asocial adjustment and prognosis in schizophrenia," *Journal of Psychiatric Research*, 7, 1969, 35–53. C. Azarcate, "Schizoid, asthenic, and inadequate personalities," in J. Lion, ed., *Personality Disorders: Diagnosis and Management* (Baltimore: Williams and Wilkins, 1974), p. 107.
   My use of *schizoid* accords with that of E. Bleuler, E. Kretschmer, and other classic writers on the topic. This is a broader usage than the one found in DSM III and DSM III-R, since it applies to many patients who would be given the diagnoses *schizotypal* and *avoidant* as well as *schizoid personality disorder* in those systems. As Manfred Bleuler states, "There still is no better term that includes all the kinds of aberrant psychiatric morbidity shared by the later schizophrenics and by many of their relatives than that of the schizoid personality" (*Schizophrenic Disorders*, p. 437; see also pp. 153–65).
   In developing DSM III, the earlier DSM II category of *schizoid personality* (which approximates the classical concept of, say, Bleuler) was divided into these three closely related clusters, with the term *schizoid* now being used in

a more narrow sense; see J. R. Lion, "A comparison between DSM III and DSM II personality disorders," in J. R. Lion, ed., *Personality Disorders: Diagnosis and Management*, 2nd ed. (Malabar, FL: Robert E. Krieger, 1986), pp. 3–4. The only significant features of these three DSM III categories *not* discussed in the present chapter are certain peculiarities of cognition and language that are included in the DSM III criteria for schizotypal personality; some of these can be thought of as milder versions of the phenomena discussed in other chapters of this book. Research by Gunderson and Siever suggests that these latter peculiarities (including magical thinking, recurrent illusions, dissociative experiences, and, probably, odd speech) may be less discriminating of individuals with a genetic predisposition to schizophrenia than are abnormalities of social adaptiveness and affective relatedness of the kind discussed in the present chapter. See L. J. Siever and J. G. Gunderson, "The search for a schizotypal personality: Historical origins and current status," *Comprehensive Psychiatry*, *24*, 1983, 199–212; J. G. Gunderson, L. J. Siever, and E. Spaulding, "The search for a schizotype: Crossing the border again," *Archives of General Psychiatry*, *40*, 1983, 15–22.

The possible affinities of schizoid, avoidant, and schizotypal personality disorders have been recognized again in DSM III-R, since the exclusion criteria that, in DSM III, had precluded assigning both the diagnoses Schizoid and Schizotypal, or Schizoid and Avoidant Personality Disorders, have now been eliminated (thus returning us, in some sense, to the classical positions of Eugen Bleuler and Kretschmer).

Re avoidant traits as possible precursors to schizophrenia, see K. S. Kendler and P. Hays, "Schizophrenia with premorbid inferiority feelings," *Archives of General Psychiatry*, *39*, 1982, 643–47. See also J. Cutting, *Psychology of Schizophrenia* (Edinburgh: Churchill Livingstone, 1985), pp. 122–24, and E. Kringlen, "An epidemiological-clinical twin study on schizophrenia," in D. Rosenthal and S. S. Kety, eds., *The Transmission of Schizophrenia* (Oxford: Pergamon, 1968), pp. 49–63 (re hypersensitivity as precursor to schizophrenia).

6. S. Wolf and J. Chick, "Schizoid personality in childhood: A controlled follow-up study," *Psychological Medicine*, *10*, 1980, 97.

7. S. Arieti, *The Interpretation of Schizophrenia*, 2nd ed. (New York: Basic Books, 1974), p. 110.

8. E. Minkowski, *La Schizophrénie* (Paris: Payot, 1927), p. 105.

9. Quotations from E. Kretschmer, *Physique and Character*, trans. W. J. H. Sprott (New York: Harcourt Brace and World, 1925), pp. 152, 157.

10. Reported to me by a colleague. "Even when I was young, I was different," said another schizophrenic patient. "I was into my own being, not other people" (also described to me by a colleague).

11. See, for example, the following quotation from an autobiographical book by the schizophrenic patient Mary Barnes:

I can remember as a child, and all through my life, having very strange feelings. I would seem to go away, right away from everything and everywhere. I didn't belong anywhere. I would jolt myself back, perhaps by touching something. . . . I was empty and not there, not anywhere. If someone spoke with me, it didn't seem to be me. It was "just a thing"—I had gone. Sometimes it was quite difficult to come back because familiar things didn't seem the same. The air had changed and everything was alien as if I was on the moon and was just something—anything, not a person, me. There was a feeling of deadness, of being in a blind alley. My soul was musty, like a cobweb in the dust. [M. Barnes and J. Berke, *Two Accounts of a Journey Through Madness* (New York: Ballantine Books, 1971), p. 17]

12. Kretschmer, *Physique and Character*, p. 182. A. Meares ("The diagnosis of prepsychotic schizophrenia," *Lancet*, January 10, 1959, 55) describes two main sources of anxiety in such persons: feelings of "lack of unity in the self" and of "loss of contact with the outside world."

13. See K. Jaspers, *General Psychopathology*, trans. J. Hoenig and M. W. Hamilton (Chicago: University of Chicago Press, 1963), p. 654.

14. E. Bleuler, quoted in Cutting, *The Psychology of Schizophrenia*, p. 122.

15. Manfred Bleuler: "Do we really know whether schizophrenia 'befalls' an individual? Perhaps it is more of a phase or a result of a personal inner development" (*Schizophrenic Disorders*, p. 188). See also discussion in J. Parnas, F. Schulsinger, H. Schulsinger, et al., "Behavioral precursors of schizophrenia spectrum," *Archives of General Psychiatry*, 39, 1982, 663.

    For certain psychoanalysts, schizophrenic symptoms involve compromise formations between instinctual desires and certain modes of psychological defense against psychic pain or anxiety; and therefore the illness is not, in this respect, fundamentally different from, say, hysteria or obsessive-compulsive disorders. Others, including psychiatrists like Eugen and Manfred Bleuler and Ernst Kretschmer (whose work will be discussed in this chapter), as well as some psychoanalytically inclined writers, have tended to place more emphasis on the role of innate temperamental characteristics in the genesis of schizophrenia. Presumably, these characteristics would have a largely biological basis; but, because they are presumed to involve tendencies present to some degree in everyone, the illness would not fall outside the domain of comprehensible "development."

16. See, for example, T. Millon, *Disorders of Personality, DSM III: Axis II* (New York: Wiley, 1981), pp. 273–85, re "intrinsic emotional blandness" and a "lack [of] the equipment for experiencing the finer shades of subtleties of emotional life"; Millon was an influential member of the task force that created the DSM III personality disorder categories. Also see the Austrian psychiatrist Stransky's notion of "intrapsychic ataxia"; "Towards an understanding of certain symptoms of dementia praecox," in J. Cutting and M. Shepherd, eds., *The Clinical Roots of the Schizophrenia Concept* (Cambridge: Cambridge University Press, 1987), pp. 37–41.

17. Psychoanalysts like W. R. D. Fairbairn, Harry Guntrip, and Masud Khan view such individuals as having a desire and capacity for human connection that is no less powerful than that of other people. In fact, it is the very intensity of this yearning, along with a characteristic emotional hypersensitivity and vulnerability (primarily derived from disappointments experienced in infancy or early childhood, though possibly with an innate component) that makes such persons turn away from the external and human world, preferring instead to withdraw to an inner world of profoundly regressive fantasy (i.e., to the stage of primary narcissism, according to most such theorists).

The current diagnostic system of the American Psychiatric Association brings these two visions of the schizoid together in a single nosological system, though in a manner that in no way reduces the purity of the two contrasting models. Thus in DSM III and DSM III-R, the traditional notion of the schizoid is subdivided into two categories that are supposedly very distinct. One of these, Avoidant Personality Disorder, is meant to include the hypersensitive and introspective type of person who desires yet fears intimacy, whereas Schizoid Personality Disorder (now defined more narrowly) includes only persons who are said to lack a capacity for or interest in such human relationships.

DSM III is supposedly based on a new respect for empirical data, and eschews the theoretical preconceptions that informed earlier diagnostic systems. The contrast between *schizoid* and *avoidant* belies this claim, however, given the paucity of research supportive of such a stark contrast between the personality types. Much of the characterization of Schizoid Personality Disorder offered by Theodore Millon (an important member of the task force that created these categories) certainly depends far more on the mechanistic vision of a simple affliction model than on any current empirical knowledge. Thus he states that such persons "engage in few complicated *unconscious* processes" (emphasis added) and that they manifest "underdevelopment of neural substrates for affectivity" (*Disorders of Personality*, pp. 273, 284, 274, 285, 293)— claims based not on any actual, perhaps not even on any conceivable, set of empirical observations. DSM III's concept of the Avoidant Personality Disorder is no less schematic and one-dimensional, though in this case consistent with the act model of British object-relations theory rather than the affliction model of biological psychiatry. Interestingly enough, Millon characterizes the DSM III Schizotypal Personality as "a more grave form of the pathologically less severe schizoid and avoidant patterns" (p. 400); and within this category he reinstates something very close to Kretschmer's original distinction between anaesthetic and hyperaesthetic schizoids (see pp. 413, 416, 428). But this would seem to call into question the validity of the sharp distinction between *avoidant* and *schizoid*. The overlapping of these two personality types is further indicated by the fact that popularization of the Avoidant Personality Disorder diagnosis of DSM III has resulted in a dropoff in the frequency with which the Schizoid Personality Disorder diagnosis is applied; see T. Millon, "Avoidant Personality Disorder: A brief review of issues and data," *Journal of Personality Disorders*, 5, 1991, 355.

It could be the case that *both* the medical-model and the object-relations views are correct, but applicable to different subpopulations. See Cutting, *Psychology of Schizophrenia* (pp. 122–24) for a discussion of research suggesting the possibility that there may be two kinds of personality that commonly precede schizophrenia (corresponding, at least roughly, to Kretschmer's two subtypes of schizoid personality, which are discussed in this chapter), and two different pathways from premorbid personality to the psychotic condition.

According to Kendler and Hays ("Schizophrenia with premorbid inferiority feelings," pp. 643–47), there is a large subset of schizophrenics who do not seem to have a strong genetic loading for schizophrenia *per se*. This group also manifests strong "premorbid inferiority feelings." It is easy enough to construct a psychogenic model that could explain their schizophrenia as, in large part, a withdrawal reaction occasioned by the interaction of such a disposition with a particularly threatening, ambivalent, or unsupportive environment.

18. E. Kretschmer, *Physique and Character*. For a review of recent findings consistent with Kretschmer's views re schizoids and schizophrenics, see G. Claridge, " 'The schizophrenias as nervous types' revisited," *British Journal of Psychiatry, 151*, 1987, 735–43. Incidentally, it is not necessary to accept the entirety of Kretschmer's position in order to profit from his characterization of schizoid phenomena. One need not, for instance, adopt his strong constitutional bias, which neglects consideration of important environmental and cultural influences on personality development, or his views about correlation of personality type with physique—for example, that the schizothymic individuals are especially likely to be ectomorphs (but see L. L. Heston, "The genetics of schizophrenic and schizoid disease," *Science, 167*, 1970, 254, who claims this correlation is present with schizophrenia).

19. Re E. Bleuler, see his article: "Die probleme der schizoidie und der syntonie," *Zeitschrift für die Gesamte Neurologie und Psychiatrie, 78*, 1922, 373–99.

20. See E. Essen-Möller, "The concept of schizoidia," *Monatsschrift für Psychiatrie und Neurologie, 112*, 1946, 260. Kretschmer notes the stiffness or jerkiness of physical movements in schizoids: "the jerkiness of the motor tempo comes out, in contra-distinction to the smooth mobility of the hypo-manic" (*Physique and Character*, p. 175).

21. Kretschmer, *Physique and Character*, p. 260.

22. E. Kretschmer, *A Textbook of Medical Psychology*, trans. E. B. Strauss (London: Hogarth Press, 1952; originally published in English in 1925, in German in 1921), p. 205.

23. M. Bleuler, *Schizophrenic Disorders*, p. 498.

24. Kretschmer, *Physique and Character*, pp. 152, 245.

25. Ibid., pp. 153–154, 172. (Strindberg epigraph—"I am hard as ice"—is quoted on p. 153.)

26. Ibid., p. 252.

27. These subtypes correspond roughly to the Avoidant and Schizoid Personality Disorders of DSM III. See also E. Bleuler, *Dementia Praecox or the Group of Schizophrenias*, trans. J. Zinkin (New York: International Universities Press, 1950), p. 65.

28. Kretschmer, *Physique and Character*, pp. 151, 152, 157, 146.

29. Ibid., pp. 152, 153. Kretschmer relates this to a similar phenomenon on the psychotic level: the fact that apparently "burnt-out," insensitive back-ward patients will, under special circumstances, show a surprising awareness and emotional intensity (p. 153). See also Bleuler, *Schizophrenic Disorders*, pp. 154, 158.

30. Interestingly enough, Kretschmer brings up Schiller's famous discussion of naive versus sentimental poetry, suggesting that this distinction corresponds to that between the cyclothymic and schizothymic dispositions (*Physique and Character*, p. 225). Schiller's notion of the so-called sentimental mode (the reflective or alienated mode) seems to correspond closely to the modernist style (or, at least, to the forms of "modernism" of concern in this book).

31. Robert Langbaum, "The theory of the avant-garde: A review," *Boundary 2, 1*, 1972, 240.

32. J. Joyce, *A Portrait of the Artist as a Young Man* (New York: Viking, 1964 [first published in 1916]), pp. 215, 247. A few years later, in Vienna, Robert Musil would characterize the creative person in similar terms: as "metaphysically restless," "contemptuous of reality," and as appearing to others to be "asocial," an "unfeeling dreamer." His description of the normal or uncreative person, by

contrast, is reminiscent of the syntonic as opposed to schizothymic disposition: "defined, true, righteous, sympathetic, social, metaphysically secure, inclusive, active, real, and committed to Sunday-ideals, illusions, realities" (quoted in D. S. Luft, *Robert Musil and the Crisis of European Culture, 1880–1942* [Berkeley: University of California Press, 1980], p. 161).

33. W. Wordsworth, "Preface to the second edition of the Lyrical Ballads" (1800), in D. Perkins, ed., *English Romantic Writers* (New York: Harcourt Brace and World, 1967), p. 324.

34. See F. Kermode, *Romantic Image* (London and Glasgow: Fontana Books, 1971).

35. In F. Kafka, *The Complete Stories* (New York: Schocken Books, 1971), p. 469.

36. Quoted in A. Blunden, "A chronology of Kafka's life," in J. P. Stern, ed., *The World of Franz Kafka* (New York: Holt, Rinehart, and Winston, 1980), p. 16.

37. R. Hayman, *Kafka: A Biography* (New York and Toronto: Oxford University Press, 1981), p. 21.

38. Quoted in Blunden, "A chronology of Kafka's life," p. 17.

39. Ibid., p. 19.

40. Another self-portrait, it would seem, is the eleventh son in the story "Eleven Sons."

41. F. Kafka, *Letter to His Father*, trans. E. Kaiser and E. Wilkins (New York: Schocken Books, 1953), pp. 11, 73, 37, 13.

42. Kretschmer, *Physique and Character*, p. 157.

43. E. Canetti, *Kafka's Other Trial: The Letters to Felice*, trans. C. Middleton (New York: Schocken Books, 1974), p. 48.

44. Quoted in Hayman, *Kafka: A Biography*, p. 21.

45. F. Kafka, *Letters to Felice* (New York: Schocken Books, 1973), p. 293.

46. Quoted in Blunden, "A chronology of Kafka's life," p. 19.

47. Quoted in Laing, *Divided Self*, p. 78.

48. Quoted in Blunden, "A chronology of Kafka's life," p. 15.

49. C. Baudelaire, *Mon Coeur Mis à Nu*, in *Fusées; Mon Coeur Mis à Nu; La Belgique Deshabillée*, ed. A. Guyaux (Paris: Gallimard, 1986), p. 94 (my translation).

50. C. Baudelaire, "One A.M.," in *Short Poems in Prose* (*Le Spleen de Paris: Petits Poémes en Prose;* originally published in 1869), trans. N. Cameron, in P. Quennell, ed., *The Essence of Laughter and Other Essays, Journals, and Letters* (New York: Meridian Books, 1956), p. 138.

51. See J.-P. Sartre, *Baudelaire* (New York: New Directions, 1950), p. 180.

52. Kretschmer, *Physique and Character*, pp. 170, 166. I have used the translation in E. Kretschmer, *Physique and Character*, 2nd rev. ed., trans. W. J. H. Sprott, with appendix by E. Miller (London: Kegan Paul, Trench, Trubner, 1936), pp. 175, 171.

53. Quoted in M. H. Abrams, "Coleridge, Baudelaire, and modernist poetics," *The Correspondent Breeze* (New York: Norton, 1984), p. 122 (my translation).

54. See "Letter to F. Desnoyer" (1855), partially quoted in Sartre, *Baudelaire*, p. 104. Baudelaire ridicules anyone who, like the nature poets, gets "worked up over plants," "believ[ing] that *the soul of the god inhabits plant life.*" ("[E]ven if it did," he declares, "I shouldn't worry much about it. I should consider my own soul of far more value than the soul of sanctified vegetables.")

55. Baudelaire quoted in Abrams, "Coleridge, Baudelaire, and modernist poetics,"

p. 128; and in J. Seigel, *Bohemian Paris* (New York: Penguin Books, 1987), p. 105. Also see C. Baudelaire, *Intimate Journals*, trans. C. Isherwood (San Francisco: City Lights Books, 1983), p. 21.

56. The intensity of this aversion was strong enough to inspire an entire book of sustained diatribe and scorn: Baudelaire's unfinished *La Belgique Deshabillée*, which mocks the nation he regarded as epitomizing the banality of normal life and "the 'little man' at his worst."

57. Baudelaire, "My heart laid bare," in *Intimate Journals*, pp. 85, 76. "Le vrai héros s'amuse tout seul" (Baudelaire, "Mon coeur mis à nu," in *Fusées; Mon Coeur Mis à Nu; La Belgique Deshabillée*, p. 95.

58. Quoted in Sartre, *Baudelaire*, p. 180.

59. Baudelaire, "My heart laid bare," p. 87.

60. Ibid., pp. 71, 87.

61. Quoted in Sartre, *Baudelaire*, p. 180. "The more a man cultivates the arts, the less he fornicates," Baudelaire declared in his intimate journals—in what may or may not be a personal confession ("My heart laid bare," p. 87).

62. Baudelaire, "The painter of modern life," in Quennell, *Essence of Laughter*, pp. 46, 50, 48; see also Seigel, *Bohemian Paris*, pp. 98–99.

63. Kretschmer, *Physique and Character*, p. 153.

64. Baudelaire, *Short Poems in Prose*, p. 139.

65. H. Deutsch, "Some forms of emotional disturbance and their relationship to schizophrenia," *Psychoanalytic Quarterly*, 11, 1942, 310, 314, 308, 316. The "as-if" personality that Deutsch discusses is commonly associated with the schizoid type (see, e.g., Millon, *Disorders of Personality*, pp. 278–80); and Deutsch herself notes that it is a frequent precursor to schizophrenia (p. 319). Re the as-if type, Nathaniel Ross states, "It is generally agreed that the 'as if' phenomenon is represented developmentally at the two–three year level of imitativeness," and he speaks of "severe retardation of ego maturation" ("The 'as if' concept," *Journal of the American Psychoanalytic Association*, 15, 1967, 80).

66. W. R. D. Fairbairn, *An Object-Relations Theory of the Personality* (New York: Basic Books, 1954), p. 10; see also pp. 13, 25.

67. H. Guntrip, *Schizoid Phenomena, Object Relations, and the Self* (New York: International Universities Press, 1968), pp. 57, 79, 50.

68. C. Lasch, *The Minimal Self* (New York: Norton, 1984), pp. 15, 182, 177.

69. Also, I am not denying that schizoid problems might in some sense (and in some cases) be rooted in infancy or early childhood. It is possible, for example, that the presence of profound feelings of insecurity and of threat from the external environment experienced during the first year of life might set up a general sense of vulnerability as well as a general inclination to defend oneself via some kind of withdrawal from the environment. However, the modes of withdrawal that are characteristic of adult schizoids seem to involve cognitive structures that are quite advanced in nature, and that cannot be accounted for through concepts of fixation or regression. My concern in this chapter (and throughout most of this book) is with what Aristotle would call the "formal cause," the pattern or essence that determines the nature of a thing. Traumatic experiences in infancy could still play a role akin to that of the efficient cause (the force or agent that produces an effect).

70. M. Bleuler, *Schizophrenic Disorders*, p. 498.

71. The psychoanalytic approaches that come closest to capturing the aspects of schizophrenia whose centrality I emphasize in this book (that is, the hyperreflexivity and alienation) are those of the British object-relations school; see, for example, W. Bion's notion of "bizarre objects," which can involve peculiar projections of self-consciousness (W. Bion, *Second Thoughts: Selected Papers on Psychoanalysis* [London: Heinemann, 1967], pp. 40, 48.); and also W. R. D. Fairbairn on schizoid "splitting" (*An Object-Relations Theory of the Personality* [New York: Basic Books, 1954], pp. 6–7, 10, 16, 20, 50–51, 57, and passim). Significantly enough, however, these are precisely the theories that are most vulnerable to the criticism of being "adultomorphic"—that is, of involving retrospective attribution to infantile consciousness of what are in fact far more advanced modes of experience and forms of knowledge (for such a criticism, see J. Frosch, *The Psychotic Process* [New York: International Universities Press, 1983], pp. 364–65; M. Eagle, *Recent Developments in Psychoanalysis* [New York: McGraw-Hill, 1984], pp. 139–40). Thus we might question whether these theorists are really *discovering* developmental precursors or origins, or rather projecting phenomena encountered in their adult schizoid and schizophrenic patients back onto the child. (This is a theoretical move that would be necessitated by the *a priori* assumption that the essential features of severe psychopathology *must* be rooted in the earliest phases of life.) It is interesting to note that schizophrenia does not develop before adolescence, which in Piaget's psychology is the stage of "formal operations," when the ability to think about thinking comes into play, along with a new sense of one's separateness as a reflective consciousness. If the essential structures of schizophrenic consciousness really were in place far earlier than this, then one might ask why we do not find this particular form of psychopathology occurring earlier in life.

72. Y.-F. Tuan, *Segmented Worlds and Self: Group Life and Individual Consciousness* (Minneapolis: University of Minnesota Press, 1982), p. 139.

73. S. Kierkegaard, *Concluding Unscientific Postscript,* trans. D. F. Swenson (Princeton, NJ: Princeton University Press, 1944), pp. 71–72.

74. Laing, *Divided Self,* p. 127.

75. N. Elias, *The History of Manners,* trans. E. Jephcott (New York: Pantheon Books, 1978), pp. 250–51.

76. Letter to Gibieuf, 1642, quoted in C. Taylor, *Sources of the Self* (Cambridge: Harvard University Press, 1989), p. 144.

77. It is true that a rejection of the Cartesian view is a central theme for both of the giants of twentieth-century philosophy, Heidegger and Wittgenstein; but this has not, it seems fair to say, had all that much impact on self-understanding in the culture at large.

78. See R. Rorty, *Philosophy and the Mirror of Nature* (Princeton, NJ: Princeton University Press, 1979), pp. 45ff.

79. W. Ong, *The Presence of the Word* (Minneapolis: University of Minnesota Press, 1981), p. 211.

80. See, for example, Clement Greenberg, "Modernist painting," in G. Battcock, ed., *The New Art: A Critical Anthology* (New York: Dutton, 1966), pp. 100–110.

81. Quoted in C. L. Griswold, "Plato's metaphilosophy: Why Plato wrote dialogues," in Griswold, ed., *Platonic Readings* (New York: Routledge, 1988), p. 150. It should be noted that I am primarily concerned with Kant as a cultural

figure, not with the details of his actual philosophical writings; the latter can be interpreted in a great variety of ways, some of these inconsistent with what I will say in these pages.

82. Friedrich Schelling, re Kant, is quoted in E. D. Hirsch, *Wordsworth and Schelling* (New Haven, CT: Yale University Press, 1960), p. 19.

Both Descartes and Kant reflected and contributed to modern alienation—to what Nietzsche described as "the strange contrast between an inner life to which nothing outward corresponds, and an outward existence unrelated to what is within" (quoted in E. Heller, *The Artist's Journey into the Interior and Other Essays* [San Diego: Harcourt Brace Jovanovich, 1976], p. 103). They offer significantly different versions of this contrast, however. In Cartesian metaphysics the mind confronts external objects that seem real, though they are distant and alien. In Kant's system, by contrast, the mind experiences objects that can feel like its own phantoms (the "phenomena") and that seem *un*real in comparison with the unseen, but somehow imagined, realm of the "noumenal" or true world. Both kinds of experiences occur in schizoids and schizophrenics.

These forms of separation and reflexivity reach one kind of culmination in the transcendental phenomenology of Edmund Husserl. Central to Husserl's philosophical method was the phenomenological reduction or *epochē*, which he himself described as a "disconnection" or "bracketing." By means of this reduction, we suspend the "natural standpoint," with its inclination to accept the real world about us "as a fact-world *that has its being out there.*" Instead we "fix our eyes steadily upon the sphere of Consciousness and study what it is that we find immanent in *it.*" But this "disconnecting of the world," as Husserl terms it, is more than simply a technique (quotations from Husserl, *Ideas: General Introduction to Pure Phenomenology*, trans. W. R. B. Gibson [New York: Collier Books, 1962; originally published in 1913], pp. 96, 102, 101). It effects a "*total change* of the natural attitude," and has a profoundly *vocational* character for modern man" (E. Husserl, *The Crisis of European Sciences and Transcendental Phenomenology*, trans. D. Carr [Evanston, IL: Northwestern University Press, 1970; written in the mid-1930s], p. 137). Re Husserl, see also chap. 9, note 48.

83. Elias, *The History of Manners*, pp. 129, 260, 253, 258. Similar tendencies toward increasing discipline, organization, and self-scrutiny are traced in Michel Foucault's *Discipline and Punish: The Birth of the Prison*, trans. A. Sheridan (New York: Vintage Books, 1979)—which pays particular attention to certain of the institutions, political organizations, and forms of architecture that are characteristic of the modern order. (Foucault's book is discussed in chapter 8.)

84. W. Ong, *The Presence of the Word* (Minneapolis: University of Minnesota Press, 1981), pp. 63, 136–37.

The shift from an oral to a literate or alphabetical culture can be seen as part of an even larger mutation with similar implications for consciousness and the self: the growing predominance of vision over other sensory modalities. The experience of premodern Europeans seems to have had more in common with that of the ancient Greeks, who thought of the universe as a kind of acoustic harmony, and also with that of tribal and peasant cultures, where the surrounding or permeating sense modalities of sound, smell, and taste have a more central role. Various scholars have written of how the "world sense" or "world presence" of virtually all premodern cultures tends in modern, technological societies to be replaced by an experience of the world as a kind of view. See W. Ong, "World as view and world as event," *American Anthropologist*, *71*, 1969, 634–47.

Noise surrounds, and it can be difficult to locate the source of a particular sound; odor permeates, obscuring the very distinction between knower and known, and often evoking the most immediate visceral reactions, including revulsion, hunger, and lust. Vision, by contrast, is the prototypical distance sense, embodying in every glance the separation of subject from object and allowing for a greater sense of control and of distance from emotional or instinctual response. Vision is also the most self-conscious sense, since it is most conducive to an awareness of one's own position in relation to the perceptual field (which seems to organize itself around perspectival sightlines emanating from one's own eyes). The ease of moving one's eyes or of shutting them, thus shifting focus or even blotting out the world at will, also makes it conducive to a feeling of sovereign control. A purely visual experience can, however, easily seem lifeless and unreal.

There seem, then, to be a number of characteristics—affectlessness, separation, sense of control—that are shared by the schizoid orientation and the visual modality. One might expect that a visually oriented culture would be especially likely to encourage, or at least to allow, the development of schizoid tendencies in its members.

85. According to George Devereux, "The ethnic personality of modern man is basically schizoid" (*Basic Problems of Ethnopsychiatry*, trans. B. M. Gulati and G. Devereux [Chicago and London: University of Chicago Press, 1980], p. 219).

86. J. Lang, "The other side of the affective aspects of schizophrenia," *Psychiatry*, *2*, 1939, 196, 197, 200. Interestingly, however, Lang also acknowledges that ideocentrism may not be an ultimate cause, but may be "the manifestation on the psychological level of underlying weaknesses in the physiological operations of the organism" (p. 201).

87. See F. Nietzsche, *Human, All Too Human*, trans. H. Zimmern and P. V. Kohn, in *The Complete Works of Friedrich Nietzsche*, ed. O. Levy, 18 vols. (New York: Macmillan, 1909–11; first published in 1878), sec. 16. Here Nietzsche was doubtless thinking of Kant's distinction of phenomenal from noumenal realms, but also of aspects of the Christian tradition of spirituality and otherworldliness (world-denial).

88. Heidegger locates the source of this subjectivism in Descartes's attempt to found being itself on the self-certainty of a representing consciousness; Heidegger, "The age of the world picture," in *The Question Concerning Technology and Other Essays*, trans. W. Lovitt (New York: Harper and Row, 1977), pp. 127, 139–41. Quotations in this paragraph from this essay, pp. 128–30, 132, 147; also, Heidegger, "The Word of Nietzsche: 'God Is Dead,'" in idem, p. 68.

89. It is in this sense that man, in Heidegger's words, "'gets into the picture' in precedence over whatever is . . . set[ting] himself up as the setting in which whatever is must henceforth set itself forth, must present itself [*sich präsentieren*], i.e., be picture" ("Age of the world picture," pp. 131–32).

90. Ibid., p. 142.

91. Heidegger quoted in H. Richter, *Dada: Art and Anti-Art* (New York and Toronto: Oxford University Press, 1965), p. 91.

92. Laing, *Divided Self*, p. 146.

93. Quoted in C. Landis, ed., *Varieties of Psychopathological Experience* (New York: Holt, Rinehart and Winston, 1964), pp. 192–93.

94. The passage continues as follows: ". . . the truth that lies closest, however, is only this, that you are beating your head against the wall of a windowless and doorless cell" (quoted in A. Hiedsieck, "Kafka's narrative ontology," *Philosophy and Literature*, 11, 1987, 249).

95. Nietzsche, *The Will to Power*, trans. W. Kaufmann and R. J. Hollingdale (New York: Vintage Books, 1968; first published in 1901), # 22 and # 23, pp. 17–18.

96. For Rorschach examples, see S. J. Blatt and C. M. Wild, *Schizophrenia: A Developmental Analysis* (New York: Academic Press, 1976), pp. 144, 149; for example, "two people in a stylized position, leaning over a pot . . . the quality of theatre about them as though somewhat acted."

97. C. Rycroft, "On the defensive function of schizophrenic thinking and delusion-formation," *Imagination and Reality* (London: Hogarth Press, 1968), pp. 86–87.

98. Laing's "inner self" is not to be confused with D. W. Winnicott's "true self": the first is primarily mental, the second highly instinctual. The schizoid is identified with the first, but alienated from the second.

99. Laing, *Divided Self*, p. 72.

100. See S. Arieti, *Interpretation of Schizophrenia*, 2nd ed. (New York: Basic Books, 1974), pp. 107–8.

101. Laing, *Divided Self*, p. 70.

102. Kretschmer, *Physique and Character*, p. 196.

103. E. Goffman, *Encounters*, excerpted in R. Sennett, ed., *The Psychology of Society* (New York: Vintage Books, 1977), p. 108.

104. See A. Macintyre, *After Virtue* (Notre Dame, IN: University of Notre Dame Press, 1981), pp. 115–19.

105. Godfrey Lienhardt, *Divinity and Experience: The Religion of the Dinka* (Oxford: Clarendon Press, 1961), pp. 149–51. Also see R. A. Schweder and E. J. Bourne, "Does the concept of the person vary cross-culturally?" in A. J. Marsella and G. M. White, *Cultural Conceptions of Mental Health and Therapy* (Dordrecht, Holland: D. Reidel, 1982, 1984), esp. pp. 105–6, 116, 127–29; and Tuan, *Segmented Worlds and Self*, pp. 139–67.

106. Francis Yates, quoted in L. Trilling, *Sincerity and Authenticity* (Cambridge: Harvard University Press, 1972), p. 19.

107. Georg Simmel and, more recently, Peter Berger are among those who have made this point; see, for example, P. Berger, B. Berger, and H. Kellner, *The Homeless Mind: Modernization and Consciousness* (New York: Vintage Books, 1974), pp. 63–82.

108. See S. Greenblatt, *Renaissance Self-Fashioning* (Chicago and London: University of Chicago Press, 1980), p. 2. Also see Trilling, *Sincerity and Authenticity*, pp. 12–16.

109. D. M. Lowe, *History of Bourgeois Perception* (Chicago: University of Chicago Press, 1982), p. 99.

110. Berger, Berger, and Kellner, *Homeless Mind*, pp. 83–96. R. Sennett makes a similar point about the reconceptualization of physical love, which replaced the Victorian notion of "eroticism" with the current notion of "sexuality." Whereas the first emphasizes social relationships, the second, he claims, emphasizes personal identity—indicating a shift "from belief in emotional actions to belief

in emotional states of being" (*The Fall of Public Man: On the Social Psychology of Capitalism* [New York: Vintage Books, 1978], pp. 7–9).

111. This is part of what Richard Sennett means by the "fall of public man" (*Fall of Public Man*).

112. Quotations in this and the following paragraph are from N. Sarraute, *The Age of Suspicion*, trans. M. Jolas (New York: Braziller, 1963), pp. 29, 61, 67, 68, 75, 82, 84, 95, 97. Sarraute is also discussed in Trilling, *Sincerity and Authenticity*, pp. 100–105.

113. Especially in those whom DSM III-R would call "avoidant."

114. M. MacLane, *I, Mary MacLane: A Diary of Human Days* (New York: Stokes, 1917), p. 31.

115. Ibid., p. 177.

116. M. MacLane, *The Story of Mary MacLane* (Chicago: Stone, 1902), pp. 138–39. Subsequent quotations are from pp. 133–36.

117. This "spirit of falseness" is so very "light and subtle," yet at the same time so all-pervasive as to undermine even itself—and she asks herself whether this "thin, fine vapor of fraud . . . so thin, so elusive, so faint" might not somehow be "itself a false thing" (ibid., pp. 134–36).

118. Laing, *Divided Self*, pp. 140, 144, 47–48.

119. Ibid., p. 53.

120. See case of Peter in ibid., p. 124.

A visual illustration of such stiltedness, where the role of scrutinizing self-consciousness is particularly evident, can be found in the work of Franz Xaver Messerschmidt, a psychotic German sculptor who lived from 1736 to 1784. See the psychoanalyst Ernst Kris's paper, "A psychotic sculptor of the eighteenth century," *Psychoanalytic Explorations in Art* (New York: Schocken Books, 1964), pp. 128–50. Messerschmidt is that rare case, an artist of considerable prominence living before the nineteenth century who exhibited distinctively schizophrenic traits (as well as paranoid ones; idem, p. 138). After a psychotic break that occurred at age thirty-five, Messerschmidt produced a series of busts showing the human face reacting to various kinds of experiences and emotions. His work clearly derives from an artistic tradition of interest in the human physiognomy that became firmly rooted in the seventeenth century; but what is striking about Messerschmidt's busts is the rigid and empty quality of the facial expressions he depicts, which lack almost entirely any feeling of authentic emotion. With the self-portrait called "The Artist How He Imagined Himself Laughing" (idem, figure 23), for example, one has the impression not of a belly laugh or even a spontaneous smile, but only of a false and masklike grinning. (These are not Messerschmidt's own titles, by the way; they were assigned after his death.)

In this, as in most of the series, Messerschmidt used himself as the model: apparently he would turn to look at himself in the mirror every half minute or so while making, as precisely as he could, whatever grimace or expression he wanted to portray. Based on his extensive study of Messerschmidt, Kris suggests that this was "an attempt to attain in a roundabout manner—as it were from the outside or the surface—a socially effective mimic expression" (p. 145). If one imagines Messerschmidt grimacing at himself before the mirror, one suspects that he may have been trying, through scrutiny and force of will, to bring on emotional states he couldn't actually feel—states from which his effortful impersonations may only have alienated him further. Under these circumstances, of course, anyone might have difficulty attaining an entirely authentic and convincing appearance. But one would expect that a sculptor who was less schizoid might have produced busts with a less masklike or "as-if" quality.

The transformative effects that behavioral self-consciousness can have are also apparent in a remarkable report by the anthropologist Edmund Carpenter: "The tribal terror of self-awareness," in P. Hockings, ed., *Principles of Visual Anthropology* (The Hague and Paris: Mouton, 1975), pp. 451–61. In the early 1970s the Territory of Papua New Guinea hired Carpenter as a communications consultant, seeking his advice on the use of various media—radio, film, and television—for communicating with small towns and villages in the remotest jungles. Carpenter was interested in how people would react if shown images of themselves for the very first time; and to this end he took cameras, tape recorders, film equipment, and a film crew to the remote Papuan Plateau, the home of the isolated Biami people, one of the few extant groups that had had virtually no experience with cameras and recorders or even with mirrors or other reflective surfaces. (Apparently the Biami had only scraps of mirrors, not large enough to reflect a decent image; and even the rivers in the area fail to provide reflections, except of foliage seen at low angles.) Predictably, on first seeing their own images in large mirrors or Polaroid photographs, the Biami were startled. At first they would cover their mouths and duck their heads in what was apparently an attempt to prevent losing their soul through their mouths. But after these almost instinctual reactions, they would typically stand transfixed, as if struck dumb and motionless before the fascinating image. And, after a few days, they grew more used to the images and would groom themselves openly before the mirror; some of the men even took to wearing their photographic portraits stuck proudly to their foreheads. But most interesting was the effect that the Biami's new visual self-consciousness seemed to have on their modes of physical activity. Whenever the people were aware of the presence of a film camera, their behavior seemed to undergo a subtle change: "Almost invariably, body movements became faster, jerky, without poise or confidence. Faces that had been relaxed now froze or alternated between twitching and rigidity," Carpenter reports (p. 455). In fact, the camera crew soon learned not to ask people to repeat actions they had failed to record; for, though the Biami would comply happily enough, their reiterated, self-conscious behavior would no longer resemble what they had done spontaneously just a moment before. "No one who ever comes to know himself with the detachment of an observer," Carpenter notes, "is ever the same again" (p. 457).

121. Laing, *Divided Self*, p. 49.
122. E. Bleuler, *Dementia Praecox*, p. 106. Bleuler's description seems to suggest, incidentally, that the hollowness of the farmers' actions was seen as a consequence of their play-acting, though it is also possible that the farmers may have made an essentially mechanistic, thus passive impression on the patient.
123. F. Nietzsche, *The Gay Science*, trans. W. Kaufmann (New York: Vintage Books, 1974; first published in 1887), # 335, p. 266.
124. Nietzsche, *The Will to Power*, # 962, p. 505.

125. Trilling, *Sincerity and Authenticity*, p. 27; see pp. 26–52. My discussion in the following pages follows Trilling's argument rather closely. The relevant pages from Hegel are in *Phenomenology of Mind*, trans. J. B. Baillie (New York: Harper and Row, 1967), pp. 509–48. Passages from Hegel not otherwise noted are quoted in Trilling, *Sincerity and Authenticity*, pp. 31, 35, 36, 38, 46.

126. Hegel, *Phenomenology of Mind*, p. 548.

127. Nor is his role-playing a fully engaged process, suggesting fixation at the stage where object-relations involve a kind of primary identification (as Helene Deutsch suggests is the case with the "as-if" personality; Deutsch, "Some forms of emotional disturbance," pp. 312, 316).

128. Hegel, *Phenomenology of Mind*, p. 546, emphasis added.

129. Quoted in Trilling, *Sincerity and Authenticity*, p. 118.

130. Baudelaire, "The dandy," in "The painter of modern life," p. 48.

131. Joseph Berze describes a schizophrenic patient whose fragmented selves are reminiscent of the varied impersonations played out by Rameau's nephew: "while leafing through an old magazine, [this patient] passed through a succession of extraordinarily different personalities, each founded on the illustrations and the images encountered in the magazine." Berze also notes that such patients typically retain a sense of separateness, distinguishing the "true self" from the series of part-personalities. "I am as I am, I am not present in any assortment," as another of Berze's patients put it (*assortment* being the term she used to refer to the "electric assortment" of persons she had within her); J. Berze, "Primary insufficiency of mental activity," in Cutting and Shepherd, *Clinical Roots of Schizophrenia Concept*, p. 54.

132. See Jaspers, *General Psychopathology*, pp. 641, 654.

133. H. C. Rümke, "The nuclear symptom of schizophrenia and the praecoxfeeling," trans. J. Neeleman, *History of Psychiatry, I*, 1990 (originally published in 1941), 336.

134. R. Rosser, "The psychopathology of feeling and thinking in a schizophrenic," *International Journal of Psychoanalysis, 60*, 1979, 178.

Kraepelin describes extremes of behavior in *dementia praecox* that are very similar to Kretschmer's hyperaesthetic and anaesthetic forms of schizoid personality. He speaks of patients who withdraw from social life, "lock[ing] themselves up to learn poems off by heart," but also of patients who seem to have lost all "delicacy of feeling," and who show disdain for all the norms of social behavior, patients who "conduct themselves in a free and easy way, laugh on serious occasions, are rude and impertinent towards their superiors" (*Dementia Praecox and Paraphrenia*, trans. R. M. Barclay [Huntington, NY: Krieger, 1971; first English edition 1919], pp. 24, 34; see also P. Barham, *Schizophrenia and Human Value* [Oxford: Blackwell, 1984], p. 4. E. Bleuler [*Dementia Praecox*, p. 65] also describes both forms of detachment as occurring in schizophrenia).

135. Erwin Stransky, Emil Kraepelin; see M. Bleuler, *Schizophrenic Disorders*, pp. 491, 499.

The affinity is, of course, also suggested by the presence of schizophreniclike concerns in schizoid patients. In a Rorschach study, M. Carsky and J. W. Bloomgarden found the responses of nonpsychotic, characterologically schizoid (or schizotypal) patients to display "bizarre" themes and concerns more reminiscent of schizophrenia than of mania or depression, including "uncertainty about identity, transformations, 'the uncanny,' grotesque mergings, or fragmentary, unintegrated thoughts or feelings" ("Subtyping in the borderline realm by means of Rorschach analysis," *Psychiatric Clinics of North America*, 4, 1981, 107–8).

136. C. Schooler and W. Caudill, "Symptomatology in Japanese and American schizophrenics," *Ethnology*, 3, 1964, 177. See also E. F. Torrey, *Schizophrenia and Civilization* (New York: Aronson, 1980), p. 153.

137. M. Bleuler, *Schizophrenic Disorders*, pp. 487–88, 499.

138. E. Bleuler, *Dementia Praecox*, pp. 192–93.

139. Manfred Bleuler's words, paraphrasing Kretschmer, in *Schizophrenic Disorders*, p. 29.

140. Bleuler, *Dementia Praecox*, p. 453. Bleuler speaks of "the affectations of the catatonic [schizophrenic], the boorish conduct of the hebephrenic, and the absurd decorum of the megalomaniac" (p. 453; see also p. 191). Schizophrenic renderings of the human figure and face also tend to have a stiff and mannered look, as Ernst Kris notes in *Psychoanalytic Explorations in Art* (pp. 107, 111–14, 128–50).

141. Bleuler, *Dementia Praecox*, p. 93.

142. Jaspers, *General Psychopathology*, p. 219. Oddly enough, Jaspers denies that Nieber can be interpreted as engaging in intentional witticisms or leg pulling of those around him; his reason is that "the patient's whole life is like this and is carried on in the institutions for decades without any efforts in earnest on their part."

143. Bleuler, *Dementia Praecox*, p. 215 (emphasis added). Bleuler mentions that the "buffooneries" of "spiteful hebephrenics" have a rather different quality. John Cutting notes that negativistic actions in schizophrenia are often difficult to distinguish from "playfulness" or "bloody-mindedness" (*The Right Cerebral Hemisphere and Psychiatric Disorders* [Oxford: Oxford University Press, 1990], p. 298).

Bleuler also mentions the posed or mannered quality that may be present in overt schizophrenia, sometimes exaggerated to the point of absurdity:

Many patients take on a certain pose. This one runs around with his arms crossed on his chest, like a prime-minister whom he had once seen in a photograph. That one apes Bismarck including his handwriting. The majority are usually content imitating something special in a general way: a pose, a facial mien, clothing, speech, handwriting. Some remain consistent in their mannerism for decades; others are constantly stepping out of their roles. Almost always there is something artificial, stilted, and pompous about their conduct. It remains inappropriate to the occasion and inadequately modifiable. Thus almost always mannerisms soon become caricatures. [E. Bleuler, *Dementia Praecox*, p. 190]

See also L. Binswanger, "Extravagance, perverseness, manneristic behavior and schizophrenia," in Cutting and Shepherd, *Clinical Roots of Schizophrenia Concept*, pp. 83–88.

144. Bleuler, *Dementia Praecox*, p. 460. See also B. Ritson and A. Forrest, "The simulation of psychosis: A contemporary presentation," *British Journal of Medical Psychology*, 43, 1970, 35, 36.

145. As E. Slater and M. Roth point out, *dissimulation* of schizophrenic symptoms by

such patients is very common, and it sometimes takes the form, described by Eugen Bleuler, "of the patient insisting that he has simulated his symptoms" (*Clinical Psychiatry*, 3rd ed. [London: Balliere, Tindall and Cassell, 1969], p. 322). Also see G. G. Hay, "Feigned psychosis—A review of the simulation of mental illness," *British Journal of Psychiatry, 143*, 1983, 8–10. In Hay's study, five of six patients thought to be feigning a schizophrenic psychosis turned out, on follow-up, to have become overtly schizophrenic. As Hay notes, this kind of malingering may be a last-ditch attempt to ward off a developing psychosis (p. 8). See also Jaspers's discussion of August Strindberg's "will to appear insane" (*Strindberg and Van Gogh,* trans. O. Grunow and D. Woloshin [Tucson: University of Arizona Press, 1977], p. 16).

146. This would be naive even for those cases where no truly psychotic illness is later found to be present. As has been noted re cases of factitious psychosis, the propensity to act crazy itself suggests serious and enduring personality disturbance; see H. G. Pope, J. M. Jonas, and B. Jones, "Factitious psychosis: Phenomenology, family history, and long-term outcome of nine patients," *American Journal of Psychiatry, 139,* 1982, 1483.

147. Schizophrenics are often said to lack "insight" into their illness, and often this is true, if by insight we mean adopting something like the psychiatric conception and evaluation of their signs and symptoms. This notion of "lack of insight" has contributed to the vision of the schizophrenic as lacking in self-awareness. In fact, however, the great majority of such patients do seem to have considerable awareness of their illness ("disease consciousness," as J. Dittmann and R. Schüttler term it ["Disease consciousness and coping strategies of patients with schizophrenic psychosis," *Acta Psychiatrica Scandinavica, 82,* 1990, 318–22]).

148. Bleuler, *Dementia Praecox,* p. 158. I am grateful to Dr. Bertram Cohen for the second example.

149. Rümke, "Nuclear symptom of schizophrenia," p. 337.

150. Bleuler, *Schizophrenic Disorders,* p. 488.

151. "Self-satisfied, self-absorbed smiling," a "lofty manner," "giggling," and "pranks" are mentioned in the ICD-9 description of the hebephrenic type of schizophrenia; printed in DSM III, p. 416. Re inappropriate giggling, see Cutting, *Right Cerebral Hemisphere,* pp. 297, 299.

152. Cleanth Brooks, "The heresy of paraphrase," in H. Adams, ed., *Critical Theory Since Plato* (San Diego: Harcourt Brace Jovanovich, 1971), p. 1039; Alan Tate, quoted in K. Burke, *A Grammar of Motives* (Berkeley and Los Angeles: University of California Press, 1969), pp. 513–14.

153. F. Schlegel, "On incomprehensibility," in K. M. Wheeler, ed., *German Aesthetic and Literary Criticism: The Romantic Ironists and Goethe* (Cambridge: Cambridge University Press, 1984), pp. 36–37. See also P. de Man, "The rhetoric of temporality," *Blindness and Insight* (Minneapolis: University of Minnesota Press, 1983), pp. 208–28.

154. Kraepelin remarks on this in *Dementia Praecox,* p. 267.

155. Rümke, "Nuclear symptom of schizophrenia," p. 338.

156. A line from a letter that Nietzsche wrote shortly after his psychotic break very effectively illustrates this disconcerting effect—where one cannot be absolutely sure whether the person is really being ironic, or, if so, in just what way the irony is intended and whether one is oneself being mocked: "Dear Herr Profes-

sor, when it comes to it I too would very much prefer a professorial chair in Basel to being God; but I did not dare to go as far in my private egoism as to refrain for its sake from the creation of the world" (quoted in E. Heller, *The Disinherited Mind* [New York and London: Harcourt Brace Jovanovich, 1975], p. 83). Nietzsche's mental illness, by the way, was in all likelihood an organic psychosis, very possibly a case of general paralysis resulting from syphilis; at least in its early stages, however, his illness did have very distinct schizo-phrenia*like* qualities, which may have been due to the strong influence of premorbid schizoid traits and tendencies.

157. R. Jakobson and G. Lübbe-Grothues, "The language of schizophrenia: Hölderlin's speech and poetry," *Poetics Today*, 2, 1980, 138–39.

158. H. S. Sullivan, *Clinical Studies in Psychiatry* (New York: Norton, 1973), p. 185.

159. Thus Freud conceived of a rational inner observer who watched the progression of the illness from some recess in the psychotic's mind; see J. E. Gedo and A. Goldberg, *Models of the Mind: A Psychoanalytic Theory* (Chicago and London: University of Chicago Press, 1973), p. 130.

160. See, for example, T. Freeman, J. Cameron, and A. McGhie, *Chronic Schizophrenia* (New York: International Universities Press, 1958), "Chapter 6: Confusion of identity," pp. 52–60; G. Kloos, "Über den witz der schizophrenen," *Zeitschrift für die gesamte Neurologie und Psychiatrie*, 172, 1941 536–77.

Chapter 4: Cognitive Slippage

1. Quoted in M. Foucault, *The Order of Things* (New York: Vintage, 1970), p. xv; from J. L. Borges, "The analytical language of John Wilkins," in *Other Inquisitions, 1937–1952*, trans. L. C. Simms (Austin, TX: University of Texas Press, 1964), p. 103.

2. Foucault, *The Order of Things*, pp. xvii, xviii.

3. See, for example, M. Hamilton, ed., *Fish's Schizophrenia*, 2nd ed. (Bristol, UK: John Wright, 1976), p. 29.

4. P. Meehl, "Schizotaxia, schizotypy, schizophrenia," *American Psychologist*, 17, 1962, 827–38.

5. E. Bleuler, *Dementia Praecox, or The Group of Schizophrenias*, trans. J. Zinkin (New York: International Universities Press, 1950), pp. 13–14. Similarly, Emil Kraepelin writes that schizophrenics "lose in a most striking way the faculty of logical ordering of their trains of thought" (*Dementia Praecox and Paraphrenia* [Edinburgh: Livingstone, 1919], p. 19).

6. To give a strict definition of this range of anomalies is, however, extremely difficult—as difficult as it would be to distinguish rigorously between thinking and other faculties of the normal mind; certainly there is considerable overlap with the perceptual and linguistic anomalies discussed elsewhere in this book.

7. F. Nietzsche, *Will to Power*, sec. 556, quoted in A. Nehamas, *Nietzsche: Life as Literature* (Cambridge: Harvard University Press, 1985) p. 81.

8. K. Goldstein, "Methodological approach to the study of schizophrenic thought disorder," in J. S. Kasanin, ed., *Language and Thought in Schizophrenia* (New York: Norton, 1964), p. 24.

9. Abstraction, according to Goldstein, requires "conscious will"—"conscious activity in the sense of reasoning, awareness and self account of one's doing" (quoted in L. J. Chapman and J. P. Chapman, *Disordered Thought in Schizophrenia* [Englewood Cliffs, NJ: Prentice-Hall, 1973], p. 144; see also p. 143). These mental functions—the capacities for choice, self-consciousness, and abstraction—are the very features that philosophers from Aquinas to Hegel have seen as constituting the essence of mind, the person, or the human soul—which means that schizophrenia, at least in its most severe form, is being viewed as a condition that is in some sense subhuman or prehuman.

10. This is akin to the view expressed in the eighteenth-century *Encyclopédie* (1750–1780), where madness is described as an absence of self-critical awareness; it was a departing from reason "with confidence and in the firm conviction that one is following it" (in Foucault, *Madness and Civilization* [New York and Toronto: New American Library, 1967], p. 91). Re the issues of doubt and certainty in the course of cultural evolution, see S. Langer, *Mind: An Essay on Human Feeling*, vol. 3 (Baltimore and London: Johns Hopkins University Press, 1982), pp. 21–25. The anthropologist Herbert Spencer, for example, whose *Principles of Sociology* had considerable influence on American social science, believed that "savages" had particularly acute sensations, but were unable to separate themselves from the sensory world in order to reflect upon or control their own behavior; see G. Stocking, "The dark-skinned savage: The image of primitive man in evolutionary anthropology," *Race, Culture, and Evolution* (Chicago and London: University of Chicago Press, 1982), p. 117. A similar view has been taken regarding the consciousness of archaic Greece; see, for example, E. R. Dodds, *The Greeks and the Irrational* (Berkeley: University of California Press, 1951). A. B. Szalita is one psychoanalyst who assimilates schizophrenia to such a conception of the mentality of archaic man; see "Regression and perception in psychotic states," *Psychiatry*, 21, 1958, 53–63, esp. 58n.

11. See, for example, S. Arieti, *The Interpretation of Schizophrenia*, 2nd ed. (New York: Basic Books, 1974), comparing the schizophrenic's supposed incapacity for abstract concepts with that of the primitive mind (pp. 250–53). See also P. Federn, *Ego Psychology and the Psychoses* (London: Maresfield Reprints, 1953/1977), citing Goldstein to assert the schizophrenic's supposed incapacity for generalization: "for the schizophrenic it is no longer possible to think generally of *the table;* he always thinks of *a specific table.* [He cannot] conceive the concept of 'the table' apart from the real table" (pp. 190–91).

12. See G. Goldstein, "Contributions of Kurt Goldstein to neuropsychology," *Clinical Neuropsychologist*, 4, 1990, 3–17, esp. pp. 8–9 re studies by Weinberger and others; see also my discussion in the appendix.

13. Von Domarus's principle is in fact very reminiscent of Freudian notions about primary process thinking—the primitive mode of cognition that is dominated by instinct and emotion and that tends to equate (logically) incompatible ideas and to treat parts as equivalent to wholes.

14. See N. Cameron, "Schizophrenic thinking in a problem-solving situation," *Journal of Mental Science*, 85, 1939, 1012–35; J. Cutting, *The Psychology of Schizophrenia* (Edinburgh: Churchill Livingstone, 1985), p. 314. "Contain atoms" is from M. H. Johnston and P. S. Holzman, *Assessing Schizophrenic Thinking* (San Francisco: Jossey-Bass, 1979), p. 76.

15. Like "concreteness," the notions of "overinclusion" and (even more obviously)

of "paleologic" also seem to involve certain conceptions of madness that have a long history in Western thought—in these latter cases, dating back to the time when the world view of the Renaissance was giving way to that of Galilean science. Foucault argues that the essence of the general epistemic mutation occurring at this time in Western history was the rejection of similarity or resemblance as the fundamental form of knowing, and a new acceptance of the logical and quantitative categories of measurement, identity, and difference; he also argues that this shift had significant implications for prevailing conceptions of madness. The initial traces of the new epistemic configuration can be found in the image of madness contained in the first great novel of Western literature, Cervantes's *Don Quixote* (1605, 1615), a book that makes endless sport of its hero's mad tendency to see sameness everywhere—to equate gaggles of geese with armies, windmills with knights, and serving maids with princesses. According to Foucault, Don Quixote served as the quintessential madman of the new age precisely because he caricatured the modes of thought of an earlier age that now needed to be disowned and subjected to ridicule. Don Quixote was thus a "disordered player of the Same and the Other," a being who "takes things for what they are not and people one for another" (*Order of Things*, p. 49). He was, we might say, a champion of the principle of similitude—the principle that had once formed the basis of knowledge but had now come to be viewed as the essential occasion of error, as a danger needing to be constantly pointed out and diligently guarded against.

Don Quixote's main characteristics—effacing distinctions between things that share a single feature, lumping things together instead of discriminating their differences—are virtually identical to the qualities of so-called paleologic and overinclusion. Foucault is therefore wrong to claim that this "man of primitive resemblances"—this person "Different only in so far as he is unaware of Difference" (idem, p. 49)—constitutes the image of the madman only from the seventeenth up to the advent of the nineteenth century; clearly, he haunts the psychiatric imagination well into the twentieth century.

16. Overinclusion has often been explained in this way, as resulting from dysfunctions in attentional processes or in the cerebral filtering of stimuli that cause a certain distractibility or an inability to exclude stimuli from awareness; see references in N. Andreasen and P. S. Powers, "Overinclusive thinking in mania and schizophrenia, *British Journal of Psychiatry, 125,* 1974, 452–56.

17. For a review of these studies, see Chapman and Chapman, *Disordered Thought in Schizophrenia.* The attempt to find a single quality that would encompass all of schizophrenic thinking has been criticized by P. S. Holzman, among others; see "Thought disorder in schizophrenia: Editor's introduction," *Schizophrenia Bulletin, 12,* 1986, 342–47. P. D. Harvey and J. M. Neale argue that the attempt to locate a central cognitive deficit has failed; see "The specificity of thought disorder to schizophrenia: Research methods in their historical perspective," in B. Maher, ed., *Progress in Experimental Personality Research,* vol. 12 (New York: Academic Press, 1983) pp. 153–80.

18. Goldstein, "Methodological approach," p. 25 and passim.

19. See Chapman and Chapman, *Disordered Thought,* p. 143.

20. Among other problems is that of confusing superficial differences of verbal style with deep-lying differences of *mentalité:* in Goldstein's system, for example, "kitchen equipment" is likely to be considered an abstract category, whereas

"things you use in the kitchen" would not be (L. S. McGaughran and L. J. Moran, " 'Conceptual level' versus 'conceptual area' analysis of object-sorting behavior of schizophrenic and nonpsychiatric groups," *Journal of Abnormal and Social Psychology*, 52, 1956, 49). Also there is the danger of confusing preferences or styles with basic cognitive capabilities. One anthropologist reports on a Kpelli informant who would categorize objects into functional complexes while commenting, "A wiseman can do no other." Only if asked, "How would a fool group the objects?" would this informant give the Westerner a (supposedly) "higher-level" response, by describing a linguistically defined equivalence structure (Glick [1968], reported in R. A. Schweder and E. J. Bourne, "Does the concept of the person vary cross-culturally?" in A. J. Marsella and G. M. White, eds., *Cultural Conceptions of Mental Health and Therapy* [Dordrecht, The Netherlands: Reidel, 1982, 1984], p. 130).

21. See, for example, McGaughran and Moran, " 'Conceptual level'," p. 50.
22. Examples quoted in I. B. Weiner, *Psychodiagnosis in Schizophrenia* (New York: Wiley, 1966), p. 98; Johnston and Holzman, *Assessing Schizophrenic Thinking*, p. 76; A. M. Shimkunas, "Conceptual deficit in schizophrenia: A reappraisal," *British Journal of Medical Psychology*, 45, 1972, 152, 155.
23. Examples quoted in M. Hamilton, *Fish's Schizophrenia*, 2nd ed., p. 34; E. Bleuler, *Dementia Praecox*, p. 74.
24. See Shimkunas, "Conceptual deficit." See also Weiner (*Psychodiagnosis in Schizophrenia*, pp. 100–102), re "inability to interpret experience at appropriate levels of abstraction" being manifest in "preoccupation with highly abstract ideas" at the expense of attending to lower-level abstractions that are more relevant. The schizophrenic preference for general and abstract terms is also noted by Minkowski, *La Schizophrénie*, p. 127; and by Barison, cited in Johnston and Holzman, *Assessing Schizophrenic Thinking*, p. 6.
25. See Cutting, *Psychology of Schizophrenia*, p. 332; Andreasen and Powers, "Overinclusive thinking." One should also note the ambiguities of the notion of "overinclusion": see, for example, J. E. Sims-Knight and R. A. Knight, "Logical and nonlogical classification systems: A look at the underlying complexity of overinclusion in schizophrenics," *Journal of Clinical Psychology*, 34, 1978, 857–65.
26. This is Cutting's conclusion; *Psychology of Schizophrenia*, pp. 336, 348.
27. D. M. Quinlan, K. D. Schultz, R. K. Davies, and M. Harrow, "Overinclusion and transactional thinking on the object sorting test of schizophrenic and nonschizophrenic patients," *Journal of Personality Assessment*, 42, 1978, 401–8.
28. The theoretical situation surrounding the topic of schizophrenic cognition is reminiscent of that which once prevailed in anthropological studies of so-called primitive cultures, where tribal man was subjected to a rather tendentious and contradictory assessment—being accused *both* of an ineptness for abstract and general conceptualization and also of a tendency to dissolve significant distinctions by using overly broad generalizations. In *The Savage Mind* (Chicago: University of Chicago Press, 1966), Claude Lévi-Strauss refers to "the supposed ineptitude of 'primitive people' for abstract thought," pointing out the tendentious character of this argument, which "becomes very apparent when one observes that the opposite state of affairs, that is, where very general terms outweigh specific names, has also been exploited to prove the intellectual pov-

erty of Savages" (p. 1). See also Schweder and Bourne, "Concept of the person," p. 109. (Re "over-abstraction" interpreted as a "cognitive deficit" in schizophrenia, see Shimkunas, "Conceptual deficit in schizophrenia," p. 156.)

29. See M. Harrow and D. M. Quinlan, *Disordered Thinking and Schizophrenic Pathology* (New York and London: Gardner Press, 1985); McGaughran and Moran, "'Conceptual level.'" See also discussion in Chapman and Chapman, *Disordered Thought,* pp. 156–57.

30. Examples from P. Ostwald and V. Zavarin, "Studies of language and schizophrenia in the USSR," in R. W. Rieber, ed., *Applied Psycholinguistics and Mental Health* (New York: Plenum, 1980), p. 81; U. F. Polyakov, "The experimental investigation of cognitive functioning in schizophrenia," in M. Cole and I. Maltzman, eds., *A Handbook of Contemporary Soviet Psychology* (New York and London: Basic Books, 1969), p. 376. Another instance is a patient who selected the parameter of "movement" to characterize a "spoon," placing together "spoon" and "automobile" as similar on this dimension; see Ostwald and Zavarin, "Studies of language," p. 81.

31. Goldstein quoted in Chapman and Chapman, *Disordered Thought,* p. 144.

32. Organic patients are, in fact, much less likely to produce bizarre responses on psychological tests like the Rorschach than are schizophrenics; see M. Lezak, *Neuropsychological Assessment,* 2nd ed. (New York: Oxford University Press, 1983), p. 606.
      Goldstein himself might, in fact, be said to have engaged in an odd but characteristic type of sorting behavior in his own interpretations of the object-sorting task. Nearly always he seems to have taken the schizophrenic's tendency to solve a problem in an unconventional way as an indication of a *failure* to generalize in an "abstract" fashion. This interpretive move—classifying unconventional ways of thinking as deficient or primitive by viewing them through a lens that equates the conventional with the "higher" or more correct—is, in fact, common among those who would emphasize either the deficient or the primitive aspect of the illness. It is perhaps the major way in which the dazzling variety of schizophrenic symptoms has been reduced to formulae that generalize at the expense of a considerable oversimplification.

33. Harrow and Quinlan report no evidence that schizophrenic thinking shows disordered logic or domination by instinctual concerns; the main feature they did find was "bizarre-idiosyncratic" speech (*Disordered Thinking,* pp. 12–13, 45, 148). For similar findings re dreams, see Arieti, *Interpretation of Schizophrenia,* pp. 594–95: Schizophrenic dreams appear to be more bizarre and uncanny than the dreams of normals, but not especially dominated by primitive aggressive or undistorted sexual themes.

34. See J. Zubin, "Problem of attention in schizophrenia," in M. L. Kietzman, S. Sutton, J. Zubin, eds., *Experimental Approaches to Psychopathology* (New York: Academic Press, 1975), pp. 139–66 (re the "goalless uniquely idiosyncratic life" and "culture" of the schizophrenic).
      See also S. Schneider ("Selective attention in schizophrenia," *Journal of Abnormal Psychology,* 85, 1976, 167–73), who found that delusional schizophrenics were especially distractible only under certain conditions, and did not differ from normals in their general *ability* to attend. Many of the thoughts schizophrenics have seem unlikely even to occur to normal individuals; this suggests that a

purported dysfunction of filtering or selective attention—a failure "to screen their own potential responses for appropriateness"—cannot fully account for their ideational anomalies; see S. Matthysee, "Why thinking is easy," in M. Spitzer and B. Maher, eds., *Philosophy and Psychopathology* (New York: Springer Verlag, 1990), p. 179. This is not to say, of course, that certain defects of attention may not play *some* role (see, e.g., my discussion of C. D. Frith's hypothesis on pages 473–75. It is also possible that some schizophrenics have difficulty with *maintaining* a focus of attention (see Cutting, *Psychology of Schizophrenia*, p. 214); but it is also not clear how this could account for their specific propensity for bizarre thinking (given that difficulties with maintenance of attention are also characteristic of patients with major affective illnesses, as the eye-tracking data show).

35. Polyakov, "Cognitive functioning," p. 376. And E. Bleuler speaks of the impossibility of describing the "endless variety" of schizophrenic peculiarities of thought (*Dementia Praecox*, p. 71).

One might wish to argue that the impressions both of overconcreteness and of overabstractness in schizophrenic thinking are mere illusions resulting from the sheer eccentricity of these patients—from the fact that their categories do not agree with the conventions followed by normal individuals. Thus one might maintain (as has been done regarding so-called primitive man; see Schweder and Bourne, "Concept of the person," p. 104) that what we are inclined to view as overconcreteness are simply instances where the patient makes a discrimination we do not deem important, at least in that context; and that apparent overabstractness involves situations where the patient fails to make a discrimination that we *are* inclined to make; but that the choice of discriminations is purely conventional, reflecting nothing fundamental about underlying modes of consciousness. No doubt this is true of at least some such instances; however, in the next chapter I suggest that some instances of seeming hyperabstractness and overconcreteness (the latter might better be termed "literalness," in my view) do reflect certain characteristic *tendencies* of the schizophrenic mind.

36. Polyakov, "Cognitive functioning," p. 374.

37. See N. Hasenfus and P. A. Magaro, "Creativity and schizophrenia: An equality of empirical constructs," *British Journal of Psychiatry, 129*, 1976, 346–49; J. A. Keefe and P. A. Magaro, "Creativity and schizophrenia: An equivalence of cognitive processing," *Journal of Abnormal Psychology, 89*, 1980, 390–98. Re the possibility of a genetic link between creativity and the predisposition to schizophrenia, see J. L. Karlsson, "Genetic association of giftedness and creativity with schizophrenia," *Hereditas, 66*, 1970, 177–82. See also remarks by Dr. Cancro in S. Wolf and B. B. Berle, eds., *The Biology of the Schizophrenic Process* (New York and London: Plenum, 1976), p. 33.

38. See Ostwald and Zavarin, "Studies of language," p. 83; Polyakov, "Cognitive functioning in schizophrenia," pp. 376–82. These findings confirm Eugen Bleuler's suggestion that the "flexibility" of the schizophrenic's associations can give him an advantage in conceiving and comprehending ideas that deviate from the normal (*Dementia Praecox*, p. 78). Henry Maudsley made similar remarks in 1871: "I have long had a suspicion . . . that mankind is indebted for much of its individuality and for certain special forms of genius to individuals [with] some indisposition to insanity. They have often taken up the bye-paths of thought,

which have been overlooked by more stable intellects. . . . There is sufficient truth in the saying 'men think in packs, as jackals hunt' to make welcome in any age, and especially in an age that seems rather to lack the originating impulse, the man who can break through the usual routine of thought and action" ("Insanity and its treatment," *Journal of Mental Science, 17,* 1871, 311–34, quoted in P. Barham, *Schizophrenia and Human Value* [Oxford: Blackwell, 1984], pp. 16–17).

39. Schizophrenics are said to tend "toward equalizing the a priori probabilities of the image hypotheses conditioned by past experience" (Polyakov, "Cognitive functioning," p. 383). They seem to be relatively free of the illusions that normal people acquire from experience. See also Ostwald and Zavarin, "Studies of language," p. 81; V. Zavarin, J. Tonkonogy, and P. Ostwald, "Cognitive processes in schizophrenia and related disorders: Experimental studies in the USSR," *The Pavlovian Journal of Biological Science, 17,* 1982, 188–203.

It would be interesting to study schizophrenic performance on some of the tasks used by the psychologists A. Tversky and D. Kahneman to study normals. Such patients may be less affected than are normal individuals by biases resulting from the "representativeness" factor (see "Judgment under uncertainty: Heuristics and biases," *Science, 185,* 1974, 1124–31) or from "topical accounts," whose role Kahneman and Tversky compare to that of "good forms" in perception and "basic-level categories" in cognition ("Choices, values, and frames," *American Psychologist, 39,* 1984, 347). D. R. Hemsley makes a similar point; see "An experimental psychological model for schizophrenia," in H. Häfner, W. F. Gattaz, and W. Janzarik, eds., *Search for the Causes of Schizophrenia* (Heidelberg: Springer Verlag, 1987), p. 181.

40. This idea is very close to Eugene Minkowski's concept of an *"affaiblissement pragmatique"* (*La Schizophrénie,* p. 229). His discussion of the case of "Paul" is particularly relevant here (see pp. 221–36).

41. Quoted in W. Woods, "Language study in schizophrenia," *Journal of Nervous and Mental Disease, 87,* 1938, 291.

42. See, for example, J. Cutting and D. Murphy, "Schizophrenic thought disorder: A psychological and organic interpretation," *British Journal of Psychiatry, 152,* 1988, 310–19; J. Cutting and D. Murphy, "Impaired ability of schizophrenics, relative to manics or depressives, to appreciate social knowledge about their culture," *British Journal of Psychiatry, 157,* 1990, 355–58. See also W. Blankenberg re the "global crisis of common sense" suffered in schizophrenia; described in J. Parnas and P. Bovet, "Autism in schizophrenia revisited," *Comprehensive Psychiatry, 32,* 1991, 7–21.

43. A similar detachment from a normal orientation toward the probable is apparent when the schizophrenic patient Henry (who is discussed in the following chapter) describes each of the two eyes of a man on a TAT card as having a different look: "It seems that the one [i.e., the eye] on the left is fatigued and the one on the right is worried and looks bitter."

At the height of the illness, many schizophrenics seem almost entirely detached from their literal circumstances, engaged almost exclusively with hypothetical actions in their delusional or quasi-delusional worlds. In their imagination, some patients seem to lead two or more of these lives at once, as if they have transcended all the intrinsic limitations of human identity and situatedness. Such experiences may well be crazy, but they are hardly "concrete"; if Goldstein's vocabulary is applicable here, we would have to speak of an exaggeration not of the concrete but of the abstract attitude.

44. S. Goldstone, "The variability of temporal judgment in psychopathology," in M. L. Kietzman, S. Sutton, and J. Zubin, eds., *Experimental Approaches to Psychopathology* (New York: Academic Press, 1975), pp. 393–419. See also discussion and references in Cutting, *Psychology of Schizophrenia*, p. 323; and p. 347 re "inconsistency, intermittent random responding and a tendency to vacillate between alternatives."

45. J. S. Kasanin, "The disturbance of conceptual thinking in schizophrenia," *Language and Thought in Schizophrenia*, p. 44; N. Cameron, "Experimental analysis of schizophrenic thinking," also in Kasanin, ibid., p. 58. See also C. D. Frith, "Consciousness, information processing, and schizophrenia," *British Journal of Psychiatry*, 134, 1979, p. 232; M. Harrow, I. Lanin-Kettering, and J. G. Miller, "Impaired perspective and thought pathology in schizophrenic and psychotic disorders," *Schizophrenia Bulletin*, 15, 1989, 618; and references in Cutting, *Psychology of Schizophrenia*, p. 323.

46. E. Bleuler, *Dementia Praecox*, p. 54.

47. Johnston and Holzman, *Assessing Schizophrenic Thinking*, pp. 93, 94.

48. See, for example, J. E. Exner, *Current Research and Advanced Interpretation*, vol. 2 of *The Rorschach: A Comprehensive System* (New York: Wiley, 1978), pp. 5, 27–28. Note that contamination responses are hardly ever found in children; see idem, *Basic Foundations*, vol. 1 of *The Rorschach*, 2nd ed. (New York: Wiley, 1986), pp. 257–89.

49. Patient quotations from Weiner, *Psychodiagnosis in Schizophrenia*, pp. 81–82; Johnston and Holzman, *Assessing Schizophrenic Thinking*, p. 99.

50. Such a response can occur in Rorschach perception also; see Johnston and Holzman, *Assessing Schizophrenic Thinking*, p. 86.

51. D. Rapaport, M. Gill, and R. Schafer, *Diagnostic Psychological Testing* (New York: International Universities Press, 1968), p. 475.

52. D. Rapaport, "Cognitive structures," *The Collected Papers of David Rapaport*, ed. M. Gill (New York: Basic Books, 1967), p. 655.

53. Re this slowing, see Frith, "Consciousness, information processing and schizophrenia," 232; and D. R. Hemsley, "Attention and information processing in schizophrenia," *British Journal of Social and Clinical Psychology*, 15, 1976, 199–209.

54. Roy Schafer describes such "dramatic" shifts as "almost distinctively schizophrenic" (*Psychoanalytic Interpretation in Rorschach Testing* [New York: Grune and Stratton, 1954], p. 107). M. Bleuler makes similar statements re the schizoid, noting that the "world he experiences undergoes a constant, renewed mental readaptation" (*Schizophrenic Disorders*, trans. S. M. Clemens [New Haven and London: Yale University Press, 1978], p. 435). In the following chapter we consider a particularly vivid example of this tendency on the Rorschach test.

55. See Cameron, "Experimental analysis," pp. 58–59 (Cameron also points out that this pattern is unlike that of the child). Similar differences between organic and schizophrenic patients have been found in their style of responding to the Wisconsin Card Sorting Test, with the former group tending to perseverate and the latter showing little continuity from trial to trial (as if the schizophrenics "have no plan, rather than being unable to shift from an incorrect plan") (A. S. Bellack, K. T. Mueser, R. L. Morrison, A. Tierney, and K. Podell, "Remediation of cognitive deficits in schizophrenia," *American Journal of Psychiatry*, 147, 1990,

1654). Goldstein's notion of loss of the abstract attitude seems to apply best to organic patients who are grossly demented or who suffer from widespread damage in cortex and subcortex (see H. Gardner, *The Shattered Mind* [New York: Vintage Books, 1974], p. 430; see also pp. 423–33). Re organic patients whose functioning may be more similar to that of schizophrenics, see appendix; see also J. Cutting, *The Right Cerebral Hemisphere and Psychiatric Disorders* (Oxford: Oxford University Press, 1990).

56. Kasanin, "Disturbance of conceptual thinking," p. 45.

57. M. R. Solovay, M. E. Shenton, and P. S. Holzman, "Comparative studies of thought disorders: I. Mania and schizophrenia," *Archives of General Psychiatry*, *44*, 1987, 14. Incongruous responses like these are common in borderline patients as well as in patients with affective psychosis.

58. For empirical findings supportive of my generalizations re schizophrenia versus mania, see P. S. Holzman, M. E. Shenton, M. R. Solovay, "Quality of thought disorder in differential diagnosis," *Schizophrenia Bulletin, 12*, 1986, 360–72. These researchers have found "combinatory thinking" (including incongruous combinations) to be far more common in mania than in schizophrenia, whereas schizophrenics were far more likely to manifest "fluid thinking" (including contaminations) and various signs of "confusion."

Something close to this distinction between the incongruous and the heteroclite is described in Andras Angyal's contribution to Kasanin's classic collection, *Language and Thought in Schizophrenia* ("Disturbances of thinking in schizophrenia," pp. 115–23). As Angyal puts it: "The thinking of the schizophrenic is not impaired so far as apprehending of relationships is concerned; the schizophrenic—when he fails in the solution of an intellectual task—fails in the apprehending of system-connections." A "relationship," for Angyal, involves the pairing of two items (like the sewing machine and the umbrella), whereas a "system" involves an indefinite number of constituents arranged "according to some unitary plan within a 'dimensional medium'" (on a given dissecting table, if you will; see pp. 117, 116 [emphasis deleted]). As synonyms for *system*, Angyal offers the following: "semantic stratum," "realm," "frame of reference," "context," "organized field" or "universe of discourse" (pp. 119–20). It is not always easy to differentiate between issues of "relationship" and of "system," and there may well be marginal cases lying in some sense between the two. Still, the distinction helps at least to distinguish between certain prototypical examples of schizophrenic versus manic thinking.

59. Thus in the DSM III-R description of "flight of ideas" (a symptom especially common in manic episodes) no reference is made to shifts of "frame of reference." Here the "abrupt changes from topic to topic" are said to be "usually based on understandable associations, distracting stimuli, or plays on words"; whereas schizophrenic disorders of form of thought are said to involve "loosening of associations, in which ideas shift from one subject to another, completely unrelated or only obliquely related subject, without the speaker's displaying any awareness that the topics are unconnected." In schizophrenia, statements that "lack a meaningful relationship may be juxtaposed, or the person may shift idiosyncratically from one *frame of reference* to another" (American Psychiatric Association, DSM III-R, pp. 397, 188 [emphasis added]). The manic's tendency always to move on to another experience, rather than to adopt, or hesitate among, several different perspectives on the same stimulus, may account for the rarity of contamination responses in their Rorschach records.

60. See S. S. Reich and J. Cutting, "Picture perception and abstract thought in schizophrenia," *Psychological Medicine, 12*, 1982, 96.

61. R. Shattuck, *The Banquet Years*, rev. ed. (New York: Vintage Books, 1968), pp. 187–252; quotations from pp. 233, 236, 202. Jarry also used circumlocutions reminiscent of some schizophrenic responses quoted earlier (see p. 125), for example, a candle called a "night illumination object." Instead of saying the word *wind*, for example, Jarry spoke of "that which blows"; instead of *bird*, of "that which chirps" (p. 212).

62. A. d'Harnoncourt, "Introduction," in A. d'Harnoncourt and K. McShine, eds., *Marcel Duchamp* (exhibition catalogue) (New York: Museum of Modern Art, 1973), p. 37. Another example of the *infra-mince:* the sound made by velvet trouser legs brushing against each other (p. 37).

63. R. Poggiolli, *The Theory of the Avant-Garde* (Cambridge: Harvard University Press, 1968), p. 196.

64. Zola quoted in J. Berger, *The Moment of Cubism and Other Essays* (New York: Pantheon Books, 1969), p. 19. De Gourmont quoted in P. Wheelright, *Metaphor and Reality* (Bloomington and London: Indiana University Press, 1962), p. 15.

65. T. S. Eliot, "Tradition and the individual talent," *Selected Essays, 1917–1932* (New York: Harcourt Brace, 1932), p. 10.

66. Blouse example reported to me by a colleague. Eugene Minkowski mentions a schizophrenic patient who had an obsession with pockets: "He wanted to know what difference there was between putting one's hands straight into a normal jacket pocket and putting them into the sloping pockets of an overcoat" (quoted in J. Cutting, "Books reconsidered: *La Schizophrénie:* E. Minkowski," *British Journal of Psychiatry, 158*, 1991, 294.

67. H. S. Sullivan, *Clinical Studies in Psychiatry* (New York: Norton, 1973), pp. 183–85.

68. See D. E. Raskin, "Bleuler and schizophrenia," *British Journal of Psychiatry, 127*, 1975, 231–34.

69. Sullivan, *Clinical Studies in Psychiatry*, pp. 184, 182.

70. Goldstein, "Methodological approach to schizophrenic thought disorder," p. 34.

71. Ibid., p. 33 (emphasis added). A similar interpretation of shifts of frame of reference as indicating weakening of boundaries (including boundaries between the person and his or her environment) is offered by Rapaport, who explicitly compares the schizophrenic phenomena to early phases of both individual and cultural development as described by Piaget and Lévy-Bruhl ("Cognitive structures," pp. 656–57).

72. For a Rorschach example, see responses of patient "B" in S. J. Blatt and C. Wild, *Schizophrenia: A Developmental Analysis* (New York: Academic Press, 1976). For instance, re Card #1: "As I look, things change. . . . They keep changing, I might as well stop. . . . At first they were moving slavic dancers, then I also see them as stationary and stylized, like Minoan painting" (p. 140). As Blatt and Wild note: "Her percepts are often accurate and well-articulated, at times even creative, but they lack stability. For her, reality seems to be in a process of continual change, and these changes occur even while she looks at an object" (p. 152).

73. Phrase from W. James, *Principles of Psychology*, vol. 1 (New York: Henry Holt, 1890), p. 488.

74. "I can go on from dimension to dimension in thinking about something," said the patient Henry, whose Rorschach is considered at length in the following chapter. He also said he felt he could very easily adopt the perspective of all the other people on the hospital ward: "I feel able to identify with everyone on the unit."

75. In his well-known (to literary scholars) discussion of the English metaphysical poets of the seventeenth century, who have strong affinities with the modernists, Samuel Johnson describes a cognitive style similar to the schizophrenic wise-cracking and slippage I have been examining. He speaks of an "analytic" and fragmenting consciousness, a "perverseness of industry" directed toward the achievement of "singular" and "surprising" insights rather than "just" or "natural" ones. Such a mode of composition is unsuited, Johnson says, to "representing or moving the affections," for such poets write "rather as beholders than partakers of human nature," as onlookers "without interest and without emotion," and paying "no regard to that uniformity of sentiment which enables us to conceive and to excite the pains and the pleasures of other minds." The metaphysical poets also presaged the modernist apotheosis of the image over the referential object (see Poggiolli, *Theory of Avant-Garde*, pp. 196–99); for, as Dr. Johnson points out, their "laboured particularities" turn the mind "more upon that from which the illustration is drawn, than that to which it is applied" (from *Life of Cowley*, in W. J. Bate, ed., *Criticism: The Major Texts* [New York and Burlingame: Harcourt, Brace and World, 1952], pp. 217–19; see also p. 201).

76. From "Vie de Henry Brulard," quoted in Shattuck, *Banquet Years*, p. 328.

77. M. H. Abrams in *Natural Supernaturalism, Tradition and Revolution in Romantic Literature* (New York: Norton, 1971), pp. 213–14.

78. U. Meyer, "Introduction," *Conceptual Art* (New York: Dutton, 1972), p. xvi.

79. Don Judd, quoted in S. Gablik, *Progress in Art* (New York: Rizzoli, 1977), p. 87.

80. Meyer, "Introduction," p. xvi.

81. The parallel between the Chinese encyclopedia and Stevens's poem is particularly close.

82. See H. Friedrich, *The Structure of Modern Poetry* (Evanston, IL: Northwestern University Press, 1974), pp. 60–62.

83. See discussions in M. Perloff, *The Futurist Moment* (Chicago and London: University of Chicago Press, 1986), pp. 44–79, and G. L. Ulmer, "The object of post-criticism," in H. Foster, ed., *The Anti-Aesthetic: Essays on Postmodern Culture* (Port Townsend, WA: Bay Press, 1983).

84. "The idea that doubt can be heroic," as Robert Hughes points out, is "one of the keys to our century, a touchstone of modernity itself" (*The Shock of the New* [New York: Knopf, 1981], p. 18).

85. See, for example, Lukacs, *Realism in Our Time* (New York: Harper and Row, 1971), pp. 33–34 and passim, re how modernism deprives literature of a sense of perspective or a hierarchy of significance.

86. Quoted in J. Tancock, "The influence of Marcel Duchamp," in d'Harnoncourt and McShine, *Marcel Duchamp*, p. 165.

87. Quoted in B. Rosenbaum and H. Sonne, *The Language of Psychosis* (New York and London: New York University Press, 1986), p. 91.

88. Quoted in J. Cutting and F. Dunne, "Subjective experiences of schizophrenia," *Schizophrenia Bulletin*, 15, 1989, 222.

89. M. Bleuler, *Schizophrenic Disorders*, p. 483.

90. M. MacLane, *I, Mary MacLane: A Diary of Human Days* (New York: Stokes, 1917), pp. 176–77.

91. It "seems to bear a persistent relation to a kind of fear," as Robert Walser remarks in his "Essay on Freedom" (*Selected Stories* [New York: Farrar, Straus and Giroux, 1982], p. 179; see also p. 181).

92. Jaspers, *General Psychopathology*, p. 294. For illustrations of such skepticism, see the short story by Robert Walser, "So, I've got you" (*Selected Stories*, pp. 105–8).

93. In this passage from *The Will to Power* (trans. W. Kaufmann [New York: Vintage Books, 1968; originally published in 1901], pp. 302–3, sec. 560), Nietzsche criticizes the hypothesis that "interpretation and subjectivity are not essential, that a thing freed from all relationships would still be a thing." He goes further: "Conversely, the apparent *objective* character of things: could it not be merely a difference of degree within the subjective?—that perhaps that which changes slowly presents itself to us as 'objectively' enduring, being, 'in-itself'—that the objective is only a false concept of a genus and an antithesis *within* the subjective?"

94. Nietzsche, *Will to Power*, p. 506.

95. Ibid., p. 221; Nietzsche quoted in S. Schwartz, *The Matrix of Modernism* (Princeton, NJ: Princeton University Press, 1985), p. 18.

96. F. Nietzsche, *On the Genealogy of Morals*, trans. W. Kaufmann and R. J. Hollingdale (New York: Vintage, 1968; originally published in 1887), 3rd essay, p. 119.

97. F. Nietzsche, *The Gay Science*, trans. W. Kaufmann (New York: Vintage Books, 1974; originally published in 1887), p. 290, sec. 347.

98. F. Nietzsche, *On the Advantage and Disadvantage of History for Life*, trans. P. Preuss (Indianapolis, IN: Hackett, 1980; originally published in 1874), pp. 50, 7, 8, 41, 10, 11, 10, 20, 24. "Basic condition of all life" is from *Beyond Good and Evil*, trans. R. J. Hollingdale (Harmondsworth, UK: Penguin Books, 1973; originally published in 1886), p. 14.

99. F. Nietzsche quoted in K. Jaspers, *Nietzsche*, trans. C. F. Wallraff and F. J. Schmitz (South Bend, IN: Regnery/Gateway, 1965), p. 392. Nietzsche seems to have known very well, on a personal level, the effects of this endless shifting of horizons, of what he called "these thought experiments with the possible" in which "we ourselves wish to be our own experiments and our own experimental animals." He felt the effects, he said, not merely as "the shaking of [a] room when a wagon goes by"; rather, "I am sitting in the wagon, and often I myself *am* the wagon" (ibid., pp. 388–89).

100. L. Aragon, quoted in A. Callinicos, *Against Postmodernism* (New York: St. Martin's, 1990), p. 29.

101. E. E. Evans-Pritchard, *Witchcraft, Oracles and Magic among the Azande* (Oxford: Oxford University Press, 1937), pp. 194–95. The same point is made in Robert Levy's study of Tahitian culture, *Tahitians: Mind and Experience in the Society Islands* (Chicago: University of Chicago Press, 1988). Interestingly, Levy found Tahitians to be "concrete" in two respects: they did not tend to shift readily among several different interpretations of a stimulus; and their style of understanding and communicating emphasized "the rich and complex

phenomenological attributes of whatever is being considered" rather than focusing on context-free attributes (pp. 258–59).

102. Musil, *Man Without Qualities*, vol. 1, trans. E. Wilkins and E. Kaiser (New York: Capricorn Books, 1965), pp. 15, 7, 71.

103. Ibid., pp. 129, 71.

104. D. S. Luft, *Robert Musil and the Crisis of European Culture, 1880–1942* (Berkeley: University of California Press, 1980), p. 231.

105. Musil, *The Man Without Qualities*, vol. 2 (London: Pan Books, 1979), pp. 275–76.

106. One colleague's patient, for example, would watch television, chuckling almost constantly at everything she saw. Re the empty smile, see H. C. Rümke, "The nuclear symptom of schizophrenia and the praecox feeling," *History of Psychiatry, 1*, 1990, 331–41. Re "meaningless hilarity," see E. Kraepelin, *Dementia Praecox*, p. 33. See also chapter 3, pages 111–15.

107. This patient was described to me by a colleague.

108. The following speech by another schizophrenic patient is not easy to follow, but it does suggest a similar kind of perspectivism: "Because I, I want to finish the second part there. And then we'll do a third, that is you know, the fourth dimension, don't you, and there are of course an infinite number of functions, and just as many visions, and then just as many dimensions, that's what I think. I can't do anything about that. Not for the moment. It's called to practice something" (from Rosenbaum and Sonne, *Language of Psychosis*, p. 59).

109. Musil quoted in P. L. Berger, "The problem of multiple realities: Alfred Schutz and Robert Musil," in M. Natanson, ed., *Phenomenology and Social Reality* (The Hague: Martinus Nijhoff, 1970), p. 216.

110. "So, I've Got You," in Walser, *Selected Stories*, pp. 105–8.

111. Patients quoted in Goldstein, "Methodological approach," p. 31.

112. D. P. Schreber, *Memoirs of My Nervous Illness*, trans. I. Macalpine and R. A. Hunter (Cambridge: Harvard University Press, 1988; originally published in German in 1903), p. 139.

113. Walser, *Selected Stories*, pp. 123–24.

114. "Hovering life within" from Musil, *Man Without Qualities*, vol. 1, p. 301 (translation slightly altered). Musil ascribes certain classic schizophrenic symptoms to Moosbrugger, including certain of the First Rank Symptoms (which I describe in chapter 7); see ibid., pp. 283–84.

   Not surprisingly, it is the more articulate and intellectual patients who offer the most eloquent descriptions of these experiences of doubt and relativism. Vacillation among competing alternatives and consequent confusion and paralysis are extremely widespread tendencies among schizophrenics, however; and it would be wrong to assume that the associated feelings of arbitrariness and relativism cannot occur in patients at many different levels of intelligence.

115. Musil even suggests that Moosbrugger, this brutish giant of a man, has a hyperaesthetic side—"a plaintive, delicately nervous over-sensitivity" that would sometimes overcome him (ibid., p. 279). Musil also suggests (p. 283) that Moosbrugger sometimes uses the ploy of feigning the feigning of symptoms (see chapter 3, pages 111–12).

116. Ibid., pp. 284–85.

117. Ibid., p. 285.

Chapter 5: Disturbances of Distance

1. See D. Rapaport, M. M. Gill, and R. Schafer, *Diagnostic Psychological Testing,* rev. ed., ed. R. Holt (New York: International Universities Press, 1968), pp. 266, 427–30, 440, 443–47, and passim.

2. Quoted in P. L. Berger, "The problem of multiple realities: Alfred Schutz and Robert Musil," in M. Natanson, ed., *Phenomenology and Social Reality* (The Hague: Nijhoff, 1970), p. 216.

3. See S. Schwartz, *The Matrix of Modernism: Pound, Eliot, and Early Twentieth Century Thought* (Princeton, NJ: Princeton University Press, 1985), pp. 12–49.

4. G. H. Hartman, *The Unmediated Vision* (New York: Harcourt, Brace and World, 1966), p. 156; and see pp. 127–73. See also M. Mandelbaum, *History, Man, and Reason: A Study in Nineteenth-Century Thought* (Baltimore and London: Johns Hopkins University Press, 1971), p. 350 and passim.

5. F. Nietzsche, *The Will to Power,* trans. W. Kaufman and R. J. Hollingdale (New York: Vintage Books, 1968; originally published in 1901), p. 307.

6. Ibid., pp. 263–64.

7. F. Nietzsche, "On truth and lies in a nonmoral sense," *Philosophy and Truth: Selections from Nietzsche's Notebooks of the Early 1870s,* trans. D. Brazeale (Atlantic Highlands, NJ: Humanities Press, 1979), p. 83.

8. Ibid., p. 84. See Mandelbaum, *History, Man, and Reason,* p. 342.

9. Nietzsche, "On truth and lies," pp. 83, 85.

10. F. Nietzsche, *The Gay Science,* trans. W. Kaufmann (New York: Vintage Books, 1974; originally published in 1887), p. 164. "Spirit of gravity" is from *Thus Spake Zarathustra.* In his essays from the early 1870s, Nietzsche writes, "there is . . . no real knowing apart from metaphor"; he disdains being "truthful" as nothing more than "employ[ing] the usual metaphors . . . the duty to lie according to fixed convention, to be with the herd and in a manner binding on everyone" (*Philosophy and Truth,* pp. 50, 84).
    These themes also emerge with particular force in the thought of Fritz Mauthner (1848–1923), the German-speaking writer and philosopher who influenced Joyce, Beckett, and Wittgenstein. Mauthner adopted a radically empiricist or sensationalist conception of human experience, along with an extreme linguistic conventionalism. Like Nietzsche in "On Truth and Lies in an Extramoral Sense," he viewed the categories of language as purely arbitrary, a kind of game "that becomes more binding as more players submit themselves to it, but which is unable either to conceive or to change the world of reality" (quoted in G. Weiler, "On Fritz Mauthner's critique of language," *Mind,* 67, 1958, 84). The only valid responses on realizing these truths are laughter and silence, according to Mauthner (see L. Ben-Zvi, "Samuel Beckett, Fritz Mauthner, and the limits of language," *PMLA,* 95, 1980, 197).

11. This illustrates both the objectivism and the subjectivism that are so characteristic of the modernist mind.

12. R. Barthes, *Mythologies,* trans. A. Lavers (New York: Hill and Wang, 1972), pp. 75, 121 (translation slightly altered). Incidentally, Barthes states that such concepts make neologism inevitable (p. 121); see chapter 6, note 56.

13. J. Cage quoted in G. L. Ulmer, "The object of post-criticism," in H. Foster, ed.,

The Anti-Aesthetic: Essays on Postmodern Culture (Port Townsend, WA: Bay Press, 1983), p. 104.

14. O. Paz, *Marcel Duchamp*, trans. R. Phillips and D. Gardner (New York: Seaver Books, 1978), p. 16.

15. Quoted in R. Shattuck, *The Banquet Years: The Origins of the Avant-Garde in France 1885–World War I*, rev. ed. (New York: Vintage Books, 1968), pp. 241–42. A similar conception is also apparent in Roland Barthes's description of the preconceptual or prelinguistic domain as an inchoate mass that "could be compared to a huge jellyfish, with uncertain articulations and contours" (quoted in F. Jameson, *The Prison-House of Language* [Princeton, NJ: Princeton University Press, 1972], p. 145).

16. J. Derrida, *Writing and Difference*, trans. A. Bass (Chicago: University of Chicago Press, 1978), p. 292.

17. C. Simon, *Triptych*, trans. H. R. Lane (London: John Calder, 1977), see pp. 7f. See discussion and quotations from Simon in C. Butler, *After the Wake: An Essay on the Contemporary Avant-Garde* (Oxford: Clarendon Press, 1980), pp. 150–54.

18. M. Lorenz, "Problems posed by schizophrenic language," *Archives of General Psychiatry*, 4, 1961, 608; originally quoted by Silvano Arieti, *The Interpretation of Schizophrenia*, 2nd ed. (New York: Basic Books, 1974), pp. 250–51. A further example of this tendency was apparent with another patient (the one preoccupied with the untrustworthiness of history): his response to the question about the similarity between "fly" and "tree" was to ask "What *kind* of fly?"—a perfectly rational, though in fact quite rare, response (my notes). For other examples, see Kurt Goldstein re patients who refused to classify a bunch of color chips simply as green, speaking instead of peacock green, emerald green, taupe green, and so on, or of "the color of the grass in Virginia, . . . of the grass in Kentucky," and so on ("Methodological approach to the study of schizophrenic thought disorder," in J. S. Kasanin, ed., *Language and Thought in Schizophrenia* [New York: Norton, 1964], p. 26).

19. Arieti, however, sees this exchange as evidence that the patient is "unable to define common words," that she "cannot cope with the task of defining the word as a symbol of a class" (*Interpretation of Schizophrenia*, p. 251).

20. This, presumably, is a canonical example of so-called illogicality, since it appears in an influential article by Nancy Andreasen as well as in DSM III-R, where it is presented as illustrating "illogical thinking" (Andreasen, "Thought, language, and communication disorders: I. Clinical assessment, definition of terms, and evaluation of their reliability," *Archives of General Psychiatry*, 36, 1979, 1320; and DSM III-R, p. 399). The diagnosis is not given, but the context implies that the patient is psychotic. Incidentally, Andreason defines "illogicality" as "a pattern of speech in which conclusions are reached that do not follow logically"; this, she says, may take the form of non sequiturs, of faulty inductive inferences (which, she says, are common among nonpatients), or that of "reaching conclusions based on faulty premises without any actual delusional thinking" (p. 1320). Interestingly enough, the DSM III-R version of the quotation is not identical to Andreasen's: the second sentence is omitted—which, it seems to me, may make it somewhat easier to hear the sentence as illogical.

21. American Psychiatric Association, *Diagnostic and Statistical Manual of Mental*

Disorders, 3rd ed., rev. (DSM III-R) (Washington, D.C.: American Psychiatric Association, 1987), p. 399.

22. For further examples, see E. Bleuler (*Dementia Praecox, or the Group of Schizophrenias*, trans. J. Zinkin [New York: International Universities Press, 1950], p. 75), who mentions several patients who treated two ideas as equivalent even though, in Bleuler's estimation, they were not really ignorant of the difference between the ideas. Another possible example of such conceptual (or linguistic) freedom is the following response to the question, "In what way are a fly and a tree alike?": "A fly has *branches*, like a tree." M. H. Johnston and P. S. Holzman offer this as an example of the category of "Queer" responses, defined as extremely peculiar responses that the "subject utters with an air of certainty, but [where] the listener has little idea of what is meant" (*Assessing Schizophrenic Thinking* [San Francisco: Jossey-Bass, 1979], p. 89). In fact, of course, branches and legs do bear an obvious metaphorical resemblance to each other; though the response may be unconventional, it is not all that difficult to conjecture what might be meant. In A. E. Goldman's study of "Symbolic representation in schizophrenia" (*Journal of Personality, 28,* 1960, 293–316), the patients demonstrated greater variability in their interpretation of a given symbol (they were shown line drawings in this study) than did the normal subjects; and at least some of the patients expressed a perspectivist awareness of this plurisignificance: ". . . depends on how I feel. Right now it means 'joy'!" said one. "It depends on what side [of the card] you look at it from," said another (pp. 307–8).

23. J. Allison, S. Blatt, and C. Zimet, *The Interpretation of Psychological Tests* (New York: Harper and Row, 1968), pp. 107–8. The response is to Card #10.

24. See E. R. Balken, "A delineation of schizophrenic language and thought in a test of imagination," *Journal of Psychology, 16,* 1943, 255; E. Minkowski, *Lived Time* (Evanston, IL: Northwestern University Press, 1970), p. 275; E. Minkowski, *La Schizophrénie* (Paris: Payot, 1927), p. 127.

25. See F. J. MacHovec, "Differentiating affective from thought disorders by semantic analysis of Rorschach responses," *Journal of Personality Assessment, 46,* 1982, 12–17. One Soviet study found a dearth of adverbs and an overabundance of adjectives in schizophrenic speech (Giliarovsky [1957], reported in P. Ostwald and V. Zavarin, "Studies of language and schizophrenia in the USSR," in R. W. Rieber, ed., *Applied Psycholinguistics and Mental Health* [New York: Plenum, 1980], p. 73). Minkowski describes a patient who wrote an autobiography in which no people or activities but only physical objects like bolts and chests were mentioned. When asked, after a visit, if she had been happy to see her mother, another patient replied: "There was movement; I don't much like that" (*La Schizophrénie*, pp. 121, 124).

26. This patient was described to me by a colleague.

27. Arieti, *Interpretation of Schizophrenia*, pp. 245–49.

28. Rapaport, Gill, and Schafer, *Diagnostic Psychological Testing*, pp. 474–75; see also pp. 428, 492, 519.

29. See, for example, D. Rapaport, "Cognitive structures," *The Collected Papers of David Rapaport*, ed. M. Gill (New York: Basic Books, 1967), pp. 656–57 (re "impairment of 'frames of reference' "). Re disturbed temporal ordering, see C. Yorke, S. Wiseberg, and T. Freeman, *Development and Psychopathology* (New Haven and London: Yale University Press, 1989), p. 215; S. Arieti, "Special logic

of schizophrenia and other types of autistic thought," *Psychiatry*, *11*, 1948, 325–38.

30. J. Ortega y Gasset, "The Dehumanization of Art," *The Dehumanization of Art and Other Essays on Art, Culture, and Literature*, trans. H. Weyl (Princeton, NJ: Princeton University Press, 1968; originally published in Spanish in 1925), p. 23.

31. Robbe-Grillet states this vision quite explicitly: "Not only do we no longer consider the world as our own, our private property, designed according to our needs and readily domesticated, but we no longer believe in its 'depth' " (*For a New Novel: Essays on Fiction*, trans. R. Howard [New York: Grove Press, 1965], p. 24).

32. Quotes from story are from A. Robbe-Grillet, "The secret room," in J. H. Pickering, ed., *Fiction 100* (New York: Macmillan, 1978; story originally published in 1962), pp. 901–3.

33. Minkowski, *Lived Time*, p. 228. Another patient quoted by Minkowski gives an eloquent account: "Everything is immobile around me. Things present themselves in isolation on their own, without evoking any response in me. . . . It is as if a pantomine were going on around me, one which I cannot take part in. . . . The value and complexity of things no longer exists. There's no link between them and me. Everything seems frozen around me" (in J. Cutting, "Books reconsidered: *La Schizophrénie*: E. Minkowski," *British Journal of Psychiatry*, *158*, 1991, 294).

34. Robbe-Grillet, *For a New Novel*, p. 19; trans. by B. Wright, in Butler, *After the Wake: An Essay on the Contemporary Avant-Garde* (Oxford: Clarendon Press, 1980), pp. 162, 166–67.

35. Re the film *Last Year at Marienbad*, on which he collaborated with Alain Resnais, Robbe-Grillet writes: "The man and woman don't start to exist until they appear on the screen for the first time; before then they were nothing, and the moment the film is over they are again nothing" (*For a New Novel*, trans. B. Wright, quoted in Butler, *After the Wake*, pp. 172–73). While insisting on the one hand that his works must be appreciated in their utmost concreteness, Robbe-Grillet also writes, "All my work is precisely engaged in the attempt to bring its own structures to light" (quoted in Butler, ibid., p. 46).

    Incidentally, Wallace Stevens's poem "Study of Two Pears"—with its denial of metaphor ("The pears are not viols, nudes or bottles") and its later indications that the pears in question are painted rather than real ("In the way they are modelled / There are bits of blue")—offers a rehearsal in miniature of many of the essential epistemological moves that occur in the *Nouveau Roman* (*Collected Poems* [New York: Knopf, 1969], pp. 196–97).

36. Interestingly enough, these fictional techniques exploited by Simon and Robbe-Grillet were to some extent inspired by the work of a severely schizoid, and perhaps even schizophrenic, writer from early in this century—Raymond Roussel. Robbe-Grillet's novel *Le Voyeur* was originally entitled *La Vue*, in homage to a work by Roussel. Roussel's involutional prose employed extensive degrees of embedding—with parentheses within parentheses within parentheses; he would shift rapidly from perspective to perspective; and he would often call attention to the fact of perspective by framing, say, a landscape description with descriptions of the circumstances of the viewer; see review by L. Sante, "Scientist of the fantastic," *New York Review of Books*, January 31, 1985, 16.

37. See F. Nietzsche, *The Will to Power*, trans. W. Kaufmann and R. J. Hollingdale (New York: Vintage Books, 1968; first version published in German in 1901), p. 267 (translation slightly altered); see also p. 264.

38. The spirit of this TAT story may be similar to that of deconstructive literary criticism, which attempts always to reveal the taken-for-granted presuppositions on which linguistic texts are based.

The failure to construct a narrative with any depth, whether of character, of time, or even perhaps of space, is also suggested by the following stories told by Robert, a schizophrenic patient I saw in psychotherapy:

Card #5 (a picture of a woman peering into a room): Looks more like a cartoon than a picture—like, "Hello is anybody there?" Looks as if nobody's there, so she'll probably turn around or come in and find something to do. That's about it.

Card B (Picasso's *La Vie*, which depicts a middle-aged woman with baby, and a naked couple): It's as if everyone is saying, "Here I am." That's about it. [What are the feelings?] I don't know. Maybe strength, I don't know.

Card 12M (young man on couch, older man leaning over him): Looks like he's saying, "Yes, I am here."

Well, that seems to be about it.

The static presentism and lack of narrative depth or thrust of these stories is patent. The reference to a cartoon (story to Card #5) seems an allusion to the card's unreality, two-dimensionality, and status as a medium of representation. Characters merely announce, "Here I am!," as if the only possible role or concern they can have (or that the storyteller will allow them to have) is that of presenting themselves to the viewer. The effect is much the same as in the novels of Claude Simon, where characters seem "explicitly fictional images," "always seen as personnages (actors) and frequently as frozen out of emotionally involving activity into some instance of static visual art" (Butler, *After the Wake*, p. 152).

In an essay on Raymond Roussel, whom he counts as one of "the direct ancestors of the modern novel," Robbe-Grillet describes the static or frozen quality of Roussel's stories, which utterly lack psychological depth (they mention only the most hackneyed of sentiments), treat reproductions or representations rather than realities, and focus on the surfaces of things, "the pure spectacle of gesture deprived of meaning." What emerges is "a *flat* and *discontinuous* universe where each thing refers only to itself" ("Enigmas and transparency in Raymond Roussel," *For a New Novel*, pp. 80–81, 82, 86).

39. J. Frank, "Spatial form in modern literature," *The Widening Gyre: Crisis and Mastery in Modern Literature* (Bloomington and London: Indiana University Press, 1968), p. 13; idem, "Spatial form: Thirty years after," in J. R. Smitten and A. Daghistany, eds., *Spatial Form in Narrative* (Ithaca and London: Cornell University Press, 1981), p. 204.

Narratives told by young children also tend to lack a tight logical or causal-temporal structure, but they do not have a timeless or reflexive quality; see A. N. Applebee, *The Child's Concept of Story* (Chicago: University of Chicago Press, 1978). It is true that the child's lived-world lacks the organized temporal structure of the adult's—a fact that has led some to equate it with the also-different world of the schizophrenic. Yet the young child is, it would seem, a kind of natural Bergsonian, caught up in an intensely dynamic, if sometimes confusing, *durée*, which has little in common with what Eugene Minkowski has aptly called the "morbid geometrism" of the schizophrenic (*Lived Time*, p. 277).

40. A close analogue to Jarry's gyroscope is Marcel Duchamp's film, *Anemic Cinema*, which does its utmost to deny, via certain reflexive tendencies, what are usually the most salient aspects of film: the opening up of a three-dimensional universe of motion and real objects; see A. Michelson, "Anemic cinema: Reflections on an emblematic work," *Artforum*, *12*, 1973, 64–69.

41. Minkowski, *Lived Time*, p. 287.

42. B. J. Freedman, "The subjective experience of perceptual and cognitive disturbances in schizophrenia," *Archives of General Psychiatry*, *30*, 1974, 338 (the quotation is from an autobiographical book by Morag Coate, *Beyond All Reason* [Philadelphia and New York: Lippincott, 1965], p. 158). See also Jaspers, *General Psychopathology*, pp. 86–87.

43. Patient quoted in Minkowski, *Lived Time*, p. 279. Ludwig Binswanger also describes the "most characteristic feature of this new [schizophrenic] world" as its abnormal temporal quality, the fact that "time virtually comes to a standstill" ("Extravagance, perverseness, manneristic behaviour and schizophrenia," in J. Cutting and M. Shepherd, eds., *The Clinical Roots of the Schizophrenia Concept*, [Cambridge: Cambridge University Press, 1987], p. 86).

44. Interestingly, Kurt Goldstein, late in his life, came to deny the defect interpretation usually given to his notion of schizophrenic "concreteness," arguing instead that their concreteness is a protective defense against anxiety (L. J. Chapman and J. P. Chapman, *Disordered Thought in Schizophrenia* [Englewood Cliffs, NJ: Prentice-Hall, 1973], pp. 147–48).

45. Frank, "Spatial form in modern literature," pp. 3–62. For a similar analysis, see Carl Schorske's discussion of Gustav Klimt, in *Fin-de-Siècle Vienna* (New York: Vintage Books, 1971), pp. 9, 270–71.

46. Minkowski, *Lived Time*, p. 288.

47. As Maurice Denis put it in 1890: "A picture—before being a warhorse, a nude woman, or some sort of anecdote—is essentially a surface covered with colours arranged in a certain order" (quoted in R. Hughes, *The Shock of the New* [New York: Knopf, 1981], p. 14).

48. C. Greenberg, "Modernist painting," in G. Battcock, ed., *The New Art: A Critical Anthology*, rev. ed. (New York: Dutton, 1966, 1973), p. 67.

49. Once one has recognized the mind's role in creating reality, a realization likely to challenge standard modes of representation, it seems possible to move in (at least) two directions. One may retreat from these forms of representation and look for sources of security in the elements of the new dualistic ontology—that is, in conceptual abstraction or in concrete sensation; or else one may continue operating in the representational mode (perhaps because one feels there is no escaping it), but now adopting a posture of constant doubt—in which one continually questions not only particular representations but the entire act of representation itself. These two options have at least a rough correspondence with what have been called "modernist" and "postmodernist" attitudes in the arts, and the distinction between them may also capture something of the difference between the attitudes adopted by the two schizophrenics whose projective test responses

I've concentrated on in this chapter: the "Before this picture . . ." TAT story seems, in this sense, more "modernist," while Henry's Rorschach responses (to be discussed) could be seen as more "postmodernist" in spirit. Whereas the TAT story tends to "bracket" or "suspend" the referent, the Rorschach responses tend rather "to problematize the activity of reference" (see C. Owens, "The allegorical impulse: Toward a theory of postmodernism," in B. Wallis, ed., *Art After Modernism: Rethinking Representation* [New York and Boston: New Museum of Contemporary Art/Godine, 1984], p. 235).

50. Quoted in J. Berger, "The moment of cubism," in *The Moment of Cubism and Other Essays* (New York: Pantheon, 1969), p. 15.
51. Last two quotations from M. R. Solovay, M. E. Shenton, and P. S. Holzman, "Comparative studies of thought disorders: I. Mania and schizophrenia," *Archives of General Psychiatry, 44,* 1987, p. 20; Johnston and Holzman, *Assessing Schizophrenic Thinking,* pp. 88–89. See also I. B. Weiner, *Psychodiagnosis in Schizophrenia* (New York: Wiley, 1966), p. 101.
52. Quoted in Rapaport, "Cognitive structures," p. 649.
53. See Roy Schafer's discussion of the radical fluctuations in the schizophrenic's mode of response on the Rorschach (*Psychoanalytic Interpretation in Rorschach Testing* [New York: Grune and Stratton, 1954], p. 107). Schafer's acceptance of the Great Chain of Being notion (the equation of abnormality with primitivity) is apparent, incidentally, in his assumption that this variability must somehow involve "regressive shifts" in "level of psychic functioning" (e.g., pp. 78–82, 93).
54. In the following passage, the writer Elias Canetti captures the essential worldliness of the manic, his or her embeddedness in a context of relatively normal motivations and pragmatic concerns, despite the heightened intensity of mood and inconsistency of goal:

The manic's transformations have a tremendous ease about them; they share the linear and roving character of the hunter's and also the disconnectedness of his aims, which change each time he fails to attain what he wants, though he nevertheless persists with the hunt. The manic also resembles the hunter in his elation; wherever he may find himself, his mood is always intense and determined; he always has *an* aim. . . . Mania is paroxysm of desire for prey. [*Crowds and Power,* trans. C. Stewart (New York: Continuum, 1962), p. 347]

55. This disengagement—along with isolating-analytic and idiosyncratic qualities—distinguishes schizophrenic thinking from the highly context-bound, holistic, and sociocentric thinking that seems more common in many non-Western cultures. The latter mode of thinking—which is oriented to "contexts and cases" and can perhaps be termed "concrete" (though not really in Goldstein's sense)—has little in common with the forms of schizophrenic literalness I am describing here. See R. A. Schweder and E. J. Bourne, "Does the concept of the person vary cross-culturally?" in A. J. Marsella and G. M. White, eds., *Cultural Conceptions of Mental Health and Therapy* (Dordrecht, The Netherlands: Reidel, 1982, 1984), pp. 105–6; R. Levy, *Tahitians: Mind and Experience in the Society Islands* (Chicago: University of Chicago Press, 1988); S. Diamond, *In Search of the Primitive* (New Brunswick, NJ: Transaction Books, 1974), pp. 146–49.
56. Such experience can be described neither as active nor as passive, in the usual sense of these terms. See Paul Federn's interesting use of the grammatical

concept of middle voice in *Ego Psychology and the Psychoses* (London: Maresfield Reprints, 1953/1977), pp. 216, 319.

57. A few moments after the above-mentioned "kinship . . . system, belief" response, he remarked, "I think this symbol is material."

58. Robert Holt is one of many who have taken such a view. In a note to Rapaport, Gill, and Schafer's *Diagnostic Psychological Testing* (p. 425), he states that Rapaport's thought-disorder categories are largely "manifestations of the primary process." Some years later Holt acknowledged some doubts about this point, but without questioning the general equation of thought disorder with developmental primitivity: he now suggests there might be regression from advanced secondary-process thinking not just to the primary process but also to "developmentally early forms of everyday thinking" ("Freud's theory of the primary process—present status," in T. Shapiro, ed., *Psychoanalysis and Contemporary Science*, vol. 5 [New York: International Universities Press, 1976], pp. 61–99). See also P.-N. Pao, *Schizophrenic Disorders* (New York: International Universities Press, 1979), pp. 292–93.

59. Rapaport, Gill, and Schafer quote a very similar response, also by a schizophrenic: "The one who drew this must have intended to represent the similarity theory of nature" (Card #8) (*Diagnostic Psychological Testing*, p. 452).

60. M. Polanyi, *Personal Knowledge: Towards a Post-Critical Philosophy* (New York and Evanston: Harper and Row, 1964), pp. 55–57. For an empirical study consistent with this view, see D. M. Houston, "The relationship between cognitive failure and self-focussed attention," *British Journal of Clinical Psychology, 28,* 1989, 85–86. For an interpretation of schizophrenic cognitive abnormalities that might be construed in Polanyi's terms, see C. D. Frith, "Consciousness, information processing, and schizophrenia," *British Journal of Psychiatry, 134,* 1979, 225–35; discussed in note 63.

61. Hughes, *The Shock of the New,* p. 17. One might also compare these Rorschach responses to the kind of writing called for by some postmodernist novelists: "a kind of discourse whose shape will be an interrogation, an endless interrogation of what it is doing while doing it, an endless denunciation of its fraudulence" (Raymond Federman quoted in C. Newman, *The Postmodern Aura* [Evanston, IL: Northwestern University Press, 1985], p. 56).

62. Quoted in M. Lorenz, "Criticism as approach to schizophrenic language," *Archives of General Psychiatry, 9,* 1963, 239.

63. *C. D. Frith's views:* Further insight into the complexities and paradoxes surrounding the role of deficiencies and intentional factors can be gleaned from a consideration of one of the more influential theories of schizophrenic cognition of recent years, a hypothesis offered by the British psychologist C. D. Frith, which has been described as "the most clearly stated position on the relationships between cognitive impairment and the core phenomena of schizophrenia" (D. R. Hemsley, "Experimental psychopathology," in P. McGuffin, M. F. Shanks, and R. J. Hodgson, eds., *The Scientific Principles of Psychopathology* [London: Academic Press, 1984], p. 583). In 1979, Frith postulated not a general inability to filter out irrelevant stimuli in the act of perception (the common "attentional dysfunction" view), but a problem of a more circumscribed and introverted sort: a specific deficit in the mechanism that allows preconscious processes to operate below the level of conscious awareness. As a result, schizo-

phrenic patients, according to Frith, become hyperaware of the "cognitive unconscious"; they become unable to prevent themselves from attending to elements of preconscious awareness that would normally remain unnoticed. This implies that the fast and automatic preconscious routines of mental life are laid open to introspection by slower, conscious processing, which operates in a far more controlled, focal, and "strategic" fashion; see C. D. Frith, "Consciousness, information processing, and schizophrenia," *British Journal of Psychiatry, 134*, 1979, 225–35, esp. p 227 (Frith assumes that this propensity must have some neurobiological basis, though he doesn't specify what this might be; other theorists have suggested that it could result from abnormalities of the septohippocampal system or from left hemisphere overactivation; see J. A. Gray, J. Feldon, J. N. P. Rawlins, et al., "The neuropsychology of schizophrenia," *Behavioral and Brain Sciences, 14,* 1991, 1–84; P. H. Venables, "Cerebral mechanisms, autonomic responsiveness, and attention in schizophrenia," *Nebraska Symposium on Motivation, 31,* 1983, 71–72).

As Frith notes, this "excessive self-awareness," an awareness of the cognitive unconscious, is hardly an advantage in most situations, since it has a disruptive and slowing effect. As he points out, hyperawareness would make one less likely to inhibit awareness of the alternative, but contextually irrelevant, meanings of ambiguous words that are normally processed only unconsciously; and this, he suggests, might lead to the schizophrenic tendency to be acutely aware of an unusual number of meanings or possibilities and thus to vacillate in problem solving.

Like many traditional theoretical approaches (e.g., the general Jacksonian model; see appendix), Frith's approach emphasizes the role of a kind of disinhibition; but in this case what is involved is a failure to suppress the activation or inhibit the awareness not of affect or impulse but of the *mental* phenomena associated with a given stimulus or idea (see A. Beech, T. Powell, J. McWilliams, and G. Claridge, "Evidence of reduced 'cognitive inhibition' in schizophrenia," *British Journal of Clinical Psychology, 28,* 1989, 111; C. D. Frith, "Schizophrenia: An abnormality of consciousness?" in G. Underwood and R. Stevens, eds., *Aspects of Consciousness,* vol. 2 [London: Academic Press, 1981], pp. 149–168, p. 161). And, instead of dementia, a tendency toward extinction of the mind and especially of the mind's capacity for self-awareness, we have a theory that postulates hyperawareness of an inner-directed kind, and what look like attempts "to perform a normally automatic process consciously" (Frith, "Schizophrenia: An abnormality," p. 156). Traditional thinkers have seen insanity as an unleashing of more primitive, automatic behavior patterns along with a decline of the capacity or tendency toward deliberation or volition. Frith's view suggests, by contrast, that schizophrenia involves an increased reliance on the more volitional or strategic (i.e., the serial) modes of mental processing, and an excessive, often paralyzing tendency toward vacillation and conscious deliberation among unsuppressed alternatives.

It seems plausible that the schizophrenic's hyperattention or hyperconsciousness, his awareness of the many part-elements involved in a given action, would often lead to an awareness of the possibility of exerting conscious and volitional control over these same elements, and would prevent these elements from simply occurring as part of the flow of some larger act. This could lend to experience a quality we might call "hyperintentionality"—described by one psychologist (not addressing himself to schizophrenia) as "a condition of extraordinarily rigid and intense directedness of behavior and of marked intensification of such normal voluntary faculties as attention, muscular control, and, on a different level, purposiveness," and often accompanied by an anxious tensing of the musculature (D. Shapiro, *Neurotic Styles* [New York: Basic Books, 1965], p. 74). Yet, paradoxically enough, such a mode of experience would, on another level of description, also imply a diminishment of intentionality—because the individual would be less able to engage in those forms of directedness and larger action patterns in which the now-conscious part-elements would normally be subsumed, almost to the point of being dissolved. The fact that the schizophrenic's behavior is, in a sense, imbued with a kind of volitionality is, then, precisely what may deprive him or her of the normal exercise of choice and self-control.

Incidentally, Frith himself no longer defends his 1979 hypothesis (see C. D. Frith and D. J. Done, "Towards a neuropsychology of schizophrenia," *British Journal of Psychiatry*, 153, 1988, 437–38). There are others, however, who continue to find the hypothesis useful (e.g., Beech et al., "Reduced 'cognitive inhibition,'" 1989), and who disagree with Frith's view that it is incompatible with the newer hypothesis he now defends (Gray et al., "Neuropsychology of schizophrenia," 1991). Frith now postulates "a defect in the internal monitoring of action," in the neural mechanism whereby we maintain awareness of our own plans and intentions (the latter being a process normally carried out by the hippocampus, at least in part). This has its most obvious application to the forms of alienation from action and thought captured in Schneider's list of First Rank Symptoms (as discussed in chapter 7); but, conceivably, it might also lead to the kinds of fragmentation in the sense of activity that we have just now been considering. (Incidentally, Gray et al. ["Neuropsychology of schizophrenia,"1991] reject the polarizing of input and output processes, of perception versus action, which causes Frith to view his two hypotheses as incompatible alternatives.)

Eye Tracking: Some well-known findings on eye-tracking patterns in psychiatric patients may have similar implications. Through using certain measuring techniques, it has been shown that two-thirds or more of schizophrenic patients manifest disorders in "smooth pursuit eye movements," these being the movements that take place as one's gaze follows a target (such as an oscillating pendulum or a car moving along a street), thereby stabilizing the moving image on the retina. Normally these movements occur in a smooth, passive, and automatic fashion—once the eyes have locked onto their target object; but in many such patients the movements tend to be interrupted by the quick jumps of the eye known as "saccades." (The neurobiological basis of this disruption remains unknown, though speculation has linked it to dysfunction of the frontal cortex and of the brain stem, as well as of the right hemisphere.) Saccadic movements, interestingly enough, are of a kind that are more subject to voluntary control— they are what occur, for example, when one actively examines a visual array, shifting fixation from one point to another; and such disruptions of smooth pursuit also tend to be increased in normals in conditions of anxiety or stress. See R. B. Lipton, D. L. Levy, P. S. Holzman, and S. Levin, "Eye movement dysfunctions in psychiatric patients: A review," *Schizophrenia Bulletin*, 9, 1983, 13–32.

Philip Holzman, the most prominent researcher in this area, has described this phenomenon in schizophrenics as a sign of "disinhibition," that is, of a failure of those inhibitory functions that would normally suppress the saccades; and he stresses that this disruption of what he calls involuntary or passive attention is itself an involuntary phenomenon, something the patient cannot control (though it does seem to be decreased when the patient is engaged more actively in a visual task, like reading numbers flashing on a swinging pendulum); see P. S. Holzman, "Cognitive impairment and cognitive stability," in G. Serban, ed., *Cognitive Defects in the Development of Mental Illness* (New York: Brunner/Mazel, 1978), pp. 361–76. It is interesting to note, however, that this disruption, involuntary though it may be, nevertheless seems likely to result in what, from the subject's standpoint, might well seem a kind of hyperintentionality—a hyperintentionality not itself under the patients' control since they cannot desist from this more volitional mode of cognition and, as it were, simply give themselves over to the world. They cannot choose not to choose, we might say (could this, perhaps, be what a patient quoted by Kraepelin meant by saying, "I have voluntary disease of the eyes"? [*Dementia Praecox*, p. 71]). Maybe this is the source of the absence of a feeling of natural harmony, of syntony with self and world, that is so characteristic of schizoid and schizophrenic individuals. (Normal subjects with poor eye-tracking have in fact been found to be characterized by "social aversiveness" and "anhedonia"; see P. H. Venables, "Cognitive and attentional disorders in the development of schizophrenia," in Hafner, Gattaz, and Janzarik, *Search for the Causes of Schizophrenia*," p. 209.)

John Cutting has proposed a similar interpretation—suggesting that in schizophrenia the brain's (left-hemisphere) "executive" or "controller" enjoys free reign because its hyperactive functioning is not restrained or directed by the needs and modes of awareness of the rest of the organism or brain (mediated by the right hemisphere); see pp. 301–3. J. Cutting, *The Right Cerebral Hemisphere and Psychiatric Disorders* (Oxford: Oxford University Press, 1990).

For more on related views and issues, see the appendix.

64. M. Bleuler, *The Schizophrenic Disorders*, trans. S. M. Clemens (New Haven and London: Yale University Press, 1978), p. 217.

65. See, for example, "Towards a newer Laocoön" (1940), *Perceptions and Judgments*, vol. 1 of *The Collected Essays and Criticism* (Chicago and London: University of Chicago Press, 1986), pp. 32, 34–35.

66. M. Fried, "Shape as form: Frank Stella's new paintings," in H. Geldzahler, ed., *New York Painting and Sculpture: 1940–1970* (New York: Dutton, 1969), pp. 404–6. Fried's views clearly reflect those of Stella himself. Thus the artist criticizes those "humanists" who believe "that there is something there besides the paint on the canvas." "My painting," he says, "is based on the fact that only what can be seen there *is* there. It really is an object. . . . What you see is what you see" ("Questions to Stella and Judd, interview by Bruce Glaser," in G. Battcock, ed., *Minimal Art* [New York: Dutton, 1968], p. 158). Stella is not the first to emphasize shape as form; an obvious precedent is Mondrian.

A more light-hearted example of the same loss of distance comes from another medium. This is the tongue-in-cheek title that an experimental filmmaker assigned to one of his own films, perhaps as a way of commenting on the state of things in that avant-garde world in the late 1970s. He called it *Film in Which*

There Appear Sprocket Holes, Edge Lettering, Dirt Particles, Etc. (George Landow, quoted in J. Hoberman, "A Freud in the dark," *The Village Voice,* December 10–16, 1980, p. 78).

67. Quoted in Kahler, *The Disintegration of Form in the Arts* (New York: Braziller, 1968), pp. 44–45. This literalist urge is particularly evident in the quasi-sculptural works exhibited at the Whitney Anti-Illusion exhibition and the St. Louis "Here and Now" exhibition of 1969; described in R. Pincus-Witten, *Postminimalism* (New York: Out of London Press, 1977), pp. 25, 30.

68. Paraphrased by J. Tancock, "The influence of Marcel Duchamp," in A. d'Harnoncourt and K. McShine, eds., *Marcel Duchamp* (exhibition catalogue) (New York: Museum of Modern Art, 1973), p. 174.

69. In 1962 Ad Reinhardt described one of his own black paintings as follows: "a pure, abstract, non-objective, timeless, spaceless, changeless, relationless, disinterested painting—an object that is self-conscious (no unconsciousness), ideal, transcendent, aware of no thing but Art (absolutely no anti-art)" (quoted in L. Nordness, ed., *Art, USA, Now* [New York: Viking, 1963], p. 269). In his essay "On the role of nature in modernist painting" (*Art and Culture* [Boston: Beacon, 1961]), Clement Greenberg connects the modernist preoccupation with the surface of the picture plane with an explicit focus on visual experience as such: thus he states that space in modernist painting (in synthetic cubism, for instance) is depicted as an "uninterrupted continuum," and that "the picture plane as a whole imitates visual experience as a whole" (p. 173).

70. Kasimir Malevich described how, in 1913, "in my desperate struggle to free art from the ballast of the objective world I fled to the form of the square and exhibited a picture which was nothing more or less than a black square upon a white ground. . . . It was no empty square which I had exhibited but rather the experience of objectlessness" (quoted in M. Shapiro, *Modern Art: 19th and 20th Centuries, Selected Papers* [New York: Braziller, 1978], p. 202).

71. S. Elizondo, *El Grafografo* (Mexico City: Joaquin Mortiz, 1972), p. 9. This translation of the passage appears as an epigraph at the beginning of M. Vargas Llosa's novel *Aunt Julia and the Scriptwriter* (New York: Farrar Straus Giroux, 1982).

72. Quoted in L. Nochlin, *Realism* (Harmondsworth, UK: Penguin Books, 1971), p. 240.

73. Rapaport, Gill, and Schafer, *Diagnostic Psychological Testing*, pp. 274–75.

74. E. Heller, "Wittgenstein and Nietzsche," *The Artist's Journey into the Interior and Other Essays* (San Diego: Harcourt Brace Jovanovich, 1976), p. 226 (quoted words are Heller's).

Chapter 6: Languages of Inwardness

1. In M. H. Johnston and P. S. Holzman, *Assessing Schizophrenic Thinking* (San Francisco: Jossey-Bass, 1979), pp. 1–2.

2. M. Bleuler, "Inconstancy of schizophrenic language and symptoms," commentary on S. Schwartz, "Is there a schizophrenic language?" *Behavioral and Brain Sciences,* 5, 1982, 591. Thus, so-called schizophrenic language really involves a heterogeneous set of behaviors that are only sporadically present in some subset

of persons bearing this diagnosis. As Eugen Bleuler noted in 1911, "The form of linguistic expression [in schizophrenia] may show every imaginable abnormality, or be absolutely correct" (*Dementia Praecox, or the Group of Schizophrenias*, trans. J. Zinkin [New York: International Universities Press, 1950], p. 148).

3. The semantic aspect of language is particularly difficult to define; here I understand it in a relatively narrow sense—as pertaining to the sorts of rules that would exclude sentences like "Colorless green ideas sleep furiously," Chomsky's famous example of a syntactically correct but semantically unacceptable sentence. Some linguists would argue, however, that semantics is ultimately inseparable from pragmatics and from the entire background of implicit knowledge about the world.

It is not, of course, that errors of phonetics, syntax, or semantics (narrowly defined) are never committed by schizophrenic speakers, but that their errors do not seem significantly different from, or more frequent than, those found in the speech of normal individuals.

4. For the most complete review of these issues, see A. R. Lecours and M. Vanier-Clement, "Schizophasia and jargonaphasia," *Brain and Language, 3*, 1976, 516–65. The aphasias, in the view of Lecours and Vanier-Clement, are characterized by poverty of production at the phonemic, morphemic, and semantic levels, whereas schizophrenic speech manifests an excessive richness at all of these levels. Re the absence of a truly linguistic deficit and of aphasialike features in the great majority of schizophrenic patients, see also S. Schwartz, "Is there a schizophrenic language?" *Behavioral and Brain Sciences, 5*, 1982, 579–88 (followed by extensive peer commentary, pp. 588–626); F. Boller, "A neurologist looks at schizophasia" (one of the peer commentaries on Schwartz, ibid., pp. 591–92); and R. Brown, "Schizophrenia, language, and reality," *American Psychologist, 28*, 1973, 395–403. That schizophrenic speech *is* a form of intermittent aphasia—not a widely held view—has been argued by E. O. Chaika; see "Schizophrenic speech, slips of the tongue, and jargonaphasia: A reply to Fromkin and to Lecours and Vanier-Clement," *Brain and Language, 4*, 1977, 464–75. A cogent critique of Chaika is presented in V. A. Fromkin, "A linguist looks at 'A linguist looks at "schizophrenic language,"'" *Brain and Language, 2*, 1975, 498–503.

5. See N. Andreasen, "The relationship between schizophrenic language and the aphasias," in F. A. Henna and H. A. Nasrallah, eds., *Schizophrenia as a Brain Disease* (New York: Oxford University Press, 1982), pp. 100, 109, 110.

6. This is in contrast to, for example, the speech of a manic or hypomanic person, which will usually be rapid, free-associative and highly circumstantial or personalized; and to that of the obsessive, who tends to be meticulous, formal, and guarded, often talking in a highly qualified, precise, and unnecessarily explicit manner.

7. Re various ways of defining what constitutes "language," see J. R. Martin, "What is language?" comment on Schwartz, "Is there a schizophrenic language?" pp. 607–8.

8. "Elbow people" and "botanized": quoted in E. Bleuler, *Dementia Praecox*, p. 155 (where Bleuler, oddly enough, offers them as examples of phrases that cannot be understood). "Side voices": J. Cutting, *The Psychology of Schizophrenia* (Edinburgh: Churchill Livingstone, 1985), p. 250. "Insinuendos":

A. C. Smith, *Schizophrenia and Madness* (London: Allen and Unwin, 1982), p. 28.

9. Quoted in S. Arieti, *Interpretation of Schizophrenia*, 2nd ed. (New York: Basic Books, 1974), p. 266. Another example: the term *northwestern* used to refer to anything pertaining to an affair one patient had had with a Scandinavian man, an experience she associated with a sense of coldness, struggle, and privation (W. L. Woods, "Language study in schizophrenia," *Journal of Nervous and Mental Disease*, 87, 1938, 302). Another patient called her spit "cage-weather juice"— due to the fact that she had to expectorate a lot because of being locked-up, that is, filled with "cage-weather" (E. Bleuler, *Dementia Praecox*, p. 152).

10. First two quotations from E. Kraepelin, *Dementia Praecox and Paraphrenia*, trans. R. M. Barclay (Huntington, NY: Robert E. Krieger, 1971; first English edition, 1919), p. 56; I have been unable to locate the source of the third quotation, which I noted down some years ago. Re this kind of ambiguity, see S. R. Rochester and J. R. Martin, *Crazy Talk: A Study of the Discourse of Schizophrenic Speakers* (New York: Plenum, 1979); B. Rosenbaum and H. Sonne, *The Language of Psychosis* (New York: New York University Press, 1986).

11. Quoted in B. D. Cohen, "Referent communication disturbances in schizophrenia," in S. Schwartz, ed., *Language and Cognition in Schizophrenia* (Hillsdale, NJ: Erlbaum, 1978, p. 29). For other examples, see S. Arieti, *Interpretation of Schizophrenia*, 2nd ed. (New York: Basic Books, 1974), pp. 249–56. Re glossomania, see Lecours and Vanier-Clement, "Schizophasia and jargonaphasia." B. D. Cohen, G. Nachmani, and S. Rosenberg noted that schizophrenics are inclined to respond to the immediately preceding verbal stimulus in their own speech rather than to the supposed referent of this speech ("Referent communication disturbances in acute schizophrenia," *Journal of Abnormal Psychology*, 1974, *83*, 1–13). Kurt Salzinger and Brendan Maher, among others, have discussed similar phenomena. For critical discussion of Salzinger, as well as Cohen, see S. Schwartz, "Language and cognition in schizophrenia: A review and synthesis," in S. Schwartz, ed., *Language and Cognition*, pp. 252–58.

    Eugen Bleuler noted the autonomy or automaticity of schizophrenic thought, remarking that one could say that "it thinks" in these patients (quoted in D. Forrest, "Poesis and the language of schizophrenia," *Psychiatry*, 28, 1965, 4).

12. Re organics, see K. Goldstein, *Human Nature in the Light of Psychopathology* (New York: Schocken Books, 1963), pp. 78, 81. Lecours and Vanier-Clement note the schizophrenic's exaggerated awareness of the polysemous nature of words: "Preoccupation with too many of the semantic features of a word in discourse" is, they say, a rare phenomenon, not characteristic of organically based jargonaphasia and observed only in volitional punning and in schizophasia (schizophrenic language) ("Schizophasia and jargonaphasia," p. 561). See p. 546 for an interesting example ("des époques d'ères, deserts d'époques") which is virtually identical to some writings by Jean-Pierre Brisset that have been of considerable influence on modernism and postmodernism; see note 107, this chapter. See also E. Chaika, "Accounting for linguistic data in schizophrenia research" (commentary on Schwartz), *Behavioral and Brain Sciences*, 5, 1982, 595.

13. Quoted in C. D. Frith, "Schizophrenia: An abnormality of consciousness?" in G. Underwood and R. Stevens, eds., *Aspects of Consciousness*, vol. 2 (London: Academic Press, 1981), p. 162. Re difficulties in understanding language, which

is fairly common in schizophrenia, see B. Freedman and L. J. Chapman, "Early subjective experience in schizophrenic episodes," *Journal of Abnormal Psychology*, 82, 1973, 46–54.

14. Quoted in M. Lorenz, "Problems posed by schizophrenic language," *Archives of General Psychiatry*, 4, 1961, 604.

15. When B. Cohen fed back descriptions of visual displays to the same schizophrenics who had originally given these descriptions, he found that these patients had just as much trouble grasping the referents of their own utterances as did normal listeners listening to these same descriptions ("Referent communication disturbances in schizophrenia," in S. Schwartz, ed., *Language and Cognition in Schizophrenia* [Hillsdale, NJ: Erlbaum, 1978], pp. 1–34).

16. First patient described to me by a colleague; second in Lecours and Vanier-Clement, "Schizophasia and jargonaphasia," p. 537.

17. P. J. Ruocchio, "First person account: Fighting the fight—the schizophrenic's nightmare," *Schizophrenia Bulletin*, 15, 1989, 163–66.

18. Quoted in J. Cutting, *The Right Cerebral Hemisphere and Psychiatric Disorders* (Oxford: Oxford University Press, 1990), p. 265.

19. Quoted in B. Maher, *Principles of Psychopathology* (New York: McGraw-Hill, 1966), p. 402.

20. E. Bleuler, *Dementia Praecox*, p. 148. Bleuler notes, however, that mutism is never absolute: most patients are capable of speaking and will do so now and then.

21. Quotations from N. Andreasen, "Thought, language, and communication disorders: I," *Archives of General Psychiatry*, 36, 1979, 1318; P. Ostwald and V. Zavarin, "Studies of language and schizophrenia in the USSR," in R. W. Rieber, ed., *Applied Psycholinguistics and Mental Health* (New York: Plenum, 1980), p. 75. In Andreasen's study of speech style in schizophrenic, manic, and depressed patients, presence of poverty of content was the feature that distinguished the language of schizophrenics most sharply from the other two groups; see Andreasen, "Thought, language, and communication disorders: II," *Archives of General Psychiatry*, 36, 1979, 1325–30. Such language has also been described as "wooly" and "pseudophilosophical" (A. C. Smith, *Schizophrenia and Madness* [London: George Allen and Unwin, 1982], p. 28). Gabrial, 1974, found abstract language and preoccupation with philosophical or pseudo-philosophical concerns to be characteristic of 54 percent of the schizophrenic patients studied (cited in Ostwald and Zavarin, "Studies of language and schizophrenia in the USSR," p. 75). (As Ostwald and Zavarin suggest, however, these findings may be tainted by the nature of the sample of "schizophrenics": the diagnosis of "sluggish schizophrenia" was sometimes applied in the Soviet Union to intellectuals and political dissidents.)

    Some research suggests, by the way, that poverty of speech and poverty of content of speech may not be part of the same syndrome; see, for example, P. F. Liddle and T. R. E. Barnes, "Syndromes of chronic schizophrenia," *British Journal of Psychiatry*, 157, 1990, 558–61.

22. Re "wooliness," see, for example, L. Wing, "Asperger's syndrome: A clinical account," *Psychological Medicine*, 11, 1981, 121. Re the murky and undifferentiated modes of cognition of the schizoid individual, see T. Millon, *Disorders of Personality* (New York: Wiley, 1981), p. 295. The supposedly undifferentiated

nature of the schizophrenic's cognition is often asserted; see, for example, H. F. Searles, *Collected Papers on Schizophrenia and Related Subjects* (New York: International Universities Press, 1965).

23. Quoted in M. Lorenz, "Problems posed," p. 604. For a more confusing (and confused) speech sample that also illustrates the abstract and reflexive quality of schizophrenic speech, see Arieti, *Interpretation of Schizophrenia*, p. 265.

24. See E. Bleuler, *Dementia Praecox*, p. 9.

25. Patient quoted in ibid., p. 157. E. Bleuler quoted in L. Binswanger, "Extravagance, perverseness, manneristic behaviour and schizophrenia," in J. Cutting and M. Shepherd, eds., *The Clinical Roots of the Schizophrenia Concept* (Cambridge: Cambridge University Press, 1987), p. 85. Also see Arieti, *Interpretation of Schizophrenia*, p. 246.

26. The phrase is from E. Bleuler, *Dementia Praecox*, pp. 156, 158; examples on p. 151. Such qualities of both emptiness and possible irony are quite apparent in the illustration of autonomization on pages 179–80, where the patient speaks rather pompously of "the subterfuge and the mistaken planned substitutions for that demanded American action."

27. B. Maher, *Principles of Psychopathology: An Experimental Approach* (New York: McGraw-Hill, 1966), p. 433.

28. P. A. Magaro, *Cognition in Schizophrenia and Paranoia* (Hillsdale, NJ: Lawrence Erlbaum, 1980), also quoted in Cutting, *Psychology of Schizophrenia*, p. 371. C. D. Frith, "The positive and negative symptoms of schizophrenia reflect impairments in the perception and initiation of action," *Psychological Medicine*, 17, 1987, 631–48.

29. C. D. Frith and U. Frith, "Elective affinities in schizophrenia and childhood autism," in P. Bebbington, ed., *Social Psychiatry: Theory, Methodology and Practice* (New Brunswick, NJ: Transaction Press, 1991).

30. See R. Hoffman, "Verbal hallucinations and language production processes in schizophrenia," *Behavioral and Brain Sciences*, 9, 1986, 503–48; E. Chaika re "sporadic disruption in the ability to match semantic features with sound strings comprising actual lexical items in the language" (quoted in Lecours and Vanier-Clement, "Schizophasia and jargonaphasia," p. 560).

31. One linguist says that discovering "a clear-cut cognitive explanation for the conversational aberrance of schizophrenics [would] show unambiguously that when speaking [schizophrenics] are operating in a cooperative manner and that the problems their hearers have are not the product of volition or a willful desire to confuse or mislead" (H. W. Buckingham, "Can listeners draw implicatures from schizophrenics?" commentary on Schwartz, "Is there a schizophrenic language?" p. 594).

32. See C. Taylor, *The Explanation of Behavior* (London: Routledge and Kegan Paul, 1964), pp. 24–25n.

33. A good example of the coarseness of such polarized thinking, which is all too common, is the following statement by the linguist Elaine Chaika:

How we view the weird speech of some schizophrenics affects how we treat them. If the speech is a way of avoiding therapy, patients must be persuaded or conditioned to accept therapy. If schizophrenics are merely being poetic or creative, then we must analyze every utterance to uncover its true meaning. If, as I think, schizophrenics who speak weirdly do so because of a linguistic problem caused by a biochemical imbalance, then the solution is biochemical. Find the proper medication and you alleviate the source of the problem. ["Crazy talk," *Psychology Today*, August 1985, 35]

34. Statements re Hölderlin are quoted in R. Jakobson and G. Lübbe-Grothues, "Two types of discourse in Hölderlin's madness," in L. Vaina and J. Hintikka, eds., *Cognitive Constraints on Communication* (Dordrecht, The Netherlands: D. Reidel, 1984), pp. 126, 121, 119–20.

35. E. Bleuler, *Dementia Praecox*, p. 89.

36. W. Thürmer, 1970, quoted in Jakobson and Lübbe-Grothues, "Two types of discourse," p. 121.

37. A literal translation, quoted in Jakobson and Lübbe-Grothues, "Two types of discourse," p. 123.

38. Ibid., pp. 121, 126.

39. See, for example, H. Friedrich, *The Structure of Modern Poetry* (Evanston, IL: Northwestern University Press, 1974), pp. 3–9.

40. Hilde Bruch, quoted in D. Forrest, "Nonsense and sense in schizophrenic language," *Schizophrenia Bulletin*, 2, 1976, 292. Similarly, Jung wrote that "the ordinary patient cannot help talking and thinking in such a way, while [James] Joyce willed it and moreover developed it with all his creative forces" (quoted in Smith, *Schizophrenia and Madness*, p. 143). This is an old view; in the eighteenth century, Swift wrote that the "mad-man . . . spoke out whatever came into his mind, and just in the confused manner as his imagination presented the ideas. [The poet on the other hand] only expressed such thoughts as his Judgement directed him to chuse" (quoted in R. Porter, *Mind Forg'd Manacles: A History of Madness in England from the Restoration to the Regency* [Cambridge: Harvard University Press, 1987], p. 102).

41. Baudelaire, 1863, "The painter of modern life," quoted in M. Calinescu, *Faces of Modernity* (Bloomington and London: Indiana University Press, 1977), p. 48. Rimbaud: "J'écrivais des silences, des nuits, je notais l'inexprimable" (quoted in N. Greene, *Antonin Artaud: Poet Without Words* [New York: Simon and Schuster, 1970], p. 222).

42. On this point, see the interesting article by Roger Cardinal, "Enigma," *Twentieth Century Studies*, 12, 1974, 42–62. For general discussion of modern literature and the distrust of language, see G. Steiner, *After Babel: Aspects of Language and Translation* (London: Oxford University Press, 1975), pp. 161–205; S. Sontag, "The aesthetics of silence," *Styles of Radical Will* (New York: Dell, 1969), pp. 3–34.

43. This is not an experience of concreteness in Goldstein's sense; I am referring to experiences akin to those of "Mere Being" and of literalness discussed in earlier chapters.

44. Another difference is that Wittgenstein wanted to block or cure the yearning for a private language.

45. Quoted in G. Steiner, *After Babel*, p. 185. See also the lovely passage from Maeterlinck that Robert Musil uses as the epigraph for his novel *Young Torless;* it begins, "In some strange way we devalue things as soon as we give utterance to them" (quoted in *Young Torless*, trans. E. Wilkins and E. Kaiser [New York: New American Library, 1964], p. 5); and T. S. Eliot's famous lines from "East

Coker" about learning to get the better of words only—"For the thing one no longer has to say, or the way in which / One is no longer disposed to say it," so that "each venture / Is a new beginning, a raid on the inarticulate / With shabby equipment always deteriorating" (*Four Quartets* [London: Faber and Faber, 1944], pp. 30–31).

46. J.-P. Sartre, *Nausea*, trans. L. Alexander (New York: New Directions, 1959), pp. 171, 174.

47. M. Sechehaye, ed., *Autobiography of a Schizophrenic Girl* (New York: New American Library, 1970), p. 40. Beckett's character Watt has a very similar experience of looking at things that seem to resist being named; he cries out "pot pot," but in vain. See pages 49 and 58.

48. R. Rosser, "The psychopathology of thinking and feeling in a schizophrenic," *International Journal of Psychoanalysis*, 60, 1979, 184–85. The absence of conventional meanings and the direct awareness of the sound qualities of words that can occur in schizophrenia may be *reminiscent* of certain aspects of early childhood; but in this instance the phenomena seem better described as *post-* rather than as *pre*verbal in nature.

49. Quotations from S. Sontag, ed., *Antonin Artaud: Selected Writings* (New York: Farrar Straus and Giroux, 1976), pp. 294–95, 84 (emphasis added). Toward the end of his life Artaud would write that "All true language is incomprehensible" (p. 549).

50. Sullivan wrote of experiences that are "so very early, so cosmically undifferentiated, if you please, that there is no expressing the content in words" (*Clinical Studies in Psychiatry* [New York: Norton, 1956], p. 328). Kurt Goldstein stressed the difficulty of capturing a highly concretistic lived-world in a conventional language that is adapted to more abstract purposes (the latter being "stereotyped and not rich in words to express the specificity of concrete situations"), or of conveying such experiences to normal individuals who presumably operate on some higher plane ("Methodological approach to the study of schizophrenic thought disorder," in J. S. Kasanin, ed., *Language and Thought in Schizophrenia* [New York: Norton, 1964], p. 29).

51. Charles Blondel, in *La Conscience Morbide* (1914), states that the normal mind is one in which cenesthesia (internal perception of our own bodies) is dominated by socialized discourse; see J. Starobinski, "A short history of body consciousness," trans. S. Matthews, in *Humanities in Review*, 1, 1982, 28–29. But in modern literature and culture, as Starobinski notes, we find a preoccupation with previously unremarked private sensations.

52. P. J. Ruocchio, "First person account: The schizophrenic inside," *Schizophrenia Bulletin*, 17, 1991, 358.

53. See S. D. Rosenberg and G. J. Tucker, "Verbal behavior and schizophrenia: The semantic dimension," *Archives of General Psychiatry*, 36, 1979, 1331 and passim; Lecours and Vanier-Clement, "Schizophasia and jargonaphasia," pp. 543, 545. Rosenberg and Tucker ask whether the expressions of "confusion, doubt, and mistrust of one's own senses and thought processes [so common in schizophrenia] derive from a sort of existential openness and awareness, or do they indicate a breakdown in baseline levels of self-integration?" (p. 1337)—a question that need not, of course, be conceived as a dichotomous choice. For an illustration of the "thread of introspection, of self-scrutiny and self-analysis" that

may run through schizophrenic discourse, see M. Lorenz, "Criticism as approach to schizophrenic language," *Archives of General Psychiatry*, 9, 1963, 236–37. Although E. Bleuler (*Dementia Praecox*, p. 150) and others have asserted that the distortions of language in schizophrenia are essentially like those occurring in dreams, detailed empirical study (involving thematic content analysis) suggests a marked difference: see, for example, the study by G. J. Tucker and S. D. Rosenberg, where schizophrenic speech was found to be distinguished from that of their dream subjects by its "heightened concern with the self in a context of distress and disorientation" ("Computer content analysis of schizophrenic speech: A preliminary report," *American Journal of Psychiatry*, *132*, 1975, 613).

54. For a discussion of this tendency in modernist art, see Sontag, "The aesthetics of silence," pp. 3–34.

55. See Woods, "Language study in schizophrenia," 87, 1938, 296–300.

56. S. Beckett, *Waiting for Godot* (New York: Grove Press, 1954), pp. 28–29.

  Another possible response to the problem of expressing something too unique or too private to be captured in conventional language (a response most suggestive, perhaps, of desocialization) is to create neologisms or use normal words in special senses (e.g., "superskeletonization," as described above)—in order, as one schizophrenic patient put it, "to give a little personal and private basis" to what one says (quoted in Lecours and Vanier-Clement, "Schizophasia and jargonaphasia," p. 536).

57. P. F. Liddle and T. R. E. Barnes report a correlation between the perceived inability to tolerate other people and apparent "poverty of speech" (and flatness of affect), suggesting that patients use withdrawal as a coping strategy ("The subjective experience of deficits in schizophrenia," *Comprehensive Psychiatry*, 29, 1988, 163).

58. The reactions of these two philosophers to this dilemma is very different, however: whereas Wittgenstein attempted to *cure* people of the temptation to speak of such ultimate, metaphysical concerns, Heidegger tried to express them in his own, rather peculiar philosophical language. Incidentally, Wittgenstein's famous concluding line in the *Tractatus Logico-Philosophicus*, "Whereof one cannot speak, thereof one must be silent," concerns primarily the ineffability of such metaphysical concerns; whereas the "private language argument" in his later work bears primarily upon the issue of ineffable particularity and uniqueness.

59. Quoted in Woods, "Language study in schizophrenia," p. 299. The markedly schizoid patient of a colleague was presented with the blank TAT card and encouraged to respond with whatever came to mind; her answer concluded as follows: "And everything in the entire world, in reality and in my imagination, recycled and compressed by an extraordinarily compact machine . . . and condensed into the size of a card."

60. Quoted in I. B. Weiner, *Psychodiagnosis in Schizophrenia* (New York: Wiley, 1966), p. 101.

61. In Sontag, *Antonin Artaud: Selected Writings*, p. 362.

62. Jaspers, *General Psychopathology*, p. 115. Patients speak of "metaphysical experiences" containing "a character of the infinite," and of experiences having "a 'cosmic character' " (pp. 114–16). Similarly, Eugen Bleuler notes the "very common preoccupation of young hebephrenics with the 'deepest questions' "—questions in which "reality has no part" (*Dementia Praecox*, p. 67n).

63. It may be that what appears to be "poor autism," a state of withdrawal seemingly devoid of an inner fantasy life, sometimes involves these all-encompassing preoccupations. Re ideas on the nature of autism, see J. Parnas and Bovet, "Autism in schizophrenia revisited," *Comprehensive Psychiatry*, 32, 1991, 7–21.

64. See J. Passmore, *A Hundred Years of Philosophy* (Harmondsworth, UK: Penguin Books, 1968), pp. 603, 477.

65. R. Rosser, "The psychopathology of feeling and thinking in a schizophrenic," *International Journal of Psychoanalysis*, 60, 1979, p. 186. See also Patricia Ruocchio re "repeated ramblings [that] are code words for things that send me into psychosis" ("First person account: The schizophrenic inside," p. 358).

   Whether Carnap was right in saying that one should not even attempt to express such sentiments in other than artistic forms (he contemptuously defined metaphysicians as "musicians without musical ability") is not the issue here; I wish only to clarify some of the reasons for what is too readily dismissed as *mere* poverty of content.

66. Incidentally, this patient's references to "being fascinated by the generative process of the mind" and to "revolving everything around me" suggest a subjectivist or even solipsistic strain to his experience—an issue examined in chapter 9, where we will once again take up the topic of the ineffability of overly general or hyperabstract concerns.

67. Quoted in Shattuck, *The Banquet Years*, p. 333.

68. Another example is the internal monologues of James Joyce, which treat the life of consciousness as something quite linguistic in nature, thereby slighting the possibility of a nonverbal domain; re some of these distinctions, see D. Cohn, *Transparent Minds: Narrative Modes for Presenting Consciousness in Fiction* (Princeton, NJ: Princeton University Press, 1978).

69. Quoted in M. Nadeau, *The History of Surrealism*, trans. R. Howard (Harmondsworth, UK: Penguin Books, 1973), p. 88.

70. Quoted in R. Poggiolli, *The Theory of the Avant-Garde*, trans. G. Fitzgerald (Cambridge and London: Harvard University Press, 1968), p. 192.

71. Most, though perhaps not all, of these features are explicitly mentioned by Vygotsky.

72. Cendrars quoted in R. Shattuck, *The Banquet Years*, p. 337; schizophrenic quoted in M. Lorenz, "Expressive form in schizophrenic language," *A.M.A. Archives of Neurology and Psychiatry*, 78, 1957, 644.

73. Quoted in Poggiolli, *Theory of the Avant-Garde*, p. 38.

74. See Nadeau, *History of Surrealism*, p. 79.

75. Quoted in N. Cameron, "Experimental analysis of schizophrenic thinking," in J. S. Kasanin, *Language and Thought*, p. 53.

76. See H. A. Allen, "Positive and negative symptoms and the thematic organisation of schizophrenic speech," *British Journal of Psychiatry*, 144, 1984, 611–17.

77. See discussion in C. D. Frith and H. A. Allen, "Language disorders in schizophrenia and their implications for neuropsychology," in P. Bebbington and P. McGuffin, eds., *Schizophrenia: The Major Issues* (Oxford: Heinemann, 1988), pp. 172–86.

78. See Cardinal, "Enigma," 12, 1974, 42–62.

79. Re the schizophrenic patient's not wanting to communicate, and re the depen-

dence of his speech style on his attitude, see E. Bleuler's remarks in *Dementia Praecox,* pp. 147, 150.

80. S. Beckett, "Imagination dead imagine," in *Collected Shorter Prose, 1945–1980* (London: John Calder, 1986), p. 145.

81. Lorenz, "Expressive form," p. 644. Another good example can be found in Lecours and Vanier-Clement, "Schizophasia and jargonaphasia," p. 543.

82. See M. Harrow and M. Prosen, "Intermingling and disordered logic as influences on schizophrenic 'thought disorders'," *Archives of General Psychiatry,* 35, 1978, 1213–18. That these researchers found little evidence of disordered logic tends to refute the notion that schizophrenic language betokens a regression to a lower level of *secondary*-process thought, as is sometimes claimed (for such a claim, see P.-N. Pao, *Schizophrenic Disorders: Theory and Treatment from a Psychodynamic Point of View* [New York: International Universities Press, 1979], pp. 291–96).

83. R. Barthes, *Writing Degree Zero* (published with *Elements of Semiology*), trans. A. Lavers and C. Smith (Boston: Beacon Press, 1970; originally published in 1953, some portions in 1947), p. 48. Epigraph ("I *see* language") from obituary of Barthes, *Newsweek,* April 7, 1980.

84. S. Mallarmé, *Crise de vers* (Paris: Éditions de la Pléiade, 1951), p. 366; quoted in E. Kahler, *Disintegration of Form in the Arts* (New York: George Braziller, 1968), pp. 75–76.

85. H. von Kleist, "On the gradual fabrication of thoughts while speaking," in P. B. Miller, ed. and trans., *An Abyss Deep Enough: Letters of Heinrich von Kleist, with a Selection of Essays and Anecdotes* (New York: Dutton, 1982; essay first published in 1805), pp. 218–22. Re Novalis (1799), see Sontag, "Aesthetics of silence," p. 26. Already in 1697 Leibniz suggested that language may not be "the vehicle of thought but its determining medium" (G. Steiner, *On Difficulty and Other Essays* [New York: Oxford University Press, 1978], p. 138).

86. See D. Messerli, "Introduction," in Messerli, ed., *Language Poetries: An Anthology* (New York: New Directions, 1987), p. 5.

87. Mallarmé quoted in S. Kern, *The Culture of Time and Space, 1880–1918* (Cambridge: Harvard University Press, 1983), p. 174; W. Fowlie, *Mallarmé* (Chicago and London: University of Chicago Press, 1953), p. 12.

88. Mallarmé had suggested that language be divided into two separate functions: a "brut" and "immédiat" type appropriate for communicating information, and an "essential" or poetic type which was strange, incantatory, and based on the isolation of the word (quoted in J. Acocella, "Photo-call with Nijinsky," *Ballet Review,* Winter, 1987, p. 68). Derrida's aestheticism, like that of many of the poststructuralists, is more totalizing, tending to deny the very possibility of Mallarmé's first function.

89. The "warmed-over Mallarmé" epithet was actually said of Derrida's follower, Paul de Man, by Northrop Frye (reported to me by Angus Fletcher). Re modernism and postmodernism, see A. Eysteinsson, *Concept of Modernism* (Ithaca and London: Cornell University Press, 1990), pp. 39–40, 47–48.

90. This line occurs in a text about Mallarmé among other topics: Derrida, "The double session," *Dissemination,* trans. B. Johnson (Chicago: University of Chicago Press, 1981), p. 177.

91. J. Derrida, "Plato's pharmacy," *Dissemination,* pp. 95–96, 129–30.

92. R. Barthes, *Writing Degree Zero*, p. 47.
93. J. Derrida, *Writing and Difference*, trans. A. Bass (Chicago: University of Chicago Press, 1978), p. 9. These lines follow just after Derrida makes a brief reference to Antonin Artaud. But it is interesting to compare this passage from Derrida with (the schizophrenic) Artaud's own more anguished description of a similar experience in a letter written in 1932. See note 96.
94. Patient quoted by P. Matussek, "Studies in delusional perception," in J. Cutting and M. Shepherd, eds., *The Clinical Roots of the Schizophrenia Concept* (Cambridge: Cambridge University Press, 1987), p. 101 (emphasis added).
95. E. Bleuler, *Dementia Praecox*, p. 14.
96. Sontag, *Antonin Artaud: Selected Writings*, p. 293. The continuation of this passage is very interesting, for it suggests that the experience of blocking results not from an excessive vitality or richness (as Derrida often seems to imply in his discussion of analogous experiences), but, in a sense, from the *lack* of any motivating force or theme:

> The brain sees . . . all the points of view it could take and all the forms with which it could invest them, a vast juxtaposition of concepts, each of which seems more necessary and also more dubious than the others . . . but if one really analyzes a state of this kind it is not by being too full that consciousness errs at these moments but by being too empty, for this prolific and above all unstable and shifting juxtaposition is an illusion. . . . If the mind has not *automatically* decided on a dominant theme it is through weakness and because at that moment nothing dominated, nothing presented itself with enough force or continuity in the field of consciousness to be recorded. The truth is, therefore, that rather than an overflow or an excess there was a deficiency; in the absence of some precise thought that was able to develop, there was slackening, confusion, fragility. [P. 293]

For other examples, see Patricia Ruocchio re what "goes on beneath the veneer of what is called 'thought blocking'," namely that these "aborted thoughts [are] not lost, but taken over by a more powerful chaos" (Ruocchio, "First person account: The schizophrenic inside," p. 357). Another schizophrenic described a similar experience, but affecting language *comprehension:* "I couldn't read them because everything that I read had a large number of associations with it . . . It seemed to start off everything I read . . . and everything that sort of caught my attention seemed to start off, bang-bang-bang, like that with an enormous number of associations moving off onto things so that it became so difficult for me to deal with that I couldn't read" (quoted in Anscombe, "The disorder of consciousness in schizophrenia," *Schizophrenia Bulletin*, 13, 1987, 253).
97. Derrida's support for the psychological reality of his universalized Mallarméan vision is extremely weak. He only shows that multitudinous traces exist potentially—"virtually"—in the linguistic system, that is, at the level of "langue," *not* that such a plethora is in fact operative in any psychological sense, that is to say, that meaning is actually *experienced* (whether consciously or unconsciously) as "infinite implication" by the individual language user engaged in normal "parole."

98. M. Merleau-Ponty, *Phenomenology of Perception*, trans. C. Smith (London: Routledge and Kegan Paul, 1962), p. 400. See also p. 403, where Merleau-Ponty compares learning the meaning of a word to learning to use a tool (which, of course, is Heidegger's famous example of something we inhabit rather than thematize or objectify).

99. Re this undifferentiated mode of experience in childhood, see L. S. Vygotsky, *Thought and Language*, trans. E. Hartmann and G. Vakar (Cambridge: MIT Press, 1962), p. 129. Silvano Arieti argues, for instance, that the patient (like the infant) experiences "the word and its characteristics . . . as identical with the thing and its characteristics"; since the word *is* the thing, by a sort of word magic it may be "substituted for the object when the latter is not available" (quoted in D. Forrest, "Poesis and the language of schizophrenia," *Psychiatry, 28,* 1965, 4).

100. Sechehaye, *Autobiography of a Schizophrenic Girl,* p. 40.

101. See Arieti, *Interpretation of Schizophrenia,* p. 369; Werner and Kaplan, *Symbol Formation* (New York: Wiley, 1963), p. 264.

102. This seems to be implied in H. Werner and B. Kaplan's analysis of this example; see *Symbol Formation,* pp. 258–60.

103. In J. Derrida, "Signature event context," *Margins of Philosophy,* trans. A. Bass (Chicago: University of Chicago Press, 1982), p. 317.

104. This mental grafting of isolated messages onto other possible contexts in fact amounts to a linguistic manifestation of the cognitive slippage discussed in an earlier chapter.

105. Similarly, one schizophrenic girl's response on a proverb-interpretation task suggested that she was paying less attention to context than is normal. To the proverb "You can't touch pitch without being tarred," she responded with a single word—"Music"—thus reacting to the word "pitch" alone rather than to the whole sentence (Woods, "Language study in schizophrenia," p. 309; see also Frith, "Schizophrenia: An abnormality," pp. 161–62). When asked to complete the sentence "The coat of the beggar was very ———," another patient offered the rather surprising answer "trite" (a response that may reflect both an ignoring of standard context *and* a certain tendency to notice the clichéd aspect of existence) (quoted in H. Oppenheimer, "On the application of Karl Jaspers' 'Verstehende' psychology to some forms of schizophrenic thought and language disorder," *Annual Review of the Schizophrenic Syndrome,* 1975, 156).

106. Derrida, "Signature event context," p. 320.

107. See the conversation between two schizophrenics quoted in J. Haley, *Strategies of Psychotherapy* (New York: Grune and Stratton, 1963), pp. 99–100. See also S. Sontag's description of the "camp" sensibility: "Notes on 'camp,' " *Against Interpretation* (New York: Dell, 1969), pp. 277–93.

Some of the writers who had a major influence on this third stream of modernist/postmodernist literary esthetics (that of the apotheosis of the word) were themselves profoundly schizoid or perhaps even schizophrenic. One of these was Raymond Roussel, the author of *Impressions d'Afrique, Locus Solus,* and other works admired by the dadaists and surrealists and later by the novelists of the *nouveau roman* school and various postmodernists and post-structuralists, including John Ashbery and Michel Foucault. In a posthumously published essay called "How I Wrote Certain of My Books," Roussel explained his methods of composition, which relied heavily on puns and other word games that foregrounded the sensory medium and the ambiguity of language. One technique was to begin with two sentences that were identical except for a single letter, yet that had radically different meanings because of this slight difference in the signifying chain, and then to concoct a plot that could lead from one sentence to the other.

Another extreme eccentric admired by some of the same writers is Jean-Pierre Brisset, who was, if anything, even more extreme in his devotion to the notion that (as he put it) "it is not I, but the Word that speaks." Brisset would scrutinize the sound of a word, a phrase, or a sentence and find different possible meanings in it. From the French word *logé* (which means "lodged"), for example, he derived the following sentences:

1. l'eau j'ai. (I have water.)
2. l'haut j'ai. (I am high.)
3. l'os j'ai. (I have a bone.)
4. loge ai. (I have a lodge.)
5. lot j'ai. (I bear my lot.)
etc.

After generating such a set, Brisset would construct an elaborate though rather arbitrary story to tie the sentences together; in this instance it was a myth of origins about the frog, who lived in the water (suggested by sentence 1) in lake villages built on posts (sentence 2) and who was carnivorous (sentence 3) and so on. Re Brisset and Roussel, see J.-J. Lecercle, *Philosophy Through the Looking Glass* (LaSalle, IL: Open Court, 1985), esp. pp. 15–27, 36–46.

One important admirer of both Roussel and Brisset was Marcel Duchamp, who declared the influence of Roussel to have been fundamentally responsible for his creation of his famous work, "The Large Glass," and who once wrote that his ideal library would contain "all Roussel's writings—Brisset, perhaps Lautreamont and Mallarmé." Duchamp seems at least to have understood how very un-Dionysian the "delirium of imagination" of Roussel and Brisset really was; for he described their work (along with that of Mallarmé) as "the direction in which art should turn: to an intellectual expression, rather than to an animal expression" (Duchamp quoted in M. Jean, ed., *The Autobiography of Surrealism* [New York: Viking, 1980], p. 414). Another schizophrenic or schizoid writer of importance in this context is Louis Wolfson (whose influence is also discussed in Lecercle, *Looking Glass*, pp. 27–31, 39–41).

108. The two issues are obviously connected, since, as philosophers of the speech act have noted, attributions of meaning are usually (some would say always) bound up with attributions of intentionality; see, for example, J. Searle, "What is a speech act?" *The Philosophy of Language* (London: Oxford University Press, 1971), pp. 39–53, esp. pp. 40–46.

109. Quoted in Lorenz, "Expressive form," p. 648.

110. It is true that even unequivocal states of mental defect or deficiency do not lead invariably to errors; such is not the case with gross neurological damage, and one should hardly expect it to be true for schizophrenia. But when such variability is so clearly nonrandom, so liable to vary with subjectively meaningful circumstances, then some other factor is very likely to be playing an important role.

There is also the possibility that some mediating factor could exacerbate or mute the expression of the defect in a fairly mechanical way, without implicating willful intentionality on the part of the patient. A once-popular theory of schizophrenia based in associationistic learning theory ascribes just such a role to anxiety—viewing it not as a signal evoking strategies of avoidance, but as a psychophysiological response that automatically increases the likelihood of emitting responses of low associative strength, such as "clang" associations in glossomanic speech (for discussion and references, see Cutting, *Psychology of Schizophrenia*, pp. 46–47, 366–67, 376). However, while such a mechanistic theory might well help to explain *some* instances of schizophrenic language disturbance, its plausibility as a general account is fairly dubious. For one thing, the deviant speech of such patients is by no means always accompanied by increased anxiety: floridly glossomanic speech may, for example, also be accompanied by a triumphant or euphoric mood. And, the circumstances under which schizophrenics will speak or act more conventionally are not necessarily those where anxiety would be expected to be low (Manfred Bleuler, for instance, mentions the sudden clarity of a patient trying to talk his way out of the hospital ["Inconstancy of schizophrenic language and symptoms," p. 591]). Also, inconsistent experimental results have kept most experimentalists from endorsing the anxiety theory, as Cutting notes (*Psychology of Schizophrenia*, pp. 366–67).

111. Lecours and Vanier-Clement, "Schizophrenia and jargonaphasia," p. 545; see also pp. 527, 532–33, 536, 554–63.

112. Letter in my files; I have added the emphasis, though the words in parentheses are, of course, those of the patient.

113. Cardinal, "Enigma," p. 44.

114. Quoted in H. Friedrich, *The Structure of Modern Poetry*, trans. J. Neugroschel (Evanston, IL: Northwestern University Press, 1974), p. 4.

115. R. D. Laing, *The Divided Self* (Harmondsworth, UK: Penguin Books, 1965), p. 164.

116. "I used some words in order to express a concept entirely different from the usual one," reported the patient. "Thus, I blithely employed the word *mangy* to mean 'gallant.' If I could not immediately find an appropriate word to express the rapid flow of ideas, I would seek release in self-invented ones, as for example *wuttas* for *doves*" (one of Forel's patients, quoted in E. Bleuler, *Dementia Praecox*, p. 150). This may also reflect a profound sense of the arbitrariness of word–meaning connections.

117. Title of an essay by J. Haley, in his *The Power Tactics of Jesus Christ and Other Essays* (New York: Avon Books, 1969), pp. 145–76.

118. See P. F. Gjerde, "Attentional capacity dysfunction and arousal in schizophrenia," *Psychological Bulletin*, 93, 1983, 68.

119. Lecours and Vanier-Clement, "Schizophasia and jargonaphasia," p. 557.

120. Phrases from Erich Heller, *The Disinherited Mind* (New York and London: Harcourt Brace Jovanovich, 1975), p. 272.

121. Re such language in modernism, see M. H. Abrams, "Coleridge, Baudelaire, and modernist poetics," *The Correspondent Breeze: Essays on English Romanticism* (New York: Norton, 1984), pp. 139–41.

Chapter 7: Loss of Self

1. R. Descartes, *Meditations and Selections from the Principles of Philosophy* (LaSalle, IL: Open Court, 1946), p. 28. Also, quotations in B. Williams, *Descartes: The Project of Pure Inquiry* (Harmondsworth, UK: Penguin Books, 1978), pp. 78–79.

2. P. F. Strawson, *The Bounds of Sense* (London: Methuen, 1966), p. 165.
3. Patients quoted in C. S. Mellor, "First rank symptoms of schizophrenia," *British Journal of Psychiatry, 117,* 1970, 16–18.
4. Patients quoted by Storch, in T. Freeman, J. Cameron, and A. McGhie, *Chronic Schizophrenia* (New York: International Universities Press, 1958), p. 54; and by H. Rosenfeld, *Psychotic States* (London: Maresfield Reprints, 1965), pp. 162, 29.
5. Jefferson quoted in S. E. Estroff, "Self, identity, and subjective experiences of schizophrenia: In search of the subject," *Schizophrenia Bulletin, 15,* 1989, 189. For more examples, see K. Jaspers, *General Psychopathology,* trans. J. Hoenig and M. W. Hamilton (Chicago: University of Chicago Press, 1963), p. 122. A particularly extreme example of a kind of multiplication of the self is a patient who announced that there was an "electric assortment" of different people inside her—"an officer of the Guard of Honor, Ernst Ritter von Poheim, Dr. K., a conference of doctors and a men's choral society" (described in J. Berze, "Primary insufficiency of mental activity," in J. Cutting and M. Shepherd, eds., *The Clinical Roots of the Schizophrenia Concept* [Cambridge: Cambridge University Press, 1987], p. 57).
6. See C. Landis, ed., *Varieties of Psychopathological Experience* (New York: Holt, Rinehart, and Winston, 1964), pp. 390–92. Such experiences help to explain why schizophrenic patients will sometimes avoid the words *I* and *me*, preferring to refer to themselves in the third person or to speak of "my person" or "my personality"; see E. Minkowski, *La Schizophrénie* (Paris: Payot, 1927), p. 126.
7. C. Geertz, *Local Knowledge* (New York: Basic Books, 1983), p. 59.
8. Jaspers had treated this loss of a sense of inhabiting one's acts as the primary example of schizophrenic incomprehensibility; see Jaspers, *General Psychopathology,* p. 578, re the "made" quality of schizophrenic experiences and acts.
9. F. Nietzsche, *Beyond Good and Evil,* trans. R. J. Hollingdale (Harmondsworth, UK: Penguin Books, 1973; originally published in 1886), pp. 28–29.
10. Mach quoted in D. S. Luft, *Robert Musil and the Crisis of European Culture: 1880–1942* (Berkeley: University of California Press, 1980), p. 82. The ancestor of this argument is, of course, Hume, in his *Treatise of Human Nature* (1739); but it was only later that it came to be a widespread vision or experience of human nature; see E. Faas, *Retreat into the Mind: Victorian Poetry and the Rise of Psychiatry* (Princeton, NJ: Princeton University Press, 1988), pp. 59–60.

   Mach's philosophy, a subjective empiricism reminiscent of Hume and especially Berkeley, amounted to a kind of phenomenalism or nominalism. He argued that it was necessary to give up all concepts associated with words like *how, because, so, in order to, suppose, as a result, although, when*—precisely the sorts of words or concepts that James saw as "carried" by the non-introspectable "transitive" elements of the stream of experience. Mach faulted such concepts for making attributions that went beyond sensational elements, for making projections onto nature, often of animistic notions derived from the observer's own felt sense of effort or will; see W. Sypher, *Loss of the Self in Modern Literature and Art* (New York: Vintage Books, 1962), pp. 79–80.
11. These symptoms are called *Ichstörungen* in German psychiatry; see M. Spitzer, "Ichstörungen: In search of a theory," in M. Spitzer, F. A. Uehlein, and G. Oepen, eds., *Psychopathology and Philosophy* (Berlin and Heidelberg: Springer-Verlag, 1988), pp. 167–83.

12. K. Schneider, *Clinical Psychopathology* (New York and London: Grune and Stratton, 1959), pp. 88–145. See also Mellor, "First rank symptoms of schizophrenia"; and K. Koehler, "First rank symptoms of schizophrenia: Questions concerning clinical boundaries," *British Journal of Psychiatry, 134,* 1979, 236–48. For an excellent, astringent critique of Schneider's critics, see J. Hoenig, "Schneider's First Rank Symptoms and the tabulators," *Comprehensive Psychiatry, 25,* 1984, 77–87.

   The First Rank Symptoms have been found to occur in some affective patients, but far less frequently than in schizophrenia. (Schneider never claimed, by the way, that these symptoms were present in all schizophrenics.) J. O'Grady found that 73 percent of schizophrenics in his sample had First Rank Symptoms (Mellor, "First rank symptoms," reports virtually the same figure), while less than 14 percent of the patients with affective disorder did. Further, in O'Grady's sample, the only affective patients who did show such symptoms (at least when Mellor's narrow definition of these symptoms was used) had the diagnosis schizoaffective psychosis, which would put them at least in the schizophrenia *spectrum* ("The prevalence and diagnostic significance of Schneiderian first-rank symptoms in a random sample of acute psychiatric in-patients," *British Journal of Psychiatry, 156,* 1990, 496–500).

13. B. O'Brien, *Operators and Things: The Inner Life of a Schizophrenic* (Cambridge, MA: Arlington Books, 1958), pp. 82–84. E. Bleuler, *Dementia Praecox, or the Group of Schizophrenias,* trans. J. Zinkin (New York: International Universities Press, 1950), p. 128.

14. American Psychiatric Association, *Diagnostic and Statistical Manual of Mental Disorders, III, Revised* (DSM III-R) (Washington, DC: American Psychiatric Association, 1987), pp. 188, 189, 194. Kraepelin also stressed distortions of selfhood, comparing schizophrenic personality to "an orchestra without a conductor," and once stating in a lecture, "There is simply no ego there" ("Da ist ein Ich einfach nicht da") (*Dementia Praecox and Paraphrenia,* trans. R. M. Barclay [Huntington, NY: Robert E. Krieger, 1971; first English ed., 1919], p. xvi); see also J. Cutting, *The Psychology of Schizophrenia* (Edinburgh: Churchill Livingstone, 1985), p. 23. For other characterizations of schizophrenia as essentially a self-disturbance, see C. Scharfetter, *General Psychopathology: An Introduction,* trans. H. Marshall (Cambridge: Cambridge University Press, 1980) (he is inclined to view all schizophrenic symptoms as "disorders of ego-consciousness"); and G. Langfeldt, "Diagnosis and prognosis of schizophrenia," *Proceedings of the Royal Society of Medicine, 53,* 1960, 1047–52.

15. V. Tausk (1919), "On the origin of the 'influencing machine' in schizophrenia," *Psychoanalytic Quarterly, 2,* 1933, 529–30.

16. "She senses all manipulations performed on the corresponding part of her own body and in the same manner. All effects and changes undergone by the apparatus take place simultaneously in the patient's body and *vice versa*" (Tausk, "The 'influencing machine,'" p. 532).

17. Ibid., p. 549. The influencing-machine delusion is one of the classic delusions of schizophrenia, described in the very first clear-cut account of this kind of psychosis, John Haslam's case study of James Tilly Matthews published in 1810; see P. K. Carpenter, "Descriptions of schizophrenia in the psychiatry of Georgian Britain: John Haslam and James Tilly Matthews," *Comprehensive Psychiatry,*

30, 1989, 332–38. For other examples of this delusion, see P. Schilder, *The Image and Appearance of the Human Body* (New York: International Universities Press, 1950), p. 223; and Freeman et al., *Chronic Schizophrenia*, pp. 64–65.

18. Tausk, "The 'influencing machine,' " p. 536*n*.
19. O. Fenichel, *The Psychoanalytic Theory of Neurosis* (New York: Norton, 1945), p. 439.
20. T. Freeman, *Psychopathology of the Psychoses* (New York: International Universities Press, 1969), pp. 137, 163.
21. A. Freud, "Preface" to Freeman, Cameron, and McGhie, *Chronic Schizophrenia*, pp. vii–viii. Other psychoanalytic interpretations of these disturbances of ego or self are summarized in Scharfetter, *General Psychopathology*, pp. 68–74. Heinz Hartmann, for example, viewed the disintegration of the ego in schizophrenia as a result of regressive submersion in "unneutralized" instinctual drives, both sexual and aggressive ("Contributions to the meta-psychology of schizophrenia," *The Psychoanalytic Study of the Child*, 8, 1953, 186–87). J. Frosch compares the fragmented body image in schizophrenia to the lack of integration characteristic of the "earliest stages in psychic development" (*The Psychotic Process* [New York: International Universities Press, 1983], p. 327*n*). See also Fenichel re schizophrenic passivization as "correlated with a primitive stage in the development of the ego" (*Psychoanalytic Theory of Neurosis*, p. 423).
22. F. Jameson, "Imaginary and Symbolic in Lacan," in S. Felman, ed., *Literature and Psychoanalysis* (Baltimore: Johns Hopkins University Press, 1982), p. 382.
23. F. Nietzsche, *The Birth of Tragedy and The Case of Wagner*, trans. W. Kaufmann (New York: Vintage Books, 1967; originally published in 1872), pp. 21, 36–37, 40–41.
24. F. Nietzsche, *The Will to Power*, trans. W. Kaufmann and R. J. Hollingdale (New York: Vintage Books, 1968; originally published in 1901), p. 267.
25. L. Bersani, *A Future for Astyanax* (New York: Columbia University Press, 1984; originally published in 1976), pp. xi, xii, 5–9, 234–66, 255–60, and passim. Leo Bersani describes "attempts to simplify character to desublimated, discontinuous scenes of the desiring imagination" (p. 263).
26. For example, Bersani asserts that "*all* serious enterprises of psychic deconstruction" involve "the pornographic tyrannies intrinsic to all desire" (*Future for Astyanax*, p. 272 [emphasis added]).
27. W. James, "The consciousness of self," *The Principles of Psychology*, vol. 1 (New York: Henry Holt, 1890), pp. 291–401; all quotes in this section not otherwise noted are from pp. 297–301, 304–5, 330.
28. See James, "Consciousness of self," p. 301. James was well aware, by the way, that his argument was similar to those of associationistic and empiricist philosophers like Hume and Herbart.
29. James, "The Stream of Thought," *Principles of Psychology*, pp. 224–90, esp. pp. 243–45. See also his reservations expressed on pp. 183–98 and 336ff of the *Principles*.
30. L. Wittgenstein, *The Blue and Brown Books* (Oxford: Blackwell, 1958), p. 66.
31. See the discussion in P. M. S. Hacker, *Insight and Illusion: Wittgenstein on Philosophy and the Metaphysics of Experience* (Oxford: Oxford University Press, 1972), pp. 126–27.

. Wittgenstein, *Philosophical Investigations*, trans. G. E. M. Anscombe (Oxrd: Blackwell, 1953), pp. 124–25.

e ibid., p. 125; Wittgenstein, *Zettel*, trans. G. E. M. Anscombe (Berkeley: University of California Press, 1970), p. 103.

34. In *The Visible and the Invisible* (trans. A. Lingis [Evanston, IL: Northwestern University Press, 1968]), Maurice Merleau-Ponty makes a similar criticism of the "movement of reflection [which] will always at first sight be convincing," yet which can engender illusions and which lacks sufficient critical self-awareness. He therefore calls for *"sur-réflexion,"* a form of reflection "that would also take itself and the changes it introduces into account," thereby reinstating both our oneness with the body and our "mute contact" with things (pp. 31, 38). See chapter 11 for further elaboration of these issues.

It is obvious, I hope, that I am not arguing in favor of *either* the traditional humanist notion *or* the nonself doctrine, which some poststructuralists and postmodernists have been inclined to defend. The implication is, rather, that each vision may have equal, though limited, validity, since each can find itself to be "true" in its own context (e.g., the contexts I have called "casual" and "exigent" introspection). From a Wittgensteinian point of view, it would be no less "metaphysical" (in the pejorative sense) to believe in the decentered subject than in its opposite, the Cartesian *cogito* and the myth of presence. It is ironic that some followers of poststructuralism should proclaim the end of metaphysics at the same time as they espouse a doctrine no less metaphysical than Cartesianism.

To an important extent, of course, such visions of human nature derive from theoretical arguments that have their own intrinsic logic and cannot be reduced to an experiential stance or mood. To account for the antihumanism implicit in poststructuralism as a simple function of exigent introspection would obviously be absurd—not to mention the fact that it would involve a rather arbitrary reduction of structuralism to phenomenology. Yet it is also true that certain lived realities are likely to accompany certain theoretical positions—sometimes as a consequence of the theory, sometimes by making the theory seem more plausible or desirable. When the theory is reified into something like a metaphysical position (as in taking the "language speaks me" idea as the final word on human subjectivity), it becomes especially useful to examine the situation or psychological stance associated with that position. The following passage by the poststructuralist critic Geoffrey Hartman, which describes the moment before putting pen to paper, suggests that something akin to the experience of exigent introspection can in fact play its part, reinforcing the vision of human nature that motivates the poststructuralist criticism of the notion of the author-God as a controlling self. (The passage is, by the way, more than a little reminiscent of Nathalie Sarraute's character, Alain, to be described in the text.):

In fact, writing teaches, paradoxically, that someone else seems to write for us: that there is a ghostwriter in every hand. . . . The blankness of starting . . . compels the one who writes to relive . . . the queasy feeling that the definitive statement one is about to make is subject to interfering thoughts that seem to come from nowhere—and often subject to words rather than thoughts, words that turn you this way or that. The very instant of writing, Pascal's fly buzzing, the book your eye chances to light on, a telephone call, the hangover of a dream, a literary echo—these are the stuff guiding the pen that claims authority. We notice, and are amused by, a slip of the tongue, and we have learned to study such parapraxes; but who can tell a slip of the pen that is always slipping on the pathless page? ["The humanities, literacy, and communication," reprinted in *Harper's*, September 1985, 33]

35. N. Sarraute, *The Age of Suspicion: Essays on the Novel*, trans. M. Jolas (New York: George Braziller, 1963), p. 57.

36. Ibid., pp. 16–17.

37. N. Sarraute, *Between Life and Death*, trans. M. Jolas (New York: Braziller, 1969), pp. 63–64, 67–68.

38. These examples of disintegrated selfhood occur at a level that is more central and profound than is the case with the forms of "uncoupling" discussed in chapter 3. The issue here is not alienation from social role, not a true-self versus false-self distinction, but alienation from one's own consciousness. Instead of insincerity and inconsistency (as with Rameau's nephew, Lionel Trilling's primary example), what seems to occur in these instances is fragmentation and dissolution of the "inner person" himself or herself.

39. "Centrifugation du Moi," in P. Valéry, *Cahiers*, vol. 2, ed. J. Robinson (Paris: Gallimard, 1974), p. 295.

40. N. Sarraute, *The Planetarium*, trans. M. Jolas (New York: Braziller, 1960), p. 296. Another example comes from Virginia Woolf's *Orlando*: "After twenty minutes the body and mind were like scraps of torn paper tumbling from a sack and, indeed, the process of motoring fast out of London so much resembles the chopping up small of body and mind, which precedes unconsciousness and perhaps death itself that it is an open question in what sense Orlando can be said to have existed at the present moment. . . . a person entirely disassembled . . . [until] her mind regained the illusion of holding things within itself" (*Orlando: A Biography* [New York: Harcourt Brace, 1928], p. 307).

Jean Starobinski notes that a focus on bodily sensation, particularly kinesthetic sensations involving the body's experience of itself, came to be emphasized in modern culture; see "A short history of body consciousness," trans. S. Matthews, *Humanities in Society*, 1, 1982, 22–39. This would be a manifestation of a potentially externalizing and self-fragmenting involution.

41. William Gass, quoted in L. Hutcheon, *Narcissistic Narrative: The Metafictional Paradox* (New York and London: Methuen, 1984), p. 33.

42. The notion of the *abyme*—so prominent in postmodernist and poststructuralist discourse—was first used as a way of designating a reflexive process in a work of art by André Gide, one of the classic modernists from earlier in the century; see J.-J. Lecercle, *Philosophy Through the Looking Glass* (LaSalle, IL: Open Court, 1985), p. 45n.

43. For discussion of tendencies toward subjectivism without a subject in the poetry of John Ashbery, see A. Williamson, *Introspection and Contemporary Poetry* (Cambridge: Harvard University Press, 1984), pp. 117–19.

And, by a strange paradox of the reflexive, language and consciousness seem, on the one hand, pathetically inadequate to the task of representing anything outside themselves and, on the other hand, immensely powerful since they seem to contain all that exists. This odd, somehow autistic combination of omnipotence and impotence emerges in postmodernist novelist Gilbert Sorrentino's description of his own writing: "These people aren't real. I'm making them up as I go along, any section that threatens to flesh them out, or make them 'walk off the page,' will be excised. They should, rather, walk into the page, and break up, disappear" (quoted in Hutcheon, *Narcissistic Narrative*, p. 87).

44. Bersani, *Future for Astyanax*, pp. 236, 272.

45. These trends correspond closely to those distinguished by Hugo von Hofmann-sthal in 1893, well before the rhetoric of the decentered self had become entrenched:

Today, two things seem to be modern: the analysis of life and the flight from life. . . . One practises anatomy on the inner life of one's mind, or one dreams. Reflection or fantasy, mirror image or dream image. . . . Modern is the dissection of a mood, a sigh, a scruple; and modern is the instinctive, almost somnambulistic surrender to every revelation of beauty, to a harmony of colours, to a glittering metaphor, to a wondrous allegory. [Quoted in J. McFarlane, "The mind of modernism," in M. Bradbury and J. McFarlane, eds., *Modernism* (Harmondsworth, UK: Penguin Books, 1976), p. 71]

For an example of what might be considered a partial synthesis of these two impulses (by means of a kind of eroticized introversion), see the discussion of William Gass's metafiction in Hutcheon, *Narcissistic Narrative*, p. 86.

The assumption that self-fragmentation must somehow be a Dionysian condition is very widespread indeed. Lionel Trilling, for example, tends to equate the (Dionysian) loss of self that is experienced, for instance, by Kurtz in Conrad's *Heart of Darkness* with the more Apollonian or Socratic fragmentation described in Wylie Sypher's *Loss of Self in Modern Literature and Art;* see Trilling, *Sincerity and Authenticity* (Cambridge: Harvard University Press, 1971), pp. 54, 106.

46. In a discussion of Rimbaud's *Illuminations,* for example, Leo Bersani points out that the loss of self is not total in this work, since complete fusion or fragmentation is prevented by the appearance of the narrator as an *element* in many of the scenic "illuminations" (though, as Bersani emphasizes, awareness of the narrator as a distinct, constituting *subjectivity* or *subject* of desire is absent). And, says Bersani, by so interrupting the dominant impulse of the work, the narrator "thereby saves himself from a *schizophrenic* failure to distinguish *at all* between the self and the alien forms into which it has been projected" (*Future for Astyanax*, p. 245 [emphasis added]).

47. Quoted in C. Landis, ed., *Varieties of Psychopathological Experience* (New York: Holt, Rinehart, and Winston, 1964), p. 193. See also "The Case of Peter," in R. D. Laing, *The Divided Self* (Harmondsworth, UK: Penguin Books, 1965), pp. 120–36.

48. For other relevant descriptions, see Rosenfeld, *Psychotic States*, pp. 13–33, 155–68; and T. Szasz, "The psychology of bodily feelings in schizophrenia," *Psychosomatic Medicine*, 19, 1957, 11–16.

49. M. Merleau-Ponty, *Phenomenology of Perception* (London: Routledge and Kegan Paul, 1962), p. xiii. Interestingly enough, a schizophrenic patient quoted by Eugene Minkowski uses almost exactly the same image: "Je ne parviens plus à donner mon activité d'une façon suffisamment vivante. Je ne puis plus passer des cordes douces aux cordes tendues . . . J'ai perdu le contact avec toutes

espèces de choses. La notion de la valeur, de la difficulté des choses a disparu. Il n'y a plus de courant entre elles et moi, je ne peux plus m'y abandonner" (*La Schizophrénie*, pp. 99–100). Re "tacit knowing," see M. Polanyi, *Personal Knowledge* (New York and Evanston: Harper and Row, 1964).

50. David Hemsley's cognitive-neurobiological theory, which emphasizes hippocampal abnormalities and the pervasiveness of a highly focused kind of attention, offers one very plausible way of accounting for this kind of exigent introspection; see D. R. Hemsley, "Cognitive abnormalities and the symptoms of schizophrenia," to appear in M. Spitzer, F. A. Uehlein, M. A. Schwartz, eds., *Phenomenology, Language, and Schizophrenia* (New York: Springer, 1992). Re a difficulty with synthetic or Gestalt-type perception which would make one prone to experiencing a perceptual field of isolated details, see discussion of Paul Matussek and Klaus Conrad in J. Cutting, *The Right Cerebral Hemisphere and Psychiatric Disorders* (Oxford: Oxford University Press, 1990), pp. 257–58.

The effects of high levels of arousal or of anxiety, or of disturbances of the ability to orient or attend to "task-relevant stimuli" (as measured, e.g., by "event-related potentials" in the brain), would provide other ways of explaining the experiential prominence of stimuli that would normally recede into the background or horizon of awareness; see P. Gjerde, "Attentional capacity dysfunction and arousal in schizophrenia," *Psychological Bulletin*, 93, 1983, 57–72; D. H. R. Blackwood and W. J. Muir, "Cognitive brain potentials and their application," *British Journal of Psychiatry*, 157, 1990, 96–101.

Another possibility is that the intensely focused, analytic mode of attention (which has such a fragmenting effect) could be a manifestation of a tendency toward overactivation of the more analytic or underactivation of the more synthetic-intuitive areas or systems of the brain (left hemisphere, right hemisphere, respectively). If so, we would have a neurobiological condition whose consequences contradict traditional assumptions about mind-body relationships: instead of suffering a straightforward decline of volitional or rational aspects of experience, such a patient would be *afflicted* with a kind of (dysfunctional) hyperintentionality or hyperrationality, while, at the same time, being deprived of the normal sense of embeddedness in spontaneous or semiautomatic action patterns; see appendix for further discussion.

Another relevant neurobiological theory is C. D. Frith's hypothesis of a disorder in the central monitoring of willed action (a process supposedly carried out largely in the hippocampus). This theory, postulating a degradation of feedback information concerning willed intentions, would provide a very direct neurophysiological explanation for the passivization experiences described by Kurt Schneider's list of First Rank Symptoms. It would seem plausible that, in the absence of such feedback, one's own actions, both bodily and mental (e.g., inner speech), could lose their normal transparency and take on a reified, thinglike, or alien quality; such phenomena would then be likely to attract a focused kind of awareness, which in turn might exacerbate still further both the reification and the passivization. See C. D. Frith and D. J. Done, "Toward a neuropsychology of schizophrenia," *British Journal of Psychiatry*, 153, 1988, 437–43. It is not clear, however, how Frith's theory, at least on its own, could explain the particular *content* of auditory hallucinations in schizophrenia, that is, the fact that (as I shall discuss) the voices heard by such patients so often involve self-monitoring, a level of meta-awareness—that is, not just thoughts aloud but voices describing ongoing activities or discussing the patient in the third person. For criticisms of Frith's hypothesis and his response to these criticisms, see C. D. Frith and J. Done, "Positive symptoms of schizophrenia," *British Journal of Psychiatry, 154,* 1989, 569–70.

See the index re other act-affliction ambiguities, and the appendix for further discussion of neurobiological aspects.

51. Patients quoted in J. Chapman, "The early symptoms of schizophrenia," *British Journal of Psychiatry, 112,* 1966, 232. Another schizophrenic patient described his body as spinning away from him: "When I am ill I lose the sense of where I am. I feel 'I' can sit in the chair, and yet my body is hurtling out and somersaulting about three feet in front of me" (quoted in J. Jaynes, *The Origin of Consciousness in the Breakdown of the Bicameral Mind* [Boston: Houghton, Mifflin, 1976], p. 418).

52. Invoking concepts from both psychoanalysis and Piaget, the psychoanalytic writers T. Freeman, J. L. Cameron, and A. McGhie argue that weakness of reflective consciousness is intimately connected with disturbances of identity, and that both are central indices of schizophrenic disturbance: "As we regard the absence of reflective awareness to be one of the chief aspects of the schizophrenic disease process, we must regard any appearance of such awareness as a therapeutically hopeful sign, signifying, as it does, that the ego is momentarily clear-cut and stable" (*Chronic Schizophrenia,* p. 95). The assumption that consciousness, ego, self, and will are all mutually supportive is very widespread. In *The Sickness unto Death* (published with *Fear and Trembling,* trans. W. Lowrie [Princeton, NJ: Princeton University Press, 1941], p. 162), Søren Kierkegaard writes as follows: "Generally speaking, consciousness, i.e., consciousness of self, is the decisive criterion of the self. The more consciousness, the more self; the more consciousness, the more will, and the more will the more self."

53. See, for example, C. Donnelly, "The observing self and the development of cohesiveness," *British Journal of Medical Psychology, 52,* 1979, 277–79.

54. See, for example, cognitive-developmental interpretations like that offered in H. Werner and B. Kaplan, *Symbol Formation* (New York: Wiley, 1963). A similar view was adopted by Joseph Berze, who argued that the central schizophrenic experiences of losing a sense of control, being influenced unduly by stimuli felt as external, and, as one patient put it, needing to make an effort to "find my own self for a few short moments," are all due to a "decline or weakness in consciousness" or a "primary insufficiency of mental activity" ("Primary insufficiency of mental activity," in Cutting and Shepherd, *Clinical Roots of Schizophrenia Concept,* pp. 51–58).

55. Jaynes, *Origin of Consciousness,* see pp. 84–85, 94–96, 404–32. See also S. Bach ("On the narcissistic state of consciousness," *International Journal of Psychoanalysis, 58,* 1977, 213), who argues that the "narcissistic" state of consciousness should be compared to that of ancient man as described by E. R. Dodds and Bruno Snell. A. Szalita ("Regression and perception in psychotic states," *Psychiatry, 21,* 1958, 58) makes a similar argument.

56. Patient quoted in A. C. Smith, *Schizophrenia and Madness* (London: George Allen and Unwin, 1982), p. 30. See also M. Hamilton, ed., *Fish's Schizophrenia,* 2nd ed. (Bristol: John Wright, 1976), pp. 92–95, 140, 157.

57. J. Lang, "The other side of hallucinations," *American Journal of Psychiatry, 94*, 1938, 1091.
58. Ibid., pp. 1091–92.
59. One man would hear his own thoughts repeated by a male voice that seemed to come from far away and was unrecognizable to him; see Cutting, *Psychology of Schizophrenia*, p. 288. Patients sometimes will hear a voice predicting their next action or criticizing an intention even before this intention comes into awareness; see E. Bleuler, *Dementia Praecox*, p. 98.
60. Eugen Bleuler remarks on this contradictory quality; see *Dementia Praecox*, pp. 95–100, 195.
61. Mellor, "First rank symptoms," p. 16.
62. C. Wallace, *Portrait of a Schizophrenic Nurse* (London: Hammond, Hammond, 1965), pp. 34, 14.
    Natalija seems to have had auditory hallucinations of the kind described by Schneider: she heard the voices of the shadowy people who were operating the influencing machine speaking about the machine and its manipulations; since the machine was modeled on Natalija herself, its motions being simulacra of Natalija's own behavior, we could say that the voices were shadowing, discussing, or criticizing Natalija's own activities.
63. Such a view is common in classical psychoanalysis. But certain views in contemporary neurobiology are not dissimilar. See N. Andreasen, "Brain imaging: Applications in psychiatry," *Science, 239*, 1382; D. R. Weinberger, K. F. Berman, and R. F. Zec, "Physiologic dysfunction of dorsolateral prefrontal cortex in schizophrenia: I. Regional cerebral blood flow evidence," *Archives of General Psychiatry, 43*, 1986, 123; and my discussion in the appendix.
64. F. Nietzsche, *The Birth of Tragedy and The Genealogy of Morals*, trans. F. Golffing (Garden City, NY: Doubleday, 1956), pp. 84–85.
65. M. Alpert and K. N. Silvers, "Perceptual characteristics distinguishing auditory hallucinations in schizophrenia and acute alcoholic psychoses," *American Journal of Psychiatry, 127*, 1970, 300.
    The auditory hallucinations can be of (at least) two kinds: they may echo a (relatively spontaneous) foundational level of thinking, or they may represent a level of meta-awareness. These correspond to Schneider's "thoughts-out-loud" and to the characteristic auditory hallucinations that he lists (a voice or voices describing the patient's ongoing action or thought, or two or more voices discussing the patient in the third person). The rendering-explicit that occurs involves a certain self-consciousness, but in the latter case it seems to be self-consciousness itself that is thematized. This duality is illustrated by Schreber's "nerves" and his "rays," discussed in the next chapter.
    During his psychotic periods, the schizophrenic dancer Vaslav Nijinsky (a major influence on avant-garde dance in the twentieth century) would hear voices saying things like the following: "I am God in you. . . . I know what you are thinking about: that he [the doctor] is here and is staring at you. I want him to look at you" (R. Nijinsky, ed., *The Diary of Vaslav Nijinsky* [Berkeley and Los Angeles: University of California Press, 1968], p. 180). Kraepelin quotes the following words that one patient spoke while carrying on a dialogue with his voices: "What does it matter to me then what you think! This has nothing to do with me, is in the highest degree indifferent to me.—What? I must think that?

That I must not think at all. I can think what I like and you better think what you like! . . . I can certainly do with my head what I will! What? I am stupid? . . . I am too clever for you" (*Dementia Praecox*, p. 56). For other examples, see Schneider, *Clinical Psychopathology*, pp. 96–97.

66. "The voices are unlike spoken voices but are as if thought," patients may say; see E. Bleuler, *Dementia Praecox*, p. 114.

67. Jaspers, *General Psychopathology*, p. 141.

68. I. R. H. Falloon and R. E. Talbot, "Persistent auditory hallucinations: Coping mechanisms and implications for management," *Psychological Medicine, 11,* 1981, 331.

69. A. Margo, D. R. Hemsley, and P. D. Slade, "The effects of varying auditory input on schizophrenic hallucinations," *British Journal of Psychiatry, 139,* 1981, 122–27.

70. J. S. Strauss, J. J. Bartko, and W. T. Carpenter, "New directions in diagnosis: The longitudinal processes of schizophrenia," *American Journal of Psychiatry, 138,* 1981, 954–58. Alpert and Silvers, "Auditory hallucinations," p. 300.

71. Quoted in J. Glass, *Delusion: Internal Dimensions of Political Life* (Chicago: University of Chicago Press, 1985), p. 193 (emphasis added).

72. J. Lang, "The other side of the ideological aspects of schizophrenia," *Psychiatry, 3,* 1940, 389, 391, 392.

73. Lang, "Other side of hallucinations," p. 1091.

74. Another patient (Lawrence, who is discussed at length in chapter 11) sometimes had the feeling he could *see* his thoughts, almost as if they appeared as subtitles at the bottom of the scene to which they pertained.

Alexander, among other philosophers, has argued that acts of consciousness cannot in fact be contemplated—that to think of them in this way is to mistakenly assimilate these processes to the things that are their objects; see J. Passmore, *A Hundred Years of Philosophy*, 2nd ed. (Harmondsworth, UK: Penguin, 1968), pp. 267–69. But the example of schizophrenics like Lang and Natalija demonstrates that such "contemplation" is possible, though it may not be normal. For, in their experience, the implicit and transparent phenomena that would normally lie close to the subject-pole of the intentional arc of consciousness have, as it were, migrated out to the endpoint of this arc, there to turn opaque. It is true, of course, that there must then be *another* act of consciousness that *is* more invisible and implicit, an "enjoyed" act that, as it were, "contemplates" the acts that have been rendered explicit. In this sense, Alexander's claim about an act of consciousness necessarily remaining implicit seems to hold true.

It is interesting, however, that the contemplated act will sometimes mimic the implicit or enjoyed one: the contemplated process will often be itself a manifestation of self-consciousness. Thus, for example, some schizophrenic patients may hear voices that express their self-consciousness. (Schreber, the famous paranoid schizophrenic written about by Freud, frequently heard voices saying, "What are you thinking of now?") In such instances, we are faced with a situation reminiscent of the *mise en abyme* so often discovered by deconstructionist readings of works of literature as infinitely reflexive artifacts. Here, as in those readings, the ultimate meaning of the "text" seems to be the expression of its own reflexivity. One schizoid young man, a visual artist, said that if he stared long enough at any painting, he realized that the canvas was like an eye that watched, while the frame was like ears. He seemed, as it were, to see seeing.

75. Phrasing borrowed from Erich Heller's discussion of Kafka in *The Disinherited Mind* (New York and London: Harcourt Brace Jovanovich, 1975), p. 202. A very similar process of introversion combined with self-alienation occurred in a schizoaffective patient who had an acute degree of insight into her condition. To the question, "Have you at times felt controlled by people or things *outside* you?" she answered: "They're always *inside* me . . . but it depends on the extent I identify with whatever is controlling me . . . inside of me . . . whether I identified with the controller, or the person *being* controlled. And what'd happen was, I wouldn't identify with *either* of them, so that . . . In other words . . . *both* of them are *me:* the person controlling and the one controlled are both me, and I didn't identify with *either* of them" (quoted in M. Stone, *The Borderline Syndromes* [New York: McGraw-Hill, 1980], p. 373).

Lang might, incidentally, be said to lack sufficient self-criticalness about his own perspective, since his objectification of tendencies of his own consciousness in the form of reified, externalized "strata" indicates a failure to be self-conscious about the effects of his own self-consciousness. In this sense, too, his position is reminiscent of that which Wittgenstein criticizes in William James. It should be noted, however, that Wittgenstein's critique concentrates on the reifications inherent in explicitly held "metaphysical" beliefs; whereas my primary concern is with the reifications inherent in a certain kind of lived-world. In some cases, like that of Jonathan Lang, such a mode of experience may also be explicitly articulated as a psychological or philosophical description. (In more than a few cases, in fact, a patient's "delusions" can be read as just such a description.) But in other instances, the mode of experience remains, in some sense, on a more prereflective level.

76. H. F. Searles, *Collected Papers on Schizophrenia and Related Subjects* (New York: International Universities Press, 1965), p. 476.

77. It may be of significance that schizophrenia generally does not have its onset before adolescence, the stage of "formal operations" when the capacity to think about thinking is acquired. If the schizophrenic can be called "egocentric," then surely it is the "higher" egocentricity of the adolescent, which involves an overvaluation of thought. See B. Inhelder and J. Piaget, *The Growth of Logical Thinking from Childhood to Adolescence* (New York: Basic Books, 1958), chap. 18.

78. Cutting quotes a similar statement by an acute schizophrenic: "My thoughts appear above my head in a bubble" (*Psychology of Schizophrenia*, p. 181).

79. See, for example, T. H. Ogden's discussion of the Kleinian vision of early forms of experience; in *Matrix of the Mind* (Northvale, NJ: Aronson, 1986), pp. 27, 31, 45. See also the works of Jean Piaget and Heinz Werner. Some recent developmental research suggests that some aspects of the sense of self may begin earlier than has previously been assumed. Daniel Stern argues, for example, that at about nine months, infants begin to sense that they have an interior subjective life of their own (*The Interpersonal World of the Infant* [New York: Basic Books, 1985], p. 9). But nothing in this work suggests that infants experience anything akin to the objectification of their own thought and action that these schizophrenic describe.

80. J. Cutting, *Right Cerebral Hemisphere*, p. 265.

81. T. Hennell, *The Witnesses* (New Hyde Park, NY: University Books, 1967), pp. 123–24.

82. Patient quoted in Chapman, "Early symptoms," p. 239.
83. A. McGhie and J. Chapman, "Disorders of attention and perception in early schizophrenia," *British Journal of Medical Psychology*, 34, 1961, 107–8 (patient #18). In the vocabulary of Martin Heidegger, the experiences quoted in the text could be described as involving a replacement of a "ready-to-hand" by a "present-at-hand" mode of experiencing components of action.

Perhaps such descriptions can help us understand why such patients sometimes find it easier to describe their experiences if they use the third, rather than the first, person. "It would be easier if we talked of a notional third person," said one. "I could more easily understand if we described this illness on a third person. Then I could understand it. I can't understand it if it is applied to myself" (Chapman, "Early symptoms," p. 228).

The two sides of these modes of awareness, the feeling of *needing* to contemplate oneself yet also of being disrupted *by* this contemplation, are suggested in the following statements from two other schizophrenics quoted by McGhie and Chapman: "If you move fast without thinking, co-ordination becomes difficult and everything becomes mechanical. I prefer to think out movements first before I do anything, then I get up slowly and do it," says one patient. But another says: "A man can walk down the street and not bother. If he stops to think about it he might look at his legs and just wonder where he is going to get the energy to move his legs. His legs will start to wobble. How does he know that his legs are going to move when he wants them to" ("Disorders of attention and perception," p. 108 [patients #12 and #17, respectively]).
84. S. Arieti, "Volition and value: A study based on catatonic schizophrenia," *On Schizophrenia, Phobias, Depression, Psychotherapy and the Farther Shores of Psychiatry* (New York: Brunner/Mazel, 1978), p. 115.
85. "At an earlier stage, sexual sensations were produced in her through manipulation of the genitalia of the machine; but now the machine no longer possesses any genitalia, though why or how they disappeared she cannot tell. Ever since the machine lost its genitalia, the patient has ceased to experience sexual sensations" (Tausk, "The 'influencing machine,' " p. 530). Oddly enough, however, both Freud and Tausk claimed—with precious little evidence—that influencing machine symbols "always [stand] for the dreamer's own genitals" (ibid., pp. 528, 534, 554–55).

In the view of some psychoanalysts, the flattened emotionality of the schizophrenic is to be explained as an indirect consequence of the id-dominated nature of the illness, since it supposedly involves an emotional shutting down in response to fear of overwhelming, primitive emotion; see, for example, McGlashan, "Intensive individual psychotherapy of schizophrenia, "*Archives of General Psychiatry*, 40, 1983, 914; Tausk, "The 'influencing machine,' " pp. 549–50. One might also consider Otto Fenichel's rather convoluted interpretation of bodily depersonalization or estrangement in schizophrenia: in accordance with a standard psychoanalytic model, Fenichel assumes that there must be an *increase* in the "libido tonus of the body," but that this is entirely suppressed—at least in conscious awareness—by means of "a special type of defense," namely, a countercathexis *against* this increase of erotic investment in one's own body (*The Psychoanalytic Theory of Neurosis* [New York: Norton, 1945], pp. 418–19). The evidence for these contentions is ambiguous to say the least. However, even if the essentially defensive origins of such depersonalization or self-estrangement *could* be established, this would hardly detract from the importance of studying these phenomena—for the latter seem, in any case, to have taken on an independent life of their own and to have given their stamp to the experience and the expression of the illness.

86. Laing, *Divided Self*, p. 109.
87. Ibid., p. 151.
88. Paul de Man quoted in F. Lentricchia, *After the New Criticism* (Chicago: University of Chicago Press, 1980), p. 179.
89. Similar processes of self-undermining scrutiny are described by Franz Kafka, who often portrays processes normally in a state of flux—such as breathing or sensations of pleasure, sound, or light—as arrested and rendered as tangible objects. A passage omitted from the published version of *The Castle* gives some hint of the fear that motivates this exigent introspection: one must have the strength, says Kafka, "to keep on staring at things without closing one's eyes . . . but if one relaxes for a single moment and closes one's eyes, then everything promptly dissolves into darkness" (quoted in M. Walser, "Kafka's novels," in J. P. Stern, ed., *The World of Franz Kafka* [New York: Holt, Rinehart, and Winston, 1980], pp. 97–98). But in a different passage, from a letter, Kafka describes the self-defeating consequences: "Since there was nothing at all I was certain of, since I needed to be provided at every instant with a new confirmation of my existence . . . naturally even the thing nearest at hand, my own body, became insecure" (quoted in A. Heidsieck, "Kafka's narrative ontology," *Philosophy and Literature, 11*, 1987, 250).
90. Quotations from S. Lotringer, "Libido unbound: The politics of 'schizophrenia,' " in "Anti-Oedipus" issue, *Semiotexte, 2*, 1977, 8–10; M. Esslin, *Antonin Artaud* (Harmondsworth, UK: Penguin Books, 1976), pp. 122–27; Bersani, *Future for Astyanax*, p. 236.
91. All quotations from Artaud in this section that are not otherwise noted are in S. Sontag, ed., *Antonin Artaud: Selected Writings* (New York: Farrar, Straus, and Giroux, 1976), pp. 72, 65, 294, 195, 82, 61, 82, 103, 59, 65, 81, 383, 382–83 (emphasis added).
92. Quoted in Esslin, *Artaud*, p. 37.
93. A. Artaud, *The Theatre and Its Double*, trans. M. C. Richards (New York: Grove Press, 1958), p. 9.
94. Ibid., pp. 11, 8.
95. Deanimation, fragmentation, and other bizarre or uncanny alterations of the body-ego are often apparent in schizophrenic responses to the Rorschach inkblot test; see A. Sugarman and L. S. Jaffe, "Body representation in paranoid and undifferentiated schizophrenics," in H. D. Lerner and P. M. Lerner, eds., *Primitive Mental States and the Rorschach* (New York: International Universities Press, 1988), p. 231.

Something akin to this experience seems to be captured in certain portraits by Francis Bacon, portraits that have been interpreted as depicting "the disintegration of the social being which takes place when one is alone in a room which has no looking-glass . . . [when] the accepted hierarchy of our features is collapsing, and . . . we are by turns all teeth, all eye, all ear, all nose . . . suddenly adrift, fragmented, and subject to strange mutation" (J. Russell, *Francis Bacon* [New York and Toronto: Oxford University Press, 1979], p. 38).

96. Patient quoted in E. Strömgren, "Autism," *European Journal of Psychiatry*, 1, 1987, 49.

97. Hennell, *The Witnesses*, p. 210.

Chapter 8: Memoirs of a Nervous Illness

1. D. P. Schreber, *Memoirs of My Nervous Illness*, trans. I. Macalpine and R. A. Hunter (Cambridge: Harvard University Press, 1988; originally published in 1903).

2. See Freud (1911), "Psychoanalytic notes upon an autobiographical account of a case of paranoia (dementia paranoides)," in *Three Case Histories*, ed. P. Rieff (New York: Collier Books, 1963), p. 180 (re "restoration of infantile autoeroticism"); see also J. Frosch, *The Psychotic Process* (New York: International Universities Press, 1983), pp. 166–67.

3. K. Jaspers, *General Psychopathology* (Chicago: University of Chicago Press, 1963), pp. 124, 141; also pp. 57, 61, 74, 106. There are also numerous references to Schreber in E. Bleuler, *Dementia Praecox, or the Group of Schizophrenias* (New York: International Universities Press, 1950).

4. See discussion of Schreber in E. Canetti, *Crowds and Power* (New York: Continuum, 1962), p. 435.

5. "The exciting cause of his illness . . . was an outburst of homosexual libido . . . and his struggles against this libidinal impulse produced the conflict which gave rise to the pathological phenomena" (Freud, "Psychoanalytic notes," p. 142).

6. Freud himself recognized this fact; see I. Macalpine and R. A. Hunter, "Translators' analysis of the case," in Schreber, *Memoirs of My Nervous Illness*, p. 374.

7. Quotations from R. B. White, "The mother-conflict in Schreber's psychosis," *International Journal of Psychoanalysis*, 42, 1961, 66; H. F. Searles, "Sexual processes in schizophrenia," in *Collected Papers on Schizophrenia and Related Subjects* (New York: International Universities Press, 1965), 431; I. Hermann, "Some aspects of psychotic regression: A Schreber study," *International Review of Psychoanalysis*, 7, 1980, 9; J. Frosch, *The Psychotic Process*, pp. 166–67.

   To Julian Jaynes, Schreber is an example of the archaic, "bicameral mind," which lacks the capacities for self-reflection and deliberation among various courses of action; see *The Origin of Consciousness in the Breakdown of the Bicameral Mind* (Boston: Houghton Mifflin, 1976), pp. 414–16.

   Actually, Freud did acknowledge the existence of a deeper regression in Schreber, a "travel[ing] back not merely to the stage of narcissism . . . but to a complete abandonment of object-love and to a restoration of infantile autoerotism," but he placed relatively little emphasis on this aspect of the case ("Psychoanalytic notes," p. 180).

8. For such a claim, see Hermann, "Some aspects of psychotic regression," p. 1.

9. See, for example, J. M. Glass, *Delusion: Internal Dimensions of Political Life* (Chicago and London: University of Chicago Press, 1985), pp. xvi, xix–xxi, 11.

10. M. Foucault, *Madness and Civilization*, trans. R. Howard (New York and

Toronto: New American Library, 1965), p. 223; Foucault quoted in J. Derrida, *Writing and Difference* (Chicago: University of Chicago Press, 1978), p. 37.

11. See M. J. Harris and D. V. Jeste, "Late-onset schizophrenia: An overview," *Schizophrenia Bulletin, 14,* 1988, 39–56. The length of Schreber's illness and bizarre nature of his delusions clearly indicate that the schizophrenia diagnosis is appropriate (see J. Cutting, *The Psychology of Schizophrenia* [Edinburgh: Churchill Livingstone, 1985], p. 356).

12. See "Introduction" to D. B. Allison, P. de Oliveira, M. S. Roberts, and A. S. Weiss, eds., *Psychosis and Sexual Identity: Toward a Post-Analytic View of the Schreber Case* (Albany: State University of New York Press, 1988), p. 2.

13. Thus, God's rays are sometimes referred to as "nerves"; and the phrase "union of all rays" refers to a union of nerves with rays.

14. Foucault quoted in P. Rabinow, ed., *The Foucault Reader* (New York: Pantheon Books, 1984), pp. 372, 8.

15. Foucault, *Discipline and Punish*, trans. A. Sheridan (New York: Vintage Books, 1979), p. 202.

16. Ibid., p. 294.

17. Ibid., p. 227.

18. Schreber's modes of subjectivity can in fact be shown to correspond to (and, no doubt, to derive from, at least in part) the upbringing to which he was subjected as a child by his pedagogue-father, an upbringing that closely resembles many of the disciplinary practices described in *Discipline and Punish*. See L. Sass, "Schreber's panopticism: Psychosis and the modern soul" (*Social Research, 54,* 1987, 112–119) for a summary of this aspect. Zvi Lothane has also described the pathogenic effects of what I would call the panoptical elements of the mental hospital in which he was incarcerated; see *In Defense of Schreber: Soul Murder and Psychiatry* (Hillsdale, NJ: Analytic Press, 1992). My focus in this chapter is exclusively on phenomenological structure, however, and I ignore questions about the genesis of Schreber's mode of consciousness. In any case, the prevalence of similar forms of subjectivity in many other schizophrenics, as well as in modernist culture (see, e.g., Valéry's Monsieur Teste, described toward the end of this chapter), shows that it is hardly necessary to experience so extreme a panoptical regimen as Schreber did in order for these kinds of symptoms to develop. See epilogue for further discussion of related issues.

19. L. S. Vygotsky, *Thought and Language,* 2nd ed., trans. E. Hanfmann and G. Vakar (Cambridge: MIT Press, 1962).

20. The rather metaphysical question, raised by structuralism and poststructuralism, of whether this sense of control is actually illusory, is not my concern here.

21. This is what Vygotsky must have meant when he wrote, "Inner speech is speech almost without words" (*Thought and Language,* p. 145)—a statement clearly intended to refer to the normal phenomenology of thinking, and not to imply that thought is in actual fact independent of language, which Vygotsky of all people obviously did not believe.

22. The phrases are taken from M. Heidegger's *History of the Concept of Time* ([Bloomington: Indiana University Press, 1985], p. 191), where one finds a useful description of the lack of objectification in normal engaged experience.

23. Freud described the tendency of schizophrenics to attend to what he called the "word-presentation" (the signifier) rather than the "thing-presentation" (the

signified) ("The unconscious," *General Psychological Theory*, ed. P. Rieff [New York: Collier Books, 1963; originally published 1915], pp. 116–50).

24. See V. Rosen, "Some aspects of Freud's theory of schizophrenic language disturbance," *Psychoanalysis and Contemporary Science*, 4, 1975, 414; V. Tausk (1919), "On the Origin of the 'Influencing Machine' in Schizophrenia," *Psychoanalytic Quarterly*, 2, 1933, 519–56. See also H. Werner and B. Kaplan, *Symbol Formation* (New York: Wiley, 1963).

25. Language as experienced by Schreber could also be compared to the "ghostly objectivity" described in Lukács's discussions of "reification." Schreber's "nerves" and "rays" seem an especially clear example of how "a man's own activity, his own labour becomes something objective and independent of him, something that controls him by virtue of an autonomy alien to man" (G. Lukacs, *History and Class Consciousness*, trans. R. Livingstone [Cambridge: MIT Press, 1985], pp. 100, 86, 87).

In *The Birth of the Clinic: An Archaeology of Medical Perception* (New York: Vintage Books, 1975), Foucault offers a closely parallel argument about the reifying, spatializing, and mortifying nature of an interior scrutiny. There, however, he is concerned with the interior of the body rather than the soul. He points out that modern medical knowledge, which derives from dissection of the dead, from a tireless illumination of every hidden corner of the body's interior, somehow transforms our lived experience: "It is when death became the concrete *a priori* of medical experience that death could detach itself from counter-nature and become *embodied* in the *living bodies* of individuals" (p. 196).

26. Notice, however, that Schreber only says that nerve-attraction is "*something like* a psychological motive power"; he refrains from the sort of explicit interpretive statement that one would expect if he experienced his own nerve-ray cosmos as merely allegorical, as but a symbolic vehicle referring to a more psychological plane of being. How, we might ask, can we account for the paradoxical fact that a person of such relentless self-consciousness should be so apparently blind to the nature and meaning of his own symbols—to the fact that these nerves and rays *are* symbols, and symbols that refer to his own mind? One way of understanding this is to see it as a consequence of the reifying process itself. When Schreber scrutinizes in his panoptical way, the phantoms of his inner cosmos become substantialized and opaque. And since, in his case, it is the parts of a mind that are turned into things, it is understandable that the phenomena that are reified become nearly unrecognizable for what they are. See R. D. Laing, *The Divided Self* (Harmondsworth, UK: Penguin Books, 1965), p. 158, re the quality of "phantom concreteness" often characteristic of schizophrenic consciousness.

Schreber's phantom concreteness should not, incidentally, be confused with literalism. He does not present his hallucinations and delusions as simple facts, but rather as images seen "in the mind's eye." To pursue this point in detail would take us far afield, into a critique of the standard psychiatric notion of "poor reality testing," a question I return to in chapter 9. Also, see my forthcoming book on Wittgenstein and the Schreber case (Ithaca, NY: Cornell University Press, 1993).

27. Sartre's critics have faulted him for polarizing subject from object and also for overemphasizing consciousness's awareness of its own nature. These, in essence, are the errors of Cartesianism—a philosophy that has been criticized (e.g., by

Heidegger) for allowing the fundamental categories of existence to be determined from the standpoint of detached contemplation (a kind of exigent introspection?) rather than from that of practical, engaged activity.

28. P. Valéry, *Monsieur Teste*, trans. J. Mathews (Princeton, NJ: Princeton University Press, 1973), pp. 148–49. The quotations from (and occasional paraphrases of) Valéry that follow in the next paragraphs of this section can be found in this same volume; see pp. 30, 119, 110, 3, 133, 118, 85, 120, 67, 149, 40, 110, 26.

29. Modernism can be viewed as, in large part, a reflection of the larger social forces of modernity; but, of course, in some respects it also involves a *rejection* of modernity (see epilogue, pages 372–73 for further discussion). If we were to accept that modernity is essentially a panoptical regime, then the withdrawal inward of a figure like Monsieur Teste could be seen as an attempt to escape from the power relations of an oppressive social order. But we would also have to acknowledge that his inner world is structurally analogous to the external panopticism he is fleeing. For brief discussion of some closely related issues, see Jameson, *Fables of Aggression* (Berkeley: University of California Press, 1979), pp. 13–14, 134; and *The Political Unconscious* (Ithaca, NY: Cornell University Press, 1981), p. 63.

30. Hermann, for example, dismisses Schreber's bellowing as a regression symptom, "the behaviour of an infant calling his mother" ("Some aspects of psychotic regression," p. 2).

31. Schreber complains that "rays did not seem to appreciate at all that a human being who actually exists *must be somewhere*. Because of the irresistible attraction of my nerves I had become an embarrassing human being for the rays (for God), in whatever position or circumstance I might be or whatever occupation I undertook" (*Memoirs of My Nervous Illness*, p. 139).

32. Valéry imagines the wife of Monsieur Teste expressing a similar willingness to collapse the competition or hierarchy of witnesses and merge her being into her husband's. And this seems to be the ultimate acquiescence to a solipsist's fantasy, for it grants her husband's consciousness a nearly divine status: "I know at every moment that I exist within a consciousness always vaster and more general than all my vigilance," says Madame Teste in Valéry's "A Letter from Madame Emilie Teste." "I may say that my life seems to me at every moment a living model of man's existence within the divine mind. I have the personal experience of being within the sphere of a being, just as all souls are in Being." Madame Teste compares herself to "a fly, flitting through its meager life in the universe of an unflinching eye . . .": "In short, I feel that I am in his hands and among his thoughts, like an object . . . I feel as if . . . a superior mind holds me captive—*by its very existence*" (*Monsieur Teste*, pp. 28–29).

33. S. Freud, "On the mechanism of paranoia," in *General Psychological Theory* (New York: Collier Books, 1963; originally published in 1911), p. 48.

34. Foucault, *Discipline and Punish*, p. 30.

35. Phrases from J. Jaynes, *Origin of Consciousness*, p. 427; T. Freeman, *Psychopathology of the Psychoses* (New York: International Universities Press, 1969), p. 163.

36. See J. H. Matthews, *Surrealism, Insanity, and Poetry* (Syracuse, NY: Syracuse University Press, 1982), pp. 4–5.

37. This is precisely the treatment for diminishing auditory hallucinations that is

recommended in P. Green and M. Preston, "Reinforcement of vocal correlates of auditory hallucinations by auditory feedback," *British Journal of Psychiatry*, 139, 1981, 204–8.

38. Renee makes a similar point in her autobiographical account: "Outwardly, however, no one suspected the inquietude or the fear. People thought I was hysterical or manic. Actually, I was indeed always agitated, cutting capers, laughing at the top of my voice, playing the fool. Yet these symptoms were not those of an excited girl, unable to control herself, but an attempt to master the fear, which, when it came over me, made me agitated, anxious, awaiting imminent misfortune. . . . Then I tried to flee the fear in excitement. I shouted and laughed, as an escape from the fear and a defense against it" (quoted in M. Sechehaye, ed., *Autobiography of a Schizophrenic Girl* [New York: New American Library, 1970], p. 26).

Chapter 9: The Morbid Dreamer

1. Quotations from H. Werner, *Comparative Psychology of Mental Development*, rev. ed. (New York: International Universities Press, 1957), p. 418; C. Landis, ed., *Varieties of Psychopathological Experience* (New York: Holt, Rinehart and Winston, 1964), pp. 53–54; P. J. Ruocchio, "First person account: The schizophrenic inside," *Schizophrenia Bulletin*, 17, 1991, 359.
   Another portion of the second patient's statement is remarkably reminiscent of Nietzsche's famous and cryptic doctrine of the eternal return: "Hasn't that which I am presently experiencing been present for countless times and doesn't it strive to again take part in a remembrance?" asked the patient. "Isn't that which one calls *history* a process of constantly returning—I don't want to say the same but similar things" (pp. 53–54).
2. M. Heidegger, "The age of the world picture," *The Question Concerning Technology and Other Essays*, trans. W. Lovitt (New York: Harper and Row, 1977), p. 142.
3. American Psychiatric Association, *Diagnostic and Statistical Manual of Mental Disorders*, 3rd ed., rev. (DSM III-R) (Washington, DC: American Psychiatric Press, 1987), pp. 404, 395, 398.
4. According to the prominent psychoanalyst Otto Kernberg, "Loss of reality testing in any one area indicates psychotic functioning . . . there is no continuum, no gradual shift from presence to absence of reality testing," and thus "there are qualitative as well as quantitative differences between the structural organization of borderline and psychotic conditions" (*Borderline Conditions and Pathological Narcissism* [New York: Jason Aronson, 1975], p. 182). See also writings by J. Frosch on the psychotic character, for example, "The psychotic character," *Psychiatric Quarterly*, 38, 1964, 81–96.
5. See G. E. Berrios, "Delusions as 'wrong beliefs': A conceptual history," *British Journal of Psychiatry*, 159 (suppl. 14), 1991, 6.
6. Quoted in A. C. Smith, *Schizophrenia and Madness* (London: Allen and Unwin, 1982), p. 84. Sources for these assumptions can be found in the ancient world (see G. Rosen, *Madness in Society* [New York and Evanston: Harper and Row, 1968], pp. 71–136), but it was during the Enlightenment that they received a decisive

formulation. Perhaps the classic definition is John Locke's description, in *An Essay Concerning Human Understanding* (1690), of madmen as those who, "having joined together some ideas very wrongly . . . mistake them for truths." "[H]aving taken their fancies for realities," supposedly, such people "make right deductions from them. Thus you shall find a distracted man fancying himself a king, with a right inference require suitable attendance, respect, and obedience; others who have thought themselves made of glass, have used the caution necessary to preserve such brittle bodies" (*The Works of John Locke*, vol. 1 [London: Henry G. Bohn, 1854], book 2, chap. 11, sec. 13, p. 276).

7. DSM III (1980), p. 188. In DSM III-R (1987), the definition of "bizarre delusions" was altered somewhat, in an effort to demonstrate greater cultural sensitivity and also to employ a more operationalizable criterion: "i.e., involving a phenomenon that the person's culture would regard as totally implausible, e.g., thought broadcasting, being controlled by a dead person" (p. 194). The DSM III version more accurately captures the impression a person judging from within his or her culture is likely to have; also, it is closer to the way "bizarreness" has traditionally been conceptualized in psychiatry. Incidentally, "impossible content" is also one of Jaspers's criteria of true delusions, the kind found in schizophrenia; see K. Jaspers, *General Psychopathology*, trans. J. Hoenig and M. W. Hamilton (Chicago: University of Chicago Press, 1963), p. 96. A. S. David gives further examples: a patient who maintained he was Shakespeare even though he knew the Bard had died in 1616 and that it was now the twentieth century; being in two places at once; having a nuclear power station inside one's body ("Insight and psychosis," *British Journal of Psychiatry*, 156, 1990, 804).

8. E. Bleuler, *Dementia Praecox, or the Group of Schizophrenias*, trans. J. Zinkin (New York: International Universities Press, 1950), p. 123.

9. K. Jaspers, *General Psychopathology*, p. 116.

10. Werner, *Comparative Psychology*, p. 464; C. Landis, ed., *Varieties of Psychopathological Experience* (New York: Holt, Rinehart, and Winston, 1964), p. 195.

11. M. Coate, *Beyond All Reason* (Philadelphia and New York: Lippincott, 1965), p. 74; E. Bleuler, *Dementia Praecox*, pp. 76, 125. See also Jaspers, *General Psychopathology*, p. 296.

12. Incidentally, most instances of Schneiderian First Rank Symptoms, discussed in chapter 7, are examples of "bizarre" delusions involving what would be considered both poor reality testing and the loss of ego boundaries.

13. Landis, *Psychopathological Experience*, pp. 180–81, 156.

14. E. Bleuler, *Dementia Praecox*, pp. 111–12.

15. My treatment of world-catastrophe fantasies as a relatively late-stage symptom contradicts a common view in psychoanalysis. See chapter 10, note 46, and this chapter, note 21.

16. D. P. Schreber, *Memoirs of My Nervous Illness*, trans. I. Macalpine and R. A. Hunter (Cambridge and London: Harvard University Press, 1988; originally published in German in 1903), pp. 103–7, 114, 115, and passim; J. Cutting, *Psychology of Schizophrenia* (Edinburgh: Churchill Livingstone, 1985), p. 292; Coate, *Beyond All Reason*, p. 56.

17. E. Minkowski, *La Schizophrénie* (Paris: Payot, 1927), p. 130.

18. T. Freeman, *Psychopathology of the Psychoses* (New York: International Universities Press, 1969), p. 49. Delusions re the end of the world seem to be

especially characteristic of schizophrenia, but they can occur in other conditions as well; see M. Hamilton, ed., *Fish's Schizophrenia*, 2nd ed. (Bristol: John Wright, 1976), p. 46.

19. S. J. Blatt and C. M. Wild, *Schizophrenia: A Developmental Analysis* (New York: Academic Press, 1976), pp. 149–50

20. Marguerite Sechehaye assumes that schizophrenics manifest the same kind of "adualism" as was described by the developmental psychologists Baldwin and Piaget: "This adualism of the regressed schizophrenic leads him to confuse interior and exterior exactly as do the dreamer and the small child" (*A New Psychotherapy in Schizophrenia*, trans. G. Rubin-Rabson [New York and London: Grune and Stratton, 1956], p. 134). In his relatively recent study, *Autonomy and Rigid Character*, even David Shapiro, one of the most open-minded and phenomenologically sensitive of psychoanalysts, simply takes this for granted, as if the issue were beyond dispute: "It is well known that the condition of schizophrenia harks back to the early lack of polarity between subject and object" ([New York: Basic Books, 1981], p. 172).

21. Jacob Arlow and Charles Brenner emphasize the projection of primitive aggression; Edith Jacobson stresses a regressive fusion of self- and object representations (see P.-N. Pao, *Schizophrenic Disorders* [New York: International Universities Press, 1979], pp. 190, 73). In his discussion of the Schreber case, Freud explains the world-catastrophe experience as the result of a "de-cathexis" of the external world that occurs when one's erotic orientation turns back toward its original object, one's own body and self; see "Psychoanalytic notes upon an autobiographical account of a case of paranoia (dementia paranoides)," *Three Case Histories* (New York: Collier Books, 1963; originally published in 1911), p. 173. According to Freud's model, this event should precede the development of hallucinations and delusions, symptoms whose primary function is the restitutive one of reengaging the psyche with objects other than itself (albeit unrealistic ones). Actually, the world catastrophe often occurs not at the outset but somewhat later in the progression of a schizophrenic illness (as is the case with Schreber, in fact). Re this issue, see chapter 10, note 46.

22. The psychoanalytic image of schizophrenic consciousness is thus captured by William James's description of the mind of the "primitive savage" and the child as "a jungle in which hallucinations, dreams, superstitions, conceptions, and sensible objects all flourish alongside of each other, unregulated except by the attention turning in this way or in that" (*The Principles of Psychology*, vol. 2 [New York: Holt, 1890], p. 299).

23. S. Langer, *Mind: An Essay on Human Feeling*, vol. 3 (Baltimore and London: Johns Hopkins University Press, 1982), p. 30. For a milder statement of a related view, see J. Flavell, "The development of children's knowledge about the appearance-reality distinction," *American Psychologist*, 41, 1986, 418–25.

Thus, according to one recent article, "there can be no phenomenological definition of delusion as, subjectively, it is an idea or product of thought which is held in the same way as any other, non-delusional, belief or idea" (A. Sims, "Delusional syndromes in ICD-10," *British Journal of Psychiatry*, 159[suppl. 4], 1991, 47). For a caustic summary of the traditional view of delusions as mistaken beliefs, susceptible to reality testing, see Berrios, "Delusions as 'wrong beliefs.'"

24. G. Santayana, *Skepticism and Animal Faith* (New York: Dover, 1955; originally published in 1923), p. 107.

25. These assumptions are clearly not independent of each other: the very awareness of fantasy as such would, for example, seem to imply a degree or kind of reflexive awareness, for it implies recognition of the occurrence of an inner or merely subjective event; therefore, given the master assumption of diminished self-awareness in schizophrenia, it is hardly likely that the purported confusion would be assumed to involve a reduction of reality to fantasy rather than the reverse.

26. T. Freeman, J. Cameron, and A. McGhie, *Chronic Schizophrenia* (New York: International Universities Press, 1958), pp. 95, 84; and Freeman, *Psychopathology of Psychoses*, p. 163. See also Freeman (p. 137) re "loss of the ability to reflect on what has just been experienced" as perhaps the most significant feature of the schizophrenic state of consciousness. In his view, this is a quality schizophrenics share with organic patients, but not with manic-depressives (pp. 137, 166).

27. M. Sechehaye, "The interpretation," *Autobiography of a Schizophrenic Girl*, trans. G. Rubin-Rabson (New York: New American Library, 1970), p. 96.

28. Jaspers, *General Psychopathology*, p. 106. Re this peculiar quality of incorrigibility in schizophrenic delusion, Jaspers says: "So far, however, we have not succeeded in defining what this is. . . . We simply give a name to something which we can neither see nor comprehend. And yet it is precisely this problem which gives us no peace" (p. 411). Re Jaspers on delusions, see C. Walker, "Delusion: What did Jaspers really say?" *British Journal of Psychiatry*, 159(suppl. 4), 1991, 94–103.

29. E. Bleuler, *Dementia Praecox*, p. 129–30. See also Jaspers, *General Psychopathology*, p. 105.

30. E. Bleuler, *Dementia Praecox*, p. 195.

31. Ibid., p. 147.

32. Sechehaye, *Autobiography of a Schizophrenic Girl*, p. 27. As the psychiatrist John Strauss remarks, "even when delusions are at their worst, there is often part of the person that does not believe them" ("The person with delusions," *British Journal of Psychiatry*, 159[suppl. 14], 1991, 59).

33. See E. Bleuler, *Dementia Praecox*, p. 127.

34. Re the difference between delusions and "overvalued ideas" (the latter common in the querulous paranoid state)—both in the quality of the patient's conviction and in the likelihood of its being acted upon, see P. J. McKenna, "Disorders with overvalued ideas," *British Journal of Psychiatry*, 145, 1984, 579.

35. E. Bleuler, *Dementia Praecox*, pp. 128–29. Bleuler notes that in the usual hallucinatory conditions (in schizophrenia), patients either continue to act in accordance with consensual reality or else do not act at all (p. 66). Bleuler also remarks on the "striking . . . indifference of patients toward their own delusional ideas and strivings," giving the following example: "In peculiar tones, a patient complains that his children are being killed: his affect is not adequate, on the one hand, because something within him knows that this is only a fantasy and, on the other hand, because a wish, not a fear . . . is at the root of his delusion" (p. 369).

36. Sechehaye, *Autobiography of a Schizophrenic Girl*, p. 42.

37. See R. L. Jenkins, "The schizophrenic sequence: Withdrawal, disorganization, psychotic reorganization," *American Journal of Orthopsychiatry*, 22, 1952, 743; I. Al-Issa, "Social and cultural aspects of hallucinations," *Psychological Bulletin*, 84, 1977, 582. Al-Issa notes that auditory hallucinations are closer to a concept

end whereas visual hallucinations are closer to a percept end of a concept/percept continuum. Auditory hallucinations are far more common than visual ones in schizophrenic patients, at least in Western cultures.

38. E. Bleuler, *Dementia Praecox,* pp. 111, 113, 103. M. Alpert and K. N. Silvers (and others) have found that the auditory hallucinations of schizophrenics had "a cognitive taint"—they lack a quality of sensory concreteness and appear like thoughts that have become audible; see "Perceptual characteristics distinguishing auditory hallucinations in schizophrenia and acute alcoholic psychoses," *American Journal of Psychiatry, 127,* 1970, 301. Jaspers notes that most hallucinations should really be conceptualized as pseudo-hallucinations (phenomena that "lack concrete reality and appear in inner subjective space"); see *General Psychopathology,* pp. 68–71. See also M. Spitzer, "Ichstörungen: In search of a theory," in M. Spitzer, F. A. Uehlein, and G. Oepen, eds., *Psychopathology and Philosophy* (Berlin and Heidelberg: Springer-Verlag, 1988), pp. 167–83, esp. p. 179n. H. Werner also acknowledges "a specific sign, a sign not found in other [what he calls] primitive types, which is characteristic of schizophrenic reality, and that is its insubstantiality"; in the onset of schizophrenia, he writes, "the invasion of the subjective forms of activity into the objective world is felt not as an enrichment of the personal life, as with normal primitive types, but as an impoverishment" (*Comparative Psychology,* p. 418).

39. Coate, *Beyond All Reason,* p. 32.

40. See W. Woods, "Language study in schizophrenia," *Journal of Nervous and Mental Disease, 87,* 1938, 304–7, 312.

41. E. Bleuler, *Dementia Praecox,* p. 128. See also the quotation from the schizophrenic patient Marie B., quoted in J.-P. Sartre, *The Psychology of Imagination,* trans. B. Frechtman (New York: Washington Square Press, 1966): "I said that I was the queen of Spain. At heart I knew well that this was untrue. . . . I lived in an imaginary world" (p. 191). Pierre Janet, with his emphasis on the ludic faculties, questioned the sincerity of many severe psychotics: "Most frequently psychotics are acting. Don't believe one fourth of what they say. They try to impress you with their grandeur or their guilt, in which they themselves believe only half-heartedly or not at all" (*L'Évolution Psychologique de la Personnalité* [Paris: Chahine, 1929], p. 328; quoted in H. F. Ellenberger, *The Discovery of the Unconscious* [New York: Basic Books, 1970], p. 351).

42. Landis, *Psychopathological Experience,* p. 354; R. D. Laing, *The Divided Self* (Harmondsworth, UK: Penguin Books, 1965), p. 86. Since Laing's patient felt guilty for having this experience of his wife, we might speculate that he did retain some skeptical distance from this delusion of the hallucinatory nature of the world.

43. Landis, *Psychopathological Experience,* p. 90. John Cutting describes a patient who seems to have believed only in what was visible to him. Thus he complained that he had "no inside of the body, but only a frame." When he eats food, it "immediately disappears. . . . The food does not reach the stomach at all but when it passes the throat it disappears" (*The Right Cerebral Hemisphere and Psychiatric Disorders* [Oxford: Oxford University Press, 1990], p. 270).

44. See Schreber, *Memoirs of My Nervous Illness,* pp. 186–87, 232–33.

45. James, *Principles of Psychology,* vol. 2, pp. 319, 287–88.

46. Schreber, *Memoirs of My Nervous Illness,* p. 232; see also pp. 32, 197.

This, incidentally, can lead to a curious feature of schizophrenic solipsism discussed in the next two chapters—the disconcerting feeling that the All one experiences is, paradoxically enough, limited or fragile in some way, and thus that it does not constitute a true plenitude of being, or a realm of absolute security and bliss.

47. Re tribal man, see Langer, *Mind: An Essay*, pp. 21, 25, 30, 69.

48. E. Husserl, *The Crisis of European Sciences and Transcendental Phenomenology*, trans. D. Carr (Evanston, IL: Northwestern University Press, 1970), pp. 137, 151, 152, 148, 137. "The world . . . has not disappeared; it is just that, during the consistently carried-out epochē, it is under our gaze purely as the correlate of the subjectivity which gives it . . . meaning, through whose validities the world 'is' at all" (p. 152). Some of the differences between this view and the approach of Heidegger are discussed in my article "Humanism, hermeneutics, and the concept of the human subject," in S. Messer, L. Sass, and R. Woolfolk, eds., *Hermeneutics and Psychological Theory* (New Brunswick, NJ: Rutgers University Press, 1988), pp. 222–71 (also in *Psychoanalysis and Contemporary Thought*, 12, 1989, 433–504).

49. See, for example, Y.-F. Tuan, *Segmented Worlds and Self: Group Life and Individual Consciousness* (Minneapolis: University of Minnesota Press, 1982), p. 107.

50. This development also marks the advent of a new objectivism. Thus it demonstrates the "necessary interplay between subjectivism and objectivism" that Heidegger sees as central to the modern age ("Age of world picture," p. 128; see also chapter 1 of this book, p. 33).

   A famous analysis of this mode of experience is Michel Foucault's discussion in *The Order of Things* ([New York: Vintage Books, 1973], pp. 3–16) of Velázquez's *Las Meninas* (which, however, is not a landscape painting). See also K. Clark, *Landscape into Art* (New York: Harper and Row, 1976).

   Heidegger writes that in archaic Greek thought, "that which is does not come into being through the fact that man first looks upon it, in the sense of a representing that has the character of subjective perception. Rather, man is the one who is looked upon by that which is . . . gathered toward presencing, by that which opens itself" ("Age of world picture," p. 131).

51. See Clement Greenberg's description of modernist painting as representing space as an "uninterrupted continuum" that shows "the unity and integrity of the visual continuum" ("On the role of nature in modernist painting," *Art and Culture: Critical Essays* [Boston: Beacon Press, 1965], p. 173).

52. For discussion, see G. Graff, *Literature Against Itself* (Chicago and London: University of Chicago Press, 1979), pp. 13–18. In postmodernism, the possibility of depicting a realistic external world is questioned or denied in a somewhat different way—by artworks that flaunt the principles of pastiche or the "simulacrum," which imply that realism is necessarily a sham, since one can never copy the real but only what is already an image or a copy; see R. Krauss, "The originality of the avant-garde: A postmodernist repetition," in B. Wallis, ed., *Art After Modernism: Rethinking Representation* (New York: New Museum of Contemporary Art/Godine, 1984), p. 27.

53. Quoted in note to line 412 of T. S. Eliot, "The Wasteland," *Selected Poems* (New York: Harcourt, Brace and World, 1934), pp. 73–74.

54. Quoted in W. Sypher, *Loss of the Self in Modern Literature and Art* (New York: Vintage Books, 1962), p. 60.

55. Valéry quoted in E. Crasnow, "Poems and fictions: Stevens, Rilke, Valéry," in M. Bradbury and J. McFarlane, eds., *Modernism: 1890–1930* (Harmondsworth, UK: Penguin Books, 1976), p. 373n.

56. J. Derrida, *Dissemination*, trans. B. Johnson (Chicago and London: University of Chicago Press, 1981), p. 324.

57. Sechehaye, *Autobiography of a Schizophrenic Girl*, p. 54.

58. Quoted in J. Glass, *Delusion: Internal Dimensions of Political Life* (Chicago and London: University of Chicago Press, 1985), p. 192. Similarly, Patricia Ruocchio describes one of her responses to what she terms her "interpersonal terror": namely, "withdrawing my consciousness back to the time when I was psychotic all the time, living in a world that existed only to me" ("First person account," p. 359).

59. Quoted in H. F. Searles, *Collected Papers on Schizophrenia and Related Subjects* (New York: International Universities Press, 1965), p. 316. Re the possibility of everything, both real and imaginary, being subsumed into the realm of the unreal, see J.-P. Sartre, *The Psychology of Imagination*, trans. B. Frechtman (New York: Washington Square Press, 1966): "If the hallucination rejoins the world of perception it does so insofar as the latter is no longer perceived but dreamed by the patient insofar as he himself has become unreal" (pp. 197–98).

60. James, *Principles of Psychology*, vol. 2, p. 286. The difficulty of describing the sense of reality has often been remarked upon. "I confess," wrote Hume, "that it is impossible perfectly to explain this feeling or manner of conception" (quoted in B. A. G. Fuller, *A History of Philosophy*, rev. ed. [New York: Henry Holt, 1945], pt. 2, p. 157).

61. See James, *Principles of Psychology*, vol. 2, p. 311.

62. See M. Alpert and K. N. Silvers, "Perceptual characteristics distinguishing auditory hallucinations in schizophrenia and acute alcoholic psychoses," *American Journal of Psychiatry*, 127, 1970, 301.

63. Sartre, *The Psychology of Imagination*, pp. 188–91.

64. See S. Arieti, *Interpretation of Schizophrenia*, 2nd ed. (New York: Basic Books, 1974), p. 574.

65. E. Kraepelin, *Dementia Praecox and Paraphrenia*, trans. R. M. Barclay and G. M. Robertson (Huntington, NY: Krieger, 1971), pp. 31–32. "As a rule also," Kraepelin writes, such patients "make no difficulties and pay no regard if any are pointed out to them, but rather hold the more to their insane ideas without further proof. 'I have innumerable proofs and not one,' said a patient" (p. 32). Kraepelin's statement about such patients not seeking explanations for their remarkable experiences is too extreme; some delusions can, in fact, be understood as providing a kind of explanation for the quality of the lived-world (e.g., the videocamera delusions discussed later in this chapter).

66. E. Bleuler, *Dementia Praecox*, pp. 82–83.

67. Thus this analysis can account, at least in part, for the fact that delusions are, as G. E. Berrios puts it, "epistemologically *manqué*": "Their so-called content," he writes, "like that of hallucinations, contains little information about the world. . . . They do have a content of sorts, but this is detached from any evidential basis" ("Delusions as 'wrong beliefs,'" p. 8).

68. The affinity with idealism was suggested in 1920 by the French psychiatrist Dr. Divry; see Minkowski, *La Schizophrénie*, pp. 128–31.

   It is difficult to know how to speak of such forms of experience, since the available vocabularies, technical as well as everyday, tend to presuppose the traditional understanding that I dispute. Because the terms are unavoidable, I will continue in this chapter to describe schizophrenic symptoms as involving "delusions," "hallucinations," and various "beliefs," but with the understanding that I do not intend these terms to imply the presence of William James's "sense of reality" or Sartre's mode of the "real" (as these psychopathological terms usually *do* imply). Rather, we shall assume that these labels allow for the subtle, yet unmistakably knowing, awareness, evident in so many schizophrenic patients, of different *kinds* of reality—such as the "double-entry bookkeeping" mode of existence, which allows an emperor to declare his sovereignty even as he matter-of-factly joins the other patients in sweeping the floors.

69. E. Bleuler, *Dementia Praecox*, pp. 123–25.

70. Werner, *Comparative Psychology*, p. 465.

71. E. Bleuler, *Dementia Praecox*, p. 54.

72. See Werner, *Comparative Psychology*, pp. 370, 464.

73. John Strauss has reported that many psychotic (including schizophrenic) patients do not seem fully convinced of their delusions but rather evince an "intermediate level of disbelief" ("Hallucinations and delusions as points on continua function," *Archives of General Psychiatry, 21*, 1969, 581–86). This is an interesting finding, but it seems mistaken to conceive the question of belief in schizophrenic patients as if it could be quantified on a single continuum. The notion of shifting between two (or more) different *modes* of experience, with (at least) two different modes of belief (which might involve experience in terms of a belief-disbelief continuum *and* experience involving suspension of belief or disbelief) can offer a better account, in my view—one that is consistent with Jaspers's observation of the certitude and imperviousness of true delusions.

74. Quoted in Cutting, *Psychology of Schizophrenia*, p. 291.

75. C. M. Wallace, *Portrait of a Schizophrenic Nurse* (London: Hammond, Hammond, 1965), p. 23; Coate, *Beyond All Reason*, p. 101; see also p. 103.

76. Patients quoted in Werner, *Comparative Psychology*, p. 464; Jaspers, *General Psychopathology*, p. 296. After all, such a patient does not, in the typical case, deny that there is still a sun overhead. As Eugen Bleuler remarks, the patient sometimes intends symbolically what "the physician [mistakenly] understands in its literal sense": "Thus a patient insisted that he could not see, that he was blind, while it was more than obvious that his eyesight was unimpaired. What he meant was that he did not experience things 'as reality' " (*Dementia Praecox*, p. 56).

77. For related discussion, see M. Merleau-Ponty, *Phenomenology of Perception*, trans. C. Smith (London: Routledge and Kegan Paul, 1962), pp. 290–91.

78. I am referring here to "lack of insight" as this diagnostic sign is conventionally defined within psychiatry, that is, as a failure to acknowledge that one's abnormal experiences are pathological in nature, the result of a mental illness, or as failure to label certain mental events as pathological (and therefore invalid). "Lack of insight" in this sense is very characteristic of schizophrenia, at least of recent-onset cases. Re these issues, see A. S. David, "Insight and psychosis,"

British Journal of Psychiatry, 156, 1990, 798–808. One can, of course, also think of insight in other ways; see last half of chapter 11.

79. Schreber, *Memoirs of My Nervous Illness*, pp. 117, 137, 227.

80. It should be noted, however, that Schreber's externalized treatment of aspects of his psyche cannot really be said to be entirely mistaken or devoid of insight. After all, many philosophers and psychologists have argued that self-consciousness is rooted in interpersonal experience, and that a correct understanding of this phenomenon reveals the presence in the human psyche of a kind of alien other; is this really so unlike the "rays" or the "God" of Schreber's *Memoirs?* A similar point could be made about his nerves and nerve-language. After all, many structuralist and poststructuralist philosophers have viewed human thought as but an epiphenomenon of language, with language in turn being seen as a process that plays itself out in the human psyche quite independently of human will. This is not *so* very different from Schreber's conception of the human soul as contained in nerves vibrating autonomously, often as a medium for sentences and sounds. All these parallels are perhaps not so surprising, given that any self-conscious mind might be expected to have—and to discover— similar structures, and to be subject to similar consequences and conditions. As Kant noted, the self in knowing itself comes to know all selves.

81. Schreber, *Memoirs of My Nervous Illness*, p. 289.

82. Jaspers would suggest that such explanations are seldom adequate: "For any true grasp of delusion, it is important to free ourselves from this prejudice that there has to be some poverty of intelligence at the root of it" (*General Psychopathology*, p. 97).

83. This is also Schreber's own view; he says, "My mind, that is to say the functioning of my intellectual powers, is as clear and healthy as any other person's; it has been unaltered since the beginning of my nervous illness. . . . I refute most decidedly that I am mentally ill if, as is usual among laymen, this word is combined with *an idea of clouded intellect*" (*Memoirs of My Nervous Illness*, pp. 285–86). We might also recall Eugen Bleuler's remark: "In no other disease is the disturbance of intelligence more inadequately designated by the terms 'dementia' and 'imbecility' than in schizophrenia" (*Dementia Praecox*, p. 71).

84. Schreber, *Memoirs of My Nervous Illness*, p. 33 and passim.

85. Merleau-Ponty, *Phenomenology of Perception*, pp. 405–6.

86. A certain amount of what is often considered evidence of concretistic thinking, primitive failure of differentiation, or inability to use symbols can easily be reinterpreted in the light of this preoccupation with the inner realm of private experience. A patient who brings his psychotherapist a canvas stool and then acts embarrassed, as if he'd brought a fecal stool, need not be assumed to have actually confused the two entities (as Hanna Segal asserts: "Some aspects of the analysis of a schizophrenic," *International Journal of Psychoanalysis, 31*, 1950, 269). It is more plausible to suppose that such a patient simply makes the mental connection (recall the acute awareness of semantic ambiguity characteristic of schizophrenia), then is less able to ignore (and takes much more seriously) what a normal person could readily dismiss from awareness as a *merely* mental association.

87. J. Baudrillard, "The precession of simulacra," in Wallis, *Art After Modernism*, p. 266.

88. In a forthcoming book (Ithaca, NY: Cornell University Press, 1993), I discuss

these and other aspects of Schreber in more detail, and from a Wittgensteinian standpoint. See also the schizophrenic Jonathan Lang's description of how persons like himself engage in "withdrawal from sensorimotor activity" and become preoccupied with "central symbolic, particularly verbal" forms of mental activity—which, by their very nature, are cut off from the realm of action or pragmatic realism (and which, we may presume, are also *felt* by the patient to be cut off in this way) ("The other side of the ideological aspects of schizophrenia," in *Psychiatry*, 3, 1940, 392, 389).

89. For a fuller discussion of these issues from a Heideggerian viewpoint, see my forthcoming article, "Heidegger, schizophrenia, and the ontological difference," *Philosophical Psychology*, 5, 1992, 109–32.

90. See F. A. Olafson, *Heidegger and the Philosophy of Mind* (New Haven and London: Yale University Press, 1987), pp. 19, 25–26, re this tendency in Husserl.

91. Ludwig Wittgenstein makes an analogous point, arguing that solipsism, subjective idealism, and other forms of metaphysical thinking stem from a confusion of empirical with transcendental issues.

92. The near-ineffability (at least in its own terms) of an ontological transformation also helps to account for another kind of misunderstanding between schizophrenics and those who treat them—this time a misunderstanding that, unlike the usual "poor-reality-testing" interpretation, results not from the patient's giving in to but from his resisting, or being indifferent to, the temptation of ontic modes of expression. This issue was already touched on in chapter 6. There I argued that some instances of so-called poverty of content of speech—a psychiatric sign defined as "speech that is adequate in amount but conveys little information because of vagueness, empty repetitions, or use of stereotyped or obscure phrases" (see DSM III-R, p. 403: "The interviewer may observe that the person has spoken at some length but has not given adequate information to answer a question") may actually be the result of attempts to give more purely ontological, and in this sense more direct, characterizations of mutations of the lived world that *are* experienced in an essentially ontological fashion. It should be evident that, because of their very nature, such mutations cannot be described by any but the most abstract or indirect phrases—phrases that, especially to the unsympathetic listener, may well seem vague, obscure, or empty, but that the speaker, in the absence of any alternative, is likely to repeat again and again in his or her (usually vain) attempt to convey the overwhelming importance of his or her theme. Rose, one of R. D. Laing's patients, for example, spoke of having no purpose, no "go," of feeling that she had "gone right down" and that she needed to get out of "it" before it was too late; she "could not hold on to herself," she said, for "it" was "slipping away" from her. She said that she "could not real-ize [people]; it is a blank feeling" (*Divided Self*, pp. 150, 152).

93. For discussion of a Cartesian lived world, see my Heideggerian analysis of Renee's *Autobiography of a Schizophrenic Girl*: L. Sass, "The truth-taking stare: A Heideggerian interpretation of a schizophrenic world," *Journal of Phenomenological Psychology*, 21, 1990, 121–49.

94. According to Wittgenstein, this kind of internal inconsistency is characteristic of solipsistic, idealistic, and sensationalist philosophies.

95. M. Bleuler, *The Schizophrenic Disorders*, trans. S. M. Clemens (New Haven: Yale University Press, 1978), p. 490.

96. Werner, *Comparative Psychology*, p. 415 (describing one of Alfred Storch's patients).

97. I make a similar argument in my article "On delusions," *Raritan, 9,* 1990, 120–41—an excerpt from my forthcoming book on Wittgenstein and the Schreber case. After writing this chapter, I came across Manfred Spitzer's excellent article, "On defining delusions," *Comprehensive Psychiatry, 31,* 1990, 377–97. Spitzer suggests we should define delusions as "statements about external reality which are uttered like statements about a mental state" (p. 391). He does not, however, speculate about the quality of the (I would say, solipsistic or quasi-solipsistic) lived world that underlies and can account for this curious mode of expression. I would disagree with Spitzer's statement, "It is not the falsity, but rather the unjustified claim for intersubjective validity that makes a belief delusional" (p. 392). Often, in fact, schizophrenics do *not* claim intersubjective validity for their delusions; also, this statement by Spitzer fails to register the fact that, on some levels at least, many schizophrenics may not experience anything like a normal intersubjective world, but rather, say, a quasi-solipsistic one.

98. The interpretation I have been suggesting can account for all the distinguishing features of what Jaspers calls "true" delusion or "delusion proper"—not only for the subjective certainty, incorrigibility, and impossible content (Jaspers's three explicit criteria), but also for two other features he sees as especially common, the "peculiarly inconsequent" attitude, and the prominence of what he calls "metaphysical delusions"; see Jaspers, *General Psychopathology*, pp. 95–96, 105, 107. (As I have suggested, the quality of "impossibility" can be understood in several ways: as deriving from the lack of constraint inherent in a purely subjective realm, as a byproduct of double bookkeeping, or as a manifestation of ontological transformations such as solipsism.)

99. See Minkowski, *La Schizophrénie*, p. 60. For exceptions to this generalization about affective illness, see E. Silber, A. C. Rey, R. Savard, and R. M. Post, "Thought disorder and affective inaccessibility," *Journal of Clinical Psychiatry, 41,* 1980, 161–65.

100. See Jaspers, *General Psychopathology*, p. 295.

101. See Hamilton, *Fish's Schizophrenia*, 2nd ed., p. 53. The anxiety the patient feels may be that of sensing the precariousness of the experiential universe itself, an issue discussed in the following chapter.

102. M. Bleuler, *Schizophrenic Disorders*, p. 490. A patient quoted by Maria Lorenz makes a similar point: "I'd like a pack of cards with four suits—morals, phantasy, reality—I'd like to get rid of the reality suit." "I've always had a sense if not of the fantastic, a fictional sense. . . . Fiction permits you so many different choices" ("Criticism as an approach to schizophrenic language," *Archives of General Psychiatry, 9,* 1963, 236, 238).

103. P. J. Ruocchio, "First person account: The schizophrenic's nightmare," *Schizophrenia Bulletin, 15,* 1989, 165.

104. See Cutting, *Psychology of Schizophrenia*, p. 302. See also Alpert and Silvers, "Perceptual characteristics," p. 301. This is not to say that the derealization experience cannot sometimes persist even during physical activity, making actions also feel unreal. One patient felt that she did not exist, she only acted as if she did: "The worst thing is that I do not exist. . . . I am so non-existent

I can neither wash nor drink." She spoke of her way of acting as "swirling"—doing something "out of non-being" (Jaspers, *General Psychopathology*, p. 122).

105. Werner, *Comparative Psychology*, p. 158.
106. Quoted in Cutting, *Psychology of Schizophrenia*, p. 390.
107. Dali quoted in M. Nadeau, *The History of Surrealism*, trans. R. Howard (Harmondsworth, UK: Penguin Books, 1973), p. 200.
108. E. M. Podvoll, "Psychosis and the mystic path," *Psychoanalytic Review*, 66, 1979, 575.
109. P. Ricoeur, "The unity of the voluntary and the involuntary as a limiting idea," trans. D. O'Connor, *The Philosophy of Paul Ricoeur: An Anthology of His Work*, ed. C. E. Reagan and D. Stewart (Boston: Beacon, 1978), p. 9.
110. In his notebooks, that exemplary modern mind Paul Valéry describes this imperialistic yet introverted movement: "Consciousness declares, therefore, that the idea of the world is relative to a perspective, which itself depends on an act or alteration whereby this perspective is subordinated, transformed into a part of itself" (*Cahiers*, vol. 2, ed. J. Robinson [Paris: Gallimard, 1974], p. 220 [my translation]).
111. P. Valéry, *Monsieur Teste* (Princeton, NJ: Princeton University Press, 1973), pp. 67–69, 104, 119.

Chapter 10: World Catastrophe

1. Hegel quoted in J. Habermas, *The Philosophical Discourse of Modernity*, trans. F. G. Lawrence (Cambridge: MIT Press, 1987), p. 18.
2. W. Stevens, "Auroras of autumn," *Collected Poems* (New York: Knopf, 1969), p. 417.
3. J. Baudrillard, "The ecstasy of communication," trans. J. Johnston, in H. Foster, ed., *The Anti-Aesthetic: Essays on Postmodern Culture* (Port Townsend, WA: Bay Press, 1983), pp. 132–33.
4. B. Russell, *History of Western Philosophy* (New York: Simon and Schuster, 1945), p. 718. Others have also associated Fichte's point of view with insanity; see T. Ziolkowski, *German Romanticism and Its Institutions* (Princeton, NJ: Princeton University Press, 1989), pp. 191, 196. For a dissenting view re Fichte's relationship to extreme subjectivism, however, see D. Henrich, "Fichte's original insight," in D. E. Christensen, M. Riedel, R. Spaemann, et al., eds., *Contemporary German Philosophy*, vol. 1 (University Park and London: Pennsylvania State University Press, 1982), pp. 15–53.
5. Johann Gottlieb Fichte, *The Vocation of Man*, trans. W. Smith (Chicago: Open Court, 1910), pp. 91, 83.
6. Ibid., pp. 28–29.
7. K. Jaspers, *General Psychopathology*, trans. J. Hoenig and M. W. Hamilton (Chicago: University of Chicago Press, 1963), p. 296.
8. Ibid., p. 296 (emphasis added). The last line, in the original German, is as follows: "Ohne Weltvertretung geht die Welt kaput" (originally quoted in K. Hilfiker, "Die schizophrene Ichauflösung im All,' *Allgemeine Zeitschrift für Psychiatrie*, 87, 1927, 440–42). The word *Vertretung* is ambiguous between

political and epistemological meanings, but in context it seems clear that episte-mological (and ontological) connotations are implied since the patient speaks of supporting, preserving, and creating the world (using words like *erstellen* and *erhalten*). This passage, incidentally, is a rich example of the wavering between ontic and ontological modes of expression that I discuss at the end of chapter 9. (I am grateful to Professor Henschel of the University of Leiden for discussion of the German connotations.)

Interestingly enough, Schreber, like Hilfiker's patient, associated his own world-destruction fantasy (which he likens to an earthquake in which the world would disappear, leaving only himself) with his own status as a "seer"—a word that implies Schreber's sense of himself as a quasi-solipsistic center or epistemological foundation of the universe (see *Memoirs of My Nervous Illness*, trans. I. Macalpine and R. A. Hunter [Cambridge: Harvard University Press, 1988; originally published in 1903], p. 97). I discuss Schreber's solipsistic aspect, with its many paradoxes, in a forthcoming book (Ithaca, NY: Cornell University Press).

9. Quoted in H. Werner, *Comparative Psychology of Mental Development*, rev. ed. (New York: International Universities Press, 1957), p. 372. M. Sechehaye, *A New Psychotherapy in Schizophrenia*, trans. G. Rubin-Rabson (New York and London: Grune and Stratton, 1956), p. 148.

10. R. Rosser, "The psychopathology of thinking and feeling in a schizophrenic," *International Journal of Psychoanalysis, 60*, 1979, 183. Another patient manifested this progression on the Rorschach: just after describing several perceptions which he saw not as things but as subjectivized "snapshots" ("I take snapshots, mind is a camera," he explained in an aside), he then described the Rorschach card as follows: "Continent that has been bombed in a nuclear holocaust. These are atomic clouds that are rising out. So this is a mutant crab" (Anthony, Card #2, my notes).

11. According to Lionel Trilling, "Preoccupation with being informs most speculation about the moral life throughout the nineteenth century"; he has also spoken of "the diminution of the sentiment of being which the nineteenth century was aware of" (*Sincerity and Authenticity* [Cambridge: Harvard University Press, 1972], p. 122). This theme is certainly no less prominent in the twentieth century—though by the time of postmodernism the very aspiration for an authentic "sentiment of being" is sometimes given up, treated almost as an object of derision.

12. Quoted in M. Wood, "Comedy of ignorance," *New York Review of Books*, April 30, 1981, 49–52.

13. S. Beckett, "Imagination dead imagine," *Collected Shorter Prose: 1945–80* (London: John Calder, 1986), p. 145. A similar passage occurs in Beckett's *Endgame*:

I once knew a madman who thought the end of the world had come. He was a painter—and engraver. . . . I used to go and see him, in the asylum. I'd take him by the hand and drag him to the window. Look! There! All that rising corn! And there! Look! The sails of the herring fleet! All that loveliness! (*Pause.*) He'd snatch away his hand and go back into his corner. Appalled. All he had seen was ashes. (*Pause.*) He alone had been spared. (*Pause.*) Forgotten. (*Pause.*) It appears the case is . . . was not so . . . so unusual (*Endgame* [New York: Grove Press, 1958], p. 44).

14. Werner, *Comparative Psychology*, pp. 371, 418.
15. Fichte, *Vocation of Man*, p. 30; see also p. 41. Elsewhere Fichte writes: "The Ego *posits* itself; and the Ego is by virtue of this mere self-positing. . . . The Ego is only, in so far as it is conscious of itself" (*Grundlage der Gesammten Wissenschaftslehre*, trans A. F. Kroeger, 1794, reprinted in D. D. Runes, ed., *Treasury of Philosophy* [New York: Philosophical Library, 1955], pp. 406–7).
16. Rosser, "Psychopathology of thinking," pp. 182, 186.
17. Patients quoted in R. D. Laing, *The Divided Self* (Harmondsworth, UK: Penguin, 1965), pp. 203–5; A. McGhie and J. Chapman, "Disorders of attention and perception in early schizophrenia," *British Journal of Medical Psychology*, 34, 1961, 109.
18. The patient whose static and subjectivistic response to one TAT card was analyzed in chapter 5 told other stories in which the possibility of world catastrophe was made explicit. See, for example, his response to Card A, where he refers to "the—er—deterioration of, of their own worlds" (quoted in R. Schafer, "How was this story told?" *Journal of Projective Techniques*, 22, 1958, 203).
19. J. L. Borges lavishly praised Casares's novella: "I have discussed with the author the details of his plot. I have reread it. To classify it as perfect is neither an imprecision nor a hyperbole" ("Prologue," in A. B. Casares, *The Invention of Morel and Other Stories*, trans. R. L. C. Simms [Austin: University of Texas Press, 1964], p. 7). I am grateful to Andy Klein for calling my attention to this story.
20. Casares, *Invention of Morel*, pp. 39, 76, 78, 56.
21. Ibid., p. 72.
22. Ibid., pp. 80, 87. Late in the diary (p. 80), the narrator asks whether Morel might also have thought to photograph the machines, thus implying that the entities that had seemed to project and thus to constitute the film images might in fact be only images themselves. By thus derealizing not just the island (which, like "reality" seemed to encompass the images), but also the machine (which, like "the subject," seemed to create them), Casares's narrator steps into Derrida's mirror-cave—a universe where there are only images, without any reality to set them off, or any point of anchorage. (And here is where Casares inserts a footnote, presented as an "editor's note," making reference to "the possibility that the world is made up exclusively of sensations" [p. 86].)
23. That the mysterious machinery and its process of recording and projecting are somehow equivalent to the protagonist's mind is suggested more than once, as when the narrator asks whether the (supposedly filmed) people he sees before him "exist[ed] only in my brain, tortured by the privations I had suffered, by the poisonous roots and the equatorial sun, were they really here on this deadly island?" (ibid., p. 39). It is significant that the preserved and repeating images are first captured in something like mirrors and that the entire process of recording, murdering, and projecting is accomplished by a device that produces light, for the phenomena of reflection and light are the most common of all metaphors for consciousness. Notice also that the process of recording or preserving operates not on the person or object, but on the reflection or image of this person or object, that is, on what stands for the experience rather than for the objective reality.
24. Ibid., p. 29. Later he compares himself to a sailor in a submarine who records in a log his slow asphyxiation at the bottom of the ocean (pp. 79, 80).

25. Ibid., pp. 72, 47, 22.
26. Ibid., pp. 89, 82. Of course, if the narrator is really Morel, then he was already recorded (alongside Faustine, e.g.), and is already in a sense dead; so this final filming of himself may seem like a contradiction. It should perhaps be read in a symbolic way, as an acknowledgment of what has already occurred. If we understand this as a psychological allegory, it is the story of a man who is realizing what his subjectivizing of life is currently doing to him, and to his entire existence.
27. Then, in the last paragraphs, there is a bursting forth of a more full-bodied existence—which can be read either as a reminder of all that has been lost or, perhaps, as a suggestion of the impossibility of ever entering entirely into the solipsistic domain. The narrator is flooded then with memories of real romances and passionate emotions: "My Venezuela, you are a piece of cassava bread as large as a shield and uninfested by insects. You are the flooded plains, with bulls, mares, and jaguars being carried along by the swift current" (ibid., p. 89). But immediately he pushes these back: "My rigid discipline must never cease to combat those ideas, for they jeopardize my ultimate calm" (p. 90).
28. Ibid., pp. 18, 70.
29. W. Stevens, "As you leave the room," Poems, selected by S. F. Morse (New York: Vintage Books, 1959), p. 168. The notion of a kind of death-in-life—a consciousness awake but not alive, a corpse with insomnia (to use Casares's image), has haunted Western literature from romanticism up until the present—from Coleridge's ancient mariner, to the speaker of Eliot's "The Wasteland," and on to Hamm and Clov in Beckett's Endgame, the denizens of a world that has already begun to "stink of corpses" (quoted in A. Alvarez, Samuel Beckett [New York: Viking, 1973], p. 90)—and in most of these, deadness is associated with a subjectivism that puts real life out of reach. A similar image occurs in Baudelaire's description of the modern individual as "a kaleidoscope endowed with consciousness" (quoted in F. Jameson, Marxism and Form [Princeton, NJ: Princeton University Press, 1971], p. 75).
30. Quoted in C. Landis, ed., Varieties of Psychopathological Experience (New York: Holt, Rinehart, and Winston, 1964), p. 166.
31. Also see the TAT stories told by "C" in S. J. Blatt and C. M. Wild, Schizophrenia: A Developmental Analysis (New York: Academic Press, 1976), esp. pp. 172, 175.
32. Casares, Invention of Morel, p. 75.
33. H. F. Searles, Collected Papers on Schizophrenia and Related Subjects (New York: International Universities Press, 1965), pp. 492–93. Natalija's delusions also offer obvious parallels to The Invention of Morel, for she too experiences the ambient world as consisting of mere illusions or sensations; and she imagines these to be creations of a mysterious machine that projects images in all sense modalities, a machine that is alienated from, and yet identified with, herself (it is mysterious and occupies another space, yet is a version of her own body).
34. M. Coate, Beyond All Reason (Philadelphia and New York: Lippincott, 1965), p. 101. Morag Coate explains the prominent role of "the idea of mirrors" in her psychotic delusions as follows: "I think the mirror was for me a symbol or form of mental shorthand to express the awareness that we see ourselves as reflections in other people's consciousness, and that our self may be distorted or damaged in the process" (pp. 150–51). Interestingly enough, in her memoir she refers to this symbolism as if it had to be something irrational in nature. Thus it seems that

she takes for granted the traditional notion that any expression of her "madness" must, like an id impulse, be something that exists in opposition to the ego's capacity for control and rationality: "As I was, perhaps through insecurity, a fanatically rational child, symbolism of this sort could only come through to consciousness when the controls were weakened" (p. 151). In my view it would be more appropriate to view the emergence of the "delusion of the mirror" (an "epistemological" delusion, after all) as something that might occur not in spite of but because of her "fanatically rational" nature.

35. From M. L. Hayward and J. E. Taylor, "A schizophrenic patient describes the action of intensive psychotherapy," *Psychiatric Quarterly, 30,* 1956; quoted in R. D. Laing, *The Divided Self* (Harmondsworth, UK: Penguin Books, 1965), p. 176.

36. E. Bleuler, *Dementia Praecox, or the Group of Schizophrenias,* trans. J. Zinkin (New York: International Universities Press, 1950), p. 123; Jaspers, *General Psychopathology,* p. 122.

37. Rosser, "Psychopathology of feeling," pp. 178, 184. A week later: "I know I'm alive because I'm breathing," p. 178.

38. Quoted in K. Jaspers, *Strindberg and Van Gogh,* trans. O. Grunow and D. Woloshin (Tucson: University of Arizona Press, 1977), p. 142.

39. Laing, *Divided Self,* p. 151.

40. Jaspers, *General Psychopathology,* p. 296. The artist Martin once experienced what he called "a sense of oneness, a kind of parapsychosis." The "curtain between myself and the world vanish[ed]," he wrote. "My ego had dissolved and my senses were allowed to mingle with noumenal reality. I was at the point of zero where I was zero or change."

41. Sechehaye, *New Psychotherapy,* p. 134. Julie, in Laing, *Divided Self,* p. 198.

42. Not surprisingly, Freud interprets the "oceanic feeling" as involving a profound regression, to the state of preverbal union with the mother (*Civilization and Its Discontents,* trans. J. Strachey [New York: Norton, 1962; first published in 1930], pp. 11–20).

43. F. Nietzsche, *The Birth of Tragedy* and *The Genealogy of Morals,* trans. F. Golffing (Garden City, NY: Doubleday, 1956), pp. 22, 25–27.

   Therefore, these experiences of merging do seem to exemplify two of the traditional assumptions I criticized at the beginning of the previous chapter: the confusion of subjective and objective and the absence of reflexive consciousness. It is by no means clear, however, that the third traditional assumption—the notion that the subjective or fantastical is assimilated by the patient to the objective or the literal—holds true of such experiences. However, it also seems dubious to interpret them as the reverse, a form of solipsism. Experiences of fusing with the wall, of one's eyes corresponding to the blue sky, or of one's pulse beat merging with the ticking of a clock would seem to suggest a world in which nothing is experienced as subjective *or* objective, inner *or* outer—and where only some intermediate or undifferentiated state exists.

44. Ibid., p. 65.

45. S. Sontag, ed., *Antonin Artaud: Selected Writings,* trans. H. Weaver (New York: Farrar, Straus, and Giroux, 1976), pp. 82, 242.

46. See G. Schmidt, "A review of the German literature on delusion between 1914 and 1939," in J. Cutting and M. Shepherd, eds., *Clinical Roots of the Schizophrenia Concept* (Cambridge: Cambridge University Press, 1987), pp. 108–9; A.

Wetzel, "Das Weltuntergangserlebnis in der Schizophrenie," *Zeitschrift für die Gesamte Neurologie und Psychiatrie*, 78, 1922, 427 and passim. In my opinion Wetzel is correct to imply that world-catastrophe experiences of the kind we will be considering generally occur only *after* the development of a schizophrenic illness is well under way. The psychoanalyst John Frosch seems to be inclined toward a similar view: "Alterations in reality may, in the psychotic extension of depersonalization, be carried to the point where the whole world appears strange and the end-of-the-world delusion may evolve" (*The Psychotic Process* [New York: International Universities Press, 1983], p. 321). This runs contrary to a widely held psychoanalytic interpretation initiated by Freud.

Beginning with his interpretation of the Schreber case, Freud argued that world-destruction experiences (and related delusions) were direct consequences and symbolic representations of a process that *initiates* and is the indispensable foundation of the psychotic experiences: withdrawal of libidinal attachments from the external world ("Psychoanalytic notes upon an autobiographical account of a case of paranoia [dementia paranoides]," *Three Case Histories*, ed. P. Rieff [New York: Collier Books, 1963; first published in 1911], pp. 171–78; see also O. Fenichel, *The Psychoanalytic Theory of Neurosis* [New York: Norton, 1945], pp. 417–18). Freud's view seems to have been driven more by theoretical presuppositions than by careful clinical observation, however. Indeed, he himself admits that the usual sequence of symptoms contradicts his theory and constitutes a possible objection to it: in "Schreber's case history, as well as [in] many others . . . the delusions of persecution . . . unquestionably made their appearance at an earlier date than the phantasy of the end of the world" ("Psychoanalytic notes," p. 176). (Freud accounts for this discrepancy rather tendentiously, by arguing that, in such cases, the withdrawal of libidinal attachments—and, presumably, the [unconscious?] beginning of the world-destruction fantasy—"happens silently; we received no intelligence of it, but can only infer it from subsequent events" [p. 174].) Also, given Freud's theory, we would expect schizophrenics to be indifferent toward the external world in early stages of a psychotic break; and we would expect virtually all such psychoses to be accompanied by world-destruction fantasies (since withdrawal of libido is supposed to be the very foundation of the psychosis). Neither of these suppositions is consistent with the clinical facts, however (Frosch, among others, has noted this [*Psychotic Process*, pp. 123–24]).

Incidentally, patients in early stages of a schizophrenic break are obviously preoccupied with disturbing alterations of mood and of the perceptual world, and they do experience a loss of a normal "sense" of reality. They may describe these nearly ineffable developments in various ways, but one should not be misled into confusing their early experiences with the far more profound world-destruction fantasies at issue in this chapter.

47. Such an interpretation is certainly consistent with the fact that this kind of world catastrophe often does occur in patients who, in earlier phases, have the alienated and reflexive experiences already discussed in this book. That the fusion experiences really do stem from these earlier symptoms is exceptionally difficult, perhaps impossible, to prove in a rigorous way. I will try to increase its plausibility by offering a theoretical account of how extreme hyperreflexivity and subjectivism might eventuate in such a catastrophic dissolution of boundaries and distinctions.

48. Fichte, *Vocation of Man*, p. 61.
49. At this point Fichte turns his attention to those entities that still retain a claim to existence—on one hand, what he calls "pictures," "representations," or "presentations" and, on the other, the "consciousness," "self," "mind," "subject," "thought," or "I" who experiences these pictures (see ibid., e.g., pp. 61–62, 66, 69–70, 79, 83–91).
50. Ibid., p. 70; see also p. 83.
51. Ibid., pp. 17–18, 89.
52. P. Valéry, *Monsieur Teste*, trans. J. Mathews (Princeton, NJ: Princeton University Press, 1973), p. 68.
53. Quoted in E. Bleuler, *Dementia Praecox*, pp. 145, 124; Landis, *Psychopathological Experience*, p. 99.
54. M. Sechehaye, ed., *Autobiography of a Schizophrenic Girl*, trans. G. Rubin-Rabson (New York: New American Library, 1970), p. 79.
55. M. Sechehaye, *New Psychotherapy*, p. 134.
    Although this decentering and derealization generally have a destabilizing effect, evoking fears of annihilation and chaos, they may also bring on a sense of relief, once all aspiration to stable or substantial selfhood is given up. This seems to have been true for one patient who had experienced every interaction as a transformation of her being. "Gradually I can no longer distinguish how much of myself is in me, and how much is already in others," she said. "I am a conglomeration, a monstrosity, modelled anew each day." But this very ephemerality also meant that what she called the "immolation" of her individuality was not so traumatic, for it too was but the dissolution of a picture: what mutated, she said, was "only snow, only a poetical image of myself" (Storch's patient, quoted in Werner, *Comparative Psychology*, p. 467).
56. Lawrence, a patient treated by a colleague.
    According to Arthur Danto, the concept of "appearance" retained currency in post-Kantian philosophy despite the denial of the existence of a Ding-an-sich (the term to which "appearance" had been counterposed) because of the fact that appearances came to be conceived not in contrast with what they were *of* but in contrast with what they appeared *to*—namely, to a consciousness; see A. C. Danto, *Jean-Paul Sartre* (New York: Viking, 1975), pp. 46–47. As we have seen, however, the notion of appearance—what Fichte in the passage just quoted refers to with the term "picture" or with the metaphor of the "dream"— may not disappear even when the ego or self has also come to be conceived as merely "appearance," and when there would thus seem to be nothing left with which to contrast the notion of "appearance." Heidegger would probably view Fichte's continued use of concepts like "appearance," "picture," or "representation" as a sign of the impossibility of escaping completely from the normal sense of worldhood, that is, from the now-hidden, but nevertheless pervasive, sense of the presence of an encompassing external world. One might say the same about those schizophrenics who continue to experience both the delusional world and normal consensual reality as being unreal, mere appearances, despite the fact that the very meaning of *appearance* would seem to have been undermined.
57. Sontag, *Antonin Artaud*, pp. 91, 96.
58. See R. Hayman, *Kafka: A Biography* (New York and Toronto: Oxford University Press, 1981), p. 164.
59. See, for example, the reaction of John Updike, who finds these prose fragments

"not merely opaque but repellent" ("Reflections: Kafka's short stories," *New Yorker, 59,* May 9, 1983, 123).

Incidentally, in the work of a number of modernist and postmodernist writers one can discern a development analogous to what occurs in this single story by Kafka—a progression, both yearned for and feared, toward a form of experience involving either world catastrophe or other, more positively toned manifestations of radical dissolution of ego boundaries. This is true of the careers of Strindberg, Joyce, Virginia Woolf, and Beckett, for instance. Perhaps the closest parallel to the schizophrenic progression can, however, be found in the development of Robbe-Grillet's fictional worlds. See R. Bogue's essay, "The twilight of relativism: Robbe-Grillet and the erasure of man," in B. J. Craige, ed., *Relativism in the Arts* (Athens, GA: University of Georgia Press, 1983), 171–98.

60. F. R. Karl, *Modern and Modernism: The Sovereignty of the Artist 1885–1925* (New York: Atheneum, 1985), p. 254.

61. "Description of a struggle," trans. T. Stern and J. Stern, F. Kafka, *The Complete Stories* (New York: Schocken Books, 1971), pp. 9–51.

62. By this point in the story most of the major characteristics of the schizoid personality have been suggested, and there are hints of the *Stimmung* that so often precedes a schizophrenic break. Elsewhere in the story is a description that suggests the "truth-taking stare" experience of objects being dissociated from their conventional names (p. 33). The narrative structure, as we shall see, suggests the quality of cognitive slippage.

63. One schizophrenic patient described a similar experience. If he walked faster, the film moved faster: "Moving is like a motion picture. If you move, the picture in front of you changes. The rate of change in the picture depends on the speed of walking. If you run, you receive the signals at a faster rate" (in S. Wolf and B. Berle, eds., *The Biology of the Schizophrenic Process* [New York: Plenum, 1976], p. 41).

64. In his monologue, the supplicant describes losing the sense of the integrity of his body-ego and of his capacity for willful action: "I was just bowing . . . when to my annoyance I noticed that my right thigh had slipped out of joint. The kneecap had also become a little loose. . . . My right leg was now giving me a lot of trouble. At first it seemed to have fallen apart completely, and only gradually did I manage to get it more or less back into shape by manipulation and careful arrangement (Kafka, *Complete Stories,* pp. 36–37).

65. Fichte, *Vocation of Man,* pp. 85, 89.

66. This is made explicit in a passage where the young man hears "someone talking beside me," a someone who uses exactly the same words that we know the young man to have used earlier in the story (Kafka, *Complete Stories,* pp. 23, 15).

67. Erich Heller has described Kafka's keenest wish as having been, from his earliest days, "to write in such a way that life, in all its deceptively convincing reality, would be seen as a dream and a nothing before the absolute" (*Franz Kafka* [Princeton, NJ: Princeton University Press, 1974], pp. 118–19).

68. Mildred, in H. A. Rosenfeld, *Psychotic States: A Psychoanalytical Approach* (London: Maresfield Reprints, 1982), p. 30.

69. Kafka seems to have verged on something like a world-catastrophe experience himself. In his biography of Kafka, R. Hayman speaks of an "experience of near-disintegration" (in August 1913) that Kafka described as follows: "My thoughts became uncontrollable, everything fell apart until, at the worst mo-

ment, the image of a Napoleonic field-marshal's black hat came to my aid, dropping over my consciousness and holding it together by force" (quoted in Hayman, *Kafka: A Biography*, p. 164). Another kind of world-catastrophe was described in a passage deleted from the text of Kafka's *The Castle:* One must have the strength "to keep on staring at things without closing one's eyes . . . but if one relaxes for a single moment and closes one's eyes, then everything promptly dissolves into darkness" (quoted by M. Walser, "On Kafka's novels," in J. P. Stern, ed., *The World of Franz Kafka* [New York: Holt, Rinehart, and Winston, 1980], p. 98).

Chapter 11   Conclusion: Paradoxes of the Reflexive

1. E. Bleuler, *Dementia Praecox, or the Group of Schizophrenias,* trans. J. Zinkin (New York: International Universities Press, 1950), p. 128.
2. Quotations from M. Spitzer, "On defining delusions," *Comprehensive Psychiatry, 31,* 1990, 393–94; J. Glass, *Delusion* (Chicago and London: University of Chicago Press, 1985), p. 147.
3. R. Rosser, "The psychopathology of feeling and thinking in a schizophrenic," *International Journal of Psychoanalysis, 60,* 182. The same phenomenon is especially clear in the following description, by a schizophrenic patient, of a bizarre but very characteristic experience: "Now the question is, cannot a human brain under certain circumstances become so perverted as to recognize for itself, and *without the volition of its bearer,* the acts of other individuals as belonging to its life, as falling within its own memory?" (quoted in C. Landis, ed., *Varieties of Psychopathological Experience* [New York: Holt, Rinehart, and Winston, 1964], p. 195 [emphasis added]). External events are somehow felt to be incorporated by the ego, owned by the self, and yet the most crucial act of all, this incorporating or owning, is not itself felt to be under one's own control.
4. L. S. Vygotsky, "The psychology of schizophrenia," *Soviet Psychology, 26,* 1987, 75.
5. E. Bleuler, *Dementia Praecox,* p. 54; K. Jaspers, *General Psychopathology,* trans. J. Hoenig and M. W. Hamilton (Chicago: University of Chicago Press, 1963), p. 413.
6. Quoted in P. K. Carpenter, "Descriptions of schizophrenia in the psychiatry of Georgian Britain: John Haslam and James Tilly Matthews," *Comprehensive Psychiatry, 30,* 1989, 332.
7. A. W. Gouldner, *The Dialectic of Ideology and Technology* (New York: Seabury, 1976), p. 49.
8. M. Foucault, *The Order of Things* (New York: Vintage Books, 1970). The next several pages are based, somewhat loosely, on pp. 294–387 of Foucault's book.
9. "Portal to the dwelling": from J. Royce, *Lectures on Modern Idealism* (New Haven, CT: Yale University Press, 1919), p. 5. "Source of the modernist project": C. Greenberg, "Modernist painting," in G. Battcock, ed., *The New Art,* rev. ed. (New York: Dutton, 1973), p. 67.
   I shall here be concerned with Kant as a cultural figure and general source of intellectual influence—with Kantianism, if you will; this need not always be the most accurate reflection of all the complexities and subtleties of what Kant actually wrote. We can think of post-Kantian idealism as "a tendency, a spirit,

a disposition to interpret life and human nature and the world in a certain general way—a tendency . . . capable of . . . expressing itself in numerous mutually hostile teachings" (J. Royce, *Lectures on Modern Idealism*, p. 2).

10. Kant did postulate a (noumenal) realm of being existing beyond the realm of human awareness; being unknowable and indescribable, however, it played little role in his philosophy, and even less in those of many of his followers.

11. Hegel described Kant's impact as: "to withdraw cognition from an interest in its objects and absorption in the study of them, and to direct it back upon itself; and so turn it to a question of form" (quoted in C. L. Griswold, Jr., "Plato's metaphilosophy: Why Plato wrote dialogues," *Platonic Readings* [New York: Routledge and Kegan Paul, 1988], p. 150).

12. *Reflection* can be defined as follows: "the act by which the ego, after having stripped away its natural immediacy and returned into itself, becomes conscious of its subjectivity in relation to counterposited objectivity, and distinguishes itself from it" (R. Gasché, *The Tain of the Mirror: Derrida and the Philosophy of Reflection* [Cambridge: Harvard University Press, 1986], p. 25).

13. A later representative of this tradition, the phenomenologist Edmund Husserl, put this (rather tautological-sounding) point as follows: "The Objective world, the world that exists for me, that always has and always will exist for me, the only world that ever can exist for me—this world, with all its Objects, I said, derives its whole sense and its existential status, which it has for me, from me myself, *from me, as the transcendental Ego*" (*Cartesian Meditations* [The Hague: Martinus Nijhoff, 1969], p. 26). In this passage, he is describing a major insight afforded by phenomenology's central methodological technique, the "bracketing" of the reality of the external world (called the "epochē").

14. M. Foucault, *The Archaeology of Knowledge and the Discourse on Language*, trans. A. M. Sheridan Smith (New York: Pantheon, 1972), p. 203.

15. I have not attempted to adhere strictly to Foucault's way of describing these paradoxes. But there is some correspondence, though only a rough one, between the issues I associate with the problems of freedom, self-creation, and lucidity, and what Foucault associates with the doubles of "the empirical and the transcendental," "the retreat and the return of the origin," and "the 'cogito' and the unthought," respectively (*Order of Things*, pp. 318, 328, 322).

16. For some of the post-Kantians, it was doubly inconceivable that mind (whose defining criterion was often said to be the presence of self-consciousness) would not be conscious of its very own nature. Thus, J. G. Fichte could argue that an object was "thoroughly transparent to thy mind's eye, because it is thy mind itself" (*The Vocation of Man* [Chicago: Open Court, 1910], p. 70).

17. Some of the post-Kantian idealists went beyond the limits Kant himself had accepted; they assumed that, since even the physical world exists as a phenomenon of our awareness, reflection on the nature of consciousness or the self is capable of revealing secrets about such matters as the difference between organic and inorganic phenomena or the essence of growth and decay (see Royce, *Lectures on Modern Idealism*, pp. 73–74). This, perhaps, is akin to the tendency of some hyperreflexive schizophrenics to think that their inner journeying can reveal the essential nature of everything, the essential principles underlying not just the mind but also physical processes and social interactions.

18. Sartre's philosophy is a particularly clear statement of these elements of the

modern episteme; see, for example, the summary in A. Danto, *Jean-Paul Sartre* (New York: Viking, 1975), pp. 66–69.

19. Not, of course, as a direct object of an inner-directed faculty of perception, but in a much more complicated way (involving the conceptual analysis of transcendental structures of experience—as in Kant's "Transcendental Analytic").

20. Foucault, *Order of Things,* p. 318.

21. A. Schopenhauer, *The Philosophy of Schopenhauer* (New York: Modern Library, 1928), p. 27 (*World as Will and Idea,* book 1, sec. 7).

22. See P. F. Strawson's discussion of the fundamental contradictions of Kant's project, which derive, in Strawson's view, from Kant's tendency to conceive of the study of necessary features of human experience on the analogy of a kind of empirical inquiry—thus implying that we could somehow get outside ourselves and think both sides of the limits of human consciousness; *The Bounds of Sense: An Essay on Kant's Critique of Pure Reason* (London: Methuen, 1966), pp. 11–44, esp. pp. 12, 15, 38, 44.

23. Freudian ideas about the unconscious mind provide a more obvious statement of the human mind's profound blindness to aspects of reality, and especially to its own nature and functioning.

24. Foucault, *Order of Things,* p. 326. This paradoxical realization was well expressed in the writings of the turn-of-the-century Austrian language philosopher Fritz Mauthner, an important influence on Wittgenstein, Joyce, and Beckett, who stressed the contingent or accidental nature of the senses: *"The world came about through our evolving senses, but the senses too come about through the evolving world. Where can there be a detached picture of the world?"* (quoted in L. Ben-Zvi, "Samuel Beckett, Fritz Mauthner, and the limits of language," *PMLA,* 95, 1980, 190).

25. This implication is not stressed by Tausk, but seems to be implicit in the structure of Natalija's delusion.

26. V. Tausk (1919), "On the origin of the 'influencing machine' in schizophrenia," *Psychoanalytic Quarterly,* 2, 1933, 521, 527.
    Incidentally, there is a close and interesting analogy between the condition implied by Natalija's delusion and the new conception of the nature of vision that developed in the early nineteenth century, at the beginning of the modern episteme; see J. Crary, *Techniques of the Observer* (Cambridge: MIT Press, 1990).

27. Foucault, *Order of Things,* p. 343.

28. Foucault says that "the human sciences . . . find themselves treating as their object what is in fact their condition of possibility" (*Order of Things,* p. 364). A discomfort with both sides of the Kantian doublet is apparent, incidentally, in P. F. Strawson's critique of Kant—in his criticism of Kant's tendencies toward psychologism regarding the fundamental principles of knowledge (*Bounds of Sense,* p. 19) and toward subjectivism (the "model of mind-made Nature" [pp. 21–22]) in his conception of the world.

29. Ibid., p. 341.

30. Tausk, "Influencing machine," p. 533.

31. This is something Tausk would surely have mentioned if it were part of her delusion. If, however, this *were* the case—had Natalija felt that she knew the machine through being shown slide images of it—then she still could not have

been sure that the slide images were accurate or that the machine itself was anything more than another illusion.

32. Lawrence was described to me by a colleague who was his therapist. Quotations are based on notes written during the sessions or immediately thereafter.

33. There is a sense in which the inner journey Lawrence undertakes (what he himself speaks of as an "odyssey") is a legitimate intellectual enterprise, and one that is even of potentially general interest (akin, perhaps, to the explorations of many Kantians and phenomenologists). The self-consciousness Lawrence both indulges and explores is a fundamental feature and potentiality of all human beings; and, to a great extent, what preoccupies him are highly abstract or general features of consciousness, not merely the idiosyncracies of his own mind. It must also be admitted, however, that the revelations he derives can seem highly repetitive, even tautologous (but, of course, there are critics who have said the same regarding parts of the Western philosophical tradition).

34. I have mentioned the tendency for post-Kantian idealism to stray beyond the obvious limits of a truly intransitive domain (see note 17, this chapter). We should not be surprised to find that many schizophrenics do this also, making claims that go outside the more legitimate boundaries of a purely subjective or inner realm. In the extent to which he resists this move, Lawrence may be exceptional. (The move beyond these limits may have something to do with what Heidegger calls a confusing of the ontological difference, a notion discussed in chapter 9.)

35. "We really were having a stimulating discussion," Lawrence said regarding a late-night conversation he had had with a member of the ward staff several days before. "I felt as if I were truly gaining back some of my intelligence . . ." Then, however, another mental health worker came up to them and used "that horrible word they use so often around here—'inappropriate.' [The mental health worker] said it was inappropriate to be having a one-on-one at that hour . . . what I seemed to be wanting to talk about was not important enough . . . And what, I ask you, could be more important than the recovery of one's mind? I tried to reason with him; and remember, I had a good deal of my intelligence back, the very intelligence that I then lost this morning."

36. He once said he used to be terrified he would think he was falling, because then he would be. On another occasion he spoke of having once arrested the deterioration of his mind simply by believing that he had reached bottom.

37. In the vocabulary of Samuel Alexander, that which is normally "enjoyed"—the mental act—comes to be "contemplated," while that which is normally "contemplated"—the object of awareness—comes to be subjectivized; see J. Passmore, *A Hundred Years of Philosophy* (Harmondsworth, UK: Penguin Books, 1968), p. 268.

38. This prospect of eventual enlightenment added a further twist, and a further source of anguish: Lawrence also worried when he did *not* sense the deterioration of his own mind, for this, he said, could mean that God was ignoring him, and that he was not in fact slated for eventual enlightenment. If we assume that, as with Schreber, "God" is in some important sense Lawrence himself, an expression of his own self-consciousness, then this fear of *not* experiencing the deterioration of his own mind (which, as we have seen, is equivalent to the objectification of his mind) would translate into a fear of losing a kind of self-consciousness on which he seems to feel profoundly dependent.

39. E. Heller, "The Romantic expectation," *The Artist's Journey into the Interior and Other Essays* (San Diego, CA: Harcourt Brace Jovanovich, 1976), p. 85.

40. See M. H. Abrams, *Natural Supernaturalism* (New York: Norton, 1971), pp. 187–88, re the tendency to equate the history of mankind with the development of mind, and in particular with "the progressive history of self-consciousness" (Schelling); see also pp. 213–14 and passim. See also J. Habermas re the post-Hegelian critique of modernity, the view that "self-relating subjectivity purchases self-consciousness only at the price of objectivating internal and external nature" (*The Philosophical Discourse of Modernity* [Cambridge: MIT Press, 1990], p. 55). See also G. Hartman, "Romanticism and anti-self-consciousness," in H. Bloom, ed., *Romanticism and Consciousness* (New York: Norton, 1970), pp. 46–56.

41. F. von Schiller, *On the Aesthetic Education of Man*, trans. R. Snell (New York: Continuum, 1989; originally published in 1795), pp. 39, 42; idem, *Naive and Sentimental Poetry* (published with *On the Sublime*), trans. J. A. Elias (New York: Frederick Ungar, 1966), pp. 116, 107. See also Abrams, *Natural Supernaturalism*, p. 214.

42. Abrams, *Natural Supernaturalism*, p. 222. Schelling's description captures the three main phenomena now included in the fashionable term *alienation*—devitalization, fragmentation, and disconnectedness. See Albert William Levi, "Existentialism and the alienation of man," in E. N. Lee and M. Mandelbaum, eds., *Phenomenology and Existentialism* (Baltimore: Johns Hopkins University Press, 1967), pp. 243–65.

43. N. Stallknecht, *Strange Seas of Thought: Studies in William Wordsworth's Philosophy of Man and Nature* (Bloomington and London: Indiana University Press, 1958/1966), p. 149. See also Abrams, *Natural Supernaturalism*, p. 459.

44. As Erich Heller (*The Disinherited Mind* [New York and London: Harcourt Brace Jovanovich, 1975], p. 322) has pointed out, the intermingling in romanticism of Rousseau's "Back to Nature" and Hegel's "Forward to Mind" led to a variety of different visions, all of which, however, shared a yearning for dissolution of alienating self-consciousness and restoration of a condition of innocence, naïveté, and spontaneity.

45. H. von Kleist, "On the puppet theater," in *An Abyss Deep Enough: Letters of Heinrich von Kleist, with a Selection of Essays and Anecdotes*, ed. and trans. P. B. Miller (New York: Dutton, 1982), p. 216.

46. Re these romantic aspirations, see Erich Heller, "The Romantic expectation." Indeed, according to some recent critics, the aspirations of romanticism were deeply self-contradictory. See, for example, T. Rajan, *Dark Interpreter: The Discourse of Romanticism* (Ithaca and London: Cornell University Press, 1980); see also Abrams, *Natural Supernaturalism*, pp. 445–47.

47. See E. D. Hirsch, *Wordsworth and Schelling* (New Haven, CT: Yale University Press, 1960), esp. chap. 2.

48. Schiller, *Naive and Sentimental*, p. 175.

49. Coleridge considered art to be "the mediatress between, and reconciler of, nature and man . . . the power of humanizing nature, of infusing the thoughts and passions of man into every thing which is the object of his contemplation." Imagination, he believed, was able "to make the external internal, the internal external, to make nature thought, and thought nature" (Coleridge's *Biographia Literaria*, quoted in Abrams, *Natural Supernaturalism*, p. 269). But for this to be

possible, consciousness had to become conscious of its own creative powers—not, however, through the splendid isolation of a purely cerebral and solipsistic mind, but through recognizing—or better, feeling—an essential embeddedness in the vital pulsations of the organic world.

50. Re the latter point, see F. Kermode, *Romantic Image* (London: Collins, 1971).

51. As in these lines from Eliot's "The Hollow Men": "Between the conception / And the creation / Between the emotion / And the response / Falls the Shadow. Between the desire / and the spasm / Between the potency / And the existence / Between the essence / And the descent / Falls the Shadow" (*Selected Poems* [New York: Harcourt, Brace and World, 1934], p. 80).

52. R. Musil, *The Man Without Qualities*, trans. E. Wilkins and E. Kaiser (New York: Perigee, 1980), pp. 129, 175.

53. J. Joyce, *A Portrait of the Artist as a Young Man* (New York: Viking, 1965; first published in 1916), pp. 212–13. Yeats and Eliot quoted in M. Perloff, *The Futurist Moment* (Chicago and London: University of Chicago Press, 1986), p. 72.

54. Raymond Federman, "Surfiction—Four propositions in the form of an introduction," in Federman, ed., *Surfiction: Fiction Now and Tomorrow* (Chicago: Swallow Press, 1975), p. 11.

55. He declared, for example, that "it's the way things happen to you in life that's unreal. The movies make emotions look so strong and real, whereas when things really do happen to you, it's like watching television—you don't feel anything." And he said: "All my films are artificial, but then everything is sort of artificial" (quoted in K. McShine, ed., *Andy Warhol: A Retrospective* [New York: Museum of Modern Art, 1989], pp. 463, 461).

56. Quoted in R. Hughes, "The rise of Andy Warhol," in B. Wallis, ed., *Art After Modernism: Rethinking Representation* (New York: New Museum of Contemporary Art/Godine, 1984), p. 48.

57. M. Merleau-Ponty, *Phenomenology of Perception*, trans. Colin Smith (London: Routledge and Kegan Paul, 1962), p. vii.

58. M. Merleau-Ponty, *The Visible and the Invisible*, trans. Alphonso Lingis (Evanston, IL: Northwestern University Press, 1968), pp. 31, 3, 43; see also pp. 28–51, and passim. Merleau-Ponty states that the philosophy of reflection—*"la philosophie réflexive"*—is "thrice untrue" in its attempts to elucidate the realities of existence: "untrue to the visible [or more generally, the perceptual] world, to him who sees it, and to his relations with the other 'visionaries' " (pp. 6, 39).

59. Ibid., p. xlvi. The translator of *Visible and Invisible* interprets *"sur-reflexion"* as "hyper-reflection" (p. 38). I have avoided the latter term because of its potential confusion with my own use of the term *hyperreflexivity*, which is meant to capture something very different, in a sense antithetical to *sur-réflexion*.

In *Phenomenology of Perception* (p. xiv), Merleau-Ponty had already spoken of what he called "radical reflection," a mode of reflection conscious of "its own dependence on an unreflective life which is its initial situation, unchanging, given once and for all."

60. Merleau-Ponty, *Visible and Invisible*, pp. 35, 38; see also pp. 28, 39.

61. Foucault generally avoids mentioning them by name, however; but see the discussion in H. Dreyfus and P. Rabinow, *Michel Foucault* (Chicago: University of Chicago Press, 1982), chap. 2.

62. A. Thiher, *Words in Reflection: Modern Language Theory and Postmodern Fiction* (Chicago and London: University of Chicago Press, 1984), p. 90.

63. Phrases from J. Derrida, *Of Grammatology* (Baltimore: Johns Hopkins University Press, 1976), pp. 12, 50; P. de Man, "The rhetoric of temporality," *Blindness and Insight* (Minneapolis: University of Minnesota Press, 1983), pp. 219, 207.

64. J. Derrida, *Margins of Philosophy*, trans. A. Bass (Chicago: University of Chicago Press, 1982), p. 130. Derrida describes the "final intention" of his book *Of Grammatology* (p. 70) as follows: "To make enigmatic what one thinks one understands by the words 'proximity,' 'immediacy,' 'presence.' "

    I am well aware that Derrida is a *critic* of the "philosophy of reflection" (a critic of the ideas of Kant and Husserl, e.g.), and that he views his critique of the metaphysics of presence as undermining this type of philosophizing (since, presumably, one would have to believe in something like "presence" or a "transcendental signified" in order to believe there was a specifiable object or truth for reflection to discover). (Re these issues, see R. Rorty, "Philosophy as a kind of writing," *Consequences of Pragmatism* [Minneapolis: University of Minnesota Press, 1982], 90–109; Gasché, *Tain of the Mirror*, pp. 5–6 and passim; J. Culler, *On Deconstruction* [Ithaca, NY: Cornell University Press, 1982], p. 205.) But though Derrida may be profoundly skeptical about the possibility that a reflective method could discover anything like truth, this hardly makes him any the less hyperreflexive (in my sense of the term) in the style of writing and point of view that he employs and encourages. His method, "deconstruction," is a reflexive and continually self-undermining movement, "a project of critical thought whose task is to locate and 'take apart' those concepts which serve as the axioms or rules for a period of thought" (D. Allison, "Translator's introduction" in Derrida, *Speech and Phenomena, and Other Essays on Husserl's Theory of Signs* [Evanston, IL: Northwestern University Press, 1973], p. xxxiin). Further, as I suggest here and in chapter 6, the philosophical positions Derrida adopts seem to give a privileged place to the "insights" that derive from detachment over those that derive from involvement; and in this sense the criticisms that Heidegger and Merleau-Ponty have directed at the "philosophy of reflection" may also apply to him (and, even more obviously, to de Man, who, as we shall see, is overt in privileging the stance of reflection over engagement). (Some of the differences between this kind of approach and that of Heidegger and Merleau-Ponty are captured in J. D. Caputo, "The thought of being and the conversation of mankind: The case of Heidegger and Rorty," *Review of Metaphysics*, 36, 1983, 661–85.)

65. Derrida, *Of Grammatology*, p. 20.

66. J. Derrida, *Dissemination*, trans. B. Johnson (Chicago: University of Chicago Press, 1981), pp. 129–30.

67. J. Derrida, *Speech and Phenomena*, p. 45n, see also p. 103; *Of Grammatology*, p. 158; *Positions*, trans. A. Bass (Chicago: University of Chicago Press, 1981), p. 111.

68. Derrida, *Writing and Difference*, p. 292 (emphasis added). In *Of Grammatology*, Derrida writes: "One could call *play* the absence of the transcendental signified as limitlessness of play, that is to say as the destruction of ontotheology and the metaphysics of presence" (p. 50).

69. Derrida's critics have therefore been able to accuse him—and with justification—both of fostering a vision of unrestrained subjective freedom and of totally effacing the active role of the subject. Thus Charles Taylor can write that what is "celebrated is the deconstructing power itself, the prodigious power of subjec-

tivity to undo all the potential allegiances which might bind it; pure untrammelled freedom" (*Sources of the Self* [Cambridge: Harvard University Press, 1989], p. 489]; whereas Paul Smith can state that deconstruction "established subjectivity as a mere passivity, a simple conductor of the hierarchy of semantic forces: 'interpretations select themselves'—'I do not select' " (these latter are quotations from Derrida) (Smith, *Discerning the Subject* [Minneapolis: University of Minnesota Press, 1988], p. 50).

As Vincent Descombes has rightly noted, "It is not hard to detect the promotion of new subjectivities in many of the communiqués announcing victory over THE SUBJECT" (*Modern French Philosophy*, trans. L. Scott-Fox and J. M. Harding [Cambridge: Cambridge University Press, 1980], p. 77). Descombes speaks of a "haemorrhage of subjectivity" which has only gotten worse during the age of the supposed "disappearance of the subject," a time when the subject's unity, but not the subject itself, has been destroyed, and when the *"for-myself"* has been reigning over *"being"* (pp. 186–90).

70. Derrida, *Writing and Difference*, p. 28.

71. There is a certain irony in the fact that Nietzsche, a strong critic of all that would undermine vitality and passion, should have been appropriated by the postmodernist and poststructuralist movements. In the following passage from an interview, Derrida describes the quality of his own writing (and that of more than a few postmodernists and poststructuralists) as a "meaning-to-say-nothing," which is "simultaneously insistent and elliptical, imprinting, as you saw, even its erasures, carrying off each concept into an interminable chain of differences, surrounding or confusing itself with so many precautions, references, notes, citations, collages, supplements" (*Positions*, p. 14). This persistent, obsessing, self-undermining, but also self-admiring, voice is hardly suggestive of the Dionysianism described in *The Birth of Tragedy*. Deconstructionism is, in fact, far more reminiscent of Socrates, Nietzsche's prototype of the "theoretical man," that almost instinctive critic who hears only voices that seek to dissuade, who is "bent on the extermination of myth" and "finds his highest satisfaction in the unveiling process itself, which proves to him his own power" (*The Birth of Tragedy and The Genealogy of Morals*, trans. F. Golffing [Garden City, NY: Doubleday, 1956], pp. 92, 84, 137, 92). It also recalls Nietzsche's characterization of the ascetic type in *The Genealogy of Morals*: "We are face to face with a deliberate split, which gloats on its own discomfiture and grows more self-assured and triumphant the more its biological energy decreases" (idem, p. 254). Re related issues, see R. C. Solomon, "Nietzsche, postmodernism, and resentment: A genealogical hypothesis," in C. Koelb, ed., *Nietzsche as Postmodernist: Essays Pro and Con* (Albany: State University of New York Press, 1990), pp. 267–93.

72. De Man, "Rhetoric of temporality," see, for example, pp. 189, 208. Actually, de Man disputes some of the traditional understanding of the romanticist point of view (e.g., p. 207). To avoid confusion, in my discussion I will continue to refer to the organicist perspectives which he criticizes as "romanticism."

73. Ibid., pp. 211, 212, 208. Heidegger is not mentioned by name, but one is certainly reminded of him when de Man compares the everyday experience of the linguistic medium to the carpenter's or cobbler's experience of a hammer (p. 213).

74. Ibid., pp. 219, 217. It must be recognized, de Man writes, that "to know inauthenticity is not the same as to be authentic" (p. 214).

75. Joyce, *Portrait of the Artist*, p. 212.

76. De Man, "Rhetoric of temporality," pp. 187–208. See, for example, C. Owens,

"The allegorical impulse: Toward a theory of postmodernism," in Wallis, *Art After Modernism*, pp. 203–35.

77. De Man, "Rhetoric of temporality," pp. 213, 218, 221.

78. Ibid., p. 216.

79. I have incorporated de Man's remarks on Hölderlin: see de Man, "Heidegger's exegeses of Hölderlin," *Blindness and Insight*, pp. 263–64. Baudelaire speaks of *"vertige de l'hyperbole,"* and de Man of *"unrelieved vertige*, dizziness to the point of madness" ("Rhetoric of temporality," p. 215).

80. Re the psychiatric concept of "insight," see A. S. David, "Insight and psychosis," *British Journal of Psychiatry, 156,* 1990, esp. 798, 799.

81. G. W. F. Hegel, *The Phenomenology of Mind,* trans. J. B. Baillie (New York: Harper and Row, 1967), p. 546.

82. Jaspers, *General Psychopathology,* p. 115.

83. D. P. Schreber, *Memoirs of My Nervous Illness,* trans. I. Macalpine and R. A. Hunter (Cambridge: Harvard University Press, 1988; originally published in 1903), p. 41.

84. Quotations from A. R. Lecours and M. Vanier-Clement, "Schizophasia and jargonaphasia," *Brain and Language, 3,* 1976, 556; M. Bleuler, *The Schizophrenic Disorders* (New Haven and London: Yale University Press, 1978), p. 490.

    As the psychotherapist Harold Searles remarks, "I have learned the hard way . . . that any chronically schizophrenic patient is in, at the beginning of our [therapeutic] work, at least as strong a position as my own"; such patients can be indifferent to help and unconscious of any psychological pain (quoted in T. McGlashan, "Intensive individual psychotherapy of schizophrenia: A review of techniques," *Archives of General Psychiatry, 40,* 1983, 913).

85. Quotations from R. D. Laing, *The Divided Self* (Harmondsworth, UK: Penguin Books, 1965), p. 146 (re his patient James); Robert Walser, "The street (1)," trans. C. Middleton, *Selected Stories* (New York: Farrar, Straus, and Giroux, 1982), p. 124; E. Meyer and L. Covi, "The experience of depersonalization: A written report by a patient," *Psychiatry, 23,* 1960, 215.

86. Hölderlin quoted in Jaspers, *General Psychopathology,* pp. 447–48.

87. See C. G. Caldwell and I. I. Gottesman, "Schizophrenics kill themselves too: A review of risk factors for suicide," *Schizophrenia Bulletin, 16,* 1990, 571–87. Suicide in schizophrenia can also have other meanings and motives, however. It may, for instance, be experienced as an ultimate declaration of power, freedom, and disdain.

88. Quotation from M. Sechehaye, ed., *Autobiography of a Schizophrenic Girl,* trans. G. Rubin-Rabson (New York: New American Library, 1968), p. 71.

89. Ibid., pp. 22, 87–89.

Notes to epilogue and appendix repeat year of publication for successive references to an article or a book. (Because of the rapidly developing nature of the fields in question, it may be useful to have ready access to dates of publication.)

Epilogue: Schizophrenia and Modern Culture

1. A. Jablensky, "Multicultural studies and the nature of schizophrenia: A review," *Journal of the Royal Society of Medicine, 80,* 1987, 162.

2. T. S. Eliot, "The metaphysical poets," in W. J. Bate, ed., *Criticism: The Major*

Texts (New York and Burlingame: Harcourt, Brace and World, 1952 [essay by Eliot first published in 1921]), pp. 529–34. Eliot describes the new poet as able only to think *or* feel, "by fits, unbalanced."

3. E. Kraepelin, *Dementia Praecox and Paraphrenia* (Huntington, NY: Krieger, 1919/1971), pp. 74–75. E. Stransky (an article from 1903) is quoted in H. C. Rümke, "The nuclear symptom of schizophrenia and the praecox feeling," trans. J. Neeleman, *History of Psychiatry, 1*, 1990 (originally published in 1941), 335n.

4. E. Jarvis, *American Journal of Insanity*, 1851–1852, quoted in G. Rosen, *Madness in Society* (New York and Evanston: Harper and Row, 1968), p. 186. G. Devereux makes a similar suggestion; see *Basic Problems of Ethnopsychiatry* (Chicago and London: University of Chicago Press, 1980), chap. 10.

5. I am following the tripartite system employed by Talcott Parsons, Clifford Geertz, and others—in which a distinction is made between culture (understood as a fabric of meaning comprising symbols, ideas, and various taken-for-granted notions), social structure (the concrete set of social relations, institutions, and practices), and the personality system of individual actors; see C. Geertz, *The Interpretation of Cultures* (New York: Basic Books, 1973), pp. 144–46, 361–62. Modernism would thus be allied with culture, modernity with social structure.

6. This refers to lifetime prevalence, the number of people in a population who suffer from the illness at some time in their lives.

7. E. F. Torrey, "Prevalence studies in schizophrenia," *British Journal of Psychiatry, 150*, 1987, 599. A. Jablensky argues that uniform incidence rates of schizophrenia suggest the illness should be viewed as "the expression of a similarly distributed liability for a 'schizophrenic' type of response rather than as a reflection of identical primary causes"—that is, as a potentiality rooted in the biopsychosocial facts of the human condition rather than as a simple consequence of extrinsic causes. And given such a conception, he argues, it would be important to understand "the psychosocial and cultural conditions that may either preclude or augment the possibility of a schizophrenic response" ("Multicultural studies," 1987, 166–67).

8. K. Birnbaum (1923) quoted in J. Cutting, *The Psychology of Schizophrenia* (Edinburgh: Churchill Livingstone, 1985), p. 94.

9. H. W. Dunham, "Society, culture and mental disorder," *Archives of General Psychiatry, 33*, 1976, 147–56.

10. Arthur Kleinman offers a critique of the "tacit professional ideology which functions to exaggerate what is universal in psychiatric disorder and de-emphasizes what is culturally particular"; he also offers a critique of the stratigraphic pathogenicity/pathoplasticity distinction which, unjustifiably, treats biology as bedrock, while relegating psychological, social, and cultural layers to the realm of the epiphenomenal ("Anthropology and psychiatry: The role of culture in cross-cultural research on illness," *British Journal of Psychiatry, 151*, 1987, 449, 450). See also E. F. Torrey, *Schizophrenia and Civilization* (New York: Aronson, 1980), pp. 56–57.

11. See R. Littlewood, "Russian dolls and Chinese boxes: An anthropological approach to the implicit models of comparative psychiatry," in J. Cox, ed., *Transcultural Psychiatry* (London: Croom Helm, 1986), pp. 47–53.

12. Summarized in Jablensky, "Multicultural studies," 1987.

13. R. Warner, *Recovery from Schizophrenia* (London and New York: Routledge

and Kegan Paul, 1985), p. 156. Fifty-eight percent of the Nigerian patients and 51 percent of the Indians had a single psychotic episode followed by complete remission; only 6 percent of those in Denmark and 27 percent of those in China did. The frequency of patients with a chronic unremitting course was 7 percent in Nigeria and 20 percent in India, versus 50 percent in Denmark and 47 percent in the United States (Jablensky, "Multicultural studies," 1987, p. 165). It should be noted that a more benign outcome was characteristic of the Third World psychotics whether or not they had a more acute onset.

14. See Warner, *Recovery from Schizophrenia*, 1985, chap. 7; N. Waxler, "Is mental illness cured in traditional societies? A theoretical analysis," *Culture, Medicine, and Psychiatry, 1*, 1977, 233–53; K. M. Lin and A. Kleinman, "Psychopathology and clinical course of schizophrenia: A cross-cultural perspective," *Schizophrenia Bulletin, 14*, 1988, 555–67.

15. Jablensky, "Multicultural studies," 1987, p. 167.

16. Issues of course and outcome were also not central to the diagnostic procedures of the later WHO study—though it should be acknowledged that a (very rough) index of one such feature, length of previous illness, *was* similar in developing and developed countries; see N. Sartorius, A. Jablensky, A. Korten, et al., "Early manifestations and first-contact incidence of schizophrenia in different cultures," *Psychological Medicine, 16*, 1986, 917.

17. Jablensky, "Multicultural studies," 1987, p. 166.

18. Ibid., p. 165; Sartorius et al., "Early manifestations," 1986, pp. 916–17.

19. The International Classification of Diseases, 9th rev. (ICD-9), printed in American Psychiatric Association, *Diagnostic and Statistical Manual of Mental Disorders*, 3rd ed. (DSM III) (Washington, DC: American Psychiatric Press, 1980), app. D, p. 417.

20. This point is forcefully argued by J. R. Stevens, "Brief psychoses: Do they contribute to the good prognosis and equal prevalence of schizophrenia in developing countries?" *British Journal of Psychiatry, 151*, 1987, 393–96.

   A similar, though somewhat more controversial, point might be made concerning the subtype "catatonic schizophrenia," which constituted about 10 percent of the "schizophrenics" in the developing countries versus only 1 percent of those in the developed countries. This subtype also has a tenuous link to schizophrenia. Though the point is controversial, a number of experts argue that a large proportion of catatonic patients are not schizophrenic at all, but are better regarded as suffering from unrelated forms of brain damage or of severe affective disorder. See Cutting, *Psychology of Schizophrenia*, 1985, pp. 95–96, 382; M. Flaum and N. Andreasen, "Diagnostic criteria for schizophrenia and related disorders: Options for DSM-IV," *Schizophrenia Bulletin, 17*, 1991, 133–42. In its criteria for "catatonic schizophrenia," ICD-9 does note that "depressive or hypomanic concomitants may be present" (quoted in American Psychiatric Association, DSM III, 1980, p. 417).

21. ICD-9, in American Psychiatric Association, DSM III, 1980, p. 416.

22. See R. Chandrasena, "Schneider's First Rank Symptoms: An international and interethnic comparison," *Acta Psychiatrica Scandinavica, 76*, 1987, 574–78.

23. Re these uncertainties about diagnosis, see K. S. Kendler's cogent article, "Toward a scientific psychiatric nosology," *Archives of General Psychiatry, 47*, 1990, 969–73.

24. The most thorough review of the literature was done by Richard Warner, who writes: "We cannot draw the definite conclusion from this analysis that schizophrenia is less common in the Third World—the data are not sound enough. We can say, however, that the evidence does *not* support the widely held belief that the prevalence of schizophrenia is similar all around the globe" (*Recovery from Schizophrenia*, 1985, p. 200). On balance, Warner is inclined to interpret the evidence as at least suggesting that schizophrenia has both a lower incidence and prevalence in less economically developed societies (p. 234).

25. Many sociologists would assert that modernization and Westernization are much the same phenomenon, since the main transformative agencies emerged first in Europe around the seventeenth century, and only later spread throughout the world. This is Weber's view, and that of the contemporary sociologist Anthony Giddens; see Giddens, *The Consequences of Modernity* (Stanford, CA: Stanford University Press, 1990), pp. 1, 174–75.

26. Jablensky notes the absence of such data; see "Multicultural studies," 1987, p. 167.

27. For reviews of this literature, see Warner, *Recovery from Schizophrenia*, 1985; and Torrey, *Schizophrenia and Civilization*, 1980.

28. Quoted in Torrey, *Schizophrenia and Civilization*, 1980, p. 46.

29. Quoted in H. Fabrega, "On the significance of an anthropological approach to schizophrenia," *Psychiatry*, 52, 1989, 49.

30. Devereux, "A sociological theory of schizophrenia," *Psychoanalytic Review, 26*, 1939, 317. See also Devereux, *Basic Problems of Ethnopsychiatry* (Chicago and London: University of Chicago Press, 1980), pp. 187, 214; Sir Andrew Halliday's account from 1828, quoted in Rosen, *Madness in Society*, 1968, p. 183; E. H. Ackerknecht, "Psychopathology, primitive medicine and primitive culture," *Bulletin of the History of Medicine, 14*, 1943, 30–67; and E. H. Ackerknecht, *A Short History of Psychiatry*, trans. S. Wolff (New York: Hafner, 1968; published in German in 1959), p. 5.

31. M. Fortes and D. Y. Mayer, "Psychosis and social change among the Tallensi of Northern Ghana," in S. H. Foulkes and G. S. Prince, eds., *Psychiatry in a Changing Society* (London: Tavistock, 1969), pp. 33–73.

32. M. J. Field, "Chronic psychosis in rural Ghana," *British Journal of Psychiatry, 114*, 1968, 31. Field, a physician/anthropologist, notes that the incidence of insanity seems to have increased throughout northern Ghana during this period; mental illness, which according to the tribal elders was almost unheard of thirty years before, had become quite common.

33. See Lin and Kleinman, "Psychopathology and clinical course," 1988, p. 55.

34. E. F. Torrey, B. B. Torrey, and B. G. Burton-Bradley, "The epidemiology of schizophrenia in Papua New Guinea," *American Journal of Psychiatry, 131*, 1974, 567–73; Torrey, "Prevalence studies," 1987, p. 603.

35. For reviews of these findings, see Warner, *Recovery from Schizophrenia*, 1985, chap. 9; A. C. Smith, *Schizophrenia and Madness* (London: Allen and Unwin, 1982), chap. 4; Torrey, *Schizophrenia and Civilization*, 1980; M. Beiser and W. G. Iacono, "An update on the epidemiology of schizophrenia," *Canadian Journal of Psychiatry, 35*, 1990, 657–68. See also H. B. M. Murphy, "Sociocultural variations in symptomatology, incidence and course of illness," in M. Shepherd and O. L. Zangwill, eds., *General Psychopathology*, vol. 1 of *Handbook of*

Psychiatry (Cambridge: Cambridge University Press, 1983), pp. 157–71; Ackerknecht, *A Short History of Psychiatry*, 1959/1968, pp. 2–7; G. Devereux, *Mohave Ethnopsychiatry: The Psychic Disturbances of an Indian Tribe* (Washington, D.C.: Smithsonian Institution Press, 1961), p. 222. Warner (p. 210) states that the evidence, though not conclusive (there are some contradictory findings), does suggest that schizophrenia is more rare in cultures where traditional lifestyles have been little touched by the cash economy.

36. E. F. Torrey and A. Bowler, "Geographical distribution of insanity in America: Evidence for an urban factor," *Schizophrenia Bulletin, 16*, 1990, 591–604.

37. H. Collomb, "Bouffées délirantes en psychiatrie africaine," *Psychopathologie Africaine, 1*, 1965, 167–239, discussed in W. G. Jilek and L. Jilek-Aall, "Transient psychoses in Africans," *Psychiatria Clinica, 3*, 1970, 337–64.

38. Jilek and Jilek-Aall, "Transient psychoses in Africans," 1970, pp. 337, 341–42.

39. Torrey, *Schizophrenia and Civilization*, 1980, p. 56. Torrey, "Prevalence studies in schizophrenia," 1987, p. 599; Stevens, "Brief psychoses," 1987, p. 394.

40. Stevens, "Brief psychoses," 1987, pp. 393, 395.

41. M. H. Hollender and S. J. Hirsch, "Hysterical psychosis," *American Journal of Psychiatry, 120*, 1964, 1066–68, 1073. Sartorius, Jablensky, Korten, and colleagues report, for example, that the symptom of "delusional mood" (equivalent to the "apophany," an aspect of the *Stimmung* described in chapter 2) was less common among patients with schizophrenia and related disorders in the Third World than in the industrialized West; see "Early manifestations of schizophrenia," 1986, pp. 920–21. Some studies—for example, J. M. Murphy's study of several deviant individuals in Yoruba and Eskimo societies ("Psychiatric labeling in cross-cultural perspective," *Science, 191*, 1976, 1019–28)—make the mistake of assuming that "crazy" behavior must necessarily be crazy in a schizophrenic way.

42. See J. Leff, "Epidemiology of mental illness across cultures," in J. Cox, ed., *Transcultural Psychiatry, 41*, 1986, 23–36; Jilek and Jilek-Aall, "Transient psychoses in Africans," 1970, pp. 344–45, 358; I. Sow, *Anthropological Studies of Madness in Black Africa* (New York: International Universities Press, 1978), pp. 25–33.

43. Devereux, *Basic Problems of Ethnopsychiatry*, 1980, pp. 219, 221. Devereux considers schizophrenia to be "the typical ethnic psychosis of complex civilized societies" (quoted in Jablensky, "Multicultural studies and schizophrenia," 1987, p. 163). Similarly, Jaspers viewed schizophrenia as the predominant mental illness of the twentieth century and hysteria as more common in earlier centuries; see Ackerknecht, *A Short History of Psychiatry*, 1959/1968, p. 3. Leff comes to a similar conclusion re hysteria; see "Epidemiology of mental illness," 1986.

A similar contrast prevails if one compares patients with hysterical personality structure in Africa and Europe. There are histrionic traits in both groups, but in Africa "a tendency to externally-oriented direct expression prevails, in contrast with more indirect and self-oriented expression patterns in the occidental group" (R. A. Pierloot and M. Ngoma, "Hysterical manifestations in Africa and Europe: A comparative study," *British Journal of Psychiatry, 152*, 1988, 115). For similar findings re depressive patients, see H. B. M. Murphy, "The advent of guilt feelings as a common depressive syndrome: A historical comparison on two continents," *Psychiatry, 41*, 1978, 229–42.

44. See Jilik and Jilek-Aall, "Transient psychoses in Africans," 1970, pp. 354, 351; see also p. 347 re E. Kretschmer and E. Bleuler re *Primitivreaktionen*.

45. For an overview of these forms of psychosis, see M. Menuck, S. Legaut, P. Schmidt, and G. Remington, "The nosological status of the remitting atypical psychoses," *Comprehensive Psychiatry*, 30, 1989, 53–73.

46. Beiser and Iacono dispute the commonly accepted view that "schizophrenia exists in a more or less invariant form in all cultures"; in their opinion the evidence suggests that "these intolerable illnesses may not be the same phenomenon everywhere," and perhaps "should not all be included under the rubric of schizophrenia" ("Update on the epidemiology," 1990, p. 663).

47. See E. Hare, "Was insanity on the increase?" *British Journal of Psychiatry*, 142, 1983, 439–55; J. Cooper and N. Sartorius, "Cultural and temporal variations in schizophrenia: A speculation on the importance of industrialization," *British Journal of Psychiatry*, 130, 1977, 50–55; E. F. Torrey, *Schizophrenia and Civilization*, 1980. For counterarguments see D. V. Jeste, R. del Carmen, J. B. Lohr, and R. J. Wyatt, "Did schizophrenia exist before the eighteenth century?" *Comprehensive Psychiatry*, 26, 1985, 493–503; and M. D. Altschule's remarks in M. D. Altschule, E. L. Bliss, R. Cancro, et al., "Historical perspective: Evolution of the concept of schizophrenia," in S. Wolf and B. B. Berle, eds., *The Biology of the Schizophrenic Process* (New York and London: Plenum, 1976), p. 3. Altschule argues (not very convincingly, in my view) that disordered thinking of the schizophrenic type is very much harder to recognize than other types of symptoms, such as mood disorders, and that it required the development of associationistic psychology in the eighteenth century before the formulation of the concept of thinking disorders (crucial to the recognition of schizophrenia, in his view) could be given direction.

    For discussion of psychopathology in relation both to cross-cultural differences and to historical change, with a particular focus on attitudes toward the self and individual responsibility, see H. B. M. Murphy's article on depressive symptoms in twentieth-century Africa and seventeenth-century England, "The advent of guilt feelings," 1978.

48. A. Gehlen, *Man in the Age of Technology*, trans. P. Lipscomb (New York: Columbia University Press, 1980), p. 94.

49. See Torrey, *Schizophrenia and Civilization*, 1980, chap. 2.

50. Hare, "Was insanity on the increase?" 1983, p. 450; Smith, *Schizophrenia and Madness*, 1982, chap. 5. Haslam in 1809 described but did not name a schizophrenialike disorder with onset at puberty and a deteriorating course. Esquirol introduced the term "intellectual monomania" in 1838. Morel wrote of *démence précoce* (which had a narrower meaning than Kraepelin's later usage of the term) in 1860. See Cutting, *Psychology of Schizophrenia*, 1985, pp. 11–15; Altschule, "Historical perspective: schizophrenia," 1976.

51. Warner, *Recovery from Schizophrenia*, 1985, p. 233.

52. Hare, "Was insanity on the increase?" 1983, pp. 450, 449. The common view, that "the incidence of schizophrenia has always been much the same," writes Hare, is "certainly not based on historical evidence" (p. 651).

53. See Smith, *Schizophrenia and Madness*, 1982, pp. 90–91, 52. See also Jilek and Jilek-Aall, "Transient psychoses in Africans," 1970, p. 357, re Stransky, who in 1907 described an apparent decrease in the Viennese population of cases of

"amentia," a concept closely analogous to transient psychoses or *bouffée déli-*
rante. Very recently, E. A. Guinness has remarked on a similar but more rapid
trend occurring among Afro-Caribbean immigrants in Britain: first, reports primarily of transient psychotic reactions, then of atypical psychosis, and finally, in
the second generation (those born in Britain to immigrant parents), a very
considerable increase of severe, unequivocal schizophrenia ("Patterns of mental
illness in the early stages of urbanisation," *British Journal of Psychiatry, 160*
[suppl. 16], 1992, 36–37; see also pp. 33–36, 66, 68).

54. See K. Jaspers, *Strindberg and Van Gogh* (Tucson: University of Arizona Press,
1977), p. 200; K. Jaspers, *General Psychopathology*, trans. J. Hoenig and M. W.
Hamilton (Chicago: University of Chicago Press, 1963), p. 733.

55. See J. H. Matthews, *Surrealism, Insanity, and Poetry* (Syracuse, NY: Syracuse
University Press, 1982); J. MacGregor, *The Discovery of the Art of the Insane*
(Princeton, NJ: Princeton University Press, 1989); J.-J. Lecercle, *Philosophy
Through the Looking Glass: Language, Nonsense, Desire* (La Salle, IL: Open
Court, 1985).

56. Re the importance of Nerval—who might better be described as "schizoaffec-
tive"—see Arthur Symons, *The Symbolist Movement in Literature* (New York:
Dutton, 1919/1958), pp. 6–21. Re Hölderlin, see H. Stierlin, "Lyrical creativity
and schizophrenic psychosis in Friedrich Hölderlin's fate," *Psychoanalysis and
Family Therapy: Collected Papers* (New York: Aronson, 1977), pp. 83–108, esp.
pp. 89, 98; and S. Tonsor, "Hölderlin and the modern sensibility," in E. E.
George, ed., *Friedrich Hölderlin: An Early Modern* (Ann Arbor: University of
Michigan Press, 1972), pp. 54–63.

57. Some issues pertaining to the influence of psychopathology on culture are discussed in R. Littlewood, "The imitation of madness: The influence of psychopathology on culture," *Social Sciences and Medicine, 19*, 1984, 705–15.

58. Torrey, *Schizophrenia and Civilization,* 1980. See also Hare ("Was insanity on
the increase?" 1983, p. 451), who suggests an infectious (viral) or dietary cause.
This view has not caught on with very many scholars and scientists, however. For
a critique, see R. Warner, *Recovery from Schizophrenia,* 1985, p. 234.

59. Yet another possibility is that the modern privatized family might pose a particular challenge to persons with schizophrenic vulnerability. It is interesting to note
that the terms used to describe this kind of family—"isolation," "emotional
overinvolvement with kin," and the like—are reminiscent of some of what is said
about families most likely to cause relapse in a schizophrenic member. See R.
Sennett, "Destructive *Gemeinschaft,*" in R. Sennett, ed., *The Psychology of
Society* (New York: Random House, 1977), pp. 192–200.

60. Jablensky, "Multicultural studies," 1987, p. 167; Murphy, "The advent of guilt
feelings," 1978, p. 240; H. Lefley, "Culture and chronic mental illness," *Hospital
and Community Psychiatry, 41,* 1990, 278. The research on "expressed emotion"
is consistent with such a view, for it indicates that a critical or blaming attitude
on the part of family members is likely to precipitate relapse into schizophrenic
psychosis; see J. Leff and C. Vaughn, eds., *Expressed Emotion in Families: Its
Significance for Mental Illness* (New York: Guilford, 1985).

The social theorist E. Gellner has argued that, in modern society, individuali-
zation and homogenization go in tandem: there is a specialization of tasks and
an emphasis on individual responsibility, but the tasks in question need to be

done in the same style, in accord with instrumental rationality. Both sides of this development might pose a particularly difficult challenge for schizophrenic persons. See Gellner, *Plough, Sword, and Book* (London: Collins Harvill, 1988), p. 262. Michel Foucault offers a similar view of modernity in *Discipline and Punish* (trans. A. Sheridan [New York: Vintage Books, 1979]).

61. This seems to be the view of H. Fabrega, "Significance of anthropological approach," 1989, pp. 60–61; and of Cooper and Sartorius, "Cultural and temporal variations," 1977.

This cultural hypothesis closely parallels one on the level of individual development that has been widely held, both in psychiatry and psychoanalysis: the notion that schizophrenia most often develops in adolescence or early adulthood because this is the stage when truly autonomous conduct begins to be expected, thereby placing overwhelming demands on a cognitive apparatus or ego structure that happens to be defective or weak and immature. One nineteenth-century alienist, for example, wrote of "the quiet collapse of jerry-built brains under the strain of their own weight or on the first contact with the responsibilities of adult life" (Hayes-Newtington, quoted in P. Barham, *Schizophrenia and Human Value* [Oxford: Blackwell, 1984], p. 38).

62. A more complete account would require, among other things, a rehearsing of nearly every feature of modernism discussed in this book, now regarding each one no longer as an affinity but as a potential influence.

63. C. Taylor, "The moral topography of the self," in S. Messer, L. Sass, and R. Woolfolk, eds., *Hermeneutics and Psychological Theory* (New Brunswick, NJ: Rutgers University Press, 1988), p. 310. See also A. R. Luria (*Cognitive Development: Its Cultural and Social Foundations*, trans. M. Lopez-Morillas and L. Solotaroff [Cambridge: Harvard University Press, 1976], p. 145), who argues that "self-awareness is a product of sociohistorical development and that reflection of external nature and social reality arises first," and that "only later, through its mediating influence, do we find self-awareness in its most complex forms."

64. See K. J. Weintraub, *The Value of the Individual: Self and Circumstance in Autobiography* (Chicago: University of Chicago Press, 1978).

65. R. M. Rilke, *The Selected Poetry of Rainer Maria Rilke*, trans. S. Mitchell (New York: Vintage Books, 1984), p. 189. See discussion in C. Taylor, *Sources of the Self* (Cambridge:. Harvard University Press, 1989), pp. 501–2 and passim.

66. P. Rieff, *Freud: The Mind of the Moralist* (Garden City, NY: Doubleday Anchor, 1961), pp. 391–92.

67. Re Gehlen and Schelsky, see A. C. Zijderveld, "The challenges of modernity," in J. D. Hunter and S. C. Ainlay, eds., *Making Sense of Modern Times* (London and New York: Routledge and Kegan Paul, 1986), pp. 57–75. See also P. Berger, "The problem of multiple realities: Alfred Schutz and Robert Musil," in M. Natanson, ed., *Phenomenology and Social Reality* (The Hague: Martinus Nijhoff, 1970), pp. 213–33. R. N. Bellah notes that until the eighteenth or even the nineteenth century, the problem of nonbelief was experienced only by a small minority of persons; *Beyond Belief: Essays on Religion in a Post-Traditional World* (New York: Harper and Row, 1970), p. 217. The views of these sociologists were anticipated by earlier writers, notably Hegel and Kierkegaard; for a summary, see M. C. Taylor, *Journeys to Selfhood: Hegel and Kierkegaard* (Berkeley: University of California Press, 1980), chap. 2.

Walter Ong emphasizes the factor of literacy, noting that psychotics (he uses the word *schizophrenics*—no doubt somewhat loosely) in oral cultures are less likely to isolate their thought processes from those of the group, and that they do not manifest systematic daydreaming, construction of private imaginary worlds, and so on; see "World as view and world as event," *American Anthropologist, 71,* 1969, 634–47.

68. Blows to self-esteem seem to be particularly common as precipitants of the schizophrenic break; see R. Grinker and P. Holzman, "Schizophrenic pathology in young adults," *Archives of General Psychiatry, 28,* 1973, 168–75.

69. For example, a propensity for inappropriate reflectiveness and rationality might be mediated by overactivation of the left hemisphere or by underactivation of the right hemisphere of the brain; or a tendency toward hyperconcentration on inner or normally unnoticed stimuli might be mediated by abnormalities of the hippocampal system (as discussed in the appendix)—and either of these tendencies might be more likely to be exacerbated, perhaps to the point of serious dysfunction, in the context of this kind of culture. If, on the other hand, one were to accept something like Weinberger's notion of hypofrontality (underactivation of part of the frontal lobes of the brain), modern culture could be important in two ways: the demand for acting on individual initiative that it imposes might be especially problematic for persons having the deficiencies associated with hypofrontality, thereby making them likely to wish to find some escape from such demands; or the culture's emphasis on inwardness and individuality might channel their mode of escape, encouraging an autistic retreat.

70. L. S. Gilles, R. Elk, O. Ben-Arie, and A. Teggin, "The Present State Examination: Experiences with Xhosa-speaking psychiatric patients," *British Journal of Psychiatry, 141,* 1982, 143–47. See discussion in H. Fabrega, "Cultural relativism and psychiatric illness," *Journal of Nervous and Mental Disease, 177,* 1989, 415–25.

71. See Giddens, *Consequences of Modernity,* 1990, pp. 4–6.

72. P. Berger, B. Berger, and H. Kellner, *The Homeless Mind: Modernization and Consciousness* (New York: Vintage Books, 1974), pt. 1, pp. 23–115.

73. Giddens, *Consequences of Modernity,* 1990, pp. 39, 176.

74. See, for example, F. Jameson, "Postmodernism and consumer society," and J. Baudrillard, "The ecstasy of communication," both in H. Foster, ed., *The Anti-Aesthetic: Essays on Postmodern Culture* (Port Townsend, WA: Bay Press, 1983), pp. 111–25, 126–34.

The debate about postmodern*ity* parallels in some respects the debate about postmodern*ism*—with some theorists (Jameson and Baudrillard, e.g.) viewing the postmodern media age as a truly new departure, and others seeing it as essentially a continuation of modernity; re the latter view, see Giddens, *Consequences of Modernity,* 1990, pp. 45–53. Some of the schizoid aspects of the media age are very well captured in Walter Benjamin's essay, "The Work of Art in the Age of Mechanical Reproduction" (*Illuminations,* trans. H. Zohn [New York: Schocken Books, 1969], pp. 217–51), where Benjamin reflects on the loss of the aura of the real and on the aesthetic pleasure modern individuals seem to take in their self-alienation, self-contemplation, and self-destruction.

75. The Marxist critic Georg Lukács took a similar view re modernism, seeing its focus on psychic moods or inner images as yet another manifestation of the "reifying" tendencies central to modern capitalist society; see F. Jameson, *Fa-*

bles of Aggression (Berkeley: University of California Press, 1979), pp. 13–14. Lukács's thought may be particularly useful for linking the domain of everyday experience with that of socioeconomic organization. His central theoretical concept is "reification," the process by which organic developments and dynamic unities are fragmented into mere collections of static and unrelated parts, thereby distorting the true nature of both natural and social reality. In his view, advanced capitalism has brought the reifying vision to ascendency—largely because such a vision echoes a widespread feeling of passivity in relationship to the inexorable social forces of the age.

Lukács did not see modernism as a truly revolutionary or critical movement (as is often claimed) but as yet one more reflection of this general societal trend. Thus, for him, modernism's focus on psychic moods or inner images was of a piece with objectivist descriptions of external events: in both cases there was a failure to appreciate the reality of historical process, the potentiality for change, or the value of engagement. He also saw the inwardness of modernism—so often felt to provide a refuge from the depersonalizing and fragmenting outer world (as, e.g., with Virginia Woolf)—as little more than a way of giving in to the isolating outer forces.

This analysis closely resembles Michel Foucault's discussion of the panoptical aspects of modernity in *Discipline and Punish*, which I discussed in chapter 8. Just as Lukács views modernist inwardness as part of a general process of fragmentation, so Foucault presents the modern focus on an inner self and sense of identity as but a reflex, and a mystification, of a general social trend toward greater discipline and control. Both Lukács and Foucault are quite one-sided in their analyses, ignoring all the potentially positive aspects of the inward turn. Their ideas are, however, particularly apt for the understanding of schizophrenic introversion: each shows to what extent both the very possibility and the form of an escape from social engagement may be laid out in advance by the society from which one retreats.

76. Quotations from Foucault's early book, *Madness and Civilization* (trans. R. Howard [New York and Toronto: New American Library, 1965], pp. 223, 226), where a Dionysian-primitivist view of insanity often seems to be assumed.

Appendix: Neurobiological Considerations

1. See, for example, E. H. Reynolds, "Structure and function in neurology and psychiatry," *British Journal of Psychiatry, 157,* 1990, 481–90; S. Rose, "Disordered molecules and diseased minds," *Journal of Psychiatric Research, 18,* 1984, 351–60; G. L. Engel, "The need for a new medical model: A challenge for biomedicine," *Science, 196*(4286), 1977, 129–36. R. C. Lewontin, S. Rose, and L. J. Kamin write as follows: "The biological and the social are neither separable, nor antithetical, nor alternatives, but complementary. All causes of the behavior of organisms . . . are simultaneously both social and biological, as they are all amenable to analysis at many levels" (*Not in Our Genes* [New York: Pantheon, 1984], p. 282).

2. Quotation from M. Foucault, *Madness and Civilization* (New York and Toronto: New American Library, 1965), p. 75. The tendency to use physicalistic-causal

language for mental illness and an idealist language, or a language of reasons, for mental health is discussed in R. Smith, "Mental disorder, criminal responsibility and the social history of theories of volition," *Psychological Medicine, 9*, 1979, 13–19. Freud seems, incidentally, to have shared this view of psychoses as involving mainly defect, rather than defense, phenomena; see P. Federn, *Ego Psychology and the Psychoses* (London: Maresfield Reprints, 1953/1977), p. 169.

3. To illustrate this viewpoint, which is very commonly held in psychology and psychiatry, let me quote from an anonymous review that I received concerning a paper I had submitted to a well-known, mainstream psychology journal:

> Portrayal of this disorder [schizophrenia] as other than an unfortunate consequence of an aberrant processing deficit would be a serious mistake. There is no more wisdom to be gained in the communication of the psychotic psychiatric patient than in the dementia of the Alzheimer's patient. Each form of disorder is a consequence of particular deficits. At best, the vicissitudes of the thought disorder may be studied in order to provide a clue to the course of the illness and its relationship to particular neurochemical changes. . . . In the schizophrenic thought disorder . . . there is little more than the tragic evidence of a mind wasted away in dementia.

4. Re the eighteenth-century view, see R. Porter, *Mind-Forged Manacles: A History of Madness in England from the Restoration to the Regency* (Cambridge: Harvard University Press, 1987), pp. 195–96. These physicalistic doctrines may have served as a way in which the alienists and mad-doctors of the period could ally themselves with more prestigious brands of medical science, while also asserting their special prerogative over the care of the insane; it has been argued that this is also the case with contemporary biological psychiatry; see R. P. Bentall, H. F. Jackson, and D. Pilgrim, "Abandoning the concept of 'schizophrenia': Some implications of validity arguments for psychological research into psychotic phenomena," *British Journal of Clinical Psychology, 27*, 1988, 315. See also Bentall, Jackson, and Pilgrim, "The concept of schizophrenia is dead: Long live the concept of schizophrenia?" *British Journal of Clinical Psychology, 27*, 1988, 329–31.

5. The philosopher Michael Oakeshott formulates this oft-stated proposition as follows: "In virtue of an agent being a reflective consciousness, his actions and utterances are the outcomes of what he understands his situation to be, and . . . this understanding cannot be 'reduced' " (quoted in Barham, *Schizophrenia and Human Value* [Oxford: Blackwell, 1984], p. 170).

6. See, for example, E. H. Reynolds, "Structure and function," 1990, p. 488: "Cerebral function is profoundly influenced by psychological and social factors."

7. In 1983 Judd Marmor noted the spreading of "the fallacy of biological determinism" as a "consequence of the remarkable advances in genetics, neurochemical, and pharmacological research" ("Systems thinking in psychiatry," *American Journal of Psychiatry, 140*, 1983, 835). Recent neuroimaging research seems to have exacerbated this tendency.

8. E. C. Johnstone, T. J. Crow, C. D. Frith, et al., "The dementia of dementia praecox," *Acta Psychiatrica Scandinavica, 57*, 1978, 305–24; E. Miller, "Neuropsychology," in P. McGuffin, M. F. Shanks, and R. J. Hodgson, eds., *The Scientific Principles of Psychopathology* (London: Academic Press, 1984), p. 448; W.

B. Lawson, I. N. Waldman, and D. R. Weinberger, "Schizophrenic dementia: Clinical and computed axial tomography correlates," *Journal of Nervous and Mental Disease*, 176, 1988, 207–12.

9. E. Kraepelin, *Dementia Praecox and Paraphrenia* (Huntington, NY: Robert E. Krieger, 1971; first English ed., 1919), p. 1.

10. Quoted in G. E. Berrios, "Positive and negative symptoms and Jackson," *Archives of General Psychiatry*, 42, 1985, 96.

11. See M. J. Clark, "The rejection of psychological approaches to mental disorder in late nineteenth-century British psychiatry," in A. Scull, ed., *Madhouses, Mad-Doctors, and Madmen: The Social History of Psychiatry in the Victorian Era* (Philadelphia: University of Pennsylvania Press, 1981), pp. 271–312, 275, 284. Re Jackson's point of view and influence, see also Berrios, "Positive and negative symptoms," 1985; Berrios, "French views on positive and negative symptoms: A conceptual history," *Comprehensive Psychiatry*, 32, 1991, 395–403; E. Stengel, "Hughlings Jackson's influence in psychiatry," *British Journal of Psychiatry*, 109, 1963, 348–55.

12. Quoted in Clark, "Rejection of psychological approaches," 1981, p. 284.

13. Ibid., p. 271.

14. Phrases from Southard (1912) in P. R. Slavney and P. R. McHugh, *Psychiatric Polarities* (Baltimore and London: Johns Hopkins University Press, 1987), p. 12. See also A. Tamburini's influential paper, "A theory of hallucinations" (1881) *History of Psychiatry*, 1, 1990, 145–56.

15. Quotations from Clark, "Rejection of psychological approaches," 1981, pp. 286, 284.

16. See M. Bleuler, *The Schizophrenic Disorders: Long-Term Patient and Family Studies*, trans. S. M. Clemens (New Haven and London: Yale University Press, 1978), p. 448. One historian of psychiatry has spoken of the "legitimation of contempt" that was brought about by these trends; see Barham, *Schizophrenia and Human Value*, 1984, p. 14.

17. A. Harrington, "Nineteenth-century ideas on hemisphere differences and 'duality of mind,'" *Behavioral and Brain Sciences*, 8, 1985, 622, 621. Also, re Kraepelin, see N. Andreasen, "Cerebral localization: Its relevance to psychiatry," *Can Schizophrenia Be Localized in the Brain?* (Washington, DC: American Psychiatric Press, 1986), p 8.

18. Quoted in Harrington, "Nineteenth-century ideas on hemisphere," 1985, p. 623. In 1879, Crichton-Browne wrote that "the cortical centers which are last organized, which are the most highly evolved and voluntary, and which are supposed to be located on the left side of the brain, might suffer first in insanity" (quoted in T. J. Crow, J. Ball, S. R. Bloom, et al., "Schizophrenia as an anomaly of development of cerebral asymmetry," *Archives of General Psychiatry*, 46, 1989, 1149). The psychoanalysts Sandor Ferenczi and Werner Wolff associated the right hemisphere with the unconscious and with libidinal fantasies; see A. Harrington, *Medicine, Mind, and the Double Brain* (Princeton, NJ: Princeton University Press, 1987), pp. 258–59.

19. See Harrington, *Medicine, Mind*, 1987.

20. E. Kraepelin, "Dementia praecox," in J. Cutting and M. Shepherd, eds., *The Clinical Roots of the Schizophrenia Concept* (Cambridge: Cambridge University Press, 1987; originally published in 1896), p. 23. Kraepelin also believed that, in

dementia praecox, "the ancestral activities offer[ed] a greater power of resistance to the morbid process than the psychic faculties belonging to the highest degrees of development, corresponding to the slighter damage done to the deeper cortical layers which are more like those of lower animals" (*Dementia Praecox*, p. 222).

21. For example, Eugene Minkowski's Bergsonian analysis, *La Schizophrénie*, published in 1927; Ludwig Binswanger's Heideggerian case studies, written just after World War II. It is a little-known fact that even Kraepelin, toward the end of his career (1920), adopted a far less monolithic and dogmatic position, acknowledging "that schizophrenic symptoms may also occur without any damage to cerebral tissue" (quoted in A. Jablensky, "Multicultural studies and the nature of schizophrenia: A review," *Journal of the Royal Society of Medicine*, 80, 1987, 167). Kurt Goldstein made a similar shift; see note 25.

22. E. Stengel, "Hughlings Jackson's influence in psychiatry," 1963, 348–55.

23. H. Luxumberger quoted in Barham, *Schizophrenia and Human Value*, 1984, p. 52.

24. The actual resemblance of these conditions to schizophrenia is rather dubious, however. As Jaspers noted, there is a "profound psychopathological difference between, for example, general paralysis and schizophrenia, between the crude organic destruction—machinery smashed up—and the distraction of mind, the cessation of organic phenomena as the [schizophrenic] process advances" (quoted in Cutting, *Psychology of Schizophrenia*, 1985, p. 30; see also p. 350). See also M. Bleuler, *Schizophrenic Disorders*, 1978, p. 453.

25. See Howard Gardner, *The Shattered Mind* (New York: Vintage Books, 1974), pp. 93–97, 143–47, 423–27; G. Goldstein, "Contributions of Kurt Goldstein to neuropsychology," *Clinical Neuropsychologist*, 4, 1990, 3–17. Kraepelin, incidentally, has also suggested that the chief defect in schizophrenia might be the loss of the capacity for abstraction (which he describes as "the process . . . which transforms perceptions to general ideas, sensations to emotions, impulses to permanent trends of volition" and which constitutes "higher psychic activity" and "the essence of the psychic personality") (*Dementia Praecox*, pp. 220–21).

    It is interesting to note that Kurt Goldstein, late in his life, actually came to deny the role of organic factors in schizophrenia, arguing that such patients' "nonuse of abstraction is a protective mechanism against the danger of catastrophe and anxiety" (quoted in Goldstein, "Contributions of Kurt Goldstein," p. 8). This is not, however, how he has usually been understood; see L. J. Chapman and J. P. Chapman, *Disordered Thought in Schizophrenia* (Englewood Cliffs, NJ: Prentice-Hall, 1973), pp. 147–48. Problems with the notion of schizophrenic concreteness have already been discussed in earlier chapters.

26. Nancy Andreasen, *The Broken Brain: The Biological Revolution in Psychiatry* (New York: Harper and Row, 1984), p. 138; Andreasen, "Brain imaging: Applications in psychiatry," *Science*, 239, 1988, 1381. I don't think anyone would claim that Andreasen, despite the importance of her empirical research, is one of the more subtle theorists of mind-body relationships; for this very reason, however, she may be the best bellweather of what has recently been the prevailing zeitgeist in biological psychiatry.

27. Berrios ("Positive and negative symptoms," 1985) questions whether contemporary uses of this distinction are truly Jacksonian, since they fail to adopt Jackson's

theoretical model (e.g., the concept of inhibition or release of lower centers, and the idea of a functional hierarchy of nervous activity). Berrios may be correct about some users of the distinction (T. J. Crow, e. g.), but he is certainly mistaken about other major figures like Weinberger and Andreasen.

28. B. G. Charlton, "Editorial: A critique of biological psychiatry," *Psychological Medicine, 20,* 1990, 4.

29. See discussion, and reference to Arvid Carlsson, in D. Healey, "D1 and D2 and D3," *British Journal of Psychiatry, 159,* 1991, 319–24.

30. For an excellent brief review, see M.-M. Mesulam, "Schizophrenia and the brain," *New England Journal of Medicine, 322*(12), March 22, 1990, 842–45.

31. See, for example, T. E. Goldberg, D. R. Weinberger, K. F. Berman, et al., "Further evidence for dementia of the prefrontal type in schizophrenia," *Archives of General Psychiatry, 44,* 1987, 1014.

32. R. Gur, "Cognitive concomitants of hemispheric dysfunction in schizophrenia," *Archives of General Psychiatry, 36,* 1979, 269. See also J. Cutting, *The Right Cerebral Hemisphere and Psychiatric Disorders* (Oxford: Oxford University Press, 1990), p. 282; M. S. Gazzaniga, "Organization of the human brain," *Science, 245,* 1989, 947–52.

33. Quotations from N. Andreasen, "Is schizophrenia a temperolimbic disease?" *Can Schizophrenia Be Localized?* 1986, pp. 39, 43; Andreason, "Brain imaging," 1988, p. 1382.

34. See D. R. Weinberger, "Implications of normal brain development for the pathogenesis of schizophrenia," *Archives of General Psychiatry, 44,* 1987, 661, 663, 665–66; Goldberg, Weinberger, Berman, et al., "Further evidence for dementia," p. 1013; D. R. Weinberger, K. F. Berman, and R. F. Zec, "Physiological dysfunction of dorsolateral prefrontal cortex in schizophrenia: I. Regional cerebral blood flow evidence," *Archives of General Psychiatry, 43,* 1986, 123.

It seems that, in contemporary biological psychiatry, only one of the three axes of the brain (cortical-subcortical) is frequently invoked to explain positive symptoms.

This classical psychodynamic formulation corresponds closely to Jackson's views regarding negative and positive symptoms—though allowing for the possibility that exaggeration of lower processes may not always be secondary to weakness of the higher ones.

35. See A. Mirsky and C. C. Duncan, "Etiology and expression of schizophrenia: Neurobiological and psychosocial factors," *Annual Review of Psychology, 37,* 1986, 297; I. Harvey, M. Williams, B. K. Toone, et al., "The ventricular-brain ratio (VBR) in functional psychoses," *Psychological Medicine, 20,* 1990, 55–62; Reynolds, "Structure and function," 1990, p. 487. From their survey of the literature, S. Rax and N. Rax report: "Studies on schizophrenia and affective disorders differed neither in the extent of reported ventriculomegaly nor in the amount of 'cortical atrophy' " ("Structural brain abnormalities in the major psychoses: A quantitative review of the evidence from computerized imaging," *Psychological Bulletin, 108,* 1990, 93). A recent study found that schizophrenics and affective-disorder patients also did not differ in reduction of temporal lobe volume; see L. I. Altschuler, A. Conrad, P. Hauser, et al., "Reduction of temporal lobe volume in bipolar disorder: A preliminary report of magnetic resonance imaging," *Archives of General Psychiatry, 48,* 1991, 482–83. B. A. Clementz and J. A. Sweeney report similar findings concerning the variable of smooth pursuit

eye movement dysfunction; see "Is eye movement dysfunction a biological marker for schizophrenia?: A methodological review," *Psychological Bulletin, 108,* 1990, 77.

36. L. J. Seidman, "Schizophrenia and brain dysfunction: An integration of recent neurodiagnostic findings," *Psychological Bulletin, 94,* 1983, 195, 223. See also H. A. Nasrallah, "Brain structure and function in schizophrenia," *Current Opinion in Psychiatry, 3,* 1990, 75–78. Most schizophrenic patients have no abnormalities on CT scan. For a critique of past findings re lateral ventricular enlargement (considered a sign of brain tissue loss), see G. N. Smith, W. F. Iacono, M. Moreau, et al., "Choice of comparison group and findings of computerised tomography in schizophrenia," *British Journal of Psychiatry, 153,* 1988, 667–74. It is unclear whether there is a brain-damaged subgroup of schizophrenics or whether it is a matter of degree, with brain abnormalities a normally distributed feature.

37. See A. Pfefferbaum, R. B. Zipursky, K. O. Lim, et al., "Computed tomographic evidence for generalized sulcal and ventricular enlargement in schizophrenia," *Archives of General Psychiatry, 45,* 1988, 633–40; A. Farmer, R. Jackson, P. McGuffin, and P. Storey, "Cerebral ventricular enlargement in chronic schizophrenia: Consistencies and contradictions," *British Journal of Psychiatry, 150,* 1987, 324–30; D. G. C. Owens, E. C. Johnstone, T. J. Crow, et al., "Lateral ventricular size in schizophrenia: Relationship to the disease process and its clinical manifestations," *Psychological Medicine, 15,* 1985, 27–41. A study by R. M. Bilder, G. Degreef, A. K. Pandurangi, and colleagues actually found better performance on neuropsychological tests in patients with more prominent brain abnormalities; "Neuropsychological deterioration and CT scan findings in chronic schizophrenia," *Schizophrenia Research, 1,* 1988, 40 (their findings were rather ambiguous, however, since there was also evidence of an apparent correlation between enlargement of ventricles and *deterioration* of functioning).

Eugen Bleuler was aware of the presence of "mild cerebral atrophy and certain histological changes" in advanced cases of schizophrenia; but he considered the implications of these findings to be unclear. As he noted, "The cerebral atrophy cannot serve as an explanation for the schizophrenic symptoms since diffuse reduction of the cortex produces entirely different manifestations." He emphasized how different the intellectual disturbances in schizophrenia are from those found in patients with dementia or imbecility (*Dementia Praecox, or the Group of Schizophrenias,* trans. J. Zinkin [New York: International Universities Press, 1950], pp. 466–67, 77).

38. See R. B. Zipursky, K. O. Lim, and A. Pfefferbaum, "Brain size in schizophrenia" (with reply by G. D. Pearlson, P. E. Barta, F. V. Schraml, et al.), *Archives of General Psychiatry, 48,* 1991, 179–81. See also N. C. Andreasen, J. C. Ehrhardt, and V. W. Swayze, et al., "Magnetic resonance imaging of the brain in schizophrenia," *Archives of General Psychiatry, 47,* 1990, 35–46.

39. See G. Goldstein, "Contributions of clinical neuropsychology to psychiatry," in P. E. Logue and J. M. Shear, eds., *Clinical Neuropsychology: A Multidisciplinary Approach* (Springfield, IL: Charles Thomas, 1984), pp. 324, 338; A. Fontana and E. Klein, "Self-presentation and the schizophrenic 'deficit,'" *Journal of Consulting and Clinical Psychology, 32,* 1968, 250–56.

40. A classic discussion of this distinction is H. Werner, "Process and achievement," *Harvard Educational Review, 7,* 1937, 353–68.

41. And it may be that the underlying feature is not in any intrinsic sense a relative deficiency. G. Claridge suggests it may be "an exquisite sensitivity of the nervous system" which, due to events, gets transformed into an "appearance of deficit" ("Schizophrenia and human individuality," in C. Blakemore and S. Greenfield, eds., *Mindwaves* [Oxford and New York: Blackwell, 1987], p. 40).

42. See, for example, R. E. Gur, D. Mozley, S. M. Resnick, et al., "Magnetic resonance imaging in schizophrenia, I: Volumetric analysis of brain and cerebrospinal fluid," *Archives of General Psychiatry, 48,* 1991, 407–12. Re taking a dimensional, rather than neurological disease, view of schizophrenia, see G. Claridge and T. Beech, "Don't leave the psyche out of neuropsychology" (commentary on Gray et al., "Neuropsychology of schizophrenia"), *Behavioral and Brain Sciences, 14,* 1991, 21.

43. See, for example, S. Levin and D. Yurgelin-Todd, "Contributions of clinical neuropsychology to the study of schizophrenia," *Journal of Abnormal Psychology, 98,* 1989, 341–56; Claridge, "Schizophrenia and human individuality," 1987; Cutting, *Right Cerebral Hemisphere,* 1990, p. 286; P. F. Gjerde, "Attentional capacity dysfunction and arousal in schizophrenia," *Psychological Bulletin, 93,* 1983, 66n.

44. On this point, see H. Ishiguro, "Skepticism and sanity," in C. Ginet and S. Shoemaker, eds., *Knowledge and Mind: Philosophical Essays* (New York and Oxford: Oxford University Press, 1983), pp. 69–70.

45. See S. Rose, "Disordered molecules and diseased minds," *Journal of Psychiatric Research, 18,* 1984, 351–60; J. Hill, "Reasons and causes: The nature of explanations in psychology and psychiatry," *Psychological Medicine, 12,* 1982, 501–14. See also discussion and references in D. Cohen and H. Cohen, "Biological theories, drug treatments, and schizophrenia: A critical assessment, *Journal of Mind and Behavior, 7,* 1986, 11–36, esp. 27–30.

46. See, for example, R. W. Sperry, "Psychology's mentalist paradigm and the religion/science tension," *American Psychologist, 43,* 1988, 609.

47. D. R. Weinberger, K. F. Berman, R. F. Zec, and M. K. Iadarola, "Effect of simulated emotional state on cortical blood flow," *Proceedings of the Thirty-ninth Annual Meeting of the Society of Biology Psychiatry,* 1984.

48. See L. Ciompi, "Is there really a schizophrenia? The long-term course of psychotic phenomena," *British Journal of Psychiatry, 145,* 1984, 639; J. L. Haracz, "Neural plasticity in schizophrenia," *Schizophrenia Bulletin, 11,* 1985, 205, 210. See also W. T. Carpenter, "Psychological and psychophysiological models of schizophrenia: Discussion," in H. Häfner, W. F. Gattaz, and W. Janzarik, eds., *Search for the Causes of Schizophrenia* (Berlin: Springer Verlag, 1987), p. 217. D. R. Weinberger raises the possibility that prolonged stress could cause a reversible pseudo-atrophy of brain tissue; "Computed tomography [CT] findings in schizophrenia: Speculation on the meaning of it all," *Journal of Psychiatric Research, 18,* 1984, 482.

49. E. Kandel, "From metapsychology to molecular biology: Explorations into the nature of anxiety," *American Journal of Psychiatry, 140,* 1983, 1278. See also the work of Gary Lynch, described in G. Johnson, *In the Palace of Memory* (New York: Knopf, 1991).

Alternatives to biological reductionism can be formulated in a number of different ways, depending on the position one takes vis-à-vis the mind-body problem. The mental or psychological realm may be understood dualistically (as a different form of existence interacting reciprocally with the physical), in an emergentist perspective (as involving systemic wholes that arise from, but are irreducible to, physical constituents existing on a lower hierarchical level), or in terms of some kind of mental-physical identity theory (here the mental is not seen as a different kind of reality; both mental and physical are understood as different languages or conceptual systems applied to a single psychophysical reality). For useful discussion of these issues in a psychiatric context, see A. Goodman, "Organic unity theory: The mind-body problem revisited," *American Journal of Psychiatry, 148,* 1991, 553–63.

50. Mercier quoted in Clark, "Rejection of psychological approaches," 1981, p. 284. M. Beiser and W. G. Iacono note that "despite protestations to the contrary, most investigations are one-sided, subscribing either to the view that a biological deficit within the individual inevitably and inexorably results in illness or that the person is at the mercy of the environment" ("An update on the epidemiology of schizophrenia," *Canadian Journal of Psychiatry, 35,* 1990, 664). According to D. Healey, current proponents of the dopamine hypothesis (e.g., T. J. Crow) ascribe virtually all features of schizophrenia to biological abnormalities, either to excess dopamine or to brain cell loss; see "Schizophrenia: Basic, release, reactive and defect processes," *Human Psychopharmacology, 5,* 1990, 105–21.

51. As Oliver Sacks has put it, "A disease is never a mere loss or excess— . . . there is always a reaction, on the part of the affected organism or individual, to restore, to replace, to compensate for and to preserve its identity, however strange the means may be" (*The Man Who Mistook His Wife for a Hat* [New York: Summit Books, 1985], p. 4).

52. H. D. Brenner, W. Böker, J. Müller, et al., "On autoprotective efforts of schizophrenics, neurotics and controls," *Acta Psychiatrica Scandinavica, 75,* 1987, 411–12. See also V. Carr, "Patients' techniques for coping with schizophrenia: An exploratory study," *British Journal of Medical Psychology, 61,* 1988, 339–52.

53. Though Kurt Goldstein stresses this point, his notion of "concreteness" has generally been understood as describing a deficit condition; see G. Goldstein, "Contributions of Kurt Goldstein," 1990, p. 7. Re these issues, see Robert Waelder, *Basic Theory of Psychoanalysis* (New York: International Universities Press, 1960), p. 204.

54. See Brenner et al., "On autoprotective efforts," 1987, pp. 412–13.

55. See E. Straus, *Von Sinn der Sinne,* discussed in E. Schachtel, *Metamorphosis* (New York: Basic Books, 1959), p. 158.

56. A. Margo, D. R. Hemsley, and P. D. Slade found that when auditory stimuli are not experienced as meaningful, they are more likely to encourage hallucinatory experience; see "The effects of varying auditory input on schizophrenic hallucinations," *British Journal of Psychiatry, 139,* 1981, 122–27. P. D. Slade showed that the intensity of auditory hallucinations decreases when patients are engaged in a complex auditory processing task, as opposed to a more passive kind of listening; see "The external control of auditory hallucinations: An information theory analysis," *British Journal of Social and Clinical Psychology, 13,* 1974, 73–79. A. Breier and J. Strauss present evidence that seems to suggest that schizophrenics are inclined to use activity to control their symptoms, whereas patients with more prominent affective features are more likely to use with-

drawal; see "Self-control in psychotic disorders," *Archives of General Psychiatry, 40,* 1983, 1141–45. C. Shagass, M. Amadeo, and D. A. Overton found that eye-tracking performance improves when schizophrenics (and other individuals) engage in a more purposeful task; see "Eye-tracking performance and engagement of attention," *Archives of General Psychiatry, 33,* 1976, 121–25. See also Cutting, *Psychology of Schizophrenia,* 1985, p. 302; R. Cohen and U. Borst, "Psychological models of schizophrenic impairment," in Häfner, Gattaz, and Janzarik, *Search for the Causes,* 1987, p. 191.

57. See D. M. Houston, "The relationship between cognitive failure and self-focused attention," *British Journal of Clinical Psychology, 28,* 1989, 85–86; J. Sternberg and J. Kolligian, eds., *Competence Reconsidered* (New Haven, CT: Yale University Press, 1990); C. D. Frith, "Schizophrenia: An abnormality of consciousness," in G. Underwood and R. Stevens, eds., *Aspects of Consciousness,* vol. 2 (London: Academic Press, 1981), p. 156.

58. See J. S. Strauss, "Subjective experiences of schizophrenia: Toward a new dynamic psychiatry-II," *Schizophrenia Bulletin, 15,* 1989, 179–87.

59. See C. Mundt (1985), discussed in W. Janzarik, "The concept of schizophrenia: History and problems," in Häfner, Gattaz, and Janzarik, *Search for the Causes,* 1987, p. 15, re "apathy syndrome." See also M. Bleuler, *Schizophrenic Disorders,* 1978, pp. 217–18, 413, 418, 480–81. The assumption that most schizophrenics deteriorate during the course of their illness has been disproven in recent years; see C. M. Harding, J. Zubin, and J. S. Strauss, "Chronicity in schizophrenia: Fact, partial fact, or artifact," *Hospital and Community Psychiatry, 38,* 1987, 477–86. Manfred Bleuler, who questions the appropriateness of the term *schizophrenic dementia,* states that he knows "of no patient who became a schizophrenic dement in slow, gradual stages . . . whose dementia did not recede appreciably again at a later time" (*Schizophrenic Disorders,* p. 418).

60. See Cutting, *Psychology of Schizophrenia,* 1985, pp. 29–30, 350. At the time Jaspers was writing, the paradigmatic organic disorders included Korsakoff's syndrome, general paralysis, senile dementia, and presenile dementia (Alzheimer's).

61. D. H. Ingvar and G. Franzen, "Abnormalities of cerebral blood flow distribution in patients with chronic schizophrenia," *Acta Psychiatrica Scandinavica, 50,* 1974, 425–62. G. Franzen and D. H. Ingvar, "Abnormal distribution of cerebral activity in chronic schizophrenia," *Journal of Psychiatric Research, 12,* 1975, 199–214.

62. J. M. Cleghorn, E. S. Garnett, C. Nahmias, et al., "Increased frontal and reduced parietal glucose metabolism in acute untreated schizophrenics," *Psychiatry Research, 28,* 1989, 119–33; R. E. Gur, S. M. Resnick, A. Alavi, et al., "Regional brain function in schizophrenia: I. A positron emission tomography study," *Archives of General Psychiatry, 44,* 1987, 119; J. L. Waddington, "Sight and insight: Regional cerebral metabolic activity in schizophrenia," *British Journal of Psychiatry, 156,* 1990, 615–19. It is also noteworthy that neuroleptic medication has been found to decrease relative frontality in some patients: see Wolkin et al. (1985), described in Andreasen, *Brain Imaging: Applications in Psychiatry,* 1989, p. 326.

63. G. Geraud, M. C. Arne-Bes, A. Guell, and A. Bes, "Reversibility of hemodynamic hypofrontality in schizophrenia," *Journal of Cerebral Blood Flow and Metabolism, 7,* 1987, 9–12. See also J. M. Cleghorn, E. S. Garnett, J. Kaplan, et

al. (1986) and, re EEG findings, P. Williamson and M. Mamelek (1987), both discussed in J. D. Russell and M. G. Roxanas, "Psychiatry and the frontal lobes," *Australian and New Zealand Journal of Psychiatry, 24,* 1990, 113–32.

Evidence of heightened activity in the schizophrenic brain and especially in the frontal regions is discussed in R. Miller, "Schizophrenia as a progressive disorder: Relations to EEG, CT, neuropathological and other evidence," *Progress in Neurobiology, 33,* 1989, 22–24; this includes EEG evidence of excessive activity in the slow frequencies (delta and theta). These frequencies have been found to be associated with inner-directed mental activity, such as reading, arithmetical calculation, and meditation; also they seem to occur prior to hallucinations in schizophrenics and prior to creative responses in normal subjects; see J. L. Whitton, H. Moldofsky, and F. Lue, "EEG frequency patterns associated with hallucinations in schizophrenia and 'creativity' in normals," *Biological Psychiatry, 13,* 1978, 124, 131. See also J. M. Morihisa, F. H. Duffy, and R. J. Wyatt, "Brain electrical activity mapping (BEAM) in schizophrenic patients," *Archives of General Psychiatry, 40,* 1983, 719–28, re increased delta activity in frontal regions in schizophrenia.

It should be noted that the hypofrontal pattern is hardly unique to schizophrenia, having also been found in patients with severe affective disorder: see M. S. Buchsbaum, J. Cappalletti, R. Ball, et al., "Positron emission tomographic image measurement in schizophrenia and affective disorders," *Annals of Neurology, 15,* 1984, 157–65; Buchsbaum, L. E. DeLisi, H. H. Holcomb, et al., "Anteroposterior gradients in cerebral glucose use in schizophrenia and affective disorders," *Archives of General Psychiatry, 41,* 1984, 1159–66. Also, the hypofrontality of schizophrenic subjects found in some studies of glucose metabolism and regional cerebral blood flow applies only to the ratio of anterior to posterior activity; absolute metabolic activity may be as high as or higher than in control subjects. Thus the finding of hypofrontality may primarily reflect elevated posterior metabolism rather than reduced frontal metabolism. See A. F. Mirsky and C. C. Duncan, "Etiology and expression of schizophrenia: Neurobiological and psychosocial factors," *Annual Review of Psychology, 37,* 1986, 291–319; M. D. Devous, "Imaging brain function by single-photon emission computer tomography," in Andreasen, *Brain Imaging,* 1989, pp. 200, 204. Ingvar and Franzen ("Abnormalities of cerebral blood flow," 1974) note that the overall mean cerebral blood flow in schizophrenics was normal, whereas in organic dementia it tends to decline.

64. See G. P. Sheppard, J. Jutai, R. Manchanda, et al., "Frontal-lobe hypofunction in schizophrenia," *Lancet,* April 28, 1984, 969–71, for a review of arguments against the hypofrontality hypothesis.

It should also be noted that evidence for structural abnormalities specifically in the frontal lobes in schizophrenia is very weak: see Russell and Roxanas, "Psychiatry and frontal lobes," 1990, pp. 125–26; Pfefferbaum, Zipursky, Lim, et al., "Computed tomographic evidence," 1988, pp. 638, 639; R. L. Suddath, M. F. Casanova, T. E. Goldberg, et al., "Temporal lobe pathology in schizophrenia: A quantitative magnetic resonance imaging study," *American Journal of Psychiatry, 146,* 1989, 464–72; Andreasen, Ehrhardt, Swayze, et al., "Magnetic resonance imaging," 1990, pp. 35–44. R. Kerwin states that "neuropathological support has been sparse" for the hypofrontality hypothesis ("How do the neuropathological changes of schizophrenia relate to pre-existing neurotransmitter and aetiological hypotheses?" *Psychological Medicine, 19,* 1989, 563–67).

Interestingly enough, there is evidence that schizophrenic patients with large frontal lesions (from leucotomy) may show an *absence* of disturbed performance on tests of attention and mental control; see D. T. Stuss, D. F. Benson, E. F. Kaplan, et al., "Leucotomized and nonleucotomized schizophrenics: Comparison on tests of attention," *Biological Psychiatry*, 16, 1981, 1085–1100. Silvano Arieti noted some time ago that an "organic defect, although limiting greatly human potentialities, may eliminate the psychoses, as, for instance, in some forms of psychosurgery" (*The Interpretation of Schizophrenia* [New York: Basic Books, 1974], p. 218).

65. See D. T. Stuss and D. F. Benson, "Neuropsychological studies of the frontal lobes," *Psychological Bulletin*, 95, 1984, 3, 17.

66. See Harrington, "Nineteenth-century ideas on hemisphere," 1985, p. 622, re this. Jackson and some other British neurologists were exceptions on this issue, by the way; see Harrington, *Medicine, Mind*, 1987, p. 225, 225n.

67. See K. F. Berman, B. P. Illowsky, and D. R. Weinberger, "Physiological dysfunction of dorsolateral prefrontal cortex in schizophrenia: IV. Further evidence for regional and behavioral specificity," *Archives of General Psychiatry*, 45, 1988, 616–22, re the Ravens Progressive Matrices test. See also E. Miller, "Intellectual function and its disorders," in M. Shepherd and O. L. Zangwill, eds., *General Psychopathology*, vol. 1 of *Handbook of Psychiatry* (Cambridge: Cambridge University Press, 1983), p. 121.

68. Stuss and Benson, "Neuropsychological studies," 1984, pp. 17–19, 22.

69. Schizophrenics have been described as having the most difficulty on "tests requiring extroversion of attention for a relatively prolonged period and the mobilization of considerable energy for their solution" (I. Kendig and W. V. Richmond [1940], quoted in T. E. Goldberg, D. R. Ragland, E. F. Torrey, et al., "Neuropsychological assessment of monozygotic twins discordant for schizophrenia," *Archives of General Psychiatry*, 47, 1990, 1070).

70. D. H. Ingvar, "Abnormal distribution of cerebral activity in chronic schizophrenia: A neurophysiological interpretation," in C. Baxter and T. Melnechuk, eds., *Perspectives in Schizophrenia Research* (New York: Raven Press, 1980), p. 107. F. B. Wood and D. L. Flowers have suggested that hypofrontal blood flow in schizophrenics may be induced by anxiety (which, they suggest, causes an active inhibition of response to novelty); see "Hypofrontal vs. hypo-Sylvian blood flow in schizophrenia," *Schizophrenia Bulletin*, 16, 1990, 419–20.

71. D. H. Ingvar and G. Franzen, "Distribution of cerebral activity in chronic schizophrenia," *Lancet*, December 21, 1974, 1484–86. Evidence of heightened activation of the posterior lobes can be found in Ingvar and Franzen, "Abnormalities of cerebral blood flow," 1974. Morihisa, Duffy, and Wyatt ("Brain electrical activity mapping," 1983, p. 726) found evidence of increased cortical arousal or activity in the postcentral regions of both medicated and drug-free schizophrenics (as indicated by increased beta activity on an EEG-related measure).

72. Some important refinements of the hypofrontality hypothesis suggested by Daniel Weinberger should be mentioned. He has argued that hypofrontality is not a constant characteristic of schizophrenics, but one that occurs only under specific conditions, namely, when a certain kind of cognitive demand is present; see, for example, D. R. Weinberger, K. F. Berman, and R. F. Zec, "Physiologic dysfunction of dorsolateral prefrontal cortex in schizophrenia: I. Regional cerebral blood flow evidence," *Archives of General Psychiatry*, 43, 1986, 114–24. Though many

empirical questions remain, Weinberger does seem to have isolated a more robust empirical phenomenon: he has been able to show that a significant subset of schizophrenics do manifest hypofrontal blood flow in a specific part of the prefrontal cortex (the dorsolateral aspect) when responding to certain card-sorting tests, tests on which they may perform particularly poorly.

(However, for various kinds of counterevidence, see Devous, "Imaging brain function," pp. 201–3, where nonparanoid schizophrenic patients failed to show the expected hypofrontality, and where half the normal control subjects *did* show such hypofrontality on the Wisconsin Card Sort. Also, R. Morice showed that manics did as poorly as schizophrenics on the WCST; see "Cognitive inflexibility and pre-frontal dysfunction in schizophrenia and mania," *British Journal of Psychiatry, 157*, 1990, 50–54. See also Levin and Yurgelin-Todd, "Contributions of clinical neuropsychology," 1989. D. L. Bratt, R. Heaton, M. Cullen, and colleagues found that a less severely ill group of outpatient schizophrenics did not perform more poorly on the WCST than did normal controls; see "Relatively normal Wisconsin card sorting results in chronic schizophrenic outpatients," *Psychopharmacology Bulletin,* in press, reported in A. S. Bellack, K. T. Mueser, R. L. Morrison, et al., "Remediation of cognitive deficits in schizophrenia," *American Journal of Psychiatry, 147*, 1990, 1653. Another study found that "abstraction," as measured by WCST performance, was one of the *least* impaired functions in a sample of unmedicated schizophrenic patients; see A. J. Saykin, R. C. Gur, R. E. Gur, et al., "Neuropsychological function in schizophrenia: Selective impairment in memory and learning," *Archives of General Psychiatry, 48*, 1991, 618–24.)

There is considerable ambiguity, however, about what this more circumscribed phenomenon might signify.

Originally, Weinberger and his co-workers equated the psychological correlate of the hypofrontality they observed with a very general loss of higher cognitive capacities, which they portrayed in terms virtually indistinguishable from Goldstein's concept of loss of the abstract attitude; see Goldberg et al., "Dementia of the prefrontal type," 1987, p. 1013. However, they did acknowledge the difficulty of ruling out the possibility that this metabolic finding could reflect motivational factors or some kind of attentional preference rather than some inherent defect—for example, a failure on the part of the schizophrenic to care about the task, or a disinterest in responding to environmental rather than internal contingencies (they speak of "diminution of the valence of external feedback" as a possible explanation; p. 1008). The difficulty of teaching schizophrenics how to improve their performance on the WCST—found by Goldberg et al., 1987—seemed to argue against such interpretations; but the sample of patients in this study was severely impaired and may not be representative of schizophrenics in general. Other investigators have found that, if properly motivated, some schizophrenics *are* able to improve their performance with training. See M. F. Green, S. Ganzell, P. Satz, et al., "Teaching the Wisconsin card sorting test to schizophrenic patients" (with reply by T. Goldberg, K. Berman, and D. Weinberger), *Archives of General Psychiatry, 47*, 1990, 91–92; Bellack et al., "Remediation of cognitive deficits," 1990. See also A. T. Summerfelt, L. D. Alphs, F. R. Funderburk, et al., "Impaired Wisconsin Card Sort performance in schizophrenia may reflect motivational deficits" (with reply by T. E. Goldberg and D. R. Weinberger), *Archives of General Psychiatry, 48*, 1991, 282–83.

Weinberger has, in any case, retreated somewhat from his rather Gold-steinian interpretation of hypofrontality, for more recently he has acknowledged that not all cognitive tasks demanding high-level abstraction and logical reasoning necessarily activate the frontal parts of the brain. On another kind of reasoning task (Ravens Progressive Matrices), the posterior lobes tend to be activated in normals, and in a study by Weinberger's group, the same pattern occurred with schizophrenic subjects; see Berman, Illowsky, and Weinberger, "Physiological dysfunction of dorsolateral prefrontal cortex in schizophrenia," 1988, pp. 616–22. (It should also be noted that many neuropsychologists do not consider sorting tasks of the kind Weinberger used to be primarily tests of abstraction or concept formation, but rather, tests only of the *application* of rules; the rules themselves may well be understood even when the patient cannot act in accordance with them; see Stuss and Benson, "Neuropsychological studies of frontal lobes," 1984, p. 18. See also E. T. Fey, "The performance of young schizophrenics and young normals on the Wisconsin Card Sort Test," *Journal of Consulting and Clinical Psychology, 15,* 1951, 313–14; and Morice, "Cognitive inflexibility," 1990, p. 53, for evidence that the WCST measures something different from either Goldstein's abstract atttitude or intelligence broadly conceived.)

It now seems appropriate to understand Weinberger's situation-specific hypofrontality as indexing not a general failure of abstraction but a more circumscribed defect, one primarily affecting more pragmatic or worldly modes of cognition (and this, of course, could easily lead to a preference for more introverted and detached modes of cognition). This would be at most an *aspect* of abstraction, if the latter term is in fact applicable. (Also, one might question whether such a circumscribed hypofrontality can account for the broad range of phenomena Weinberger ascribes to it—including failures of inhibition.) For a critique of Weinberger, see Miller, "Schizophrenia as a progressive disorder," 1989, pp. 36–37.

73. Hayes-Newtington quoted in Barham, *Schizophrenia and Human Value*, 1984, p. 38.

74. J. Lang, "The other side of the ideological aspects of schizophrenia," *Psychiatry, 3,* 1940, 392, 389, 393 (emphasis added). Lang points out that on "the ideological level, the ideocentric schizophrene uses abstractions"; indeed, he says, "One of the chief quests of his thought is the search for abstractions" (p. 393).

75. Re cortical hyperarousal, see P. H. Venables, "Psychophysiological aspects of schizophrenia," *British Journal of Medicine, 39,* 1966, 289–97; see also Gjerde, "Attentional capacity dysfunction," 1983, p. 65.

This would be consistent with research on animals, where acute stress seems to increase brain dopamine turnover, especially in the cortex; see R. J. Wyatt, R. C. Alexander, M. F. Egan, and D. G. Kirch, "Schizophrenia, just the facts: What do we know, how well do we know it?" *Schizophrenia Research, 1,* 1988, 15. Weinberger himself describes the condition of cortical dopaminergic hypofunction and subcortical hyperfunction, which he postulates as being a "paradoxical" and "peculiar" state, and he admits there is no direct evidence for such hypofunction in schizophrenia. See D. R. Weinberger and K. F. Berman, "Speculation on the meaning of cerebral metabolic hypofrontality in schizophrenia," *Schizophrenia Bulletin, 14,* 1988, 165; and D. R. Weinberger, "Implications of normal brain development," 1987, p. 664. Studies of the so-called cortical-subcortical ratio of activation have been equivocal and contradictory; see S. M. Resnick, R. E. Gur, A. Alavi, et al., "Positron emission tomography and subcortical glucose metabolism in schizophrenia," *Psychiatry Research, 24,* 1988, 9. Certainly there is considerable evidence (albeit inconsistent—as with nearly everything about schizophrenia) of an increase in neural activity in the schizophrenic forebrain. Partly, this could result from heightened activity of subcortical structures such as the hippocampus (the forebrain includes both cortical and subcortical areas), but it seems unlikely that the increase can be wholly explained in this way. Several investigators have in fact found evidence of heightened neural activity specifically in the cortex in schizophrenia (as measured by dendritic activation and glucose utilization; see C. R. Mukundan, "Computed EEG in schizophrenics," *Biological Psychiatry, 21,* 1986, 1227, re EEG evidence); and there are also interesting suggestions that the calming effect of neuroleptic drugs may sometimes be associated with a *decrease* in cortical activity along with a relatively constant level of subcortical metabolism; see R. E. Gur, S. M. Resnick, R. C. Gur, et al., "Regional brain function in schizophrenia: II. Repeated evaluation with positron emission tomography," *Archives of General Psychiatry, 44,* 1987, 129.

76. This is the most likely meaning of the common finding of enlarged ventricles in the schizophrenic brain; see review in G. W. Roberts, "Schizophrenia: A neurological perspective," *British Journal of Psychiatry, 158,* 1991, 8–17. See also, for example, R. Brown, N. Colter, J. A. N. Corsellis, et al., "Postmortem evidence of structural brain changes in schizophrenia," *Archives of General Psychiatry, 43,* 1986, 36–42; B. Bogerts, E. Meertz, and R. Schonfeldt-Bausch, "Basal ganglia and limbic system pathology in schizophrenia," *Archives of General Psychiatry, 42,* 1985, 784–91; M.-M. Mesulam, "Schizophrenia and the brain," 1990, 842–45. However, a recent postmortem study found changes in temporal lobe structures in suicide as well as schizophrenic brains, which raises questions as to how specific to schizophrenia these changes really are; see L. I. Altschuler, M. F. Casanova, T. E. Goldberg, and J. E. Kleinman, "The hippocampus and parahippocampus in schizophrenic, suicide, and control brains," *Archives of General Psychiatry, 47,* 1990, 1029–34.

77. R. L. Suddath, G. S. Christison, E. F. Torrey, et al., "Anatomical abnormalities in the brains of monozygotic twins discordant for schizophrenia," *New England Journal of Medicine,* 322(12), 1990, 789–94. For conflicting results, however, see S. Heckers, H. Heinson, and H. Beckmann, "Reply" to B. Bogerts, P. Falkai, and B. Greve, "Evidence of reduced temporolimbic structure volumes in schizophrenia," *Archives of General Psychiatry, 48,* 1991, 956–58. Also, a neurophysiological study by J. Gruzelier, K. Seymour, L. Wilson, and associates found patterns of deficits "suggestive of focal impairments involving hippocampal systems in many [schizophrenic] patients" ("Impairments on neuropsychologic tests of temporohippocampal and frontohippocampal functions and word fluency in remitting schizophrenia and affective disorders," *Archives of General Psychiatry, 45,* 1988, 629).

78. E. F. Torrey and M. R. Peterson, "Schizophrenia and the limbic system," *Lancet,* October 19, 1974, 943. One study found hypermetabolism of the left temporal lobe in schizophrenic patients; M. Kurachi, K. Kobayashi, R. Matsubara, et al., "Regional cerebral blood flow in schizophrenic disorders," *European Neurology,*

24, 1985, 176–81. Another study found relative hyperactivity in the hippocampal areas of patients who were having auditory hallucinations (many of whom were schizophrenic); see M. Musalek, I. Podreka, H. Walter, et al., "Regional brain function in hallucinations: A study of regional cerebral blood flow," *Comprehensive Psychiatry, 30,* 1989, 99–108.

79. This combination of functional and structural anomalies—on the one hand, overactivation, and, on the other, diminished size, lesions, or abnormalities of neuronal morphology and packaging—may seem paradoxical at first, but various hypotheses can account for it: loss of neuronal mass in the hippocampus could affect a regulatory center, thereby allowing other parts of the structure to become overactive; a lesion could be of the irritative type, causing spontaneous discharge; alternatively, the overactivation itself could cause the cell loss or disorganization, perhaps by causing the internal release of neurotoxic substances. See Andreasen, "Brain imaging," 1988, p. 1382; J. R. Stevens, "Epilepsy, psychosis and schizophrenia," *Schizophrenia Research, 1,* 1988, 79–89; Miller, "Schizophrenia as a progressive disorder," 1989, pp. 24, 26, 35, 37.

80. Quotations from R. L. Isaacson and K. H. Pribram, eds., *The Hippocampus,* vol. 4 (New York and London: Plenum, 1986), p. 329. J. A. Gray speaks of the literature on the hippocampus as "a maddening confusion" ("Précis of *The neuropsychology of anxiety: An enquiry into the functions of the septohippocampal system*" [with peer commentary], *Behavioral and Brain Sciences, 3,* 1982, 516). D. V. Jeste and J. B. Lohr describe its functions as mostly unknown; "Hippocampal pathologic findings in schizophrenia," *Archives of General Psychiatry, 46,* 1989, 1023.

81. See Bogerts, Meertz, and Schonfeldt-Bausch, "Basal ganglia and limbic system," 1985, pp. 789–90. Contemporary neurobiologists seem less inclined to make a sharp distinction between the kinds of functions served by cortical and subcortical areas. It is recognized that the connections existing between the cortex, especially the frontal cortex, and the limbic system, especially the hippocampal formation, are extremely prolific; and some of the most sophisticated recent models of schizophrenia postulate abnormalities of neural systems that incorporate both limbic *and* cortical structures, such as a hyperactivation occurring in both areas. Given the new understanding of the functions of the limbic system, it is hardly necessary to conceptualize this intimate interaction as a matter of one region (the cortex) exercising cognitive control while the other serves only as the source of motivating energies or affective response.

82. See, for example, Gray, "Précis of *Neuropsychology of Anxiety,*" 1982, p. 516.

83. A. J. Saykin, R. C. Gur, R. E. Gur, and colleagues found in schizophrenics a selective deficit in memory and learning compared to other psychological functions, a finding they interpret as consistent with particular disturbance of the temporal-hippocampal system (against a background of diffuse dysfunction); see "Neuropsychological function in schizophrenia: Selective impairment in memory and learning," *Archives of General Psychiatry, 48,* 1991, 618–24.

84. See J. A. Gray, J. Feldon, J. N. P. Rawlins, et al., "The neuropsychology of schizophrenia" (with peer commentary), *Behavioral and Brain Sciences, 14,* 1991, 1–84, esp. 4, 11, 19; J. A. Gray, *The Neuropsychology of Anxiety* (Oxford: Oxford University Press, 1982).

85. See Gray et al., "The neuropsychology of schizophrenia," 1991, p. 18. Possible consequences of abnormalities of hippocampal function, including aspects of delusion formation, are ingeniously described in D. R. Hemsley, "Cognitive abnormalities and the symptoms of schizophrenia," and in H. M. Emrich, "Sub-

jectivity, error correction capacity, and the pathogenesis of delusions of refer-
ence," both to appear in M. Spitzer, F. A. Uehlein, M. A. Schwartz, and C.
Mundt, eds., *Phenomenology, Language, and Schizophrenia* (New York:
Springer, 1992).

The so-called septohippocampal system also seems to mediate the integration
of motivation (or affect) with informational input—which suggests that dysfunction of this system might be relevant to aspects of the splitting between cognitive
and affective processes that is so prominent in schizophrenia (as described, for
example, by Stransky's concept of "intrapsychic ataxia").

86. P. V. Simonov, "On the role of the hippocampus in the integrative activity of the
brain," *Acta Neurobiologiae Experimentalis*, 34, 1974, 37–38; see also D. T. D.
James, "The evolution of hesitation, doubt, and mapmaking (response to Gray),"
Behavioral and Brain Sciences, 3, 1982, 488–89.

87. The neurobiologist R. Miller has proposed that this kind of activation—"generated in the hippocampus, [but] entraining other parts of the hemisphere,"
including the frontal lobes—could also account for the (seemingly paradoxical)
finding of smaller hippocampal size ("Schizophrenia as a progressive disorder,"
1989, p. 37 and passim); for it is known that an increase of this kind of activation
(manifest in increased power of theta rhythm [Simonov, "On role of hippocampus," 1974]) can cause cell loss. This speculative hypothesis suggests the intriguing possibility of a unified theory of schizophrenia—one that would associate
"positive symptoms" with limbic-hippocampal hyperactivity occurring in early
stages of the illness, and "negative symptoms" like emotional flatness and indifference to the environment with later stages, when the hippocampal formation
would have suffered significant cell loss, largely because of this very hyperactivity. See also J. R. Stevens, "Epilepsy, psychosis and schizophrenia," *Schizophrenia Research*, 1, 1988, 81, 84, 87.

Such damage to the hippocampus and related areas could, incidentally, account for certain findings that Weinberger ascribes to hypofrontality. Instead of
viewing the tendency to perseverate on the Wisconsin Card Sorting task (found
primarily in chronic schizophrenic patients) as being a sign of inability to abstract—as Weinberger has sometimes suggested—one could ascribe it to certain
tendencies that have been found associated with hippocampal damage: for
example, with "inability to suppress well-established patterns of learned behavior in response to changed environmental contingencies" (M. Gabriel, "Homun-
culus in the subiculum [response to Gray]," *Behavioral and Brain Sciences*, 3,
1982, 485–86; see also Gray, "Précis of *Neuropsychology of Anxiety*," 1982, p.
517) or with a "relative insensitivity to contextual manipulations and alterations
of task contingencies" (Issacson and Pribram, *The Hippocampus*, vol. 4, 1986, p.
28).

88. I am, of course, speaking of the usual hemispheric asymmetry, that characteristic
of right-handed persons. For overviews of laterality theories of schizophrenia,
see H. A. Nasrallah, "Is schizophrenia a left hemisphere disease?" in N. Andreasen, *Can Schizophrenia Be Localized*, 1986, pp. 55–74; Seidman, "Schizophrenia and brain dysfunction," 1983, pp. 215–18.

89. Sacks, *Man Who Mistook*, 1985, p. 2.

90. Cutting, *Right Cerebral Hemisphere*, 1990, p. 282.

91. The left-brain interpreter, Gazzaniga writes, is what "allows the organism to
generate hypotheses about the nature of its responses, and, by doing so, not only
presents the human species with a mechanism to both form and modify beliefs,
but perhaps also frees the human agent from the shackles of environmental

stimuli"; it is the part of the mind that makes inferences and perceives causal relationships, and that "tries to bring order and unity to our conscious lives" ("Organization of human brain," 1989, pp. 951, 947).

92. See, for example, J. C. Eccles, "The self-conscious mind and the brain," in K. R. Popper and J. C. Eccles, eds., *The Self and Its Brain* (New York: Springer International, 1977), pp. 355–76.

93. According to Andreasen (*Broken Brain*, 1984, p. 122), it is the prominence of disturbances of language and logical thought in schizophrenia that has suggested its association with left-brain dysfunction, whereas affective disorders, as diseases of emotion, have naturally been assumed to be due to right-hemisphere abnormalities.

94. Re the right-hemisphere dysfunction hypothesis, see Cutting, *Psychology of Schizophrenia*, 1985, and *Right Cerebral Hemisphere*, 1990; see also references in Nasrallah, "Is schizophrenia left hemisphere disease?" 1986, p. 65.

95. See S. Wolff, " 'Schizoid' personality in childhood and adult life, I: Vagaries of diagnostic labelling," *British Journal of Psychiatry*, 159, 617.

96. W. Wapner, S. Hamby, and H. Gardner, "The role of the right hemisphere in the apprehension of complex linguistic materials," *Brain and Language, 14,* 1981, 15–33.

97. Cutting, *Right Cerebral Hemisphere,* 1990, p. 218.

98. See J. Cutting and D. Murphy, "Schizophrenic thought disorder: A psychological and organic interpretation," *British Journal of Psychiatry, 152,* 1988, 310–19. See also Wapner, Hamby, and Gardner ("Role of right hemisphere," 1981), re how schizophrenics may manifest "difficulties in respecting the boundaries of a fictive entity" (p. 15): in retelling stories read to them, for instance, they will often be uncertain about the difference between what actually did happen and events that only could have happened but were not part of the story's account ("it could have happened" was, for several such patients, sufficient justification for embellishments to the story [p. 24]). See also D. W. Zaidel and A. Kasher, "Hemispheric memory for surrealistic versus realistic paintings," *Cortex, 25,* 1989, 617–41, an interesting study that shows that, in normal subjects, memory for scenes incongruous with known reality (e.g., surrealistic scenes) was better in the left than in the right brain.

99. See, for example, R. Knight, P. Youard, and I. Wooles, "Visual information-processing deficits in chronic schizophrenic subjects using tasks matched for discriminating power," *Journal of Abnormal Psychology, 94,* 1985, 453–59, re Gestalt perception being replaced by analytic perception, by "the more elaborate processing usually specific" for what is meaningful. See also S. Gessler, J. Cutting, C. D. Frith, and J. Weinman, "Schizophrenic inability to judge facial emotion: A controlled study," *British Journal of Clinical Psychology, 28,* 1989, 19–29, where it was found that schizophrenics seem to "bypass Gestalt processing and rely on feature analysis" (p. 27).

100. See N. D. Cook, "Toward a central dogma for psychology," *New Ideas in Psychology, 7,* 1989, 1–18. Kosslyn, in 1987, and Hecaen, in 1964, have offered similar views; see Cutting, *Right Cerebral Hemisphere,* 1990, pp. 95, 143. See also P. H. Venables, "Cerebral mechanisms, autonomic responsiveness, and attention in schizophrenia," *Nebraska Symposium on Motivation, 31,* 1983, 75–78. Current conceptualizations of the brain suggest that this stabilizing

function may be mediated largely by the septohippocampal system or by the right hemisphere, for both have been said to provide a general sense of context; in the first instance this is described as a matter of providing a context of familiarity within which novelty can be noticed and assimilated, and, in the second, as a grounding or orienting context within which focal knowing can take place.

101. Sacks, *Man Who Mistook*, 1985, p. 3.
102. One argument against left-sided dysfunction is that the cognitive style and the typical pattern of errors made by schizophrenic patients are not really very similar to the overall pattern of those of organic patients known to have damaged or malfunctioning left hemispheres; see E. Walker and M. McGuire, "Intra- and interhemispheric information processing in schizophrenia," *Psychological Bulletin*, 92, 1982, 701.
103. See Venables, "Cerebral mechanisms in schizophrenia," 1983, pp. 60–63; Walker and McGuire, "Intra- and interhemispheric information," 1982; Cutting, *Right Cerebral Hemisphere*, 1990, pp. 341–42. See also Levin and Yurgelin-Todd, "Contributions of clinical neuropsychology," 1989.
104. See A. Raine and D. Manders, "Schizoid personality, inter-hemispheric transfer, and left hemisphere over-activation," *British Journal of Clinical Psychology*, 27, 1988, 333–47; A. Raine, H. Andrews, C. Sheard, et al., "Interhemispheric transfer in schizophrenics, depressives, and normals with schizoid tendencies," *Journal of Abnormal Psychology*, 98, 1989, 35–41.
105. See, for example, R. E. Gur, S. M. Resnick, A. Alavi, et al., "Regional brain function in schizophrenia: I. A positron emission tomography study," *Archives of General Psychiatry*, 44, 1987, 119–25; see also R. E. Gur, S. M. Resnick, R. C. Gur, et al., "Regional brain function in schizophrenia: II, 1987, 126–29. R. E. Gur, R. C. Gur, B. E. Skolnick, et al. ("Brain function in psychiatric disorders," *Archives of General Psychiatry*, 42, 1985, 329–34) found abnormally high resting blood flow in the left hemisphere of severely disturbed schizophrenics. See also Cleghorn (1988, mentioned in Miller, "Schizophrenia as progressive disorder," 1989, p. 23) re early acute cases; and L. Schweitzer, E. Becker, and H. Welsh, "Abnormalities of cerebral lateralization in schizophrenia patients," *Archives of General Psychiatry*, 35, 1978, 982–85.
106. M. Lezak, *Neuropsychological Assessment*, 2nd ed. (New York: Oxford University Press, 1983), p. 58; M. S. Myslobodsky, M. Mintz, and R. Tomer, "Neuroleptic effects and the site of abnormality in schizophrenia," in M. Myslobodsky, ed., *Hemisyndromes* (New York: Academic Press, 1983), p. 374.
107. See discussion in Cutting, *Psychology of Schizophrenia*, 1985, pp. 294–300, 305.
108. Quoted in R. Rosser, "The psychopathology of thinking and feeling in a schizophrenic," *International Journal of Psychoanalysis*, 60, 1979, 182.
109. E. Minkowski, *Lived Time* (Evanston, IL: Northwestern University Press, 1970), p. 278. Such patients distinctly recall Nietzsche's descriptions of the Apollonian, and particularly of the Socratic, mindsets. Apollo enjoins the practice of self-knowledge through detached contemplation, while Socrates transforms this into "logical schematism" (*The Birth of Tragedy and The Genealogy of Morals*, trans. F. Golffing [Garden City, NY: Doubleday, 1956], pp. 65, 88).
110. Schweitzer, Becker, and Welsh, "Abnormalities of cerebral lateralization," 1978, p. 984.

111. See G. Schmidt, "A review of the German literature on delusions," in Cutting and Shepherd, *Clinical Roots*, 1987, p. 106. See also J. Cutting, "The phenomenology of acute organic psychosis: Comparison with acute schizophrenia," *British Journal of Psychiatry, 151,* 328.

112. Quoted in Harrington, *Medicine, Mind,* 1987, pp. 211, 219 (the latter phrases are Jackson quoting Herbert Spencer).

113. It is even possible that some forms of brain damage might *protect* against the development of schizophrenia in a predisposed individual. See S. W. Lewis, I. Harvey, M. Ron, et al., "Can brain damage protect against schizophrenia?" *British Journal of Psychiatry, 157,* 1990, 600–603. See also Stuss et al., "Leucotomized and nonleucotomized schizophrenics," 1981, pp. 1085–1100.

114. See, for example, Seidman, "Schizophrenia and brain dysfunction," 1983, pp. 223–29. The importance of possible cortico-limbic interplay is stressed in D. R. Weinberger, K. F. Berman, and R. F. Zec, "Physiologic dysfunction of dorsolateral prefrontal cortex in schizophrenia: I. Regional cerebral blood flow evidence," *Archives of General Psychiatry, 43,* 1986, 122; and in R. Miller, "Cortico-hippocampal interplay: self-organizing phase-locked loops for indexing memory," *Psychobiology, 17,* 1989, 115–28.

115. It should be noted, however, that there is increasing evidence that genetic factors may play a less prominent role than was previously believed; see Beiser and Iacano, "An update on the epidemiology of schizophrenia," 1990, p. 664. In the view of both Manfred Bleuler (*Schizophrenic Disorders,* 1978, p. 419) and Karl Leonhard ("Contradictory issues in the origin of schizophrenia," *British Journal of Psychiatry, 136,* 1980, 437–44), there is, surprisingly enough, less evidence of a genetic loading for severe or "systematic" schizophrenias than for the more episodic or benign cases.

Baldwin, J. M., 510n20
Balken, E. R., 468n24
Ball, J., 546n18
Ball, R., 552–53n63
Balzac, Honoré de, 365, 420n87
Barham, P., 415n53, 450n134, 458–59n38, 542n61, 545n5, 546n16, 547n23, 556n73
Barnes, Djuna, 34
Barnes, Mary, 438–39n11
Barnes, T. R. E., 480n21, 484n57
Barta, P. E., 549n38
Barthelme, Donald, 417–18n66
Barthes, Roland, 28, 151, 198, 200, 419n84, 427–28n58, 467n15
Bartko, J. J., 500n70
Baruch, J., 436n111
Bate, W. J., 463n75, 536n2
Battcock, G., 419n75, 420n94, 444n80, 471n48, 476–77n66, 527–28n9
Battie, William, 270
Baudelaire, Charles, 82, 85–90, 105–6, 185, 207, 349, 350–51, 367, 401–2n22, 443n55–56, 482n41, 535n79
Baudrillard, Jean, 291, 301, 543n74
Baxter, C., 554n70
Bebbington, P., 436n107, 481n29, 485n77
Becker, E., 561n105, 561n110
Beckett, Samuel, 34, 36, 56, 58, 69, 189, 197, 208, 297, 303–4, 344–45, 367, 419n78, 434n97, 483n47, 522n29, 525–26n59
Beckmann, H., 557n77
Beebe, Maurice, 422n103, 422n109
Beech, A., 473–76n63
Beech, T., 550n42
Beiser, M., 538–39n35, 540n46, 551n50, 562n115
Bell, D., 422n106
Bellack, A. S., 460–61n55, 554–56n72
Bellah, R. N., 542–43n67
Ben-Arie, O., 543n70
Benjamin, Walter, 543n74
Benn, Gottfried, 422–23n111
Bennett, J., 399n2
Benson, D. F., 553–54n64–65, 554n68, 554–56n72

Bentall, R. P., 545n4
Bentham, Jeremy, 251, 254, 255
Ben-Zvi, L., 466n10, 529n24
Berger, Brigitte, 371, 447n107, 447–48n110
Berger, J., 462n64, 472n50
Berger, Peter L., 371, 447n107, 447–48n110, 465n109, 466n2, 542–43n67
Berke, J., 438–39n11
Berkeley, George, 269, 491n10
Berle, B. B., 458n37, 526n63, 540n47
Berman, K. F., 499n63, 548n31, 548n34, 550n47, 554n67, 554–56n72, 556–57n75, 562n114
Berner, P., 427n44
Berrios, G. E., 426n40, 508n5, 510n23, 514n67, 546n10–11, 547–48n27
Bersani, Leo, 493n25, 496n44, 496n46, 503n90
Berze, Joseph, 409n17, 416n59, 450n131, 491n5, 498n54
Bes, A., 552–53n63
Bilder, R. M., 549n37
Binswanger, Ludwig, 416n57, 451n143, 471n43, 481n25, 547n21
Bion, W., 444n71
Birnbaum, K., 536n8
Blackwood, D. H. R., 497–98n50
Blakemore, C., 415n48, 549–50n41
Blanc, Charles, 172
Blanck, G., 412–13n33
Blanck, R., 412–13n33
Blankenberg, W., 459n42
Blatt, Sidney J., 410–11n29, 447n96, 462n72, 468n23, 510n19, 522n31
Bleuler, Eugen, 14, 19–20, 24, 76, 80, 110–11, 121, 126–27, 129, 135, 175, 180–81, 183, 201, 243, 270, 274, 275–76, 295, 325, 379, 396, 402–3n28, 405–7n48, 409n16, 409n25, 416n54, 416n56, 416n59, 425n25, 437–38n4–5, 439n14–15, 441n27, 449n122, 450n134, 451–52n145, 456n23, 458n35, 458–59n38, 468n22, 478–79n8–9, 479n11, 480n20, 481n24, 481n26, 483–84n53, 484–85n62, 486n79, 490n116, 492n13, 499n59–60, 500n66, 509n11, 509n14, 511n30,

511n33, 512n41, 514n66, 515n69, 515n71, 515n76, 516n83, 523n36, 525n53, 527n1, 540n44, 549n37

Bleuler, Manfred, 110–12, 139–40, 175, 268, 407n3, 408n5, 408n7, 409n18, 414n47, 415n49, 435–36n105, 437–38n4–5, 439n15, 441n23, 441n29, 444n70, 450–51n135, 452n150, 460n54, 476n64, 489–90n110, 517n95, 518n102, 535n84, 546n16, 547n24, 552n59, 562n115

Bliss, E. L., 540n47

Blondel, Charles, 483n51

Bloom, Harold, 422n105, 531n40

Bloom, S. R., 546n18

Bloomgarden, J. W., 450–51n135

Blunden, A., 442n36, 442n38, 442n46, 442n48

Bogerts, B., 557n76, 557n77, 558n81

Bogue, R., 525–26n59

Böker, W., 435–36n105, 551n52

Boller, F., 478n4

Borges, Jorge Luis, 119–22, 132, 151, 159, 305, 417–18n66

Borst, U., 551–52n56

Bourne, E. J., 447n105, 455–56n20, 456–57n28, 458n35, 472–73n55

Bovet, P., 459n42, 485n63

Bowers, M., 431n73

Bowler, A., 539n36

Bradbury, M., 416–17n64–65, 432n78, 496n45, 514n55

Bradley, F. H., 280, 281

Bratt, D. L., 554–56n72

Breier, A., 436n113, 551–52n56

Brenner, Charles, 510n21, 551n54

Brenner, H. D., 410–11n29, 435–36n105, 551n52

Breton, André, 22, 45, 65, 72, 106, 184, 193, 194, 265

Brisset, Jean-Pierre, 367, 479n12, 488–89n107

Broadbent, D. E., 426n42

Brooks, Cleanth, 452n152

Broustra, Jean, 413n37

Brown, Norman O., 22, 401n17

Brown, R., 478n4, 557n76

Bruch, Hilde, 482n40

Brundage, B. E., 426n38

Büchner, Georg, 365

Buchsbaum, M. S., 552–53n63

Buckingham, H. W., 481n31

Burke, K., 452n152

Burton-Bradley, B. G., 538n34

Butler, C., 419–20n85, 467n17, 469n34–35, 470n38

Bynum, W. F., 399–400n5, 401–2n22

Cage, John, 151, 417–18n66

Caldwell, C. G., 535n87

Calinescu, M., 482n41

Callinicos, A., 464n100

Calvino, Italo, 35

Cameron, J. L., 399–400n5, 410–12n28–30, 413n35, 453n160, 460–61n55, 491n4, 493n21, 498n52, 511n26

Cameron, Norman, 123, 125, 429n68, 460n45, 485n75

Camus, Albert, 34, 420n87

Cancro, R., 540n47

Canetti, Elias, 416n57, 442n43, 472n54, 504n4

Cappalletti, J., 552–53n63

Caputo, J. D., 533n64

Cardinal, Roger, 482n42, 485n78, 490n113

Carl (case example), 131, 298, 395

Carlsson, Arvid, 548n29

Carmen, R. del, 540n47

Carnap, Rudolph, 192

Carne-Ross, D. S., 419n84

Carothers, John, 363

Carpenter, E., 448–49n120

Carpenter, P. K., 492–93n17, 527n6

Carpenter, W. T., 500n70, 550n48

Carr, V., 435–36n105, 551n52

Carsky, M., 450–51n135

Casacchia, M., 405–7n48

Casanova, M. F., 553–54n64, 557n76

Casares, Adolfo Bioy, 305–11, 318, 521n22, 522n32

Cassirer, Ernst, 22

Caudill, W., 451n136

Cendrars, Blaise, 194–95, 197

Deleuze, Gilles, 22
DeLisi, L. E., 552–53n63
de Man, Paul, 345, 347, 349–51, 401–2n22, 452n153, 486n89, 503n88, 533n63–64
Denis, Maurice, 471n47
Derrida, Jacques, 151, 199–205, 208, 280–81, 308, 315, 345, 347–49, 352, 394, 486n88, 504–5n10, 521n22
Descartes, René, 23, 75, 91–93, 213–15, 269, 292, 294, 298, 369, 392, 445n82, 446n88
Descombes, Vincent, 533–34n69
Deutsch, Helene, 89, 400n13, 450n127
Devereux, George, 362, 364, 446n85, 536n4, 538–39n35
Devous, M. D., 552–53n63, 554–56n72
Diamond, S., 472–73n55
Diderot, Denis, 104, 114
Ditmann, J., 452n147
Dodds, E. R., 454n10, 498n55
Domarus, E. von, 123
Done, D. J., 435n102, 473–76n63, 497–98n50
Donnelly, C., 498n53
Dostoevsky, Fyodor, 4, 318
Dreyfus, H., 532n61
Dubuffet, Jean, 38, 413n37
Duchamp, Marcel, 36, 66, 113, 119, 135, 139, 151, 164, 171, 350, 417–18n66, 471n40, 488–89n107
Duffy, F. H., 552–53n63, 554n71
Duncan, C. C., 548–49n35, 552–53n63
Dunham, H. W., 536n9
Dunne, F., 424n9, 425n26, 434n96, 464n88
Durkheim, Émile, 371

Eagle, M., 410–11n29, 444n71
Eccles, J. C., 560n92
Edwards, P., 399n4
Egan, M. F., 556–57n75
Ehrhardt, J. C., 549n38, 553–54n64
Eissler, K. R., 430–31n70
Elias, Norbert, 90–93
Eliot, T. S., 28, 86, 135, 137, 186, 260, 280, 344, 357, 419n78, 421n96, 482–83n45, 522n29, 532n51
Elizondo, Salvador, 171–72
Elk, R., 543n70
Ellenberger, H. F., 512n41
Ellman, R., 435n104
Emrich, H. M., 431n73, 432n79, 558–59n85
Emrich, W., 416–17n65
Engel, G. L., 544n1
Erlich, V., 429n62, 432n78, 432n80, 432–33n84
Esquirol, J., 540n50
Essen-Möller, E., 441n20
Esslin, M., 503n90, 503n92
Estroff, S. E., 491n5
Evans-Pritchard, Edward, 142
Exner, J. E., 414n43, 436n109, 460n47
Eysteinsson, A., 416–18n65–66, 418n70, 420n93, 486n89

Faas, E., 401–2n22, 491n10
Fabrega, H., 538n29, 542n61, 543n70
Fairbairn, W. R. D., 89, 439–40n17, 444n71
Falkai, P., 557n77
Falloon, I. R. H., 500n68
Farmer, A., 549n37
Faulkner, William, 31, 34
Federman, J. Raymond, 473n61, 532n54
Federn, Paul, 55, 410–11n29, 454n11, 473n56, 544–45n2
Feigenberg, I. M., 127
Feldon, J., 434n98, 473–76n63, 558n84
Felman, S., 493n22
Fenichel, Otto, 412–13n33, 493n19, 493n21, 502–3n85, 523–24n46
Ferenczi, Sandor, 410n27, 546n18
Fey, E. T., 554–56n72
Fichte, Johann Gottlieb, 82, 302, 304, 313–17, 320, 321, 525n56, 528n16
Field, M. J., 538n32
Fischer, Franz, 160
Flaubert, Gustave, 35, 138–39
Flaum, M., 405–7n48, 537n20
Flavell, J., 510n23

Fletcher, Angus, 486n89
Flowers, D. L., 554n70
Fontana, A. F., 435–36n105, 549n39
Ford, Ford Madox, 31, 100
Forel, August, 276
Forrest, A., 451n144
Forrest, D., 479n11, 482n40, 488n99
Fortes, Meyer, 362
Foster, H., 463n83, 467n13, 543n74
Foucault, Michel, 119–21, 130, 131, 159,
    213, 243, 246, 250–53, 256, 265, 295,
    327–32, 334, 338, 347, 365, 373, 400n8,
    400n10, 402n27, 413n37, 414n41,
    420n91, 445n83, 454n10, 454–55n15,
    488–89n107, 506n25, 513n50, 541–
    42n60, 543–44n75–76, 544–45n2
Foulkes, S. H., 538n31
Fowlie, W., 486n87
Frank (case example), 233, 282
Frank, Joseph, 34, 159, 161, 170
Franzen, G., 552n61, 552–53n63, 554n71
Freedman, B. J., 471n42, 479–80n13
Freeman, Thomas, 399–400n5, 410–
    12n28–30, 413n35, 453n160, 468–
    69n29, 491n4, 492–93n17, 493n20–21,
    498n52, 507n35, 509–10n18, 511n26
Freud, Anna, 21, 218, 411–12n30
Freud, Sigmund, 19–21, 55, 105, 217,
    218, 243–45, 265, 379, 400n14, 403n32,
    411–12n30, 413–14n40, 416n60, 430–
    31n70, 453n159, 473n58, 500–501n74,
    502–3n85, 504n7, 505–6n23, 523n42,
    523–24n46, 544–45n2
Fried, Michael, 170–71
Friedrich, H., 463n82, 482n39, 490n114
Frith, C. D., 217, 396, 435n102, 436n107,
    457–58n34, 460n45, 460n53, 473n60,
    473–76n63, 479–80n13, 481n28–29,
    485n77, 488n105, 497–98n50, 545–
    46n8, 552n57, 560n99
Frith, U., 481n29
Fromkin, V. A., 478n4
Frosch, John, 407n1, 410–12n29–30,
    416n60, 429n67, 444n71, 493n21,
    504n2, 504n7, 508n4, 523–24n46
Frye, Northrop, 486n89
Fuller, B. A. G., 514n60
Funderburk, F. R., 554–56n72

Gablik, S., 463n79
Gabrial, T. M., 480n21
Gabriel, M., 559n87
Galileo, 417–18n66
Ganzell, S., 554–56n72
Gardner, Howard, 460–61n55, 547n25,
    560n96, 560n98
Garnett, E. S., 552–53n62–63
Gasché, R., 528n12, 533n64
Gascoyne, D., 401–2n22, 415n50
Gass, William, 495n41, 496n45
Gattaz, W. F., 434n98, 459n39, 473–
    76n63, 550n48, 551–52n56, 552n59
Gauguin, Paul, 422–23n111
Gauss, Karl Friedrich, 96
Gazzaniga, Michael S., 392, 395, 548n32
Gedo, J. E., 409n18, 411–12n30, 453n159
Geertz, Clifford, 10, 215, 404n41, 536n5
Gehlen, Arnold, 370, 540n48
Geldzahler, H., 476–77n66
Gellner, E., 541–42n60
Genet, Jean, 219, 226
George, E. E., 541n56
Geraud, G., 552–53n63
Gessler, S., 560n99
Gibieuf, 444n76
Giddens, Anthony, 371–72, 538n25,
    543n74
Gide, André, 495n42
Gie, Robert, 230
Giliarovsky, V. A., 468n25
Gill, M. M., 156, 460n51, 466n1,
    473n58–59, 477n73
Gilles, L. S., 543n70
Ginet, C., 550n44
Gittelman-Klein, R., 437–38n5
Gjerde, P. F., 434n94, 434–35n100,
    490n118, 497–98n50, 550n43, 556–
    57n75
Glaser, Bruce, 476–77n66
Glass, J. M., 500n71, 504n9, 514n58,
    527n2
Glick, J., 455–56n20
Glucksmann, A., 414n41
Goffman, Erving, 98
Gogh, Vincent van, 56, 367
Goldberg, A., 409n18, 411–12n30,
    453n159

Heidegger *(Continued)*
444n77, 488n98, 502n83, 505n22, 506–7n27, 513n50, 517n89, 533n64
Heidsieck, A., 403n36, 503n89
Heinson, H., 557n77
Heller, Erich, 10, 58, 173, 418n69, 419n80, 420n89, 422n104, 445n82, 452–53n156, 490n120, 501n75, 526n67, 531n39, 531n44, 531n46
Hemingway, Ernest, 420n87
Hemsley, David R., 431n73, 432n79, 434n98, 436n107, 436n111, 459n39, 460n53, 473–76n63, 497–98n50, 500n69, 551–52n56, 558–59n85
Henna, F. A., 478n5
Hennell, Thomas, 236, 241, 426n39
Henrich, D., 519n4
Henry (case example), 96, 166–69, 168–70
Heraclitus, 2, 20
Herbart, J. F., 493n28
Hermann, I., 504n7–8, 507n30
Heston, L. L., 441n18
Hiedsieck, A., 447n94
Hilfiker, K., 519–20n8
Hill, J., 550n45
Hintikka, J., 482n34
Hirsch, E. D., 445n82, 531n47
Hirsch, S. J., 539n41
Hirsch, S. R., 409n18
Hobbes, Thomas, 3
Hoberman, J., 476–77n66
Hockings, P., 448–49n120
Hockney, David, 433n86
Hodgson, R. J., 473–76n63, 545–46n8
Hoenig, J., 405–7n48, 409n25, 492n12
Hoffman, R., 481n30
Hofmannsthal, Hugo von, 45, 56–57, 62, 75, 185–86, 187, 193, 198, 427n51–55, 432n77, 496n45
Holcomb, H. H., 552–53n63
Hölderlin, Friedrich, 24–25, 82, 84, 114, 183–84, 310, 353, 357, 367
Holland, Henry, 401–2n22
Hollender, M. H., 539n41
Holt, Robert, 412–13n33, 466n1, 473n58
Holzman, Philip S., 396, 405–7n48, 414n47, 435n101, 436n106, 454n14,

455n17, 456n22, 456n24, 460n47, 460n49–50, 461n57–58, 468n22, 472n51, 473–76n63, 477n1, 543n68
Hosek, C., 421n98
Houston, D. M., 473n60, 552n57
Howe, Irving, 416–17n65
Hughes, Robert, 463n84, 471n47, 473n61, 532n56
Humboldt, Alexander von, 81
Hume, David, 491n10, 493n28, 514n60
Hunter, J. D., 542–43n67
Hunter, R. A., 407n1, 504n6
Husserl, Edmund, 279, 292, 445n82, 517n90, 528n13, 533n64
Hutcheon, L., 422n105, 495n41, 495–96n43, 496n45
Huyssen, A., 417–18n66
Hyde, G. M., 432n78

Iacono, W. F., 549n36
Iacono, W. G., 538–39n35, 540n46, 551n50, 562n115
Iadarola, M. K., 550n47
Illowsky, B. P., 554n67, 554–56n72
Ingvar, D. H., 552n61, 552–53n63, 554n70–71
Inhelder, B., 428n60, 501n77
Ionesco, Eugène, 56, 186, 189, 193, 194, 198
Isaacson, R. L., 558n80, 559n87
Ishiguro, H., 550n44

Jablensky, Assen, 358, 360, 535n1, 536–37n12–13, 537n15–16, 537n17, 538n26, 539n41, 539n43, 541–42n60, 547n21
Jackson, H. F., 545n4
Jackson, J. Hughlings, 377–78, 380–82, 392, 395, 400n14, 546n11, 554n66, 562n112
Jackson, R., 549n37
Jacobson, Edith, 510n21
Jaffe, L. S., 503–4n95

Jakobson, Roman, 183, 432n80, 453n157, 482n34, 482n37
James (case example), 95, 102–3, 106
James, D. T. D., 559n86
James, William, 220–23, 226–27, 228, 234–35, 261, 277–78, 283, 346, 463n73, 491n10, 501n75, 510n22, 515n68
Jameson, F., 413n37, 419n72, 419n79, 420n92, 421n98, 432n80, 467n15, 493n22, 507n29, 522n29, 543n74, 543–44n75
Janet, Pierre, 376, 409n16, 409n18, 416n59, 512n41
Janzarik, W., 405–7n48, 434n98, 459n39, 473–76n63, 550n48, 551–52n56, 552n59
Jarry, Alfred, 32–33, 106, 113, 134, 135, 151, 160, 350, 367, 421n101
Jarvis, E., 536n4
Jaspers, Karl, 7, 13, 16–19, 26, 27, 52–53, 60–61, 78, 108–9, 111, 140, 148, 191, 215, 216, 241, 243–44, 268, 274, 295, 324, 325, 366–67, 388, 400n6, 402n26, 404–5n44, 405–7n48, 407n4, 408n9, 408n13, 409n22, 409n25, 416n56, 423n3, 424n10, 434n92, 436n113, 451–52n145, 464n92, 464n99, 471n42, 488n105, 491n5, 500n67, 509n7, 509n9, 509n11, 511n29, 512n38, 515n73, 515n76, 516n82, 518n98, 518n100, 519n7, 523n36, 523n38, 523n40, 535n82, 539n43, 541n54, 547n24
Jaynes, Julian, 229–31, 233, 498n51, 504n7, 507n35
Jean, M., 424n12, 424n14, 424n18, 427n49, 488–89n107
Jefferson, Lara, 215
Jenkins, R. L., 511–12n37
Jeste, D. V., 505n11, 540n47, 558n80
Jilek, W. G., 539n37, 539n38, 539n42, 540n44, 540–41n53
Jilek-Aall, L., 539n37, 539n38, 539n42, 540n44, 540–41n53
Joan (case example), 310
Johns, Jasper, 417–18n66
Johnson, G., 550–51n49
Johnson, Samuel, 463n75

Johnston, M. H., 436n106, 454n14, 456n22, 456n24, 460n47, 460n49, 460n50, 468n22, 477n1
Johnstone, E. C., 545–46n8, 549n37
Jonas, J. M., 452n146
Jones, B., 452n146
Jones, S. H., 436n107
Joubert, Nicolas, 3
Joyce, James, 34, 70–71, 82, 344, 350, 428–29n61, 435n103, 482n40, 485n68, 525–26n59
Judd, Don, 463n79
Jung, Carl G., 70–71, 243, 409n19, 412–13n33, 422n107, 482n40
Jung, Lucia, 70–71
Jutai, J., 553–54n64

Kafka, Franz, 8, 45, 82–90, 95, 317–23, 330–31, 357, 367, 501n75, 503n89, 525–26n59
Kahlbaum, K., 365
Kahler, Erich, 59, 67, 401n16, 424n15, 424n17, 433n87, 477n67, 486n84
Kahn, C. H., 399n4
Kahn, E., 408n14
Kahneman, D., 459n39
Kamin, L. J., 544n1
Kandel, Eric, 385
Kant, Immanuel, 31, 82, 91–94, 137, 163, 292, 302, 327–32, 341, 369, 445n82, 446n87, 516n80, 527–28n9, 529n22, 529n28, 533n64
Kaplan, B., 411–12n30, 429n67, 488n102, 498n54, 506n24
Kaplan, E. F., 553–54n64
Kaplan, J., 552–53n63
Karl, Frederick R., 417–18n66, 526n60
Karlsson, J. L., 458n37
Kasanin, J. S., 453n8, 460n45, 461n56, 461n58, 467n18, 483n50, 485n75
Kasher, A., 560n98
Katharina (artist), 219
Katt, Ernst (case example), 98
Keefe, J. A., 458n37
Kellner, Hansfried, 371, 447n107, 447–48n110

Kendig, I., 554n69

Kendler, K. S., 317n23, 399–400n5, 405–7n48, 437–38n5, 439–40n17

Kermode, Frank, 417–18n66, 442n34, 532n50

Kern, S., 486n87

Kernberg, Otto, 410–11n29, 508n4

Kerwin, R., 553–54n64

Kety, S. S., 437–38n5

Khan, Masud, 439–40n17

Kierkegaard, Søren, 90, 367, 444n73, 498n52, 542–43n67

Kietzman, M. L., 436n109, 457–58n34, 460n44

Kinsbourne, M., 434n99

Kirch, D. G., 556–57n75

Klein, D. F., 437–38n5

Klein, E. B., 435–36n105, 549n39

Klein, Melanie, 410–11n29

Kleinman, Arthur, 536n10, 537n14, 538n33

Kleinman, J. E., 557n76

Kleist, Heinrich von, 198, 342–43, 346, 401–2n22, 486n85

Klimt, Gustav, 471n45

Kloos, G., 453n160

Knight, R. A., 456n25, 560n99

Kobayashi, K., 557–58n78

Koehler, K., 492n12

Koelb, C., 534n71

Koestenbaum, P., 414n44

Kohut, Heinz, 410–11n29

Kolakowski, L., 409n20

Kolligian, J., 552n57

Korten, A., 537n16, 539n41

Kosslyn, S. M., 560–61n100

Koyré, A., 412–13n33

Kraepelin, Emil, 13–14, 17–20, 24, 108, 175, 284, 357, 360, 376, 379, 380, 408n15, 409n21, 409n25, 414n46, 416n62, 450–51n134–35, 452n154, 453n5, 465n106, 473–76n63, 479n10, 492n14, 499–500n65, 540n50, 546n17, 547n21, 547n25

Krauss, R., 513n52

Kretschmer, Ernst, 79–86, 88, 98, 100, 108, 109, 396, 437–38n5, 438n9, 439n12, 439n15, 439–40n17, 441n18, 441n20, 451n139, 540n44

Kringlen, E., 437–38n5

Kris, Ernst, 70, 435n103, 448–49n120, 451n140

Kristeva, Julia, 417–18n66

Kurachi, M., 557–58n78

Laing, R. D., 22, 76, 90, 95, 97, 102–3, 106, 207, 402n23–24, 409n23, 416n60, 442n47, 449n121, 496n47, 503n86, 506n26, 512n42, 517n92, 521n17, 523n35, 523n39, 535n85

Lamb, Charles, 70, 435n103

Landis, C., 447n93, 491n6, 496n47, 508n1, 509n10, 509n13, 512n42–43, 522n30, 525n53, 527n3

Landow, George, 476–77n66

Lang, Jonathan, 94, 231–32, 233–35, 237, 241, 390, 499n57, 500–501n74–75, 516–17n88, 556n74

Langbaum, Robert, 441n31

Lange, Carl, 132

Langer, S., 454n10, 510n23, 513n47

Langfeldt, G., 492n14

Lanin-Kettering, I., 460n45

Lasch, Christopher, 89

Lautréamont, 38, 120, 219, 226, 488–89n107

Lawrence (case example), 68, 78, 156, 207, 333–39, 352, 500–501n74

Lawrence, D. H., 38

Lawson, W. B., 545–46n8

Lecercle, J.-J., 488–89n107, 495n42, 541n55

Lecours, A. R., 478n4, 479n11–12, 480n16, 481n30, 483–84n53, 484n56, 486n81, 490n111, 490n119, 535n84

Lee, E. N., 531n42

Leff, J., 539n42–43, 541–42n60

Lefley, H., 541–42n60

Legaut, S., 540n45

Leibniz, G. W. von, 486n85

Lentricchia, F., 503n88

Leon, J. de, 437n4

Leonhard, Karl, 562n115

Lerner, H. D., 503–4n95

Lerner, P. M., 503–4n95

Lesage, Augustin, 163

Levenson, M. H., 419n78, 422n104

Levi, Albert William, 531n42
Levin, S., 473–76n63, 550n43, 554–56n72, 561n103
Lévi-Strauss, Claude, 19, 258, 403n30, 421–22n102, 456–57n28
Levy, D. L., 473–76n63
Levy, J., 434n99
Levy, O., 446n87
Levy, Robert, 464–65n101, 472–73n55
Lévy-Bruhl, Lucien, 22, 462n71
Lewis, C. S., 28
Lewis, S. W., 562n113
Lewis, Wyndham, 32
Lewontin, R. C., 544n1
Lezak, M., 457n32, 561n106
Liddle, P. F., 480n21, 484n57
Lieberman, P., 405–7n48
Lienhardt, Godfrey, 447n105
Lim, K. O., 549n37–38, 553–54n64
Lin, K. M., 537n14, 538n33
Lion, J. R., 437–38n5
Lipton, R. B., 473–76n63
Littlewood, R., 536n11, 541n57
Locke, John, 10, 369, 508–9n6
Logue, P. E., 549n39
Lohr, J. B., 540n47, 558n80
Lorenz, Maria, 152, 205–6, 473n62, 480n14, 481n23, 483–84n53, 485n72, 486n81, 518n102
Lothane, Zvi, 505n18
Lotringer, S., 503n90
Lowe, D. M., 447n109
Lübbe-Grothues, G., 453n157, 482n34, 482n36–37
Lue, F., 552–53n63
Luft, D. S., 441–42n32, 465n104, 491n10
Lukach, J. M., 424n11
Lukács, Georg, 139, 422–23n111, 506n25, 543–44n75
Luria, A. R., 542n63
Luxumberger, H., 547n23
Lynch, Gary, 550–51n49
Lyotard, Jean-François, 185, 417–18n66

Macalpine, I., 407n1, 504n6
MacGregor, J., 541n55
Mach, Ernst, 216

MacHovec, F. J., 468n25
Macintyre, A., 447n104
MacLane, Mary, 101–2, 140
Maeterlinck, M., 482–83n45
Magaro, P. A., 458n37, 481n28
Magritte, René, 298, 299
Maher, Brendan, 455n17, 457–58n34, 479n11, 480n19, 481n27
Maj, M., 405–7n48
Malevich, Kasimir, 477n70
Mallarmé, Stéphane, 32, 184, 198–99, 208, 213, 419n83, 488–89n107
Maltzman, I., 457n30
Mamelek, M., 552–53n63
Manchanda, R., 553–54n64
Mandelbaum, M., 466n4, 466n8, 531n42
Manders, D., 561n104
Mann, Thomas, 418–19n71
Margo, A., 500n69, 551–52n56
Marian (case example), 174–76
Marmor, Judd, 545n7
Marsella, A. J., 447n105, 455–56n20, 472–73n55
Martin (case example), 93–94, 96, 136, 235, 274–76, 305, 316, 332–33, 352
Martin, J. R., 478n7, 479n10
Marx, Karl, 371
Matsubara, R., 557–58n78
Matthews, J. H., 413n37, 507n36, 541n55
Matthews, James Tilly, 492–93n17, 527n6
Matthysee, S., 457–58n34
Matussek, Paul, 54, 71–72, 426n31, 426–27n43–44, 431n74, 433n86, 436n110, 487n94
Maudsley, Henry, 365, 378, 379, 401–2n22, 458–59n38
Mauthner, Fritz, 466n10, 529n24
Mayer, Doris, 362
McFarlane, J., 416–17n64–65, 432n78, 496n45, 514n55
McGaughran, L. S., 455–56n20–21, 457n29
McGhie, Andrew, 54, 399–400n5, 410–12n28–30, 413n35, 426n42, 427n44, 434n95, 436n107, 453n160, 491n4, 493n21, 498n52, 502n83, 511n26, 521n17

McGill, D., 433n86

McGlashan, T. H., 412n32, 416n60, 430–31n70, 502–3n85, 535n84

McGuffin, P., 436n107, 473–76n63, 485n77, 545–46n8, 549n37

McGuire, M., 561n102–3

McHugh, P. R., 546n14

McKenna, P. J., 511n34

McShine, K., 462n62, 463n86, 477n68, 532n55

McWilliams, J., 473–76n63

Meares, A., 439n12

Meehl, Paul, 121

Meertz, E., 557n76, 558n81

Megill, A., 404n42

Mellor, C. S., 491n3, 492n12, 499n61

Melnechuk, T., 554n70

Menuck, M., 540n45

Mercier, Charles, 377–78, 385–86

Merleau-Ponty, Maurice, 202–3, 228, 290, 305, 345–47, 349, 428–29n61, 433n86, 435n102, 494–95n34, 515n77, 533n64

Messer, S., 513n47, 542n63

Messerli, D., 486n86

Messerschmidt, Franz Xaver, 448–49n120

Mesulam, M.-M., 548n30, 557n76

Meyer, Adolf, 243

Meyer, E., 408n10, 535n85

Meyer, U., 463n78, 463n80

Michelson, A., 471n40

Miller, E., 545–46n8, 554n67

Miller, J. G., 460n45

Miller, J. Hillis, 422n105

Miller, P. B., 486n85

Miller, R., 552–53n63, 554–56n72, 558n79, 559n87, 561n105, 562n114

Millon, T., 439–40n16–17, 443n65, 480–81n22

Minkowski, Eugene, 119, 160, 268, 395, 402n23–24, 408n6, 414n47, 416n55, 438n8, 456n24, 459n40, 462n66, 468n24, 469n33, 470–71n39, 471n46, 491n6, 496–97n49, 509n17, 515n68, 518n99, 547n21

Mintz, M., 561n106

Mirsky, A. F., 548–49n35, 552–53n63

Moldofsky, H., 552–53n63

Mondrian, P., 28

Monk, R., 403n37, 404n40

Monro, John, 399n3

Moran, L. J., 455–56n20–21, 457n29

Moreau, M., 549n36

Morel, Benedict-Augustin, 308–9, 540n50

Morice, R., 554–56n72

Morihisa, J. M., 552–53n63, 554n71

Morrison, R. L., 460–61n55, 554–56n72

Morse, S. F., 522n29

Mozley, D., 550n42

Mueser, K. T., 460–61n55, 554–56n72

Muir, W. J., 497–98n50

Mukărovsky, Jan, 63

Mukundan, C. R., 556–57n75

Müller, Heinrich Anton, 128

Müller, J., 435–36n105, 551n52

Mundt, C., 431n73, 552n59, 558–59n85

Murphy, D., 459n42, 560n98

Murphy, H. B. M., 538–39n35, 539n43, 540n47, 541–42n60

Murphy, J. M., 539n41

Musalek, M., 557–58n78

Musil, Robert, 16, 45, 57–58, 140, 142–47, 149, 186, 344, 441–42n32, 465n105, 465n109, 466n2, 542–43n67

Myslobodsky, M. S., 561n106

Nachmani, G., 479n11

Nadeau, Maurice, 413n37, 421n101, 424n13, 429n64, 432n81, 485n69, 485n74, 519n107

Nahmias, C., 552n62

Nannarello, J. J., 437n4

Narcissus, 68

Nasrallah, H. A., 478n5, 549n36, 559n88, 560n94

Natalija (case example), 217–18, 227, 233, 235, 237, 241, 286–87, 311, 331–33, 499n62, 500–501n74, 522n33, 529n26, 529–30n31

Natanson, M., 542–43n67

Nauman, Bruce, 171

Nayrac, P., 409n18

Neale, J. M., 455n17
Nehamas, A., 453n7
Nerval, Gérard de, 6, 367, 426n39
Newman, C., 473n61
Newton, Isaac, 417–18n66
Ngoma, M., 539n43
Nieber, R. H., 111, 451n142
Nietzsche, Friedrich, 4, 10, 22, 31, 37, 38, 45, 94–96, 103, 107, 119, 122, 140–42, 148–53, 158, 159, 161, 164, 167, 173, 216, 218–19, 232–33, 261, 300, 312, 317, 324, 367, 419n77, 424n18, 445n82, 452–53n156, 464n95, 464n98, 466n5–10, 493n24, 508n1, 534n71
Nijinsky, R., 408n13, 499–500n65
Nijinsky, Vaslav, 17, 367, 499–500n65
Nochlin, Linda, 172
Noland, R. W., 422–23n111
Nordness, L., 477n69
Novalis, F. von H., 198, 486n85

Oakeshott, Michael, 545n5
O'Brien, B., 492n13
O'Connor, D., 519n109
Oepen, G., 491–92n11, 512n38
Ogden, T. H., 410–11n29, 501n78
O'Grady, J., 492n12
Olafson, F. A., 517n90
Oldenburg, Claes, 63–64
Oliveira, P. de, 505n12
Ong, Walter, 93, 278–79, 444n79, 542–43n67
Oppenheimer, H., 488n105
Ortega y Gasset, José, 35–36, 38, 157, 421n97
Ostwald, P., 457n30, 458–59n38–39, 468n25, 480n21
Overton, D. A., 551–52n56
Owens, C., 420n93, 471–72n49, 534–35n76
Owens, D. G. C., 549n37

Pandurangi, A. K., 549n37
Pao, Ping-Nie, 410–11n29, 473n58, 486n82

Parker, P., 421n98
Parnas, J., 439n15, 459n42, 485n63
Parsons, Talcott, 536n5
Passmore, J., 485n64, 500–501n74, 530n37
Paz, Octavio, 30, 74, 467n14
Pearlson, G. D., 549n38
Peckham, Morse, 422n105
Peralta, V., 437n4
Perkins, D., 442n33
Perloff, M., 417–18n66, 419n84, 463n83, 532n53
Peters, F. (case example), 277–78
Peterson, M. R., 557–58n78
Pfefferbaum, A., 549n37–38, 553–54n64
Philip (case example), 106–8, 140, 178, 206
Phillips, William, 422n107
Philo Judaeus of Alexandria, 3
Piaget, Jean, 273, 428–29n60–61, 444n71, 462n71, 498n52, 501n77–78, 510n20
Picasso, Pablo, 137, 138
Pickering, J. H., 469n32
Picon, G., 424n16
Pierloot, R. A., 539n43
Pilgrim, D., 545n4
Pincus-Witten, P., 477n67
Pinel, Philippe, 365
Pirandello, Luigi, 114
Plato, 1, 3, 20, 200, 280, 281, 294, 336, 340, 445n81, 528n11
Plokker, J. H., 423n4
Podell, K., 460–61n55
Podreka, I., 557–58n78
Podvoll, E. M., 519n108
Poggiolli, R., 418n67, 423n112, 432n76, 462n63, 463n75, 485n70, 485n73
Polanyi, Michael, 168, 473n60, 496–97n49
Pollack, W. S., 412–13n33
Pollock, Jackson, 279
Polyakov, U. F., 127, 457n30, 458n35–36
Pope, H. G., 452n146
Popper, K. R., 560n92
Porter, R., 401–2n22, 482n40, 545n4
Post, R. M., 518n99
Pound, Ezra, 34, 419n84

Powell, T., 473–76n63
Powers, P. S., 455n16, 456n25
Preston, M., 507–8n37
Pribram, K. H., 558n80, 559n87
Prince, G. S., 538n31
Prosen, M., 486n82
Proust, Marcel, 280
Pynchon, Thomas, 417–18n66

Quennell, P., 442n50, 443n62
Quinlan, D. M., 456n27, 457n29, 457n33

Rabinow, P., 505n14, 532n61
Ragland, D. R., 554n69
Raine, A., 561n104
Rajan, T., 421n99, 531n46
Rakfeldt, J., 405–7n48
Rameau, 450n131, 495n38
Rank, O., 410n27
Rapaport, David, 130, 149, 156, 168, 172, 409n24, 460n52, 462n71, 468–69n29, 472n52, 473n58–59
Raskin, D. E., 414n46, 462n68
Rauschenberg, Robert, 417–18n66
Rawlins, J. N. P., 434n98, 473–76n63, 558n84
Rax, N., 548–49n35
Rax, S., 548–49n35
Read, Herbert, 28
Reagan, C. E., 519n109
Reeve, Basil, 404n40
Reich, S. S., 462n60
Reinhardt, Ad, 477n69
Reitmann, F., 425n30
Remington, G., 540n45
Renee (case example), 46–50, 54–56, 60, 62, 67, 73, 74, 187, 203, 273, 275, 278, 281–82, 315, 353–54, 429–30n69, 508n38, 517n93
Resnais, Alain, 305, 469n35
Resnick, S. M., 550n42, 552n62, 556–57n75, 561n105
Rey, A. C., 518n99
Reynolds, E. H., 544n1, 545n6, 548–49n35

Richmond, W. V., 554n69
Richter, Hans, 171
Ricoeur, Paul, 298
Rieber, R. W., 457n30, 480n21
Riedel, M., 519n4
Rieff, P., 504n2, 505–6n23, 523–24n46, 542n66
Rilke, Rainer Maria, 45, 58, 62, 186, 369–70, 370, 432n77
Rimbaud, Arthur, 29–30, 38, 137, 184, 185, 194, 196, 197, 208, 219, 226, 238, 482n41, 496n46
Ritson, B., 451n144
Robbe-Grillet, Alain, 32, 33, 157–58, 305, 417–18n66, 420n87, 525–26n59
Robert (case example), 144, 189, 326, 470n38
Roberts, G. W., 557n76
Roberts, M. S., 505n12
Robinson, J., 437n2
Roccatagliata, G., 400n9
Rochester, S. R., 479n10
Ron, M., 562n113
Rorty, R., 444n78, 533n64
Rose, S., 544n1, 550n45
Rosen, G., 400n9, 401–2n22, 508–9n6, 536n4, 538n30
Rosen, V., 506n24
Rosenbaum, B., 463n87, 465n108, 479n10
Rosenberg, Harold, 403n35, 416n63, 419n73
Rosenberg, S. D., 479n11, 483–84n53
Rosenfeld, H. A., 491n4, 496n48, 526n68
Rosenthal, D., 437–38n5
Ross, Nathaniel, 443n65
Rosser, Rachel, 51, 109, 303, 304, 310, 325, 395, 415n51, 483n48, 485n65, 561n108
Rossi, A., 405–7n48
Roth, M., 451–52n145
Rothenberg, D., 432–33n84
Rothenberg, J., 432–33n84
Rousseau, Jean-Jacques, 99–100, 531n44
Roussel, Raymond, 367, 469–70n36, 470n38, 488–89n107
Roxanas, M. G., 552–54n63–64
Royce, J., 527–28n9, 528n17

Rubin, W., 424n11, 429–30n69
Rümke, H. C., 109, 112, 113, 408n12, 465n106, 536n3
Ruocchio, Patricia J., 188, 480n17, 485n65, 487n96, 508n1, 514n58, 518n103
Russell, Bertrand, 96, 302
Russell, C., 418n70
Russell, J. D., 552–54n63–64
Rycroft, Charles, 96–97
Ryle, Gilbert, 91

Sacks, Oliver, 402n25, 551n51, 559n89, 561n101
Salzinger, Kurt, 479n11
Santayana, George, 273
Sante, L., 469–70n36
Sarraute, Nathalie, 31, 100–101, 223–26, 234, 448n112, 494–95n34
Sartorius, N., 537n16, 537n18, 539n41, 540n47, 542n61
Sartre, Jean-Paul, 45, 49, 50, 66–67, 72, 186–87, 190, 192, 194, 259–60, 283–84, 297, 311, 402n24, 419n84, 424n15, 437n1, 442n51, 442–43n54, 443n58, 443n61, 506–7n27, 512n41, 514n59, 515n68, 528–29n18
Sass, Louis, 505n18, 513n47, 517n93, 542n63
Satz, P., 554–56n72
Saussure, René de, 63, 202
Sauvages, François Boissier de, 3
Savard, R., 518n99
Saykin, A. J., 554–56n72, 558n83
Scadding, J. G., 405–7n48
Schachtel, E., 428–29n61, 551n55
Schafer, Roy, 156, 460n51, 460n54, 466n1, 472n53, 473n58–59, 477n73, 521n18
Scharfetter, C., 492n14, 493n21
Schelling, Friedrich W. J. von, 342, 343, 445n82
Schelsky, Helmut, 370
Schilder, P., 408n8, 492–93n17
Schiller, Friedrich von, 38, 82, 137, 341, 343, 349, 422–23n111, 441n30

Schlegel, August, 36
Schlegel, Friedrich, 36, 113
Schmidt, G., 523–24n46, 562n111
Schmidt, P., 540n45
Schneider, Kurt, 53, 78, 109, 216–17, 230–31, 244, 405–7n48, 409n25, 427n55, 431n71–72, 473–76n63, 497–98n50, 499n62, 499–500n65
Schneider, S. J., 436n107, 457–58n34
Schonfeldt-Bausch, R., 557n76, 558n81
Schooler, C., 451n136
Schopenhauer, Arthur, 329, 432n79
Schorske, Carl, 471n45
Schraml, F. V., 549n38
Schreber, Daniel Paul. See Subject Index
Schulsinger, F., 439n15
Schulsinger, H., 439n15
Schultz, K. D., 456n27
Schütter, R., 452n147
Schutz, Alfred, 465n109, 466n2, 542–43n67
Schwartz, M. A., 405–7n48, 431n73, 497–98n50, 558–59n85
Schwartz, S., 464n95, 466n3, 477–78n2, 478n4, 478n7, 479n11, 480n15, 481n31
Schweder, R. A., 447n105, 455–56n20, 456–57n28, 458n35, 472–73n55
Schweitzer, L., 561n105, 561n110
Scull, A., 399n3, 399–400n5, 400n12, 546n11
Searle, J., 489n108
Searles, Harold F., 410–11n29, 480–81n22, 501n76, 504n7, 514n59, 522n33, 535n84
Sechehaye, Marguerite, 22, 54–55, 60, 273, 408n7, 408n9, 424n20–24, 425n28–30, 434n91, 436n112, 437n114–16, 483n47, 488n100, 508n38, 510n20, 511n32, 511n36, 520n9, 523n41, 525n54–55, 535n88
Sedlmayr, Hans, 403n33
Segal, Hanna, 410–11n29, 516n86
Seidman, L. J., 549n36, 562n114
Seigel, J., 443n55
Seligman, Curt, 362
Senghor, Leopold, 432–33n84
Sennett, Richard, 447–48n110–11, 541n59

Serban, G., 414n47, 435n101, 473–76n63

Seymour, K., 557n77

Shagass, C., 551–52n56

Shanks, M. F., 473–76n63, 545–46n8

Shapiro, David, 434n94, 473–76n63, 510n20

Shapiro, Meyer, 32, 477n70

Shapiro, T., 473n58

Shattuck, Roger, 159–60, 193, 419n83, 420n95, 422n103, 462n61, 463n76, 467n15, 485n72

Shear, J. M., 549n39

Sheard, D., 561n104

Shenton, M. E., 405–7n48, 461n57–58, 472n51

Shepherd, M., 401–2n22, 408n15, 409n18, 415n49, 416n57, 416n59, 423n2, 426n31, 439n16, 450n131, 451n143, 471n43, 481n25, 487n94, 491n5, 498n54, 523–24n46, 538–39n35, 546–47n20, 554n67, 562n111

Sheppard, G. P., 553–54n64

Shimkunas, A. M., 456n22, 456n24, 456–57n28

Shklovsky, Viktor, 63

Shoemaker, S., 550n44

Siever, L. J., 437–38n5

Silber, E., 518n99

Silk, M. S., 404n42

Silvers, K. N., 499–500n65, 500n70, 512n38, 514n62, 518–19n104

Simmel, Georg, 447n107

Simon, B., 401–2n22

Simon, Claude, 151, 158–59

Simonov, P. V., 559n86, 559n87

Sims-Knight, J. E., 456n25

Sinclair, I. von, 415n50

Skolnick, B. E., 561n105

Skultans, V., 399n1, 400–401n15, 401–2n22

Slade, P. D., 500n69, 551–52n56

Slater, E., 451–52n145

Slavney, P. R., 546n14

Smith, A. C., 478–79n8, 480n21, 482n40, 499n56, 508–9n6, 538–39n35, 540n50, 540–41n53

Smith, G. N., 549n36

Smith, Paul, 533–34n69

Smith, R., 544–45n2

Smith, W. L., 434n99

Smitten, J. R., 470–71n39

Snell, Bruno, 498n55

Snyder, S., 402–3n28

Soby, James, 424n12

Solomon, R. C., 534n71

Solovay, M. R., 405–7n48, 461n57–58, 472n51

Sonne, H., 463n87, 465n108, 479n10

Sontag, Susan, 66, 418n69, 421n101, 422n105, 482n42, 483n49, 484n54, 484n61, 486n85, 487n96, 488–89n107, 503n91, 523n45

Sophocles, 3

Sorrentino, Gilbert, 495–96n43

Southard, E. E., 546n14

Sow, I., 539n42

Spaemann, R., 519n4

Spaulding, E., 437–38n5

Spears, M. K., 422n106

Spencer, Herbert, 454n10, 562n112

Sperry, R. W., 550n46

Spichtig, L., 435–36n105

Spitzer, Manfred, 405–7n48, 431n73, 432n79, 457–58n34, 491–92n11, 497–98n50, 512n38, 518n97, 527n1, 558–59n85

Spitzer, R. L., 399–400n5

Stallknecht, N., 531n43

Starobinski, Jean, 483n51, 495n40

Stein, Gertrude, 34, 198

Steiner, George, 28, 418n69, 482n42, 482–83n45, 486n85

Stella, Frank, 170–71

Stendhal, H. B., 137, 139, 224

Stengel, E., 546n11, 547n22

Stern, Daniel, 501n78

Stern, J. P., 404n42, 442n36, 503n89, 526–27n69

Sternberg, J., 552n57

Stevens, J. R., 537n20, 539n39–40, 558n79, 559n87

Stevens, R., 473–76n63, 479–80n13, 552n57

Stevens, Wallace, 137, 301, 308, 463n81, 469n35, 519n2, 522n29

Stewart, D., 519n109

Stierlin, H., 409n25, 541n56
Stocking, G., 413n39, 454n10
Stone, M., 405–7n48, 501n75
Storch, Alfred, 285, 491n4, 518n96
Storey, P., 549n37
Störring, G., 423n2
Stransky, Erwin, 357, 416n59, 439n16, 450–51n135, 558–59n85
Straus, E., 551n55
Strauss, John S., 405–7n48, 435–36n105, 436n113, 500n70, 511n32, 515n73, 551–52n56, 552n58–59
Strawson, P. F., 214, 529n22, 529n28
Strindberg, August, 75, 78, 357, 367, 451–52n145, 525–26n59
Strömgren, E., 504n96
Stuss, D. T., 553–54n64–65, 554n68, 554–56n72, 562n113
Suddath, R. L., 553–54n64, 557n77
Sugarman, A., 503–4n95
Sullivan, Harry Stack, 114, 135–36, 187, 412–13n33, 453n158
Summerfelt, A. T., 554–56n72
Sutton, S., 436n109, 457–58n34, 460n44
Swayze, V. W., 549n38, 553–54n64
Sweeney, J. A., 548–49n35
Symons, Arthur, 426n39, 541n56
Sypher, Wylie, 413n37, 420n95, 491n10, 496n45, 514n54
Szalita, A. B., 454n10, 498n55
Szasz, T., 496n48

Talbot, R. E., 500n68
Talfourd, T. N., 435n103
Tamburini, A., 546n14
Tancock, J., 463n86, 477n68
Tanguy, Yves, 64
Tate, Alan, 452n152
Tausk, Victor, 217–18, 227–28, 331–33, 502–3n85, 506n24
Taylor, Charles, 444n76, 481n32, 533–34n69, 542n63, 542n65
Taylor, J. E., 523n35
Taylor, M. C., 542–43n67
Teggin, A., 543n70

Thiher, A., 532n62
Thürmer, W., 482n36
Tierney, A., 460–61n55
Tomer, R., 561n106
Tonkonogy, J., 459n39
Tonsor, S., 541n56
Toone, B. K., 548–49n35
Torrey, B. B., 538n34
Torrey, E. Fuller, 358, 368, 451n136, 536n10, 538n27, 538n28, 538n34, 538–39n35–36, 539n39, 540n47, 540n49, 554n69, 557–58n77–78
Trilling, Lionel, 36, 99, 104, 419n73, 447n106, 447n108, 448n112, 450n129, 495n38, 496n45, 520n11
Tuan, Y.-F., 444n72, 513n49
Tucker, G. J., 483–84n53
Turner, William, 279
Tversky, A., 459n39
Tzara, Tristan, 30

Uehlein, F. A., 431n73, 491–92n11, 497–98n50, 512n38, 558–59n85
Ulmer, G. L., 463n83, 467n13
Underwood, G., 473–76n63, 479–80n13, 552n57
Updike, John, 525–26n59

Vaché, Jacques, 350, 421n101
Vaina, L., 482n34
Valéry, Paul, 35, 76, 225, 260–61, 280, 289, 298–300, 315, 437n1, 505n18
Vanier-Clement, M., 478n4, 479n11–12, 480n16, 481n30, 483–84n53, 484n56, 486n81, 490n111, 490n119, 535n84
van Praag, H. M., 416n61
Vargas Llosa, M., 477n71
Varghese, F. T., 408n13
Vaughn, C., 541–42n60
Velázquez, D. R. de S., 513n50
Venables, P. H., 473–76n63, 556–57n75, 560–61n100, 561n103
Villon, Jacques, 210

Vinchon, Jean, 436n106
Vonèche, J. J., 428n60
Vygotsky, Lev S., 194, 256–57, 325, 488n99

Waddington, J. L., 552n62
Waelder, Robert, 551n53
Wain, Louis, 161, 162
Waldman, I. N., 545–46n8
Walker, C., 511n28
Walker, E., 561n102, 561n103
Wallace, Clare, 232, 499n62, 515n75
Wallis, B., 471–72n49, 513n52, 532n56, 534–35n76
Walser, M., 503n89, 526–27n69
Walser, Robert, 140, 144–45, 464n92, 535n85
Walter, H., 557–58n78
Wapner, W., 560n96, 560n98
Warhol, Andy, 106, 344–45, 417–18n66
Warner, Richard, 536–37n13–14, 538n24, 538n27, 538–39n35, 541n58
Waxler, N., 537n14
Weber, Max, 11, 371, 372, 417–18n66, 538n25
Weiler, G., 466n10
Weinberger, Daniel R., 368, 382, 383, 389–90, 392, 396, 454n12, 499n63, 543n69, 545–46n8, 548n31, 548n34, 550n47–48, 554n67, 554–56n72, 559n87, 562n114
Weiner, I. B., 456n22, 456n24, 460n49, 472n51, 484n60
Weinman, J., 560n99
Weintraub, K. J., 542n64
Weiss, A. S., 505n12
Welsh, H., 561n105, 561n110
Werner, Heinz, 295, 428–29n61, 429n67, 488n102, 498n54, 501n78, 506n24, 508n1, 509n10, 512n38, 515n70, 515n72, 515n76, 519n105, 520n9, 521n14, 549n40
Wetzel, A., 312–13, 523–24n46
Wheeler, K. M., 452n153
White, G. M., 447n105, 455–56n20, 472–73n55

White, R. B., 504n7
Whitton, J. L., 552–53n63
Wiggins, O. P., 405–7n48
Wild, Cynthia M., 410–11n29, 447n96, 462n72, 510n19, 522n31
Wilde, Oscar, 105–6
Wilkins, John, 453n1
Williams, B., 490–91n1
Williams, J. B. W., 399–400n5, 405–7n48
Williams, M., 548–49n35
Williams, Raymond, 422–23n111
Williams, Tennessee, 4
Williamson, A., 421–22n102, 495–96n43
Williamson, P., 552–53n63
Wilson, L., 557n77
Wilson, Scottie, 133
Wing, L., 480–81n22
Winnicott, D. W., 410–11n29, 447n98
Wiseberg, S., 468–69n29
Wittgenstein, Ludwig, 2, 9, 21, 28, 68–69, 173, 186, 188, 190, 222–23, 292, 294, 295, 345–47, 367, 444n77, 484n58, 501n75, 506n26, 517n91, 517n94, 518n97
Wolf, S., 458n37, 526n63, 540n47
Wolff, S., 438n6, 560n95
Wolff, Werner, 546n18
Wölfli, Adolf, 116, 132, 259
Wolfson, Louis, 367, 488–89n107
Wolkin, 552n62
Wood, F. B., 554n70
Wood, M., 520n12
Woods, W. L., 459n41, 479n9, 484n55, 484n59, 488n105, 512n40
Wooles, I., 560n99
Woolf, Virginia, 28, 30–31, 100, 495n40, 525–26n59, 543–44n75
Woolfolk, R., 513n47, 542n63
Wordsworth, William, 82, 99–100
Worringer, William, 161, 170
Würgler, S., 435–36n105
Wyatt, R. J., 540n47, 552–53n63, 554n71, 556–57n75

Yates, Francis, 447n106
Yeats, William Butler, 344
Yorke, C., 468–69n29

Youard, P., 560n99
Yurgelin-Todd, D., 550n43, 554–56n72, 561n103

Zaidel, D. W., 560n98
Zangwill, O. L., 538–39n35, 554n67
Zavarin, V., 457n30, 458–59n38–39, 468n25, 480n21

Zec, R. F., 499n63, 548n34, 550n47, 554–56n72, 562n114
Zijderveld, A. C., 542–43n67
Zimet, C., 468n23
Ziolkowski, T., 401–2n22, 519n4
Zipursky, R. B., 549n37, 549n38, 553–54n64
Zola, Émile, 81, 135
Zubin, J., 436n109, 457–58n34, 460n44, 552n59

S U B J E C T I N D E X

anxiety *(Continued)*
nia, 127, 236–37; world-catastrophe experience and, 301–10
apathy. *See* indifference
aphasia, language in, 176, 178, 206
Apollo and Apollonianism, 10, 37, 74, 312, 349, 422*n*103, 561*n*109; described, 404*n*42; modernism and, 37, 38
apophany experience, 539*n*41; in modernism, 56, 57–58, 64–66; in schizophrenia, 52–55, 60–61; traditional interpretations of, 53–55
aporia. *See mise en abyme*
arche-writing (Derrida), 202–3, 348
arousal disorder, 434–35*n*100, 497–98*n*50
"as-if" quality, 77, 98. *See also* public self (and false self)
attention. *See* cognitive psychology; eye-tracking research; selective attention theories
atypical psychosis, 361, 363
auditory hallucinations, 229, 231–35, 243, 247, 249, 250, 254, 256, 275–76, 382, 386–87, 499–500*n*65
authenticity, 99; inauthenticity vs., 103–8
autism, 291
Autobiography of a Schizophrenic Girl (Sechehaye), 46–50, 60, 187, 203
automatic writing, 194
autonomization of schizophrenic language, 176, 178–80, 198–205, 348
avant-gardism, 135, 421–22*n*102; in modernism, 29–30, 134–35, 367; view of schizophrenia, 21–23, 218–20
avoidant personality, 405–7*n*48, 437–38*n*5, 439–40*n*17. *See also* schizoid personality
awkwardness, physical, 102, 236, 342, 448–49*n*120

Bald Soprano, The (Ionesco), 189
Banquet Years, The (Shattuck), 193
Being and Time (Heidegger), 294

Between Life and Death (Sarraute), 224–25
Birth of Tragedy, The (Nietzsche), 4, 10, 22, 38, 232–33, 312
bizarre delusions, 270, 399–400*n*5, 509*n*7, 509*n*12
bizarreness, 16–17, 133, 270, 366; of modernism, 28–38; nature of, 26–27. *See also* incomprehensibility; praecox-feeling
blocking, of thought or speech, 26, 180, 201, 487*n*96
Blue Book (Wittgenstein), 222–23
bouffée délirante, 363, 405–7*n*48
brain. *See* neurobiological aspects of schizophrenia; organic brain syndromes
brief reactive psychosis, 361, 363
Broken Brain, The: The Biological Revolution in Psychiatry (Andreasen), 380

catatonia, and catatonic schizophrenia, 14–15, 47, 111, 231, 236, 303, 365, 537*n*20
causes, of schizophrenia. *See* schizophrenia, causes of
cave myth (Plato), 280–81, 336
Les Chants de Maldoror (Lautréamont), 120
childhood origins of schizophrenia, 405*n*46, 443–44*n*69
child's lived-world, 58–59, 136, 277, 470–71*n*39, 483*n*48. *See also* animistic perception
Chinese encyclopedia (Borges), 121–22, 126, 131, 132–33, 159
Civilization and Its Discontents (Freud), 105
Cogito (*Cogito ergo sum*), 23, 91–92, 213–15, 298, 392
cognitive function in schizophrenia. *See* perceptual abnormalities; selective attention theories; thinking, in schizophrenia
cognitive psychology: language in, 181–82, 195; models of schizophrenia in, 69–70; self-disturbances and, 228;

Stimmung and, 53–54. *See also* selective attention theories

cognitive slippage, 119–47, 204, 370. *See also* thinking, in schizophrenia

"Colours" (von Hofmannsthal), 56

command hallucination, 231–35

comparator function, 391, 432n79

concrete attitude/concretistic thinking, 25, 122–23, 124–26, 131, 151–52, 157, 165–67, 389. *See also* phantom concreteness

consciousness: de Man on, 349–51; Derrida on, 348–49; Descartes on, 75, 91–92, 214–15; division of, 233–34; features of, 75, 376; Fichte on, 313–15; Foucault on, 329–32; Heidegger on, 292, 345–46, 347; James on, 220–23, 226–27, 234–35; Kant on, 91–92, 328–29, 331–322; Merleau-Ponty on, 346–47; in "primitive" cultures, 22, 142, 464–65n101, 472–73n55; Proust on, 280; Sarraute on, 224–26; Sartre on, 311; Schreber and, 246–51, 254–55, 257, 260, 261, 266; Wittgenstein on, 223

contamination in thought or perception, 130, 131, 137

contradictory aspects of schizophrenia, 8–10, 25–26, 324–27, 416n56. *See also* paradoxes of reflexivity

cortical-subcortical axis of brain. *See* vertical axis of brain

creativity: schizoid personality and, 81; schizophrenia and, 127

criminal behavior, 146–47

cubism, 28, 137–38, 169, 279

cultural influences, 9–10; cross-cultural dimension, 358–64; historical dimension, 364–66; possible role in genesis of schizophrenia, 355–73; schizoid personality and, 82, 88–108; schizophrenia as, 366–69; world-as-view and, 278–81. *See also* modernism

dadaism, 28, 135, 151, 171

death: madness as, 3; schizophrenia as, 7–8

deautomatization, in modernism, 63

deconstructionism, 347–51, 394, 533n64. *See also* Derrida, Jacques *in* Name Index

defamiliarization, 63

defect (or deficit) view of schizophrenia, 2–3, 18–19, 53–54, 71–72, 89, 182, 368, 375–76, 380, 386, 408n14

dehumanization, 157; in modernism, 31–32, 35–36, 157

"Dehumanization of Art, The" (Ortega y Gasset), 35–36, 157

deictic aspect of speech, 177

delusional mood, 370

delusional percept, 44; *Stimmung* and, 44–45, 52–53, 61

delusional tension, 53

delusions, 14, 44, 53, 268–99, 382, 384, 387; anomalous features of, 274–78; apathy toward, 295–97; bizarre, 270, 399–400n5, 509n7, 509n12; epistemological, 285–88, 291–95; formation of, 60–61; influencing-machine, 217–18, 229–30, 233, 235, 237, 284, 286–87, 307, 311, 331–33, 499n62; mood-congruent vs. incongruent, 270–71; ontological issues in, 286–87, 288, 291–95, 298; reality-testing and, 270–71, 283, 284; realm of the imaginary in, 282, 283–85; realm of the real in, 283, 288–91; of Schreber, 244–45, 246–51, 253–58; of world-catastrophe, 271–72, 300–23. *See also* hallucinations; *Stimmung*

dementia, 3, 4, 5, 11, 15, 18, 380, 383, 405–7n48

dementia in schizophrenia, 17–18, 24, 376, 378, 384. *See also* defect (or deficit) view of schizophrenia

dementia praecox, 13–14, 17–18, 24, 70, 108, 145, 365; as term, 357, 379

Dementia Praecox or the Group of Schizophrenias (E. Bleuler), 121, 379

depression, 11, 166. *See also* affective disorders

derealization, 370; in modernism, 32–33. *See also* solipsism; subjectivism; unworlding of the world

"Description of a Struggle" (Kafka), 317–23, 330–31

desocialization of schizophrenic language, 176–78, 193–97

detachment, 23–24, 75–76, 106, 369, 429–30n69; from emotion, 370; estrangement from face or body, 44, 105, 227–29, 239–40, 252–53, 265, 433n86, 433–34n88, 435n102, 448–49n120; in modernism, 35–38, 59–60, 65–67; in schizoid personality, 78; from self (uncoupling), 90, 97–108, 344, 371; from world (disconnection), 59–60, 90–97. *See also* irony

diagnosis of schizophrenia. *See* schizophrenia, concept of

Diagnostic and Statistical Manual (DSM III and DSM III-R), 152–53, 270, 273, 360–361, 399–400n5, 439–40n 17

Dionysus and Dionysianism, 2, 4, 5, 8, 10, 22, 23, 147, 181, 197, 218, 226, 238–39, 298, 312, 317, 342, 349; described, 404n42; modernism and, 37, 38

Discipline and Punish (Foucault), 243, 246, 250–51

disconnection. *See* detachment

disdain for convention. *See* antinomianism

disengagement. *See* detachment

"dissociation of sensibility" (T. S. Eliot), 357

disturbances of distance, 148–73; narrative and visual form and, 154–73; verbal concepts and, 150–54

Divided Self, The (Laing), 76

doctrine of the abyss, 18–19

dopamine hypothesis, 381, 382, 384, 551n50

double (or multiple) bookkeeping, 275, 285, 515n68

doublet of modern thought, 327–33; deconstructionism and, 348–49; hypermodernism (or postmodernism) and, 345; parallel in schizophrenic case, 333–40; romanticism and, 341–42

doubt. *See* skepticism

dreaming as model for schizophrenia, 3, 400n14

DSM III, 270, 360–61, 399–400n5, 439–40n17

DSM III-R, 152–53, 270, 273, 361, 399–400n5

eccentricity, in schizophrenic thinking, 124–29, 364, 366. *See also* thinking, in schizophrenia

echolalia, 189

ego boundaries, loss of, 217–18, 269, 271, 272, 311–23, 410–11n29; Fichte and, 313–17, 321; Kafka and, 317–323; Schreber and, 244–45; *Stimmung* and, 55, 60

egocentricity, 181, 195, 278; radical, 273

egoism, 37

epilepsy, 391

episteme, modern, 365. *See also* doublet of modern thought

epistemological delusions, 285–88, 291–95

estrangement. *See* detachment

etiquette, schizoid personality and, 92–93, 110–11

evolutionism, 3, 22, 377

external reality (worldhood), as experienced in schizophrenia, 269–74

eye-tracking research, 435n101, 473–76n63

false self. *See* public self (and false self)

La Femme Visible (Dali), 297

First Rank Symptoms of schizophrenia, 216–17, 230–31, 244, 273, 359, 361, 364, 492n12

fixation. *See* primitivity view of schizophrenia; psychoanalytic model

flatness in painting, 161–64, 170, 171, 477n69

flatness (or inappropriateness) of affect, 23–24, 112–15, 296, 363, 364. *See also* affective abnormalities in schizophrenia

flight of ideas, 166, 461–62n59

impressionism, 279

inauthenticity, 103–8

incidence and prevalence of schizophrenia, 13; cross-cultural comparisons, 358–64, 370–71; historical comparisons, 364–66

incomprehensibility, 215, 243, 408n13, 409n20, 409n22; in modernism, 8, 30; in schizophrenia, 15–17, 18, 19, 26–27. See also bizarreness; language in schizophrenia, obscurity of; praecox-feeling

incongruous affect, in schizophrenia, 143–44

incongruous responses, 119–21, 461n58

inconsistency, in thinking, 129–34

indifference, 275, 387; in schizoid personality, 77. See also detachment

individualism, 370, 541–42n60

industrialization, 365, 368, 371

ineffability, relevance for language in modernism and in schizophrenia, 185–93

infantile autoeroticism, 20, 243, 272

influencing-machine delusion, 217–18, 229–30, 233, 235, 237, 284, 286–87, 307, 311, 331–33, 499n62

infra-mince (Duchamp), 135

"Inner Eye" of the Mind (Descartes), 91, 93

inner speech, 184, 193–97, 206–7; of Schreber, 247, 255–58

insight, 6–7, 351–54, 452n147, 515–516n78, 516n80, 530n33

intentional aspects of schizophrenia. See act-affliction issue

intrapsychic ataxia (Stransky), 26, 109, 357

introspection, 222, 223–26, 227, 228, 229, 240–41; morbid, 401–2n22

introversion. See schizoid personality

Invention of Morel, The (Casares), 305–11, 318

irony, 351; in modernism, 35–36, 113; in schizoid personality, 88, 106–8; in schizophrenia, 26, 111–15. See also detachment; humor, in schizophrenia

irrationality, 399–400n5; mental illness

as, 378–79; in traditional concepts of madness, 1–7. See also rationality

Korsakoff's syndrome, 380, 552n60

Labyrinth of Solitude, The (Paz), 74

language in modernism, 57, 184–205, 207; Hölderlin and, 24–25, 114, 183–84

language in schizophrenia, 25, 50–51, 174–209; act-affliction issue and, 175, 182–85, 196, 205–8; autonomization of, 176, 178–80, 198–205, 348; desocialization of, 176–78, 193–97; Hölderlin and, 24–25, 114, 183–84; irony in, 112–15; obscurity in, 174–78, 196, 206–7; poverty of, 176, 180–81, 185–93, 405–7n48, 517n92; Schreber and, 244–45, 247–50, 255–57; traditional theories of, 181–84; trends in, 176–81

"language poetry" movement, 198–99

lateral axis of brain, 378–79, 381–82, 392–96, 497–98n50

laughter, in schizophrenia, 24, 108, 112–14, 135–36, 143–44, 247, 351. See also humor, in schizophrenia

Lectures on Clinical Psychiatry (Kraepelin), 24

"Lenz" (Büchner), 365

"Letter of Lord Chandos, The" (von Hofmannsthal), 56–57, 185–86, 187

Letter to His Father (Kafka), 83–84

limbic system, 382, 385, 390–92

literacy, schizoid personality and, 93–94

literalism, 156–57, 159, 164–65, 166, 170–71

looseness of association, 121, 407n49

loss of self. See self-disturbances

"Louis Lambert" (Balzac), 365

Love's Body (Brown), 22

"Love Song of J. Alfred Prufrock, The" (Eliot), 344

lowering of mental level, 18, 70, 376, 380, 384, 388, 401–2n22 madness: traditional conceptions or images of, 1–7, 403–4n39, 454–55n15. *See also entries beginning with* schizophrenia

Madness and Civilization (Foucault), 246

mania, 17, 73, 131, 472n54; delusions in, 275; reality-testing in, 270; in schizoaffective disorders, 11; schizophrenia vs., 131–32. *See also* affective disorders

manic-depressive illness, 5, 14, 25, 79, 80; delusions in, 296. *See also* affective disorders

mannered behavior in schizophrenia, 110–11, 180–81, 205, 451n143

Man Without Qualities, The (Musil), 16, 57–58, 142–43, 145–47, 344

Medico-Psychological Association (Great Britain), 365–66

Meditations on First Philosophy (Descartes), 213–15

Memoirs of My Nervous Illness (Schreber), 242–51, 253–60, 261–67, 289–91

mental automatism, 18

mental microscopy, 59, 67

"mere being" experience: in modernism, 56–57, 64; in schizophrenia, 48–49, 50–52, 54

minimalism, 170

mise en abyme, 226, 238, 241, 500–501n74

Mrs. Dalloway (Woolf), 30

modernism: adversarial stance of, 29–30, 134–35, 367; aesthetic self-referentiality in, 34–35, 163; anti-epiphany in, 44, 55–60, 70–71; antinomianism in, 134–35; apophany experience in, 56, 57–58, 64–66; avant-gardism of, 29–30, 134–35, 367; creative illusion in, 151–53, 158, 167; dehumanization in, 31–32, 35–36, 157; derealization in, 32–33; dissolution of ego boundaries and, 311–23; distinguished from postmodernism, 8, 29, 30, 32, 35, 36, 417–18n66, 471–72n49; disturbances of distance in, 170–73; fragmentation in,

31, 57, 141–42; hyperawareness/hyperconsciousness in, 37–38, 59, 65, 67, 74; hypermodernist, 341, 343–45, 349–51; immediacy in, 150–51, 158, 167; impoverishment and ineffability of language in, 185–93; independence of language and, 184, 198–205; influence of schizophrenia on, 366–69; inner speech in, 184, 193–97; irony and detachment in, 35–38, 59–60, 65–67, 113; language in schizophrenia and, 184–205, 207; nature of, 8–9, 28–38, 421–22n102; as negative category, 36–37; ontological insecurity in, 305–11; origins of, 28; paradoxes of reflexivity in, 340–51; perspectivism and relativism in, 30–31, 122, 137–39, 141–47; postromantic, 341, 343–47, 349–51; reflexivity in, 35, 161–64; schizoid personality and, 82, 88–108; schizophrenia and, 37–38, 134–47; self-disturbances and, 223–26, 238–40; self-fragmentation or dissolution in, 16, 31–32, 216, 220–26; spatial form in, 33–34, 155–56, 158; *Stimmung* and, 58–60, 62–67, 72; subjectivism in, 32–35, 37, 38, 171–72; as term, 8, 11–12, 29, 31; thinking in schizophrenia and, 134–47; world-as-view in, 278–81. *See also* cultural influences; postmodernism

modernity, 90–91, 92–93, 356, 357, 368, 371–73

monitoring of willed action, 497–98n50

morbid geometrism, 26, 161–63

"morbid introspection," 401–2n22

music, poetry as, 199

My Heart Laid Bare (Baudelaire), 86

Nadja (Breton), 65, 72

narcissism, 89, 226; transcendental, 328, 334, 338

narrative form, 150–61; schizophrenia and, 154–57; spatial form and, 159–64

Nausea (Sartre), 49, 66–67, 72, 186–87, 190, 192

negative symptoms, 377–78, 380–81,

negative symptoms *(Continued)* 387, 405–7n48. *See also* positive symptoms

neologisms, 71, 175, 177, 206, 207, 466–67n12, 484n56

neoprimitivism, 38

Nerve Meter, The (Artaud), 239

neurobiological aspects of schizophrenia, 16–19, 69–70, 228, 370, 374–97, 432n79, 434n100, 435n102; alternatives to traditional models concerning, 387–96; assumptions concerning, 375–77; criticism of traditional views concerning, 384–97; historical sources, 377–84

neuroimaging techniques, 381

neuroleptic drugs, 394

Nightwood (Barnes), 34

nihilism, 94–96, 311

Notes from the Underground (Dostoevsky), 4, 318

nouveau roman school, 100, 151, 157–59, 171, 305

objectivism, 161, 346, 422n104, 422n105, 466n11; in modernism, 31–32, 33, 34, 37, 38; romanticists and, 342. *See also* subjectivism

object-relations theory, 79, 410–11n29, 444n71

object-sorting tests, 125–26, 129

obscurity in schizophrenic language, 174–78, 196, 206–7

Observations on Insanity (Haslam), 365

observing ego, 20, 114, 221, 222, 229

obsessive-compulsive disorder, 25

omnipotence, 296–99, 300, 324–26; in modernism, 31; in schizophrenia, 26. *See also* solipsism

"On Naive and Sentimental Poetry" (Schiller), 341

On the Essence of Laughter (Baudelaire), 351

"On the Puppet Theater" (Kleist), 342–43

ontic issues, 293–95, 302

ontological insecurity, 67, 301–10

ontological issues, 190–92, 302, 530n34; in delusions, 286–287, 288, 291–95, 298

Order of Things, The (Foucault), 119–21, 327, 330

organic brain syndromes, 5, 14, 15, 386, 460–61n55, 511n26, 549n37; aphasia in, 176, 178, 206; hyperintentionality and, 69–70; lesions in limbic system, 390, 391; lesions on frontal lobes, 389; right-hemisphere damage, 393; Rorschach test and, 164, 166, 457n32; thought disorders in, 122, 131, 134

overinclusive thinking, 123, 125, 152

paleological thinking, 123, 152

panopticism, 248–51, 252–56, 258–59, 266, 315, 373, 507n29

Panopticon, 251–54, 258

paradoxes of reflexivity, 120, 324–54; consciousness machine and, 331–33; doublet of modern thought as, 327–40; Lawrence (case example), 333–39; in modernism, 340–51; Natalija (case example), 331–33; in schizophrenia, 324–27, 331–40, 351–54. *See also* reflexivity

paralogical thinking. *See* paleological thinking

paranoia, and paranoid psychosis, 14, 17, 61; delusions in, 275; reality-testing in, 270

paranoid features in schizophrenia, 145, 231, 235–36, 245, 285–88. *See also* Schreber, Daniel Paul

passivization, 64–66, 72, 203, 208, 235, 244–45, 258, 390

pathogenic-pathoplastic distinction, 358–60, 368–69

Paysan de Paris (Aragon), 65

perceptual abnormalities, 43–74

perspectival shifting: in modernism, 136, 137–39; in schizophrenia, 130, 131

"Perspective, The" (Hölderlin), 183

perspectivism, 122, 141–47; in modernism, 30–31, 122, 137–39; of Musil, 142–43, 145–47; of Nietzsche, 141–42; in schizophrenia, 131, 139–40. *See also* relativism

Phaedrus (Plato), 200, 340

phantom concreteness, 506*n*26

phenomenological approach, 9, 10–11, 355–57, 374, 383, 404–5*n*44; described, 403*n*38

phenomenologist's attitude (Husserl), 96, 279, 445*n*82, 528*n*13; Merleau-Ponty on, 228

Phenomenology of Mind (Hegel), 103–5

Philosophical Investigations (Wittgenstein), 223

phonological rules, 176

physicalism, 376, 380, 385

Physique and Character (Kretschmer), 79–82

picture-arrangement tests, 129

Planetarium, The (Sarraute), 225

Politics of Experience, The (Laing), 22

poor reality-testing. *See* reality-testing, disturbances in

Portrait of the Artist as a Young Man (Joyce), 82

positive symptoms, 377–78, 379, 380–81, 382, 387, 548*n*34. *See also* negative symptoms

postmodernism, 8, 12, 29–37, 151, 269, 280, 345–51, 367, 420*n*93, 494–95*n*34, 520*n*11, 534*n*71; distinguished from modernism, 8, 29, 30, 32, 35, 36, 417–18*n*66, 471–72*n*49; as term, 344–45. *See also* modernism

postmodernity, 372

postromanticism, 341, 343–47, 349–51

poststructuralism, 198–205, 269, 280, 345–51, 367, 494–95*n*34, 543*n*71

poverty of content of speech, 180, 189, 191–92, 517*n*92

poverty of language, in modernism, 185–93

poverty of speech, 180, 189, 405–7*n*48

praecox-feeling, 14, 16–17, 109, 133, 174, 217, 241, 248, 317, 363, 416*n*60; defined, 45. *See also* bizarreness; incomprehensibility

premorbid personality. *See* schizoid personality

prereflective mode of experience, 345, 347, 349, 353–54

presentism, 155, 158, 470*n*38; in modernism, 34

prevalence, of schizophrenia. *See* incidence and prevalence of schizophrenia

primary process, 20, 167, 407*n*49, 454*n*13, 473*n*58

"primitive" cultures, 98, 239, 361–64, 370–71; consciousness in, 22, 142, 464–65*n*101, 472–73*n*55

primitivism, 38, 267

primitivity view of schizoid personality, 89–90

primitivity view of schizophrenia, 4, 19–21, 22, 58–60, 372, 379–80, 407*n*49, 409–10*n*26, 410–11*n*28–30, 427*n*44, 472*n*53, 473*n*58; language in, 181, 187, 188, 203; reality-testing, 270; Schreber and, 243–46, 253–58, 262; self-disturbances and, 217–18, 229–30, 232, 243–45; *Stimmung* and, 54–55; thinking and, 135–36; worldhood in, 272–73. *See also* psychoanalytic model

Principles of Psychology, The (James), 220–23, 277–78, 283

prisons, 251–53

projective tests: described, 153–54. *See also* Rorschach test; Thematic Apperception Test (TAT)

psychiatric model, 3, 16–19, 69–70, 334, 351, 358, 370, 374–97; self-disturbances in, 216–17; thinking in schizophrenia and, 386–87; worldhood of schizophrenic, 273–74. *See also* cognitive psychology; neurobiological aspects of schizophrenia

psychoanalytic model, 3, 379–80; conception of madness, 11, 20–21, 23, 54–55, 409–13*n*26–33, 430–31*n*70, 502–3*n*85; language and, 181, 187, 188, 203; object-relations theory, 79, 410–11*n*29, 444*n*71; reality-testing and, 270; schizoid personality and, 89–90; Schreber and, 243–46, 253–58, 262;

psychoanalytic model *(Continued)*
self-disturbances in, 217–18; *Stimmung* and, 54–55; world-catastrophe symptom and, 311–23, 509n15, 510n21, 523–24n46; worldhood in, 272–73. *See also* primitivity view of schizophrenia
Psychology of Imagination, The (Sartre), 283–84
psychosis: atypical, 361, 363; cross-cultural studies, 358–64, 370–71; historical perspective, 364–66, 403–4n39; manic-depressive illness, 5, 14, 25, 79, 80, 296; paranoid delusions in, 285–86; traditional views of, 1–5, 377–80; World Health Organization studies, 359–61
psychotic, defined, 270, 273
public self (and false self), 77, 98; abdication of, 100–103; private self vs., 97–100; unconventionality and inauthenticity in, 103–8, 110–12, 139–40

regression model of schizophrenia. *See* primitivity view of schizophrenia; psychoanalytic model of schizophrenia
relativism, 164, 370; in modernism, 30–31; of Musil, 142–43, 145–47; of Nietzsche, 141–42. *See also* perspectivism
Republic, The (Plato), 3
"Rhetoric of Temporality, The" (de Man), 349–51
risk-taking behavior, 239, 310
role distance, in schizoid personality, 97–100
romanticism, 5, 29, 36, 82, 135, 340–44, 349, 350, 369, 422n105
Rorschach test, 129–31, 139, 172, 457n32, 503–4n95; contamination responses to, 137; described, 129, 154; instructions for, 164; schizophrenic-type responses to, 164–70, 191; vacilation in, 129–31; world-catastrophe experience and, 272
Russian formalists, 63, 65
Russian futurists, 63, 198

Rameau's Nephew (Diderot), 104
rationality, 1–2, 23, 326, 370, 376; absence of, as negative, 2–3; antirationalism, 3–4, 238–40; as term, 2, 399n2. *See also* irrationality
rationalization, 371, 373
reading, schizoid personality and, 93–94
real, realm of the, 282, 283, 288–91
reality-testing, disturbances in, 268–99
reason. *See* irrationality; rationality
rebelliousness. *See* antinomianism; avant-gardism; modernism, adversarial stance of
reductionistic model of insanity (biological reductionism), 375–84, 404–5n44; assumptions of, 375–77; critique of, 384–87; historical sources, 377–84
reflexivity: Cartesian, 91–92; defined, 326–27, 421–22n102, 528n12; Kantian, 91–92; in modernism, 35, 159, 161–64; paradoxes of, 8, 120, 324–54; in schizophrenia, 156, 161, 165. *See also* hyperreflexivity; *mise en abyme*

schizaesthesia, 59, 67
schizoaffective disorders, 9, 11, 405–7n48; *Stimmung* in, 45. *See also* affective disorders
schizoid personality, 9, 11, 75–115, 369, 396, 405–7n48; abdication of public self and, 100–103; act-affliction issue and, 79–82, 439–40n17; anaesthetic, 80–81, 85–88, 103–8, 109; Baudelaire as, 85–90; characteristics of, 77–82, 437–38n5, 439–40n17; critical stance of, 7; cultural influences and, 82, 88–108; de Chirico as, 43, 44–46, 52; hyperaesthetic, 80–81, 82–85, 100–103, 109; interiorizing trends and, 90–94; irony in, 88, 106–8; Kafka as, 82–85, 87, 88–90, 95, 317–23; Kretschmer on, 79–86, 88; loss of reality and, 94–97; modernism and, 82, 88–108; object-relations theory and, 79, 444n71; parallels with modern culture, 82, 88–108; primitivity view of, 89–90; rela-

tionship to schizophrenia, 78–79, 108–15; role distance in, 97–100; Rorschach test and, 164–65; *Stimmung* in, 45; unconventionality and inauthenticity in, 103–8

schizophrenia, causes of, 9–10; cross-cultural dimension and, 358–64; etiological hypotheses (involving cultural and social factors), 366–73; historical dimension and, 364–66; neurobiological approach to (pathogenesis), 374–97. *See also* childhood origins of schizophrenia

schizophrenia, concept of, 11, 13–27, 405n47; avant-gardist model, 21–23, 218–20; defining, 13–14; as heightened awareness, 5–7, 10–11, 70–74, 357; ideal-type (concept adopted in this book), 11, 405–7n48; psychiatric model, 16–19, 69–70, 351, 358, 360, 370, 374–97; schizoid personality and, 78–79, 108–15. *See also* primitivity view of schizophrenia; psychoanalytic model

schizophrenia, symptoms of, 13–14, 23–27, 359, 360–61, 364, 386; cognitive disturbances, 24–25; disturbances of reality-testing, 269–71; ego boundary loss, 269, 271, 311–23; external reality (worldhood) and, 269–74; First Rank Symptoms, 216–17, 230–31, 244, 273, 359, 361, 364, 492n12; flatness of affect, 23–24, 112–15, 296, 363, 364; heterogeneity of, 25–27, 76, 106, 125, 133, 165, 175, 206–8, 324–25; hyperawareness/hyperconsciousness, 68–70, 473–76n63; negative, 377–78, 380–81, 387, 405–7n48; positive, 377–78, 387, 548n34; "unreality" experience, 47–48, 50–52, 54, 60, 62, 73, 354; variability of, 24–25, 175, 415n49, 489–90n110; world-catastrophe experience, 271–72, 300–23. *See also* delusions; hallucinations; language in schizophrenia; reality-testing, disturbances in; self-disturbances in schizophrenia; *Stimmung*; thinking, in schizophrenia

schizophreniform disorders, 9, 360–61, 405–7n48; *Stimmung* in, 45

schizothymic tendency, 79, 80–81

schizotypal personality, 9, 405–7n48, 437–38n5

Schneider's First Rank Symptoms of schizophrenia, 216–17, 230–31, 244, 273, 359, 361, 364, 492n12

Schreber, Daniel Paul, 242–51, 253–60, 261–67; auditory hallucinations of, 243, 247–49, 250, 254, 256, 499–500n65, 500–501n74; boundary confusion of, 244–45; compulsive thinking of, 68, 248–50, 255–60, 262, 264–65, 530n38; delusions of, 145, 246–51, 271, 277, 278, 289–91, 516n80, 518n97; diagnosis, 402n26; experience of reality of, 289–91, 352; father of, 505n18; panopticism of, 248–51, 253–54, 258–59, 266, 315, 373, 507n29; passivization of, 244–45, 258; soul-voluptuousness of, 262–64, 312; wife of, 264; world-catastrophe experience and, 510n21, 519–20n8, 523–24n46

"Seascape" (Rimbaud), 137

"Secret Room, The" (Robbe-Grillet), 157–58

selective attention theories, 54, 123–24, 126, 368, 386, 436n107, 436n109. *See also* eye-tracking research

self-consciousness. *See* hyperreflexivity; reflexivity; self-referentiality, aesthetic

self-disturbances in schizophrenia, 15–16, 31–32, 213–41, 242–67, 408n15; act-affliction issue and, 228, 240–41, 297–99, 385–87, 395, 405–7n48, 439–40n17, 473–76n63; auditory hallucinations, 229, 231–35, 243, 247, 249, 250, 254, 256; avant-gardist view, 218–19; dispossession and furtive abductions, 235–40; influencing-machine and, 217–18, 229–30, 233, 235, 237, 284, 286–87, 307, 311, 331–33, 499n62; James on, 220–23, 226–27; modernism and, 223–26, 238–40; psychiatric view, 216–17; psychoanalytic view, 217–18,

self-disturbances *(Continued)*
229–30, 232, 243–45; Schreber and, 242–51, 253–60, 261–67
self-fragmentation (or dissolution) in modern art and experience, 16, 31–32, 216, 220–26
self-mutilation, 239, 310
self-referentiality, aesthetic, 163–64, 344; in modernism, 34–35, 37
semantic rules, 176
semiotic relationships, 154, 155–57
senile dementia, 15, 18, 380
sexuality: schizoid personality and, 77, 87, 107–8; in schizophrenia, 237, 245, 265, 285, 502–3*n*85
"Signature Event Context" (Derrida), 204–5
similarities tests, 125, 126
sincerity and authenticity, 99, 103–8, 110–12
skepticism, 128–29, 136–40; in cultural evolution, 372, 454*n*10; Musil and, 142–43; Nietzsche and, 141–42; in schizophrenia, 236
sleep, madness as, 3
Socrates and Socratic mode, 10, 37, 74, 200, 232–33, 534*n*71, 561*n*109; described, 404*n*42; modernism and, 37, 38
solipsism, 32–33, 37, 96, 278, 288, 291, 294, 300–301, 311–14, 325, 334, 485*n*66; in modernism, 297–99; in schizophrenia, 295–99
Sound and the Fury, The (Faulkner), 31, 34
spatial form, 159–64; flatness in painting, 161–64, 170, 171, 477*n*69; in modernism, 33–34, 157–63; in schizophrenia, 48, 155–56, 158; time-space alterations and, 159–61
"Spatial Form in Modern Literature" (Frank), 159
speech, writing vs., 201–3
Stimmung, 43–74, 227, 526*n*62; as act vs. as affliction, 68–74; apophany in, 52–55, 60–61; defined, 45; delusional percept in, 44–45, 52–53, 61; descriptions of schizophrenic, 46–55; fragmenta-

tion of perceptual world in, 49–52; "mere being" in, 48–49; modernism and, 58–60, 62–67, 72; traditional interpretations of, 53–55; "unreality" in, 47–48
subjectivism, 139, 161, 226, 235, 251, 300, 328, 341, 346, 370, 422*n*104, 422*n*105, 464*n*93, 466*n*11, 529*n*28; Cartesian, 214–15; Fichte on, 313–15, 321; loss of reality and, 94–97; in modernism, 32–35, 37, 38, 171–72; in modern world-as-view, 278–81; ontological uncertainty and, 67, 301–10; in schizophrenic delusions, 275–78, 281–95. *See also* objectivism
suicide, 106, 270, 353
superior performance, by schizophrenics, 72, 127, 384–85, 415*n*48, 458–59*n*38
sur-réflexion, 346–47, 350
surrealism, 28, 45, 106, 135, 137, 194, 367; pursuit of *Stimmung* in, 63–66, 72
"Surrealist Manifesto" (Breton), 22
symbiosis, 252–53
syntonic tendency, 80, 84, 115, 396, 473–76*n*63

telegraphic speech, 177, 194
Tel Quel group, 198–99
Theatre and Its Double, The (Artaud), 238–39
Thematic Apperception Test (TAT), 96; described, 154; instructions for, 154–55; schizophrenic-type responses to, 155–57, 159, 470*n*38
thinking, in schizophrenia, 24–25, 119–47, 150–53; abstract, 125–26, 129, 151, 165–67, 191–93, 364, 366, 370, 371; cognitive style, 394–95; doublet of modern thought in, 331–40; eccentricity of perspective in, 124–29, 364, 366; lowering of mental level, 18, 70, 376, 380, 384, 388, 401–2*n*22; narrative form and, 154–57; neurobiological approach and, 386–87; Nietzschean dualism and, 150–54, 158, 167; parallels

with modernism, 134–47; psychoanalytic view, 135–36; Schreber and, 248–50, 255–60, 262, 264–65; spatial form and, 48, 155–56, 158; time and, 156–57; traditional theories of, 122–24; vacillation and inconsistency in, 129–34, 169

"Thirteen Ways of Looking at a Blackbird" (Stevens), 137

Thought and Language (Vygotsky), 194, 256–57

thought disorder, formal, 24–25, 119–47, 148–73, 382. *See also* abstract attitude; blocking, of thought or speech; concrete attitude/concretistic thinking; thinking, in schizophrenia

time, 159–64; modernism and, 159–60; schizoid personality and, 159–60; schizophrenia and, 156–57, 158, 160–61

transcendental narcissism (Foucault), 328, 334, 338

Treatise on Madness (Battie), 270

Trema, 43–44, 47, 49, 50, 51, 52; traditional interpretations of, 53–55. *See also Stimmung*

tribal cultures. *See* "primitive" cultures

Triptych (Simon), 151, 158–59

truth-taking stare, 43–74, 187, 191, 240, 526n62; defined, 44. *See also Stimmung*

Ubu Roi (Jarry), 134

Ulysses (Joyce), 34, 70–71

Umbilicus of Limbo, The (Artaud), 239

"uncanny" experience, 55

unconventionality. *See* antinomianism; avant-gardism; modernism, adversarial stance of

uncoupling. *See* detachment

understandability, as diagnostic criterion. *See* bizarreness; incomprehensibility; praecox-feeling

"unreality" experience, 44, 425n26; in modernism, 64; in schizophrenia, 47–

48, 50–52, 54, 60, 62, 73, 354, 523–24n46

unworlding of the world, 32–33. *See also* objectivism

vacillation, 129–34, 169

variability of schizophrenic symptoms, 24–25, 175, 415n49, 489–90n110

vertical axis of brain, 378–79, 381, 390–92, 400–401n15

viral hypothesis, 368

Visible and the Invisible, The (Merleau-Ponty), 346–47

visual modality, dominance of, 445–46n84

Vocation of Man, The (Fichte), 302, 313–15

volitional aspect of schizophrenic symptoms. *See* act-affliction issue

Waiting for Godot (Beckett), 189, 208

"Wasteland, The" (Eliot), 137, 280, 344

Watt (Beckett), 69

Waves, The (Woolf), 31

Wildman image of schizophrenia, 1, 3, 4, 16, 21–23, 134, 238–239, 262, 413n37

Will to Power, The (Nietzsche), 103

Witnesses, The (Hennell), 236

word association tests, 204

word definition tests, 152, 178–79

world-as-view, 32, 278–81, 307, 345–46

world-catastrophe experience, 269, 272–73, 300–23; dissolution of ego boundaries and, 311–23; ontological insecurity and, 301–10

World Health Organization (WHO) studies, 359–61

writing, speech vs., 201–3

Writing Degree Zero (Barthes), 198

Young Torless (Musil), 58